The Heston Model and Its Extensions in Matlab and C#

Founded in 1807, John Wiley & Sons is the oldest independent publishing company in the United States. With offices in North America, Europe, Australia, and Asia, Wiley is globally committed to developing and marketing print and electronic products and services for our customers' professional and personal knowledge and understanding.

The Wiley Finance series contains books written specifically for finance and investment professionals as well as sophisticated individual investors and their financial advisors. Book topics range from portfolio management to e-commerce, risk management, financial engineering, valuation, and financial instrument analysis, as well as much more.

For a list of available titles, visit our website at www.WileyFinance.com

The Heston Model and Its Extensions in Matlab and C#

FABRICE DOUGLAS ROUAH

WILEY

Cover illustration: Gilles Gheerbrant, "1 2 3 4 au hasard" (1976);
© Gilles Gheerbrant
Cover design: Gilles Gheerbrant

Published by John Wiley & Sons, Inc., Hoboken, New Jersey.

Published simultaneously in Canada.

Library of Congress Cataloging-in-Publication Data:

Rouah, Fabrice, 1964-
The Heston model and its extensions in Matlab and C# / Fabrice Douglas Rouah.
pages cm. – (Wiley finance series)
Includes bibliographical references and index.
ISBN 978-1-118-54825-7 (paper); ISBN 978-1-118-69518-0 (ebk); ISBN 978-1-118-69517-3 (ebk)
1. Options (Finance)–Mathematical models. 2. Options (Finance)–Prices. 3. Finance–Mathematical models. 4. MATLAB. 5. C# (Computer program language) I. Title.
HG6024.A3R6777 2013
332.64′53028553–dc23

2013019475

Printed in the United States of America.

10 9 8 7 6 5 4 3 2 1

Contents

Foreword

I am pleased to introduce The Heston Model and Its Extensions in Matlab and C# by Fabrice Rouah. Although I was already familiar with his previous book entitled Option Pricing Models and Volatility Using Excel/VBA, I was pleasantly surprised to discover he had written a book devoted exclusively to the model that I developed in 1993 and to the many enhancements that have been brought to the original model in the twenty years since its introduction. Obviously, this focus makes the book more specialized than his previous work. Indeed, it contains detailed analyses and extensive computer implementations that will appeal to careful, interested readers. This book should interest a broad audience of practitioners and academics, including graduate students, quants on trading desks and in risk management, and researchers in option pricing and financial engineering.

There are existing computer programs for calculating option prices, such as those in Rouah's prior book or those available on Bloomberg systems. But this book offers more. In particular, it contains detailed theoretical analyses in addition to practical Matlab and C# code for implementing not only the original model, but also the many extensions that academics and practitioners have developed specifically for the model. The book analyzes numerical integration, the calculation of Greeks, American options, many simulation-based methods for pricing, finite difference numerical schemes, and recent developments such as the introduction of time-dependent parameters and the double version of the model. The breadth of methods covered in this book provides comprehensive support for implementation by practitioners and empirical researchers who need fast and reliable computations.

The methods covered in this book are not limited to the specific application of option pricing. The techniques apply to many option and financial engineering models. The book also illustrates how implementation of seemingly straightforward mathematical models can raise many questions. For example, one colleague noted that a common question on the Wilmott forums was how to calculate a complex logarithm while still guaranteeing that the option model produces real values. Obviously, an imaginary option value will cause problems in practice! This book resolves many similar difficulties and will reward the dedicated reader with clear answers and practical solutions. I hope you enjoy reading it as much as I did.

Professor Steven L. Heston
Robert H. Smith School of Business
University of Maryland
January 3, 2013

Preface

In the twenty years since its introduction in 1993, the Heston model has become one of the most important models, if not the single most important model, in a then-revolutionary approach to pricing options known as stochastic volatility modeling. To understand why this model has become so important, we must revisit an event that shook financial markets around the world: the stock market crash of October 1987 and its subsequent impact on mathematical models to price options.

The exacerbation of smiles and skews in the implied volatility surface that resulted from the crash brought into question the ability of the Black-Scholes model to provide adequate prices in a new regime of volatility skews, and served to highlight the restrictive assumptions underlying the model. The most tenuous of these assumptions is that of continuously compounded stock returns being normally distributed with constant volatility. An abundance of empirical studies since the 1987 crash have shown that this assumption does not hold in equities markets. It is now a stylized fact in these markets that returns distributions are not normal. Returns exhibit skewness, and kurtosis—fat tails—that normality cannot account for. Volatility is not constant in time, but tends to be inversely related to price, with high stock prices usually showing lower volatility than low stock prices. A number of researchers have sought to eliminate this assumption in their models, by allowing volatility to be time-varying.

One popular approach for allowing time-varying volatility is to specify that volatility be driven by its own stochastic process. The models that use this approach, including the Heston (1993) model, are known as stochastic volatility models. The models of Hull and White (1987), Scott (1987), Wiggins (1987), Chensey and Scott (1989), and Stein and Stein (1991) are among the most significant stochastic volatility models that pre-date Steve Heston's model. The Heston model was not the first stochastic volatility model to be introduced to the problem of pricing options, but it has emerged as the most important and now serves as a benchmark against which many other stochastic volatility models are compared.

Allowing for non-normality can be done by introducing skewness and kurtosis in the option price directly, as done, for example, by Jarrow and Rudd (1982), Corrado and Su (1997), and Backus, Foresi, and Wu (2004). In these models, skewness and kurtosis are specified in Edgeworth expansions or Gram-Charlier expansions. In stochastic volatility models, skewness can be induced by allowing correlation between the processes driving the stock price and the process driving its volatility. Alternatively, skewness can arise by introducing jumps into the stochastic process driving the underlying asset price.

The parameters of the Heston model are able to induce skewness and kurtosis, and produce a smile or skew in implied volatilities extracted from option prices generated by the model. The model easily allows for the inverse relationship between price level and volatility in a manner that is intuitive and easy to understand. Moreover, the call price in the Heston model is available in closed form, up to an integral that must be evaluated numerically. For these reasons, the Heston model has become the most popular stochastic volatility model for pricing equity options.

Another reason the Heston model is so important is that it is the first to exploit characteristic functions in option pricing, by recognizing that the terminal price density need not be known, only its characteristic function. This crucial line of reasoning was the genesis for a new approach for pricing options, known as pricing by characteristic functions. See Zhu (2010) for a discussion.

In this book, we present a treatment of the classical Heston model, but also of the many extensions that researchers from the academic and practitioner communities have contributed to this model since its inception. In Chapter 1, we derive the characteristic function and call price of Heston's (1993) original derivation. Chapter 2 deals with some of the issues around the model such as integrand discontinuities, and also shows how to model implied and local volatility in the model. Chapter 3 presents several Fourier transform methods for the model, and Chapter 4 deals exclusively with Alan Lewis' (2000, 2001) approach to stochastic volatility modeling, as it applies to the Heston model. Chapter 5 presents a variety of numerical integration schemes and explains how integration can be speeded up. Chapter 6 deals with parameter estimation, and Chapter 7 presents classical simulation schemes applied to the model and several simulation schemes designed specifically for the model. Chapter 8 deals with pricing American options in the Heston model. Chapter 9 presents models in which the parameters of the original Heston model are allowed to be piecewise constant. Chapter 10 presents methods for obtaining the call price that rely on solving the Heston partial differential equation with finite differences. Chapter 11 presents the Greeks in the Heston model. Finally, Chapter 12 presents the double Heston model, which introduces an additional stochastic process for variance and thus allows the model to provide a better fit to the volatility surface.

All of the models presented in this book have been coded in Matlab and C#.

Acknowledgments

I would like to thank Steve Heston not only for having bestowed his model to the financial engineering community, but also for contributing the Foreword to this book and to Leif B.G. Andersen, Marco Avellaneda, Peter Christoffersen, Jim Gatheral, Espen Gaarder Haug, Andrew Lesniewski, and Alan Lewis for their generous endorsement. And to my team at Wiley—Bill Falloon, Meg Freeborn, Steven Kyritz, and Tiffany Charbonier—thank you. I am also grateful to Gilles Gheerbrant for his strikingly beautiful cover design.

Special thanks also to a group who offered moral support, advice, and technical reviews of the material in this book: Amir Atiya, Sébastien Bossu, Carl Chiarella, Elton Daal, Redouane El-Kamhi, Judith Farer, Jacqueline Gheerbrant, Emmanuel Gobet, Greg N. Gregoriou, Antoine Jacquier, Dominique Legros, Pierre Leignadier, Alexey Medvedev, Sanjay K. Nawalkha, Razvan Pascalau, Jean Rouah, Olivier Scaillet, Martin Schmelzle, and Giovanna Sestito. Lastly, a special mention to Kevin Samborn at Sapient Global Markets for his help and support.

The Heston Model and Its Extensions in Matlab and C#

CHAPTER 1

The Heston Model for European Options

Abstract

In this chapter, we present a complete derivation of the European call price under the Heston model. We first present the model and obtain the various partial differential equations (PDEs) that arise in the derivation. We show that the call price in the Heston model can be expressed as the sum of two terms that each contains an in-the-money probability, but obtained under a separate measure, a result demonstrated by Bakshi and Madan (2000). We show how to obtain the characteristic function for the Heston model, and how to solve the Riccati equation from which the characteristic function is derived. We then show how to incorporate a continuous dividend yield and how to compute the price of a European put, and demonstrate that the numerical integration can be speeded up by consolidating the two numerical integrals into a single integral. Finally, we derive the Black-Scholes model as a special case of the Heston model.

MODEL DYNAMICS

The Heston model assumes that the underlying stock price, S_t, follows a Black-Scholes–type stochastic process, but with a stochastic variance v_t that follows a Cox, Ingersoll, and Ross (1985) process. Hence, the Heston model is represented by the bivariate system of stochastic differential equations (SDEs)

$$\begin{aligned} dS_t &= \mu S_t dt + \sqrt{v_t} S_t dW_{1,t} \\ dv_t &= \kappa(\theta - v_t)dt + \sigma\sqrt{v_t}dW_{2,t} \end{aligned} \tag{1.1}$$

where $E^{\mathbb{P}}[dW_{1,t}dW_{2,t}] = \rho dt$.

We will sometimes drop the time index and write $S = S_t$, $v = v_t$, $W_1 = W_{1,t}$ and $W_2 = W_{2,t}$ for notational convenience. The parameters of the model are

- μ the drift of the process for the stock;
- $\kappa > 0$ the mean reversion speed for the variance;
- $\theta > 0$ the mean reversion level for the variance;
- $\sigma > 0$ the volatility of the variance;
- $v_0 > 0$ the initial (time zero) level of the variance;

$\rho \in [-1, 1]$ the correlation between the two Brownian motions W_1 and W_2; and
λ the volatility risk parameter. We define this parameter in the next section and explain why we set this parameter to zero.

We will see in Chapter 2 that these parameters affect the distribution of the terminal stock price in a manner that is intuitive. Some authors refer to v_0 as an unobserved initial state variable, rather than a parameter. Because volatility cannot be observed, only estimated, and because v_0 represents this state variable at time zero, this characterization is sensible. For the purposes of estimation, however, many authors treat v_0 as a parameter like any other. Parameter estimation is covered in Chapter 6.

It is important to note that the volatility $\sqrt{v_t}$ is not modeled directly in the Heston model, but rather through the variance v_t. The process for the variance arises from the Ornstein-Uhlenbeck process for the volatility $h_t = \sqrt{v_t}$ given by

$$dh_t = -\beta h_t dt + \delta dW_{2,t}. \tag{1.2}$$

Applying Itō's lemma, $v_t = h_t^2$ follows the process

$$dv_t = (\delta^2 - 2\beta v_t)dt + 2\delta\sqrt{v_t}dW_{2,t}. \tag{1.3}$$

Defining $\kappa = 2\beta$, $\theta = \delta^2/(2\beta)$, and $\sigma = 2\delta$ expresses dv_t from Equation (1.1) as (1.3).

The stock price and variance follow the processes in Equation (1.1) under the historical measure $\mathbb{P}$, also called the physical measure. For pricing purposes, however, we need the processes for (S_t, v_t) under the risk-neutral measure $\mathbb{Q}$. In the Heston model, this is done by modifying each SDE in Equation (1.1) separately by an application of Girsanov's theorem. The risk-neutral process for the stock price is

$$dS_t = rS_t dt + \sqrt{v_t}S_t d\widetilde{W}_{1,t} \tag{1.4}$$

where

$$\widetilde{W}_{1,t} = \left(W_{1,t} + \frac{\mu - r}{\sqrt{v_t}}t\right).$$

It is sometimes convenient to express the price process in terms of the log price instead of the price itself. By an application of Itō's lemma, the log price process is

$$d\ln S_t = \left(\mu - \frac{1}{2}\right)dt + \sqrt{v_t}dW_{1,t}.$$

The risk-neutral process for the log price is

$$d\ln S_t = \left(r - \frac{1}{2}\right)dt + \sqrt{v_t}d\widetilde{W}_{1,t}. \tag{1.5}$$

If the stock pays a continuous dividend yield, q, then in Equations (1.4) and (1.5) we replace r by $r - q$.

The risk-neutral process for the variance is obtained by introducing a function $\lambda(S_t, v_t, t)$ into the drift of dv_t in Equation (1.1), as follows

$$dv_t = [\kappa(\theta - v_t) - \lambda(S_t, v_t, t)]dt + \sigma\sqrt{v_t}d\widetilde{W}_{2,t} \tag{1.6}$$

where

$$\widetilde{W}_{2,t} = \left(W_{2,t} + \frac{\lambda(S_t, v_t, t)}{\sigma\sqrt{v_t}}t\right). \tag{1.7}$$

The function $\lambda(S, v, t)$ is called the volatility risk premium. As explained in Heston (1993), Breeden's (1979) consumption model yields a premium proportional to the variance, so that $\lambda(S, v, t) = \lambda v_t$, where λ is a constant. Substituting for λv_t in Equation (1.6), the risk-neutral version of the variance process is

$$dv_t = \kappa^*(\theta^* - v_t)dt + \sigma\sqrt{v_t}d\widetilde{W}_{2,t} \tag{1.8}$$

where $\kappa^* = \kappa + \lambda$ and $\theta^* = \kappa\theta/(\kappa + \lambda)$ are the risk-neutral parameters of the variance process.

To summarize, the risk-neutral process is

$$\begin{aligned} dS_t &= rS_t dt + \sqrt{v_t}S_t d\widetilde{W}_{1,t} \\ dv_t &= \kappa^*(\theta^* - v_t)dt + \sigma\sqrt{v_t}d\widetilde{W}_{2,t} \end{aligned} \tag{1.9}$$

where $E^{\mathbb{Q}}[d\widetilde{W}_{1,t}d\widetilde{W}_{2,t}] = \rho dt$ and with $\mathbb{Q}$ the risk-neutral measure.

Note that, when $\lambda = 0$, we have $\kappa^* = \kappa$ and $\theta^* = \theta$ so that these parameters under the physical and risk-neutral measures are the same. Throughout this book, we set $\lambda = 0$, but this is not always needed. Indeed, λ is embedded in the risk-neutral parameters κ^* and θ^*. Hence, when we estimate the risk-neutral parameters to price options we do not need to estimate λ. Estimation of λ is the subject of its own research, such as that by Bollerslev et al. (2011). For notational simplicity, throughout this book we will drop the asterisk on the parameters and the tilde on the Brownian motion when it is obvious that we are dealing with the risk-neutral measure.

Properties of the Variance Process

The properties of v_t are described by Cox, Ingersoll, and Ross (1985) and Brigo and Mercurio (2006), among others. It is well-known that conditional on a realized value of v_s, the random variable $2c_t v_t$ (for $t > s$) follows a non-central chi-square distribution with $d = 4\kappa\theta/\sigma^2$ degrees of freedom and non-centrality parameter $2c_t v_s e^{-\kappa(t-s)}$, where

$$c_t = \frac{2\kappa}{\sigma^2(1 - e^{-\kappa(t-s)})} \tag{1.10}$$

and with $t > s$. The mean and variance of v_t, conditional on the value v_s are, respectively

$$\begin{aligned} m &= E[v_t|v_s] = \theta + (v_s - \theta)e^{-\kappa(t-s)}, \\ S^2 &= \mathrm{Var}[v_t|v_s] = \frac{v_s\sigma^2 e^{-\kappa(t-s)}}{\kappa}(1 - e^{-\kappa(t-s)}) + \frac{\theta\sigma^2}{2\kappa}(1 - e^{-\kappa(t-s)})^2. \end{aligned} \tag{1.11}$$

The effect of the mean reversion speed κ on the moments is intuitive and explained in Cox, Ingersoll, and Ross (1985). When $\kappa \to \infty$ the mean m approaches the mean reversion rate θ and the variance S^2 approaches zero. As $\kappa \to 0$ the mean approaches the current level of variance, v_s, and the variance approaches $\sigma^2 v_t(t-s)$.

If the condition $2\kappa\theta > \sigma^2$ holds, then the drift is sufficiently large for the variance process to be guaranteed positive and not reach zero. This condition is known as the Feller condition.

THE EUROPEAN CALL PRICE

In this section, we show that the call price in the Heston model can be expressed in a manner which resembles the call price in the Black-Scholes model, which we present in Equation (1.76). Authors sometimes refer to this characterization of the call price as "Black-Scholes–like" or "à la Black-Scholes." The time-t price of a European call on a non-dividend paying stock with spot price S_t, when the strike is K and the time to maturity is $\tau = T - t$, is the discounted expected value of the payoff under the risk-neutral measure $\mathbb{Q}$

$$\begin{aligned} C(K) &= e^{-r\tau} E^{\mathbb{Q}}[(S_T - K)^+] \\ &= e^{-r\tau} E^{\mathbb{Q}}[(S_T - K)\mathbf{1}_{S_T>K}] \\ &= e^{-r\tau} E^{\mathbb{Q}}[S_T \mathbf{1}_{S_T>K}] - Ke^{-r\tau} E^{\mathbb{Q}}[\mathbf{1}_{S_T>K}] \\ &= S_t P_1 - Ke^{-r\tau} P_2 \end{aligned} \tag{1.12}$$

where $\mathbf{1}$ is the indicator function. The last line of (1.12) is the "Black-Scholes–like" call price formula, with P_1 replacing $\Phi(d_1)$, and P_2 replacing $\Phi(d_2)$ in the Black-Scholes call price (1.76). In this section, we explain how the last line of (1.12) can be derived from the third line. The quantities P_1 and P_2 each represent the probability of the call expiring in-the-money, conditional on the value $S_t = e^{x_t}$ of the stock and on the value v_t of the volatility at time t. Hence

$$P_j = \Pr(\ln S_T > \ln K) \tag{1.13}$$

for $j = 1, 2$. These probabilities are obtained under different probability measures. In Equation (1.12), the expected value $E^{\mathbb{Q}}[\mathbf{1}_{S_T>K}]$ is the probability of the call expiring in-the-money under the measure $\mathbb{Q}$ that makes W_1 and W_2 in the risk-neutral version of Equation (1.1) Brownian motion. We can therefore write

$$E^{\mathbb{Q}}[\mathbf{1}_{S_T>K}] = \mathbb{Q}(S_T > K) = \mathbb{Q}(\ln S_T > \ln K) = P_2.$$

Evaluating $e^{-r\tau} E^{\mathbb{Q}}[S_T \mathbf{1}_{S_T>K}]$ in (1.12) requires changing the original measure $\mathbb{Q}$ to another measure $\mathbb{Q}^S$. Consider the Radon-Nikodym derivative

$$\frac{d\mathbb{Q}}{d\mathbb{Q}^S} = \frac{B_T/B_t}{S_T/S_t} = \frac{E^{\mathbb{Q}}[e^{x_T}]}{e^{x_T}} \tag{1.14}$$

where

$$B_t = \exp\left(\int_0^t r\,du\right) = e^{rt}.$$

In (1.14), we have written $S_t e^{r(T-t)} = E^{\mathbb{Q}}[e^{x_T}]$, since under $\mathbb{Q}$ assets grow at the risk-free rate, r. The first expectation in the third line of (1.12) can therefore be written as

$$
\begin{aligned}
e^{-r(T-t)}E^{\mathbb{Q}}[S_T \mathbf{1}_{S_T>K}] &= S_t E^{\mathbb{Q}}\left[\frac{S_T/S_t}{B_T/B_t}\mathbf{1}_{S_T>K}\right] = S_t E^{\mathbb{Q}^S}\left[\frac{S_T/S_t}{B_T/B_t}\mathbf{1}_{S_T>K}\frac{d\mathbb{Q}}{d\mathbb{Q}^S}\right] \\
&= S_t E^{\mathbb{Q}^S}[\mathbf{1}_{S_T>K}] = S_t \mathbb{Q}^S(S_T > K) = S_t P_1.
\end{aligned} \tag{1.15}
$$

This implies that the European call price of Equation (1.12) can be written in terms of both measures as

$$
C(K) = S_t \mathbb{Q}^S(S_T > K) - Ke^{-r\tau}\mathbb{Q}(S_T > K). \tag{1.16}
$$

The measure $\mathbb{Q}$ uses the bond B_t as the numeraire, while the measure $\mathbb{Q}^S$ uses the stock price S_t. Bakshi and Madan (2000) present a derivation of the call price expressed as (1.16), but under a general setup. As shown in their paper, the change of measure that leads to (1.16) is valid for a wide range of models, including the Black-Scholes and Heston models. We will see later in this chapter that when S_T follows the lognormal distribution specified in the Black-Scholes model, then $\mathbb{Q}^S(S_T > K) = \Phi(d_1)$ and $\mathbb{Q}(S_T > K) = \Phi(d_2)$. Hence, the characteristic function approach to pricing options, pioneered by Heston (1993), applies to the Black-Scholes model also.

THE HESTON PDE

In this section, we explain how to derive the PDE for the Heston model. This derivation is a special case of a PDE for general stochastic volatility models, described in books by Gatheral (2006), Lewis (2000), Musiela and Rutkowski (2011), Joshi (2008), and others. The argument is similar to the hedging argument that uses a single derivative to derive the Black-Scholes PDE. In the Black-Scholes model, a portfolio is formed with the underlying stock, plus a single derivative which is used to hedge the stock and render the portfolio riskless. In the Heston model, however, an additional derivative is required in the portfolio, to hedge the volatility. Hence, we form a portfolio consisting of one option $V = V(S, v, t)$, Δ units of the stock, and φ units of another option $U(S, v, t)$ for the volatility hedge. The portfolio has value

$$
\Pi = V + \Delta S + \varphi U
$$

where the t subscripts are omitted for convenience. Assuming the portfolio is self-financing, the change in portfolio value is

$$
d\Pi = dV + \Delta dS + \varphi dU. \tag{1.17}
$$

The strategy is similar to that for the Black-Scholes case. We apply Itō's lemma to obtain the processes for U and V, which allows us to find the process for Π. We then find the values of Δ and φ that makes the portfolio riskless, and we use the result to derive the Heston PDE.

Setting Up the Hedging Portfolio

To form the hedging portfolio, first apply Itō's lemma to the value of the first derivative, $V(S, v, t)$. We must differentiate V with respect to the variables t, S, and v, and form a second-order Taylor series expansion. The result is that dV follows the process

$$\begin{aligned} dV = {} & \frac{\partial V}{\partial t}dt + \frac{\partial V}{\partial S}dS + \frac{\partial V}{\partial v}dv + \frac{1}{2}vS^2\frac{\partial^2 V}{\partial S^2}dt \\ & + \frac{1}{2}v\sigma^2\frac{\partial^2 V}{\partial v^2}dt + \sigma\rho vS\frac{\partial^2 V}{\partial S\partial v}dt. \end{aligned} \tag{1.18}$$

We have used the fact that $(dS)^2 = vS^2(dW_1)^2 = vS^2dt$, that $(dv)^2 = \sigma^2 vdt$, and that $dSdv = \sigma vSdW_1dW_2 = \sigma\rho vSdt$. We have also used $(dt)^2 = 0$ and $dW_1dt = dW_2dt = 0$. Applying Itō's lemma to the second derivative, $U(S, v, t)$, produces an expression identical to (1.18), but in terms of U. Substituting these two expressions into (1.17), the change in portfolio value can be written

$$\begin{aligned} d\Pi &= dV + \Delta dS + \varphi dU \\ &= \left[\frac{\partial V}{\partial t} + \frac{1}{2}vS^2\frac{\partial^2 V}{\partial S^2} + \rho\sigma vS\frac{\partial^2 V}{\partial v\partial S} + \frac{1}{2}\sigma^2 v\frac{\partial^2 V}{\partial v^2}\right]dt \\ &\quad + \varphi\left[\frac{\partial U}{\partial t} + \frac{1}{2}vS^2\frac{\partial^2 U}{\partial S^2} + \rho\sigma vS\frac{\partial^2 U}{\partial v\partial S} + \frac{1}{2}\sigma^2 v\frac{\partial^2 U}{\partial v^2}\right]dt \\ &\quad + \left[\frac{\partial V}{\partial S} + \varphi\frac{\partial U}{\partial S} + \Delta\right]dS + \left[\frac{\partial V}{\partial v} + \varphi\frac{\partial U}{\partial v}\right]dv. \end{aligned} \tag{1.19}$$

In order for the portfolio to be hedged against movements in both the stock and volatility, the last two terms in Equation (1.19) must be zero. This implies that the hedge parameters must be

$$\varphi = -\frac{\partial V}{\partial v}\Big/\frac{\partial U}{\partial v}, \qquad \Delta = -\varphi\frac{\partial U}{\partial S} - \frac{\partial V}{\partial S}. \tag{1.20}$$

Substitute these values of φ and Δ into (1.19) to produce

$$\begin{aligned} d\Pi = {} & \left[\frac{\partial V}{\partial t} + \frac{1}{2}vS^2\frac{\partial^2 V}{\partial S^2} + \rho\sigma vS\frac{\partial^2 V}{\partial S\partial v} + \frac{1}{2}\sigma^2 v\frac{\partial^2 V}{\partial v^2}\right]dt \\ & + \varphi\left[\frac{\partial U}{\partial t} + \frac{1}{2}vS^2\frac{\partial^2 U}{\partial S^2} + \rho\sigma vS\frac{\partial^2 U}{\partial S\partial v} + \frac{1}{2}\sigma^2 v\frac{\partial^2 U}{\partial v^2}\right]dt. \end{aligned} \tag{1.21}$$

The condition that the portfolio earn the risk-free rate, r, implies that the change in portfolio value is $d\Pi = r\Pi dt$. Equation (1.17) thus becomes

$$d\Pi = r(V + \Delta S + \varphi U)dt. \tag{1.22}$$

Now equate Equation (1.22) with (1.21), substitute for φ and Δ, drop the dt term and re-arrange. This yields

$$\frac{\left[\frac{\partial V}{\partial t}+\frac{1}{2}vS^2\frac{\partial^2 V}{\partial S^2}+\rho\sigma vS\frac{\partial^2 V}{\partial S\partial v}+\frac{1}{2}\sigma^2 v\frac{\partial^2 V}{\partial v^2}\right]-rV+rS\frac{\partial V}{\partial S}}{\frac{\partial V}{\partial v}}$$
$$=\frac{\left[\frac{\partial U}{\partial t}+\frac{1}{2}vS^2\frac{\partial^2 U}{\partial S^2}+\rho\sigma vS\frac{\partial^2 U}{\partial S\partial v}+\frac{1}{2}\sigma^2 v\frac{\partial^2 U}{\partial v^2}\right]-rU+rS\frac{\partial U}{\partial S}}{\frac{\partial U}{\partial v}} \tag{1.23}$$

which we exploit in the next section.

The PDE for the Option Price

The left-hand side of Equation (1.23) is a function of V only, and the right-hand side is a function of U only. This implies that both sides can be written as a function $f(S, v, t)$. Following Heston (1993), specify this function as

$$f(S, v, t) = -\kappa(\theta - v) + \lambda(S, v, t)$$

where $\lambda(S, v, t)$ is the price of volatility risk. An application of Breeden's (1979) consumption model yields a price of volatility risk that is a linear function of volatility, so that $\lambda(S, v, t) = \lambda v$, where λ is a constant. Substitute for $f(S, v, t)$ in the left-hand side of Equation (1.23)

$$-\kappa\,(\theta - v) + \lambda(S, v, t)$$
$$=\frac{\left[\frac{\partial U}{\partial t}+\frac{1}{2}vS^2\frac{\partial^2 U}{\partial S^2}+\rho\sigma vS\frac{\partial^2 U}{\partial S\partial v}+\frac{1}{2}\sigma^2 v\frac{\partial^2 U}{\partial v^2}\right]-rU+rS\frac{\partial U}{\partial S}}{\frac{\partial U}{\partial v}}$$

Rearrange to produce the Heston PDE expressed in terms of the price S

$$\begin{aligned}&\frac{\partial U}{\partial t}+\frac{1}{2}vS^2\frac{\partial^2 U}{\partial S^2}+\rho\sigma vS\frac{\partial^2 U}{\partial v\partial S}+\frac{1}{2}\sigma^2 v\frac{\partial^2 U}{\partial v^2}\\&-rU+rS\frac{\partial U}{\partial S}+[\kappa(\theta-v)-\lambda(S,v,t)]\frac{\partial U}{\partial v}=0.\end{aligned} \tag{1.24}$$

This is Equation (6) of Heston (1993).

The following boundary conditions on the PDE in Equation (1.24) hold for a European call option with maturity T and strike K. At maturity, the call is worth its intrinsic value

$$U(S, v, T) = \max(0, S - K). \tag{1.25}$$

When the stock price is zero, the call is worthless. As the stock price increases, delta approaches one, and when the volatility increases, the call option becomes equal to the stock price. This implies the following three boundary conditions

$$U(0, v, t) = 0, \quad \frac{\partial U}{\partial S}(\infty, v, t) = 1, \quad U(S, \infty, t) = S. \tag{1.26}$$

Finally, note that the PDE (1.24) can be written

$$\frac{\partial U}{\partial t} + \mathcal{A}U - rU = 0 \tag{1.27}$$

where

$$\begin{aligned}\mathcal{A} &= rS\frac{\partial}{\partial S} + \frac{1}{2}vS^2\frac{\partial^2}{\partial S^2} \\ &+ [\kappa(\theta - v) - \lambda(S,v,t)]\frac{\partial}{\partial v} + \frac{1}{2}\sigma^2 v\frac{\partial^2}{\partial v^2} + \rho\sigma vS\frac{\partial^2}{\partial S\partial v}\end{aligned} \tag{1.28}$$

is the generator of the Heston model. As explained by Lewis (2000), the first line in Equation (1.28) is the generator of the Black-Scholes model, with $v = \sqrt{\sigma_{BS}}$, where σ_{BS} is the Black-Scholes volatility. The second line augments the PDE for stochastic volatility.

We can define the log price $x = \ln S$ and express the PDE in terms of (x, v, t) instead of (S, v, t). This leads to a simpler form of the PDE in which the spot price S does not appear. This simplification requires the following derivatives. By the chain rule

$$\frac{\partial U}{\partial S} = \frac{\partial U}{\partial x}\frac{1}{S}, \qquad \frac{\partial^2 U}{\partial v \partial S} = \frac{\partial}{\partial v}\left(\frac{1}{S}\frac{\partial U}{\partial x}\right) = \frac{1}{S}\frac{\partial^2 U}{\partial v \partial x}.$$

Using the product rule,

$$\frac{\partial^2 U}{\partial S^2} = \frac{\partial}{\partial S}\left(\frac{1}{S}\frac{\partial U}{\partial x}\right) = -\frac{1}{S^2}\frac{\partial U}{\partial x} + \frac{1}{S}\frac{\partial^2 U}{\partial S \partial x} = -\frac{1}{S^2}\frac{\partial U}{\partial x} + \frac{1}{S^2}\frac{\partial^2 U}{\partial x^2}.$$

Substitute these expressions into the Heston PDE in (1.24). All the S terms cancel, and we obtain the Heston PDE in terms of the log price $x = \ln S$

$$\begin{aligned}&\frac{\partial U}{\partial t} + \frac{1}{2}v\frac{\partial^2 U}{\partial x^2} + \left(r - \frac{1}{2}v\right)\frac{\partial U}{\partial x} + \rho\sigma v\frac{\partial^2 U}{\partial v \partial x} \\ &+ \frac{1}{2}\sigma^2 v\frac{\partial^2 U}{\partial v^2} - rU + [\kappa(\theta - v) - \lambda v]\frac{\partial U}{\partial v} = 0\end{aligned} \tag{1.29}$$

where we have substituted $\lambda(S, v, t) = \lambda v$. The modern approach to obtaining the PDE in (1.29) is by an application of the Feynman-Kac theorem, which we will encounter in Chapter 12 in the context of the double Heston model of Christoffersen et al. (2009).

The PDE for P_1 and P_2

Recall Equation (1.16) for the European call price, written here using $x = x_t = \ln S_t$

$$C(K) = e^x P_1 - Ke^{-r\tau}P_2. \tag{1.30}$$

Equation (1.30) expresses $C(K)$ in terms of the in-the-money probabilities $P_1 = \mathbb{Q}^S(S_T > K)$ and $P_2 = \mathbb{Q}(S_T > K)$. Since the European call satisfies the PDE (1.29), we can find the required derivatives of Equation (1.30), substitute them into the PDE, and express the PDE in terms of P_1 and P_2. The derivative of $C(K)$ with respect to t is

$$\frac{\partial C}{\partial t} = e^x \frac{\partial P_1}{\partial t} - Ke^{-r\tau}\left[rP_2 + \frac{\partial P_2}{\partial t}\right]. \tag{1.31}$$

With respect to x

$$\frac{\partial C}{\partial x} = e^x \left[P_1 + \frac{\partial P_1}{\partial x}\right] - Ke^{-r\tau}\frac{\partial P_2}{\partial x}. \tag{1.32}$$

With respect to x^2

$$\begin{aligned}\frac{\partial^2 C}{\partial x^2} &= e^x P_1 + 2e^x \frac{\partial P_1}{\partial x} + e^x \frac{\partial^2 P_1}{\partial x^2} - Ke^{-r\tau}\frac{\partial^2 P_2}{\partial x^2} \\ &= e^x\left[P_1 + 2\frac{\partial P_1}{\partial x} + \frac{\partial^2 P_1}{\partial x^2}\right] - Ke^{-r\tau}\frac{\partial^2 P_2}{\partial x^2}.\end{aligned} \tag{1.33}$$

With respect to v, and v^2

$$\frac{\partial C}{\partial v} = e^x \frac{\partial P_1}{\partial v} - Ke^{-r\tau}\frac{\partial P_2}{\partial v}, \quad \frac{\partial^2 C}{\partial v^2} = e^x \frac{\partial^2 P_1}{\partial v^2} - Ke^{-r\tau}\frac{\partial^2 P_2}{\partial v^2}. \tag{1.34}$$

With respect to v and x

$$\frac{\partial^2 C}{\partial x \partial v} = e^x\left[\frac{\partial P_1}{\partial v} + \frac{\partial^2 P_1}{\partial x \partial v}\right] - Ke^{-r\tau}\frac{\partial^2 P_2}{\partial x \partial v}. \tag{1.35}$$

As mentioned earlier, since the European call $C(K)$ is a financial derivative, it also satisfies the Heston PDE in (1.29), which we write here in terms of $C(K)$

$$\begin{aligned}&\frac{\partial C}{\partial t} + \frac{1}{2}v\frac{\partial^2 C}{\partial x^2} + \left(r - \frac{1}{2}v\right)\frac{\partial C}{\partial x} + \rho\sigma v\frac{\partial^2 C}{\partial v \partial x} \\ &+ \frac{1}{2}\sigma^2 v\frac{\partial^2 C}{\partial v^2} - rC + [\kappa(\theta - v) - \lambda v]\frac{\partial C}{\partial v} = 0.\end{aligned} \tag{1.36}$$

To obtain the Heston PDE for P_1 and P_2, Heston (1993) argues that the PDE in (1.36) holds for any contractual features of $C(K)$, in particular, for any strike price $K \geq 0$, for any value of $S \geq 0$, and for any value $r \geq 0$ of the risk-free rate. Setting $K = 0$ and $S = 1$ in the call price in Equation (1.12) produces an option whose price is simply P_1. This option will also follow the PDE in (1.36). Similarly, setting $S = 0$, $K = 1$, and $r = 0$ in (1.12) produces an option whose price is $-P_2$. Since $-P_2$ follows the PDE, so does P_2.

In Equations (1.31) through (1.35), regroup terms common to P_1, cancel e^x, and substitute the terms into the PDE in (1.36) to obtain

$$\begin{aligned}&\frac{\partial P_1}{\partial t} + \frac{1}{2}v\left[P_1 + 2\frac{\partial P_1}{\partial x} + \frac{\partial^2 P_1}{\partial x^2}\right] + \left(r - \frac{1}{2}v\right)\left[P_1 + \frac{\partial P_1}{\partial x}\right] + \rho\sigma v\left[\frac{\partial P_1}{\partial v} + \frac{\partial^2 P_1}{\partial x \partial v}\right] \\ &+ \frac{1}{2}\sigma^2 v\frac{\partial^2 P_1}{\partial v^2} - rP_1 + [\kappa(\theta - v) - \lambda v]\frac{\partial P_1}{\partial v} = 0.\end{aligned} \tag{1.37}$$

Simplifying, (1.37) becomes

$$\begin{aligned}&\frac{\partial P_1}{\partial t}+\left(r+\frac{1}{2}v\right)\frac{\partial P_1}{\partial x}+\frac{1}{2}v\frac{\partial^2 P_1}{\partial x^2}+\rho\sigma v\frac{\partial^2 P_1}{\partial x\partial v}\\&+[\rho\sigma v+\kappa(\theta-v)-\lambda v]\frac{\partial P_1}{\partial v}+\frac{1}{2}\sigma^2 v\frac{\partial^2 P_1}{\partial v^2}=0.\end{aligned}\tag{1.38}$$

Similarly, in Equations (1.31) through (1.35) regroup terms common to P_2, cancel $-Ke^{-r\tau}$, and substitute the terms into the PDE in Equation (1.36) to obtain

$$\begin{aligned}&\frac{\partial P_2}{\partial t}+\frac{1}{2}v\frac{\partial^2 P_2}{\partial x^2}+\left(r-\frac{1}{2}v\right)\frac{\partial P_2}{\partial x}+\rho\sigma v\frac{\partial^2 P_2}{\partial v\partial x}\\&+\frac{1}{2}\sigma^2 v\frac{\partial^2 P_2}{\partial v^2}+[\kappa(\theta-v)-\lambda v]\frac{\partial P_2}{\partial v}=0.\end{aligned}\tag{1.39}$$

For notational convenience, combine Equations (1.38) and (1.39) into a single expression

$$\begin{aligned}&\frac{\partial P_j}{\partial t}+\rho\sigma v\frac{\partial^2 P_j}{\partial v\partial x}+\frac{1}{2}v\frac{\partial^2 P_j}{\partial x^2}+\frac{1}{2}\sigma^2 v\frac{\partial^2 P_j}{\partial v^2}\\&+(r+u_j v)\frac{\partial P_j}{\partial x}+(a-b_j v)\frac{\partial P_j}{\partial v}=0\end{aligned}\tag{1.40}$$

for $j=1,2$ and where $u_1=\frac{1}{2}$, $u_2=-\frac{1}{2}$, $a=\kappa\theta$, $b_1=\kappa+\lambda-\rho\sigma$, and $b_2=\kappa+\lambda$. This is Equation (12) of Heston (1993).

OBTAINING THE HESTON CHARACTERISTIC FUNCTIONS

When the characteristic functions $f_j(\phi;x,v)$ are known, each in-the-money probability P_j can be recovered from the characteristic function via the Gil-Pelaez (1951) inversion theorem, as

$$P_j=\Pr(\ln S_T>\ln K)=\frac{1}{2}+\frac{1}{\pi}\int_0^\infty \mathrm{Re}\left[\frac{e^{-i\phi\ln K}f_j(\phi;x,v)}{i\phi}\right]d\phi.\tag{1.41}$$

Inversion theorems can be found in many textbooks, such as that by Stuart (2010). The inversion theorem in (1.41) will be demonstrated in Chapter 3. A discussion of how the theorem relates to option pricing in stochastic volatility models appears in Jondeau et al. (2007).

At maturity, the probabilities are subject to the terminal condition

$$P_j=\mathbf{1}_{x_T>\ln K}\tag{1.42}$$

where $\mathbf{1}$ is the indicator function. Equation (1.42) simply states that, when $S_T>K$ at expiry, the probability of the call being in-the-money is unity. Heston (1993) postulates that the characteristic functions for the logarithm of the terminal stock price, $x_T=\ln S_T$, are of the log linear form

$$f_j(\phi;x_t,v_t)=\exp(C_j(\tau,\phi)+D_j(\tau,\phi)v_t+i\phi x_t)\tag{1.43}$$

where $i = \sqrt{-1}$ is the imaginary, unit, C_j and D_j are coefficients and $\tau = T - t$ is the time to maturity.

The characteristic functions f_j will follow the PDE in Equation (1.40). This is a consequence of the Feynman-Kac theorem, which stipulates that, if a function $f(\mathbf{x}_t, t)$ of the Heston bivariate system of SDEs $\mathbf{x}_t = (x_t, v_t) = (\ln S_t, v_t)$ satisfies the PDE $\partial f / \partial t - rf + \mathcal{A}f = 0$, where $\mathcal{A}$ is the Heston generator from (1.28), then the solution to $f(\mathbf{x}_t, t)$ is the conditional expectation

$$f(\mathbf{x}_t, t) = E[f(\mathbf{x}_T, T)|\mathcal{F}_t].$$

Using $f(\mathbf{x}_t, t) = \exp(i\phi \ln S_t)$ produces the solution

$$f(\mathbf{x}_t, t) = E[e^{i\phi \ln S_T}|x_t, v_t]$$

which is the characteristic function for $x_T = \ln S_T$. Hence, the PDE for the characteristic function is, from Equation (1.40)

$$\begin{aligned} &-\frac{\partial f_j}{\partial \tau} + \rho\sigma v \frac{\partial^2 f_j}{\partial v \partial x} + \frac{1}{2} v \frac{\partial^2 f_j}{\partial x^2} + \frac{1}{2}\sigma^2 v \frac{\partial^2 f_j}{\partial v^2} \\ &+ (r + u_j v)\frac{\partial f_j}{\partial x} + (a - b_j v)\frac{\partial f_j}{\partial v} = 0. \end{aligned} \tag{1.44}$$

Note the transformation from t to τ, which explains the negative sign in front of the first term in the PDE (1.44). The following derivatives are required to evaluate (1.44)

$$\begin{aligned} &\frac{\partial f_j}{\partial \tau} = \left(\frac{\partial C_j}{\partial \tau} + \frac{\partial D_j}{\partial \tau} v\right) f_j, \quad \frac{\partial f_j}{\partial x} = i\phi f_j, \quad \frac{\partial f_j}{\partial v} = D_j f_j, \\ &\frac{\partial^2 f_j}{\partial x^2} = -\phi^2 f_j, \quad \frac{\partial^2 f_j}{\partial v^2} = D_j^2 f_j, \quad \frac{\partial^2 f_j}{\partial v \partial x} = i\phi D_j f_j. \end{aligned}$$

Substitute these derivatives into (1.44) and drop the f_j terms to obtain

$$\begin{aligned} &-\left(\frac{\partial C_j}{\partial \tau} + v\frac{\partial D_j}{\partial \tau}\right) + \rho\sigma v i\phi D_j - \frac{1}{2} v\phi^2 + \frac{1}{2} v\sigma^2 D_j^2 \\ &+ (r + u_j v)i\phi + (a - b_j v)D_j = 0, \end{aligned} \tag{1.45}$$

or equivalently

$$v\left(-\frac{\partial D_j}{\partial \tau} + \rho\sigma i\phi D_j - \frac{1}{2}\phi^2 + \frac{1}{2}\sigma^2 D_j^2 + u_j i\phi - b_j D_j\right) - \frac{\partial C_j}{\partial \tau} + ri\phi + aD_j = 0. \tag{1.46}$$

This produces two differential equations

$$\begin{aligned} \frac{\partial D_j}{\partial \tau} &= \rho\sigma i\phi D_j - \frac{1}{2}\phi^2 + \frac{1}{2}\sigma^2 D_j^2 + u_j i\phi - b_j D_j \\ \frac{\partial C_j}{\partial \tau} &= ri\phi + aD_j. \end{aligned} \tag{1.47}$$

These are Equations (A7) in Heston (1993). The first equation in (1.47) is a Riccati equation in D_j, while the second is an ordinary derivative for C_j that can solved using straightforward integration once D_j is obtained. Solving these equations requires two initial conditions. Recall from (1.43) that the characteristic function is

$$f_j(\phi; x_t, v_t) = E[e^{i\phi x_T}] = \exp(C_j(\tau, \phi) + D_j(\tau, \phi)v_t + i\phi x_t). \tag{1.48}$$

At maturity ($\tau = 0$), the value of $x_T = \ln S_T$ is known, so the expectation in (1.48) will disappear, and consequently the right-hand side will reduce to simply $\exp(i\phi x_T)$. This implies that the initial conditions at maturity are $D_j(0, \phi) = 0$ and $C_j(0, \phi) = 0$.

Finally, when we compute the characteristic function, we use x_t as the log spot price of the underlying asset, and v_t as its unobserved initial variance. This last quantity is the parameter v_0 described earlier in this chapter, and must be estimated. We sometimes write (x_0, v_0) for (x_t, v_t), or simply (x, v).

SOLVING THE HESTON RICCATI EQUATION

In this section, we explain how the expressions in Equation (1.47) can be solved to yield the call price. First, we introduce the Riccati equation and explain how its solution is obtained. The solution can be found in many textbooks on differential equations, such as that by Zwillinger (1997).

The Riccati Equation in a General Setting

The Riccati equation for $y(t)$ with coefficients $P(t)$, $Q(t)$, and $R(t)$ is defined as

$$\frac{dy(t)}{dt} = P(t) + Q(t)y(t) + R(t)y(t)^2. \tag{1.49}$$

The equation can be solved by considering the following second-order ordinary differential equation (ODE) for $w(t)$

$$w'' - \left[\frac{P'}{P} + Q\right]w' + PRw = 0 \tag{1.50}$$

which can be written $w'' + bw' + cw = 0$. The solution to Equation (1.49) is then

$$y(t) = -\frac{w'(t)}{w(t)}\frac{1}{R(t)}.$$

The ODE in (1.50) can be solved via the auxiliary equation $r^2 + br + c = 0$, which has two solutions α and β given by

$$\alpha = \frac{-b + \sqrt{b^2 - 4c}}{2}, \quad \beta = \frac{-b - \sqrt{b^2 - 4c}}{2}.$$

The solution to the second-order ODE in (1.50) is

$$w(t) = Me^{\alpha t} + Ne^{\beta t}$$

where M and N are constants. The solution to the Riccati equation is therefore

$$y(t) = -\frac{M\alpha e^{\alpha t} + N\beta e^{\beta t}}{Me^{\alpha t} + Ne^{\beta t}} \frac{1}{R(t)}.$$

Solution of the Heston Riccati Equation

From Equation (1.47), the Heston Riccati equation can be written

$$\frac{\partial D_j}{\partial \tau} = P_j - Q_j D_j + RD_j^2 \tag{1.51}$$

where

$$P_j = u_j i\phi - \frac{1}{2}\phi^2, \quad Q_j = b_j - \rho\sigma i\phi, \quad R = \frac{1}{2}\sigma^2. \tag{1.52}$$

The corresponding second-order ODE is

$$w'' + Q_j w' + P_j R w = 0 \tag{1.53}$$

so that $D_j = -\frac{1}{R}\frac{w'}{w}$. The auxiliary equation is $r^2 + Q_j r + P_j R = 0$, which has roots

$$\alpha_j = \frac{-Q_j + \sqrt{Q_j^2 - 4P_jR}}{2} = \frac{-Q_j + d_j}{2}$$

$$\beta_j = \frac{-Q_j - \sqrt{Q_j^2 - 4P_jR}}{2} = \frac{-Q_j - d_j}{2}$$

where

$$\begin{aligned} d_j &= \alpha_j - \beta_j = \sqrt{Q_j^2 - 4P_jR} \\ &= \sqrt{(\rho\sigma i\phi - b_j)^2 - \sigma^2(2u_j i\phi - \phi^2)}. \end{aligned} \tag{1.54}$$

For notational simplicity, we sometimes omit the "j" subscript on some of the variables. The solution to the Heston Riccati equation is therefore

$$D_j = -\frac{1}{R}\frac{w'}{w} = -\frac{1}{R}\left(\frac{M\alpha e^{\alpha\tau} + N\beta e^{\beta\tau}}{Me^{\alpha\tau} + Ne^{\beta\tau}}\right) = -\frac{1}{R}\left(\frac{K\alpha e^{\alpha\tau} + \beta e^{\beta\tau}}{Ke^{\alpha\tau} + e^{\beta\tau}}\right) \tag{1.55}$$

where $K = M/N$. The initial condition $D_j(0,\phi) = 0$ implies that, when $\tau = 0$ is substituted in (1.55), the numerator becomes $K\alpha + \beta = 0$, from which $K = -\beta/\alpha$. The solution for D_j becomes

$$\begin{aligned} D_j &= -\frac{\beta}{R}\left(\frac{-e^{\alpha\tau} + e^{\beta\tau}}{-g_j e^{\alpha\tau} + e^{\beta\tau}}\right) = -\frac{\beta}{R}\left(\frac{1 - e^{d_j\tau}}{1 - g_j e^{d_j\tau}}\right) \\ &= \frac{Q_j + d_j}{2R}\left(\frac{1 - e^{d_j\tau}}{1 - g_j e^{d_j\tau}}\right) \end{aligned} \tag{1.56}$$

where

$$g_j = -K = \frac{\beta}{\alpha} = \frac{b_j - \rho\sigma i\phi + d_j}{b_j - \rho\sigma i\phi - d_j} = \frac{Q_j - d_j}{Q_j + d_j}. \tag{1.57}$$

The solution for D_j can, therefore, be written

$$D_j(\tau,\phi) = \frac{b_j - \rho\sigma i\phi + d_j}{\sigma^2}\left(\frac{1-e^{d_j\tau}}{1-g_je^{d_j\tau}}\right). \tag{1.58}$$

The solution for C_j is found by integrating the second equation in (1.47)

$$C_j = \int_0^\tau ri\phi dy + a\left(\frac{Q_j+d_j}{\sigma^2}\right)\int_0^\tau\left(\frac{1-e^{d_jy}}{1-g_je^{d_jy}}\right)dy + K_1 \tag{1.59}$$

where K_1 is a constant. The first integral is $ri\phi\tau$ and the second integral can be found by substitution, using $x = \exp(d_jy)$, from which $dx = d_j\exp(d_jy)dy$ and $dy = dx/(xd_j)$. Equation (1.59) becomes

$$C_j = ri\phi\tau + \frac{a}{d_j}\left(\frac{Q_j+d_j}{\sigma^2}\right)\int_1^{\exp(d_j\tau)}\left(\frac{1-x}{1-g_jx}\right)\frac{1}{x}dx + K_1. \tag{1.60}$$

The integral in (1.60) can be evaluated by partial fractions

$$\begin{aligned}\int_1^{\exp(d_j\tau)}\frac{1-x}{x(1-g_jx)}dx &= \int_1^{\exp(d_j\tau)}\left[\frac{1}{x} - \frac{1-g_j}{1-g_jx}\right]dx \\ &= \left[\ln x + \frac{1-g_j}{g_j}\ln(1-g_jx)\right]_{x=1}^{x=\exp(d_j\tau)} \\ &= \left[d_j\tau + \frac{1-g_j}{g_j}\ln\left(\frac{1-g_je^{d_j\tau}}{1-g_j}\right)\right].\end{aligned} \tag{1.61}$$

Substituting the integral back into (1.60), and substituting for d_j, Q_j, and g_j, produces the solution for C_j

$$C_j(\tau,\phi) = ri\phi\tau + \frac{a}{\sigma^2}\left[(b_j - \rho\sigma i\phi + d_j)\tau - 2\ln\left(\frac{1-g_je^{d_j\tau}}{1-g_j}\right)\right] \tag{1.62}$$

where $a = \kappa\theta$. Note that we have used the initial condition $C_j(0,\phi) = 0$, which results in $K_1 = 0$. This completes the original derivation of the Heston model.

We use two functions to implement the model in Matlab, HestonProb.m and HestonPrice.m. The first function calculates the characteristic functions and returns the real part of the integrand. The function allows for the Albrecher et al. (2007) "Little Trap" formulation for the characteristic function, which is introduced in Chapter 2. The functions allow to price calls or puts, and allow for a dividend yield, as explained in the following section. To conserve space parts of the functions have been omitted.

```
function y = HestonProb(phi,...,Trap);
x = log(S);
a = kappa*theta;
d = sqrt((rho*sigma*i*phi - b)^2 - sigma^2*(2*u*i*phi - phi^2));
g = (b - rho*sigma*i*phi + d) / (b - rho*sigma*i*phi - d);
if Trap==1
    c = 1/g;
    D = (b - rho*sigma*i*phi - d)/sigma^2*((1-exp(-d*tau)) ...;
    G = (1 - c*exp(-d*tau))/(1-c);
    C = (r-q)*i*phi*tau + a/sigma^2*((b-rho*sigma*i*phi-d)...;
elseif Trap==0
    G = (1 - g*exp(d*tau))/(1-g);
    C = (r-q)*i*phi*tau + a/sigma^2*((b - rho*sigma*i*phi + d) ...;
    D = (b - rho*sigma*i*phi + d)/sigma^2*((1-exp(d*tau)) ...;
end
f = exp(C + D*v0 + i*phi*x);
y = real(exp(-i*phi*log(K))*f/i/phi);
```

The second function calculates the price of a European call $C(K)$, or European put $P(K)$, by put-call parity in Equation (1.67). The function calls the HestonProb.m function at every point of the integration grid and uses the trapezoidal rule for integration when all the integration points have been calculated, using the built-in Matlab function trapz.m. Chapter 5 presents alternate numerical integration schemes that do not rely on built-in Matlab functions.

```
function y = HestonPrice(PutCall,...,trap,Lphi,Uphi,dphi)
phi = [Lphi:dphi:Uphi];
N = length(PHI);
for k=1:N;
    int1(k) = HestonProb(phi(k),...,1);
    int2(k) = HestonProb(phi(k),...,2,);
end
I1 = trapz(int1)*dphi;
I2 = trapz(int2)*dphi;
P1 = 1/2 + 1/pi*I1;
P2 = 1/2 + 1/pi*I2;
HestonC = S*exp(-q*T)*P1 - K*exp(-r*T)*P2;
HestonP = HestonC - S*exp(-q*T) + K*exp(-r*T);
```

Pricing European calls and puts is straightforward. For example, the price a 6-month European put with strike $K = 100$ on a dividend-paying stock with spot price $S = 100$ and yield $q = 0.02$, when the risk-free rate is $r = 0.03$ and using the parameters $\kappa = 5$, $\sigma = 0.5$, $\rho = -0.8$, $\theta = v_0 = 0.05$, and $\lambda = 0$, along with the integration grid $\phi \in [0.00001, 50]$ in increments of 0.001 is 5.7590. The price of the call with identical features is 6.2528. If there is no dividend yield so that $q = 0$, then as expected, the put price decreases, to 5.3790, and the call price increases, to 6.8678.

Some applications require Matlab code for the Heston characteristic function. The HestonProb.m function can be modified to return the characteristic function itself, instead of the integrand. In certain instances, the integrand for P_j

$$\text{Re}\left[\frac{e^{-i\phi\ln K}f_j(\phi; x, v)}{i\phi}\right] \tag{1.63}$$

is well-behaved in that it poses no difficulties in numerical integration. This corresponds to an integrand that does not oscillate much, that dampens quickly so that a large upper limit in the numerical integration is not required, and that does not contain portions that are excessively steep. In other instances, the integrand is not well-behaved, and numerical integration loses precision. To illustrate, we plot the second integrand ($j = 2$) in Equation (1.63), using the settings $S = 7$, $K = 10$, and $r = q = 0$, with parameter values $\kappa = 10$, $\theta = v_0 = 0.07$, $\sigma = 0.3$, and $\rho = -0.9$. The plot uses the domain $-50 < \phi < 50$ over maturities running from 1 week to 3 months. This plot appears in Figure 1.1. The integrand has a discontinuity at $\phi = 0$, but this does not show up in the figure.

The plot indicates an integrand that has a fair amount of oscillation, especially at short maturities, and that is steep near the origin. In Chapter 2, we investigate other problems that can arise with the Heston integrand.

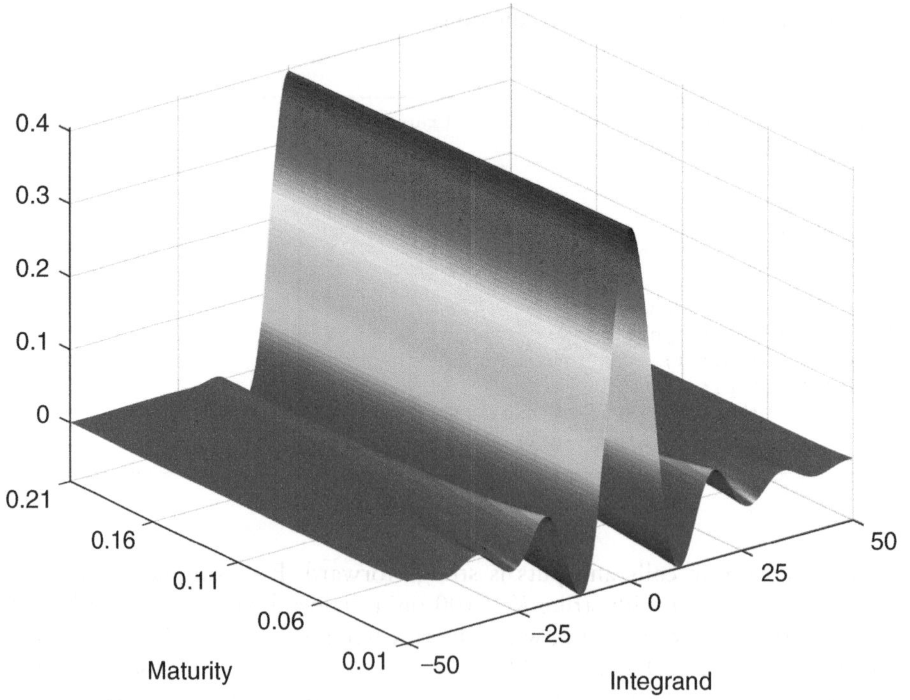

FIGURE 1.1 Heston Integrand and Maturity

DIVIDEND YIELD AND THE PUT PRICE

It is straightforward to include dividends into the model if it can be assumed that the dividend payment is a continuous yield, q. In that case, r is replaced by $r - q$ in Equation (1.4) for the stock price process

$$dS_t = (r - q)S_t dt + \sqrt{v_t} S_t d\widetilde{W}_{1,t}. \tag{1.64}$$

The solution for C_j in Equation (1.62) becomes

$$C_j = (r - q)i\phi\tau + \frac{\kappa\theta}{\sigma^2}\left[(b_j - \rho\sigma i\phi + d_j)\tau - 2\ln\left(\frac{1 - g_j e^{d_j\tau}}{1 - g_j}\right)\right]. \tag{1.65}$$

To obtain the price $P(K)$ of a European put, first obtain the price $C(K)$ of a European call, using a slight modification of Equation (1.12) to include the term $e^{-q\tau}$ for the dividend yield, as explained by Whaley (2006)

$$C(K) = S_t e^{-q\tau} P_1 - K e^{-r\tau} P_2. \tag{1.66}$$

The put price is found by put-call parity

$$P(K) = C(K) + Ke^{-r\tau} - S_t e^{-q\tau}. \tag{1.67}$$

Alternatively, as in Zhu (2010) the put price can be obtained explicitly as

$$P(K) = Ke^{-r\tau} P_2^c - S_t e^{-q\tau} P_1^c. \tag{1.68}$$

The put expires in-the-money if $x_T < \ln K$. The in-the-money probabilities in (1.68) are, therefore, the complement of those in (1.41)

$$P_j^c = \Pr(\ln S_T < \ln K) = \frac{1}{2} - \frac{1}{\pi}\int_0^\infty \text{Re}\left[\frac{e^{-i\phi\ln K} f_j(\phi; x, v)}{i\phi}\right] d\phi. \tag{1.69}$$

It is straightforward to show the equivalence of Equations (1.67) and (1.68). Finally, by an application of the Feynman-Kac theorem, which will be introduced in Chapter 12, the PDE for $x = \ln S$ is

$$\begin{aligned} &\frac{\partial U}{\partial t} + \frac{1}{2}v\frac{\partial^2 U}{\partial x^2} + \left(r - q - \frac{1}{2}v\right)\frac{\partial U}{\partial x} + \rho\sigma v\frac{\partial^2 U}{\partial v \partial x} \\ &\quad + \frac{1}{2}\sigma^2 v\frac{\partial^2 U}{\partial v^2} - rU + [\kappa(\theta - v) - \lambda v]\frac{\partial U}{\partial v} = 0. \end{aligned} \tag{1.70}$$

Equation (1.70) is simply (1.29), but with $(r - v/2)$ in the third term replaced by $(r - q - v/2)$.

CONSOLIDATING THE INTEGRALS

It is possible to regroup the integrals for the probabilities P_1 and P_2 into a single integral, which will speed up the numerical integration required in the call price calculation. Substituting the expressions for P_j from Equation (1.41) into the call price in (1.66) and re-arranging produces

$$
\begin{aligned}
C(K) &= \frac{1}{2}S_t e^{-q\tau} - \frac{1}{2}Ke^{-r\tau} \\
&+ \frac{1}{\pi}\int_0^\infty \text{Re}\left[\frac{e^{-i\phi \ln K}}{i\phi}\left(S_t e^{-q\tau} f_1(\phi; x, v) - Ke^{-r\tau} f_2(\phi; x, v)\right)\right] d\phi.
\end{aligned}
\tag{1.71}
$$

The advantage of this consolidation is that only a single numerical integration is required instead of two, so the computation time will be reduced by almost one-half. The put price can be obtained by using put-call parity, with the call price calculated using (1.71).

The integrand of the consolidated form is in the function HestonProbConsol.m.

```
function y = HestonProbConsol(phi,...,Pnum,Trap);
% First characteristic function f1
u1 = 0.5;
b1 = kappa + lambda - rho*sigma;
d1 = sqrt((rho*sigma*i*phi - b1)^2 - sigma^2*(2*u1*i*phi - phi^2));
g1 = (b1 - rho*sigma*i*phi + d1) / (b1 - rho*sigma*i*phi - d1);
G1 = (1 - g1*exp(d1*tau))/(1-g1);
C1 = (r-q)*i*phi*tau + a/sigma^2 * ...;
D1 = (b1 - rho*sigma*i*phi + d1)/sigma^2 * ...;
f1 = exp(C1 + D1*v0 + i*phi*x);
% Second characteristic function f1
f2 = exp(C2 + D2*v0 + i*phi*x);
% Return the real part of the integrand
y = real(exp(-i*phi*log(K))/i/phi*(S*exp(-q*tau)*f1 - K*exp(-r*tau)*f2));
```

This function is then fed into the HestonPriceConsol.m function, which calculates the call price in accordance with Equation (1.71).

```
function y = HestonPriceConsol(PutCall,...,trap,Lphi,Uphi,dphi)
% Build the integration grid
phi = [Lphi:dphi:Uphi];
N = length(phi);
for k=1:N;
    inte(k) = HestonProbConsol(phi(k),...,1,trap);
end
I = trapz(inte)*dphi;
% The call price
HestonC = (1/2)*S*exp(-q*T) - (1/2)*K*exp(-r*T) + I/pi;
% The put price by put-call parity
HestonP = HestonC - S*exp(-q*T) + K*exp(-r*T);
```

The consolidated form produces exactly the same prices for the call and the put, but requires roughly one-half of the computation time only.

BLACK-SCHOLES AS A SPECIAL CASE

With a little manipulation, it is straightforward to show that the Black-Scholes model is nested inside the Heston model. The Black-Scholes model assumes the following dynamics for the underlying price S_t under the risk-neutral measure $\mathbb{Q}$

$$dS_t = rS_t + \sigma_{BS} S_t d\widetilde{W}_t. \tag{1.72}$$

It is shown in many textbooks, such as that by Hull (2011) or Chriss (1996) that (1.72) can be solved for the spot price S_t. This is done in two steps. First, apply Itō's lemma to obtain the process for $d \ln S_t$, which produces a stochastic process that is no longer an SDE since its drift and volatility no longer depend on S_t. Second, integrate the stochastic process to produce

$$S_t = S_0 \exp([r - \sigma_{BS}^2/2]t + \sigma_{BS} \widetilde{W}_t). \tag{1.73}$$

This implies that, at time t, the natural logarithm of the stock price at expiry $\ln S_T$ is distributed as a normal random variable with mean $\ln S_t + \left(r - \frac{1}{2}\sigma_{BS}^2\right)\tau$ and variance $\sigma_{BS}^2 \tau$, where $\tau = T - t$ is the time to expiry. Consequently, the characteristic function of $\ln S_T$ in the Black-Scholes model is

$$E[e^{i\phi \ln S_T}] = \exp\left(i\phi\left[\ln S_t + \left(r - \frac{1}{2}\sigma_{BS}^2\right)\tau\right] - \frac{1}{2}\phi^2 \sigma_{BS}^2 \tau\right). \tag{1.74}$$

The Black-Scholes PDE is

$$\frac{\partial U}{\partial t} + \frac{1}{2}\sigma_{BS}^2 S^2 \frac{\partial^2 U}{\partial S^2} + rS\frac{\partial U}{\partial S} - rU = 0. \tag{1.75}$$

The Black-Scholes call price is given by

$$C_{BS}(K) = S_t \Phi(d_1) - Ke^{-r\tau}\Phi(d_2) \tag{1.76}$$

with

$$\begin{aligned} d_1 &= \frac{\ln(S_t/K) + (r + \sigma_{BS}^2/2)\tau}{\sigma_{BS}\sqrt{\tau}}, \\ d_2 &= \frac{\ln(S_t/K) + (r - \sigma_{BS}^2/2)\tau}{\sigma_{BS}\sqrt{\tau}} = d_1 - \sigma_{BS}\sqrt{\tau} \end{aligned} \tag{1.77}$$

where $\Phi(x)$ is the standard normal cumulative distribution function. The volatility σ_{BS} is assumed to be constant.

If we set $\sigma = 0$, the volatility of variance parameter in the Heston model, then the Brownian component of the variance process in Equation (1.1) drops out. Consequently, from (1.11) we obtain $\text{Var}[v_t|v_0] = 0$. This will produce volatility that is time-varying, but deterministic. If we further set $\theta = v_0$, then from (1.11) we get $E[v_t|v_0] = v_0$, which is time independent. This will produce volatility that is constant. Hence, setting $\sigma = 0$ and $\theta = v_0$ in the Heston model leads us to expect the same price as that produced by the Black Scholes model, with $\sigma_{BS} = \sqrt{v_0}$ as the Black Scholes implied volatility. Indeed, substituting $\sigma = 0$ and $\theta = v_0$ into the Heston PDE (1.24) along with $\lambda = 0$ produces the Black-Scholes PDE in (1.75) with $\sigma_{BS} = \sqrt{v_0}$. Consequently, the Heston price under these parameter values will be the Black-Scholes price.

To implement the Black-Scholes model as a special case of the Heston model, we cannot simply substitute $\sigma = 0$ into the pricing functions, because that will lead to division by zero in the expressions for $C_j(\tau,\phi)$ in Equation (1.62) and $D_j(\tau,\phi)$ in (1.58). Instead, we must start with the set of equations in (1.47). With $\sigma = 0$, the Riccati equation in (1.51) reduces to the ordinary first-order differential equation

$$\frac{\partial D_j}{\partial \tau} = P_j - Q_j D_j,$$

where $P_j = u_j i\phi - \frac{1}{2}\phi^2$ and $Q_j = b_j$. The solution of this ODE is

$$D_j(\tau,\phi) = \frac{\left(u_j i\phi - \frac{1}{2}\phi^2\right)\left(1 - e^{-b_j\tau}\right)}{b_j}. \tag{1.78}$$

As for the general case $\sigma > 0$, substitute (1.78) into the expression for C_j in the second equation of (1.47) and integrate to obtain

$$\begin{aligned} C_j(\tau,\phi) &= ri\phi\tau + a\int_0^\tau \frac{\left(u_j i\phi - \frac{1}{2}\phi^2\right)\left(1 - e^{-b_j y}\right)}{b_j} dy + K_1 \\ &= ri\phi\tau + \frac{a\left(u_j i\phi - \frac{1}{2}\phi^2\right)}{b_j}\left[\tau - \frac{\left(1 - e^{-b_j\tau}\right)}{b_j}\right] \end{aligned} \tag{1.79}$$

where the initial condition $C_j(0,\phi) = 0$ has been applied, which produces $K_1 = 0$ for the integration constant. Now substitute C_j and D_j from Equations (1.79) and (1.78) into the characteristic function in (1.43), and proceed exactly as in the case $\sigma > 0$. Note that the correlation coefficient, ρ, no longer appears in the expressions for C_j and D_j, which is sensible since it is no longer relevant.

Now consider the case $j = 2$. Substitute for $u_2 = -\frac{1}{2}$ and $b_2 = \kappa$ (with $\lambda = 0$) in Equations (1.78) and (1.79), set $\theta = v_0$, and substitute the resulting expressions for $D_2(\tau,\phi)$ and $C_2(\tau,\phi)$ into the characteristic function in (1.48). The second characteristic function is reduced to

$$f_2(\phi) = \exp\left(i\phi\left[x_0 + \left(r - \frac{1}{2}v_0\right)\tau\right] - \frac{1}{2}\phi^2 v_0\tau\right) \tag{1.80}$$

where $x_0 = \ln S_0$ is the log spot stock price and v_0 is the spot variance (at $t = 0$). Equation (1.80) is recognized to be (1.74), the characteristic function of $x_T = \ln S_T$ under the Black-Scholes model, with the Black-Scholes volatility as $\sigma_{BS} = \sqrt{v_0}$, as required by (1.77).

The Black-Scholes call price can also be derived using the characteristic function approach to pricing options detailed by Bakshi and Madan (2000), in accordance with Equation (1.16). If a random variable Y is distributed lognormal with mean μ and variance σ^2, its cumulative density function is

$$F_Y(y) = \Pr(Y < y) = \Phi\left(\frac{\ln y - \mu}{\sigma}\right). \tag{1.81}$$

The expectation of Y, conditional on $Y > y$ is

$$L_Y(y) = E(Y|Y > y) = \exp\left(\mu + \frac{\sigma^2}{2}\right)\Phi\left(\frac{-\ln y + \mu + \sigma^2}{\sigma}\right). \tag{1.82}$$

See, for example, Hogg and Klugman (1984) for a derivation of these formulas, which are straightforward. Under the risk-neutral measure $\mathbb{Q}$, S_T is distributed as lognormal with mean $\ln S_t + \left(r - \frac{1}{2}\sigma_{BS}^2\right)\tau$ and variance $\sigma_{BS}^2\tau$, as described earlier in this section. Substituting this mean and variance into (1.81) produces

$$\mathbb{Q}(S_T > K) = \Phi\left(\frac{\mu - \ln K}{\sigma}\right) = \Phi\left(\frac{\ln\left(S_t/K\right) + \left(r - \frac{1}{2}\sigma_{BS}^2\right)\tau}{\sigma_{BS}\sqrt{\tau}}\right) = \Phi(d_2) \tag{1.83}$$

where $1 - \Phi(x) = \Phi(-x)$ has been exploited. To obtain the other probability, apply the Radon-Nikodym derivative (1.14)

$$\begin{aligned}\mathbb{Q}^S(S_T > K) &= \int_K^\infty d\mathbb{Q}^S = \int_K^\infty \frac{d\mathbb{Q}^S}{d\mathbb{Q}}d\mathbb{Q} = \frac{e^{-r(T-t)}}{S_t}\int_K^\infty S_T q_T(x)dx \\ &= \frac{e^{-r\tau}}{S_t}E^{\mathbb{Q}}[S_T|S_T > K]\end{aligned} \tag{1.84}$$

where $q_T(x)$ is the probability density function for S_T. Substitute the mean and variance of S_T into Equation (1.82), and substitute the resulting expression in the last line of (1.84) to obtain

$$\mathbb{Q}^S(S_T > K) = \Phi\left(\frac{\ln\left(S_t/K\right) + \left(r + \frac{1}{2}\sigma_{BS}^2\right)\tau}{\sigma_{BS}\sqrt{\tau}}\right) = \Phi(d_1). \tag{1.85}$$

The Black-Scholes call price can therefore be written as the form in Equation (1.16)

$$C(K) = S_t\mathbb{Q}^S(S_T > K) - Ke^{-r\tau}\mathbb{Q}(S_T > K).$$

To obtain the result with a continuous dividend yield, replace r by $r - q$ in all the required expressions and the result follows.

The fact that $f_2(\phi)$ in Equation (1.80) is the Black-Scholes characteristic function, and not $f_1(\phi)$, is the desired result. Indeed, we will see in Chapter 2 that $f_2(\phi)$ is the "true" characteristic function in the Heston model, because it is the one obtained under the risk-neutral measure $\mathbb{Q}$. As shown by Bakshi and Madan (2000) and others, $f_1(\phi)$ can be expressed in terms of $f_2(\phi)$, so a separate expression for $f_1(\phi)$ is not required.

The function HestonProbZeroSigma.m is used to implement the Black-Scholes model as a special case of the Heston model (when $\sigma = 0$). To conserve space, only the crucial portions of the function are presented.

```
function y = HestonProbZeroSigma(phi,...,Pnum)
D = (u*i*phi - phi^2/2)*(1-exp(-b*tau))/b;
C = (r-q)*i*phi*tau + a*(u*i*phi-0.5*phi^2)/b * ...;
f = exp(C + D*theta + i*phi*x);
y = real(exp(-i*phi*log(K))*f/i/phi);
```

The function HestonPriceZeroSigma.m is used to obtain the price when $\sigma = 0$. The following Matlab code illustrates this point, using the same settings as stated earlier. Again, only the relevant parts of the code are presented.

```
d1 = (log(S/K) + (r-q+theta/2)*T)/sqrt(theta*T);
d2 = d1 - sqrt(theta*T);
BSCall = S*exp(-q*T)*normcdf(d1)  - K*exp(-r*T)*normcdf(d2);
BSPut  = K*exp(-r*T)*normcdf(-d2) - S*exp(-q*T)*normcdf(-d1);
HCall = HestonPriceZeroSigma('C',...);
HPut  = HestonPriceZeroSigma('P',...);
```

With the settings $\tau = 0.5$, $S = K = 100$, $q = 0.02$, $r = 0.03$, $\kappa = 5$, $v_0 = \theta = 0.05$, and $\lambda = 0$, the Heston model and Black-Scholes model with $\sigma_{BS} = \sqrt{v_0}$ each return 6.4730 for the price of the call and 5.9792 for the price of the put.

SUMMARY OF THE CALL PRICE

From Equation (1.66), the call price is of the form

$$C(K) = S_t e^{-q\tau} P_1 - K e^{-r\tau} P_2 \tag{1.86}$$

with in-the-money probabilities P_1 and P_2 from Equation (1.41)

$$P_j = \Pr(\ln S_T > \ln K) = \frac{1}{2} + \frac{1}{\pi}\int_0^\infty \text{Re}\left[\frac{e^{-i\phi \ln K} f_j(\phi; x, v)}{i\phi}\right] d\phi. \tag{1.87}$$

These probabilities are derived from the characteristic functions f_1 and f_2 for the logarithm of the terminal stock price, $x_T = \ln S_T$

$$f_j(\phi; x_t, v_t) = \exp(C_j(\tau, \phi) + D_j(\tau, \phi)v_t + i\phi x_t) \tag{1.88}$$

where $x_t = \ln S_t$ is the log spot price of the underlying asset, and v_t is its unobserved initial variance, which is estimated as the parameter v_0.

To obtain the price of a European call, we use the expressions for C_j and D_j in Equations (1.65) and (1.58) to obtain the two characteristic functions. To obtain the price of a European put, we use put-call parity in (1.67).

CONCLUSION

In this chapter, we have presented the original derivation of the Heston (1993) model, including the PDEs from the model, the characteristic functions, and the European call and put prices. We have also shown how the Black-Scholes model arises as a special case of the Heston model.

The Heston model has become the most popular stochastic volatility model for pricing equity options. This is in part due to the fact that the call price in the model is available in closed form. Some authors refer to the call price as being in "semi-closed" form because of the numerical integration required to obtain P_1 and P_2. But the Black-Scholes model also requires numerical integration, to obtain $\Phi(d_1)$ and $\Phi(d_2)$. In this sense, the Heston model produces call prices that are no less closed than those produced by the Black-Scholes model. The difference is that programming languages often have built-in routines for calculating the standard normal cumulative distribution function, $\Phi(\cdot)$ (usually by employing a polynomial approximation), whereas the Heston probabilities are not built-in and must be obtained using numerical integration. In the next chapter, we investigate some of the problems that can arise in numerical integration when the integrand

$$\text{Re}\left[\frac{e^{-i\phi \ln K} f_j(\phi; x, v)}{i\phi}\right]$$

is not well-behaved. We encountered an example of such an integrand in Figure 1.1.

CHAPTER 2

Integration Issues, Parameter Effects, and Variance Modeling

Abstract

In this chapter, we investigate several issues around the Heston model. First, following Bakshi and Madan (2000), we show that the Heston call price can be expressed in terms of a single characteristic function. It is well-known that the integrand for the call price can sometimes show high oscillation, can dampen very slowly along the integration axis, and can show discontinuities. All of these problems can introduce inaccuracies in numerical integration. The "Little Trap" formulation of Albrecher et al. (2007) provides an easy fix to many of these problems. Next, we examine the effects of the Heston parameters on implied volatilities extracted from option prices generated with the Heston model. Borrowing from Gatheral (2006), we examine how the fair strike of a variance swap can be derived under the model and present approximations to local volatility and implied volatility from the model. Finally, we examine moment explosions derived by Andersen and Piterbarg (2007) and bounds on implied volatility of Lee (2004b).

REMARKS ON THE CHARACTERISTIC FUNCTIONS

In Chapter 1, it was shown that the in-the-money probabilities P_1 and P_2 are obtained by the inverse Fourier transform of the characteristic functions f_1 and f_2

$$P_j = \Pr(\ln S_T > \ln K) = \frac{1}{2} + \frac{1}{\pi}\int_0^\infty \text{Re}\left[\frac{e^{-i\phi \ln K} f_j(\phi; x, v)}{i\phi}\right] d\phi. \tag{2.1}$$

This form of inversion is due to Gil-Pelaez (1951) and will be derived in Chapter 3. It makes sense that two characteristic functions f_1 and f_2 be associated with the Heston model, because P_1 and P_2 are obtained under different measures. On the other hand, it also seems that only a single characteristic function ought to exist, because there is only one underlying stock price in the model. Indeed, some authors write the probabilities P_1 and P_2 in terms of a single characteristic function $f(\phi) = f(\phi; x, v)$, as

$$P_1 = \frac{1}{2} + \frac{1}{\pi}\int_0^\infty \text{Re}\left[\frac{e^{-i\phi \ln K} f(\phi - i)}{i\phi f(-i)}\right] d\phi \tag{2.2}$$

and

$$P_2 = \frac{1}{2} + \frac{1}{\pi}\int_0^\infty \mathrm{Re}\left[\frac{e^{-i\phi \ln K} f(\phi)}{i\phi}\right] d\phi \tag{2.3}$$

which suggests that $f_2(\phi) = f(\phi)$ and $f_1(\phi) = f(\phi - i)/f(-i)$. In this section, it is shown that the expressions for P_j in Equations (2.2) and (2.3) are identical to (2.1). This is explained in Bakshi and Madan (2000), and a simplified version of their result follows.

First, note that P_2 in Equation (2.3) is identical to (2.1) with $j = 2$, but P_1 is not identical to (2.1) with $j = 1$. The "true" characteristic function is actually f_2, since it is associated with the probability measure $\mathbb{Q}$ that makes $W_{1,t}$ and $W_{2,t}$ in the risk-neutral stochastic differential equations (SDEs) for S_t and v_t Brownian motion and for which the bond serves as numeraire. Hence, in the call price

$$C(K) = S_t P_1 - e^{-r\tau} K P_2$$

we can use $q(x)$, the probability density function for $\ln S_T$, to write

$$P_2 = \mathbb{Q}(x_T > \ln K) = \int_{\ln K}^\infty q(x)dx$$

where $x_T = \ln S_T$.

To evaluate P_2, express the cumulative distribution function $\mathbb{Q}(x_T < x)$ in terms of the characteristic function $f(\phi)$ as

$$\mathbb{Q}(x_T < x) = \frac{1}{2} - \frac{1}{2\pi}\int_{-\infty}^\infty \frac{e^{-i\phi x} f(\phi)}{i\phi} d\phi. \tag{2.4}$$

The density $q(x)$ is obtained by differentiation with respect to x

$$q(x) = \frac{1}{2\pi}\int_{-\infty}^\infty e^{-i\phi x} f(\phi) d\phi.$$

It is well-known that the real part of the characteristic function $f(\phi)$ is even, and the imaginary part is odd. This important fact implies that, when integrated over the entire real line, the imaginary part of $e^{-i\phi x} f(\phi)$ will cancel out, which must happen anyway since $q(x)$ is real. Hence, we can simply integrate over the real part, and since the real part is even, the integral over $(0, \infty)$ will be equal to twice the integral over $(-\infty, 0)$. This implies that the density can be written

$$q(x) = \frac{1}{2\pi}\int_{-\infty}^\infty \mathrm{Re}\left[e^{-i\phi x} f(\phi)\right] d\phi = \frac{1}{\pi}\int_0^\infty \mathrm{Re}\left[e^{-i\phi x} f(\phi)\right] d\phi \tag{2.5}$$

and that $\mathbb{Q}(x_T < x)$ can be written from Equation (2.4) as

$$\mathbb{Q}(x_T < x) = \frac{1}{2} - \frac{1}{\pi}\int_0^\infty \mathrm{Re}\left[\frac{e^{-i\phi x} f(\phi)}{i\phi}\right] d\phi. \tag{2.6}$$

The in-the-money probability P_2 is the complement of (2.6), evaluated at $\ln K$

$$P_2 = \mathbb{Q}(x_T > \ln K) = \frac{1}{2} + \frac{1}{\pi}\int_0^\infty \text{Re}\left[\frac{e^{-i\phi \ln K} f(\phi)}{i\phi}\right] d\phi \tag{2.7}$$

which is identical to Equation (2.3). To obtain P_1, invoke a change of numeraire. Recall the Radon-Nikodym derivative from Chapter 1

$$\frac{d\mathbb{Q}^S}{d\mathbb{Q}} = \frac{S_T/S_t}{B_T/B_t} = \frac{e^{x_T}}{E^{\mathbb{Q}}[e^{x_T}]}. \tag{2.8}$$

We can write $S_t e^{r(T-t)} = E^{\mathbb{Q}}[S_T]$, since under the risk-neutral measure $\mathbb{Q}$, the stock price grows at the risk-free rate, r. Equation (2.8) suggests that a new density function $q^S(x)$ should be defined from $q(x)$ via the Radon-Nikodym derivative as

$$q^S(x)dx = \frac{e^x}{E^{\mathbb{Q}}[e^{x_T}]} q(x)dx.$$

The characteristic function for $q^S(x)$ is, therefore

$$E^{\mathbb{Q}^S}[e^{i\phi x_T}] = \int_{-\infty}^{\infty} e^{i\phi x} q^S(x)dx = \frac{1}{E^{\mathbb{Q}}[e^{x_T}]}\int_{-\infty}^{\infty} e^{i\phi x} e^x q(x)dx. \tag{2.9}$$

Note that $E^{\mathbb{Q}}[e^{x_T}]$ is a constant and can be taken out of the integral. Note also that, since the characteristic function for x_T is $f(\phi) = E^{\mathbb{Q}}[e^{i\phi x_T}]$, then

$$E^{\mathbb{Q}}[e^{x_T}] = f(-i) = S_t e^{r(T-t)}.$$

Finally, the integral in the right-hand side of Equation (2.9) can be written

$$\int_{-\infty}^{\infty} e^{i(\phi - i)x} q(x)dx = E^{\mathbb{Q}}[e^{i(\phi - i)x_T}].$$

This last expression is the characteristic function for x_T, evaluated at $\phi - i$. Hence, the characteristic function for the density $q^S(x)$ can be expressed in terms of the characteristic function for $q(x)$ evaluated at the points $-i$ and $\phi - i$ as

$$E^{\mathbb{Q}^S}[e^{i\phi x_T}] = \frac{f(\phi - i)}{f(-i)} = \frac{f(\phi - i)}{S_t e^{r(T-t)}}. \tag{2.10}$$

When the stock pays a continuous dividend yield q, the denominator of (2.10) becomes $e^{(r-q)(T-t)}S_t$. It was shown in Chapter 1 that

$$e^{-r\tau} E^{\mathbb{Q}}[S_T \mathbf{1}_{S_T > K}] = S_t \mathbb{Q}^S(S_T > K).$$

To show that $\mathbb{Q}^S(x_T > \ln K)$ can be expressed in the form of Equation (2.2), apply the inversion theorem to the characteristic function in (2.10)

$$P_1 = \mathbb{Q}^S(x_T > \ln K) = \frac{1}{2} + \frac{1}{\pi}\int_0^\infty \text{Re}\left[\frac{e^{-i\phi \ln K} f(\phi - i)}{i\phi f(-i)}\right] d\phi \tag{2.11}$$

which is Equation (2.2). What remains to be demonstrated is that $q^S(x)$ can serve as a density function, which requires that $q^S(x) \geq 0$ and that $q^S(x)$ integrate to unity. To show the first requirement, note from Equation (2.8) that

$$q^S(x) = \frac{S_T/S_t}{B_T/S_t} q(x) > 0.$$

Now consider the integral of $q^S(x)$ over $(0, \infty)$

$$\int_0^\infty q^S(x)dx = \frac{\int_0^\infty e^x q(x)dx}{E^{\mathbb{Q}}[e^{x_T}]} = \frac{E^{\mathbb{Q}}[e^{x_T}]}{E^{\mathbb{Q}}[e^{x_T}]} = 1.$$

The result is that the call price can be written as

$$C(K) = S_t P_1 - e^{-r(T-t)} K P_2$$

with P_1 in Equation (2.11) and P_2 in Equation (2.7) each obtained from the characteristic function for $x_T = \ln S_T$. This is a general setup that is valid for many models, not only the Heston model, as shown in Bakshi and Madan (2000). It is commonly referred to as the characteristic function approach for option pricing.

To illustrate, it was shown in Chapter 1 that, in the Black-Scholes model, x_T is normally distributed with mean $\ln(S_t) + (r - \sigma_{BS}^2/2)\tau$ and variance $\sigma_{BS}^2\tau$, so that the characteristic function for x_T is

$$f(\phi) = \exp\left(i\phi \left[\ln S_t + \left(r - \frac{1}{2}\sigma_{BS}^2 \right) \tau \right] - \frac{1}{2}\phi^2 \sigma_{BS}^2 \tau \right).$$

Substituting $f(\phi)$ into the expressions for P_1 and P_2 and evaluating the integrals numerically will produce the same call price as the closed form solution for the Black-Scholes call price, up to approximation error.

The relationship among the characteristic functions can be easily illustrated in the Heston model by showing that

$$f_1(\phi) = \frac{f_2(\phi - i)}{f_2(-i)}. \tag{2.12}$$

Because of the log-linear form of the characteristic function, this is equivalent to showing that

$$C_1(\tau, \phi) = C_2(\tau, \phi - i) - C_2(\tau, -i)$$
$$D_1(\tau, \phi) = D_2(\tau, \phi - i) - D_2(\tau, -i).$$

With these identities, it is straightforward to show that (2.12) holds, and consequently, that the probabilities P_1 and P_2 can be written in terms of Equation (2.1) or equivalently in terms of (2.2) and (2.3). This can be illustrated with the following code, which calculates the integrands using either formulation of the characteristic functions described in this section.

```
for k=1:length(x);
  phi    = x(k);
  weight = w(k);
  f2(k)  = HestonCF(phi,...,2,trap);
  if CF==1
    f1(k)  = HestonCF(phi,...,1,trap);
  elseif CF==2
    f1(k)  = HestonCF(phi-i,...,2,trap)/(S*exp((r-q)*T));
  end
  int2(k)  = weight * real(exp(-i*phi*log(K))*f2(k)/i/phi);
  int1(k)  = weight * real(exp(-i*phi*log(K))*f1(k)/i/phi);
end
```

It is easy to verify that both methods produce the same option price.

PROBLEMS WITH THE INTEGRAND

Recall from Chapter 1 that the integrand from which the probabilities P_j are obtained is

$$F_j(\phi) = \text{Re}\left[\frac{e^{-i\phi \ln K} f_j(\phi; x, v)}{i\phi}\right] \tag{2.13}$$

for $\phi > 0$. In some instances, the integrand is well-behaved and the integration poses no numerical problems. In other cases, however, the integrand is not well-behaved so numerical integration can be problematic.

The first problem is that the integrand is not defined at the point $\phi = 0$, even though the integration range is $[0, \infty)$. This implies that the integration must begin at a very small point close to zero. In order to avoid inaccuracies due to the removal of the origin, the integrand must not be too steep there.

The second problem is that the integrand may contain discontinuities. To illustrate, Figure 2.1 plots two integrands for f_1 in the range $\phi \in (0, 10]$. The first integrand has a maturity of $\tau = 3$ years and $\sigma = 0.75$, and the second has $\tau = 1$ year and $\sigma = 0.09$. Both integrands use $\kappa = 10$, $\theta = v_0 = 0.05$, $\rho = -0.9$, $r = 0$, along with spot $S_0 = 100$ and strike $K = 100$.

The first integrand (red line) is smooth and shows no particular numerical instability. The second integrand (black line), on the other hand, has discontinuities near the points $\phi = 1.7$ and $\phi = 5$, and it is steep near 1.7. In later sections, we present a simple modification of the integrand by Albrecher et al. (2007) which is effective at eliminating these discontinuities.

Finally, the third problem that can arise is that of an integrand that oscillates wildly. In Figure 2.2, the first integrand has a maturity of $\tau = 1/52$ years and uses $\sigma = 0.175$, $\theta = v_0 = 0.01$, and a spot $S_0 = 7$. The second has $\tau = 1$ year and uses $\sigma = 0.09$, $\theta = v_0 = 0.07$, and a spot $S_0 = 10$. Both use $\rho = -0.9$, $\kappa = 10$, $r = 0$, and a strike of $K = 10$. The plots are over the integration range $\phi \in (0, 100]$.

The first integrand (black line) shows high oscillation, which is still not damped at $\phi = 100$. This implies that the numerical integral needs to extend much further

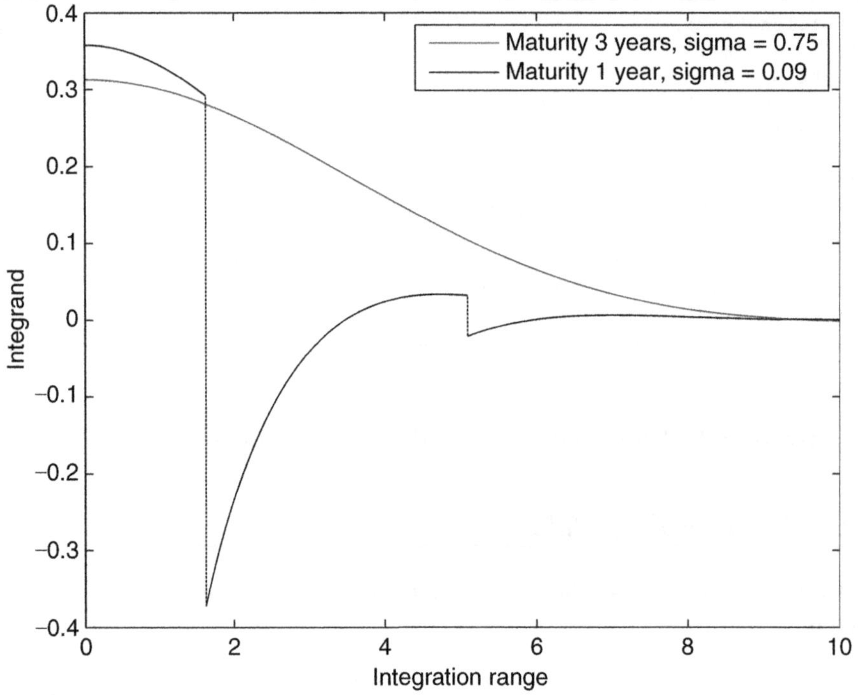

FIGURE 2.1 Discontinuities in the Heston Integrand

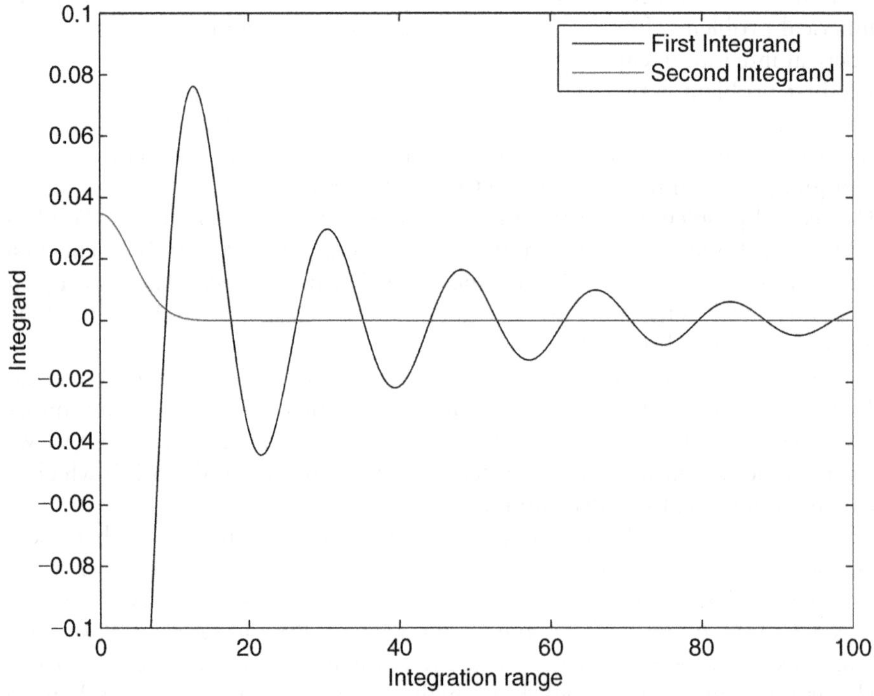

FIGURE 2.2 Oscillations in the Heston Integrand

beyond $\phi = 100$ to converge. Moreover, the integrand is very steep near the origin, which requires a very fine grid for the numerical integral. The second integrand (red line) is well-behaved and would pose no numerical difficulties. Indeed, it does not oscillate, is not steep anywhere, and rapidly dampens to zero, starting at around $\phi = 10$. High oscillation of the integrand is usually associated with short-maturity options.

THE LITTLE HESTON TRAP

Albrecher et al. (2007) explain that the academic literature on the Heston model embodies two different formulations of the Heston characteristic function. The first is the original formulation of Heston (1993), while the second has a slightly different form. Albrecher et al. (2007) show that these two formulations are equivalent, but that the second leads to a characteristic function that is much better behaved and, therefore, better suited for numerical integration.

The original formulation of the Heston characteristic function was derived in Chapter 1. To derive the second formulation, first note that the solution to D_j in Chapter 1 can be multiplied by $\exp(-d_j\tau)$ in the numerator and denominator, which leads to the equivalent form

$$D_j = \frac{b_j - \rho\sigma i\phi + d_j}{g_j\sigma^2}\left(\frac{1-e^{-d_j\tau}}{1-e^{-d_j\tau}/g_j}\right) = \frac{b_j - \rho\sigma i\phi - d_j}{\sigma^2}\left(\frac{1-e^{-d_j\tau}}{1-c_je^{-d_j\tau}}\right) \tag{2.14}$$

where

$$c_j = \frac{1}{g_j} = \frac{b_j - \rho\sigma i\phi - d_j}{b_j - \rho\sigma i\phi + d_j}. \tag{2.15}$$

The logarithm in the solution to C_j can be written

$$\begin{aligned} d_j\tau - 2\ln\left[\frac{1-g_je^{d_j\tau}}{1-g_j}\right] &= d_j\tau - 2\ln\left[e^{d_j\tau}\left(\frac{e^{-d_j\tau}-g_j}{1-g_j}\right)\right] \\ &= d_j\tau - 2d_j\tau - 2\ln\left[\frac{e^{-d_j\tau}-g_j}{1-g_j}\right] \\ &= -d_j\tau - 2\ln\left[\frac{1-c_je^{-d_j\tau}}{1-c_j}\right]. \end{aligned} \tag{2.16}$$

This implies that C_j can be written in the equivalent form

$$C_j = ri\phi\tau + \frac{\kappa\theta}{\sigma^2}\left[(b_j - \rho\sigma i\phi - d_j)\tau - 2\ln\left(\frac{1-c_je^{-d_j\tau}}{1-c_j}\right)\right]. \tag{2.17}$$

Implementing this formulation is very simple and involves only replacing C_j and D_j with the slightly different forms in Equations (2.17) and (2.14). The function HestonIntegrand.m, which follows, computes the characteristic function using the original Heston (1993) formulation, and the Albrecher et al. (2007) "Little Trap" formulation. To conserve space, parts of the function are omitted.

```
function y = HestonIntegrand(phi,...,Trap)
d = sqrt((rho*sigma*i*phi - b)^2 - ...;
g = (b - rho*sigma*i*phi + d) / ....;
if Trap==1
    % "Little Heston Trap" formulation
    c = 1/g;
    D = (b - rho*sigma*i*phi - d)/sigma^2 * ...;
    G = (1 - c*exp(-d*tau))/(1-c);
    C = r*i*phi*tau + a/sigma^2*((b-rho*sigma*i*phi-d) * ...;
elseif Trap==0
    % Original Heston formulation.
    G = (1 - g*exp(d*tau))/(1-g);
    C = r*i*phi*tau + a/sigma^2 * ...;
    D = (b - rho*sigma*i*phi + d)/sigma^2 * ...;
end
% The characteristic function.
f = exp(C + D*v0 + i*phi*x);
% Return the real part of the integrand.
y = real(exp(-i*phi*log(K))*f/i/phi);
```

The implementation in C# is done using the HestonProb() function and is very similar. The C# code is therefore not presented here.

Albrecher et al. (2007) explain that, although Heston's original formulation and their formulation are identical, their formulation causes fewer numerical problems in the implementation of the model. This is illustrated by plotting the integrand

$$\text{Re}\left[\frac{e^{-i\phi\ln K}f_j(\phi;x,v)}{i\phi}\right]$$

for the characteristic function f_1. The same parameter values as Albrecher et al. (2007) were used, namely $\kappa = 1.5768$, $\sigma = 0.5751$, $\rho = -0.5711$, $\theta = 0.0398$, and $v_0 = 0.0175$. In addition, we use $S = K = 100$ and a maturity of $\tau = 5$ years. Figure 2.3 reproduces the figure for f_1 in their article. The integrand uses the integration range $\phi = (0, 10]$.

The original Heston (1993) formulation (black line) shows a discontinuity at $\phi \approx 3.5$, which is corrected with the Albrecher et al. (2007) formulation in the red line. The following code uses the HestonIntegrand.m function to generate Figure 2.3 and can also be used to generate the figure for f_2 in Albrecher et al. (2007).

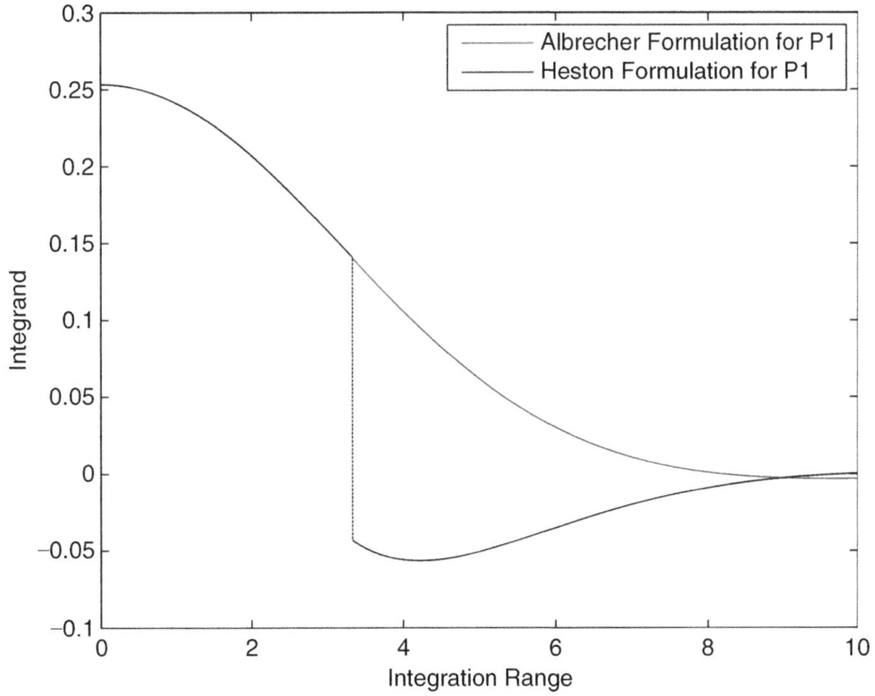

FIGURE 2.3 Integrand for P_1, Original and Little Trap Formulations

```
phi = 0.0001:.01:10;
Pnum = 1;
% Illustration of the integrand for P1
for x=1:N
    HestonP1(x)     = HestonIntegrand(phi(x),...,Pnum,0);
    AlbrecherP1(x)  = HestonIntegrand(phi(x),...,Pnum,1);
end;
Pnum = 2;
% Illustration of the integrand for P2
for x=1:N
    HestonP2(x)     = HestonIntegrand(phi(x),...,Pnum,0);
    AlbrecherP2(x)  = HestonIntegrand(phi(x),...,Pnum,1);
end;
```

Finally, the rotation algorithm of Kahl and Jäckel (2005) can be used to overcome the discontinuities brought on by the original Heston formulation. We do not cover the rotation algorithm in this book, but we refer interested readers to Kahl and Jäckel (2005), and also to the book by Zhu (2010) for alternate algorithms. Note, however, that since the "Little Trap" formulation always works, these and other algorithms are somewhat obsolete.

EFFECT OF THE HESTON PARAMETERS

Heston Terminal Spot Price

Under the Heston model, the distribution of the log stock price at maturity, $\ln S_T$, is able to exhibit skewness and excess kurtosis, depending on the parameter settings. In the following section, the effect of the correlation ρ and the volatility of variance σ on the distribution of $\ln S_T$ are investigated.

Effect of Correlation and Volatility of Variance

The correlation parameter ρ controls the skewness of the density of $\ln S_T$ and of the continuously compounded return $\ln(S_T/S_0)$ over $[0, T]$. When $\rho > 0$, the probability densities will be positively skewed, and when $\rho < 0$, the densities will be negatively skewed. The figures in this section use the parameter settings from Table 1 of Heston (1993) to demonstrate this. The parameter settings are $v_0 = 0.01$, $\kappa = 2$, $\theta = 0.01$, $\lambda = 0$, and $\sigma = 0.1$. The density of $\ln S_T$ can be recovered by inverting its characteristic function $f_2(\phi)$, as in Equation (2.5), and applying a numerical integration scheme. The densities in Figure 2.4 use $\rho = -0.8$, $\rho = 0$, and $\rho = 0.8$. The figure is similar to Figure 1 of Heston (1993) and clearly indicates the relationship between correlation and skewness.

As explained by Heston (1993), positive correlation implies a rise in variance when the stock price rises. This has the effect of fattening the right tail of the

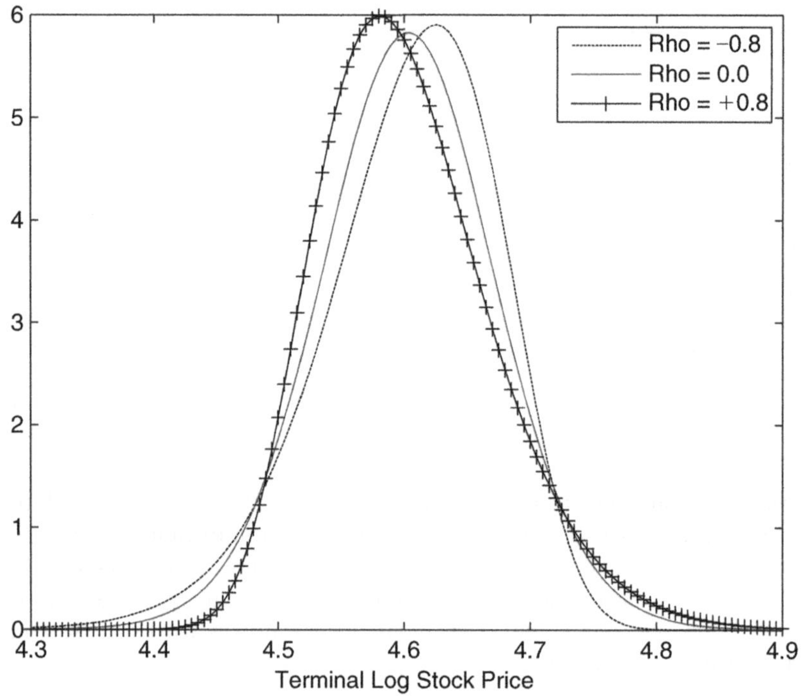

FIGURE 2.4 Effect of Correlation on Density

distribution, and thinning the left tail. When the correlation is negative, the opposite happens. It will be shown in the next section that a negative correlation results in deep in-of-the-money calls being priced higher in the Heston model than in the Black-Scholes model.

The volatility of variance parameter σ controls the kurtosis. When σ is high, the variance process is highly dispersed, so we expect the distribution of returns to have higher kurtosis and fatter tails than when σ is small. This is illustrated in Figure 2.5 for $\sigma \approx 0$, $\sigma = 0.2$, and $\sigma = 0.4$. The figure is similar to Figure 3 of Heston (1993).

Comparison With Black-Scholes Prices

The results illustrated in Figures 2.4 and 2.5 suggest that, because of the skew in returns produced by the Heston model, option prices generated by the Heston model should differ from those generated by the Black-Scholes model in a way that is sensible. In this section, we investigate the effect of the correlation parameter ρ and the volatility of variance parameter σ on call prices in this regard.

When $\rho > 0$, the skew in the distribution of $\ln S_T$ is positive, so more weight is assigned to the right tail of the distribution. Out-of-the-money (OTM) calls have a strike price that lies in the right tail. This implies that, when $\rho > 0$, deep OTM calls produced by the Heston model should be more expensive than those produced by the Black-Scholes model. In-the-money (ITM) calls have a strike price that lies in the left tail. Since less weight is assigned to the left tail, deep ITM calls from the Heston model should be less expensive than those produced by Black-Scholes. Similarly,

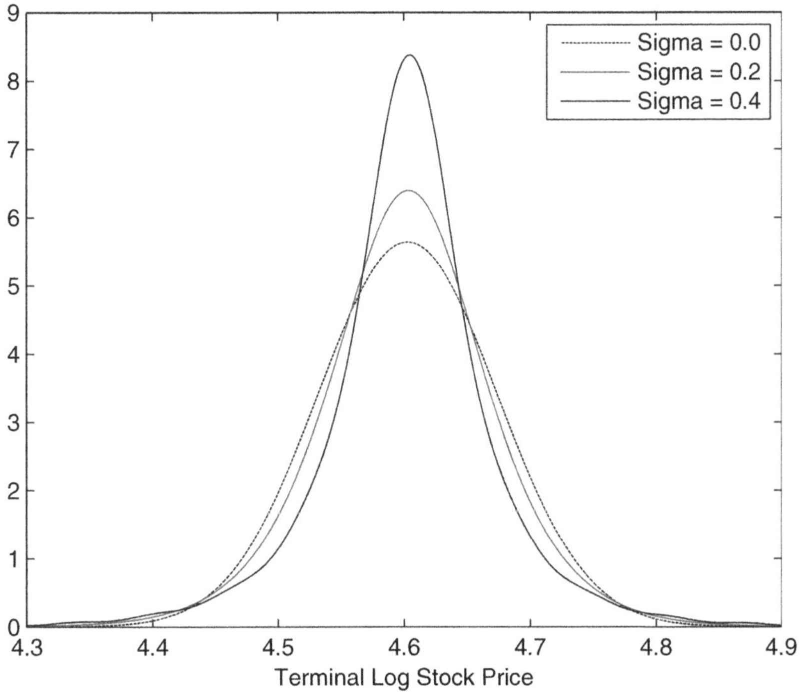

FIGURE 2.5 Effect of Volatility of Variance on Density

TABLE 2.1 Price Comparisons Under Different Correlations

	ρ > 0	ρ < 0
OTM Calls	Heston > BS	Heston < BS
ITM Calls	Heston < BS	Heston > BS

when $\rho < 0$, the distribution of $\ln S_T$ is negatively skewed and the opposite happens: more weight is assigned to the left tail, and less in the right tail. This implies that deep ITM calls from the Heston model should be more expensive than those produced by the Black-Scholes model, and deep OTM calls should be less expensive. Table 2.1 summarizes these observations.

Figure 2.6 reproduces Figure 2 from Heston (1993). It plots the difference between call prices from both models (Heston price minus Black-Scholes price), as the spot price varies from \$70 to \$140. We use the same parameter settings as the example earlier in this section, corresponding to those in Table 1 of Heston (1993). In order for the Heston and Black-Scholes price comparisons to be valid, however, the Black-Scholes volatilities must be matched to the Heston prices. This can be done by defining the Black-Scholes volatility σ_{BS} in terms of the standard deviation of the distribution of the returns $\ln(S_T/S_0)$. The moments of the returns can be

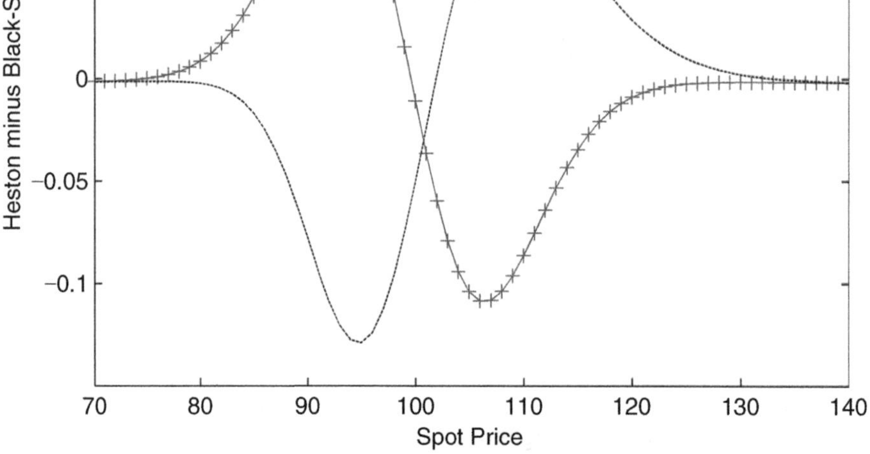

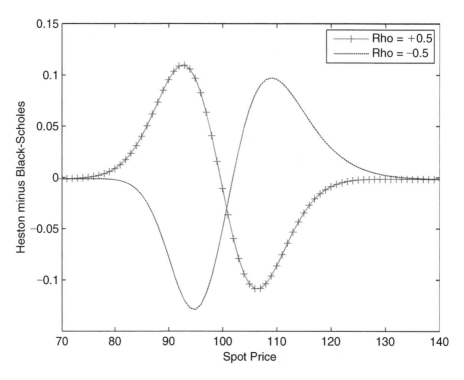

FIGURE 2.6 Effect of Correlation on Heston Prices Relative to Black-Scholes

obtained from the moments of $x_T = \ln S_T$, which are available by differentiation of the characteristic function $f_2(\phi)$

$$E[x_T^n] = i^{-n}\left[\frac{d^n}{d\phi^n}f_2(\phi)\right]_{\phi=0}. \tag{2.18}$$

The Matlab file MomentMatching.m approximates (2.18) using finite differences.

```
rho = [-0.5 0.0 0.5];
dphi = 1e-4;
for k=1:3
    param.rho = rho(k);
    dfp = HestonCF(+dphi,param,tau,S,r,q,trap);
    dfm = HestonCF(-dphi,param,tau,S,r,q,trap);
    df = (dfp - dfm)/2/dphi;
    EX = df/i;
    dfpp = HestonCF(+2*dphi,param,tau,S,r,q,trap);
    dfmm = HestonCF(-2*dphi,param,tau,S,r,q,trap);
    dff1 = (dfpp - dfp)/dphi;
    dff2 = (dfm - dfmm)/dphi;
    ddf  = (dff1 - dff2)/3/dphi;
    EX2 = ddf/i^2;
    var = EX2 - EX^2;
    BSvol(k) = sqrt(var);
end;
```

The results of the approximation suggest that, when $\rho = -0.5$, we use $\sigma_{BS} = \sqrt{2} \times 0.0710$ to generate the Black-Scholes prices, and when $\rho = +0.5$, we use $\sigma_{BS} = \sqrt{2} \times 0.0704$.

The left portion of Figure 2.6 corresponds to low stock prices and OTM calls, and the right portion to high stock prices and ITM calls. Clearly, when correlation is positive, Heston OTM calls are more expensive than Black-Scholes OTM calls, due to the thickness in the right tail of the distribution of $\ln S_T$ generated by the Heston model. When correlation is negative, the difference is positive in the ITM call region. Heston ITM calls are more expensive than Black-Scholes ITM calls, due to the thickness in the left tail of the distribution of $\ln S_T$ generated by the Heston model. Similar arguments can be made for negative differences.

The effect of increasing σ is to increase kurtosis. This makes sense, since a high volatility of variance will increase the range of terminal stock price values. This is illustrated in Figure 2.7, which compares the difference between the Heston and Black-Scholes call prices with $\rho = 0$, and when $\sigma = 0.1$ and $\sigma = 0.2$. It indicates that Heston prices are higher than Black-Scholes prices in ITM and OTM regions but lower in the at-the-money region. These two observations are consistent with thicker tails of the distribution of $\ln S_T$ generated by the Heston model. Not surprisingly, the difference is more pronounced when σ is higher. Figure 2.7 is similar to Figure 4 of Heston (1993).

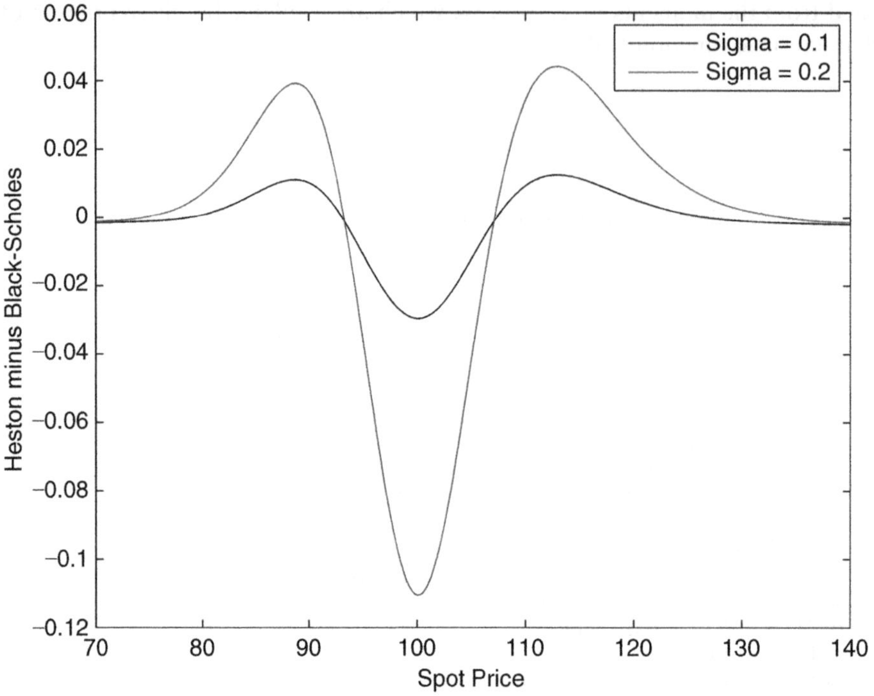

FIGURE 2.7 Effect of Volatility of Variance on Heston Prices Relative to Black-Scholes

Heston Implied Volatility

Another feature of the Heston model is that implied volatilities extracted from option prices generated by the model will show a smile or skew. The shape of the skew is driven by the values of the parameters. The correlation parameter ρ determines the direction of skew, with $\rho > 0$ corresponding to a positive slope, and $\rho < 0$ corresponding to a negative slope. This is illustrated in the first panel of Figure 2.8 by generating implied volatilities using $S = 100$, $r = 0.05$, $\tau = 0.25$, $\kappa = 2$, $\theta = 0.01$, $\lambda = 0$, and $v_0 = 0.01$ over the strike range 95 to 105.

Equity options usually show a negative slope in their implied volatilities. Not surprisingly, when options data are used to estimate the parameters of the Heston model, the correlation will in most cases turn out to be negative.

Increasing values of the volatility of variance σ increases the curvature of the smile. This is illustrated in the second panel of Figure 2.8, which uses the same settings but with $\rho = 0$. Finally, the parameters κ, θ and v_0 control the level of the smile, as illustrated in the remaining panels of Figure 2.8. The mean reversion speed κ also controls the curvature, to a certain extent, with higher values of κ flattening the implied volatility.

To generate the implied volatilities, we first create Heston prices using the Matlab function HestonPriceGaussLaguerre.m over a range of strikes K. This function uses the Gauss-Laguerre quadrature for numerical integration, which we cover in Chapter 5.

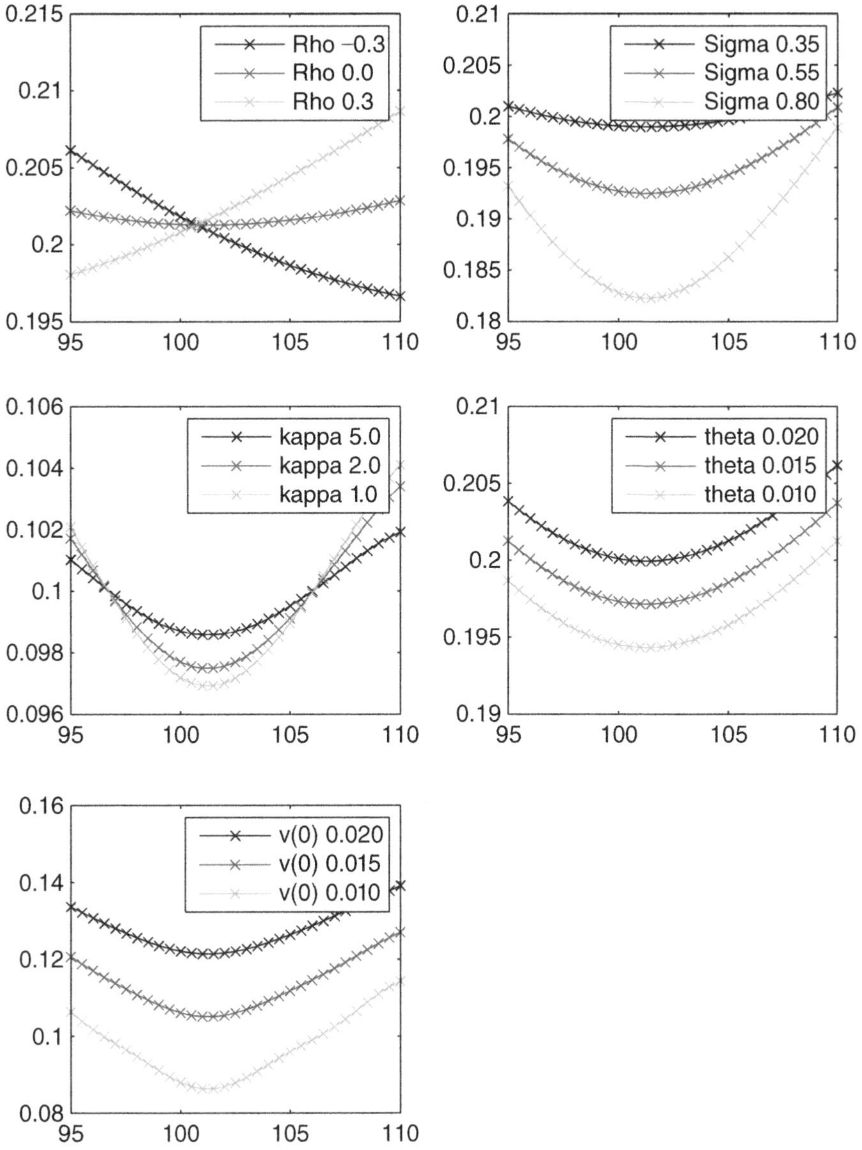

FIGURE 2.8 Effect of Heston Parameters on Implied Volatility

```
sigma = [0.35 0.55 0.80];
for j=1:length(sigma);
    for i=1:length(K);
        HCallS(i,j) = HestonPriceGaussLaguerre
                          (K(i),sigma(j),...);
        IVS(i,j) = BisecBSIV(HCallS(i,j),...);
    end
end
```

The earlier code invokes the Matlab function BisecBSIV.m that uses the bisection algorithm to find the implied volatilities once the prices are generated. The first part of the function defines a function handle for calculating the price of calls under the Black-Scholes model. The main part of the function calculates the Black-Scholes call price at the midpoint of the two endpoints, and compares the difference between this call price and the market price. If the difference is greater than the user-specified tolerance, the function updates one of the endpoints with the midpoint and passes through the iteration again. To conserve space, parts of the function have been omitted.

```
function y = BisecBSIVMktPrice,Tol,MaxIter,...)
% Black Scholes call
BSC = @(s,K,rf,q,v,T) (s.*normcdf((log(s./K) + ...;
lowCdif  = MktPrice - BSC(S,K,rf,q,a,T);
highCdif = MktPrice - BSC(S,K,rf,q,b,T);
if lowCdif*highCdif > 0 y = -1;
else
    for x=1:MaxIter
        midP = (a+b)/2;
        midCdif = MktPrice - BSC(S,K,rf,q,midP,T);
        if abs(midCdif)<Tol
            break
        else
            if midCdif>0 a = midP;
            else b = midP;
            end
        end
    end
    y = midP;
end
```

The bisection algorithm in C# is very similar and is coded in the function BisecBSIV(). The difference is that we must create a separate C# function, NormCDF(), to calculate the standard normal distribution function.

```
static double BisecBSIV(string PutCall,...){
double lowCdif = MktPrice - BlackScholes(a,...);
double highCdif = MktPrice - BlackScholes(b,...);
double BSIV = 0.0;
double midP;
if (lowCdif*highCdif > 0.0)
    BSIV = -1.0;
else {
    for (int x=0; x>=MaxIter; x++) {
        midP = (a+b)/2.0;
        double midCdif = MktPrice - BlackScholes(midP,...);
        if (Math.Abs(midCdif) < Tol){
            break; }
        else {
            if (midCdif > 0.0) a = midP;
            else b = midP; }
    BSIV = midP;  } }
return BSIV; }
```

We use the approximation to the standard normal distribution function $\Phi(x)$ due to Bagby (1995). The approximation to the integral

$$P(x) = \frac{1}{\sqrt{2\pi}} \int_0^x e^{-t^2/2} dt$$

for $x > 0$, is based on

$$Q(x) = \frac{1}{2}\left\{1 - \frac{1}{30}\left[7e^{-x^2/2} + 16e^{-x^2(2-\sqrt{2})} + \left(7 + \frac{\pi x^2}{4}\right)e^{-x^2}\right]\right\}^{1/2}.$$

Hence, Bagby's (1995) approximation is

$$\Phi(x) \approx \begin{cases} 0.5 + Q(x) & \text{for } x > 0 \\ 0.5 - Q(x) & \text{for } x < 0. \end{cases}$$

```
static double NormCDF(double x) {
double x1 = 7.0*Math.Exp(-0.5*x*x);
double x2 = 16.0*Math.Exp(-x*x*(2.0 - Math.Sqrt(2.0)));
double x3 = (7.0 + 0.25*Math.PI*x*x)*Math.Exp(-x*x);
double Q = 0.5*Math.Sqrt(1.0 - (x1 + x2 + x3)/30.0);
if(x > 0)
    return 0.5 + Q;
else
    return 0.5 - Q; }
```

This function is fed into the C# function BlackScholes(), which calculates the Black-Scholes price of a European vanilla option. The price is used in the BisecBSIV() function.

```
static double BlackScholes(double S,double K,...) {
double d1 = (Math.Log(S/K) + (rf-q+v*v/2.0)*T) / v / Math.Sqrt(T);
double d2 = d1 - v*Math.Sqrt(T);
double BSCall = S*Math.Exp(-q*T)*NormCDF(d1) -
                K*Math.Exp(-rf*T)*NormCDF(d2);
double Price = 0.0;
if(PutCall == "C")
    Price = BSCall;
else if(PutCall == "P")
    Price = BSCall - S*Math.Exp(-q*T) + K*Math.Exp(-rf*T);
return Price; }
```

All the figures in this section can be generated using the earlier snippets of Matlab code. Figure 2.9, for example, presents a surface of implied volatilities and local volatilities extracted from Heston call prices. It is generated using the following Matlab code.

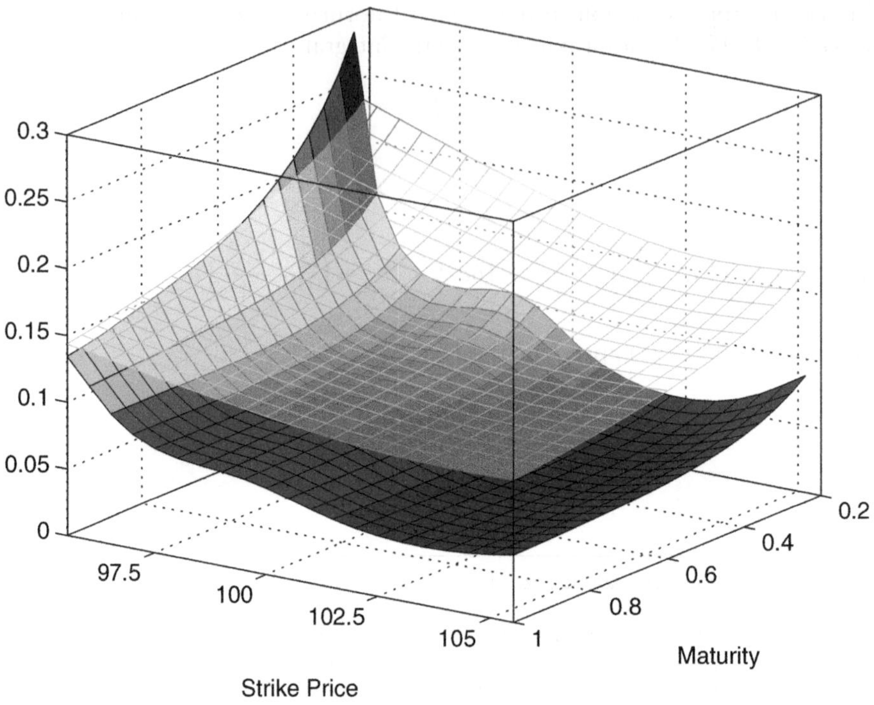

FIGURE 2.9 Heston Implied Volatility and Local Volatility Surfaces

```
for t=1:NT;
    for k=1:NK;
        % Heston prices
        Price = HestonCallGaussLaguerre(K(k),T(t),...);
        % Implied volatility
        IV(k,t) = BisecBSIV(K(k),T(t),...);
        % Local variance
        CT  = HestonCallGaussLaguerre(K(k),T(t)+dt,...);
        CT_ = HestonCallGaussLaguerre(K(k),T(t)-dt,...);
        dCdT =  (CT - CT_) / (2*dt);
        CK  = HestonCallGaussLaguerre(S,K(k)+dK,T(t),...);
        CK0 = HestonCallGaussLaguerre(S,K(k)    ,T(t),...);
        CK_ = HestonCallGaussLaguerre(S,K(k)-dK,T(t),...);
        dC2dK2 = (CK - 2*CK0 + CK_) / (dK)^2;
        LocalVar = 2*dCdT / (K(k)^2*dC2dK2);
        % Local volatility
        LV(k,t) = sqrt(LocalVar);
    end
end
% Transparent mesh for implied volatility
mesh(IV)
% Surface plot for local volatility
hold on
surf(LV)
```

In Figure 2.9, implied volatility is represented by the transparent mesh, and local volatility is represented by the solid surface underneath the mesh. The figure reflects the observation of Derman et al. (1995) that local volatility tends to show more variability than implied volatility. Local volatility is covered in the next section.

VARIANCE MODELING IN THE HESTON MODEL

Variance Swap

Recall from Chapter 1 that the volatility of the Heston model is driven by the CIR process

$$dv_t = \kappa(\theta - v_t)dt + \sigma\sqrt{v_t}dW_{2,t}$$

and consequently, that the expected value of v_t conditional on v_s $(s < t)$ is

$$E[v_t|v_s] = v_s e^{-\kappa(t-s)} + \theta(1 - e^{-\kappa(t-s)}) = (v_s - \theta)e^{-\kappa(t-s)} + \theta. \tag{2.19}$$

In the following section, we make use of $E[v_t|v_s]$ but with $s = 0$. It is useful to denote this quantity as $\hat{v}_t$

$$\hat{v}_t = E[v_t|v_0] = (v_0 - \theta)e^{-\kappa t} + \theta. \tag{2.20}$$

It is also useful to define the total (integrated) variance $\hat{w}_t$ as

$$\hat{w}_t = \int_0^t \hat{v}_s ds = (v_0 - \theta)\left(\frac{1 - e^{-\kappa t}}{\kappa}\right) + \theta t. \tag{2.21}$$

As explained by Gatheral (2006), a variance swap requires an estimate of the future variance over the $(0, T)$ time period. This can be obtained as the conditional expectation of the integrated variance. A fair estimate of the total variance is therefore

$$\begin{aligned} E\left[\int_0^T v_t dt|v_0\right] &= \int_0^T E\left[v_t|v_0\right]dt = \int_0^T \left[\theta + (v_0 - \theta)\, e^{-\kappa t}\right]dt \\ &= (v_0 - \theta)\left(\frac{1 - e^{-\kappa T}}{\kappa}\right) + \theta T \end{aligned} \tag{2.22}$$

which is simply $\hat{w}_T$. Since this represents the total variance over $(0, T)$, it must be scaled by T in order to represent a fair estimate of annual variance (assuming that T is expressed in years.) Hence, the strike variance K^2_{var} for a variance swap is obtained by dividing this last expression by T

$$K^2_{\text{var}} = \frac{\hat{w}_T}{T} = (v_0 - \theta)\left(\frac{1 - e^{-\kappa T}}{\kappa T}\right) + \theta. \tag{2.23}$$

This is the expression on page 138 of Gatheral (2006).

We can use a strip of market prices for options with identical maturities to estimate the Heston parameters and obtain the fair strike variance from Equation (2.23). If the replication algorithm described in Demeterfi et al. (1999) and others is applied to the same set of options, we should obtain a fair strike that is identical, in principle at least. The level of agreement between both strikes will depend on how well the Heston model fits the options, and on the interpolation and extrapolation methods used in the replication algorithm.[1]

The Matlab file VarianceSwap.m implements the replication algorithm of Demeterfi et al. (1999). The function requires vectors of OTM calls and puts and their implied volatilities.

```
function y = VarianceSwap(KCI,CallVI,KPI,PutVI,S,T,rf,q)
Sb = S;  % Take ATM as the boundary point
f = @(S, Sb, T) 2/T*((S - Sb) / Sb - log(S/Sb));
% Calls
for i=1:n-1
    Temp(i) = (f(KCI(i+1),Sb,T) - f(KCI(i),Sb,T)) ...;
    if i==1
        CallWeight(1) = Temp(1);
    end
    CallValue(i) = BSC(S,KCI(i),rf,0,CallVI(i),T);
    if i>1
        CallWeight(i) = Temp(i) - Temp(i-1);
    end;
    CallContrib(i) = CallValue(i)*CallWeight(i);
end
Pi1 = sum(CallContrib);
% Puts
n = length(PutVI);
KPI   = fliplr(KPI);
PutVI = fliplr(PutVI);
for i=1:n-1
    Temp2(i) = (f(KPI(i+1),Sb,T) - f(KPI(i),Sb,T)) ...;
    if i==1
        PutWeight(1) = Temp2(1);
    end;
    PutValue(i) = BSP(S,KPI(i),rf,0,PutVI(i),T);
    if i>1
        PutWeight(i) = Temp2(i) - Temp2(i-1);
    end
    PutContrib(i) = PutValue(i) * PutWeight(i);
end
Pi2 = sum(PutContrib);
Pi_CP = Pi1 + Pi2;
Kvar = 2/T*(rf*T - (S/Sb*exp(rf*T) - 1) + ....;
y = Kvar;
```

The replication algorithm of Demeterfi et al. (1999) is coded in the C# function VarianceSwap(). The code is very similar and is, therefore, not presented here. The

[1]We thank Jim Gatheral for pointing this out.

VarianceSwap() function does need, however, a C# function for linear interpolation. This is achieved with the interp1() function.

```
static double interp1(double[] X,double[] Y,double xi) {
int x1 = 0;
int x2 = 0;
double yi = 0.0;
// Look for xi on the end points
if(xi == X[0]) yi = Y[0];
else if(xi == X[N-1]) yi = Y[N-1];
else
    for(int i=1;i<=N-1;i++)
        if((X[i-1] <= xi) & (xi < X[i])) {
            x1 = i-1;
            x2 = i;
            double p = (xi - Convert.ToDouble(X[x1])) ...;
            yi = (1-p)*Y[x1] + p*Y[x2]; }
return yi; }
```

To illustrate, we use a strip of options from the Dow Jones Industrial Average ETF (ticker DIA) with 15 days to maturity, and obtain the parameter estimates $\kappa = 3.000$, $\theta = 0.063$, $\sigma = 0.502$, $v_0 = 0.104$, and $\rho = -0.901$. Parameter estimation will be covered in Chapter 6. Using Equation (2.23), we obtain $K^2_{\text{var}} = 0.101$; using the replication algorithm on the market option quotes, we obtain $K^2_{\text{var}} = 0.085$.

Dupire Local Volatility

Dupire's (1994) formula for local volatility is

$$\sigma_L(K,T) = \sqrt{\frac{\dfrac{\partial C}{\partial T}}{\dfrac{1}{2}K^2\dfrac{\partial^2 C}{\partial K^2}}} \tag{2.24}$$

where $C = C(K)$ is the time- t call price with strike K and maturity T when the spot price is S_t.

Equation (2.24) stipulates that, given a set of option prices, the local volatility for a strike K and maturity T is obtained with first- and second-order derivatives of the call price. These derivatives can be obtained by finite differences, which we present in the next section. Finite differences, however, can be both computationally extensive and numerically unstable. In the Heston model, the derivatives required to evaluate (2.24) can be obtained analytically by straightforward differentiation.[2] Recall that the Heston call price is

$$C(K) = S_t P_1 - Ke^{-rT} P_2.$$

[2]See Chapter 11, "The Heston Greeks," for more on these derivatives.

The derivative with respect to T is obtained using the product rule

$$\frac{\partial C}{\partial T} = S_t \frac{\partial P_1}{\partial T} - Ke^{-rT}\left(-rP_2 + \frac{\partial P_2}{\partial T}\right) \tag{2.25}$$

where

$$\frac{\partial P_j}{\partial T} = \frac{1}{\pi}\int_0^\infty \text{Re}\left[\frac{K^{-i\phi}\partial f_j/\partial T}{i\phi}\right] d\phi. \tag{2.26}$$

Differentiating the characteristic function $f_j = f_j(\phi)$ produces

$$\frac{\partial f_j}{\partial T} = \exp(C_j + D_j v_0 + i\phi x)\left(\frac{\partial C_j}{\partial T} + \frac{\partial D_j}{\partial T} v_0\right) \tag{2.27}$$

where $C_j = C_j(T,\phi)$ and $D_j = D_j(T,\phi)$. Differentiating C_j produces

$$\frac{\partial C_j}{\partial T} = ri\phi + \frac{\kappa\theta}{\sigma^2}\left[(b_j - \rho\sigma i\phi + d_j) + 2\left(\frac{g_j d_j e^{d_j T}}{1 - g_j e^{d_j T}}\right)\right] \tag{2.28}$$

while differentiating D_j produces

$$\frac{\partial D_j}{\partial T} = \left(\frac{b_j - \rho\sigma i\phi + d_j}{\sigma^2}\right)\left[\frac{d_j e^{d_j T}(g_j e^{d_j T} - 1) + (1 - e^{d_j T}) g_j d_j e^{d_j T}}{(1 - g_j e^{d_j T})^2}\right]. \tag{2.29}$$

Hence, $\partial C/\partial T$ is found by substituting Equations (2.27), (2.28), and (2.29) into (2.26) and substituting the result into (2.25). Note that $\partial C/\partial T$ obtained in this way requires only one numerical integration for each P_j, while $\partial C/\partial T$ obtained by finite differences requires two numerical integrals for each P_j.

The second-order derivative $\partial^2 C/\partial K^2$ is

$$\frac{\partial^2 C}{\partial K^2} = S_t \frac{\partial^2 P_1}{\partial K^2} - e^{-rT}\left(2\frac{\partial P_2}{\partial K} + K\frac{\partial^2 P_2}{\partial K^2}\right). \tag{2.30}$$

The required derivatives are

$$\frac{\partial P_j}{\partial K} = -\frac{1}{\pi}\int_0^\infty \text{Re}\left[K^{-i\phi-1} f_j(\phi)\right] d\phi \tag{2.31}$$

and

$$\frac{\partial^2 P_j}{\partial K^2} = \frac{1}{\pi}\int_0^\infty \text{Re}\left[(i\phi + 1) K^{-i\phi-2} f_j(\phi)\right] d\phi. \tag{2.32}$$

The bracketed expression on the right-hand side of (2.30) is therefore

$$2\frac{\partial P_2}{\partial K} + K\frac{\partial^2 P_2}{\partial K^2} = \frac{1}{\pi}\int_0^\infty \text{Re}\left[(i\phi - 1) K^{-i\phi-1} f_2(\phi)\right] d\phi. \tag{2.33}$$

Note that $\partial^2 C/\partial K^2$ obtained in this way does not save computation time compared to finite differences, since two sets of numerical integrals are required under both methods.

If the "Little Trap" formulation of Albrecher et al. (2007) for C_j and D_j in Equations (2.17) and (2.14) is used, then

$$\frac{\partial C_j}{\partial T} = ri\phi + \frac{\kappa\theta}{\sigma^2}\left[\left(b_j - \rho\sigma i\phi - d_j\right) - 2\left(\frac{c_j d_j e^{-d_j T}}{1 - c_j e^{-d_j T}}\right)\right] \tag{2.34}$$

and

$$\frac{\partial D_j}{\partial T} = \left(\frac{b_j - \rho\sigma i\phi - d_j}{\sigma^2}\right)\left[\frac{d_j e^{-d_j T}\left(1 - c_j e^{-d_j T}\right) - (1 - e^{-d_j T})c_j d_j e^{-d_j T}}{(1 - c_j e^{d_j T})^2}\right]. \tag{2.35}$$

The other derivatives are the same, except that C_j and D_j in those derivatives take the "Little Trap" formulation.

The Matlab function dPjdT.m implements the integrand that is used to obtain the derivatives $\partial P_j/\partial T$ in Equation (2.26) using $\partial f_j/\partial T$ from Equation (2.27). It allows for the original Heston (1993) formulation for C_j and D_j and their derivatives, or for the "Little Trap" formulation in (2.17), (2.14), (2.34), and (2.35). To conserve space, parts of the function are omitted.

```
function y = dPjdT(Pnum,phi,...);
if Trap==1
    % Little Trap formulation
    c = 1/g;
    edT = exp(-d*T);
    dDdT = (b - rho*sigma*i*phi - d)/sigma^2 * ...;
    dCdT = rf*i*phi + kappa*theta/sigma^2  *...;
    G = (1 - c*edT)/(1-c);
    D = (b - rho*sigma*i*phi - d)/sigma^2 * ...;
    C = rf*i*phi*T + kappa*theta/sigma^2 * ...;
else
    % Original Heston formulation.
    edT = exp(d*T);
    dDdT = (b - rho*sigma*i*phi + d)/sigma^2 * ...;
    dCdT = rf*i*phi + kappa*theta/sigma^2 *...;
    G = (1 - g*edT)/(1-g);
    C = rf*i*phi*T + kappa*theta/sigma^2 * ...;
    D = (b - rho*sigma*i*phi + d)/sigma^2 * ....;
end
dfdT = exp(C + D*v0 + i*phi*x)*(dCdT + dDdT*v0);
y = real(K^(-i*phi)*dfdT/i/phi);
```

The function is then passed to the Matlab function dCdT.m for implementing the derivatives $\partial C/\partial T$ in Equation (2.25), using, in this case, Gauss-Laguerre weights and abscissas stored in the vectors x and w, respectively.

```
function y = dCdT(...);
for k=1:length(x)
    int1(k)  = w(k)*dPjdT(1,x(k),...);
    int2(k)  = w(k)*dPjdT(2,x(k),...);
    int3(k)  = w(k)*HestonProb(x(k),...,2);
end
dP1dT = (1/pi)*sum(int1);
dP2dT = (1/pi)*sum(int2);
P2    = (1/2) + (1/pi)*sum(int3);
y = S*dP1dT - K*exp(-rf*T)*(-rf*P2 + dP2dT);
```

The Matlab function d2P1dK2.m implements the integrand that is used to obtain the derivative $\partial^2 P_1/\partial K^2$ (for P_1 only) in Equation (2.32).

```
function y = d2P1dK2(phi,...);
d = sqrt((rho*sigma*i*phi - b)^2 - ...;
g = (b - rho*sigma*i*phi + d) / ...;
% Original Heston formulation.
G = (1 - g*exp(d*T))/(1-g);
C = rf*i*phi*T + kappa*sigma/sigma^2 * ...;
D = (b - rho*sigma*i*phi + d)/sigma^2 * ...;
% The cf and real part of the integrand
f1 = exp(C + D*v0 + i*phi*x);
y = real((i*phi+1) * K^(-i*phi-2) * f1);
```

The last function needed is that for $2\partial P_2/\partial K + K\partial^2 P_2/\partial K^2$ in Equation (2.33). This is the dP2dK2_2.m Matlab function.

```
function y = dP2dK2_2(phi,...);
% Original Heston formulation.
G = (1 - g*exp(d*T))/(1-g);
C = rf*i*phi*T + kappa*sigma/sigma^2 * ...;
D = (b - rho*sigma*i*phi + d)/sigma^2 * ...;
% The cf and real part of the integrand
f2 = exp(C + D*v0 + i*phi*x);
y = real((i*phi-1) * K^(-i*phi-1) * f2);
```

Finally, the function HestonLVAnalytic.m regroups these functions and obtains the analytic expression for local volatility $\sigma_L(K, T)$ in the Heston model, using Equation (2.24).

```
function y = HestonLVAnalytic(...);
for k=1:length(x)
    int1(k)  = w(k)*dPjdT(1,x(k),...);
    int2(k)  = w(k)*dPjdT(2,x(k),...);
    int3(k)  = w(k)*HestonProb(x(k),...,2);
```

```
    int4(k) = w(k)*d2P1dK2(x(k),...);
    int5(k) = w(k)*dP2dK2_2(x(k),...);
end
dP1dT = (1/pi)*sum(int1);
dP2dT = (1/pi)*sum(int2);
P2    = (1/2) + (1/pi)*sum(int3);
% dC/dT : derivative with respect to T
dCdT = S*dP1dT - K*exp(-rf*T)*(-rf*P2 + dP2dT);
dP1dK2 = (1/pi)*sum(int4);
TwodP2dK2 = (1/pi)*sum(int5);
% d2C/dK2 : 2nd derivative with respect to K^2
d2CdK2 = S*dP1dK2 - exp(-rf*T)*TwodP2dK2;
% Local Variance and Local Volatility
LocalVar = 2*dCdT / (K^2*d2CdK2);
y = sqrt(LocalVar);
```

The C# functions for obtaining the derivatives and the analytic local volatility $\sigma_L(K,T)$ in Equation (2.24) are very similar to the Matlab functions and are not presented here.

Instead of expressing the derivatives of Equation (2.24) analytically, we can use approximate these derivatives using finite differences. This is the approach used to obtain local volatility in the next section.

Local Volatility With Finite Differences

The analytic expressions for the derivatives required of the Dupire (1994) local volatility formula require extensive coding, as illustrated in the previous section. From a coding point of view, it is simpler to approximate the derivatives using finite differences. Write $C(K) = C(K,T)$ to emphasize the dependence of the European call price on the maturity T. We use a small time increment dt and approximate the time derivative as the central difference

$$\frac{\partial C}{\partial T} \approx \frac{C(K,T+dt) - C(K,T-dt)}{2dt}. \tag{2.36}$$

Similarly, we can use a small strike increment dK and approximate the second-order strike derivative as the central difference

$$\frac{\partial^2 C}{\partial K^2} \approx \frac{C(K-dK,T) - 2C(K,T) + C(K+dK,T)}{(dK)^2}. \tag{2.37}$$

The function HestonLVFD.m obtains local volatility $\sigma_L(K,T)$ in the Heston model using the central difference approximation to the derivatives.

```
function y = HestonLVFD(...,dt,dK);
% dC/dT by central finite difference
CT_1 = HestonCallGaussLaguerre(S,K,T-dt,...,x,w);
CT1  = HestonCallGaussLaguerre(S,K,T+dt,...,x,w);
dCdT =  (CT1 - CT_1) / (2*dt);
```

```
% dC2/dK2 by central finite differences
CK_1  = HestonCallGaussLaguerre(S,K-dK,...,x,w);
CK0   = HestonCallGaussLaguerre(S,K    ,...,x,w);
CK1   = HestonCallGaussLaguerre(S,K+dK,...,x,w);
dC2dK2 = (CK_1 - 2*CK0 + CK1) / (dK)^2;
% Local variance and local volatility
LocalVar = 2*dCdT / (K^2*dC2dK2);
y = sqrt(LocalVar);
```

The C# code for approximating the first- and second-order derivatives required in $\sigma_L(K,T)$ is very similar and is not presented here.

The code for $\sigma_L(K,T)$ in this section is indeed much simpler and more compact than the code in the previous section that uses analytic derivatives. The disadvantage is that, since finite differences require multiple calculations of the call price, the code that uses finite differences will run slower. Moreover, finite differences can cause numerical instability in the second-order derivative. Finally, finite differences are only approximations to the derivatives, whereas the analytic expressions are exact.

Approximate Local Volatility

In his excellent book, *The Volatility Surface: A Practitioner's Guide*, Gatheral (2006) derives an approximation to local volatility in the Heston model that is valid when $\rho \approx \pm 1$. In this section, we present his results and fill in the details of his derivation. Recall that in the bivariate system of SDEs that characterize the Heston model, $W_{1,t}$ and $W_{2,t}$ are dependent Brownian motions with correlation ρ. It is well-known that $W_{1,t}$ and $W_{2,t}$ can be replaced by a Cholesky decomposition of two independent Brownian motions Z_t and B_t, by defining $W_{1,t} = B_t$ and $W_{2,t} = \rho B_t + \sqrt{1-\rho^2} Z_t$.

Gatheral (2006) derives approximate local volatility in terms of log-moneyness $x_t = \ln(S_t/K)$, and using a zero drift, so that $\mu = 0$. The process for x_t can be obtained using Itō's lemma. Together with the Cholesky decomposition, we can write the Heston SDEs as

$$\begin{aligned} dx_t &= -\frac{v_t}{2}dt + \sqrt{v_t}dB_t \\ dv_t &= \kappa(\theta - v_t)dt + \sigma\sqrt{v_t}(\rho dB_t + \sqrt{1-\rho^2}dZ_t) \end{aligned} \tag{2.38}$$

where $E[dB_t dZ_t] = 0$. In the process for v_t in (2.38), replace the term involving $\sqrt{v_t}dB_t$ with that appearing in the process for x_t, and assume that $\rho \approx \pm 1$ so that the term involving $1-\rho^2$ vanishes. This produces

$$dv_t = \kappa(\theta - v_t)dt + \rho\sigma\left(dx_t + \frac{1}{2}v_t dt\right). \tag{2.39}$$

Gatheral defines $u_t = E[v_t | x_T]$ to denote the expected value of the time-t instantaneous variance conditional on the value of log-moneyness at time T.

Moreover, he assumes that the following ansatz, loosely defined as an educated guess, holds

$$E[x_t|x_T] = \frac{x_T}{\hat{w}_T}\hat{w}_t.$$

Taking the conditional expectation of (2.39) and applying the ansatz produces

$$du_t = \kappa(\theta - u_t)dt + \rho\sigma\left(\frac{x_T}{\hat{w}_T}\hat{v}_t dt + \frac{1}{2}u_t dt\right)$$

since according to the ansatz, $E[dx_t|x_T] = (x_T/\hat{w}_T)d\hat{w}_t$, and from Equation (2.21), $d\hat{w}_t = \hat{v}_t dt$. Rearranging terms produces

$$du_t = \kappa'(\theta' - u_t)dt + \rho\sigma\frac{x_T}{\hat{w}_T}\hat{v}_t dt \tag{2.40}$$

where $\kappa' = \kappa - \rho\sigma/2$ and $\theta' = \theta\kappa/\kappa'$. We can write (2.40) as

$$\frac{du_t}{dt} + \kappa' u_t = \rho\sigma\frac{x_T}{\hat{w}_T}\hat{v}_t + \kappa'\theta'.$$

We recognize this as a first-order differential equation of the form $du_t/dt + P_t u_t = Q_t$, whose solution u_T at time T is given by

$$u_T \exp\left(\int_0^T P_t dt\right) = \int_0^T Q_t \exp\left(\int_0^t P_s ds\right) dt + C_1$$

where C_1 is a constant.

Substituting for $P_t = \kappa'$ and $Q_t = \rho\sigma v_t x_T/\hat{w}_T + \kappa'\theta'$, multiplying both sides by $e^{-\kappa' T}$ and performing the integration produces

$$u_T = \rho\sigma\frac{x_T}{\hat{w}_T}\int_0^T \hat{v}_t e^{-\kappa'(T-t)}dt + \theta'(1 - e^{-\kappa' T}) + C_1 e^{-\kappa' T}. \tag{2.41}$$

The initial condition is that $u_0 = E[v_0|x_T] = v_0$, the initial variance. Setting $T = 0$ in Equation (2.41) implies that $u_0 = C_1 = v_0$. The approximation to local variance when $\rho \approx \pm 1$, u_T is, therefore

$$u_T = \hat{v}'_T + \rho\sigma\frac{x_T}{\hat{w}_T}\int_0^T \hat{v}_t e^{-\kappa'(T-t)}dt \tag{2.42}$$

where

$$\hat{v}'_T - (v_0 - \theta')e^{-\kappa' T} + \theta' \tag{2.43}$$

analogous to (2.20). Equation (2.42) is Equation (3.15) of Gatheral (2006), and can be further integrated to produce

$$u_T = \hat{v}'_T + \rho\sigma\frac{x_T}{\hat{w}_T}e^{\kappa' T}\left[\frac{v_0 - \theta}{\kappa' - \kappa}\left(e^{(\kappa' - \kappa)T} - 1\right) + \frac{\theta}{\kappa'}(e^{\kappa' T} - 1)\right]. \tag{2.44}$$

The Matlab function HestonLVApprox.m implements Gatheral's (2006) approximation to local volatility $\sigma_L(K,T)$ in the Heston model, in accordance with (2.44).

```
function y = HestonLVApprox(...);
% Modified parameters kappa' and theta'
kappa_ = kappa - rho*sigma/2;
theta_ = theta*kappa/kappa_;
% wT and vT'
xT = log(K/S);
wT = (v0-theta)*(1-exp(-kappa*T))/kappa + theta*T;
vT = (v0-theta_)*exp(-kappa_*T) + theta_;
% Integral
F1 = (v0-theta)/(kappa_-kappa);
E1 = exp((kappa_-kappa)*T) - 1;
F2 = theta/kappa_;
E2 = exp(kappa_*T) - 1;
Integral = exp(-kappa_*T)*(F1*E1 + F2*E2);
% Local Variance and Local Volatility
uT = vT + rho*sigma*xT/wT*Integral;
y = sqrt(uT);
```

The C# code is very similar and is therefore not presented here.

Numerical Illustration of Local Volatility

We illustrate local volatility in the Heston model using a set of put options with 222 days to expiry, when the spot price is $S_t = 30.67$. The Heston parameters associated with this set of options were estimated as $\theta = 0.007$, $\kappa = 6.45 \times 10^{-6}$, $\sigma = 0.639$, $v_0 = 0.579$, and $\rho = -0.805$. We obtain exact local volatility $\sigma_L(K,T)$ in (2.24) using analytic derivatives and finite difference approximations and we also obtain Gatheral's (2006) approximate local volatility in (2.44), for $T = 222/365$ and for strikes running from $K = 15$ to $K = 65$. We have also added the implied volatility from Heston put prices generated with the parameter estimates. The results are illustrated in Figure 2.10.

Figure 2.10 illustrates the observation of Gatheral (2006) that the approximate form of local volatility (solid red line) tends to be less curved than the exact form. The figure also shows that the exact form using the analytic formulation (solid black line) and finite difference approximation (black circles) produce local volatilities that are nearly identical. Finally, the slope of local volatility is roughly 1.9 times that of implied volatility, on average, which is consistent with the rule of thumb of Derman et al. (1995) that local volatility is roughly twice as steep as implied volatility. Figure 2.10 is generated using the following code, which makes use of the functions described earlier in this section.

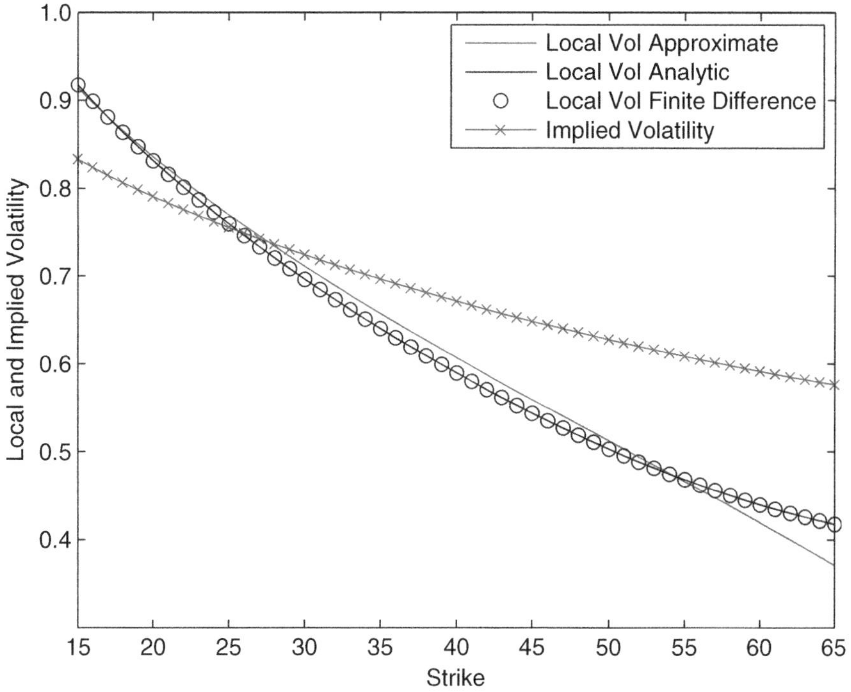

FIGURE 2.10 Heston Local Volatility and Implied Volatility

```
% Local volatilities
for k=1:length(K)
    LVFD(k) = HestonLVFD(K(k),...,dt,dK);
    LVAN(k) = HestonLVAnalytic(K(k),...);
    LVAP(k) = HestonLVApprox(K(k),...);
end
% Implied volatilities
PutCall = 'P';
a = 0.001;    b = 10;   Tol = 1e-10; MaxIter = 1000;
for k=1:length(K)
    CallPrice = HestonCallGaussLaguerre(K(k),...);
    ModelPrice(k) = CallPrice - S0 + exp(-rf*T)*K(k);
    IVm(k) = BisecBSIV(K(k),ModelPrice(k),...);
end
plot(K,LVAP,K,LVAN,K,LVFD,K,IVm)
```

We can also apply our three estimates of local volatility–analytic and finite differences in Equation (2.24), and approximate in (2.44)–to SPX options data. This appears in Figure 2.11.

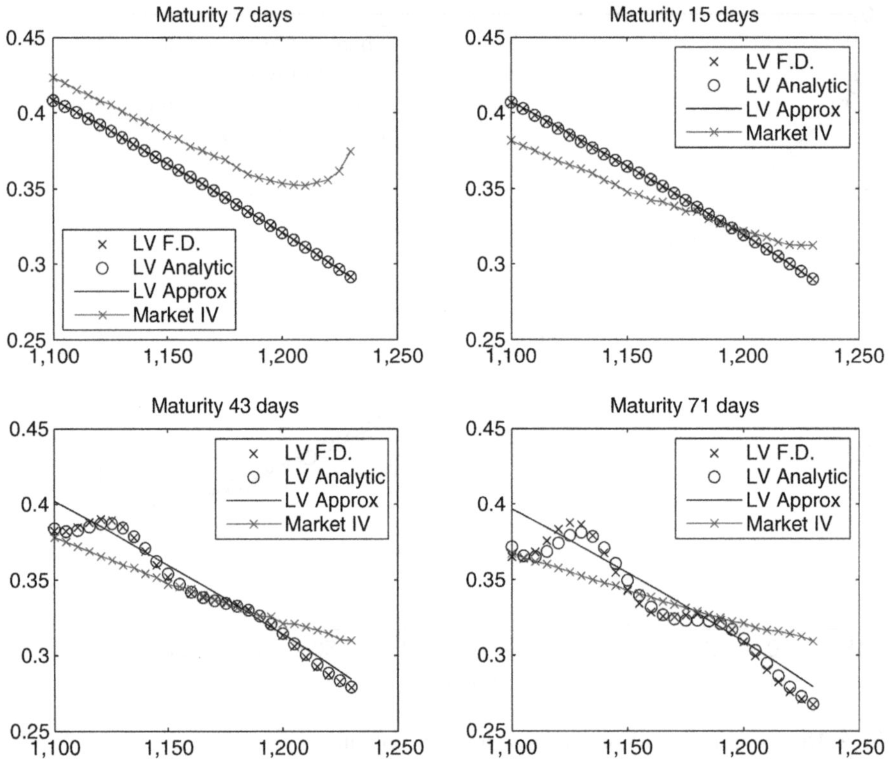

FIGURE 2.11 Market Implied Volatility and Heston Volatility, S&P 500 Index

As expected, and consistent with Figure 2.10, local volatility is generally steeper and more erratic than implied volatility. The approximation to local volatility preserves the steeper slope, but does not preserve the erratic behavior. The analytic and finite difference local volatilities are very close, except for the maturity of 71 days, where the finite difference approximation breaks down slightly.

Implied Volatility

We noted earlier in this chapter that option prices obtained with the Heston model have an implied volatility smile that is built in, in the sense that implied volatilities extracted from those prices will exhibit an implied volatility smile. Moreover, the parameters ρ and σ have an effect on the skew and steepness of the smile.

In practice, implied volatilities extracted from Heston model prices will sometimes show a poor fit to market implied volatilities for short maturities. For longer maturities, however, the fit is better. We illustrate this by using put options on the Dow Jones Industrial Average ETF (ticker DIA) with four maturities (37, 72, 135, and 226 days). The closing price for DIA was \$129.14. We obtained the parameter estimates $\kappa = 8.8799$, $\theta = 0.0674$, $\sigma = 3.6706$, $v_0 = 0.0435$, and $\rho = -0.4171$. Parameter estimation methods for the Heston model are dealt with in Chapter 6. For simplicity, we set $r = q = 0$. Figure 2.12 presents market implied volatilities from the DIA, and implied volatilities obtained using the bisection algorithm on Heston prices generated with the earlier parameter estimates.

Figure 2.12 clearly indicates that, at the short maturity, the Heston implied volatilities to the market implied volatilities is poor. For longer maturities, however, the Heston model provides a very good fit.

The bisection algorithm is used to obtain market and Heston implied volatilities. The Matlab function BisecBSIV.m and the C# function BisecBSIV() for this algorithm were presented earlier in this chapter. The algorithm finds the implied volatility by finding the zero of the difference between the market price and the Black-Scholes price. The advantage of using this algorithm is that a solution will always be found, provided that the function is continuous, and that the two initial endpoints of the interval are selected so that one value produces a negative difference, and the other produces a positive difference, indicating the presence of a root within the interval. Since option prices are monotone increasing in volatility, we can always use a very small value for the first initial endpoint (say 0.1 percent), and a very large value for the second endpoint (say 500 percent).

We have used the following Matlab code to generate Figure 2.12. We hard-code the parameter values, which we obtained from Matlab code in Chapter 6.

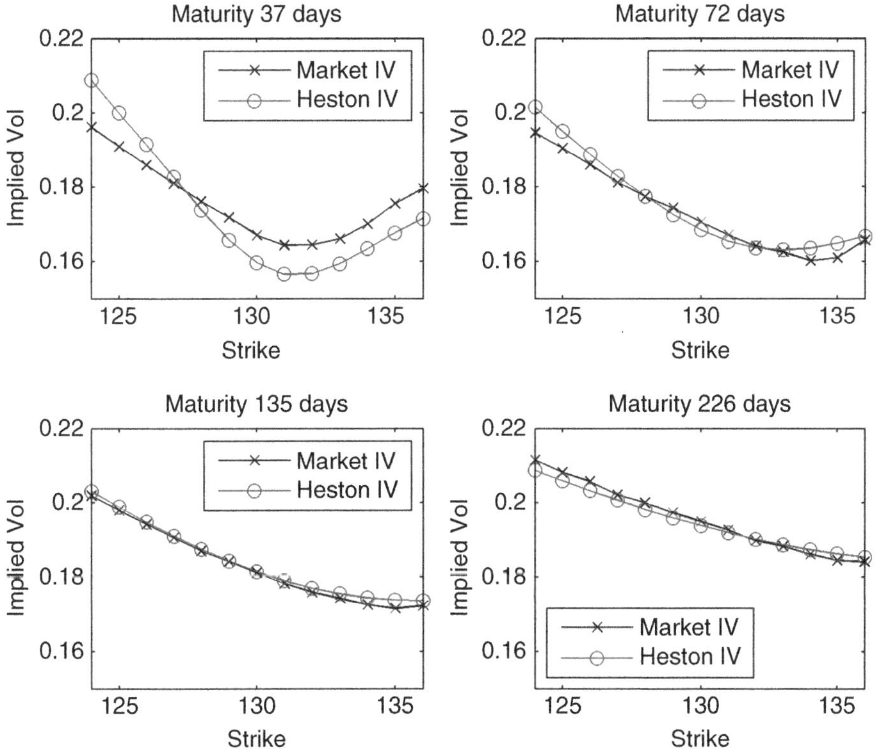

FIGURE 2.12 Market and Heston Implied Volatilities from Puts on DIA

```
param = [8.8799, 0.0674, 3.6706, 0.0435, -0.4171];
for k=1:NK
    for t=1:NT
        CallPrice = HestonCallGaussLaguerre(K(k),T(t),...);
        ModelPrice(k,t) = CallPrice - S0 + exp(-rf*T(t))*K(k);
    end
end
for k=1:NK
    for t=1:NT
        IVm(k,t) = BisecBSIV(K(k),T(t),ModelPrice(k,t),...);
    end
end
for t=1:NT
    subplot(2,2,t);
    plot(K,IV(:,t),K,IVm(:,t))
end
```

MOMENT EXPLOSIONS

Andersen and Piterbarg (2007) derive conditions under which the moments of the terminal stock price, $E[S_T^\omega]$, explode (become infinite) within a finite amount of time. The results of their paper can be used to find values of $\omega > 1$ for which $E[S_T^\omega]$ remains finite for all $T > 0$, using their analytic expressions for the time to moment explosion $T^* = \sup\{t : E[S_t^\omega] < \infty\}$. The moment will be finite for $T < T^*$ but will explode to infinity for $T > T^*$. Define the quantities

$$k = \frac{\lambda_L^2}{2}\omega(\omega-1), \quad b = \frac{2k}{\sigma^2}, \quad a = \frac{2}{\sigma^2}(\rho\sigma\lambda_L\omega - \kappa), \quad D = a^2 - 4b. \tag{2.45}$$

The value of T^* arises from one of three possible cases:

Case 1. $D \geq 0$ and $a < 0$

$$T^* = \infty.$$

Case 2. $D \geq 0$ and $a > 0$

$$T^* = \frac{1}{\gamma\sigma^2}\ln\left(\frac{a/2+\gamma}{a/2-\gamma}\right), \text{ where } \gamma = \frac{\sqrt{D}}{2}.$$

Case 3. $D < 0$

$$T^* = \frac{2}{\beta\sigma^2}(\pi \mathbf{1}_{a<0} + \arctan(2\beta/a)), \text{ where } \beta = \frac{\sqrt{-D}}{2}.$$

In these equations, we can set $\lambda_L = 1$ (see, for example, Forde and Jacquier, 2009). Case 1 is the most desirable, since it implies that the time to moment explosion will never be reached.

The Matlab function MomentExplode.m finds the time to moment explosion.

```
function y = MomentExplode(w,lambda,sigma,kappa,rho)
if D>=0 & a>0
    T = inf;
elseif D>=0 & a>0
    g = sqrt(D)/2;
    T = log((a/2+g)/(a/2-g))/g/sigma^2;
elseif D<0
    beta = sqrt(-D)/2;
    if a<0 PI = pi;
    else PI = 0;
    end
    T = 2*(PI + atan(2*beta/a))/beta/sigma^2;
end
y = T;
```

The C# code is very similar to the Matlab code and, therefore, not presented here. To illustrate, suppose that $\kappa = 0.1$ and $\sigma = 0.3$. If $\rho = -0.7$, the second moment ($\omega = 2$) will explode after $T^* = 5.14$ years; if $\rho = 0.7$, the second moment will never explode.

BOUNDS ON IMPLIED VOLATILITY SLOPE

One problem that arises in modeling the implied volatility surface is that extrapolation of the surface beyond observable strikes is often arbitrary. Lee (2004b) provides guidance on this issue, by deriving the slopes of the implied volatility at extreme strikes. These slopes were subsequently refined by Benaim and Friz (2008).

Define the log-moneyness to be $k = \ln(K/F)$ where $F = E[S_T]$ is the forward price, and let $\sigma(k, T)$ denote implied volatility at log-moneyness k and at maturity T. The extreme strike tail of the implied variance can be written as a linear function of $|k|$ for some value of the slope coefficient

$$\sigma^2(k, T) = \text{Coefficient} \times \frac{|k|}{T}. \tag{2.46}$$

The first moment formula is for implied variance for extreme strikes on the right-hand side of the tail, as $k \to \infty$. In this case, the tail slope is bounded above by 2, so that $\sigma^2(k, T) < 2|k|/T$. The actual value of the slope coefficient is found in the limit as

$$\beta_R = \limsup_{k\to\infty} \frac{\sigma^2(k, T)}{|k|/T}, \tag{2.47}$$

with $0 \leq \beta_R \leq 2$. Hence, as $k \to \infty$, we have that $\sigma^2(k, T) \to \beta_R |k|/T$. The result of Lee (2004b) is that β_R can be obtained as

$$\beta_R = 2 - 4\left(\sqrt{\tilde{p}^2 + \tilde{p}} - \tilde{p}\right) \tag{2.48}$$

where $\tilde{p} - 1$ is the largest finite moment of S_T, namely

$$\tilde{p} = \sup\left\{p : E\left[S_T^{1+p}\right] < \infty\right\}. \tag{2.49}$$

The second moment formula is for implied variance for extreme strikes on the left-hand side of the tail, as $k \to -\infty$. The limiting value of the slope coefficient in this case is

$$\beta_L = \limsup_{k\to-\infty} \frac{\sigma^2(k,T)}{|k|/T}, \tag{2.50}$$

with $0 \le \beta_L \le 2$ given by

$$\beta_L = 2 - 4(\sqrt{\tilde{q}^2 + \tilde{q}} - \tilde{q}) \tag{2.51}$$

and with

$$\tilde{q} = \sup\left\{q : E\left[S_T^{-q}\right] < \infty\right\}. \tag{2.52}$$

Hence, β_R and β_L represent the slopes that must be respected when we extrapolate the implied variance at large and small strikes, respectively.

The first step to finding these coefficients is to find the bounds on finite moments, $\tilde{p}$ and $\tilde{q}$. We can find these using the moment explosion formula of Andersen and Piterbarg (2007). We move away from $\omega > 1$ in increments and calculate T^* at each step, and stop when we encounter $T^* < \infty$. Alternatively, we can use the characteristic function $f_2(\phi) = E[S_T^{i\phi}]$ by noting that the moments are $E[S_T^{\omega}] = f_2(-i\omega)$. Again, we move away from $\omega > 1$ in increments and calculate $f_2(-i\omega)$ until we encounter a complex value.

Both of these approaches to finding the bounds on finite moments are implemented in the Matlab function FindLeeBounds.m. The first part of the function uses the result of Andersen and Piterbarg (2007) to find the bounds on finite moments. To find the moment $\omega > 1$ at which $T^* < \infty$, we start with a wide grid $1 < \omega < 10$ and loop through the values to identify where $T^* < \infty$. We then reduce the size of the grid for ω and repeat. After several iterations we have a fairly accurate estimate of the upper moment at which T^* starts to become finite. To find the lower moment, we use $-10 < \omega < 0$ and apply the same methodology.

```
function [bR bL LowerAP UpAP LoCF UpCF] = FindLeeBounds(...)
lambda = 1;
% Upper and lower moment bounds using Andersen and Piterbarg
W = [1:HiLimit];
for k=1:15
    j = 1;
    T = Inf;
    while(T == inf)
        j = j+1;
        T = MomentExplode(W(j),lambda,sigma,kappa,rho);
    end
    e = 1/10^k;
    W = [W(j-1):e:W(j+1)];
    clear T
```

```
end
UpperAP = W(j);
% Lower moment bound
W = [LoLimit:0];
for k=1:15
    j = 1;
    T(j) = 0;
    while(T(j) < inf)
        j = j+1;
        T(j) = MomentExplode(W(j),lambda,sigma,kappa,rho);
    end
    e = 1/10^k;
    W = [W(j-1):e:W(j+1)];
    clear T
end
LowerAP = W(j);
```

To find the moment bounds using the characteristic function, we loop through values of ω until a complex value of the characteristic function is returned. This is accomplished with the middle part of the FindLeeBounds.m function.

```
% Upper Moment.  Loop through until imag(CF) is encountered
CF = 0;
e = 1e-5;
W = 0.9*UpperAP;
while isreal(CF)
    phi = -i*W;
    CF = HestonCF(phi,kappa,theta,0,rho,sigma,tau,S,r,q,v0,trap);
    W = W+e;
end
UpperCF = W;
% Lower Moment.  Loop through until imag(CF) is encountered
CF = 0;
e = -1e-5;
W = 0.9*LowerAP;
while isreal(CF)
    phi = -i*W;
    CF = HestonCF(phi,kappa,theta,0,rho,sigma,tau,S,r,q,v0,trap);
    W = W+e;
end
LowerCF = W;
```

Finally, the last part of the function returns the Lee (2004b) bounds on the volatility slope.

```
p =  UpperAP - 1;
q = -LowerAP;
bR = 2 - 4*(sqrt(p^2 + p) - p);
bL = 2 - 4*(sqrt(q^2 + q) - q);
```

The C# code is similar and not presented. To illustrate, we use the parameter estimates from put options on the Dow Jones Industrial Average (DJIA) with maturity 37 days. The spot price is \$129.14. The parameter estimates are $\kappa = 4.52$, $\sigma = 2.11$, $\rho = -0.27$. The upper moment bound is 3.6842, so $\tilde{p} = 2.6842$. The lower moment bound is -1.3376, so $\tilde{q} = 1.3376$. We substitute the values of $\tilde{p}$ and $\tilde{q}$ into Equations (2.48) and (2.51) to obtain the limiting slope coefficients $\beta_L = 0.2773$ and $\beta_R = 0.1580$.

We can use these limiting slope coefficients to find the slope of the implied volatility at extreme strikes for the set of 37-day maturity puts on the DJIA that were used to generate them. This is illustrated in Figure 2.13.

The range of observed strikes is $[124, 136]$ in increments of \$1, and the spot is $S_t = 129.14$, so the range of observed log-moneyness is $[-0.0406, 0.0518]$. We fit Heston prices to the expanded range of strikes $[120, 140]$, corresponding to the range of log-moneyness $[-0.0734, 0.0807]$, and extract implied volatilities from those prices. Finally, we expand the log-moneyness range to $[-0.1534, 0.1407]$ and use β_L and β_R to obtain the slopes at the extreme values of log-moneyness. Note that the slopes of the implied volatility at the extreme strikes in Figure 2.13 are not β_L and β_R, since these are the slopes for variance.

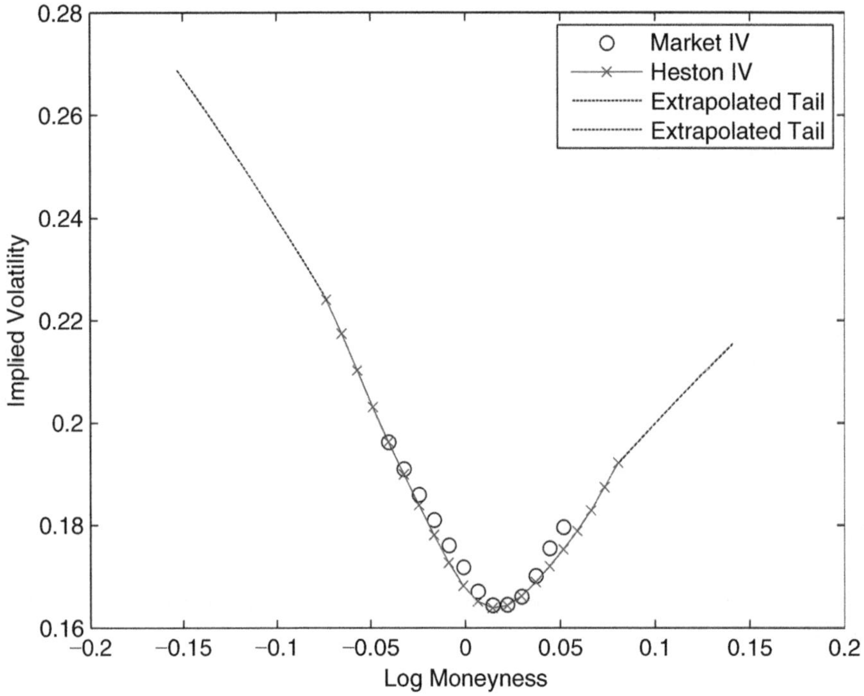

FIGURE 2.13 Implied Volatility at Extreme Strikes, DJIA Puts

CONCLUSION

In this chapter, we showed that the Heston call price can be expressed in terms of a single characteristic function and that the Heston model fits into the framework described by Bakshi and Madan (2000). Next, we presented the "Little Trap" formulation of Albrecher et al. (2007) that can remedy many of the problems with the numerical integration that arise when the integrand is discontinuous. We then examined the effect of the Heston parameters on the implied volatilities, and showed that varying these parameters can induce substantial changes in the pattern of implied volatility smiles and skews. We also presented Gatheral's (2006) fair strike of a variance swap under the Heston model, his approximation to local and implied volatility in the model, and formulas for analytical local volatility and finite difference approximations to local volatility. Finally, we showed how the moment explosion times of Andersen and Piterbarg (2007) can be used to find the bounds on implied volatility due to Lee (2004b) and illustrated the value of these bounds on extreme strikes in an implied volatility smile.

The formulas for the Heston call price have so far involved inversion of the characteristic function to obtain the probabilities P_1 and P_2. In the next chapter, we present a popular method to obtain the call price due to Carr and Madan (1999) that uses the Fourier transform of the call price itself. We also present an alternate derivation of the Heston call price due to Gatheral (2006) that makes use of Fourier transforms of P_1 and P_2. Finally, we present a call price formula due to Attari (2004) that makes use of a single integral that decays very quickly and, therefore, requires a short integration domain.

CHAPTER 3

Derivations Using the Fourier Transform

Abstract

The Heston model laid the foundation for the popularity of Fourier transforms in mathematical finance. Fourier transforms have now earned their place as crucial tools in pricing models for equity derivatives. This owes to the fact that, in most cases, the terminal price density has no analytic structure. The characteristic function, on the other hand, is often readily available for many models, including the Heston model. The Heston model is a perfect illustration of why Fourier transforms are useful. Indeed, if the characteristic function is available for the price process, then the Fourier transform can be used to extract the probabilities from the characteristic function and obtain the call price using the Black-Scholes–style representation described in Chapter 2.

The application of Fourier transforms to option pricing is not limited to obtaining probabilities, as is done in Heston's (1993) original derivation. As explained by Wu (2008), the literature approaches Fourier transforms in option pricing in two broad ways. The first approach considers option prices to be analogous to cumulative distribution functions. This is the approach adopted by Heston (1993), Carr and Madan (1999), Bakshi and Madan (2000), and others. The second approach considers option prices to be analogous to probability density functions. This is the approach of Lewis (2000, 2001) that we cover in Chapter 4.

In this chapter, we show how to derive the Heston call price using the Fourier transform. We follow the derivations described by Gatheral (2006) and Attari (2004). Next, we present the Carr and Madan (1999) representation of the Heston call price, a method in which the Fourier transform plays a key role. We also discuss the optimal choice of the damping factor that is required of their method.

THE FOURIER TRANSFORM

There are several definition of the Fourier transform $\hat{f}$ of a function f. The one usually encountered in the mathematical finance literature and used by Carr and Madan (1999), Duffie, Pan, and Singleton (2000), and Zhu (2010), among others, is

$$\hat{f}(u) = \int_{-\infty}^{\infty} e^{iux} f(x)\, dx \tag{3.1}$$

where $i = \sqrt{-1}$ is the imaginary unit. See, for example, Shephard (1991). The original function f can be recovered from $\hat{f}$ via the inverse Fourier transform

$$f(x) = \frac{1}{2\pi}\int_{-\infty}^{\infty} e^{-iux}\hat{f}(u)\,du. \tag{3.2}$$

Differentiation in the Fourier transform is an easy operation, because it is converted into multiplication. The Fourier transform of the derivative of f is

$$\widehat{f'(u)} = \int_{-\infty}^{\infty} e^{iux}f'(x)\,dx. \tag{3.3}$$

Perform integration by parts to obtain

$$\widehat{f'(u)} = e^{iux}f(x)\Big|_{x=-\infty}^{x=\infty} - iu\int_{-\infty}^{\infty} e^{iux}f(x)\,dx = -iu\hat{f}(u). \tag{3.4}$$

Applying integration by parts once more shows that $\widehat{f''(u)} = (-iu)^2\hat{f}(u)$, while a repeated application shows that the Fourier transform of the derivative of order n is $(-iu)^n\hat{f}(u)$.

The derivative of the Fourier transform is obtained by differentiating inside the integral of Equation (3.1)

$$\frac{d\hat{f}(u)}{du} = \int_{-\infty}^{\infty}\frac{d}{du}(e^{iux}f(x))dx = \int_{-\infty}^{\infty} ixe^{iux}f(x)dx = i\hat{g}(u) \tag{3.5}$$

where $g(x) = xf(x)$.

The representation in (3.1) is convenient when $f(x)$ represents the density of a random variable X. In that case, the Fourier transform is the characteristic function for X

$$\hat{f}(u) = E[e^{iux}].$$

Using Euler's identity, $e^{ix} = \cos x + i\sin x$, the characteristic function $\varphi(u)$ can be written

$$\varphi(u) = E[e^{iux}] = E[\cos ux] + iE[\sin ux]. \tag{3.6}$$

The following property of the characteristic function is useful. Since $\cos(x)$ is an even function, while $\sin(x)$ is odd, we can write

$$\begin{aligned}\varphi(-u) &= E[\cos(-ux)] + iE[\sin(-ux)]\\ &= E[\cos ux] - iE[\sin ux] = \overline{\varphi(u)}\end{aligned} \tag{3.7}$$

where $\bar{z}$ denotes the complex conjugate of z.

RECOVERY OF PROBABILITIES WITH GIL-PELAEZ FOURIER INVERSION

Recall from Chapters 1 and 2 that the in-the-money probabilities are

$$\Pr(\ln S_T > k) = \frac{1}{2} + \frac{1}{\pi}\int_0^{\infty} \text{Re}\left[\frac{e^{-iuk}\varphi(u)}{iu}\right] du \tag{3.8}$$

where $k = \ln K$.

We have suppressed the j index, and we have denoted $\varphi(u)$ to be the characteristic function for $\ln S_T$ evaluated at u. The probabilities expressed in the form of Equation (3.8) were derived by Gil-Pelaez (1951) using the inversion theorem for Fourier transforms. The sign function sgn α plays in an important role in this derivation. It is defined as

$$\text{sgn}\,\alpha = \begin{cases} \alpha/|\alpha| & \alpha \neq 0 \\ 0 & \alpha = 0 \end{cases} \tag{3.9}$$

so that $\text{sgn}\,\alpha = 1$ for $\alpha > 0$, $\text{sgn}\,\alpha = -1$ for $\alpha < 0$, and $\text{sgn}\,\alpha = 0$ for $\alpha = 0$. The sign function has the integral representation

$$\text{sgn}\,\alpha = \frac{1}{\pi}\int_{-\infty}^{\infty} \frac{\sin \alpha x}{x} dx. \tag{3.10}$$

See, for example, Stuart (2010) for a derivation or Chacon (1991) for an introduction. Denote $f(x)$ to be the density of $\ln S_T$, and $F(x)$ to be its distribution. Using the definition of the sign function in (3.9), we can write for a fixed y

$$\begin{aligned}\int_{-\infty}^{\infty} \text{sgn}(x-y)f(x)dx &= \int_{y}^{\infty} \text{sgn}(x-y)f(x)dx - \int_{-\infty}^{y} \text{sgn}(y-x)f(x)dx \\ &= [1-F(y)] - F(y) = 1 - 2F(y).\end{aligned} \tag{3.11}$$

To evaluate (3.11), we have broken up the integration range at y and we have exploited the sign of $x - y$ over each region.

To begin the derivation of Equation (3.8), note that $f(x)$ can be recovered from $\varphi(u)$ by inversion, as in (3.2)

$$f(x) = \frac{1}{2\pi}\int_{-\infty}^{\infty} e^{-iux}\varphi(u)\,du. \tag{3.12}$$

We can express $\Pr(\ln S_T > k)$ using the density, and then substitute Equation (3.12) to obtain

$$\begin{aligned}\Pr(\ln S_T > k) &= \int_k^{\infty} f(x)dx = \frac{1}{2\pi}\int_k^{\infty}\left(\int_{-\infty}^{\infty} e^{-iux}\varphi(u)\,du\right)dx \\ &= \frac{1}{2\pi}\int_{-\infty}^{\infty}\varphi(u)\left(\int_k^{\infty} e^{-iux}dx\right)du.\end{aligned} \tag{3.13}$$

The last equality is obtained by reversing the order of integration. Now evaluate the inner integral in the second line of (3.13), which results in

$$\Pr(\ln S_T > k) = \frac{1}{2\pi}\int_{-\infty}^{\infty} \varphi(u)\frac{e^{-iuk}}{iu}du - \frac{1}{2\pi}\lim_{R\to\infty}\int_{-\infty}^{\infty} \varphi(u)\frac{e^{-iuR}}{iu}du. \tag{3.14}$$

In the second integrand of (3.14), express $\varphi(u)$ as a Fourier transform and apply the results developed earlier in this section. This produces

$$\begin{aligned}
&\frac{1}{2\pi}\lim_{R\to\infty}\int_{-\infty}^{\infty}\left(\int_{-\infty}^{\infty} e^{iux}f(x)\,dx\right)\frac{e^{-iuR}}{iu}du \\
&= \frac{1}{2\pi}\lim_{R\to\infty}\int_{-\infty}^{\infty} f(x)\left(\int_{-\infty}^{\infty}\frac{e^{iu(x-R)}}{iu}du\right)dx \\
&= \frac{1}{2\pi}\lim_{R\to\infty}\int_{-\infty}^{\infty}\pi\,\mathrm{sgn}(x-R)f(x)\,dx \\
&= \frac{1}{2}\lim_{R\to\infty}(1-2F(R)) = -\frac{1}{2}.
\end{aligned} \tag{3.15}$$

To obtain the second line in Equation (3.15), we have applied (3.11), and we have used the fact the inner integrand can be written using Euler's identity in (3.6)

$$\frac{e^{iu(x-R)}}{iu} = \frac{1}{i}\frac{\cos(u(x-R))}{u} + \frac{\sin(u(x-R))}{u}. \tag{3.16}$$

The first term is an odd function in u, so it will disappear when integrated over $(-\infty, \infty)$, while the second term will integrate to $\pi\,\mathrm{sgn}(x-R)$. Substituting the result of (3.15) into Equation (3.14) produces

$$\Pr(\ln S_T > k) = \frac{1}{2} + \frac{1}{2\pi}\int_{-\infty}^{\infty}\varphi(u)\frac{e^{-iuk}}{iu}du. \tag{3.17}$$

By applying Euler's identity to both $\varphi(u)$ and $e^{-iu\ln K}$, we can see that the integrand in (3.17) is odd in its imaginary part and even in its real part. Hence, we can use the real part only, restrict the integration range to $(0, \infty)$ and multiply the result by 2, and we obtain the desired expression for the probability in Equation (3.8). Alternatively, we can argue that, since $\Pr(\ln S_T > k)$ is real, we need only consider the real portion of the integrand in (3.17) and arrive at the same result.

Finally, we can use Euler's identity to express the real part of the integrand in (3.17) explicitly, which produces an alternate form for the probability

$$\Pr(\ln S_T > \ln K) = \frac{1}{2} + \frac{1}{\pi}\int_0^{\infty}\left[\frac{\mathrm{Im}\left[\varphi\left(u\right)\right]\cos(uk) - \mathrm{Re}[\varphi(u)]\cos(uk)}{u}\right]du \tag{3.18}$$

where $\mathrm{Im}[\varphi(u)]$ and $\mathrm{Re}[\varphi(u)]$ denote the imaginary and real parts of $\varphi(u)$, respectively. To obtain Equation (3.18) we have exploited the fact that $1/i = -i$. This expression is used in the Attari (2004) formulation of the call price, which we cover later in this chapter.

DERIVATION OF GATHERAL (2006)

Gatheral (2006) derives the Albrecher et al. (2007) formulation of the Heston (1993) characteristic function by working with the log-moneyness of the forward price, $x_t = \ln(F_{t,T}/K)$, where K is the strike price of the option and where $F_{t,T} = S_t e^{\mu(T-t)}$ is the forward price of the stock. His derivation is slightly different than that of Heston (1993) since Gatheral works with the Fourier transforms of the in-the-money probabilities P_1 and P_2 directly.

Consider again the SDE for the variance v_t, defined in Chapter 1

$$dv_t = \kappa(\theta - v_t)dt + \sigma\sqrt{v_t}dW_{2,t}.$$

Applying Itō's lemma shows that x_t follows the stochastic process

$$dx_t = -\frac{1}{2}v_t dt + \sqrt{v_t}dW_{2,t}.$$

Gatheral (2006) assumes the market price of volatility risk to be zero, so that $\lambda(S,v,t) = 0$. With x_t defined as $x_t = \ln(F_{t,T}/K)$ instead of $x_t = \ln S_t$, the terminal condition for the in-the-money probabilities defined in Chapter 1 becomes

$$P_j(x,v,0) = \mathbf{1}_{x>0} \tag{3.19}$$

for $j = 1,2$. With these modifications, the partial differential equation (PDE) for P_j becomes

$$\begin{aligned} -\frac{\partial P_j}{\partial \tau} + \rho\sigma v\frac{\partial^2 P_j}{\partial x \partial v} + \frac{1}{2}v\frac{\partial^2 P_j}{\partial x^2} + \frac{1}{2}v\sigma^2\frac{\partial^2 P_j}{\partial v^2} + \\ u_j v\frac{\partial P_j}{\partial x} + (a - b_j v)\frac{\partial P_j}{\partial v} = 0 \end{aligned} \tag{3.20}$$

where $u_1 = \frac{1}{2}$, $u_2 = -\frac{1}{2}$ and $a = \kappa\theta$. The parameters u_1, u_2 and a remain the same as in Chapter 1, but $b_1 = \kappa - \rho\sigma$, and $b_2 = \kappa$ are redefined since it is assumed that $\lambda = 0$. The transformation of the PDE from t to the time to maturity $\tau = T - t$ explains the minus sign in front of the maturity derivative in Equation (3.20).

In this section, it is more convenient to denote the integration variable by k rather than by u. The form of the Fourier transform used by Gatheral (2006) is slightly different than that in Equation (3.1). It replaces e^{iux} with e^{-ikx} in (3.1), and replaces e^{-iux} with e^{ikx} in the inverse Fourier transform (3.2). The derivative in (3.4) is thus $\widehat{f'(k)} = ik\hat{f}(k)$.

Consider the Fourier transform $\hat{P}_j$ of the probabilities $P_j = P_j(x,v,\tau)$

$$\hat{P}_j(k,v,\tau) = \int_{-\infty}^{\infty} e^{-ikx}P_j(x,v,\tau)\,dx.$$

Using the terminal condition (3.19) we have

$$\hat{P}_j(k,v,0) = \int_{-\infty}^{\infty} e^{-ikx}\mathbf{1}_{x>0}\,dx = -\frac{1}{ik}e^{-ikx}\Big|_{x=0}^{x=\infty} = \frac{1}{ik}.$$

Remembering that differentiation of the Fourier transform $\hat{P}_j$ with respect to x corresponds to multiplication by ik, the PDE in Equation (3.20) for $\hat{P}_j$ is

$$-\frac{\partial \hat{P}_j}{\partial \tau} + \rho\sigma v ik \frac{\partial \hat{P}_j}{\partial v} - \frac{1}{2} v k^2 \hat{P}_j + \frac{1}{2} v \sigma^2 \frac{\partial^2 \hat{P}_j}{\partial v^2} + u_j v ik \hat{P}_j + (a - b_j v) \frac{\partial \hat{P}_j}{\partial v} = 0. \quad (3.21)$$

Rearranging, we obtain

$$v \left\{ \alpha_j \hat{P}_j - \beta_j \frac{\partial \hat{P}_j}{\partial v} + \gamma \frac{\partial^2 \hat{P}_j}{\partial v^2} \right\} + a \frac{\partial \hat{P}_j}{\partial v} - \frac{\partial \hat{P}_j}{\partial \tau} = 0 \quad (3.22)$$

where

$$\alpha_j = u_j ik - \frac{k^2}{2}, \quad \beta_j = b_j - \rho\sigma ik, \quad \gamma = \frac{\sigma^2}{2}.$$

Note that these coefficients are identical to the coefficients P, Q, and R for the Riccati equation in Chapter 1, except that k replaces ϕ. The ansatz is that the $\hat{P}_j$ are of the form

$$\begin{aligned} \hat{P}_j(k, v, \tau) &= \exp[C_j(k,\tau)\theta + D_j(k,\tau)v]\hat{P}_j(k, v, 0) \\ &= \frac{1}{ik}[C_j(k,\tau)\theta + D_j(k,\tau)v]. \end{aligned} \quad (3.23)$$

Take the following derivatives of (3.23)

$$\frac{\partial \hat{P}_j}{\partial \tau} = \left[\frac{\partial C_j}{\partial \tau}\theta + \frac{\partial D_j}{\partial \tau} v \right] \hat{P}_j, \quad \frac{\partial \hat{P}_j}{\partial v} = D_j \hat{P}_j, \quad \frac{\partial^2 \hat{P}_j}{\partial v^2} = D_j^2 \hat{P}_j.$$

Substituting these derivatives back into the PDE in (3.22) and dropping the $\hat{P}_j$ terms produces

$$v\{\alpha_j - \beta_j D_j + \gamma D_j^2\} + aD_j - \left[\frac{\partial C_j}{\partial \tau}\theta + \frac{\partial D_j}{\partial \tau} v \right] = 0. \quad (3.24)$$

This implies that the following two equations must be satisfied, which appear as Equation (2.11) in Gatheral (2006)

$$\begin{aligned} \frac{\partial C_j}{\partial \tau} &= \kappa D_j \\ \frac{\partial D_j}{\partial \tau} &= \alpha_j - \beta_j D_j + \gamma D_j^2. \end{aligned} \quad (3.25)$$

The first equation holds since $a = \kappa\theta$ so that θ cancels out. The second equation is identical to the Riccati equation in Chapter 1. The two roots r_-^j and r_+^j of this quadratic equation are

$$r_\pm^j = \frac{\beta_j \pm \sqrt{\beta_j^2 - 4\alpha_j\gamma}}{2\alpha_j} = \frac{b_j - \rho\sigma ik \pm d_j}{\sigma^2}$$

where

$$d_j = \sqrt{(\rho\sigma ik - b_j)^2 - \sigma^2(2u_j ik - k^2)}.$$

This expression for d_j is identical to that obtained in Chapter 1, with ϕ replaced by k. The solution for D_j is obtained using the solution of the Riccati equation in Chapter 1, as

$$D_j = r_-^j \left(\frac{1 - e^{-d_j\tau}}{1 - c_j e^{-d_j\tau}} \right) \tag{3.26}$$

where $c_j = r_-^j / r_+^j$ is identical to that in the "Little Trap" formulation of Albrecher et al. (2007), which we encountered in Chapter 2, but with ϕ replaced by k. The solution for C_j is, remembering that $r = 0$ in this derivation

$$\begin{aligned} C_j &= \frac{\kappa}{\sigma^2}\left[(b_j - \rho\sigma i\phi - d_j)\,\tau - 2\ln\left(\frac{1 - c_j e^{-d_j\tau}}{1 - c_j}\right)\right] \\ &= \kappa\left[r_-^j \tau - \frac{2}{\sigma^2}\ln\left(\frac{1 - c_j e^{-d_j\tau}}{1 - c_j}\right)\right] \end{aligned} \tag{3.27}$$

since θ cancels out. The expressions for D_j and C_j in (3.26) and (3.27) are Equation (2.12) in Gatheral (2006). The resulting characteristic function for the Heston model in Equation (2.15) of Gatheral (2006) is identical to the "Little Trap" formulation of Albrecher et al. (2007), but with $r = 0$.

ATTARI (2004) REPRESENTATION

Attari (2004) presents an alternate formula for the Heston call price. The formula is similar to that proposed earlier by Lewis (2001), which we present in the next chapter. What follows is a simplified version of Attari's derivation.

Attari (2004) writes the terminal stock price as $S_T = S_t e^{r\tau + x(t,T)}$, where $x = x(t,T)$ now denotes the stochastic component of the stock price process. The call price is, as in Chapter 1

$$\begin{aligned} C(K) &= e^{-r\tau} E^{\mathbb{Q}}[S_T | S_T > K] - K e^{-r\tau} E^{\mathbb{Q}}[\mathbf{1}_{S_T > K}] \\ &= S_t E^{\mathbb{Q}}[e^x | x > \ell] - K e^{-r\tau} E^{\mathbb{Q}}[\mathbf{1}_{x>\ell}] \\ &= S_t \Pi_1 - K e^{-r\tau} \Pi_2 \end{aligned} \tag{3.28}$$

where $\ell = \ln(Ke^{-r\tau}/S_t)$. The two expectations are taken under the risk-neutral density for x, $q(x)$. The probabilities are, therefore,

$$\begin{aligned} \Pi_1 &= E^{\mathbb{Q}}[e^x | x > \ell] = \int_\ell^\infty e^x q(x)\,dx = \int_\ell^\infty p(x)\,dx \\ \Pi_2 &= E^{\mathbb{Q}}[\mathbf{1}_{x>\ell}] = \int_\ell^\infty q(x)\,dx. \end{aligned} \tag{3.29}$$

Since $e^x q(x) > 0$ and $0 \leq \Pi_1 \leq 1$, then $e^x q(x) = p(x)$ can be treated as a density function. The characteristic function for $q(x)$ is denoted $\varphi_2(u)$, and that for $p(x)$ is denoted $\varphi_1(u)$. Using the definition of the characteristic function and performing the required integrations, we have $\varphi_1(u) = \varphi_2(u - i)$. Indeed,

$$\varphi_1(u) = \int_{-\infty}^{\infty} e^{iux} p(x)\,dx = \int_{-\infty}^{\infty} e^{iux} e^x q(x)\,dx = \int_{-\infty}^{\infty} e^{i(u-i)x} q(x)\,dx = \varphi_2(u - i). \quad (3.30)$$

Now, write Π_1 using the representation in Equation (3.13)

$$\Pi_1 = \frac{1}{2\pi}\int_{-\infty}^{\infty} \varphi_1(v)\left(\int_{\ell}^{\infty} e^{-ivx}\,dx\right)dv = \frac{1}{2\pi}\int_{-\infty}^{\infty} \varphi_2(v - i)\left(\int_{\ell}^{\infty} e^{-ivx}\,dx\right)dv. \quad (3.31)$$

Perform the change of variable $u = v - i$ so that (3.31) becomes

$$\Pi_1 = \frac{1}{2\pi}\int_{-\infty}^{\infty} \varphi_2(u)\left(\int_{\ell}^{\infty} e^{-i(u+i)x}\,dx\right)du \quad (3.32)$$

which is Equation (8) of Attari (2004). Now evaluate the inner integral in Equation (3.32), as was done in (3.14). This produces

$$\begin{aligned}\Pi_1 &= \frac{1}{2\pi}\int_{-\infty}^{\infty} \varphi_2(u)\frac{e^{-i(u+i)\ell}}{i(u+i)}\,du - \frac{1}{2\pi}\lim_{R\to\infty}\int_{-\infty}^{\infty} \varphi_2(u)\frac{e^{-i(u+i)R}}{i(u+i)}\,du \\ &= I_1 - I_2.\end{aligned} \quad (3.33)$$

The second integral is a complex integral with a pole at $u = -i$. The residue there is, therefore, $\varphi_2(-i)/i$. Applying the Residue Theorem, we obtain[1]

$$I_2 = \lim_{R\to\infty}\frac{1}{2\pi}\left[-2\pi i \times \frac{\varphi_2(-i)}{i}\right] = -\varphi_2(-i) = -\varphi_1(0) = -1. \quad (3.34)$$

Substituting the resulting Equation (3.34) into (3.33) produces

$$\Pi_1 = \frac{e^{\ell}}{2\pi}\int_{-\infty}^{\infty} \varphi_2(u)\frac{e^{-iu\ell}}{i(u+i)}\,du + 1 \quad (3.35)$$

which is Equation (12) of Attari (2004). For Π_2, we use the Gil-Pelaez (1951) form in (3.17)

$$\Pi_2 = \frac{1}{2} + \frac{1}{2\pi}\int_{-\infty}^{\infty} \varphi_2(u)\frac{e^{-iu\ell}}{iu}\,du. \quad (3.36)$$

[1]The Residue Theorem will be introduced in Chapter 4.

Substitute for Π_1 and Π_2 into the last line of Equation (3.28) for the call price

$$\begin{aligned}C(K) &= S_t\left[1+\frac{e^{\ell}}{2\pi}\int_{-\infty}^{\infty}\varphi_2(u)\frac{e^{-iu\ell}}{i(u+i)}du\right]-Ke^{-r\tau}\left[\frac{1}{2}+\frac{1}{2\pi}\int_{-\infty}^{\infty}\varphi_2(u)\frac{e^{-iu\ell}}{iu}du\right]\\&= S_t-\frac{1}{2}Ke^{-r\tau}-\frac{Ke^{-r\tau}}{\pi}\int_0^{\infty}\text{Re}\left[\varphi_2(u)e^{-iu\ell}\left(\frac{1}{iu}-\frac{1}{i(u+i)}\right)\right]du. \qquad (3.37)\end{aligned}$$

We have substituted for $\ell = Ke^{-r\tau}/S_t$ and have used the fact that we only need to consider the real part of the integrals. In the bracketed term of the last integral in (3.37), multiply the second fraction by $u-i$ in the numerator and denominator. The integrand becomes

$$\text{Re}\left[\varphi_2(u)e^{-iu\ell}\left(\frac{1-i/u}{u^2+1}\right)\right]. \qquad (3.38)$$

Now expand $\varphi_2(u) = R_2(u)+iI_2(u)$ where $R_2(u)$ and $I_2(u)$ are the real and imaginary parts of $\varphi_2(u)$, respectively, and expand $e^{-iu\ell} = \cos(u\ell)-i\sin(u\ell)$. Substitute into the integrand (3.38) and regroup the real terms. The integrand becomes

$$A(u) = \frac{\left(R_2(u)+\dfrac{I_2(u)}{u}\right)\cos(u\ell)+\left(I_2(u)-\dfrac{R_2(u)}{u}\right)\sin(u\ell)}{1+u^2}. \qquad (3.39)$$

Attari's (2004) formula for the call price is, therefore,

$$C(K) = S_t-\frac{1}{2}Ke^{-r\tau}-\frac{Ke^{-r\tau}}{\pi}\int_0^{\infty}A(u)du. \qquad (3.40)$$

Recall that in Attari (2004), the logarithm of the terminal stock price is $\ln S_T = \ln S_t + r\tau + x(t,T)$ and the characteristic function $\varphi_2(u)$ is for $x = x(t,T)$ and not for $\ln S_T$. Consequently, to express the integrand in Equation (3.39) in terms of the Heston (1993) characteristic function for $\ln S_T$, we use the fact that

$$E^{\mathbb{Q}}[e^{iux(t,T)}] = E^{\mathbb{Q}}[e^{iu\ln S_T}]\exp[-iu(\ln S_t+r\tau)].$$

Hence, in (3.39) we set

$$\begin{aligned}\varphi_2(u) &= f_2(u)\times\exp[-iu(\ln S_t+r\tau)]\\&= \exp(C_2(\tau,u)+D_2(\tau,u)v_0-iur\tau)\end{aligned}$$

where $f_2(u)$ is the Heston (1993) characteristic function defined in Chapter 1, with $j=2$. Note that the Attari (2004) characteristic function $\varphi_2(u)$ is identical to $f_2(u)$, except that the term $iu\ln S_t$ in $f_2(u)$ is replaced with $-iur\tau$. This means that $\varphi_2(u)$ is independent of the spot price S_t. The main advantage of Attari's representation is that a single numerical integration only is required to produce the call price. Moreover, the u^2 term in the denominator of $A(u)$ causes the integrand to dampen quickly, so that truncation of the upper limit in the integral for the purposes of numerical integration causes less loss of precision. This is illustrated in Figure 3.1

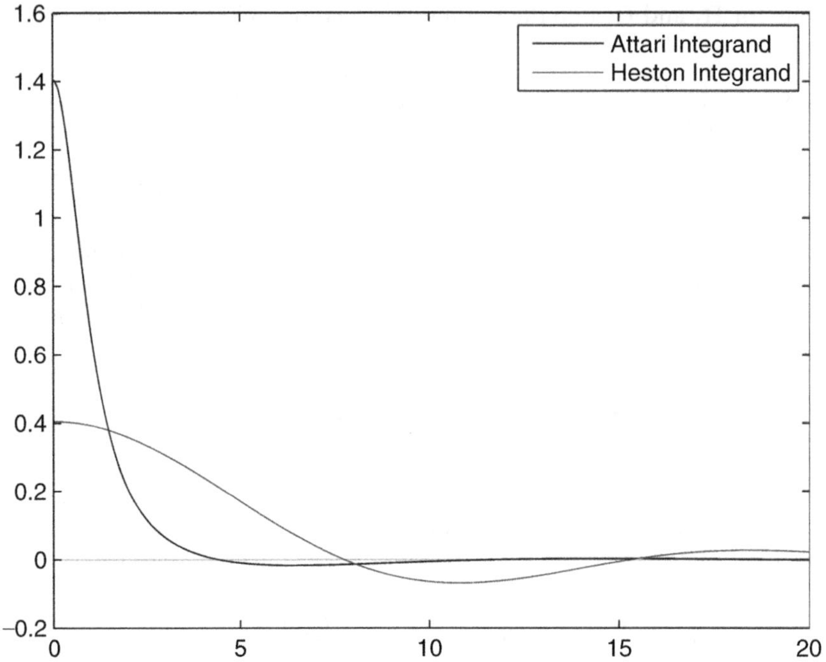

FIGURE 3.1 Attari (2004) and Heston (1993) Integrands

using $S = 30$, $K = 20$, $r = 0.01$, $q = 0$, a maturity of 1 month, along with the parameter values $\kappa = 1.4$, $\theta = v_0 = 0.05$, $\sigma = 0.3$, and $\rho = -0.8$. The figure shows that the Attari integrand decays must faster than the Heston integrand, but that it is much steeper at the origin. Consequently, there exists the potential for problems in numerical integration in that region.

The Matlab function AttariProb.m implements the integrand in Equation (3.39). It is based on the same function used to implement the Heston characteristic function $f_2(\phi)$ and is, therefore, not presented in its entirety.

```
function y = AttariProb(phi,...,Trap);
f = exp(C + D*v - i*phi*r*tau);
L = log(exp(-r*tau)*K/S);
y = ((real(f) + imag(f)/phi)*cos(L*phi)
    + (imag(f) - real(f)/phi)*sin(L*phi)) / (1+phi^2);
```

The function AttariPriceGaussLaguerre.m returns the call price in Equation (3.40) or the put price by put-call parity.

```
function y = AttariPriceGaussLaguerre(...)
for k=1:length(x);
    int1(k) = w(k) * AttariProb(x(k),...);
end
HestonC = S*exp(-q*T) - K*exp(-r*T)*(1/2 + sum(int1)/pi);
```

The C# code for the Attari (2004) model is very similar and not presented here.

To illustrate pricing with the Attari (2004) method, we use the same settings as those in Figure 3.1, along with 32-point Gauss-Laguerre integration. The Heston price is 10.0152 and the Attari price is 10.0167, which is very close.

CARR AND MADAN (1999) REPRESENTATION

Carr and Madan (1999) present a derivation of the call price based on the Fourier transform. It offers advantages in terms of reduced computation time and an integrand that decays faster than the integrand of the original Heston (1993) formulation. Their method requires a modification of the call price that incorporates a damping factor. The Fourier transform of the modified call price is obtained, and inverted. The call price can be then be recovered by removing the damping factor from the modified call price.

Define $k = \ln K$ and $x = x_T = \ln S_T$, and let $q(x)$ denote the density function for S_T. We saw in Chapter 1 that the call price can be written

$$\begin{aligned} C(k) &= e^{-r\tau} E^{\mathbb{Q}}[(S_T - K)^+] \\ &= e^{-r\tau} \int_k^\infty (e^x - e^k) q(x)\, dx \qquad (3.41) \\ &= e^{x_t} \mathbb{Q}^S(S_T > e^k) - K e^{-r\tau} \mathbb{Q}(S_T > e^k). \end{aligned}$$

In (3.41), $\mathbb{Q}^S(S_T > e^k)$ and $\mathbb{Q}(S_T > e^k)$ are found by inverting a characteristic function. This inversion obviously requires that the characteristic function be integrable. Since

$$\begin{aligned} \lim_{k\to-\infty} C(k) &= \lim_{k\to-\infty} e^{-r\tau} \int_k^\infty (e^x - e^k) q(x) dx \\ &= e^{-r\tau} E^{\mathbb{Q}}[e^x] - 0 \\ &= S_t \end{aligned}$$

which is not zero, $C(k)$ is not integrable L^1, and its Fourier transform will not exist. Carr and Madan (1999) rectify this by defining the modified call price $c(k)$ as

$$c(k) = e^{\alpha k} C(k)$$

which includes the damping factor $e^{\alpha k}$ on $C(k)$. Since

$$\begin{aligned} \lim_{k\to-\infty} c(k) &= \lim_{k\to-\infty} e^{-r\tau} \int_k^\infty (e^{\alpha k + x} - e^{(\alpha+1)k}) q(x) dx \\ &= \lim_{k\to-\infty} e^{-r\tau} \int_k^\infty e^{\alpha k + x} q(x) dx - \lim_{k\to-\infty} e^{-r\tau + (\alpha+1)k} \int_k^\infty q(x) dx \\ &= e^{-r\tau}[0] - 0 \end{aligned}$$

which is zero, $c(k)$ is integrable L^1 and the Fourier transform for $c(k)$ can be found. The idea of Carr and Madan (1999) is to first find the Fourier transform $\hat{c}(v)$ of $c(k)$, invert the Fourier transform to yield $c(k)$ and remove the damping factor to recover $C(k)$. The Fourier transform of $c(k)$ is, using Equation (3.41)

$$\begin{aligned}\hat{c}(v) &= \int_{-\infty}^{\infty} e^{ivk} c(k)\, dk = \int_{-\infty}^{\infty} e^{ivk} e^{\alpha k} C(k)\, dk \\ &= e^{-r\tau} \int_{-\infty}^{\infty} e^{(\alpha+iv)k} \left[\int_{k}^{\infty} \left(e^{x} - e^{k}\right) q(x)\, dx \right] dk.\end{aligned} \tag{3.42}$$

The area of integration $-\infty < k < \infty$ and $k < x < \infty$ is equivalent to $-\infty < x < \infty$ and $-\infty < k < x$, so (3.42) can be written as

$$\begin{aligned}\hat{c}(v) &= e^{-r\tau} \int_{-\infty}^{\infty} q(x) \left[\int_{-\infty}^{x} \left(e^{(\alpha+iv)k+x} - e^{(\alpha+iv+1)k} \right) dk \right] dx \\ &= e^{-r\tau} \int_{-\infty}^{\infty} q(x) \left[\frac{e^{(\alpha+iv)k+x}}{\alpha+iv} - \frac{e^{(\alpha+iv+1)k}}{\alpha+iv+1} \Bigg|_{k=-\infty}^{k=x} \right] dx \\ &= e^{-r\tau} \int_{-\infty}^{\infty} q(x) \left[\frac{e^{(\alpha+iv+1)x}}{\alpha^2+\alpha-v^2+iv(2\alpha+1)} \right] dx \\ &= \frac{e^{-r\tau}\varphi(v-(\alpha+1)i)}{\alpha^2+\alpha-v^2+iv(2\alpha+1)}.\end{aligned} \tag{3.43}$$

The last equality holds because

$$\varphi(u) = E^{\mathbb{Q}}[e^{iux}] = \int_{-\infty}^{\infty} e^{iux} q(x)\, dx$$

is the characteristic function of $x = \ln S_T$, which we have denoted $f_2(\phi)$ in previous chapters. The call price is found through the inverse Fourier transform of the modified call price

$$\begin{aligned}C(k) &= e^{-\alpha k} c(k) = \frac{e^{-\alpha k}}{2\pi} \int_{-\infty}^{\infty} e^{-ivk} \hat{c}(v)\, dv \\ &= \frac{e^{-\alpha k}}{\pi} \int_{0}^{\infty} \text{Re}[e^{-ivk}\hat{c}(v)]\, dv.\end{aligned} \tag{3.44}$$

The last equality holds, because while the integrand $e^{-ivk}\hat{c}(v)$ is a complex number, the call price $C(k)$ in Equation (3.44) is a real number. This implies that we can ignore the imaginary part of the integrand, and work only with the real part, which is even-valued. Lord and Kahl (2007) point out at least three advantages to the representation of the call price in (3.44). First, only a single numerical integration scheme is required, instead of two. Second, the denominator in the integrand in (3.43) is a quadratic function of the integration variable, v, and thus decays faster than the integrands in the original Heston formulation, in which the denominators are linear functions of the integration variable. This implies that truncation of the integration domain from $(0, \infty)$ to some finite range $(0, M)$, where $M < \infty$, is less problematic in (3.44). Finally, there is computational accuracy to be gained from the representation, provided that the damping factor α is appropriately chosen. We address this issue in a later section of this chapter.

The function CarrMadanIntegrand.m returns the Carr and Madan (1999) integrand in Equation (3.43). It calls the function HestonCF.m, which returns the Heston characteristic function.

```
function y = CarrMadanIntegrand(u,...);
I = exp(-i*u*log(K))*exp(-r*tau)*HestonCF(u-(alpha+1)*i,...) /...;
y = real(I);
```

The function HestonCallGaussLaguerre.m implements the call price using either the original Heston form, or the Carr-Madan form in (3.44).

```
function y = HestonCallGaussLaguerre(Integrand,...)
if strcmp(Integrand,'Heston') % Heston formulation
    for k=1:length(x);
        int1(k)  = w(k)*HestonIntegrand(x(k),...,1);
        int2(k)  = w(k)*HestonIntegrand(x(k),...,2);
    end
    % The in-the-money probabilities P1 and P2
    P1 = 1/2 + 1/pi*sum(int1);
    P2 = 1/2 + 1/pi*sum(int2);
    % The Call price
    y = S*exp(-q*T)*P1 - K*exp(-r*T)*P2;
elseif strcmp(Integrand,'CarrMadan') % Carr-Madan form
    for k=1:length(x);
        int1(k)  = w(k)*CarrMadanIntegrand(x(k),...);
    end
    % The Call Price
    y = exp(-alpha*log(K))*sum(int1)/pi;
end
```

To illustrate, in the following Matlab example we use $S = K = 100$, $r = 0.10$, $q = 0.07$ and a maturity of 6 months, with $\kappa = 2, \theta = v_0 = 0.06, \sigma = 0.1, \rho = -0.7$, and the damping factor $\alpha = 1.75$.

```
% The call price using the Heston integrand
CallHeston = HestonCallGaussLaguerre('Heston',...);
% The call price using the Carr-Madan integrand
S = S*exp(-q*T);
CallCarrMadan = HestonCallGaussLaguerre('CarrMadan',...);
```

Matlab returns the call prices as 7.3461 for both the Heston and Carr-Madan representations.

Note that to implement the Carr-Madan price on the stock paying continuous dividend yield, q, we have replaced the spot price S by $Se^{-q\tau}$ before passing the price to the function. See Whaley (2006) for an explanation. Finally, the C# code to implement the Carr and Madan (2009) method is similar to the Matlab code and is not presented here.

BOUNDS ON THE CARR-MADAN DAMPING FACTOR AND OPTIMAL VALUE

Carr and Madan (1999) demonstrate that a sufficient condition for $c(k)$ to be integrable is that $\hat{c}(0)$ in Equation (3.43) be finite. By setting $v = 0$ in (3.43), we can see that this is guaranteed when the characteristic function evaluated at $-(\alpha+1)i$ is finite, namely when $\varphi(-(\alpha+1)i) < \infty$. Since $\varphi(v) = E[e^{iv \ln S_T}] = E[S_T^{iv}]$, the condition that $\varphi(-(\alpha+1)i) < \infty$ is equivalent to the existence of the $(\alpha+1)$-st moment of S_T, namely $E[S_T^{\alpha+1}] < \infty$. For some models, it is possible to find $\alpha_{\max}$, the maximum value for α, by setting the condition $E[S_T^{\alpha+1}]$ in the characteristic function and solving for α analytically. Carr and Madan (1999) suggest using $\alpha = \alpha_{\max}/4$ and illustrate this for the Variance Gamma model, for which they chose $\alpha = 1.5$ (see also Carr, Madan, and Chang, 1998). Other studies, such as those by Raible (2000), Schoutens et al. (2004), and Borak et al. (2011) have used ad-hoc choices ranging from $\alpha = 0.75$ to $\alpha = 25$.

While ad-hoc values of the damping factor α can serve as a general guide, it is more useful to have a range of admissible values for α. To this end, Lee (2004a) shows how minimum and maximum values for α can be obtained. Denote by $A_X = (a_-, a_+)$ the interval of allowable values for $\alpha+1$, where $a_- < 0$ and $a_+ > 1$, so that α can be selected from anywhere in the interval $(a_- - 1, a_+ - 1) = (\alpha_{\min}, \alpha_{\max})$. The values of a_- and a_+ can be found by solving the following equality for a

$$g(-ia)e^{d(-ia)\tau} = 1 \tag{3.45}$$

where $g(\phi)$ and $d(\phi)$ are g_2 and d_2 of the Heston characteristic function ($j = 2$), with $\lambda = 0$, that is

$$g(\phi) = \frac{\kappa - \rho\sigma\phi i + d(\phi)}{\kappa - \rho\sigma\phi i - d(\phi)}, \qquad d(\phi) = \sqrt{(\kappa - \rho\sigma\phi i)^2 + \sigma^2(\phi i + \phi^2)}.$$

Solving Equation (3.45) for a requires a non-linear search algorithm and will generate multiple solutions, but we need only two solutions, $a_- < 0$ and $a_+ > 1$. When $\kappa - \rho\sigma > 0$, we can define a_- to be the largest solution in $(-\infty, y_-)$ and a_+ to be the smallest solution in (y_+, ∞), where

$$y_\pm = \frac{\sigma - 2\kappa\rho \pm \sqrt{\sigma^2 - 4\kappa\rho\sigma + 4\kappa^2}}{2\sigma(1-\rho^2)}. \tag{3.46}$$

This simply means that, given multiple negative solutions to (3.45), we select $a_- < 0$ to be the one closest to y_-, and given multiple solutions greater than unity, we select $a_+ > 1$ to be the one closest to y_+. The interval of allowable values for α is then $\alpha \in (a_- - 1, a_+ - 1)$. The roots $y_\pm$ arise as the roots of $d(-i\phi)^2$

$$\begin{aligned} d(-i\phi)^2 &= (\kappa - \rho\sigma\phi)^2 + \sigma^2(\phi - \phi^2) \\ &= \phi^2(\rho^2\sigma^2 - \sigma^2) + \phi(\sigma^2 - 2\kappa\rho\sigma) + \kappa^2 \end{aligned}$$

which is a second-order polynomial in ϕ. For example, using the settings in Lord and Kahl (2007), namely $S = 1, r = 0, K = 1.2, \rho = -0.7, v_0 = \theta = 0.1, \kappa = \sigma = 1$, and $\tau = 1$ produces $(y_-, y_+) = (-0.3852, 5.0910)$. By repeated application of a nonlinear search algorithm, and visual inspection, we find the function in (3.45) to have the negative solutions -0.3852, -2.3068, -9.4823, etc., and the positive solutions 5.0910, 10.0600, 18.2763, etc. Hence, we select $A_X = (-2.3068, 10.0600)$, since the lower limit of A_X should be less than $y_- = -0.3852$, while the upper limit of A_X should be greater than $y_+ = 5.0910$. The range of admissible values for α is, therefore, $(\alpha_{\min}, \alpha_{\max}) = (-3.3068, 9.0600)$.

Optimal Damping Factor

While $(\alpha_{\min}, \alpha_{\max})$ forms a region of admissible values for the damping factor α, it does not indicate which value of α in the region is optimal, in the sense that an optimal value produces an integrand in Equation (3.44) that oscillates as little as possible. Recall that the Carr and Madan (1999) representation of the call price is

$$C(k) = \frac{e^{-\alpha k}}{\pi} \int_0^\infty \psi(v, \alpha) dv$$

where the integrand is

$$\begin{aligned} \psi(v, \alpha) &= \text{Re}[e^{-ivk} \hat{c}(v)] \\ &= \text{Re}\left[\frac{e^{-ivk} e^{-r\tau} \varphi\,(v - (\alpha + 1)\, i)}{\alpha^2 + \alpha - v^2 + iv(2\alpha + 1)}\right]. \end{aligned} \tag{3.47}$$

Lord and Kahl (2007) argue that the optimal α^* is that which reduces the total variation of the integrand $\psi(v, \alpha)$ over the integration domain $[0, \infty)$. Under the assumption that $\psi(v, \alpha)$ is monotone in v on $[0, \infty)$, they show that the optimal α is given by

$$\alpha^* = \underset{\alpha_{\min} \leq \alpha \leq \alpha_{\max}}{\arg\min} \left[-\alpha k + \frac{1}{2} \ln\left(\psi(v, \alpha)^2\right)\right] \tag{3.48}$$

which they define as the function $\Psi(\alpha, k)$. Using the settings from the example in the previous section and running the optimization in Equation (3.48) produces $\alpha^* = 6.6233$. Note that this optimal value is within the range of admissible values $(\alpha_{\min}, \alpha_{\max}) = (-3.3068, 9.0600)$ obtained in the previous section.

Numerical Implementation and Illustration

We continue to illustrate the bounds on α and the optimal α^* using the settings for the previous example, namely $S = 1$, $r = 0$, $K = 1.2$, $\rho = -0.7$, $v_0 = \theta = 0.1$, $\kappa = \sigma = 1$, and $\tau = 1$.

The Matlab function RogerLeeGExpD.m defines an objective function as the squared difference from both sides of Equation (3.45).

```
function y = RogerLeeGExpD(phi,kappa,rho,sigma,tau);
A = (rho*sigma*phi*i - kappa);
B = sigma^2*(phi*i + phi^2);
d = sqrt(A^2 + B);
g = (kappa - rho*sigma*phi*i + d) / ...;
E = real(g*exp(d*tau));
y = (E - 1)^2;
```

The fminsearch.m function in Matlab is used to find $y_{-} = -2.3069$ and $y_{+} = 10.0600$.

```
% Find y-
[yneg feval] = fminsearch(@(a) RogerLeeGExpD(-i*a,...), start);
% Find y+
[ypos feval] = fminsearch(@(a) RogerLeeGExpD(-i*a,...), start);
% The range for Ax
Ax = [yneg ypos];
AlphaMax = ypos - 1;
AlphaMin = yneg - 1;
```

The average of the returned values $\alpha_{\min} = -3.3069$ and $\alpha_{\max} = 9.0600$ can be used as starting values to find α^*, the optimal damping factor.

```
start = (AlphaMin + AlphaMax)/2;
[aOpt eval] = fminsearch(@(alpha)LordKahlFindAlpha(alpha,...),...);
```

The above snippet of code uses the function LordKahlFindAlpha.m, which defines the objective function in the minimization in Equation (3.48).

```
function y = LordKahlFindAlpha(alpha,...)
PSI = HestonPsi(0,alpha,...);
y = -alpha*log(K)  + (1/2)*log(PSI^2);
```

The optimal alpha is $\alpha^* = 6.6233$. In Figure 3.2, we plot the optimal alpha function $\Psi(\alpha, k)$ and its derivative, and identify visually the local minima of $\Psi(\alpha, k)$.

Figure 3.2 is generated using the following code. The first part defines the admissible range for α and generates the $\Psi(\alpha, k)$ function and its derivative using central differences.

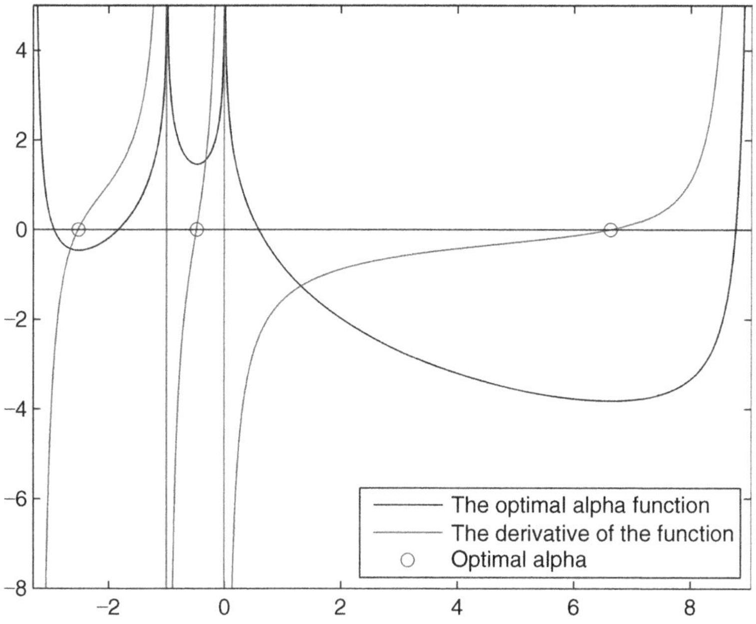

FIGURE 3.2 Lord and Kahl Optimal Alpha

```
A = [AlphaMin:dA:AlphaMax];
N = length(A);
% The function for optimal alpha and its derivative
for x=1:N
    f(x) = LordKahlFindAlpha(A(x),...);
end
dA = 0.001;
for x=2:N-1
    der(x) = (f(x+1) - f(x-1))/(2*dA);
end
der = der(2:N-1);
```

The second part finds the local minima for $\Psi(\alpha, k)$ by finding points along the α-axis where the derivative switches sign.

```
% Find the points where the derivative switches sign.
optim = zeros(N-3,1);
for x=2:N-2
    if sign(der(x)) ~= sign(der(x-1)) & abs(der(x)) < .1;
        optim(x) = 1;
    end
end
% Identify the local minima along the x-axis
Op = find(optim==1);
Opy = zeros(1,length(Op));
Opx = (A(Op) + A(Op+1))/2;
AlphaOptimalSet = Opx;
```

Finally, the last portion plots $\Psi(\alpha, k)$, its derivative, and the optimal points indicated with circles in Figure 3.2.

```
z = zeros(length(A),1);
plot(A, f,'k-',A(1:N-2),der,'r-',Opx,Opy,'bo',A,z,'k')
axis([A(1) A(end) -8 5])
```

The function $\Psi(\alpha, k)$ illustrated in Figure 3.2 has three local minima, at values of $\alpha = -2.5194$, $\alpha = -0.4778$, and $\alpha = 6.6233$ indicated by the circles. Lord and Kahl (2007) explain that since $\Psi(\alpha, k)$ explodes to infinity when $\alpha = -1$ or 0, which is reflected in Figure 3.2, $\Psi(\alpha, k)$ will have local minima in the intervals $(\alpha_{\min}, 0)$, $(-1, 0)$, and $(0, \alpha_{\max})$. Since our range of admissible values is $\alpha \in (-3.3068, 9.0600)$, we select $\alpha^* = 6.6233$. To ascertain whether this choice of α^* actually leads to a well-behaved integrand, in Figure 3.3 we plot the integrand in Equation (3.44) for three values of the damping factor, $\alpha = 1.6582$, $\alpha = 7.8417$, and the optimal value $\alpha^* = 6.6233$.

The graph indicates that the integrand with the optimal value of $\alpha^* = 6.6233$ behaves better than the other integrands, which have non-optimal values of α, in the sense that the integrand with optimal alpha oscillates less, is flatter at the origin, and converges to zero at least as quickly as the others.

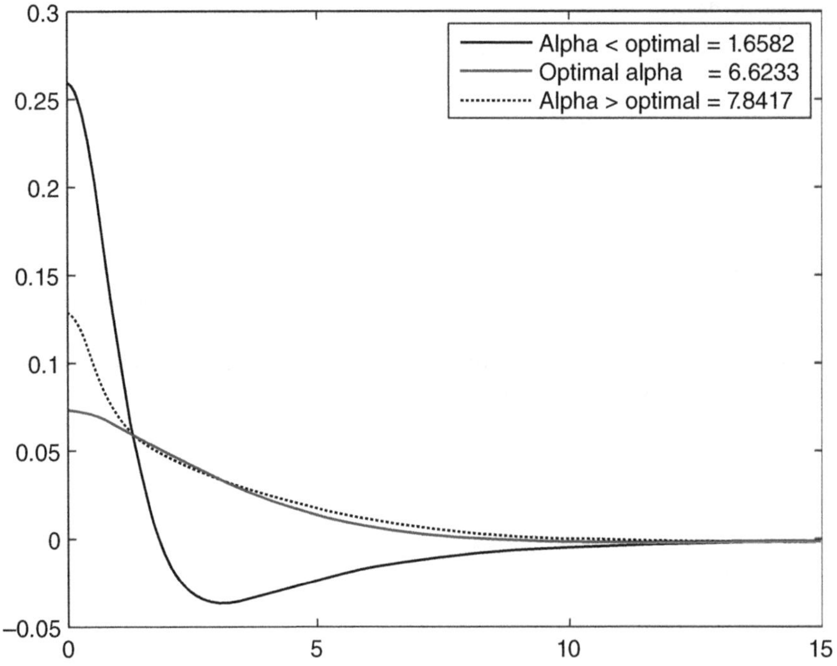

FIGURE 3.3 Carr-Madan Integrands

Lee (2004b) also suggests selecting the damping factor with a minimization procedure. In his approach, α is chosen by simultaneously minimizing two errors that occur when the integral in Equation (3.44) is evaluated numerically: truncation error, which arises since the upper limit of the numeric integral is finite, and sampling error, which arises because the integrand is evaluated only the grid points of any numerical integration scheme. Readers are referred to his paper for details.

Finally, the C# code to find $A_X = (a_-, a_+)$ and α^* is similar to the Matlab code. We need to invoke the Nelder-Mead algorithm twice, once with an objective function based on Equation (3.45) to find a_- and a_+, and again with the objective function in (3.48) to find α^*. Hence, in C#, we need the following code to select the objective function that we subsequently pass to the NelderMead() function, which is presented in Chapter 6.

```
// Objective function is Roger Lee's G*exp(d*Tau) function
// or Lord and Kahl's optimal alpha function
static double f(double[] x,double[] param) {
    if(GlobalVars.ObjFunChoice == "RogerLee") {
        return RogerLeeGExpD(x[0],kappa,rho,sigma,tau);}
    else if(GlobalVars.ObjFunChoice == "LordKahl") {
        return LordKahlFindAlpha(x[0],...);}
}
```

We select Lee's (2004a) function as the objective function and find $A_X = (a_-, a_+)$ with the following code.

```
// Select the Roger Lee function as the obj fun
GlobalVars.ObjFunChoice = "RogerLee";
// Calculate lower limit of the the range Ax
double[] AxLo = NelderMead(f,s1,...);
// Calculate upper limit of the the range Ax
double[] AxHi = NelderMead(f,s2,...);
```

Next, we select Lord and Kahl's (2007) function as the objective function and find α^* with the following code.

```
// Select the KahlLord function as the obj fun
GlobalVars.ObjFunChoice = "LordKahl";
// Lord and Kahl optimal alpha
double[] AlphaOptimal = NelderMead(f,s3,...);
```

With the settings used at the beginning of this section, the C# returns the same optimal value of $\alpha^* = 6.6233$.

THE CARR-MADAN REPRESENTATION FOR PUTS

We can always use put-call parity to find the value of the put, or we can apply a damping factor to the put price and find a representation for the put itself. The put price $P(k)$ is

$$\begin{aligned} P(k) &= e^{-r\tau} E^{\mathbb{Q}}[(K - S_T)^+] \\ &= e^{-r\tau} \int_{-\infty}^{k} (e^k - e^x) q(x)\, dx \end{aligned} \tag{3.49}$$

which again does not have a Fourier transform since it is not L^1. Indeed,

$$\lim_{k\to+\infty} P(k) = \lim_{k\to+\infty} e^{-r\tau} \int_{-\infty}^{k} (e^k - e^x) q(x)\, dx = \infty.$$

Note that, since the upper limit is $+\infty$, we will need a damping factor with a negative exponent. Schmelzle (2010) uses the modified put price defined by

$$p(k) = e^{-\alpha k} P(k)$$

which is L^1 because

$$\lim_{k\to+\infty} p(k) = \lim_{k\to+\infty} e^{-r\tau} \int_{-\infty}^{k} \left(e^{(-\alpha+1)k} - e^{-\alpha k + x}\right) q(x)\, dx = 0 - 0.$$

The Fourier transform of the modified put price is

$$\begin{aligned} \hat{p}(v) &= \int_{-\infty}^{\infty} e^{ivk} p(k)\, dk = \int_{-\infty}^{\infty} e^{ivk} e^{-\alpha k} P(k)\, dk \\ &= e^{-r\tau} \int_{-\infty}^{\infty} e^{(-\alpha+iv)k} \left[\int_{-\infty}^{k} \left(e^k - e^x\right) q(x)\, dx \right] dk. \end{aligned}$$

The area of integration $-\infty < k < \infty$ and $-\infty < x < k$ is equivalent to $-\infty < x < \infty$ and $x < k < \infty$, so we can write

$$\begin{aligned} \hat{p}(v) &= e^{-r\tau} \int_{-\infty}^{\infty} q(x) \left[\int_{x}^{\infty} \left(e^{(-\alpha+iv+1)k} - e^{(-\alpha+iv)k+x}\right) dk \right] dx \\ &= e^{-r\tau} \int_{-\infty}^{\infty} q(x) \left[\frac{e^{(-\alpha+iv+1)x}}{\alpha^2 - \alpha - v^2 + iv(1-2\alpha)} \right] dx \\ &= \frac{e^{-r\tau} \varphi(v + (\alpha-1)i)}{\alpha^2 - \alpha - v^2 + iv(1-2\alpha)} \end{aligned}$$

provided that the damping factor is such that $-\alpha + 1 < 0$, or $\alpha > 1$, in order for the upper limit of the inner integral to vanish. The put price is, therefore, obtained by the inverse Fourier transform, analogous to what was done for the call in Equation (3.44)

$$P(k) = e^{\alpha k} p(k) = \frac{e^{\alpha k}}{2\pi} \int_{-\infty}^{\infty} e^{-ivk} \hat{p}(v)\, dv = \frac{e^{-\alpha k}}{\pi} \int_{0}^{\infty} \text{Re}[e^{-ivk} \hat{p}(v)]\, dv. \tag{3.50}$$

To implement the Carr-Madan representation for puts in Matlab, we modify the CarrMadanIntegrand.m function presented earlier in this chapter to include a subroutine for puts. This function can handle calls also.

```
function y = CarrMadanIntegrand(u,...,PutCall);
if strcmp(PutCall,'C')
    I = exp(-i*u*log(K))*HestonCF(u-(alpha+1)*i,...) / ...;
else
    I = exp(-i*u*log(K))*HestonCF(u-(-alpha+1)*i,...) / ...;
end
y = exp(-r*tau)*real(I);
```

We also use a more general function for the Heston price, which can return the price of either a call or a put, using the Heston or Carr-Madan representation. In this function, we use Gauss-Laguerre integration, which is covered in Chapter 5. The function uses put-call parity to return the put price under the Heston representation, but uses Equation (3.50) to return the put price under the Carr-Madan representation.

```
function y = HestonPriceGaussLaguerre(Integrand,...)
if strcmp(Integrand,'Heston')
    for k=1:length(x);
        int1(k) = w(k)*HestonIntegrand(x(k),1,...);
        int2(k) = w(k)*HestonIntegrand(x(k),2,...);
    end
    P1 = 1/2 + 1/pi*sum(int1);
    P2 = 1/2 + 1/pi*sum(int2);
    Call = S*exp(-q*T)*P1 - K*exp(-r*T)*P2;
    if strcmp(PutCall,'C')
        y = Call;
    else
        y = Call - S*exp(-q*T) + K*exp(-r*T);
    end
elseif strcmp(Integrand,'CarrMadan')
    for k=1:length(x);
        int1(k) =
          w(k)*CarrMadanIntegrand(x(k),...,PutCall);
    end
    if strcmp(PutCall,'C')
        y = exp(-alpha*log(K))*sum(int1)/pi;
    else
        y = exp( alpha*log(K))*sum(int1)/pi;
    end
end
```

Using the same settings as the example presented earlier in this chapter, we obtain the put price as 5.9085 with the Heston form, and 5.9083 with the Carr-Madan form. The C# code to implement the Carr and Madan (2009) put price is similar to the Matlab code and is not presented.

THE REPRESENTATION FOR OTM OPTIONS

Carr and Madan (1999) emphasize the fact that, for very short maturities, the call value approaches its intrinsic value $(S_T - K)^+$, and this causes the integrand in the Fourier inversion in Equation (3.44) to be highly oscillatory and, therefore, difficult to integrate. This was illustrated with figures in Chapters 1 and 2. Carr and Madan (1999) define $z(k)$ to be the time-t price of out-of-the-money (OTM) calls and puts with strike $K = e^k$. For convenience, they assume that $S_t = 1$, but their argument can be easily generalized to other values of S_t, as shown in the following section. The regions $K < S_t$ and $K > S_t$ correspond to OTM puts and calls, respectively. Hence, the price is

$$\begin{aligned} z(k) &= \begin{cases} \text{OTM Put Price when } k < 0 \\ \text{OTM Call Price when } k > 0 \end{cases} \\ &= e^{-r\tau} \int_{-\infty}^{\infty} \left[\left(e^k - e^x\right)^+ + (e^x - e^k)^+ \right] q(x)\, dx \\ &= e^{-r\tau} \int_{-\infty}^{k} (e^k - e^x) \mathbf{1}_{k<0}\, q(x)\, dx + e^{-r\tau} \int_{k}^{\infty} (e^x - e^k) \mathbf{1}_{k>0}\, q(x)\, dx \end{aligned} \tag{3.51}$$

with Fourier transform

$$\begin{aligned} \hat{z}(v) &= e^{-r\tau} \int_{-\infty}^{\infty} e^{ivk} z(k)\, dk \\ &= e^{-r\tau} \int_{-\infty}^{\infty} e^{ivk} \int_{-\infty}^{k} (e^k - e^x) \mathbf{1}_{k<0}\, q(x)\, dxdk \\ &\quad + e^{-r\tau} \int_{-\infty}^{\infty} e^{ivk} \int_{k}^{\infty} (e^x - e^k) \mathbf{1}_{k>0}\, q(x)\, dxdk \\ &= e^{-r\tau} \int_{-\infty}^{0} e^{ivk} \int_{-\infty}^{k} (e^k - e^x) q(x) dxdk + e^{-r\tau} \int_{0}^{\infty} e^{ivk} \int_{k}^{\infty} (e^x - e^k) q(x) dxdk. \end{aligned} \tag{3.52}$$

Now, reserve the order of integration in (3.52) to obtain

$$\begin{aligned} \hat{z}(v) &= e^{-r\tau} \int_{-\infty}^{0} q(x) \int_{x}^{0} \left(e^{(iv+1)k} - e^{ivk+x}\right) dkdx \\ &\quad + e^{-r\tau} \int_{0}^{\infty} q(x) \int_{0}^{x} \left(e^{ivk+x} - e^{(iv+1)k}\right) dkdx. \end{aligned} \tag{3.53}$$

It is evident that the two inner integrals in (3.53), for which k is the integration variable, are identical except for opposite signs. Indeed, we can reverse the limits of integration in the second inner integral and change its sign, which will produce the first inner integral. We can, therefore, regroup the two outer integrals to arrive at

$$\hat{z}(v) = e^{-r\tau} \int_{-\infty}^{\infty} \left(\int_{x}^{0} \left(e^{(iv+1)k} - e^{ivk+x} \right) dk \right) q(x)\, dx. \tag{3.54}$$

The inner integral in (3.54) evaluates to

$$\frac{e^{x(iv+1)}}{iv(iv+1)} - \frac{e^x}{iv} + \frac{1}{iv+1}.$$

The Fourier transform in (3.54) can, therefore, be expressed in terms of expectations under the risk-neutral density $q(x)$ as

$$\hat{z}(v) = e^{-r\tau} \left(\frac{E^{\mathbb{Q}}\left[e^{x(iv+1)}\right]}{iv(iv+1)} - \frac{E^{\mathbb{Q}}[e^x]}{iv} + \frac{1}{iv+1} \right).$$

Since the characteristic function is $\varphi(v) = E^{\mathbb{Q}}[e^{ivx}]$, we have that $E^{\mathbb{Q}}[e^{x(iv+1)}] = \varphi(v - i)$. Moreover, since $q(x)$ is the risk-neutral density for $x = \ln S_T$, we have that $E^{\mathbb{Q}}[e^x] = S_t e^{r\tau} = e^{r\tau}$, since we have assumed that $S_t = 1$. This implies that the Fourier transform of $z(k)$ can be written

$$\hat{z}(v) = e^{-r\tau} \left(\frac{1}{iv+1} - \frac{e^{r\tau}}{iv} + \frac{\varphi(v-i)}{v^2 - iv} \right). \tag{3.55}$$

Finally, the price $z(k)$ of an OTM option with strike $K = e^k$ is obtained with the inverse Fourier transform, in a manner analogous to what was done for the call in Equation (3.44) and for the put in Equation (3.50)

$$z(k) = \frac{1}{2\pi} \int_{-\infty}^{\infty} e^{-ivk} \hat{z}(v) dv = \frac{1}{\pi} \int_{0}^{\infty} \mathrm{Re}[e^{-ivk} \hat{z}(v)]\, dv. \tag{3.56}$$

Carr and Madan (1999) point out that the integrand $\hat{z}(v)$ can become highly oscillatory for short maturities and for $k \approx 0$. Instead of basing their derivation on $z(k)$, Carr and Madan suggest basing it on $y(k) = z(k)\sinh(\alpha k)$, which makes use of the dampening factor α, through the hyperbolic sin function $\sinh(x) = \frac{1}{2}(e^x - e^{-x})$. The Fourier transform of $y(k)$ is

$$\begin{aligned} \hat{y}(v) &= \int_{-\infty}^{\infty} e^{ivk} y(k)\, dk = \int_{-\infty}^{\infty} e^{ivk} \left(\frac{e^{\alpha k} - e^{-\alpha k}}{2} \right) z(k)\, dk \\ &= \frac{1}{2} \int_{-\infty}^{\infty} e^{(iv+\alpha)k} z(k)\, dk - \frac{1}{2} \int_{-\infty}^{\infty} e^{(iv-\alpha)k} z(k)\, dk. \end{aligned}$$

Recall that

$$\hat{z}(v) = \int_{-\infty}^{\infty} e^{ivk} z(k) dk.$$

We can, therefore, express $\hat{y}(v)$ in terms of $\hat{z}(v)$, as

$$\hat{y}(v) = \frac{\hat{z}(v - i\alpha) - \hat{z}(v + i\alpha)}{2}. \tag{3.57}$$

The OTM option price is then obtained by Fourier inversion, analogous to Equation (3.56)

$$\begin{aligned} z(k) &= \frac{1}{\sinh(\alpha k)} y(k) = \frac{1}{2\pi \sin(\alpha k)} \int_{-\infty}^{\infty} e^{-ivk}\, \hat{y}(v)\, dv \\ &= \frac{1}{2\pi \sin(\alpha k)} \int_{0}^{\infty} \text{Re}[e^{-ivk} \hat{y}(v)]\, dv. \end{aligned} \tag{3.58}$$

The damped and regular integrands $\hat{y}(v)$ and $\hat{z}(v)$ are each illustrated in Figure 3.4, which reproduces the figure in Carr and Madan (1999). We use the settings $S_t = 1$, $K = 0.96$, maturities running from 1 to 4 weeks, $r = 0.03$, $\kappa = 2$, $\theta = 0.25$, $\sigma = 0.3$, $v_0 = 0.05$ and $\rho = -0.8$, and $\alpha = 1.1$. The integrand for $\hat{z}(v)$ uses Equation (3.60), while the damped integrand for $\hat{y}(v)$ uses (3.57) but with $\hat{z}(v)$ from (3.60).

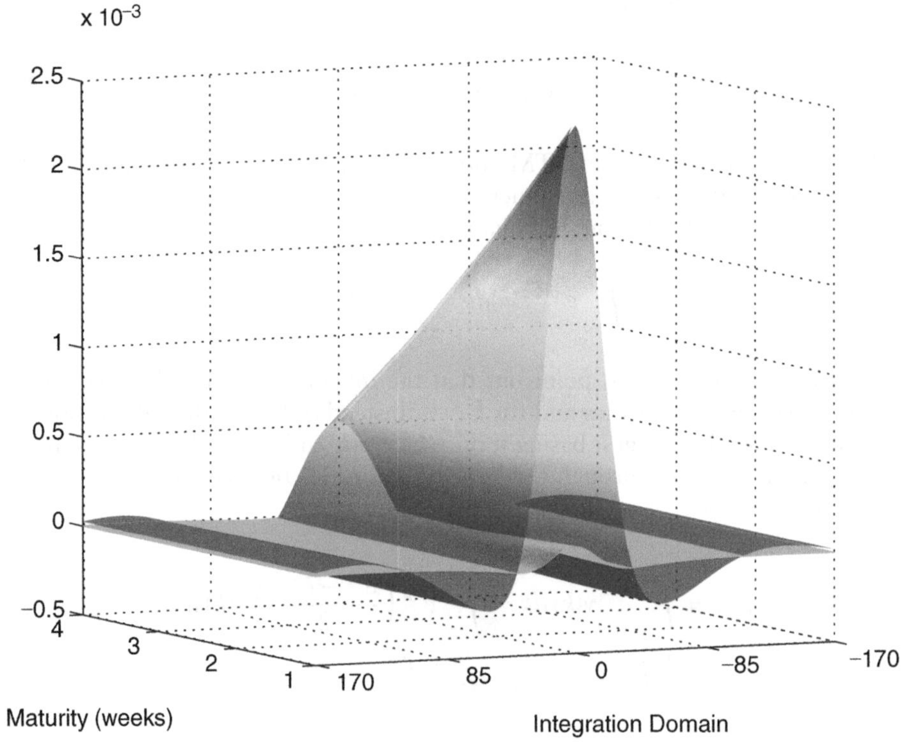

FIGURE 3.4 Carr-Madan Integrands for OTM Options

The damped integrand is represented by the flat green surface in Figure 3.4, and the un-damped integrand by the colored surface. Clearly, adding a damping factor leads to an integrand that is much less oscillatory and on which it is much easier to apply a numerical integration scheme.

The prices of OTM options in Equations (3.56) and (3.58) are designed for $S_t = 1$ only. It is desirable to obtain these formulas for any value of $S_t > 0$. This is the subject of the following section.

Generalization of the OTM Representation

It is straightforward to generalize the OTM representation for any value of $S_t > 0$ because that only involves changing the limits in the required integrals. For $S_t > 0$, the indicator function in Equation (3.51) is based on the OTM cutoff $x_t = \ln S_t$ so that $z(k)$ is

$$z(k) = e^{-r\tau}\int_{-\infty}^{k}(e^k - e^x)\mathbf{1}_{k<x_t}\,q(x)\,dx + e^{-r\tau}\int_{k}^{\infty}(e^x - e^k)\mathbf{1}_{k>x_t}\,q(x)\,dx.$$

Using (3.52), the Fourier transform of $z(k)$ takes the form

$$\hat{z}(v) = e^{-r\tau}\int_{-\infty}^{x_0} e^{ivk}\int_{-\infty}^{k}(e^k - e^x)q(x)dxdk + e^{-r\tau}\int_{x_0}^{\infty} e^{ivk}\int_{k}^{\infty}(e^x - e^k)q(x)dxdk.$$

We proceed exactly in the same fashion: by reversing the order of integration, by noting that the inner integrals are identical, and by regrouping the two outer integrals. The result is a generalization of Equation (3.54)

$$\hat{z}(v) = e^{-r\tau}\int_{-\infty}^{\infty}\left(\int_{x}^{x_t}\left(e^{(iv+1)k} - e^{ivk+x}\right)dk\right)q(x)\,dx. \tag{3.59}$$

The only thing changed is the upper limit in the inner integral, which becomes $k = x_t$ instead of $k = 0$. The inner integral is now

$$\frac{e^{x(iv+1)}}{iv(iv+1)} - \frac{e^{ivx_t+x}}{iv} + \frac{e^{(iv+1)x_t}}{iv+1}.$$

Again, we express $\hat{z}(v)$ in terms of expectations and the characteristic function

$$\hat{z}(v) = e^{-r\tau}\left(\frac{S_t^{iv+1}}{iv+1} - \frac{e^{r\tau}S_t^{iv+1}}{iv} - \frac{\varphi\,(v-i)}{v^2 - iv}\right). \tag{3.60}$$

To obtain the OTM option price for general S_t, we substitute the Fourier transform (3.60) into Equation (3.56) and apply a numerical integration technique. For the damped version, we substitute (3.60) into Equations (3.57) and (3.58).

The following Matlab functions implement, respectively, the OTM Carr-Madan integrand in the OTM price of Equation (3.56), and its damped version in (3.58). These functions are for general values of S_t, so they use (3.60) for $\hat{z}(v)$.

```
function z = CarrMadanIntegrandOTM(u,...)
% Calculate the integrand
phi = HestonCF(u-i,kappa,theta,lambda,rho,sigma,tau,K,S,r,v0,Trap);
I = exp(-i*u*log(K)) * exp(-r*tau) ...
  * (S^(i*u+1)/(1+i*u) - exp(r*tau)*S^(i*u+1)/(i*u)
  - phi/(u^2-i*u));
% Return the real part
z = real(I);
```

```
function y = CarrMadanDampedIntegrandOTM(v, alpha,...)
% Calculate z(v-ia)
u   = v - i*alpha;
phi = HestonCF(u-i,...);
z1  = exp(-r*tau)*(S^(i*u+1)/(1+i*u) - ...);
% Calculate z(v+ia)
clear u phi
u   = v + i*alpha;
phi = HestonCF(u-i,...);
z2  = exp(-r*tau)*(S^(i*u+1)/(1+i*u) - ...);
% Calculate the Fourier transform of y
y = exp(-i*u*log(K)) * (z1 - z2)/2;
% Return the real part only
y = real(y);
```

These functions are passed to the pricing function HestonPriceLaguerre.m, which in this version accepts the OTM integrand. Only the relevant portion of the function is presented here.

```
function y = HestonPriceGaussLaguerre(Integrand,...)
elseif strcmp(Integrand,'CarrMadan') % Carr-Madan
    for k=1:length(x);
        int1(k) = w(k)*CarrMadanIntegrandOTM(x(k),...);
    end
    % The Option Price
    y = sum(int1)/pi;
elseif strcmp(Integrand,'CarrMadanDamped')
    % Carr-Madan damped
    for k=1:length(x);
        int1(k) =  w(k)*CarrMadanDampedIntegrandOTM(x(k),...);
    end
    % The Option Price
    y = 1/sinh(alpha*log(K)) * sum(int1)/pi;
end
```

TABLE 3.1 OTM Pricing Using the Heston and Carr-Madan Method

	OTM Put	OTM Call
$S_t = 1$	$K = 0.95$	$K = 1.05$
Heston	0.1170	0.1485
Carr-Madan	0.1175	0.1473
Carr-Madan Damped	0.1108	0.1575
$S_t = 25$	$K = 20$	$K = 30$
Carr-Madan	1.4944	2.3819
Carr-Madan	1.4888	2.4166

The C# code for pricing OTM calls and puts using the damped and undamped Carr and Madan (1999) integrands is very similar to the Matlab code and is not presented here.

We illustrate the pricing of OTM options using a spot price of $S_t = 1$ and maturity $\tau = 1$ year, and using $r = 0.03$, $\kappa = 2$, $\theta = 0.25$, $\sigma = 0.3$, $v_0 = 0.05$, $\rho = -0.8$, and $\alpha = 1.1$. The strike prices are $K = 0.95$ for the puts and $K = 1.05$ for the calls. To illustrate the pricing of OTM using a general value for the spot price S_t, we use the same parameter and option settings except that we set $S_t = 25$ and change the strike prices to $K = 20$ and $K = 30$. This is accomplished with the following code. The results are in Table 3.1. All integration is done using 32-point Gauss-Laguerre integration.

```
S = 25;
% Price an OTM put
Kp = 20;
PutCall = 'P';
HestonOTMPut = HestonPriceGaussLaguerre('Heston',Kp,...);
CarrMadanOTMPut = HestonPriceGaussLaguerre('CarrMadan',Kp,...);
% Price an OTM Call
Kc = 30;
PutCall = 'C';
HestonOTMCall = HestonPriceGaussLaguerre('Heston',Kc,...);
CarrMadanOTMCall = HestonPriceGaussLaguerre('CarrMadan',Kc,...);
```

CONCLUSION

In this chapter, we have presented the expressions for the in-the-money probabilities that are most often associated with the Heston model. These expressions are based on the form of inversion due to Gil-Pelaez (1951). We have illustrated the derivation of the Heston model by Gatheral (2006), which uses Fourier transforms of the probabilities, and have we presented the Attari (2004) version of the Heston call price, which is based on a modification of the Gil-Pelaez-style probabilities. Finally, we have presented the Carr-Madan (1999) representation, which relies on the Fourier transform of the entire call price, along with optimal choices for, and bounds on, the damping factor and optimal choices of the damping factor. In Chapter 5, we present the fast Fourier transform (FFT) of Carr and Madan (1999), and the fractional FFT of Chourdakis (2005), both of which allow for a very fast calculation of a large set of option prices.

Fourier methods have been applied to option pricing by other authors. Among these, for example, are the cosine method of Fang and Oosterlee (2008), the convolution method of Lord et al. (2008), and the methods of Lewis (2000, 2001). The Lewis methods are the subject of the next chapter.

CHAPTER 4

The Fundamental Transform for Pricing Options

Abstract

In his excellent book, *Option Valuation Under Stochastic Volatility: With Mathematica Code*, Alan Lewis (2000) offers a powerful valuation approach that is applicable to a wide range of European options. His method requires that the fundamental transform, a generalization of the characteristic function that allows complex arguments, be available. It also requires the Fourier transform of the option payoff. Since payoff transforms are available for a wide set of options, however, Lewis' approach is readily applicable to path independent European options of various sorts. The advantage of this approach over other approaches that use Fourier transforms is that, once the fundamental transform of a given model is obtained, it can be used repeatedly to price European options for which the payoff transform is known. This greatly simplifies pricing, since payoff transforms are much easier to obtain than the Fourier transform of the option price itself.

In this chapter, we explain Lewis' fundamental transform approach for option valuation, and we also present his subsequent paper (Lewis, 2001) that uses Parseval's identity to obtain option prices. In that paper, simple variations in the contours of integrations give rise to different forms of the call price encountered in the literature. Finally, we present Lewis' (2000) volatility of volatility series expansion, an approximation that allows the Heston price of European options to be calculated very quickly and without the need for numerical integration.

THE PAYOFF TRANSFORM

In the following sections, we present the fundamental transform approach of Lewis (2000) for pricing options. In his approach, the Fourier transform of the option value is not required, only the Fourier transform of the option payoff. This simplification allows for the pricing of a variety of options under a general setting. The approach, however, does require the fundamental transform. The Lewis (2000) recipe for pricing options thus requires two transforms

1. The payoff transform for a given option, which is model independent and does not depend on the fundamental transform.
2. The fundamental transform for a given model, which is model dependent and analogous to the characteristic function.

The first element required for Lewis' (2000) fundamental transform approach to option valuation is the generalized Fourier transform $\hat{f}(k,t)$ of the derivative value $f(x,t)$ at time t

$$\hat{f}(k,t) = \int_{-\infty}^{\infty} e^{ikx} f(x,t)\, dx \tag{4.1}$$

where $x = \ln S_t$ since we are at time t. Equation (4.1) is identical to the Fourier transform, except that the argument k is allowed to be complex, so that $k = k_r + ik_i$ where k_r and k_i are real numbers. The simplest solution for $\hat{f}(k,t)$ is for European options at expiry time T, for which the payoff $f(x,T)$ is known explicitly. The generalized Fourier transform at expiry, $\hat{f}(x,T)$, is called the payoff transform.

For example, the payoff of a European call option is $f(x,T) = (S_T - K)^+$ so its payoff transform is

$$\hat{f}(k,T) = \int_{-\infty}^{\infty} e^{ikx}(e^x - K)^+ dx = \left(\frac{e^{(ik+1)x}}{ik+1} - \frac{Ke^{ikx}}{ik} \right]_{x=\ln K}^{x=\infty} = -\frac{K^{ik+1}}{k^2 - ik} \tag{4.2}$$

where the last equality holds provided that $k_i > 1$. In Equation (4.2), we now denote $x = \ln S_T$, since we are at maturity. The condition $k_i > 1$ is required because in order for the integrand in Equation (4.2) to not explode at the upper limit $x = \infty$, we must have e^{ikx} decaying faster than e^x grows as $x \to \infty$. To see why the condition works, we can write the term $e^{(ik+1)x}$ in (4.2) as $\exp[(ik_r - k_i + 1)x]$. This term does not explode at $x = \infty$ when $k_i > 1$ so the upper limit of integration in (4.2) is well-defined. It is straightforward to show that $\hat{f}(k,T)$ for the put option is identical to that for the call, except that the admissible region is $k_i < 0$. Payoff transforms for other options are in Table 2.2.1 of Lewis (2000).

To illustrate, in Figure 4.1, we reproduce Figure 4 of Schmelzle (2010) and plot the real portion payoff for the put, over the integration range $-1 < k_i < 0$ and $-4 < k_r < 0$.

Since $\hat{f}(k,t)$ in Equation (4.1) is the generalized Fourier transform, its inverse transform is

$$f(x,t) = \frac{1}{2\pi} \int_{ik_i-\infty}^{ik_i+\infty} e^{-ikx} \hat{f}(k,t)\, dk. \tag{4.3}$$

The generalized Fourier transform is slightly different from the regular Fourier transform, which assumes that k is real only. The generalized Fourier transform is obtained by integrating Equation (4.3) along the strip of regularity. For most derivative payoffs, this strip of regularity is defined as $\alpha < k_i < \beta$, as in Table 2.2.1 of Lewis (2000). For the payoff of the European call, the strip is $k_i > 1$, and for the put it is $k_i < 0$.

THE FUNDAMENTAL TRANSFORM AND THE OPTION PRICE

The second element required for Lewis' (2000) approach is the fundamental transform itself. In this section, we illustrate how Lewis derives the fundamental transform, and we present his recipe for obtaining option prices under his

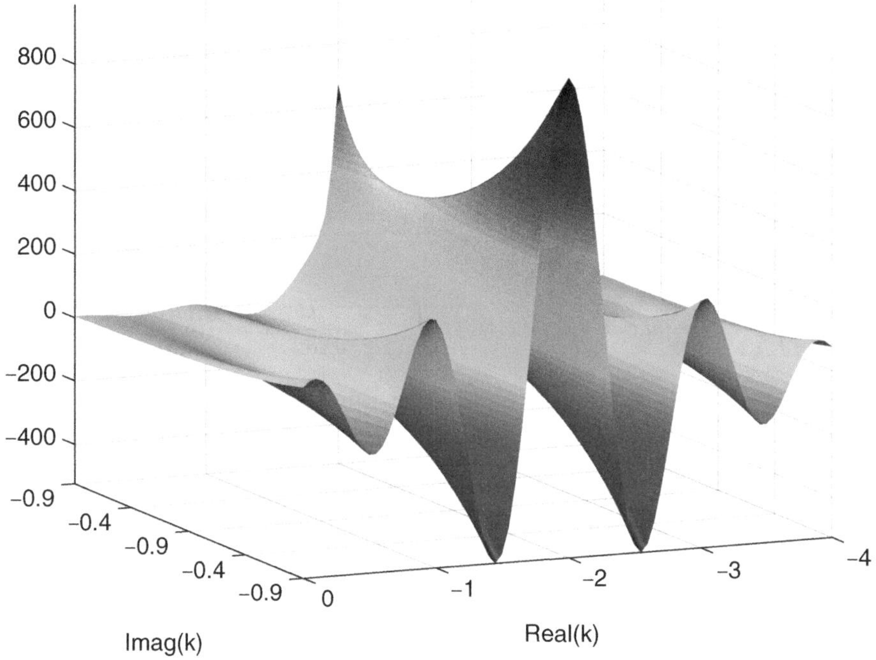

FIGURE 4.1 Real Part of the Put Payoff Transform

method. Lewis (2000) derives the fundamental transform for a general class of stochastic volatility models, but we restrict his derivation to the Heston model.

The Heston partial differential equation (PDE) for the value of the derivative, $U = U(x, t)$, was derived in Chapter 1, reproduced here with a continuous dividend yield, q, and re-arranged as

$$-\frac{\partial U}{\partial t} = -rU + \left(r - q - \frac{1}{2}v\right)\frac{\partial U}{\partial x} + \frac{1}{2}v\frac{\partial^2 U}{\partial x^2} + [\kappa(\theta - v) - \lambda v]\frac{\partial U}{\partial v} + \frac{1}{2}\sigma^2 v\frac{\partial^2 U}{\partial v^2} + \rho\sigma v\frac{\partial^2 U}{\partial v \partial x}. \tag{4.4}$$

To express this PDE in terms of the Fourier transform $\hat{U}$, differentiate (4.1) with respect to t and apply (4.4). This produces

$$-\frac{\partial \hat{U}}{\partial t} = \int_{-\infty}^{\infty} e^{ikx}\left\{-\frac{\partial U}{\partial t}\right\}dx = \int_{-\infty}^{\infty} e^{ikx}\left\{-rU + \left(r - q - \frac{1}{2}v\right)\frac{\partial U}{\partial x} + \frac{1}{2}v\frac{\partial^2 U}{\partial x^2} + [\kappa(\theta - v) - \lambda v]\frac{\partial U}{\partial v} + \frac{1}{2}\sigma^2 v\frac{\partial^2 U}{\partial v^2} + \rho\sigma v\frac{\partial^2 U}{\partial v \partial x}\right\}dx. \tag{4.5}$$

To evaluate (4.5), perform integration by parts and ignore the boundary terms. For example

$$\int_{-\infty}^{\infty} e^{ikx}\frac{\partial U}{\partial x}dx = e^{ikx}U(x,t)|_{x=-\infty}^{x=\infty} - ik\int_{-\infty}^{\infty} e^{ikx}U(x,t)dx = -ik\hat{U}(x,t) \tag{4.6}$$

where the boundary term $e^{ikx}U(x,t)|_{x=-\infty}^{x=\infty}$ has been set to zero. Lewis (2000) explains why this can be done. The other terms in Equation (4.5) are evaluated in a similar fashion. We end up with

$$\int_{-\infty}^{\infty} e^{ikx}\frac{\partial^2 U}{\partial x^2}dx = -k^2\hat{U}(x,t), \qquad \int_{-\infty}^{\infty} e^{ikx}\frac{\partial^2 U}{\partial x\partial v}dx = -ik\frac{\partial\hat{U}}{\partial v}$$

and obviously

$$\int_{-\infty}^{\infty} e^{ikx}\frac{\partial U}{\partial v}dx = \frac{\partial\hat{U}}{\partial v}, \qquad \int_{-\infty}^{\infty} e^{ikx}\frac{\partial^2 U}{\partial v^2}dx = \frac{\partial^2\hat{U}}{\partial v^2}.$$

Substituting these derivatives into (4.5) produces the PDE for $\hat{U}$

$$\begin{aligned} -\frac{\partial\hat{U}}{\partial t} &= [-r - ik(r-q)]\hat{U} - \frac{1}{2}v(k^2 - ik)\hat{U} \\ &\quad + [\kappa(\theta - v) - \lambda v - ik\rho\sigma v]\frac{\partial\hat{U}}{\partial v} + \frac{1}{2}\sigma^2 v\frac{\partial^2\hat{U}}{\partial v^2}. \end{aligned} \tag{4.7}$$

In Equation (2.2.6) of Lewis (2000), the transform in (4.1) is written in the form

$$\hat{U}(k,t) = \exp([-r - ik(r-q)]\tau) \times \hat{H}(k,v,\tau) \tag{4.8}$$

where $\tau = T - t$ is the time to maturity. The function $\hat{H}$ is obtained as the solution of a PDE that is constructed by differentiating Equation (4.8). We thus need the following derivatives

$$-\frac{\partial\hat{U}}{\partial t} = \frac{\partial\hat{U}}{\partial\tau} = [-r - ik(r-q)]e^{[-r-ik(r-q)]\tau}\hat{H}(k,v,\tau) + e^{[-r-ik(r-q)]\tau}\frac{\partial\hat{H}}{\partial\tau}$$

and

$$\frac{\partial\hat{U}}{\partial v} = e^{[-r-ik(r-q)]\tau}\frac{\partial\hat{H}}{\partial v}, \qquad \frac{\partial^2\hat{U}}{\partial v^2} = e^{[-r-ik(r-q)]\tau}\frac{\partial^2\hat{H}}{\partial v^2}.$$

Substituting these derivatives of $\hat{U}$ expressed in terms of $\hat{H}$ into Equation (4.7) and canceling terms produces the PDE for $\hat{H}$

$$\frac{\partial\hat{H}}{\partial\tau} = \frac{1}{2}\sigma^2 v\frac{\partial^2\hat{H}}{\partial v^2} + [\kappa(\theta - v) - \lambda v - ik\rho\sigma v]\frac{\partial\hat{H}}{\partial v} - vc(k)\hat{H}(k,v,\tau) \tag{4.9}$$

where $c(k) = \frac{1}{2}(k^2 - ik)$. Equation (4.9) is Equation (2.2.7) of Lewis (2000), but for the Heston model. Lewis explains that only the special case of a payoff of 1, namely $\hat{H}(k, v, 0) = 1$, need be considered. All other payoffs can be handled by multiplying $\hat{H}(k, v, 0)$ by the appropriate payoff transform. A solution $\hat{H}(k, v, \tau)$ to the PDE in Equation (4.9) that satisfies the initial condition $\hat{H}(k, v, 0) = 1$ is called a fundamental transform. The fundamental transform is called regular if it is regular in k within the strip $\alpha < k_i < \beta$, where $k_i = \text{Im}[k]$, the imaginary part of k.

Once the fundamental transform has been found by solving Equation (4.9), Lewis' (2000) recipe to calculate option prices is straightforward. All that is required is that the payoff transform be known, such as that for the European call in (4.2), for example. The recipe is as follows.

- Multiply the fundamental transform $\hat{H}(k, v, \tau)$ by the payoff transform $\hat{f}(k, T)$. The payoff transform depends on the option under consideration, but the fundamental transform does not.
- Multiply the result by the term $\exp([-r - ik(r - q)]\tau)$.
- Pass the resulting expression through the inversion formula in Equation (4.3) and evaluate the integral, taking care to respect the strip of regularity.

Recall that, in the Carr and Madan (1999) approach, which was covered in Chapter 3, the Fourier transform of the derivative price is required. The consequence is that a separate Fourier transform is required for each type of option for which we need a price. To further aggravate matters, Fourier transforms of prices can be complicated. The advantage of the Lewis (2000) recipe is that once the fundamental transform is obtained, only the transform of the derivative payoffs are required. Since the fundamental transform is model dependent, but not payoff dependent, the same fundamental transform can be applied to value many different European options; all that is required is that their payoff transforms be available analytically. Moreover, since payoffs are specified in options contracts and therefore known explicitly, their Fourier transforms are much easier to obtain than the Fourier transforms of the option prices themselves.

In the next sections, we illustrate the Lewis recipe for a European call. First, we present the fundamental transform for the Heston model.

THE FUNDAMENTAL TRANSFORM FOR THE HESTON MODEL

From Equation (4.9), the PDE for $\hat{H}(k, v, \tau)$ using $\lambda = 0$ is

$$\frac{\partial \hat{H}}{\partial \tau} = \frac{1}{2}\sigma^2 v \frac{\partial^2 \hat{H}}{\partial v^2} + [\kappa(\theta - v) - ik\rho\sigma v]\frac{\partial \hat{H}}{\partial v} - c(k) v \hat{H}(k, v, \tau). \tag{4.10}$$

This PDE must be converted into a form similar to the Riccati equation for which the solution is known. Following Chapter 11 of Lewis (2000), define $t = \sigma^2\tau/2$ so that

$$\frac{\partial \hat{H}}{\partial \tau} = \frac{2}{\sigma^2}\frac{\partial \hat{H}}{\partial t}$$

Equation (4.10) becomes

$$\begin{aligned}\frac{\partial \hat{H}}{\partial t} &= v\frac{\partial^2 \hat{H}}{\partial v^2} + \frac{2}{\sigma^2}[\kappa(\theta - v) - ik\rho\sigma v]\frac{\partial \hat{H}}{\partial v} - \frac{2c(k)}{\sigma^2}v\hat{H}(k, v, \tau)\\ &= v\frac{\partial^2 \hat{H}}{\partial v^2} + \tilde{\kappa}(\tilde{\theta} - v)\frac{\partial \hat{H}}{\partial v} - \tilde{c}(k)v\hat{H}(k, v, \tau)\end{aligned} \tag{4.11}$$

where

$$\tilde{\kappa} = \frac{2(\kappa + ik\rho\sigma)}{\sigma^2}, \quad \tilde{\theta} = \frac{\kappa\theta}{\kappa + ik\rho\sigma}$$

and where $\tilde{c}(k) = 2c(k)/\sigma^2 = (k^2 - ik)/\sigma^2$. The second equation in (4.11) is a parabolic equation in v, and has a solution of the form

$$f(v, t) = \exp(C(t) + D(t)v)$$

with initial condition $C(0) = D(0) = 0$. Take the derivatives of $f(v, t)$, substitute into (4.11), and cancel f on both sides. This produces

$$\frac{\partial C}{\partial t} + \frac{\partial D}{\partial t}v = vD^2 + \tilde{\kappa}(\tilde{\theta} - v)D - \tilde{c}v.$$

Now equate terms in v, which produces the set of equations

$$\frac{\partial D}{\partial t} = D^2 - \tilde{\kappa}D - \tilde{c}, \quad \frac{\partial C}{\partial t} = \tilde{\kappa}\tilde{\theta}D. \tag{4.12}$$

Solving these equations is done in exactly the same manner as was done in the original Heston (1993) derivation covered in Chapter 1. The first equation in (4.12) is the Riccati equation from Chapter 1 with $P(t) = -\tilde{c}$, $Q(t) = -\tilde{\kappa}$, and $R(t) = 1$. To solve it, we apply exactly the same procedure. We set up the second-order ODE

$$w'' + \tilde{\kappa}w' - \tilde{c}w = 0$$

and define

$$\alpha = \frac{-\tilde{\kappa} + d}{2}, \quad \beta = \frac{-\tilde{\kappa} - d}{2}$$

where $d = \sqrt{\tilde{\kappa} + 4\tilde{c}}$. The solution to the Riccati equation in (4.12) is, therefore,

$$D = -\frac{1}{R}\left(\frac{K\alpha e^{\alpha t} + \beta e^{\beta t}}{Ke^{\alpha t} + e^{\beta t}}\right).$$

The initial condition $D(0) = 0$ implies that, by setting $t = 0$ in the numerator, we obtain $K = -\beta/\alpha = (\tilde{\kappa} + d)/(-\tilde{\kappa} + d)$. This produces

$$D(t) = \frac{\tilde{\kappa} + d}{2}\left(\frac{1 - e^{dt}}{1 - ge^{dt}}\right) \tag{4.13}$$

where $g = -K = (\tilde{\kappa} + d)/(\tilde{\kappa} - d)$ and $\alpha - \beta = d$. The solution for $C(t)$ is found by integration. The integral of $D(t)$ is

$$\begin{aligned}\int_0^t D(y)dy &= \frac{\tilde{\kappa} + d}{2}\int_0^t \left(\frac{1 - e^{dy}}{1 - ge^{dy}}\right) dy + K_1 \\ &= \frac{\tilde{\kappa} + d}{2d}\left[dt + \frac{1-g}{g}\ln\left(\frac{1 - ge^{dy}}{1-g}\right)\right] + K_1 \\ &= \left[\frac{\tilde{\kappa} + d}{2}t - \ln\left(\frac{1 - ge^{dt}}{1-g}\right)\right] + K_1\end{aligned}$$

where K_1 is an integration constant. Hence,

$$C(t) = \tilde{\kappa}\tilde{\theta}\left[\frac{\tilde{\kappa} + d}{2}t - \ln\left(\frac{1 - ge^{dt}}{1-g}\right)\right] \tag{4.14}$$

where we have applied the initial condition $C(0)$ so that $K_1 = 0$. The fundamental transform of the Heston model is, therefore,

$$\hat{H}(k, v, \tau) = \exp(C(t) + D(t)v) \tag{4.15}$$

where $D(t)$ is given by Equation (4.13), and $C(t)$ by (4.14). The initial condition at $t = 0$ implies that we set $v = v_0$, the parameter for the initial variance, in (4.15).

The fundamental transform in (4.15) is identical to the characteristic function derived in Chapter 1, with the notation $C(t)$ and $D(t)$ denoting $C(\tau, \phi)$ and $D(\tau, \phi)$. Lewis (2000, Section 2.4) describes the conditions under which $\hat{H}(k, v, \tau)$ is an analytic characteristic function.

The Call Price Using the Fundamental Transform

Recall that the Lewis recipe requires the payoff transform for the option being priced. To apply the Lewis recipe to the European call price, we use the payoff transform obtained in Equation (4.2). The integral to solve is, therefore,

$$C_1(K) = \frac{1}{2\pi}\int_{ik_i-\infty}^{ik_i+\infty} e^{-ikx} \times e^{[-r-ik(r-q)]\tau} \times \hat{H}(k, v, \tau) \times \left(\frac{-K^{ik+1}}{k^2 - ik}\right) dk \tag{4.16}$$

where $x = \ln S_t$. Defining $X = \ln(S_t/K) + (r - q)\tau$, the call price can be written in the form of Equation (2.2.8) in Lewis (2000), namely

$$C_1(K) = -\frac{Ke^{-r\tau}}{2\pi}\int_{ik_i-\infty}^{ik_i+\infty} e^{-ikX}\frac{1}{k^2 - ik}\hat{H}(k, v, \tau)\, dk \tag{4.17}$$

where the integral is defined for $1 < k_i < \beta$. Indeed, the strip of regularity for $\hat{H}(k, v, \tau)$ is $\alpha < k_i < \beta$, and the strip of regularity for the payoff transform is $k_i > 1$. Hence, $C_1(K)$ is defined on the intersection of these two strips, namely $1 < k_i < \beta$.

Equations (4.17) and (4.19) for the call price each depend on the analytical form of the fundamental transform $\hat{H}(k, v, \tau)$ and are, therefore, valid for a wide set of models, including the Heston model. Lewis (2000) derives analytical expressions for $\hat{H}(k, v, \tau)$ for several models, including the Heston model, which we covered in the previous section.

Lewis (2000) also finds an alternative solution to the call price in (4.17), based on put-call parity and a covered call, which has the payoff $\min(S_T, K)$. This solution is valid under the simpler restriction that $0 < k_i < 1$. The payoff of the covered call is

$$\min(S_T, K) = K - (K - S_T)^+.$$

Taking expectations on both sides and discounting, the time t price of the covered call is

$$e^{-r\tau}E[\min(S_T, K)] = Ke^{-r\tau} - P(K)$$

where $P(K)$ is the time t value of a European put struck at K. Put-call parity

$$C(K) = S_t e^{-q\tau} - [Ke^{-r\tau} - P(K)] \tag{4.18}$$

implies that the call price can be expressed in terms of the spot price and the covered call. Hence, to find the second solution, we need to apply Alan Lewis' recipe to the covered call, which has the payoff transform

$$\hat{f}(k, T) = \int_{-\infty}^{\infty} e^{ikx}[K - (K - e^x)^+]dx = K\int_{\ln K}^{\infty} e^{ikx}dx + \int_{-\infty}^{\ln K} e^{(ik+1)x}dx$$

$$= K\left(\left.\frac{e^{ikx}}{ik}\right]_{x=\ln K}^{x=\infty}\right) + \left(\left.\frac{e^{(ik+1)x}}{ik+1}\right]_{x=-\infty}^{x=\ln K}\right) = -\frac{K^{ik+1}}{ik} + \frac{K^{ik+1}}{ik+1} = \frac{K^{ik+1}}{k^2 - ik}$$

where the strip is $0 < k_i < 1$ because the first integral requires $k_i > 0$, while the second requires $k_i < 1$. Hence, the payoff transform for the covered call is identical to that for the call, except for the absence of a minus sign, and the restriction $0 < k_i < 1$, which is easier to deal with than the restriction $k_i > 1$ for the call. Applying the Lewis (2000) recipe to the covered call and using put-call parity in Equation (4.18), the second solution is, therefore,

$$C_2(K) = S_t e^{-q\tau} - \frac{Ke^{-r\tau}}{2\pi}\int_{ik_i-\infty}^{ik_i+\infty} e^{-ikX}\frac{1}{k^2 - ik}\hat{H}(k, v, \tau)\,dk \tag{4.19}$$

where $\max(0, \alpha) < k_i < \min(1, \beta)$. The value $C_2(K)$ is identical to $C_1(K)$ in (4.17) except for the presence of the term $S_t e^{-q\tau}$ and a different strip. Indeed, the strip for the transform $\hat{f}(k, T)$ of the covered call is $0 < k_i < 1$ and the strip for $\hat{H}(k, v, \tau)$ is $\alpha < k_i < \beta$. Hence, $C_2(K)$ is defined on the intersection of these two strips,

$\max(0,\alpha) < k_i < \min(1,\beta)$. Equation (4.19) for the call price is easier to deal with than (4.17), because in (4.19), we can simply select $k_i = 1/2$. Equation (4.19) is Equation (2.2.10) in Lewis (2000).

The integral for the call price $C_1(K)$ in (4.17) or for $C_2(K)$ in (4.19) can be simplified by noting that the integrand is also even in its real part, and odd in its imaginary part. Hence, the expressions for the call price can be written

$$C_1(K) = -\frac{Ke^{-r\tau}}{\pi}\int_0^{\infty} \mathrm{Re}\left[e^{-ikX}\frac{1}{k^2 - ik}\hat{H}(k, v, \tau)\right] dk \tag{4.20}$$

where $1 < k_i < \beta$, and

$$C_2(K) = S_t e^{-q\tau} - \frac{Ke^{-r\tau}}{\pi}\int_0^{\infty} \mathrm{Re}\left[e^{-ikX}\frac{1}{k^2 - ik}\hat{H}(k, v, \tau)\right] dk \tag{4.21}$$

where $\max(0,\alpha) < k_i < \min(1,\beta)$ and where $X = \ln(S_t/K) + (r-q)\tau$. The solutions in Equations (4.20) and (4.21) are identical, except that the expression for $C_2(K)$ includes the term $S_t e^{-q\tau}$ while that for $C_1(K)$ does not. Hence, it seems unintuitive that both would produce the same call value. Remember, however, that the integration strips are different. Indeed, in $C_2(K)$, we can take $k_i = 1/2$, but in $C_1(K)$ we must take $k_i > 1$. This difference means that the integrals will have different values; the net effect is that $C_1(K) = C_2(K)$.

When a numerical integration scheme is applied to the integrals in Equations (4.20) and (4.21), their upper limits are often truncated and replaced by a large number. Lewis uses the range $(0, k_{\max})$ where $k_{\max} = \max(1000, 10/\sqrt{v_0\tau})$. We return to this issue in Chapter 5.

The Matlab function LewisIntegrand.m implements the fundamental transform $\hat{H}(k, v, \tau)$ from Equation (4.15).

```
function y = LewisIntegrand(k,X,...)
kappa = 2*(kappa + i*k*rho*sigma)/sigma^2;
theta = kappa*theta/(kappa + i*k*rho*sigma);
t = tau*sigma^2/2;
c = (k^2-i*k)/sigma^2;
d = sqrt(kappa^2 + 4*c);
alpha = (-kappa + d)/2;
beta  = (-kappa - d)/2;
g = beta/alpha;
B = (kappa+d)*(1-exp(d*t)) / (1 - g*exp(d*t))/2;
A = kappa*theta*((kappa+d)*t/2 - log((1-g*exp(d*t))/(1-g)) );
H = exp(A + B*v0);
y = real(exp(-X*i*k)/(k^2 - i*k)*H);
```

This function is then used passed to the function HestonLewisCallPrice.m, which calculates either $C_1(K)$ from Equation (4.20), or $C_2(K)$ from (4.21). The function can use either the trapezoidal integration rule, or Gauss Laguerre integration.

TABLE 4.1 Comparison of Call Prices

Call Price Formula	Integration Rule	Call Price
Original Heston Formulation	Gauss-Laguerre	4.939490
$C_1(K)$ in (4.20)	Trapezoidal	4.932314
$C_1(K)$ in (4.20)	Gauss-Laguerre	4.934282
$C_2(K)$ in (4.21)	Trapezoidal	4.932314
$C_2(K)$ in (4.21)	Gauss-Laguerre	4.928201

```
function y = HestonLewisCallPrice(...)
kmax = floor(max(1000,10/sqrt(v0*tau)));
X = log(S/K) + (r-q)*tau;
if IntRule==1                    % Trapezoidal Rule
    h = (b-a)/(N-1);
    phi = [a:h:b];
    wt = h.*[1/2 ones(1,N-2) 1/2];
    for k = 1:N;
        u = phi(k) + i*ki;
        int(k) = wt(k)*LewisIntegrand(u,...);
    end
    Integral = sum(int);
else                              % 32-point Gauss Laguerre
    for k = 1:length(x);
        u = x(k) + i*ki;
        int(k) = w(k)*LewisIntegrand(u,...);
    end
    Integral = sum(int);
end
if form==2
    y = S*exp(-q*tau) - (1/pi)*K*exp(-r*tau)*Integral;
else
    y = - (1/pi)*K*exp(-r*tau)*Integral;
end
```

The C# code to implement $C_1(K)$ and $C_2(K)$ is similar to the Matlab code and not presented.

We illustrate with call prices obtained using Lewis' (2000) recipe, using $S_t = K = 100$, $r = 0.05$, $q = 0.01$ and a maturity of 3 months, along with parameter values $\kappa = 2$, $\theta = v_0 = 0.05$, $\sigma = 0.1$, and $\rho = -0.9$. For the trapezoidal rule, we choose an upper limit of integration of 100 and 10,000 integration points. Gauss-Laguerre integration uses 32 points. The results are in Table 4.1 and indicate high agreement between the call prices $C_1(K)$ and $C_2(K)$ in Equations (4.20) and (4.21), respectively, and those of the original Heston (1993) formulation, regardless of the integration rule chosen.

OPTION PRICES USING PARSEVAL'S IDENTITY

In the follow-up paper to his book, Lewis (2001) makes use of Parseval's identity to obtain option prices that are valid under any Lévy price process for which the characteristic function is known, including the Heston model. In this section, we describe and implement his approach. First, we present Parseval's identity for Fourier transforms.

Parseval's Identity

This is a key identity for the application of Fourier transforms to option pricing. It is described in textbooks such as that by Rudin (1986). Define the scalar product of two functions f and g integrable on $(-\infty, \infty)$ as

$$\langle f, g\rangle = \int_{-\infty}^{\infty} f(x)\overline{g(x)}\, dx$$

where $\overline{g(x)}$ is the complex conjugate of $g(x)$. Parseval's identity states that the scalar product is preserved under Fourier transforms, so that $\langle f, g\rangle = \frac{1}{2\pi}\langle \hat{f}, \hat{g}\rangle$. Hence Parseval's identity is

$$\int_{-\infty}^{\infty} f(x)\overline{g(x)}\, dx = \frac{1}{2\pi}\int_{-\infty}^{\infty} \hat{f}(k)\overline{\hat{g}(k)}\, dk.$$

If we consider $\langle f, \overline{g}\rangle$ instead, then we have

$$\int_{-\infty}^{\infty} f(x)g(x)\, dx = \frac{1}{2\pi}\int_{-\infty}^{\infty} \hat{f}(k)\hat{g}(-k)\, dk. \tag{4.22}$$

The fact that $\hat{g}(-k)$ rather than $\hat{g}(k)$ appears in the integral on the right-hand side of (4.22) is a consequence of the convolution theorem for Fourier transforms. See, for example, Section 7.2.5 of Beerends et al. (2003).

If we need the generalized Fourier transform, which allows complex values for k so that $k = k_r + ik_i$, Parseval's identity in Equation (4.22) becomes

$$\int_{-\infty}^{\infty} f(x)g(x)\, dx = \frac{1}{2\pi}\int_{ik_i-\infty}^{ik_i+\infty} \hat{f}(k)\hat{g}(-k)\, dk. \tag{4.23}$$

The Option Price Using Parseval's Identity

Writing $x_t = \ln S_t$, the time-t value $f(x_t, t)$ of a derivative with payoff $w(x_T)$ can be written

$$f(x_t, t) = e^{-r\tau}E^{\mathbb{Q}}[w(x_T)] = e^{-r\tau}\int_{-\infty}^{\infty} w(x)q(x)\, dx = \frac{e^{-r\tau}}{2\pi}\int_{-\infty}^{\infty} \hat{w}(k)\hat{q}(-k)\, dk,$$

where the last equality follows from Equation (4.22). Since $\hat{q}(k)$ is the Fourier transform of the density for $\ln S_T$, it is also the characteristic function, $\varphi(k)$. Hence, the derivative value can be expressed in terms of the characteristic function and the Fourier transform of the payoff. When k is a complex number the option value is, using Parseval's identity in Equation (4.23)

$$f(x_t, t) = \frac{e^{-r\tau}}{2\pi}\int_{ik_i-\infty}^{ik_i+\infty} \hat{w}(k)\hat{q}(-k)\, dk = \frac{e^{-r\tau}}{2\pi}\int_{ik_i-\infty}^{ik_i+\infty} \hat{w}(k)\varphi(-k)\, dk. \tag{4.24}$$

Parseval's Identity for the Heston Model

Lewis (2001) derives an option pricing formula under a general setup for the stock price. Suppose that the stock price S_T at time T evolves from S_0 at time $t = 0$ as

$$S_T = S_0 e^{(r-q)T+X_T} \tag{4.25}$$

where T is the exercise time of the option, r is the risk-free rate, q is the dividend yield, and X_T is a Lévy process for which $E[e^{X_T}] = 1$. Under certain regularity conditions, the option price $U(S_0)$ at time $t = 0$ is

$$U(S_0) = \frac{e^{-rT}}{2\pi} \int_{ik_i-\infty}^{ik_i+\infty} e^{-ikY} \varphi(-k)\hat{w}(k)\, dk \tag{4.26}$$

where $Y = \ln S_0 + (r - q)T$, where $\hat{w}(k)$ is the Fourier transform of the payoff $w(x_T)$, and where $\varphi(k)$ is the characteristic function of the Lévy process X_T evaluated at the complex number $k = k_r + ik_i$. Lewis (2001) assumes that $\varphi(k)$ is regular in the strip $S_X = \{k : a < k_i < b\}$ such that $a < -1$ and $b > 0$. To show how Equation (4.26) is derived, use the inverse transform of the payoff in (4.3), writing $w(x)$ for $f(x, t)$ and $\hat{w}(k)$ for $\hat{f}(k, t)$

$$w(x) = \frac{1}{2\pi} \int_{ik_i-\infty}^{ik_i+\infty} e^{-ikx} \hat{w}(k)\, dk = \frac{1}{2\pi} \int_{ik_i-\infty}^{ik_i+\infty} S_T^{-ik} \hat{w}(k)\, dk \tag{4.27}$$

since $x = \ln S_T$. The no-arbitrage price of the option is

$$\begin{aligned} U(S_0) &= e^{-rT} E^{\mathbb{Q}}[w(x)] \\ &= \frac{e^{-rT}}{2\pi} E^{\mathbb{Q}} \left[\int_{ik_i-\infty}^{ik_i+\infty} \left(S_0 e^{(r-q)T+X_T}\right)^{-ik} \hat{w}(k)\, dk \right] \\ &= \frac{e^{-rT}}{2\pi} \int_{ik_i-\infty}^{ik_i+\infty} e^{-ikY} E^{\mathbb{Q}}[e^{-ikX_T}] \hat{w}(k)\, dk \\ &= \frac{e^{-rT}}{2\pi} \int_{ik_i-\infty}^{ik_i+\infty} e^{-ikY} \varphi(-k)\hat{w}(k)\, dk \end{aligned} \tag{4.28}$$

since $\varphi(-k) = E^{\mathbb{Q}}[e^{-ikX_T}]$ is the characteristic function for X_T, evaluated at $-k$. Note that, in the last line of (4.28), the term $e^{-ikY}\varphi(-k)$ can be written

$$e^{-ikY}\varphi(-k) = E^{\mathbb{Q}}[e^{-ik(Y+X_T)}] = E^{\mathbb{Q}}[e^{-ik \ln S_T}] = f_2(-k) \tag{4.29}$$

which is the Heston (1993) characteristic function for $\ln S_T$, evaluated at $-k$.

The valuation formula (4.28) is Equation (3.5) in Lewis (2001) and the main result of that paper. Lewis (2000) explains that (4.28) is applicable to a wide range of models, including the Variance Gamma model, the Heston model, and many others. All that is needed is the characteristic function and its strip of regularity.

The transform $\hat{w}(k)$ is defined in the region S_w so that for the call option we have $S_w^{Call} = \{k : k_i > 1\}$ and for the put option we have $S_w^{Put} = \{k : k_i < 0\}$, as explained

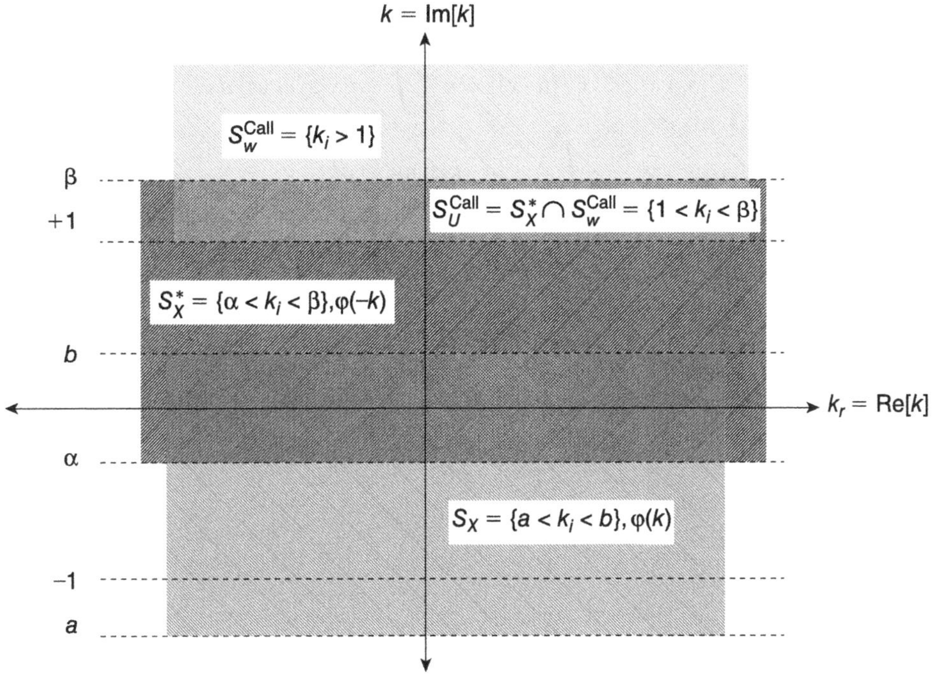

FIGURE 4.2 Integration Strip for the Call Option

earlier in this chapter. Moreover, the characteristic function $\varphi(k)$ is regular in the strip S_X. This implies that $\varphi(-k)$ is defined in the strip S_X^*, which reflects S_X across the real axis and flips it across the imaginary axis. The conclusion is that the integral in Equation (4.28) is defined in the intersection of these two regions, namely $S_U = S_w \cap S_X^*$. For the call option, we have $S_U^{Call} = \{k : 1 < k_i < \beta\}$ as illustrated in Figure 4.2.

By a similar argument, for the put option, we have $S_U^{Put} = \{k : \alpha < k_i < 0\}$.

Lewis (2001) provides an alternate derivation using the complex form of Parseval's identity in (4.23). Define $s_T = \ln S_T$ and $s_0 = \ln S_0$, and the cumulative distribution functions $Q(x|s_0) = \Pr(s_T < x|x_0)$ and $P(x) = \Pr(X_T < x)$. Using $Y = s_0 + (r - q)T$, it is straightforward to show that

$$\Pr(s_T < x|s_0) = \Pr(X_T < x - Y)$$

so that by differentiation, we have $q(s_T|s_0) = p(x - Y)$ where q and p are the densities corresponding to Q and P. Using the definition of the Fourier transform, making a change of variable to evaluate the integral, and recalling that $s_T = Y + X_T$, we have

$$\hat{q}(k|s_0) = \int_{ik_i-\infty}^{ik_i+\infty} e^{iks_T} q(s_T|s_0)ds_T = \int_{ik_i-\infty}^{ik_i+\infty} e^{ik(Y+X_T)} p(X_T|s_0)dX_T = e^{ikY}\hat{p}(k).$$

Furthermore, we can write $\hat{q}(k|s_0) = e^{ikY}\varphi(k)$, since $\hat{p}(k)$ is the characteristic function for X_T, which we denoted $\varphi(k)$. Note that $\hat{q}(k|s_0)$ is the characteristic function for $s_T = \ln S_T$. By an application of Parseval's identity in Equation (4.22), we have

$$\begin{aligned} U(S_0) &= e^{-rT} E^{\mathbb{Q}}[w(x)] = e^{-rT} \int_{-\infty}^{\infty} q(x|s_0) w(x)\, dx \\ &= \frac{e^{-rT}}{2\pi} \int_{ik_i-\infty}^{ik_i+\infty} \hat{q}(-k|s_0)\hat{w}(k)\, dk \\ &= \frac{e^{-rT}}{2\pi} \int_{ik_i-\infty}^{ik_i+\infty} e^{-ikY} \varphi(-k)\hat{w}(k)\, dk. \end{aligned} \tag{4.30}$$

Substituting for payoff transforms $\hat{w}(x)$ produces valuation formulas corresponding to those payoffs. The call option has payoff transform $\hat{w}(x)$ given in Equation (4.2). Hence, the call price $C(S_0)$ is found by substituting for $\hat{w}(x)$ into (4.30)

$$\begin{aligned} C(S_0) &= -\frac{e^{-rT}}{2\pi} \int_{ik_i-\infty}^{ik_i+\infty} e^{-ikY} \varphi(-k) \frac{K^{ik+1}}{k^2 - ik} dk \\ &= -\frac{Ke^{-rT}}{2\pi} \int_{ik_i-\infty}^{ik_i+\infty} e^{-ikW} \varphi(-k) \frac{1}{k^2 - ik} dk \end{aligned} \tag{4.31}$$

for $1 < k_i < \beta$ and where $W = \ln(S_0/K) + (r - q)T$, which we denoted by X earlier in this chapter. The second line of (4.31) is Equation (3.9) of Lewis (2001). Recall that the condition $k_i > 1$ must hold in order for the call option payoff transform to be defined (where $k_i = \text{Im}[k]$). Note the identical forms of the call price in Equation (4.31) and the call price $C_1(K)$ in (4.17), which shows that

$$\hat{H}(k, v, \tau) = \varphi(-k).$$

Contour Variations and the Call Price

The residue of a complex-valued function $f(k)$ at a simple pole c is defined as

$$\text{Res}(c) = \lim_{k \to c} f(k)(k - c).$$

The residue theorem stipulates that a complex integral evaluated along a contour is equal to $2\pi i$ times the sum of the residues at all poles contained within the contour. This greatly simplifies the evaluation of a complex integral, since we only need to know the value of the residues at the poles. The integral in Equation (4.31) is not defined at the poles $k = 0$ and $k = i$, since both of these values produce zero in the denominator. The residue at $k = 0$ for the integrand in (4.31) is

$$\text{Res}(0) = \lim_{k \to 0} \left[-\frac{Ke^{-rT-ikW}\varphi(-k)}{2\pi k(k - i)} k \right] = -\frac{Ke^{-rT} i}{2\pi}$$

since $\varphi(0) = 1$ and $1/i = -i$. Similarly, the residue at $k = i$ is

$$\text{Res}(i) = \lim_{k \to i} \left[-\frac{Ke^{-rT-ikW}\varphi(-k)}{2\pi (k^2 - ik)} (k - i) \right] = \frac{S_0 e^{-qT} i}{2\pi}$$

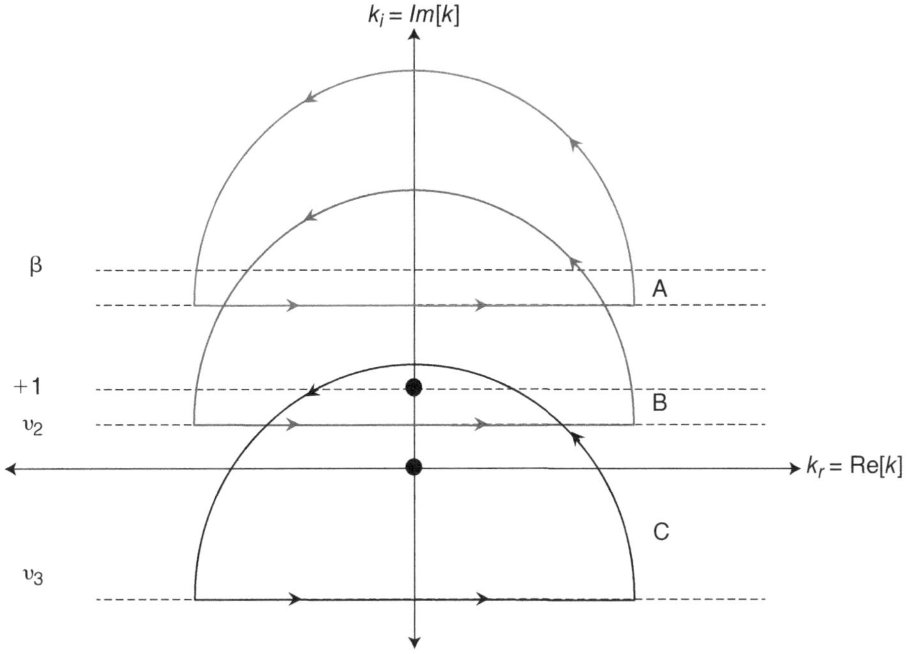

FIGURE 4.3 Contours of Integration

since $\varphi(-i) = E[e^{X_T}]$, and $E[e^{X_T}] = 1$ is a requirement on the Lévy process X_T made in (4.25).

To integrate Equation (4.31), we can select a contour comprised of a horizontal line just above $k_i = 1$ but below β, and a semi-circle above. Since there are no poles in this region, we do not apply the residue theorem and the call price $C(S_0)$ is obtained by direct integration of (4.31). This is illustrated by the blue semi-circle A in Figure 4.3. The poles are indicated by solid dots. The pole $k = 0$ lies at the origin, and the pole $k = i$ lies at the point $(k_r, k_i) = (0, 1)$.

Lewis (2001) shows how variations on the call price arise by modifying the contour. If we move the integration contour in Equation (4.31) down to another value $\upsilon_2 \in (0, 1)$, say, instead of at $\beta > 1$, then we include the pole at $k_i = 1$ in the integration contour, as illustrated by the red semi-circle B in Figure 4.3. By the residue theorem, $C(S_0)$ will be equal to the integral evaluated along this new integration contour, minus $2\pi i$ times the residue at i, which has been excluded. Hence, Equation (4.31) becomes

$$\begin{aligned} C(S_0) &= -\frac{Ke^{-rT}}{2\pi}\int_{i\upsilon_2-\infty}^{i\upsilon_2+\infty} e^{-ikW}\varphi(-k)\frac{1}{k^2-ik}\,dk - 2\pi i\left(\frac{S_0e^{-qT}i}{2\pi}\right) \\ &= S_0e^{-qT} - \frac{Ke^{-rT}}{2\pi}\int_{i\upsilon_2-\infty}^{i\upsilon_2+\infty} e^{-ikW}\varphi(-k)\frac{1}{k^2-ik}\,dk \end{aligned} \tag{4.32}$$

for $\upsilon_2 \in (0, 1)$. The second line of (4.32) is Equation (3.10) of Lewis (2001).

Finally, Lewis (2001) shows that, if the integration contour is moved to $v_3 \in (\alpha, 0)$, with $\alpha < 0$, then both poles are included, as shown by the black semi-circle C in Figure 4.3. Applying the residue theorem again, $C(S_0)$ will be equal to the integral along this new contour, minus $2\pi i$ times the sum of both residues. Recall that the payoff transform for the put is

$$\hat{w}(k) = \frac{K^{ik+1}}{k^2 - ik}$$

which is identical to that for the call, except that the admissible region is $k_i < 0$. Hence, when we take the contour at v_3 in Equation (4.31), we end up with $P(S_0)$, the value of the put. By the residue theorem, the call option is the integral in (4.31) along the new contour, minus $2\pi i$ times the sum of the two residues

$$C(S_0) = P(S_0) - 2\pi i \left(\frac{S_0 e^{-qT} i}{2\pi} - \frac{K e^{-rT} i}{2\pi} \right) = P(S_0) + S_0 e^{-qT} - K e^{-rT}$$

which is the price of the call by put-call parity.

If we choose $v_2 = \frac{1}{2}$ in Equation (4.32), then we are integrating along the line $k_i = \frac{1}{2}$ in between the two poles in Figure 4.3. Writing $k = u + \frac{1}{2}i$ so that $k^2 - ik = u^2 + \frac{1}{4}$, we can express (4.32) as

$$\begin{aligned}
C(S_0) &= S_0 e^{-qT} - \frac{K e^{-rT}}{2\pi} \int_{i/2-\infty}^{i/2+\infty} e^{-i\left(u+\frac{1}{2}i\right)W} \varphi\left(-u - \tfrac{1}{2}i\right) \frac{1}{u^2 + \frac{1}{4}} du \\
&= S_0 e^{-qT} - \frac{\sqrt{K S_0} e^{-(r+q)T/2}}{2\pi} \int_{i/2-\infty}^{i/2+\infty} e^{-iuW} \varphi\left(-u - \tfrac{1}{2}i\right) \frac{1}{u^2 + \frac{1}{4}} du \\
&= S_0 e^{-qT} - \frac{\sqrt{K S_0} e^{-(r+q)T/2}}{\pi} \int_0^{\infty} \text{Re}\left[e^{iuW} \varphi\left(u - \tfrac{1}{2}i\right) \frac{1}{u^2 + \frac{1}{4}} \right] du. \qquad (4.33)
\end{aligned}$$

The first line uses $u + \frac{1}{2}i$ substituted for k, and uses $W = \ln(S_0/K) + (r - q)T$, while the last line uses the fact that

$$\text{Re}\left[e^{-iuW} \varphi\left(-u - \tfrac{1}{2}i\right)\right] = \text{Re}\left[e^{iuW} \varphi\left(u - \tfrac{1}{2}i\right)\right].$$

This last expression is easily demonstrated, by expressing e^{iuW} and $\varphi(u)$ as complex numbers, and using the property of the complex conjugate of the characteristic function, namely that $\varphi(-u) = \overline{\varphi(u)}$. The last line of (4.33) is Equation (3.11) of Lewis (2001). See Itkin (2010) for a similar derivation, under the Variance Gamma model. An expression similar to (4.33) was derived by Lipton (2002) for foreign exchange options.

Recall from Equation (4.25) that $\ln S_T = \ln S_0 + (r - q)T + X_T = Y + X_T$. To implement the call price in (4.33), it is useful to write $\varphi(u)$, the characteristic function for X_T, as we did in (4.29), namely

$$\varphi(u) = E[e^{iuX_T}] = E[e^{iu \ln S_T}] e^{-iuY} = f_2(u) e^{-iuY} \qquad (4.34)$$

where $f_2(u)$ is the Heston characteristic function evaluated at u.

The following Matlab code implements the call price in Equation (4.33). The Matlab function LewisIntegrand311.m calculates $\varphi(u)$ using $f_2(u)$, in accordance with (4.34). Only the last part of this function is presented later. Since we are passing $u - i/2$ to this function, in the last part, we need to remove $i/2$ from u in order to calculate e^{iuW} and u^2 properly in the last line of the function.

```
function y = LewisIntegrand311(u,...)
% The Heston characteristic function for ln S(T)
CFlnST = exp(C + D*v0 + i*u*x);
% The cf for XT
Y = log(S) + (r-q)*tau;
CFXT = exp(-i*u*Y)*CFlnST;
% The integrand
u = u + i/2;
W = Y - log(K);
y = exp(i*u*W)*CFXT/(u^2 + 1/4);
```

The function LewisPrice311.m calculates the call price using the integration weights w and the abscissas x passed to the function. It is similar to the function HestonLewisCallPrice.m defined earlier in this chapter, except that it passes the integration points $u_j = x_j - i/2$ to the integrand.

```
function y = LewisPrice311(...)
lambda = 0;
Y = log(S) + (r-q)*T;
W = Y - log(K);
% Compute the integral.
for j=1:length(x);
    u = x(j) - (1/2)*i;
    int(j) = w(j)*LewisIntegrand311(u,...);
end
Integral = sum(int);
% Equation (3.11) in Lewis (2011)
y = S*exp(-q*T) - (1/pi)*sqrt(K*S)*exp(-(r+q)*T/2)*Integral;
```

The C# code to implement the call price in Equation (4.33) is similar and not presented here.

To illustrate, we use the same settings as those used to generate Table 4.1 to generate call prices using (4.33) for strikes ranging from $K = 95$ to $K = 105$. We use 32-point Gauss Laguerre integration to obtain the call prices using the original Heston (1993) formulation and Equation (3.11) of Lewis (2001). The results in Table 4.2 indicate high agreement between both sets of prices.

TABLE 4.2 Comparison of Call Prices

Strike	Equation (4.33)	Original Heston	Percent Error
95	7.9798	7.9835	0.047
96	7.3047	7.3085	0.052
97	6.6618	6.6656	0.057
98	6.0520	6.0559	0.064
99	5.4763	5.4802	0.072
100	4.9350	4.9391	0.081
101	4.4286	4.4327	0.092
102	3.9571	3.9613	0.105
103	3.5201	3.5244	0.120
104	3.1173	3.1216	0.138
105	2.7477	2.7521	0.158

VOLATILITY OF VOLATILITY SERIES EXPANSION

Lewis (2000) derives a volatility of volatility series expansion for the call price and for the implied volatility that are valid under a general class of stochastic volatility models. In this section, we present this expansion for the Heston model only. Obtaining the Heston call price with this method is very fast, because numerical integration is not required. The name is derived from the fact that both series expansions are in terms of powers of the volatility of variance parameter, σ. The first series is based on an expansion about the Black-Scholes price evaluated at the average variance $\overline{v}$

$$C_{BS}(S_0, \overline{v}, T) = S_0 e^{-qT}\Phi(d_1) - Ke^{-rT}\Phi(d_2) \tag{4.35}$$

where

$$d_1 = \frac{\log(S_0/K) + \left(r - q + \frac{\overline{v}}{2}\right)T}{\sqrt{\overline{v}T}}$$

and with $d_2 = d_1 - \sqrt{\overline{v}T}$. The quantity $\overline{v}$ denotes the average expected variance over $(0, T)$ of the CIR process that we first encountered in Chapter 2

$$\begin{aligned}\overline{v} &= E\left[\frac{1}{T}\int_0^T v_t dt \middle| v_0\right] = \frac{1}{T}\int_0^T E[v_t|v_0]dt \\ &= \frac{1}{T}\int_0^T [\theta + (v_0 - \theta)e^{-\kappa t}]dt = (v_0 - \theta)\left(\frac{1 - e^{-\kappa T}}{\kappa T}\right) + \theta.\end{aligned} \tag{4.36}$$

The average expected variance $\overline{v}$ is also the fair strike of a variance swap in the Heston model, as demonstrated by Gatheral (2006), which we denoted $K_{var}^2 = \hat{w}_T/T$ in Chapter 2. The first series expansion uses the derivative of the Black-Scholes call price with respect to the variance v, again evaluated at $\overline{v}$

$$C_v(S_0, \overline{v}, T) = \left.\frac{\partial C_{BS}}{\partial v}\right|_{v=\overline{v}} = \sqrt{\frac{T}{8\pi\overline{v}}} S_0 e^{-qT} \exp\left(-\tfrac{1}{2}d_1^2\right). \tag{4.37}$$

Both expansions make use of the integrals J_1, J_3, and J_4, which in the Heston model take the following form, using $\varphi = \frac{1}{2}$ in Equations (3.3.7), (3.3.8), and (3.3.9) on page 86 of Lewis (2000).

$$\begin{aligned} J_1(v,T) &= \frac{\rho}{\kappa}\int_0^T (1-e^{-\kappa(T-s)})(\theta + e^{-\kappa s}(v-\theta))ds \\ &= \frac{\rho}{\kappa}\left[\theta T + \left(1-e^{-\kappa T}\right)\left(\frac{v}{\kappa} - \frac{2\theta}{\kappa}\right) - e^{-\kappa T}(v-\theta)T\right]. \end{aligned} \tag{4.38}$$

$$\begin{aligned} J_3(v,T) &= \frac{1}{2\kappa^2}\int_0^T \left(1-e^{-\kappa(T-s)}\right)^2(\theta + e^{-\kappa s}(v-\theta))ds \\ &= \frac{\theta}{2\kappa^2}\left[T + \frac{1}{2\kappa}\left(1-e^{-2\kappa T}\right) - \frac{2}{\kappa}\left(1-e^{-\kappa T}\right)\right] \\ &+ \frac{(v-\theta)}{2\kappa^2}\left[\frac{1}{\kappa}\left(1-e^{-2\kappa T}\right) - 2Te^{-\kappa T}\right]. \end{aligned} \tag{4.39}$$

$$\begin{aligned} J_4(v,T) &= \frac{\rho^2}{\kappa^2}\int_0^T (\theta + e^{-\kappa(T-s)}(v-\theta))\left(\frac{1}{\kappa}\left(1-e^{-\kappa s}\right) - se^{-\kappa s}\right)ds \\ &= \frac{\rho^2\theta}{\kappa^3}\left[T\left(1+e^{-\kappa T}\right) - \frac{2}{\kappa}\left(1-e^{-\kappa T}\right)\right] \\ &- \frac{\rho^2}{2\kappa^2}T^2e^{-\kappa T}(v-\theta) + \frac{\rho^2(v-\theta)}{\kappa^3}\left[\frac{1}{\kappa}\left(1-e^{-\kappa T}\right) - Te^{-\kappa T}\right]. \end{aligned} \tag{4.40}$$

Finally, the following ratios of Black-Scholes derivatives are needed

$$\begin{aligned} R^{1,2} &= \left[\frac{1}{2} - W\right], \quad R^{1,2} = \left[W^2 - W - \frac{4-Z}{Z}\right], \\ R^{2,0} &= T\left[\frac{W^2}{2} - \frac{1}{2Z} - \frac{1}{8}\right], \\ R^{2,2} &= T\left[\frac{W^4}{2} - \frac{W^3}{2} - \frac{3X^2}{Z^3} + \frac{X(12+Z)}{8Z^3} + \frac{48-Z^2}{32Z^2}\right]. \end{aligned} \tag{4.41}$$

In these ratios, Lewis (2000) defines $W = X/Z$, $X = \log(S_0/K) + (r-q)T$ as in the previous sections of this chapter, and $Z = \overline{v}T$. The first series expansion produces Heston call prices directly, while the second series produces an implied variance that is then fed into the Black-Scholes model to produce the Heston call price. The first expansion (Series I) produces the call price $C_I(S_0, v_0, T)$ directly

$$\begin{aligned} C_I(S_0,v_0,T) &\approx C_{BS}(S_0,\overline{v},T) + \sigma\frac{J_1}{T}R^{1,1}C_v(S_0,\overline{v},T) + \\ &\sigma^2 C_v(S_0,\overline{v},T)\left[\frac{J_2}{T} + \frac{J_3R^{2,0}}{T^2} + \frac{J_4R^{1,2}}{T} + \frac{(J_1)^2R^{2,2}}{2T^2}\right]. \end{aligned} \tag{4.42}$$

The second expansion (Series II) produces the implied variance

$$v_{imp} \approx \overline{v} + \sigma \frac{J_1}{T} R^{1,1} + \sigma^2 \left[\frac{J_2}{T} + \frac{J_3 R^{2,0}}{T^2} + \frac{J_4 R^{1,2}}{T} + \frac{(J_1)^2}{2T^2} \left(R^{2,2} - \left(R^{1,1}\right)^2 R^{2,0} \right) \right] \tag{4.43}$$

which is then fed into the Black-Scholes call formula in (4.35) to produce $C_{II}(S_0, v_0, T)$, the Heston call price under Series II. In other words, we use (4.35) to obtain the call price, but we replace $\overline{v}$ with v_{imp} from (4.43)

$$C_{II}(S_0, v_0, T) = C_{BS}(S_0, v_{imp}, T). \tag{4.44}$$

Finally, in the expressions for the call price in Equations (4.42) and (4.44) the integrals J_1, J_3, and J_4 are all evaluated at the initial variance v_0, so that v is replaced by Heston parameter v_0 everywhere in (4.38), (4.39), and (4.40).

The deterministic variance in Equation (4.36) and Black-Scholes price in (4.35) are easy to implement in Matlab, using user-defined functions. This is illustrated with the following code snippet.

```
v = theta + (v0-theta)*(1-exp(-kappa*T))/(kappa*T);
BSC = @(S,K,rf,q,v,T) (S*exp(-q*T)*normcdf((log(S/K) + ...);
BSPrice = BSC(S,K,rf,q,v,T);
```

The functions $J_1(v,T)$ through $J_4(v,T)$ in Equations (4.38) through (4.40) are implemented in a single Matlab function J.m.

```
function y = J(rho,theta,k,T,v0,Number)
if Number==1
    y = (theta*T + (1-exp(-k*T))*(v0/k - 2*theta/k) - ....;
    y = y*rho/k;
elseif Number==3
    y = theta*T + theta/2/k*(1-exp(-2*k*T)) - ...;
    y = y/2/k^2;
elseif Number==4
    y = theta/k*(T*(1+exp(-k*T)) - 2/k*(1-exp(-k*T))) + ... ;
    y = y*rho^2/k;
end
```

The functions $R^{p,q}$ in Equation (4.41) are also implemented in a single function, R.m.

```
function y = R(p,q,X,Z,T)
if p==2 & q==0
    y = T*(0.5*(X/Z)^2 - 0.5/Z - 1/8);
elseif p==1 & q==1
    y = -X/Z + 0.5;
elseif p==1 & q==2
    y = (X/Z)^2 - X/Z - 0.25/Z*(4-Z);
elseif p==2 & q==2
    y = T*(0.5*(X/Z)^4 - 0.5*(X/Z)^3 - 3*(X^2/Z^3) + ...;
end
```

The function SeriesICall.m returns the Series I call price in Equation (4.42). It uses functions for the Black-Scholes price in (4.35) and its variance derivative in (4.37).

```
function y = SeriesICall(...);
BSC = @(S,K,rf,q,v,T) (S*exp(-q*T)*normcdf(...)...);
BSV = @(S,K,rf,q,v,T) (sqrt(T/8/pi/v)*S*exp(-q*T)*exp(-0.5*(...);
J1 = J(rho,theta,kappa,T,v0,1);
J3 = J(rho,theta,kappa,T,v0,3);
J4 = J(rho,theta,kappa,T,v0,4);
v = theta + (v0-theta)*(1-exp(-kappa*T))/(kappa*T);
X = log(S*exp((rf-q)*T)/K);
Z = v*T;
R20 = R(2,0,X,Z,T);
R11 = R(1,1,X,Z,T);
R12 = R(1,2,X,Z,T);
R22 = R(2,2,X,Z,T);
C  = BSC(S,K,rf,q,v,T);
cv = BSV(S,K,rf,q,v,T);
y = c + sigma/T*J1*R11*cv + sigma^2*(J3*R20/T^2 + ...;
```

The function SeriesIICall.m returns the implied volatility in Equation (4.43) and the Series II call price in (4.44).

```
function [ivx y] = SeriesIICall(...);
BSC = @(S,K,rf,q,v,T) (S*exp(-q*T)*normcdf(...)...);
J1 = J(rho,theta,kappa,T,v0,1);
J3 = J(rho,theta,kappa,T,v0,3);
J4 = J(rho,theta,kappa,T,v0,4);
v = theta + (v0-theta)*(1-exp(-kappa*T))/(kappa*T);
X = log(S*exp((rf-q)*T)/K);
Z = v*T;
R20 = R(2,0,X,Z,T);
R11 = R(1,1,X,Z,T);
```

```
R12 = R(1,2,X,Z,T);
R22 = R(2,2,X,Z,T);
iv = v + sigma/T*J1*R11 + sigma^2*(J3*R20/T^2 + ...;
y = BSC(S,K,rf,q,iv,T);
ivx = sqrt(iv);
```

The C# code to generate the Series I call price in Equation (4.42), the implied variance in (4.43) and the Series II call price in (4.44) is similar and not presented here. The difference is that we need the C# function NormCDF() to calculate the standard normal distribution function. Please refer to Chapter 2 for details of that function.

To illustrate, we calculate the prices of out-of-the money calls with 3 months to maturity, using $S_0 = 100$, $K = 105$, $r = 0.05$, $q = 0.01$. For the Heston parameters, we use $\kappa = 10$, $\theta = 0.07$, $v_0 = 0.06$, $\sigma = 0.9$, and $\rho = 0.9$. With these settings the average expected variance $\overline{v}$ from Equation (4.36) is $\overline{v} = 0.06633$, which when used in (4.35), produces $C_{BS}(S_0, \overline{v}, T) = 3.48426$ for the Black-Scholes price. The exact Heston price using 10,000 points in the trapezoidal rule is $C(K) = 3.65090$. The Series I and Series II prices in Equations (4.42) and (4.44) are $C_I(S_0, v_0, T) = 3.65218$ and $C_{II}(S_0, v_0, T) = 3.66106$, which are very close to the closed-form price. The Series II implied variance in (4.43) is $v_{imp} = 0.26667$. The time average of deterministic variance is $\overline{v} = 0.25754$.

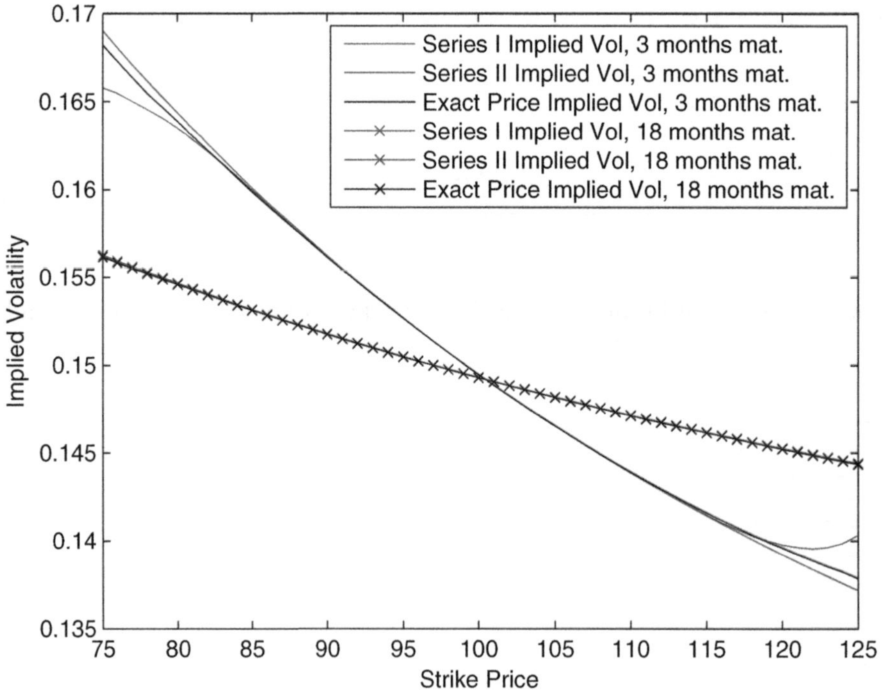

FIGURE 4.4 Reproduction of Figure 3.3.1. of Lewis (2000)

With the parameter values used in Table 3.3.1 of Lewis (2000), namely $\rho = -0.5$, $v_0 = 0.0225$, $\kappa = 4$, $\theta = 0.09/4$, $\sigma = 0.1$, as well as $T = 0.25$ and $S = K = 100$, we obtain from (4.36) the average variance $\overline{v} = 0.0225$. The Matlab program Lewis_Table_Figure.m reproduces the entries in Table 3.3.1 on page 81 of Lewis (2000), and Figure 3.3.1 on page 80. His figure is reproduced in Figure 4.4, along with the additional maturity of 18 months.

As indicated in Lewis (2000), for the 3-month maturity, the Series II expansion implied volatility (dashed line) is more accurate than the Series I expansion implied volatility (dotted line), since it is closer to the implied volatility extracted from the exact price (solid line). For the 18-month maturity, however, both series are accurate.

CONCLUSION

In this chapter, we have presented several powerful and novel approaches developed by Alan Lewis (2000, 2001) for pricing options under stochastic volatility. The fundamental transform is extremely convenient, because once the fundamental transform for a given stochastic volatility model is obtained, European option prices under the model are readily obtained via their payoff transform. Moreover, in Lewis (2000), the fundamental transform is available for a wide range of models, and not restricted to the Heston model. We also examine the approach of Lewis (2001) for pricing options using Parseval's identity. Finally, we present the volatility of volatility series expansion of Lewis (2001), which approximates the Heston (1993) call price with a sum of analytic terms. The chief advantage of this expansion is that numerical integration is not required, so option prices can be calculated very quickly.

Most models encountered in this book, however, require numerical integration. This poses challenges along several fronts, among which the integration domain $[0, \infty)$ that must often be reduced to a more manageable domain and possible extreme oscillations in the integrand. A desirable numerical integration scheme is one that both overcomes these difficulties and requires little computational time. This is the subject of the next chapter.

CHAPTER 5

Numerical Integration Schemes

Abstract

The calculation of the call price in the Heston model often requires the evaluation of an integral. This is true for most of the formulations of the call price we have encountered, that by Heston (1993), Lewis (2000, 2001), Carr and Madan (1999), or Attari (2004). Integration usually involves finding the anti-derivative of the integrand, and applying the Fundamental Theorem of Calculus, according to which the value of the integral can be expressed in terms of the anti-derivative evaluated at the endpoints of the integration domain. Unfortunately, in the Heston model, the anti-derivative of the integrals for the probabilities P_j cannot be found and the integrals must be approximated numerically.

Quadratures approximate an integral on $[a, b]$ as the sum of functional values evaluated at discrete points along the integration domain, and multiplied by a weight

$$\int_a^b f(x)dx \approx \sum_{j=1}^{N} w_j f(x_j). \tag{5.1}$$

The points $(x_1, \ldots, x_N)$ are called nodes, points, or abscissas, and the points $(w_1, \ldots, w_N)$ are called weights or coefficients. In this chapter, we present two general classes of quadratures, Newton-Cotes formulas and Gaussian quadrature. Newton-Cotes formulas are easy to implement, but they assume equally spaced abscissas. This means that many abscissas are required in order for the approximation in Equation (5.1) to be accurate, especially if there are regions in the integration range where the function is steep or highly oscillatory. The consequence is that the computing time required to evaluate the sum in (5.1) can be dramatically increased. Gaussian quadrature requires far fewer abscissas, sometimes as little as 10, but they are more difficult to understand, and the abscissas and weights are not easy to obtain. Once these are obtained, however, they can be stored and used when needed. In this chapter, we present Newton-Cotes formulas and Gaussian quadrature, and we also show how they can be used to approximate double integrals.

The probabilities P_j in the Heston (1993) model require the integration domain $(0, \infty)$ so that $a = 0$ and $b = \infty$ are required as the limits of the integral in (5.1). When we use Newton-Cotes formulas, however, we must truncate the upper limit. This chapter shows how this can be done sensibly using multi-domain integration described by Zhu (2010). Alternatively, Kahl and Jäckel (2005) transform the domain of integration to $[0, 1]$, which eliminates the need for truncation altogether. Finally, in the last two sections of this chapter, we present the fast Fourier transform

(FFT) pioneered by Carr and Madan (1999) and the fractional FFT of Chourdakis (2005), a refinement to the FFT that is more flexible than its predecessor. These methods are both very fast because they are able to produce a set of option prices along a grid of strikes in a single calculation.

THE INTEGRAND IN NUMERICAL INTEGRATION

Authors often denote by x_0 the first abscissa in the numerical approximation of Equation (5.1). To make our notation consistent with that for Gaussian quadratures, we sometimes denote the first abscissa x_1. Furthermore, since array indexing in Matlab starts with 1, it can be convenient for the abscissas to start at 1 also. The literature on numerical integration method is rich and extensive, and there are many excellent textbooks on the subject, such as those by Burden and Faires (2010) and Cohen (2011).

In (5.1), the abscissas are denoted x_j, but in the formulas for the integrals of the Heston model, the integration variable is denoted ϕ, so the abscissas should be denoted ϕ_j. The form of the integrand depends on which formula we are using to obtain the Heston call price. If we are using the original Heston (1993) formulation, the integrand in (5.1) for P_j is

$$f(\phi_j) = \text{Re}\left[\frac{e^{-i\phi_j \ln K} f_k(\phi_j; x, v)}{i\phi_j}\right] \quad \text{for } k = 1, 2. \tag{5.2}$$

If we are using the fundamental transform of Lewis (2000) covered in Chapter 4, the integrand is

$$f(\phi_j) = \text{Re}\left[e^{-i\phi_j X}\frac{1}{\phi_j^2 - i\phi_j}\hat{H}(\phi_j, v, \tau)\right]. \tag{5.3}$$

Finally, if we are using the Carr and Madan (1999) formulation covered in Chapter 3, the integrand in (5.1) becomes

$$f(\phi_j) = \text{Re}[e^{-i\phi_j \ln K}\psi(\phi_j)] \tag{5.4}$$

where

$$\psi(\phi_j) = \frac{e^{-rT} f_2(\phi_j - (\alpha+1)i; x, v)}{\alpha^2 + \alpha - \phi_j^2 + i(2\alpha+1)\phi_j}$$

and where f_2 is the characteristic function of the Heston model.

NEWTON-COTES FORMULAS

Newton-Cotes are the simplest integration rules, but also the ones that require the most computing power. Closed Newton-Cotes formulas partition the domain of integration $[a, b]$ into equally spaced subintervals using the abscissas $x_1, x_2, \ldots, x_N$.

The definition of the abscissas depends on the formula being used. We consider four types of Newton-Cotes formulas: the mid-point rule, the trapezoidal rule, Simpson's rule, and Simpson's three-eighths rule. We consider the closed version of these rules only, so-called because the endpoints a and b are used as abscissas.

In the Heston model, we usually require an integral evaluated over the integration domain $(0, \infty)$. This means that, when we apply Newton-Cotes formulas, we must select the domain as $[\phi_{\min}, \phi_{\max}]$, where $\phi_{\min}$ is a small number and $\phi_{\max}$ is a large number. We saw in Chapter 1 that the Heston integrand can sometimes be highly oscillatory. Hence, when we select $\phi_{\max}$, we must ensure that it is large enough so that the integrand is sufficiently damped to not cause a loss of accuracy in the approximation in Equation (5.1). Since the Heston integrand is not defined at $\phi = 0$, instead we use $\phi_{\min}$ as the lower limit of the integration domain.

One exception to the requirement of the integration domain $(0, \infty)$ is due to Kahl and Jäckel (2005). They transform the domain $(0, \infty)$ to the closed interval $[0, 1]$. Hence, in their approach, we need not worry about choosing $\phi_{\min}$ or $\phi_{\max}$. We will see in this chapter that their transformation is particularly well-suited to Gauss-Lobatto quadrature, rather than Newton-Cotes formulas.

Mid-point Rule

This is the simplest of the Newton-Cotes formulas we present. It approximates the integral in Equation (5.1) as the sum of rectangles, each with equal width $x_{j+1} - x_j$, and with height given by the integrand $f(x)$ evaluated at the mid-point of the interval (x_j, x_{j+1}). Define the abscissas $x_j = a + (j-1)h$ for $j = 1, \ldots, N$, where $h = (b-a)/(N-1)$ so that $x_1 = a$ and $x_N = b$. Since there are $N-1$ subintervals, the approximation involves $N-1$ terms

$$\int_a^b f(x)dx \approx h\sum_{j=1}^{N-1} f\left(\frac{x_j + x_{j+1}}{2}\right).$$

The mid-point rule formula thus uses the weights $w_j = h$ for $j = 1, \ldots, N-1$, and $w_N = 0$. The following code implements the mid-point rule in Matlab. It is taken from the Matlab function HestonPriceNewtonCotes.m.

```
h = (b-a)/(N-1);
phi = [a:h:b];
wt = h.*ones(1,N);
for k=1:N-1;
    mid(k)  = (phi(k) + phi(k+1))/2;
    int1(k) = wt(k)*HestonProb(mid(k),...,1);
    int2(k) = wt(k)*HestonProb(mid(k),...,2);
end
I1 = sum(int1);
I2 = sum(int2);
P1 = 1/2 + 1/pi*I1;
P2 = 1/2 + 1/pi*I2;
```

Trapezoidal Rule

This rule is only slightly more complicated as it approximates the integral in Equation (5.1) as the sum of trapezoids, each with equal width $x_{j+1} - x_j$, but with height defined by the value of $f(x)$ at each of the endpoints. The trapezoids are constructed by joining the line segments at $f(x_j)$ and $f(x_{j+1})$. Define the abscissas as in the mid-point rule in the previous section. The trapezoidal rule uses the weights $w_1 = w_N = h/2$ and $w_j = h$ for $j = 2, \ldots, N-1$. Hence, the approximation in (5.1) is

$$\int_a^b f(x)dx \approx \frac{h}{2}f(x_1) + h\sum_{j=2}^{N-1} f(x_j) + \frac{h}{2}f(x_N).$$

The Matlab code for implementing the trapezoidal rule is straightforward also. It appears in the Matlab function HestonPriceNewtonCotes.m.

```
wt = h.*[1/2 ones(1,N-2) 1/2];
for k=1:N;
    int1(k) = wt(k)*HestonProb(phi(k),...,1);
    int2(k) = wt(k)*HestonProb(phi(k),...,2);
end
```

Trapezoidal Rule for Double Integrals

In Chapter 8, we will encounter the model of Chiarella and Ziogas (2006) for pricing American call options in the Heston (1993) model. Their method requires a routine for the numerical evaluation of a double integral. One of the simplest methods for double integration is the composite trapezoidal rule described by Burden and Faires (2010). Suppose we wish to evaluate a double integral on the domain $[a, b] \times [c, d]$. The composite trapezoidal rule approximates the integral as

$$\begin{aligned}
&\int_a^b \left(\int_c^d f(x, y)\, dy \right) dx \\
&\approx \frac{(b-a)(d-c)}{16} \times \left[f(a,c) + f(a,d) + f(b,c) + f(b,d) + 2\left(f\left(\frac{a+b}{2}, c\right) \right.\right. \\
&\left.\left. + f\left(\frac{a+b}{2}, d\right) + f\left(a, \frac{c+d}{2}\right) + f\left(b, \frac{c+d}{2}\right)\right) + 4f\left(\frac{a+b}{2}, \frac{c+d}{2}\right)\right].
\end{aligned} \tag{5.5}$$

The Matlab function DoubleTrapz.m implements the composite trapezoidal rule, in accordance with Equation (5.5).

```
function y = DoubleTrapz(f,X,Y)
Nx = length(X);
Ny = length(Y);
for y=2:Ny
```

```
        a = Y(y-1);
        b = Y(y);
        for x=2:Nx
            c = X(x-1);
            d = X(x);
            term1 = f(a,c) + f(a,d) + f(b,c) + f(b,d);
            term2 = f((a+b)/2,c) + f((a+b)/2,d) + ...;
            term3 = f((a+b)/2,(c+d)/2);
            Int(x,y) = (b-a)*(d-c)/16*(...);
        end
    end
    y = sum(sum(Int));
```

To invoke the function, we create an integration grid for $[a, b] \times [c, d]$, create a function for $f(x, y)$, and then pass the function to the DoubleTrapz.m function in the first argument. To illustrate, we run the following code to evaluate the standard normal bivariate distribution.

```
f = @(x,y) (0.5/pi*exp(-(x^2+y^2)/2));
for j=1:NX;
    X(j) = LoX + j*dx;
end
for j=1:NY;
    Y(j) = LoY + j*dy;
end
TrapValue = DoubleTrapz(f,X,Y);
```

The DoubleTrapz.m function returns the value 0.18075 for the value of the standard normal bivariate distribution function at the point $(x, y) = (-0.515, 0.243)$, which is very close to the value obtained using the Matlab function mvncdf.m. The C# code for the composite trapezoidal rule is very similar and not presented here.

Simpson's Rule

Simpson's rule is more complicated than either the mid-point rule or the trapezoidal rule, since it uses quadratic polynomials in the approximation in Equation (5.1), rather than straight lines. As such, however, it is much more accurate. Simpson's rule uses the same abscissas as the mid-point and trapezoidal rules, but defines the weights as $w_1 = w_N = h/3$, along with $w_j = 4h/3$ when j is even, and $w_j = 2h/3$ when j is odd. Hence, we can represent the approximation (5.1) as

$$\int_a^b f(x)dx \approx \frac{h}{3}f(x_1) + \frac{4h}{3}\sum_{j=1}^{N/2-1} f(x_{2j}) + \frac{2h}{3}\sum_{j=1}^{N/2} f(x_{2j-1}) + \frac{h}{3}f(x_N).$$

Implementing Simpson's rule in Matlab is no more complicated than implementing the mid-point or trapezoidal rule. We need only be careful of the alternating nature of the weights that depend on whether j is even or odd. The following code, taken from the Matlab function HestonPriceNewtonCotes.m, is used to implement this rule.

```
wt = (h/3).*[1 (3+(-1).^[2:N-1]) 1];
for k=1:N;
    int1(k) = wt(k)*HestonProb(phi(k),...,1);
    int2(k) = wt(k)*HestonProb(phi(k),...,2);
end
```

Simpson's Three-Eighths Rule

Simpson's three-eighths rule is a refinement to Simpson's rule. It uses cubic polynomials in the approximation in Equation (5.1), rather than quadratic polynomials. To implement Simpson's three-eighths rule, it is more convenient to start the abscissas at x_0 and define them as $x_j = a + ih$ for $i = 0, \ldots, N$ where N is a number divisible by three and with $h = (b-a)/N$. The weights w_j for Simpson's three-eighths rule depend on whether j is divisible by three

$$w_j = \begin{cases} 3h/8 & \text{if } j = 0 \text{ or } j = N \\ 6h/8 & \text{if } j = 3, 6, 9, \ldots \\ 9h/8 & \text{otherwise.} \end{cases}$$

For example, with $N = 12$, the weights are

j	0	1	2	3	4	5	6	7	8	9	10	11	12
w_j	$\frac{3h}{8}$	$\frac{9h}{8}$	$\frac{9h}{8}$	$\frac{6h}{8}$	$\frac{9h}{8}$	$\frac{9h}{8}$	$\frac{6h}{8}$	$\frac{9h}{8}$	$\frac{9h}{8}$	$\frac{6h}{8}$	$\frac{9h}{8}$	$\frac{9h}{8}$	$\frac{3h}{8}$

Simpson's three-eighths rule is, therefore,

$$\int_a^b f(x)dx \approx \frac{3h}{8}f(x_0) + \frac{6h}{8}\sum_{j=3,6,9,\ldots}^{N-3} f(x_j) + \frac{9h}{8}\sum_{j\neq 3,6,9,\ldots}^{N-1} f(x_j) + \frac{3h}{8}f(x_N).$$

The following snippet of code implements Simpson's three-eighths rule. It is taken from the Matlab function HestonPriceNewtonCotes.m.

```
N = N-mod(N,3)+1;
h = (b-a)/(N-1);
wt = (3*h/8).*[[1 3 3] repmat([2 3 3],1,(N-1)/3-1) 1];
phi = [a:h:b];
for k=1:N
    int1(k) = wt(k)*HestonProb(phi(k),...,1);
    int2(k) = wt(k)*HestonProb(phi(k),...,2);
end
```

Because of the array indexing, which starts at one and not zero, to implement this rule in Matlab we need to ensure that $N-1$ is divisible by three. The first part of the code ensures that this holds. We use the Matlab function repmat.m to construct the weights, and proceed as in the previous rules.

GAUSSIAN QUADRATURE

In Newton-Cotes formulas, the abscissas are fixed and usually spaced equally. Gaussian quadrature uses unequally spaced abscissas, and weights which can easily be computed in Matlab. Gaussian quadrature is more accurate than Newton-Cotes quadrature and requires far fewer abscissas. Moreover, since the abscissas are specified for us in advance, we need not worry about selecting the upper and lower limits $\phi_{\min}$ and $\phi_{\max}$ for the integration range $(0,\infty)$.

Gaussian quadrature approximates the integral over the range $[a,b]$ by the weighted sum of the integrand evaluated at the abscissas, as in Equation (5.1), reproduced here for convenience

$$\int_a^b f(x)dx \approx \sum_{k=1}^{N} w_k f(x_k).$$

Similar to Newton-Cotes formulas, Gaussian quadrature requires a set of abscissas $(x_1,\ldots,x_N)$ along with a set of weights $(w_1,\ldots,w_N)$. The values of the abscissas and weights depends on the choice of quadrature and on the choice of N. For our purposes, the choice of method depends largely on the integration range for which the quadrature is designed. Quadratures are described in many textbooks on the subject, such as that by Cohen (2011), Stroud and Secrest (1966), or on the Wolfram website (www.mathworld.wolfram.com). In the following sections, we describe Gauss-Laguerre, Gauss-Legendre, and Gauss-Lobatto quadratures, and present algorithms for finding the weights and abscissas of each method.

Gauss-Laguerre Quadrature

Gauss-Laguerre quadrature is especially relevant for the purposes of evaluating the integral for the Heston model, because it is designed for integrals over the integration domain $(0,\infty)$. Suppose we wish to apply Gauss-Laguerre quadrature with N points. The abscissas $(x_1,\ldots,x_N)$ are the roots of the Laguerre polynomial $L_N(x)$ of order N defined as

$$L_N(x) = \sum_{k=0}^{N} \frac{(-1)^k}{k!} \binom{N}{k} x^k \tag{5.6}$$

where $\binom{N}{k}$ is the binomial coefficient. There are N roots in all. The weights $(w_1,\ldots,w_N)$ are obtained with the derivative of $L_N(x)$ evaluated at each of the N abscissas

$$L'_N(x_j) = \sum_{k=1}^{N} \frac{(-1)^k}{(k-1)!} \binom{N}{k} x_j^{k-1} \quad \text{for } j = 1,\ldots,N. \tag{5.7}$$

We then define each weight as

$$w_j = \frac{(n!)^2 e^{x_j}}{x_j[L'_N(x_j)]^2} \quad \text{for } j = 1, \ldots, N.$$

Note that the Laguerre polynomial in Equation (5.6) has $N + 1$ terms, but its derivative (5.7) has N terms, which is the correct number of terms required for the approximation in (5.1).

It is straightforward to use Matlab to calculate the abscissas and weights for any N. This is accomplished with the GenerateGaussLaguerre.m function, which returns the abscissas and weights in the vectors x and w, respectively.

```
function [x w] = GenerateGaussLaguerre(n)
for k=0:n
    L(k+1) = (-1)^k/factorial(k)*nchoosek(n,k);
end
L = fliplr(L);
x = flipud(roots(L));
w = zeros(n,1);
for j=1:n
    for k=1:n
        dL(k,j) = (-1)^k/factorial(k-1)*nchoosek(n,k)*...;
    end
    w(j) = 1/x(j)/sum(dL(:,j))^2;
    w(j) = w(j)*exp(x(j));
end
```

To numerically evaluate the Heston integrals for P_1 and P_2 using Gauss-Laguerre integration, we first generate abscissas and weights, evaluate the integrand at each abscissa, apply the weight, and take the sum. This is implemented as part of the Matlab function HestonPriceGaussLaguerre.m, which returns the call price, or the put price by put-call parity. To conserve space, parts of the function are omitted.

```
function y = HestonPriceGaussLaguerre(PutCall,...)
for k=1:length(x);
    int1(k) = w(k)*HestonProb(x(k),...,1);
    int2(k) = w(k)*HestonProb(x(k),...,2);
end
P1 = 1/2 + 1/pi*sum(int1);
P2 = 1/2 + 1/pi*sum(int2);
HestonC = S*exp(-q*T)*P1 - K*exp(-r*T)*P2;
```

To illustrate, suppose that $S = K = 100$, $T = 1.5$, $r = 0.05$, $q = 0.01$, $\kappa = 2$, $\sigma = 0.3$, $\theta = v_0 = 0.05$, and $\rho = 0.45$. The Matlab code

```
[x w] = GenerateGaussLaguerre(32);
HestonPriceGaussLaguerre('C',100,100,1.5,0.05,0.01,2,0.05,0.3,0,
   0.05,0.45,1,x,w)
```

returns a call price of 13.2561.

Gauss-Legendre Quadrature

Gauss-Legendre quadrature is designed for integrals over the integration domain $[-1, +1]$, but this can be modified to accept any finite domain $[a, b]$ through the transformation

$$\int_a^b f(x)dx = \frac{b-a}{2}\int_{-1}^{1} f\left(\frac{b-a}{2}x + \frac{a+b}{2}\right) dx. \tag{5.8}$$

Since the endpoints a and b are not included in the abscissas, to implement Gauss-Legendre quadrature for the Heston model, we can select $a = 0$. We must, however, still set $b = \phi_{\max}$, a large number. In Gauss-Legendre quadrature with N points, the abscissas $(x_1, \ldots, x_N)$ are the roots of the Legendre polynomial $P_N(x)$ defined as

$$P_N(x) = \frac{1}{2^N}\sum_{k=0}^{\lfloor N/2 \rfloor} (-1)^k \binom{N}{k}\binom{2N-2k}{N} x^{N-2k} \tag{5.9}$$

where $\lfloor\ \rfloor$ is the floor function. The weights $(w_1, \ldots, w_N)$ are obtained with the derivative of $P_N(x)$ evaluated at the abscissas. Similar to what is done for Gauss-Laguerre quadrature, we evaluate the derivative at each of the N abscissas

$$P'_N(x) = \frac{1}{2^N}\sum_{k=0}^{\lfloor N/2 \rfloor} (-1)^k \binom{N}{k}\binom{2N-2k}{N} (N-2k)x^{N-2k-1}. \tag{5.10}$$

We then define each weight as

$$w_j = \frac{2}{(1-x_j^2)[P'_N(x_j)]^2} \quad \text{for } j = 1, \ldots, N.$$

The binomial coefficients grow very quickly, so for numerical implementation, it is best to replace Equations (5.9) and (5.10) with, respectively

$$P_N(x) = \frac{1}{2^N}\sum_{k=0}^{\lfloor N/2 \rfloor} (-1)^k \frac{(2N-2k)!}{k!(N-k)!(N-2k)!} x^{N-2k}$$

and

$$P'_N(x) = \frac{1}{2^N}\sum_{k=0}^{\lfloor N/2 \rfloor}(-1)^k \frac{(2N-2k)!}{k!(N-k)!(N-2k)!}(N-2k)x^{N-2k-1}.$$

The Legendre polynomials $P_N(x)$ are defined in such a way that some of the coefficients are zero. Indeed, when N is even, $P_N(x)$ contains only even powers of x, and when N is odd, $P_N(x)$ contains only odd powers. For $N = 3$ and $N = 6$, for example, the Legendre polynomials are

$$\begin{aligned}
P_3(x) &= \frac{1}{2}(5x^3 - 3x) \\
&= \frac{1}{2}(5x^3 + 0x^2 - 3x^1 + 0x^0), \\
P_6(x) &= \frac{1}{16}(231x^6 - 315x^4 + 105x^2 - 5) \\
&= \frac{1}{16}(231x^6 + 0x^5 - 315x^4 + 0x^3 + 105x^2 + 0x^1 - 5x^0).
\end{aligned}$$

Hence, when we calculate Legendre polynomials in Matlab, we must ensure that we include these zero values when we apply the roots.m Matlab function to find its roots. This is illustrated in the Matlab function GenerateGaussLegendre.m, which generates the abscissas and weights for a given number of points.

```
function [x w] = GenerateGaussLegendre(n)
m = floor(n/2);
for k=0:m
    L(k+1) = (1/2^n)*(-1)^k*factorial(2*n-2*k) ...;
end
for k=1:n+1
    if mod(k,2)==0
        P(k)=0;
    else
        P(k) = L((k+1)/2);
    end
end
x = sortrows(roots(P));
w = zeros(n,1);
for j=1:n
    for k=0:m
        dC(k+1,j) = (1/2^n)*(-1)^k*factorial(2*n-2*k) ...;
    end
    w(j) = 2/(1-x(j)^2)/sum(dC(:,j))^2;
end
```

To numerically evaluate the Heston integrals for P_1 and P_2 using Gauss-Legendre integration, we proceed in the same way as we did earlier for Gauss-Laguerre integration. We first generate abscissas and weights, evaluate the integrand at each abscissa, apply the weight, and take the sum. We must ensure, however, that the transformation in (5.8) is correctly applied. This is implemented as part of the Matlab function HestonPriceGaussLegendre.m.

```
function y = HestonPriceGaussLegendre(...,x,w,a,b)
for k=1:length(x);
    X = (a+b)/2 + (b-a)/2*x(k);
    int1(k) = w(k)*HestonProb(X,...,1);
    int2(k) = w(k)*HestonProb(X,...,2);
end
P1 = 1/2 + 1/pi*sum(int1)*(b-a)/2;
P2 = 1/2 + 1/pi*sum(int2)*(b-a)/2;
HestonC = S*exp(-q*T)*P1 - K*exp(-r*T)*P2;
```

The difference with Gauss-Laguerre integration is that we need to specify the upper and lower limits a and b of the integrand. Since the endpoints are not part of the abscissas, we can specify $a = 0$, and for b we can select a large number, such as $b = 100$. For example, the Matlab code

```
[x w] = GenerateGaussLegendre(32);
HestonPriceGaussLegendre('C',100,100,1.5,0.05,0.01,2,0.05,0.3,0,
  0.05,0.45,1,x,w,0,100)
```

produces a call price of 13.2561, which is identical to the call price obtained using 32-point Gauss-Laguerre integration in the previous section.

Gauss-Lobatto Quadrature

Gauss-Lobatto quadrature is also designed for integrals over the integration range $[-1, +1]$ and can be modified to accept any finite range $[a, b]$ through the transformation in Equation (5.8). The quadrature can be easily constructed from Legendre polynomials. The advantage of Gauss-Lobatto quadrature over the Gauss-Laguerre and Gauss-Legendre quadrature is that the endpoints of the interval, a and b, are included in the set of abscissas, so that $x_1 = a$ and $x_N = b$. The remaining $N - 2$ abscissas $(x_2, \ldots, x_{N-1})$ are the roots of $P'_{N-1}(x)$, the derivative of the Legendre polynomial in (5.10), but of order $N - 1$. The weights of the abscissas $(x_2, \ldots, x_{N-1})$ are given as in terms of the Legendre polynomials $P_{N-1}(x)$ in (5.9) as

$$w_j = \frac{2}{N(N-1)[P_{N-1}(x_j)]^2} \quad \text{for } j = 2, \ldots, N-1.$$

The weights at the endpoints are

$$w_1 = \frac{2}{N(N-1)}$$

and $w_N = w_1$.

The Matlab function GenerateGaussLobatto.m generates the abscissas and weights for a given number of points.

```
function [x w] = GenerateGaussLobatto(N)
n = N-1;
m = floor(n/2);
for k=0:m
    L(k+1)  = (1/2^n)*(-1)^k*factorial(2*n-2*k) ...;
    dL(k+1) = (1/2^n)*(-1)^k*factorial(2*n-2*k) ...;
end
for k=1:n+1
    if mod(k,2)==0
        P(k)=0;
        dP(k) = dL(k/2);
    else
        P(k) = L((k+1)/2);
        dP(k) = 0;
    end
end
x = sortrows(roots(dP));
x = [-1 x' 1]';
w = zeros(n+1,1);
for j=2:n+1
    for k=1:n+1
        Poly(k) = P(k)*x(j)^(n+1-k);
    end
    w(j) = 2/N/(N-1)/sum(Poly)^2;
end
w(1) = 2/N/(N-1);
w(n+1) = w(1);
```

To implement Gauss-Lobatto quadrature for the Heston call or put price, we can use the HestonPriceGaussLegendre.m function described earlier. We simply pass the Gauss-Lobatto weights and abscissas to the function, instead of the Gauss-Legendre weights and abscissas. Since the endpoints a and b form part of the abscissas, however, we cannot specify $a = 0$ but must select a small number instead. Continuing with the example, the code

```
[x w] = GenerateGaussLobatto(32);
HestonPriceGaussLegendre('C',100,100,1.5,0.05,0.01,2,0.05,0.3,0,
  0.05,0.45,1,x,w,1e-5,100)
```

produces a call price of 13.2561, which is identical to the call price obtained in the previous sections.

Gaussian Quadrature for Double Integrals

The generalization of Gaussian quadrature to double integrals is straightforward. We illustrate using Gauss-Legendre quadrature, since it can be used for integrals over a general domain of integration, using the transformation in Equation (5.8).

Burden and Faires (2010) show that Gauss-Legendre approximation to the double integral over the domain $[a, b] \times [c, d]$ is

$$\int_a^b \left(\int_c^d f(x, y)\, dy \right) dx \approx \sum_{j=1}^{N_2} \sum_{i=1}^{N_1} h_1 k_1 w_{i,1} w_{j,2} \cdot f(h_1 x_{i,1} + h_2, k_1 x_{j,2} + k_2). \quad (5.11)$$

The approximation uses two sets of Gauss-Legendre abscissas and weights, of sizes N_1 and N_2. In (5.11), $w_{i,1}$ and $w_{j,2}$ are the weights, $x_{i,1}$ and $x_{j,2}$ are the abscissas, and $h_1 = (b - a)/2$, $h_2 = (b + a)/2$, $k_1 = (d - c)/2$, and $k_2 = (d + c)/2$. The approximation in (5.11) is implemented with the DoubleGaussLegendre.m function.

```
function y = DoubleGaussLegendre(f,a,b,c,d,x1,w1,x2,w2)
h1 = (b-a)/2;    h2 = (b+a)/2;
k1 = (d-c)/2;    k2 = (d+c)/2;
for i=1:N1;
    for j=1:N2
        Int(i,j) = h1*k1*w1(i)*w2(j) * f(h1*x1(i)+h2,k1*x2(j)+k2);
    end
end
y = sum(sum(Int));
```

We use the following code to implement the same example of the standard normal bivariate distribution used to illustrate the composite trapezoidal rule.

```
f = @(x,y) (0.5/pi*exp(-(x^2+y^2)/2));
[x1 w1] = GenerateGaussLegendre(12);
[x2 w2] = GenerateGaussLegendre(14);
a = -5;
b = -0.515;
c = -5;
d =  0.243;
GLeValue = DoubleGaussLegendre(f,a,b,c,d,x1,w1,x2,w2);
```

The code returns a value of 0.18075, which is very close to the true value.

Gaussian Quadrature in C#

The C# code to generate the abscissas and weights of the Gauss-Laguerre quadrature is similar to the Matlab code presented in this chapter. We need, however, a C# routine to find the roots of the Laguerre polynomial $L_N(x)$ defined in Equation (5.6). One simple way to obtain the roots of $L_N(x)$ is to first obtain the Sturm sequence of polynomials for $L_N(x)$, then find the regions in x over which the Sturm polynomials change sign, aggregate the sign changes, and find the regions over which the number of sign changes decreases. This will identify the regions in x over which $L_N(x)$ changes sign, and consequently, where the roots are located. This approach to finding roots of polynomials is described in textbooks such as that by McNamee (2007).

To implement this method in C#, we first need the polyrem() function for obtaining the remainder of polynomial division, adapted from the C++ code in Press et al. (2007).

```
static double[] polyrem(double[] P,double[] Q){
int nP = P.Length - 1;
int nQ = Q.Length - 1;
while(nQ >= 0 && Q[nQ] == 0) nQ--;
double[] rem = new double[nP+1];
Array.Copy(P,rem,nP+1);
double[] quo = new double[P.Length];
for(int k=nP-nQ;k>=0;k--) {
    quo[k] = rem[nQ+k]/Q[nQ];
    for(int j=nQ+k-1;j>=k;j--)
        rem[j] -= quo[k]*Q[j-k];
    }
    for(int j=nQ;j<=nP;j++)
        rem[j] = 0.0;
return rem;}
```

The sturm() C# function generates the Sturm sequence of polynomials. It uses the polydiff() function, which returns the first-order derivative of a polynomial. Since the Sturm sequence is comprised of polynomials of different degrees, the sequence is stored in a jagged array in C#.

```
static double[][] sturm(double[] p) {
int N = p.Length;
double[][] P = new double[N][];
P[0] = p;
P[1] = polydiff(p);
for(int j=2;j<=N-1;j++){
    P[j] = polyrem(P[j-2],P[j-1]);
    for(int k=0;k<P[j].Length;k++)
        P[j][k] = -P[j][k];}
return P;}
```

Finally, the findroot() function returns a vector of roots of a polynomial. The function uses the C# function findintervals(), which returns the intervals on which the polynomial changes sign, in the form two vectors: one each for the left and right endpoints of each interval. These endpoints are in the vectors StartInt[] and EndInt[], respectively, which are returned as part of the C# structure SturmRoots. The left and right endpoints produce values of the polynomial that are opposite in sign, so the root is contained within the interval defined by the endpoints. These endpoints are used as inputs to the Bisection() function, which uses the bisection algorithm to find the root.

```
static double[] findroot(double[] C,...) {
// Find the Sturm sequence
double[][] Sturm = sturm(C);
int nS = C.Length;
// Find the signs of the Sturm sequences over intervals
SturmRoots sr = findintervals(a,b,nI,C,Sturm,nS);
// Number of roots and start/end of the intervals
int NRoots = sr.NRoots;
List<double> StartInt = sr.StartInt;
List<double> EndInt = sr.EndInt;
// Apply the bisection algorithm to find the roots
double[] root = new double[NRoots];
for(int i=0;i<=NRoots-1;i++) {
    a = StartInt[i];
    b = EndInt[i];
    root[i] = Bisection(C,a,b,Tol,MaxIter);}
return root;}
```

To illustrate, suppose that $N=5$ so that the Laguerre polynomial in Equation (5.6) is

$$L_5(x) = 1 - 5x + 5x^2 - \frac{5}{3}x^3 + \frac{5}{24}x^4 - \frac{1}{120}x^5. \tag{5.12}$$

This polynomial is plotted in Figure 5.1. The figure indicates the location of the five roots of $L_5(x)$ with circles. Table 5.1 lists the left and right endpoints

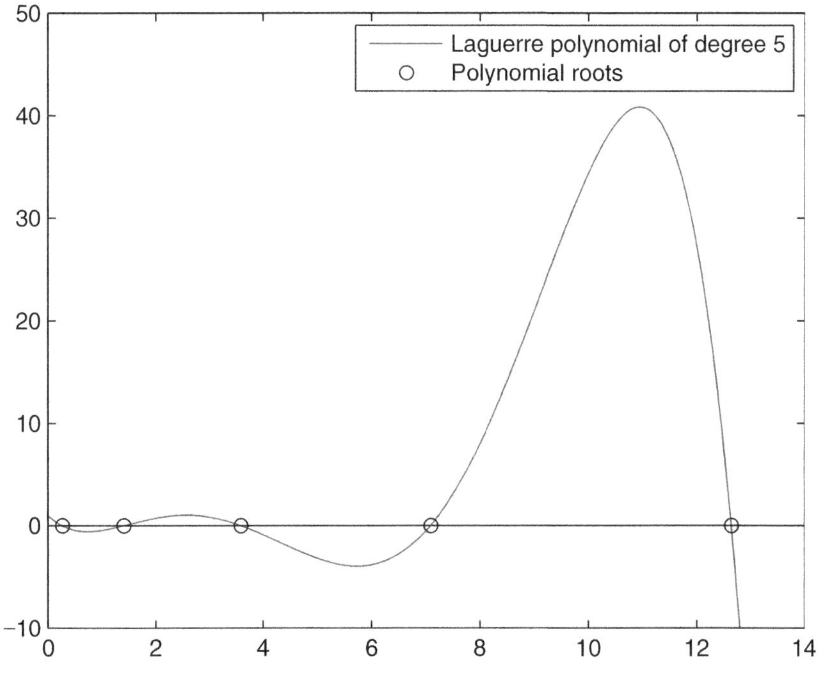

FIGURE 5.1 Laguerre Polynomial of Fifth Order

TABLE 5.1 Roots and Weights of the Fifth Order Laguerre Polynomial

Number	Left Endpoint	Right Endpoint	Root	Weight
1	0.2500	0.3300	0.2636	0.6791
2	1.3699	1.4499	1.4134	1.6385
3	3.5297	3.0697	3.5964	2.7694
4	7.0494	7.1294	7.0858	4.3157
5	12.5690	12.6489	12.6408	7.2192

of the intervals containing the roots. These are produced by the findintervals() function. It also lists the roots from the findroots() function, and the weights from the GaussLaguerre() function.

We use the following code snippet to generate Gauss-Laguerre abscissas and weights for $N = 32$ points.

```
int n = 32;
// Settings for bisection algorithm
double Tol = 1e-10;
int MaxIter = 5000;
// Starting and ending values for interval
double a = 0.0;
double b = 120.0;
int nI = 1500;
// Gauss Laguerre abscissas and weights
XW xw = GaussLaguerre(n,a,b,nI,Tol,MaxIter);
```

In the code, we select $[a, b] = [0, 120]$ as the range that contains all the roots of $L_{32}(x)$, and consequently, all the abscissas.

The code to generate weights and abscissas for Gauss-Legendre and Gauss-Lobatto quadrature is very similar to the C# code in this chapter and is not presented here. We note, however, that since the roots of $P_N(x)$ defined in Equation (5.9) are all contained in $[-1, 1]$, we select $[a, b] = [-1, 1]$ as the range for both of these quadratures.

INTEGRATION LIMITS AND KAHL AND JÄCKEL TRANSFORMATION

When we implement Gauss-Laguerre integration, the abscissas are provided to us, so we need not worry about choosing the lower and upper limits of integration. When we implement the Newton-Cotes formulas and Gauss-Legendre or Gauss-Lobattao quadratures, however, we need to provide the limits. The lower limit required in Equation (5.1) is $a = 0$, but if we use the original Heston formulation of the integrand in (5.2) then we cannot use zero since the integrand is undefined there. We therefore must use a small number $\phi_{\min}$ for a. The upper limit required in (5.1) is $b = \infty$, so we must truncate the integration domain and choose a large number $b = \phi_{\max}$ for the upper limit. How large a number depends on how fast the integrand, which typically oscillates, decays to zero. In general, the oscillation and the speed of decay both vary inversely with maturity, so that short maturities oscillate substantially and require a large number for the upper limit. This is illustrated in Figure 5.2 for typical values of Heston parameters and option settings.

In general, it is not wise to use ad-hoc choices for the upper integration limit, but rather, use a choice that takes into consideration the speed of decay of the integrand, as illustrated in Figure 5.2. For example, in his Mathematica code, Lewis (2000) uses $\phi_{\max} = \max[1000, 10/\sqrt{v_0\tau}]$.

We can also use the multi-domain integration approach described by Zhu (2010) to select the upper integration limit. In this method, the domain of integration is separated into subdomains $(a_0, a_1]$, $(a_1, a_2]$, $(a_2, a_3]$ and so on, where $a_0 = 0$ and $a_0 < a_1 < a_2 < a_3 < \cdots$. The integral for the probability P_j is constructed by aggregating the integrals over each subdomain, as

$$\sum_{k\geq 0} \int_{a_k}^{a_{k+1}} \text{Re}\left[\frac{e^{-i\phi \ln K} f_j(\phi; x, v)}{i\phi}\right] d\phi.$$

The summation stops when the subdomain integrals cease to contribute to the sum. In other words, when we observe

$$\left| \int_{a_M}^{a_{M+1}} \text{Re}\left[\frac{e^{-i\phi \ln K} f_j(\phi; x, v)}{i\phi}\right] d\phi \right| < \varepsilon \tag{5.13}$$

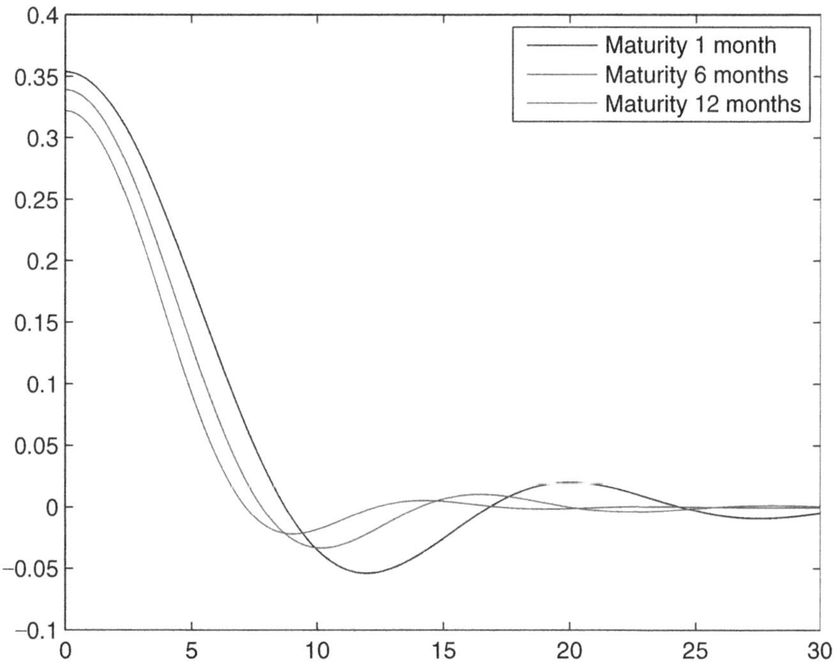

FIGURE 5.2 Integrand Decay and Maturity

for some integer M, where ε is a tolerance level. The integration domain is thus $(0, a_M]$ so that $\phi_{\max} = a_M$. Zhu (2010) explains that this method has the advantage of assigning the upper limit optimally, with the ability to adapt to different strikes, maturities, and parameter values. Moreover, the method will automatically assign a wider domain to shorter maturity options, for which the integrand tends to oscillate, and a narrower domain to longer maturity options, for which the integrand is better behaved. The method is thus able to reduce computation time by avoiding domains that are needlessly wide. It also increases accuracy by assigning a wide domain to those integrals that require it.

Gauss-Legendre or Gauss-Lobatto quadrature is particularly well-suited for this method, since both can accommodate integrals on any domain, by using the transformation in Equation (5.8). Hence, to apply the multi-domain integration method of Zhu (2010), we can generate abscissas and weights once, and use these to obtain the integrals on the subdomains, applying the transformation each time. We stop when the condition in (5.13) is satisfied. The Matlab function HestonPriceGaussLegendreMD.m implements the multi-domain integration method.

```
function [Price D N] = HestonPriceGaussLegendreMD(...,xGLe,wGLe)
for j=2:length(A);
    for k=1:length(xGLe);
        % Lower and upper limits
        a = A(j-1);
        b = A(j);
        X = (a+b)/2 + (b-a)/2*xGLe(k);
        % The integrals
        int1(j,k) = wGLe(k)*HestonProb(X,...,1)*(b-a)/2;
        int2(j,k) = wGLe(k)*HestonProb(X,...,2)*(b-a)/2;
        % Sum the integrals over each subdomain
        sum1(j) = sum(int1(j,:));
        sum2(j) = sum(int2(j,:));
    end
    % Stopping criterion
    if abs(sum1(j))<tol && abs(sum2(j))<tol
        break;
    end
end
P1 = 1/2 + 1/pi*sum(sum1);
P2 = 1/2 + 1/pi*sum(sum2);
HestonC = S*exp(-q*T)*P1 - K*exp(-r*T)*P2;
% Integration domain and points
D = [A(1) A(j)];
N = length(A(1:j));
```

The function accepts as input a set of points defining the subdomains. It outputs the call price, or the put price by put-call parity. It also outputs the resulting domain of integration and the number of points used. The C# function to implement this method is very similar to the Matlab code and is not presented here.

To illustrate the multi-domain integration of Zhu (2010), we use the settings for the example that illustrates Gaussian quadrature throughout this chapter.

Recall that the maturity in this example is $\tau = 1.5$. The following code implements the multi-domain integration. We separate the integration domain $(0, 150]$ into 10 subdomains.

```
[xGLe wGLe] = GenerateGaussLegendre(32);
% The domain of integration and the tolerance
lo = 1e-10; hi = 150;
N  = 10;
dA = (hi - lo)/N;
A = [lo:dA:hi];
tol = 1e-6;
% Calculate the "true" option price using Newton-Cotes
N = 10000;
method = 3;
a = 1e-20;
b = 150;
PriceSimpson = HestonPriceNewtonCoates(...,method,a,b,N);
% Calculate the price using a multi-domain of integration
[PriceMD Domain Npoints] = HestonPriceGaussLegendreMD(...,xGLe,wGLe);
```

The price using multi-domain integration with a tolerance level of $\varepsilon = 10^{-6}$ is 13.2563, which is very close to the price of 13.2561 using Simpson's rule with 10,000 points and an integration range of $(0, 150]$. With this tolerance level, the algorithm returns $\phi_{\max} = 21.45$, so the integration range is substantially narrower and the computation time is decreased. If we reduce the maturity to $\tau = 0.5$, the price drops to 7.1026, which again is very accurate. The algorithm returns $\phi_{\max} = 35.4$, however, so the domain of integration is substantially wider than that for $\tau = 1.5$ and the computation time is increased.

Another approach to finding an adequate domain of integration is to transform the domain $\phi \in [0, \infty)$ to a more manageable interval $x \in [0, 1]$, as suggested by Kahl and Jäckel (2005). In their method, the argument ϕ in the Heston integrand

$$\text{Re}\left[\frac{e^{-i\phi \ln K} f_j(\phi; x, v)}{i\phi}\right]$$

is replaced by $-\ln x / C_\infty$, where $C_\infty = \sqrt{1-\rho^2}(v_0 + \kappa\theta\tau)/\sigma^2$ and where τ is the time to maturity, and the integrands are divided by xC_∞. The call price becomes

$$C(K) = e^{-r\tau} \int_0^1 y(x)dx \tag{5.14}$$

where

$$y(x) = \frac{1}{2}(F - K) + \frac{Ff_1(-\ln x/C_\infty) - Kf_2(-\ln x/C_\infty)}{x\pi C_\infty} \tag{5.15}$$

and where $F = e^{(r-q)\tau}$. In the form of (5.15) the integral $y(x)$ is not defined at the endpoints $x = 0$ and $x = 1$, which implies that the integration can only be done over the range $(0,1)$. However, Kahl and Jäckel (2005) derive the limits of the integrand analytically

$$\lim_{x\to 0} y(x) = \frac{1}{2}(F-K)$$

$$\lim_{x\to 1} y(x) = \frac{1}{2}(F-K) + \frac{F\lim_{u\to 0} f_1(u) - K\lim_{u\to 0} f_2(u)}{\pi C_\infty}.$$

The expressions for $\lim_{u\to 0} f_j(u)$ are given in their Equations (44) and (50). Hence,

$$\lim_{u\to 0} f_1(u) = \ln(F/K) + \text{Im}[C'(-i)] + \text{Im}[D'(-i)]v_0 \tag{5.16}$$

and

$$\lim_{u\to 0} f_2(u) = \ln(F/K) + \text{Im}[C'(0)] + \text{Im}[D'(0)]v_0. \tag{5.17}$$

In this last expression, we have

$$\text{Im}[C'(0)] = -\frac{e^{-\kappa\tau}\theta\kappa + \theta\kappa(\kappa\tau - 1)}{2\kappa^2}, \quad \text{Im}[D'(0)] = \frac{e^{-\kappa\tau/2} - 1}{2\kappa}.$$

In Equation (5.16), when $\kappa - \rho\sigma \neq 0$, we have

$$\text{Im}[C'(-i)] = \frac{e^{(\rho\sigma-\kappa)\tau}\theta\kappa + \theta\kappa((\kappa-\rho\sigma)\tau - 1)}{2(\kappa-\rho\sigma)^2}$$

$$\text{Im}[D'(-i)] = \frac{1 - e^{-(\kappa-\rho\sigma)\tau}}{2(\kappa-\rho\sigma)}$$

but when $\kappa - \rho\sigma = 0$, these simplify to

$$\text{Im}[C'(-i)] = \frac{\kappa\theta\tau^2}{4}, \quad \text{Im}[D'(-i)] = \frac{\tau}{2}.$$

Kahl and Jäckel (2005) recommend the use of Gauss-Lobatto quadrature for the integral in Equation (5.14). This is sensible, because this quadrature includes in the abscissas the endpoints of the integration domain $[-1,+1]$. When the transformation in (5.8) is applied, the result is that the endpoints of the transformed domain $[0,1]$ required of the Kahl and Jäckel method are included in the abscissas.

The Matlab function HestonPriceKahlJackel.m implements the call price in (5.14) and returns the call price or the put price by put-call parity.

```
function y = HestonPriceKahlJackel(...)
for u = 1:length(X);
    % Transformation of the abscissa
    x = 0.5*X(u) + 0.5;
    if x == 0;
        % Integrand at left abscissa 0
        y(u) = 0.5*(F-K);
```

```
    elseif x == 1
        % Integrand at right abscissa 1
        f1 = log(F/K) + ImC1 + ImD1*v0;
        f2 = log(F/K) + ImC2 + ImD2*v0;
        y(u) = 0.5*(F-K) + (F*f1 - K*f1)/(pi*Cinf);
    else
        % Integrand at remaining abscissas
        f1 = HestonProb(-log(x)/Cinf,...,1);
        f2 = HestonProb(-log(x)/Cinf,...,2);
        y(u) = 0.5*(F-K) + (F*f1 - K*f2)/(x*pi*Cinf);
    end
    % Multiply by the weights
    z(u) = W(u)*y(u);
end
% The call price
KJCall = exp(-rf*T)*(1/2)*sum(z);
```

To illustrate, we use the following settings: $S = 10$, $K = 7$, $r = 0.06$, $q = 0.04$, a maturity of 1 month, and the parameters $\kappa = 1$, $\theta = 0.06$, $\sigma = 0.5$, $v_0 = 0.06$, and $\rho = -0.8$. Gauss-Laguerre and Gauss-Lobatto integration using the Heston formulation and 32 abscissas produce a call price of 3.0006 and 3.0017, respectively. The same Gauss-Lobatto weights used along with the Kahl and Jäckel (2005) formulation produces a price of 2.9992.

Kahl and Jäckel's integrand is plotted in Figure 5.3 along with the values of the integrand at the 32 Gauss-Lobatto abscissas. The integral is highly

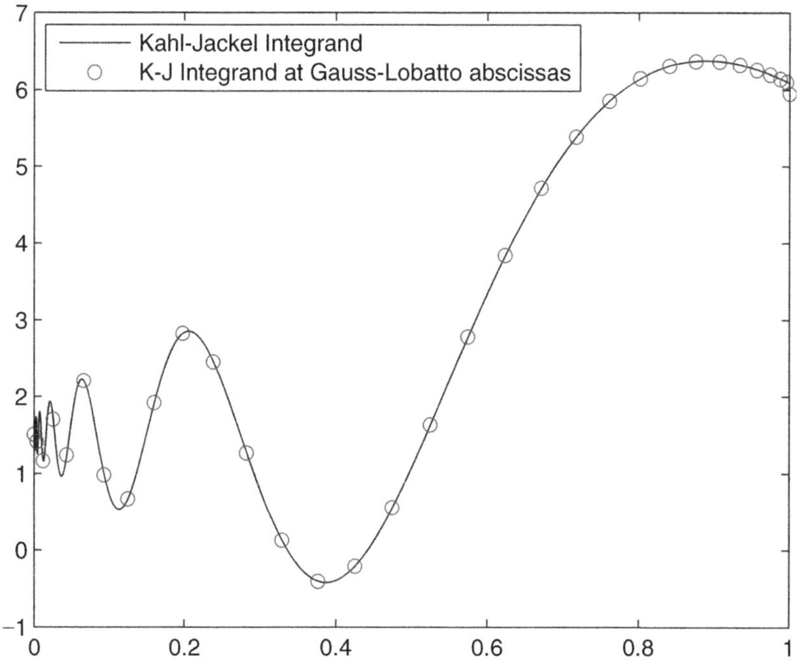

FIGURE 5.3 Kahl and Jäckel (2005) Integrand

oscillatory, but since it dampens quickly, the oscillation causes a negligible loss of precision only.

ILLUSTRATION OF NUMERICAL INTEGRATION

The Matlab function HestonPriceNewtonCotes.m contains all the code necessary to implement the four Newton-Cotes formulas in this chapter, while the functions HestonPriceGaussLaguerre.m and HestonPriceGaussLegendre.m are used for Gaussian quadrature. In the following example, we calculate the price of 1-month European calls and puts when the spot is $S = 100$ and with $r = 0.03$ and $q = 0.02$. We use common parameter settings. We use 100 abscissas for the Newton Cotes formulas, but only 5 abscissas for the Gaussian quadrature. The prices for strikes ranging from $K = 98$ to $K = 102$ are in Table 5.2 for the calls and in Table 5.3 for the puts, along with the mean absolute error in the last column.

The results indicate that the four Newton-Cotes formulas produce prices that are fairly accurate. The Gauss-Legendre and Gauss-Lobatto quadratures are also very accurate, especially in light of the fact that they use five abscissas only. The Gauss-Laguerre quadrature is the least accurate of all the methods.

TABLE 5.2 Comparison of Quadratures on Call Prices

Method	$K = 98$	$K = 99$	$K = 100$	$K = 101$	$K = 102$	Error
True Price	2.70	1.97	1.37	0.86	0.43	
100-pt. Mid-Point	2.71	2.04	1.41	0.84	0.39	0.0369
100-pt. Trapezoidal	2.71	2.04	1.41	0.84	0.39	0.0369
100-pt. Simpson's	2.71	2.04	1.41	0.84	0.39	0.0375
100-pt. Simpson's 3/8	2.71	2.04	1.41	0.84	0.39	0.0369
5-pt. Gauss Laguerre	1.80	1.16	0.61	0.16	−0.21	0.7634
5-pt. Gauss Legendre	2.71	2.04	1.41	0.83	0.38	0.0376
5-pt. Gauss Lobatto	2.71	2.04	1.41	0.84	0.39	0.0372

TABLE 5.3 Comparison of Quadratures on Put Prices

Method	$K = 98$	$K = 99$	$K = 100$	$K = 101$	$K = 102$	Error
True Price	0.87	1.14	1.54	2.03	2.59	
100-pt. Mid-Point	0.88	1.21	1.58	2.00	2.55	0.0369
100-pt. Trapezoidal	0.88	1.21	1.58	2.00	2.55	0.0369
100-pt. Simpson's	0.88	1.21	1.58	2.00	2.55	0.0375
100-pt. Simpson's 3/8	0.88	1.21	1.58	2.00	2.55	0.0369
5-pt. Gauss Laguerre	−0.03	0.32	0.78	1.32	1.96	0.7634
5-pt. Gauss Legendre	0.88	1.21	1.58	2.00	2.54	0.0376
5-pt. Gauss Lobatto	0.88	1.21	1.58	2.00	2.55	0.0372

FAST FOURIER TRANSFORM

The fast Fourier transform (FFT) was applied by Carr and Madan (1999) to speed up the computation of option prices. The discrete Fourier transform maps a vector of points $\mathbf{x} = (x_1, \ldots, x_N)$ to another vector of points $\hat{\mathbf{x}} = (\hat{x}_1, \ldots, \hat{x}_N)$ via the relation

$$\hat{x}_k = \sum_{j=1}^{N} e^{-i\frac{2\pi}{N}(j-1)(k-1)} x_j \quad \text{for } k = 1, \ldots, N. \tag{5.18}$$

Computing these sums independently of one another would require N^2 steps. The fast Fourier transform computes these sums simultaneously, which requires $N\log_2 N$ steps. Recall from Chapter 3 that the Carr and Madan (1999) representation for the call price for a value of the log strike $k = \ln K$ is

$$C(k) = \frac{e^{-\alpha k}}{\pi} \int_0^\infty \text{Re}[e^{-ivk}\psi(v)]dv \tag{5.19}$$

where

$$\psi(v) = \frac{e^{-r\tau} f_2(v - (\alpha + 1)i)}{\alpha^2 + \alpha - v^2 + iv(2\alpha + 1)}$$

and where f_2 is the Heston characteristic function. The objective of the FFT is to discretize the expression for the call price $C(k)$ in Equation (5.19) and express it in terms of (5.18).

Note that the inverse FFT of $\hat{\mathbf{x}} = (\hat{x}_1, \ldots, \hat{x}_N)$ is the vector $\mathbf{x} = (x_1, \ldots, x_N)$ defined as

$$x_k = \frac{1}{N} \sum_{j=1}^{N} e^{i\frac{2\pi}{N}(j-1)(k-1)} \hat{x}_j \quad \text{for } k = 1, \ldots, N. \tag{5.20}$$

The FFT and inverse FFT are intuitive discrete analogues of their continuous counterparts. We can denote the FFT that maps $\mathbf{x}$ to $\hat{\mathbf{x}}$ as the function $\hat{\mathbf{x}} = D(\mathbf{x})$ and the inverse FFT that maps $\hat{\mathbf{x}}$ back to $\mathbf{x}$ by $\mathbf{x} = D^{-1}(\hat{\mathbf{x}})$. We will use this notation when we describe the fractional fast Fourier transform (FRFT) later in this chapter.

Discretization of the Integration Range and of the Strike Range

Evaluation of the call price in Equation (5.19) requires the discretization of the range of strikes and of the integration domain. We can approximate the call price by the trapezoidal rule over the truncated integration domain $[0, b]$ for v, using N equidistant points

$$v_j = (j - 1)\eta \quad \text{for } j = 1, \ldots, N \tag{5.21}$$

where η is the increment. The trapezoidal rule approximates the call price $C(k)$ as

$$\begin{aligned} C(k) &\approx \frac{e^{-\alpha k}}{\pi} \text{Re}\left[\frac{1}{2} e^{-iv_1 k} \psi(v_1) + e^{-iv_2 k} \psi(v_2) + \cdots \right. \\ &\qquad \left. + e^{-iv_{N-1} k} \psi(v_{N-1}) + \frac{1}{2} e^{-iv_N k} \psi(v_N)\right] \\ &= \frac{\eta e^{-\alpha k}}{\pi} \sum_{j=1}^{N} \text{Re}\left[e^{-iv_j k} \psi(v_j)\right] w_j \end{aligned} \tag{5.22}$$

where the weights are $w_1 = w_N = \frac{1}{2}$ and $w_j = 1$ for $j = 2, \ldots, N-1$. If Simpson's rule is used instead of the trapezoidal rule, we set $w_1 = w_N = \frac{1}{3}$ and $w_j = \frac{4}{3}$ when j is even, and $w_j = \frac{2}{3}$ when j is odd.

We are interested in strikes near the money, so we need to define the discretization range of the log strikes so that it is centered about the log spot price $\log S_t$. Carr and Madan (1999) assume that the spot price is $S_t = 1$, but it is straightforward to generalize the discretization for general values of S_t. The strike range is, thus, discretized using the N equidistant points as

$$k_u = -b + (u-1)\lambda + \ln S_t \quad \text{for } u = 1, \ldots, N \tag{5.23}$$

where λ is the increment and $b = N\lambda/2$. This produces log strikes over the range $[\ln S_t - b, \ln S_t + b - \lambda]$. For a log strike value k_u on the grid, we can write Equation (5.22) for the price of the call as

$$C(k_u) \approx \frac{\eta e^{-\alpha k_u}}{\pi} \sum_{j=1}^{N} \text{Re}\left[e^{-iv_j k_u} \psi(v_j)\right] w_j. \tag{5.24}$$

Substitute for v_j and k_u

$$\begin{aligned} C(k_u) &\approx \frac{\eta e^{-\alpha k_u}}{\pi} \sum_{j=1}^{N} \text{Re}\left[e^{-i(j-1)\eta[-b+(u-1)\lambda+\ln S_t]} \psi(v_j)\right] w_j \\ &= \frac{\eta e^{-\alpha k_u}}{\pi} \sum_{j=1}^{N} \text{Re}\left[e^{-i\lambda\eta(j-1)(u-1)} e^{i(b-\ln S_t)v_j} \psi(v_j)\right] w_j. \end{aligned} \tag{5.25}$$

In order to express Equation (5.25) in terms of the discrete FFT in (5.18), we must have the following constraint on the increments η and λ

$$\lambda\eta = \frac{2\pi}{N}.$$

This is an important limitation of the FFT, since it entails a trade-off between the grid sizes. For a fixed N, choosing a fine grid for the integration range will produce a coarse grid for the log strikes range, and vice-versa. The only way to increase the granularity of both grids is to increase N, and consequently, the computation time.

Summary of the FFT

Recall that the Carr and Madan (1999) price of the call at the log strike $k = \ln K$ is

$$C(k) = \frac{e^{-\alpha k}}{\pi}\int_0^\infty \text{Re}[e^{-ivk}\psi(v)]dv.$$

To implement the FFT on the call price, first create the integration grid $\{v_j\}_{j=1}^N$ and the log-strike grid $\{k_u\}_{u=1}^N$. Define the points x_j for $j = 1, \ldots, N$ as

$$x_j = e^{i(b-\ln S_t)v_j}\psi(v_j)w_j \tag{5.26}$$

with $b = N\lambda/2$. In (5.26), $\psi(v_j)$ is the function ψ evaluated at the grid point v_j

$$\psi(v_j) = \frac{e^{-r\tau}f_2(v_j - (\alpha+1)i)}{\alpha^2 + \alpha - v_j^2 + iv_j(2\alpha+1)}$$

where $f_2(v_j - (\alpha+1)i)$ is the Heston characteristic function evaluated at $v_j - (\alpha+1)i$. Define $\hat{x}_u = C(k_u)$, the call price evaluated at the log-strike point k_u. Each call price $\hat{x}_u$ can be obtained from the set $\{x_j\}_{j=1}^N$ via the fast Fourier transform as the sum

$$\hat{x}_u = \frac{\eta e^{-\alpha k_u}}{\pi}\sum_{j=1}^N \text{Re}\left[e^{-i\frac{2\pi}{N}(j-1)(u-1)}x_j\right] \quad \text{for } u = 1, \ldots, N. \tag{5.27}$$

Call prices are obtained from (5.27) directly. Hence, $C(k_u) = \hat{x}_u$ is the price of the call struck at $\exp(k_u)$.

The fast Fourier transform for the Heston call price is implemented using the Matlab function HestonCallFFT.m. The function calls the HestonCF.m function, which constructs the Heston characteristic function $f_2(\phi; x, v)$. The function implements the FFT in one of two ways: a fast version which makes use of vectorization and a slow version which uses a loop. To conserve space, only the main part of the function is presented.

```
function [CallFFT K lambdainc eta] = HestonCallFFT(...);
if fast==1
    % Implement the FFT - fast algorithm
    U = [0:N-1];
    J = [0:N-1];
    psi = HestonCF(v-(alpha+1).*i,...,Trap);
    phi = exp(-r*tau).*psi ./ (alpha.^2 + alpha - v.^2 + ...;
    x = exp(i.*(b-s0).*v).*phi.*w;
    e = exp(-i*2*pi/N.*(U'*J))*x;
    CallFFT = eta.*exp(-alpha.*k)./pi .* real(e);
elseif fast==0
    % Implement the FFT - slow algorithm
    for u=1:N
        for j=1:N
            psi(j) = HestonCF(v(j)-(alpha+1)*i,...,Trap);
            phi(j) = exp(-r*tau)*psi(j)/(alpha^2 + alpha - ...;
```

```
            x(j) = exp(i*(b-s0)*v(j))*phi(j)*w(j);
            e(j) = exp(-i*2*pi/N*(j-1)*(u-1))*x(j);
        end
        CallFFT(u) = eta*exp(-alpha*k(u))/pi * real(sum(e));
    end
end
```

The implementation of the FFT in C# is done without vectorization, using the function HestonFFT(), which is very similar to the second portion of the Matlab function HestonCallFFT.m.

```
static double[,] HestonFFT(HParam param,OpSet settings,...)
for(int u=0;u<=N-1;u++) {
    for(int j=0;j<=N-1;j++) {
        psi[j] = HestonCF(v[j]-(alpha+1.0)*i,param,settings);
        phi[j] = Complex.Exp(-r*tau)*psi[j] ...;
        x[j]   = Complex.Exp(i*(b-s0)*v[j])*phi[j]*w[j];
        e[j]   = Complex.Exp(-i*2*pi/Convert.ToDouble(N)*j*u)*x[j];
        sume[u] += e[j].Real;}
    CallFFT[u] = eta*Math.Exp(-alpha*k[u])/pi * sume[u]; }
```

To illustrate, suppose that the spot price is $S_t = 50$ and that the Heston parameters are $\kappa = 0.2$, $v_0 = \theta = 0.05$, $\sigma = 0.3$, and $\rho = -0.7$. Suppose that the maturity is 6 months, that the risk-free rate is $r = 0.03$, and that the dividend yield is $q = 0.05$. Using $N = 2^{10} = 1,024$ and a damping parameter of $\alpha = 1.5$, we obtain the call prices in Table 5.4 along with the approximation error relative to the exact price, which is obtained using 32-point Gauss-Laguerre integration.

The FFT produces prices that are very accurate, regardless of whether Simpson's rule or the trapezoidal rule is used. Indeed, with $N = 1,024$ points, the mean absolute percent error is 0.0394 percent for both Simpson's rule and the trapezoidal rule. In this example, the integration increment is $\eta = 0.0977$ and the log-strike increment is $\lambda = 0.0628$.

TABLE 5.4 Comparison of FFT Call Prices

Strike	Exact Price	Trapezoidal FFT Price	Simpson's FFT Price	Trapezoidal Error	Simpson's Error
41.4102	8.6378	8.6381	8.6381	0.0010	0.0040
44.0956	6.4765	6.4761	6.4761	−0.0072	−0.0072
46.9551	4.4453	4.4454	4.4454	0.0014	0.0014
50.0000	2.6778	2.6782	2.6782	0.0118	0.0118
53.2424	1.3269	1.3267	1.3267	−0.0152	−0.0152
56.6950	0.5020	0.5018	0.5018	−0.0421	−0.0421
60.3716	0.1421	0.1424	0.1424	0.1938	0.1938

FRACTIONAL FAST FOURIER TRANSFORM

The fractional fast Fourier transform (FRFT) was applied to option pricing by Chourdakis (2005). The FRFT is a refinement of the FFT that relaxes the restrictive constraint $\lambda\eta = 2\pi/N$ on the grid size parameters, so that the term $1/N$ in the exponent of the fast Fourier transform is replaced with a general term β. Hence, Equation (5.27) becomes

$$\hat{x}_u = \frac{\eta e^{-\alpha k_u}}{\pi} \sum_{j=1}^{N} \mathrm{Re}\left[e^{-i2\pi\beta(j-1)(u-1)} x_j\right] \quad \text{for } u = 1, \ldots, N. \tag{5.28}$$

The relationship between the grid size parameters λ and η becomes $\lambda\eta = 2\pi\beta$. We can, thus, choose the grid size parameters freely, and then set

$$\beta = \frac{\lambda\eta}{2\pi}.$$

The FFT arises as the special case $\beta = 1/N$. To implement the FRFT on a set of points $x_1, \ldots, x_N$, first define the vectors $\mathbf{y}$ and $\mathbf{z}$, each of dimension $2N$

$$\mathbf{y} = \left(\left\{e^{-i\pi(j-1)^2\beta_j} x_j\right\}_{j=1}^{N}, \quad \{0\}_{j=1}^{N}\right)$$

$$\mathbf{z} = \left(\left\{e^{i\pi(j-1)^2\beta_j}\right\}_{j=1}^{N}, \quad \left\{e^{i\pi(N-j+1)^2\beta}\right\}_{j=1}^{N}\right).$$

Next, take the FFT of $\mathbf{y}$ and $\mathbf{z}$ to obtain the vectors $\hat{\mathbf{y}} = D(\mathbf{y})$ and $\hat{\mathbf{z}} = D(\mathbf{z})$, and take their product element by element, which produces the vector $\hat{\mathbf{h}}$ of dimension $2N$ defined as

$$\hat{\mathbf{h}} = \hat{\mathbf{y}} \odot \hat{\mathbf{z}} = \{y_j z_j\}_{j=1}^{2N}.$$

Now take the inverse FFT of $\hat{\mathbf{h}}$ to produce the vector $\mathbf{h} = D^{-1}(\hat{\mathbf{h}})$ of dimension $2N$. Finally, multiply element by element the resulting vector with the vector $\mathbf{e}$ of dimension $2N$ defined as

$$\mathbf{e} = \left(\left\{e^{-i\pi(j-1)^2\beta}\right\}_{j=1}^{N}, \quad \{0\}_{j=1}^{N}\right).$$

Hence, we can write the fractional FFT in compact form as

$$\begin{aligned}\hat{\mathbf{x}} &= \mathbf{e} \odot D^{-1}(\hat{\mathbf{h}}) = \mathbf{e} \odot D^{-1}(\hat{\mathbf{y}} \odot \hat{\mathbf{z}}) \\ &= \mathbf{e} \odot D^{-1}(D(\mathbf{y}) \odot D(\mathbf{z})).\end{aligned}$$

The first N elements of $\hat{\mathbf{x}}$ are retained and the remaining N elements are discarded, as these are zeros. Note that similar to the FFT, the FRFT takes the N-vector $\mathbf{x}$ and maps it to the N-vector $\hat{\mathbf{x}}$. The FRFT, however, uses the intermediate $2N$-vectors $\mathbf{y}$ and $\mathbf{z}$, and requires that two FFTs be computed in the intermediate steps. Nevertheless, the increase in computational time required by the two intermediate

FFTs is usually offset by the increase in accuracy due to being able to choose the integration and strike grids independently and as arbitrarily small as we wish.

To implement the FRFT, we choose an arbitrary number of points, N, an integration increment, η, and a log-strike increment, λ. We then set $\beta = \lambda\eta/(2\pi)$ and proceed as described in this section. For the points x_j that appear in the vector $\mathbf{z}$ in Equation (5.29), we use $x_j = \exp[i(b - \ln S_t)v_j]\psi(v_j)w_j$, exactly the same points as in (5.26) for the FFT. Finally, the integration grid $\{v_j\}_{j=1}^N$ and log-strike grid $\{k_u\}_{u=1}^N$ are built exactly as in (5.21) and (5.23), with $b = N\lambda/2$, as before.

The Matlab function FRFT takes an input vector $\mathbf{x}$ and an increment parameter β and returns the FRFT $\hat{\mathbf{x}}$ from (5.30), using the built-in Matlab functions fft.m for the fast Fourier transform and ifft.m for the inverse fast Fourier transform.

```
function xhat = FRFT(x,beta);
N = length(x);
y = [exp(-i.*pi.*(0:N-1).^2.*beta).*x, zeros(1,N)];
z = [exp( i.*pi.*(0:N-1).^2.*beta)    , ...];
Dy = fft(y);
Dz = fft(z);
h = Dy.*Dz;
ih = ifft(h);
e = [exp(-i.*pi.*(0:N-1).^2.*beta), zeros(1,N)];
xhat = e.*ih;
xhat = xhat(1:N);
```

This function is used in the HestonCallFRFT.m function, which implements the FRFT.

```
function [CallFRFT K lambdainc eta] = HestonCallFRFT(...);
b = N*lambdainc/2;
v = eta.*[0:N-1]';
k = -b + lambdainc.*[0:N-1]' + s0;
K = exp(k);
CallFRFT = zeros(N,1);
beta = lambdainc*eta/2/pi;
psi = HestonCF(v-(alpha+1).*i,...,Trap);
psi = conj(psi);
phi = exp(-r*tau).*psi./conj(alpha.^2 + alpha - v.^2 + ...;
x = conj(exp(i.*(b-s0).*v)).*phi.*w;
y = real(FRFT(x',beta));
CallFRFT = eta.*exp(-alpha.*k).*y'./pi;
```

The C# function to implement the FRFT is done using the FRFT() function, which is very similar to the Matlab function FRFT.m. The difference is that vectorization is not employed, and built-in functions for the FFT and the inverse FFT must be coded separately, since these are not available as standard functions in C#.

```
static Complex[] FRFT(Complex[] x,double beta) {
for(int j=0;j<=N-1;j++) {
    double J = Convert.ToDouble(j);
    y[j] = Complex.Exp(-i*pi*J*J*beta) * x[j];
    z[j] = Complex.Exp(i*pi*J*J*beta); }
for(int j=N;j<=2*N-1;j++) {
    y[j] = 0.0;
    double M = Convert.ToDouble(2*N-j);
    z[j] = Complex.Exp(i*pi*M*M*beta); }
Dy = FFT(y);
Dz = FFT(z);
for(int j=0;j<=2*N-1;j++)
    h[j] = Dy[j]*Dz[j];
ih = IFFT(h);
for(int j=0;j<=N-1;j++) {
    double J = Convert.ToDouble(j);
    e[j] = Complex.Exp(-i*pi*J*J*beta); }
for(int j=0;j<=N-1;j++)
    xhat[j] = e[j] * ih[j];
return xhat;}
```

The C# function FFT() implements the fast Fourier transform.

```
static Complex[] FFT(Complex[] x) {
int N = x.Length;
double pi = Math.PI;
for(int k=0;k<=N-1;k++) {
    coeff = 0.0;
    for(int j=0;j<=N-1;j++) {
        double K = Convert.ToDouble(k);
        double J = Convert.ToDouble(j);
        double M = Convert.ToDouble(N);
        coeff += Complex.Exp(-i*2*pi*J*K/M) * x[j]; }
    xhat[k] = coeff;}
return xhat;}
```

The C# function IFFT() implements inverse FFT.

```
static Complex[] IFFT(Complex[] xhat) {
int N = xhat.Length;
double pi = Math.PI;
for(int k=0;k<=N-1;k++) {
    coeff = 0.0;
    for(int j=0;j<=N-1;j++) {
        double K = Convert.ToDouble(k);
        double J = Convert.ToDouble(j);
        double M = Convert.ToDouble(N);
        coeff += Complex.Exp(i*2*pi*J*K/M) * xhat[j]; }
    x[k] = coeff / Convert.ToDouble(N); }
return x;}
```

Finally, the C# function HestonFRFT() returns a vector of strikes and a vector of call prices evaluated at each strike.

```
static double[,] HestonFRFT(HParam param,OpSet settings,...) {
double b = Convert.ToDouble(N)*lambdainc/2.0;
for(int j=0;j<=N-1;j++)
    v[j] = eta * j;
for(int j=0;j<=N-1;j++) {
    k[j] = -b + lambdainc*Convert.ToDouble(j) + s0;
    K[j] = Math.Exp(k[j]); }
double beta = lambdainc*eta/2.0/pi;
for(int j=0;j<=N-1;j++) {
    psi[j] = HestonCF(v[j]-(alpha+1.0)*i,param,settings);
    phi[j] = Complex.Exp(-r*tau)*psi[j] ...;
    x[j]   = Complex.Exp(i*(b-s0)*v[j]) * phi[j] * w[j]; }
y = FRFT(x,beta);
for(int u=0;u<=N-1;u++) {
        Call = eta*Complex.Exp(-alpha*k[u])*y[u]/pi;
        CallFRFT[u] = Call.Real;}
for(int j=0;j<=N-1;j++) {
    output[j,0] = K[j];
    output[j,1] = CallFRFT[j]; }
return output; }
```

To illustrate, we use the same settings at those used to produce the FFT prices in Table 5.3, but using $\lambda = \eta = 0.01$ for the grid increments and increasing the integration points to $N = 2^{12}$. The results are presented in Table 5.5, along with the errors relative to the exact prices, which are obtained using 32-point Gauss-Laguerre integration.

The FRFT prices are less accurate than the FFT prices in Table 5.3, with a mean absolute percent error of 2.55 percent for each rule. One advantage of using the FRFT is that we are able to choose the log-strike grid size and obtain call prices in increments of roughly \$0.50 in Table 5.4. Compare that to the call

TABLE 5.5 Comparison of FRFT Call Prices

Strike	Exact Price	Trapezoidal FRFT Price	Simpson's FRFT Price	Trapezoidal Error	Simpson's Error
48.5223	3.4792	3.4798	3.4798	0.0180	0.0181
49.0099	3.2025	3.2032	3.2032	0.0213	0.0213
49.5025	2.9352	2.9358	2.9358	0.0219	0.0219
50.0000	2.6778	2.6784	2.6784	0.0193	0.0193
50.5025	2.4311	2.4314	2.4314	0.0133	0.0133
51.0101	2.1956	2.1957	2.1957	0.0042	0.0042
51.5227	1.9719	1.9717	1.9717	−0.0069	−0.0069

TABLE 5.6 Comparison of FRFT Call Prices, Small Strike Grid

Strike	Exact Price	Trapezoidal FRFT Price	Simpson's FRFT Price	Trapezoidal Error	Simpson's Error
49.9329	2.7118	2.7123	2.7123	0.0199	0.0199
49.9553	2.7004	2.7010	2.7010	0.0197	0.0197
49.9776	2.6891	2.6897	2.6897	0.0195	0.0195
50.0000	2.6778	2.6784	2.6784	0.0193	0.0193
50.0224	2.6666	2.6671	2.6671	0.0191	0.0191
50.0448	2.6553	2.6558	2.6558	0.0189	0.0189
50.0672	2.6441	2.6446	2.6446	0.0187	0.0187

prices in Table 5.3, which are in increments that are much coarser, roughly \$3.00. Moreover, the FRFT is much faster than the FFT for the same number of points, $N = 2^{12}$.

Another advantage of the FRFT is that we can restrict the range of strikes on which the algorithm is applied. Suppose we want the range of strikes to begin at K'. From Equation (5.23), selecting the log-strike increment λ as

$$\lambda = \frac{2}{N} \log(S_t/K') \tag{5.31}$$

will guarantee that the first log strike will be $k_1 = \log K'$ and that the last strike will be approximately $k_N \approx S_t^2/K'$. Hence, by selecting K' close to S_t we can make λ as small as we wish, and obtain a very narrow discretization range for the strike price. We then select an arbitrary value for the integration grid size η. This is illustrated in Table 5.6, where we have used $K' = 20$ (recall that $S_t = 50$). The FRFT constructs the strike grid in increments of approximately \$0.02 in the near-the-money region.

We could also apply Equation (5.31) to construct a narrow strike range for the FFT itself, but since we are constrained in the relationship between λ and η, this would result in a large value for η, and consequently a very coarse integration grid.

CONCLUSION

In this chapter, we have presented a variety of numerical integration methods, all of which work reasonably well. Newton-Cotes formulas are easy to understand and implement, but require more abscissas and, therefore, more computing time, than Gaussian quadrature. Among these methods, Gauss-Laguerre quadrature is well-suited to the Heston model. Gauss-Lobatto quadrature, however, works very well for the Kahl and Jäckel (2005) transformation of the integration domain. Implementing Gaussian quadrature in C# is more involved than in Matlab because we must create C# functions to find polynomial roots. We also showed that it is straightforward to adapt Newton-Cotes formulas and Gaussian quadrature for the approximation of double integrals. Finally, we presented the fast Fourier transform

(FFT) and the fractional fast Fourier transform (FRFT). Both of these methods work very well for the Heston model, and produce a large set of option prices very quickly. In Chapter 11, we will show that the FFT and FRFT can be applied to calculate Greeks also.

All of the methods to produce option prices in the Heston model that we have encountered require a set of parameter values. Up to now, we have assumed these values to be given. In reality, parameters must be estimated from market data. In the next chapter, we explain how this is done.

CHAPTER 6

Parameter Estimation

Abstract

All of the pricing methodologies we have covered have assumed the Heston model parameters to be given. In this chapter, we describe how to estimate these parameters. We first present the most common estimation method, the loss function approach, in which parameters are selected so that the quoted option prices are as close as possible to the model option prices. Alternatively, quoted and model implied volatilities can be used instead of prices. Next, we summarize the Nelder and Mead (1965) minimization algorithm and we show how to code it in C#. Then we describe the "Smart Parameter" method of Gauthier and Rivaille (2009) to select starting values and the Strike-Vector Computation of Kilin (2007), which constructs the loss function in a way that greatly speeds up the estimation. We then present the Differential Evolution algorithm, which has been shown by Vollrath and Wendland (2009) to be effective in the Heston model. Finally, we present a method due to Atiya and Wall (2009) to obtain maximum likelihood estimates of the Heston model parameters. Throughout this chapter, the Heston parameters are represented as the vector $\Theta = (\kappa, \theta, \sigma, v_0, \rho)$, and their corresponding estimates, as $\hat{\Theta}$.

ESTIMATION USING LOSS FUNCTIONS

The most popular way to estimate the parameters of the Heston model is with loss functions. This method uses the error between quoted market prices and model prices, or between market and model implied volatilities. The parameter estimates $\hat{\Theta}$ are those values which minimize the value of the loss function, so that the model prices or implied volatilities are as close as possible to their market counterparts. A constrained minimization algorithm must be used in this regard so that the constraints on the parameters

$$\kappa > 0, \quad \theta > 0, \quad \sigma > 0, \quad v_0 > 0, \quad \rho \in [-1, +1] \tag{6.1}$$

are respected. Since loss functions use market option prices (or implied volatility derived from those prices) as inputs, they produce estimates of the risk-neutral parameters of the Heston model.

Suppose we have a set of N_T maturities τ_i $(t = 1, \ldots, N_T)$ and a set of N_K strikes K_k $(k = 1, \ldots, N_K)$. For each maturity-strike combination (τ_t, K_k), we have a market price $C(\tau_t, K_k) = C_{tk}$ and a corresponding model price $C(\tau_t, K_k; \Theta) = C_{tk}^{\Theta}$ generated by the Heston model. Attached to each option is an optional weight w_{tk}. There are many possible ways to define a loss function, but they usually fall into one of two categories: those based on prices, and those based on implied volatilities.

The first category of loss functions are those that minimize the error between quoted and model prices. The error is usually defined as the squared difference between the quoted and model prices, or the absolute value of the difference; relative errors can also be used. For example, parameter estimates obtained using the mean error sum of squares (MSE) loss function are obtained by minimizing

$$\frac{1}{N}\sum_{t,k} w_{tk}(C_{tk} - C_{tk}^{\Theta})^2 \tag{6.2}$$

with respect to Θ, where N is the number of quotes. The relative mean error sum of squares (RMSE) parameter estimates are obtained with the loss function

$$\frac{1}{N}\sum_{t,k} w_{tk}\frac{(C_{tk} - C_{tk}^{\Theta})^2}{C_{tk}}. \tag{6.3}$$

Alternatively, we can define the error in terms of the absolute value, so that $|C_{tk} - C_{tk}^{\Theta}|$, and set up a loss function as in Equations (6.2) and (6.3).

One well-known disadvantage of the MSE loss function is that short maturity, deep out-of-the money options with very little value contribute little to the sum in (6.2). Hence, the optimization will tend to fit long maturity, in-the-money options well, at the detriment of the other options. One remedy is to use in-the-money options only, so that, in (6.2), call options are used for strikes less than the spot price, and put options are used for strikes greater than the spot price. The other remedy is to use the RMSE loss function in (6.3). The problem with RMSE, however, is that the opposite effect occurs. Indeed, because of the presence of C_{tk} in the denominator, options with low market value will over-contribute to the sum in (6.3). The over- and under-contribution, however, can be mitigated by assigning weights w_{tk} to the individual terms in the objective function, although the choice of the weights is usually subjective.

The second category of loss functions are those that minimize the error between quoted and model implied volatilities. Again, the error is usually defined as the squared difference, absolute difference, or relative difference, between quoted and model implied volatilities. This category of loss function is sensible, since options are often quoted in terms of implied volatility, and since the fit of model is often assessed by comparing quoted and model implied volatilities. Hence, for example, the implied volatility mean error sum of squares (IVMSE) parameter estimates are based on the loss function

$$\frac{1}{N}\sum_{t,k} w_{tk}(IV_{tk} - IV_{tk}^{\Theta})^2 \tag{6.4}$$

where $IV_{tk} = IV(\tau_t, K_k)$ and $IV_{tk}^{\Theta} = IV(\tau_t, K_k; \Theta)$ are the quoted and model implied volatilities, respectively. The relative and absolute versions can also be used.

The main disadvantage of Equation (6.4) is that it is numerically intensive. Indeed, at each iteration of the optimization, we must first obtain every Heston price C_{tk}^{Θ}, and then apply a root-finding algorithm such as the bisection algorithm to extract the implied volatility IV_{tk}^{Θ} from C_{tk}^{Θ} so that the quantity $(IV_{tk} - IV_{tk}^{\Theta})^2$ can be constructed. One remedy is to use the approximated implied volatility from Lewis' (2000) Series II expansion described in Chapter 4, and use that instead of IV_{tk}^{Θ}. This allows us to bypass the bisection algorithm entirely. Another remedy is to use the loss function described in Christoffersen et al. (2009), which serves as an approximation to the IVMSE in (6.4). It uses the reciprocal of the squared Black-Scholes vega as the weight in (6.2). The parameter estimates from their method are, therefore, based on the loss function

$$\frac{1}{N}\sum_{t,k}\frac{(C_{tk} - C_{tk}^{\Theta})^2}{\text{BSVega}_{tk}^2} \tag{6.5}$$

where BSVega_{tk} is the Black-Scholes sensitivity of the option price with respect to the market implied volatility IV_{tk}, evaluated at the maturity τ_t and the strike K_k

$$\text{BSVega}_{tk} = S\exp(-q\tau_t)n(d_{tk})\sqrt{\tau_t}$$

with

$$d_{tk} = \frac{\log(S/K_k) + (r - q + IV_{tk}^2/2)\tau_t}{IV_{tk}\sqrt{\tau_t}}$$

and where $n(x) = \exp(-x^2/2)/\sqrt{2\pi}$ is the standard normal density. The chief advantage of loss functions based on the approximations of Lewis (2000) or Christoffersen et al. (2009) is that a considerable amount of computation time is saved, albeit at the expense of a loss in precision in the parameter estimates.

Estimation of the Heston model parameters by loss functions has been used by Bakshi, Cao, and Chen (1997), Bams et al. (2009), Christoffersen and Jacobs (2004), Mikhailov and Nögel, (2003), and many others. There is no consensus on which loss function is the best one, but Christoffersen and Jacobs (2004) point out that the same loss function should be used for parameter estimation and for evaluating model fit.

The Matlab function HestonObjFun.m implements the loss functions covered in this section. If we set Method=2, then we obtain the implied volatility directly from the Lewis (2000) approximation, so we do not need to calculate the implied volatility with the bisection algorithm. The function can be easily modified to add more loss functions.

```
function y = HestonObjFun(ObjFun,...);
for k=1:NK
    for t=1:NT
        % Select the method for obtaining the price
        if Method==1
            CallPrice = HestonPriceGaussLaguerre
                        (K(k),T(t),...,);
```

```
        elseif Method==2
            [iv CallPrice] = SeriesIICall(K(k),T(t),...);
        elseif Method==3
            CallPrice = SeriesICall(K(k),T(t),...);
        end
        % Obtain the call price or put price
        if PutCall(k,t)=='C'
            ModelPrice(k,t) = CallPrice;
        else
            ModelPrice(k,t) = CallPrice - S*exp(-q*T(t)) + ...;
        end
        % Select the objective function
        if ObjFun == 1
            error(k,t) = (MktPrice(k,t) - ModelPrice(k,t))^2;
        elseif ObjFun == 2
            error(k,t) = (MktPrice(k,t) -
                          ModelPrice(k,t))^2 ...;
        elseif ObjFun == 3
            if Method==2
                ModelIV = iv;
            else
                ModelIV = BisecBSIV(K(k),T(t),
                          ModelPrice(k,t)...);
            end
            error(k,t) = (ModelIV - MktIV(k,t))^2;
        elseif ObjFun == 4
            d = (log(S/K(k)) + (rf-q+MktIV(k,t)^2/2)*T(t)) ...;
            Vega(k,t) = S*normpdf(d)*sqrt(T(t));
            error(k,t) = (ModelPrice(k,t) -
                          MktPrice(k,t))^2 ...;
        end
    end
end
y = sum(sum(error)) / (NT*NK);
```

To obtain the parameter estimates, we pass the HestonObjFun.m function to the Matlab function fmincon.m. This Matlab function allows for constrained optimization so that the conditions in (6.1) are met.

```
e = 1e-5;
lb = [e   e  e  e -.999];  % Lower bound on the estimates
ub = [100 10 10 10 .999];  % Upper bound on the estimates
[param feval] = fmincon(@(p) HestonObjFun(...),...,lb,ub)
```

The C# code to implement the loss functions is similar to the Matlab code and is presented in the next section. One crucial difference is that the standard normal density must be calculated when loss the function (6.5) is used. This is done with the C# variable NormPDF in the following code snippet.

```
case 4:
    double d = (Math.Log(S/K[k]) +
                (r-q+MktIV[k,t]*MktIV[k,t]/2.0)...;
    double NormPDF = Math.Exp(-0.5*d*d)/Math.Sqrt(2.0*pi);
    Vega = S*NormPDF*Math.Sqrt(T[t]);
    Error += Math.Pow(ModelPrice[k,t] - MktPrice[k,t],2)
            /Vega/Vega/Convert.ToDouble(NT*NK);
break;
```

Another difference is that the C# function NormCDF() presented in Chapter 2 must be used to calculate the standard normal distribution function when implied volatilities are used in the objective function. Please refer to Chapter 2 for a description of the NormCDF() function.

To illustrate, we estimate the Heston parameters using options collected on April 13, 2012, on the S&P500 index for four maturities: 45, 98, 261, and 348 days, and seven strikes, running from 120 to 150 in increments of 5. We use 32-point Gauss-Laguerre integration to obtain the model price C_{tk}^{Θ} (by setting Method=1 in the Matlab function HestonObjFunction.m), and we compare the parameter estimates from the MSE loss function (6.2), the RMSE loss function (6.3), the IVMSE loss function (6.4), and the Christoffersen, Heston, and Jacobs (CHJ) (2009) loss function (6.5). We also report the IVMSE between the model and the quoted implied volatilities. The results are in Table 6.1.

The parameter estimates vary, and MSE seems to provide the best fit to the implied volatilities. As is usually the case, ρ is negative. The plots of quoted implied volatilities and implied volatilities generated from Heston prices that use MSE parameter estimates are presented in Figure 6.1. These indicate that the fit of implied volatilities is slightly better for longer term options than for shorter term ones.

The parameter estimates in Table 6.1 were obtained using the risk-free rate and dividend yield implied from the prices of the puts and the calls. See Shimko (1993) for details.

Nelder-Mead Algorithm in C#

Parameter estimation in C# requires a routine to minimize the loss function we select among those described in the previous section. We use the Nelder-Mead algorithm, which is suitable for unconstrained minimization. The algorithm can be adapted for constrained minimization, however, by including a penalty function for

TABLE 6.1 Results of Estimation With Various Objective Functions

Loss Function	IVMSE	$\hat{\kappa}$	$\hat{\theta}$	$\hat{\sigma}$	$\hat{v}_0$	$\hat{\rho}$
MSE (6.2)	6.79×10^{-6}	1.9214	0.0904	1.0193	0.0344	−0.7799
RMSE (6.3)	5.79×10^{-5}	8.9931	0.0571	2.0000	0.0405	−0.7899
IVMSE (6.4)	9.33×10^{-4}	9.0000	0.0420	0.3044	0.0405	−0.8038
CHJ (2009) (6.5)	5.06×10^{-5}	8.9655	0.0602	1.7142	0.0250	−0.7913

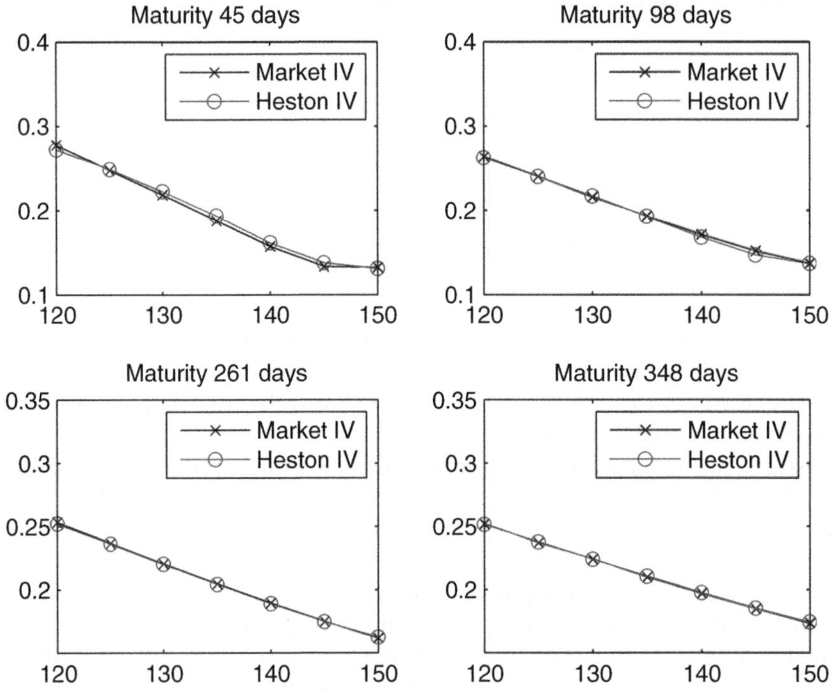

FIGURE 6.1 S&P500 Market and Heston Implied Volatilities Estimated Using MSE

inadmissible parameter values. The Nelder-Mead algorithm is the method of choice for the built-in Matlab function fminsearch.m.

The Nelder-Mead algorithm is designed to find the global minimum of an objective function $f(\mathbf{x}) : \mathbb{R}^n \to \mathbb{R}$. The algorithm requires a set of $n+1$ starting values, each of which is a vector of dimension n. At each iteration, the algorithm replaces the vector that produces the worst value of f (namely, the largest value) with a vector that produces a smaller value of f. The Nelder-Mead algorithm is explained in Nelder and Mead (1965) and in many other sources, such as Dréo, Nunes, and Siarry (2009), for example. The algorithm consists of the following steps.

Step 0. Initialization. Define the $n+1$ vertices $\mathbf{x}_0, \mathbf{x}_1, \ldots, \mathbf{x}_n$ in terms of ranked values of the objective function

$$f(\mathbf{x}_0) \le f(\mathbf{x}_1) \le \cdots \le f(\mathbf{x}_{n-1}) \le f(\mathbf{x}_n).$$

Hence, $\mathbf{x}_0$ is the best point, since it has the lowest value of the objective function, and $\mathbf{x}_n$ is the worst point. Calculate the mean $\overline{\mathbf{x}} = (\mathbf{x}_0 + \mathbf{x}_1 + \cdots + \mathbf{x}_{n-1})/n$. Note that $\overline{\mathbf{x}}$ excludes the worst point $\mathbf{x}_n$.

Step 1. Reflection Rule. Calculate the reflection point $\mathbf{x}_r$ as

$$\mathbf{x}_r = \overline{\mathbf{x}} + \rho(\overline{\mathbf{x}} - \mathbf{x}_n).$$

If $f(\mathbf{x}_1) \le f(\mathbf{x}_r) \le f(\mathbf{x}_n)$, then replace $\mathbf{x}_n$ with the reflection point $\mathbf{x}_r$ and proceed to the next iteration in Step 0. Otherwise, continue to Step 2.

Step 2. Expansion Rule. If $f(\mathbf{x}_r) \leq f(\mathbf{x}_0)$, calculate the expansion point

$$\mathbf{x}_e = \overline{\mathbf{x}} + \chi(\mathbf{x}_r - \overline{\mathbf{x}}).$$

If $f(\mathbf{x}_e) \leq f(\mathbf{x}_r)$, then replace $\mathbf{x}_n$ with the expansion point $\mathbf{x}_e$ and proceed to the next iteration in Step 0. If $f(\mathbf{x}_e) > f(\mathbf{x}_r)$, then replace $\mathbf{x}_n$ with the reflection point $\mathbf{x}_r$ and proceed to the next iteration.

If $f(\mathbf{x}_r) > f(\mathbf{x}_0)$, then continue to Step 3.

Step 3. Outside Contraction Rule. Calculate the outside contraction point

$$\mathbf{x}_{oc} = \overline{\mathbf{x}} + \gamma(\mathbf{x}_r - \overline{\mathbf{x}}).$$

If $f(\mathbf{x}_{n-1}) \leq f(\mathbf{x}_r) < f(\mathbf{x}_n)$ and $f(\mathbf{x}_{oc}) < f(\mathbf{x}_n)$, then replace $\mathbf{x}_n$ with $\mathbf{x}_{oc}$ and proceed to the next iteration in Step 0. Otherwise, continue to Step 4.

Step 4. Inside Contraction Rule. Calculate the inside contraction point

$$\mathbf{x}_{ic} = \overline{\mathbf{x}} + \gamma(\mathbf{x}_n - \overline{\mathbf{x}}).$$

If $f(\mathbf{x}_n) \leq f(\mathbf{x}_r)$ and $f(\mathbf{x}_{ic}) < f(\mathbf{x}_{n+1})$, then replace $\mathbf{x}_n$ with $\mathbf{x}_{ic}$ and proceed to the next iteration in Step 0. Otherwise, continue to Step 5.

Step 5. Shrinkage. Replace $\mathbf{x}_i$ with $\mathbf{x}_i + \sigma(\mathbf{x}_0 - \mathbf{x}_i)$ for $i = 1, \ldots, n$. Note that the best point $\mathbf{x}_0$ does not undergo shrinkage.

Standard values for the coefficients in the steps described earlier are $\rho = 1$ for reflection, $\chi = 2$ for expansion, $\gamma = 1/2$ for contraction, and $\sigma = 1/2$ for shrinkage.

The Nelder-Mead algorithm stops when the number of iterations reaches a specified value, or when the absolute difference between the best and worst function values, $|f(\mathbf{x}_0) - f(\mathbf{x}_n)|$, reaches a specified tolerance level.

The algorithm is implemented in C# using the NelderMead() function. The following snippet of code contains Steps 1 through 5 described earlier. The reflection, expansion, and inside and outside contraction points are calculated earlier in the function and are not presented here. The last part of the function returns the parameter estimates, the value of the objective function, and the number of iterations used in the minimization.

```
static double[] NelderMead(ObjFun f, NMSet nmsettings,
                           double[,] x) {
   while((NumIters <= MaxIters) && (Math.Abs(f1-fn1)
         >= Tolerance)) {
   // Step 1. Reflection Rule
   if((f1<=fr) && (fr<fn)) {
      for(j=0;j<=N-1;j++)
         for(i=0;i<=N-1;i++) x[i,j] = y[i,j];
      for(i=0;i<=N-1;i++) x[i,N] = xr[i];
      goto step0;}
   // Step 2.  Expansion Rule
   if(fr<f1) {
   for(j=0;j<=N-1;j++)
```

```
            for(i=0;i<=N-1;i++) x[i,j] = y[i,j];
        if(fe<fr)
            for(i=0;i<=N-1;i++) x[i,N] = xe[i];
        else
            for(i=0;i<=N-1;i++) x[i,N] = xr[i];
        goto step0; }
        // Step 3.  Outside contraction Rule
        if((fn<=fr) && (fr<fn1) && (foc<=fr)) {
            for(j=0;j<=N-1;j++)
                for(i=0;i<=N-1;i++) x[i,j] = y[i,j];
                    for(i=0;i<=N-1;i++) x[i,N] = xoc[i];
            goto step0; }
        // Step 4.  Inside contraction Rule
        if((fr>=fn1) && (fic<fn1)){
        for(j=0;j<=N-1;j++)
            for(i=0;i<=N-1;i++) x[i,j] = y[i,j];
                for(i=0;i<=N-1;i++) x[i,N] = xic[i];
                        goto step0; }
        // Step 5. Shrink Step
        for(i=0;i<=N-1;i++) x[i,0] = y[i,0];
        for(i=0;i<=N-1;i++)
            for(j=1;j<=N;j++) x[i,j] = 0.5*(y[i,j] + x[i,0]);
        goto step0;
        }
    // Output component
    double[] outvec = new Double[N+2];
    for(i=0;i<=N-1;i++)
        outvec[i] = x1[i];
    outvec[N] = f1;
    outvec[N+1] = NumIters;
    return outvec; }
```

To use the Nelder-Mead algorithm for finding parameter estimates, we create the objective function by defining the f() function in C#, which returns the loss function of choice. As usual, parts of the function have been omitted. Since the Nelder-Mead function is designed for unconstrained optimization, in the first part of the function we include a penalty, so that a very large number (1×10^{50}) is returned if an inadmissible parameter value is encountered. Inadmissible values are those that fall outside of specified lower and upper bounds on the parameters, as described in (6.1).

```
static double f(double[] param,OFSet ofset) {
// Penalty for inadmissible parameter values
if((param2.kappa<=kappaLB) || (param2.theta<=thetaLB) ...
   Error = 1e50;
else {
   for(int k=0;k<NK;k++) {
      for(int t=0;t<NT;t++) {
         ModelPrice[k,t] = HestonPriceGaussLaguerre(K[k],T[t],...);
         switch(LossFunction) {
         case 1:
            // MSE Loss Function
            Error += Math.Pow(ModelPrice[k,t] - MktPrice[k,t],2) ...;
```

```
            break;
            case 2:
               // RMSE Loss Function
               Error += Math.Pow(ModelPrice[k,t] - MktPrice[k,t],2) ...;
            break; } } }
   return Error;}
```

The Heston parameter estimates are obtained using the following C# code. The first portion creates the starting values, the vertices, using initial values and random increments around these initial values. The last portion calls the NelderMead() function.

```
double kappaS = 9.00;
double thetaS = 0.05;
double sigmaS = 0.30;
double v0S = 0.05;
double rhoS = -0.80;
int N = nmsettings.N;
double[,] s = new double[N,N+1];
for(int j=0;j<=N;j++) {
    s[0,j] = kappaS + RandomNum(-0.01,0.01);
    s[1,j] = thetaS + RandomNum(-0.01,0.01);
    s[2,j] = sigmaS + RandomNum(-0.01,0.01);
    s[3,j] = v0S    + RandomNum(-0.01,0.01);
    s[4,j] = rhoS   + RandomNum(-0.01,0.01); }
// Obtain the parameter estimates
double[] B = NelderMead(f,nmsettings,s);
```

In the C# code for the Nelder-Mead algorithm, we have created a series of structures that allow for inputs to be passed to the functions in a more compact form. These structures contain settings for the Nelder-Mead algorithm, for the objective function, for the Heston model parameters, and for the option price. The C# code also makes use of several functions for adding and subtracting vectors and for obtaining the average of vector elements. These structures and functions are not presented here but are included with the C# code.

Starting Values

Recall that the constraints (6.1) on the Heston parameters are $\kappa > 0$, $\theta > 0$, $\sigma > 0$, $v_0 > 0$, and $|\rho| \leq 1$. As described earlier in this chapter, we use the Matlab function fmincon.m to minimize the objective function under these constraints, which requires upper and lower bounds on the parameters. This function uses a variety of methods for constrained optimization, which are explained on the MathWorks website (www.mathworks.com). We can also use the Matlab function fminsearch.m to minimize the objective function, but this function uses the Nelder-Mead algorithm, and as such is designed for unconstrained optimization only. One simple way to incorporate a constraint is to impose a penalty, as we did for the C# code in the previous section.

TABLE 6.2 Parameter Estimates From the Literature

Source	$\hat{\kappa}$	$\hat{\theta}$	$\hat{\sigma}$	$\hat{v}_0$	$\hat{\rho}$	Data, Date
GS (2012)[a]	0.3369	0.0551	0.1927	0.0746	−1.000	S&P500, 09/2008
Forde *et al.* (2010)	1.7609	0.0494	0.4086	0.0464	−0.5195	Eurostoxx 50, 02/2006
Gatheral (2006)	1.3253	0.0354	0.3877	0.0174	−0.7165	S&P500, 09/2005
CHJ (2009)[b]	1.6048	0.0464	0.3796	n/a	−0.7670	S&P500, 2004
SST (2004)[c]	0.6067	0.0707	0.2928	0.0654	−0.7571	Eurostoxx 50, 10/2003
BCC (1997)[d]	1.15	0.04	0.39	0.0348	−0.64	S&P500, 1988–1991

[a]Guillaume and Schoutens (2012)
[b]Christoffersen, Jacobs, and Heston (2009)
[c]Schoutens, Simons, and Tistaert (2004)
[d]Bakshi, Cao, and Chen (1997)
n/a = not applicable

The functions fmincon.m and fminsearch.m each require a set of starting values for the parameters. As with any optimization, it is important that these starting values lie not too far away from the true values. We can look to estimates from the empirical literature, such as those in Table 6.2, for clues on appropriate starting values.

We must also apply good judgment when selecting starting values. For example, volatility and price are usually negatively correlated, so we may specify for the starting value for the correlation to lie in $(-1, 0)$. Aït-Sahalia and Kimmel (2007) use 30-day at-the-money implied volatility as a proxy for instantaneous unobserved volatility, so we can use that value as a starting estimate for v_0.

To find starting values of ρ and σ, we can use the "Smart Parameter" method of Gauthier and Rivaille (2009), which is described in the remainder of this section. Their method is based on the approximation of the option price by expansion developed by Benhamou et al. (2010). Gauthier and Rivaille (2009) express the approximation in terms of the call price, but it can also be expressed in terms of the put price, which is consistent with the original development of Benhamou et al. (2010) that we will cover in Chapter 9. Gauthier and Rivaille rewrite the approximated Heston put price as

$$\text{Put} = A + B\sigma^2 + C\rho\sigma + D\rho^2\sigma^2 \tag{6.6}$$

where

$$\begin{aligned}
A &= P_{BS}(x, \hat{w}_\tau), \quad B = (r_0 v_0 + \theta r_1)\frac{\partial^2 P_{BS}}{\partial y^2}, \quad C = (v_0 p_0 + \theta p_1)\frac{\partial^2 P_{BS}}{\partial x \partial y}, \\
D &= \left[(v_0 q_0 + \theta q_1)\frac{\partial^3 P_{BS}}{\partial x^2 \partial y} + \frac{1}{2}(r_0 p_0 + \theta p_1)\frac{\partial^4 P_{BS}}{\partial x^2 \partial y^2}\right].
\end{aligned} \tag{6.7}$$

In Equation (6.7), the derivatives of the Black-Scholes put $P_{BS}(x, \hat{w}_\tau)$ are in terms of the log-stock price $x = \ln S_t$ and the total integrated variance $\hat{w}_\tau$ we encountered in Chapter 2

$$\hat{w}_\tau = (v_0 - \theta)\left(\frac{1 - e^{-\kappa\tau}}{\kappa}\right) + \theta.$$

Formulas for these derivatives are presented in Chapter 9. The other quantities we need for the coefficients in (6.7), namely m_0, m_1, p_0, p_1, q_0, q_1, r_0 and r_1 can be found in Gauthier and Rivaille (2009) or in Benhamou et al. (2010).

The method of Gauthier and Rivaille is built on the idea that given two quoted puts with the same maturity τ, namely $P(K_1)$ with strike K_1 and $P(K_2)$ with strike K_2, we can form the system of two equations in two unknowns

$$\begin{aligned} P(K_1) &= A(K_1) + B(K_1)\sigma^2 + C(K_1)\rho\sigma + D(K_1)\rho^2\sigma^2 \\ P(K_2) &= A(K_2) + B(K_2)\sigma^2 + C(K_2)\rho\sigma + D(K_2)\rho^2\sigma^2 \end{aligned} \tag{6.8}$$

and solve for (ρ,σ). In order for this to work, we must fix values of κ, θ, and v_0 in the coefficients. We can solve for (ρ,σ) by using the symbolic toolbox in Matlab. In general, four solutions will be produced, but only one will be admissible, with both $|\rho| \leq 1$ and $\sigma > 0$.

Alternatively, we can find the values of (ρ,σ) that minimize the objective function

$$\begin{aligned} f(\rho,\sigma) = {} & (A(K_1) + B(K_1)\sigma^2 + C(K_1)\rho\sigma + D(K_1)\rho^2\sigma^2 - P(K_1))^2 \\ & + (A(K_2) + B(K_2)\sigma^2 + C(K_2)\rho\sigma + D(K_2)\rho^2\sigma^2 - P(K_2))^2. \end{aligned} \tag{6.9}$$

Implementing this method in Matlab is straightforward. The Matlab file BlackScholesDerivatives.m contains the required derivatives for the coefficients in Equation (6.7). This function is passed to GauthierCoefficients.m function, which calculates the coefficients in (6.7).

```
function [A B C D] = GauthierCoefficients(...);
% Generate the Black-Scholes derivatives
[P11 P21 P02 P22] = BlackScholesDerivatives(...);
% Black Scholes Put Price
BSPut = K*exp(-rf*T)*normcdf(f) - S*exp(-q*T)*normcdf(g);
% Return the coefficients
A = BSPut;
B = (v0*r0 + theta*r1)*P02;
C = (v0*p0 + theta*p1)*P11;
D = (v0*q0 + theta*q1)*P21 + 0.5*(v0*p0 + theta*p1)^2*P22;
```

Finally, these coefficients are passed to the GetGauthierValues.m function, which calculates sigma and rho in one of two ways: using closed-form values obtained with Matlab's symbolic calculator, or using the objective function in Equation (6.9).

```
function [sigma rho] = GetGauthierValues(K1,K2,Put1,Put2,...,method)
% Find the Gauthier coefficients for each strike
[A1 B1 C1 D1] = GauthierCoefficients(K1,...);
[A2 B2 C2 D2] = GauthierCoefficients(K2,...);
```

```
if method==1
    % Closed form expressions for sigma and rho
    Rho(1) = -(-1/2*(-C1^2*D2*B2-B1*C2^2*D1 ...;
    Rho(2) =    (-1/2*(-C1^2*D2*B2-B1*C2^2*D1 ...;
    Sigma(1) =  1/2*2^(1/2)*((-C1^2*D2*B2-B1 ...;
    Sigma(2) = -1/2*2^(1/2)*((-C1^2*D2*B2-B1 ...;
    % Find sigma, rho constrained optimization
    for i=1:4
        if abs(Rho(i))<1 && Sigma(i)>0;
            rho = Rho(i);
            sigma = Sigma(i);
        end
    end
elseif method==2
    % Find sigma, rho constrained optimization
    Coeff1 = [A1 B1 C1 D1];
    Coeff2 = [A2 B2 C2 D2];
    [SigmaRho] = fmincon(@(p) GauthierObjFun(p,...),start,...);
    sigma = SigmaRho(1);
    rho   = SigmaRho(2);
end
```

The objective function in (6.9) is implemented using the GauthierObjFun.m function.

```
function y = GauthierObjFun(param,Coeff1,Coeff2,Put1,Put2)
sigma = param(1);
rho   = param(2);
y = (A1 + B1*sigma^2 + C1*rho*sigma + D1*rho^2*sigma^2
        - Put1)^2 ...
  + (A2 + B2*sigma^2 + C2*rho*sigma + D2*rho^2*sigma^2
        - Put2)^2;
```

The C# code to implement the "Smart Parameter" method of Gauthier and Rivaille (2009) is very similar to the code snippets presented earlier, and is not presented here. The difference is that, since we do not have a symbolic calculator in C#, the code uses only the second method to find (ρ, σ), via the objective function (6.9).

SPEEDING UP THE ESTIMATION

One drawback of loss function estimation is that it can be very time consuming, especially if many maturities and strikes are used. Kilin (2007) suggests a very simple trick for speeding up the optimization routines required of loss function estimation. Recall that the integrand for the in-the-money probabilities P_j $(j = 1, 2)$ is

$$\operatorname{Re}\left[\frac{e^{-i\phi \ln K} f_j(\phi)}{i\phi}\right]. \tag{6.10}$$

Kilin (2007) notes that the characteristic function $f_j(\phi)$ does not depend on the strike K, but it does depend on the maturity τ. This implies that, in the optimization, the values of $f_1(\phi)$ and $f_2(\phi)$ can be calculated once for each maturity, cached, and used repeatedly for the different strikes. This is important because the term $f_j(\phi)$ is by far the one that requires the most computation time in the integrand, as it contains a number of complex operations, including logarithms, exponents, and square roots. Zhu (2010) refers to Kilin's trick as Strike Vector Computation, and Schmelzle (2010) calls it the caching technique. Kilin (2007) points out that, in order for this to work, the outer loop of the optimization must be for the maturities and the inner loop for the strikes. When coupled with a pricing formula that requires a single integrand, such as those by Attari (2004) or Lewis (2001), or by consolidating the Heston integrals into a single integral, as we did in Chapter 1, the caching technique leads to an estimation time that is considerably reduced.

The Matlab file HestonObjFunSVC.m implements the method of Kilin (2007) using Gauss-Laguerre integration. Parts of the function have been removed to conserve space. The function allows for original Heston (1993) or Attari (2004) formulation of the characteristic function. The outer loop is for maturities and the inner loop is for strikes. At the beginning of each strike loop, we calculate the value of the characteristic functions f_1 and f_2 at the Gauss-Laguerre abscissas ϕ_j. We then retain these values, form the integrand at each of the strikes, and calculate the call or put prices.

```
function y = HestonObjFunSVC(param,...,x,w,CF)
for t=1:NT
    for j=1:length(x)
        % Store the c.f. at each time step
        phi = x(j);
        if strcmp(CF,'Heston')
            f2(j) = HestonCF(phi   ,...);
            f1(j) = HestonCF(phi-i,...) / (S*exp((rf-q)*T(t)));
        elseif strcmp(CF,'Attari')
            f(j) = AttariCF(phi,...);
        end
    end
    for k=1:NK
        L = log(exp(-rf*T(t))*K(k)/S);
        for j=1:length(x);
            phi = x(j);
            if strcmp(CF,'Heston')
                int1(j) = w(j) * real
                          (exp(-i*phi*log(K(k)))*f1(j)/i/phi);
                int2(j) = w(j) * real
                          (exp(-i*phi*log(K(k)))*f2(j)/i/phi);
            elseif strcmp(CF,'Attari')
                int1(j) = w(j) * ((real(f(j)) + imag(f(j))/phi)
                                 *cos(L*phi)...);
            end
        end
        % The call price
        if strcmp(CF,'Heston')
            P1 = 1/2 + 1/pi*sum(int1);
            P2 = 1/2 + 1/pi*sum(int2);
```

```
            CallPrice = S*exp(-q*T(t))*P1 - ...;
        elseif strcmp(CF,'Attari')
            CallPrice = S*exp(-q*T(t)) - K(k)*exp(-rf*T(t))...;
        end
        if strcmp(PutCall(k,t),'C')
            ModelPrice(k,t) = CallPrice;
        else
            ModelPrice(k,t) = CallPrice - S*exp(-q*T(t)) + ...;
        end
        % Select the objective function
        if ObjFun == 1
            % MSE
            error(k,t) = (MktPrice(k,t) - ModelPrice(k,t))^2;
        end
    end
clear f1 f2
end
y = sum(sum(error)) / (NT*NK);
```

The C# code to generate the objective functions using Kilin's (2007) Strike Vector Computation is similar to the Matlab code shown above and is not presented here.

We will see in Table 6.3 that the Strike Vector Computation substantially reduces the computation time required for calibration, with little effect on the parameter estimates.

One recent trend to improve the speed of estimation is to reduce the set of parameters to estimate. We will see in Chapter 11, for example, that the sensitivity of the Heston option price to changes in κ is low. Hence, we can fix κ at an arbitrary, but reasonable, value. In their version of the Heston model with time-dependent parameters, which we cover in Chapter 9, Benhamou et al. (2010) allow the parameters to be piecewise constant, but restrict κ to a single value. Aït-Sahalia and Kimmel (2007) use short-term (30-day) at-the-money (ATM) implied volatility to proxy instantaneous volatility. Janek et al. (2010) and Zhu (2010) calibrate v_0 to the ATM implied volatility in the FX market, and suggest setting κ large enough so that Feller's condition $2\kappa\theta > \sigma^2$ is satisfied. This leaves only the parameters set (θ, σ, ρ) to estimate. Guillaume and Schoutens (2012) calibrate v_0 and θ to the VIX, and estimate (κ, σ, ρ) only.

Modifying the Matlab files for parameter estimation in which one or more of the parameters is fixed is straightforward. In the first argument to the objective function, we pass only those parameters to be optimized, and we pass the fixed parameters as additional arguments to the function.

Finally, we can use the fast Fourier transform (FFT) or the fractional fast Fourier transform (FRFT) to estimate the parameters. Both will reduce considerably the computation time required. The Matlab file HestonObjFunFRFT.m constructs the loss functions described in the first section of this chapter, but using the FRFT to obtain model prices. The function calls the HestonCallFRFT.m function described in Chapter 5 to calculate model prices, and then uses the built-in Matlab function interp1.m to apply linear interpolation to obtain the call prices at the desired strikes. The setting for this function can be changed to "spline" to implement cubic splines, but this increases the computation time and does not increase the accuracy by much, in light of the fine granularity of the strike grid employed.

```
function y = HestonObjFunFRFT(param,S,K1,...,eta,alpha,rule)
lambdainc = 2/N*log(S/K1);
for t=1:NT
    [CallFRFT KK lambdainc eta] = HestonCallFRFT(N,T(t),...);
    CallPrice = LinearInterpolate(KK,CallFRFT,K);
    for k=1:NK
        if strcmp(PutCall(k,t),'C')
            ModelPrice(k,t) = CallPrice(k);
        else
            ModelPrice(k,t) = CallPrice(k) - S*exp(-q*T(t)) + ...;
        end
    end
    % Select the objective function
    if ObjFun == 1
        error(:,t) = (MktPrice(:,t) - ModelPrice(:,t)).^2;
    end
end
y = sum(sum(error)) / (NT*NK);
```

In the earlier code, we use our own function for linear interpolation, LinearInterpolate.m, which runs faster than the built-in Matlab function interp1.m.

```
function Yi = LinearInterpolate(X,Y,Xi)
N = length(X);
M = length(Xi);
for j=1:M
    k = find(Xi(j)<=X);
    k = k(1)-1;
    Yi(j) = Y(k+1)*(Xi(j)-X(k))/(X(k+1)-X(k)) + ...;
end
```

We use the S&P500 data used to generate the parameter estimates in Table 6.1 to compare the speed of estimation using the MSE loss function. We implement the estimation using 32-point Gauss-Laguerre integration and the ordinary objective function HestonObjFun.m, using the Strike Vector Computation (SVC) with the Heston (1993) characteristic function and the Attari (2004) characteristic function, and using the FRFT. The results are in Table 6.3.

TABLE 6.3 Comparison of Estimation Methods

Estimation Method	IVMSE	$\hat{\kappa}$	$\hat{\theta}$	$\hat{\sigma}$	$\hat{v}_0$	$\hat{\rho}$	Estimation Time (sec)
Ordinary	6.79×10^{-6}	1.9214	0.0904	1.0193	0.0344	−0.7799	33.51
SVC-Heston	6.79×10^{-6}	1.9643	0.0895	1.0268	0.0344	−0.7816	8.19
SVC-Attari	9.47×10^{-6}	1.5359	0.0986	0.9436	0.0345	−0.7729	6.12
FRFT	9.57×10^{-6}	1.6691	0.0932	0.9076	0.0339	−0.8013	2.35

The ordinary objective function produces exactly the same parameter estimates as in the first row of Table 6.1, as expected. The SVC objective function using either the Heston or the Attari characteristic functions are comparable in terms of computation time. Finally, the FRFT returns the parameter estimates very quickly, requiring less than 10 percent of the time than the ordinary objective function. The parameter estimates from the different estimation methods, as well as the values of IVMSE, are very close.

The conclusion is evident: when possible, the SVC method or the FRFT should be used to estimate the Heston parameters. Note however, that the FRFT settings must be used with care. Setting the number of points too high in the FRFT function will slow down the FRFT estimation, with little or no gain in precision.

DIFFERENTIAL EVOLUTION

The Differential Algorithm of Storn and Price (1997) has been applied to option pricing by Nykvist (2009) and Gilli and Schumann (2011). Vollrath and Wendland (2009) have applied the algorithm to the Heston model and have found the algorithm effective in identifying the global minimum in the parameter space, albeit at the expense of high computation time. The algorithm updates a randomly chosen population of parameter values by creating a new candidate member from each existing member in the population. Each existing member is compared to its candidate, and the candidate replaces the member in the population if the candidate's objective function is smaller than the member's. A new population is thus created, and the process is repeated over successive iterations, or generations. In the final generation, the member with the smallest value of the objective function is chosen as the solution.

The DE algorithm can thus be implemented in the following steps.

Step 1. Initial selection of the population. Form a matrix of size $5 \times N_P$ of randomly chosen parameter values, where N_P is the number of population members. The matrix must be constructed so that each row respects the constraints on the parameters. Lower and upper bounds can be chosen so that the random values for the parameters are reasonable, for example, $0 < \kappa < 20$, $0 < \theta, v_0, \sigma < 2$, and $-1 < \rho < 0$. In order for Step 2 to work, we must have $N_P \geq 4$. This implies we have the population

$$\underset{(5\times N_P)}{\mathbf{P}} = \begin{pmatrix} \mathbf{x}_1 & \mathbf{x}_2 & \cdots & \mathbf{x}_{N_P} \end{pmatrix} \tag{6.11}$$

where each member of $\mathbf{P}$ is a vector of parameters, namely $\mathbf{x}_i = (\kappa_i, \theta_i, \sigma_i, v_{0i}, \rho_i)^T$.

Step 2. Mutation of the population members. For each member $\mathbf{x}_i$ of the population ($i = 1, \ldots, N_P$), randomly select three other members $\mathbf{x}_{r1}$, $\mathbf{x}_{r2}$, and $\mathbf{x}_{r3}$ distinct from each other and from $\mathbf{x}_i$ as well. This implies that we must select the indices r_1, r_2, and r_3 so that $i \neq r_1 \neq r_2 \neq r_3$. For each member, form a donor member defined by

$$\mathbf{y}_i = \mathbf{x}_{r1} + F(\mathbf{x}_{r2} - \mathbf{x}_{r3}) \tag{6.12}$$

where $F \in [0, 2]$ is a constant mutation factor. The elements of the donor member $\mathbf{y}_i$ are used to construct a candidate member that may or may not replace $\mathbf{x}_i$, based on the results of Steps 3 and 4.

Step 3. Recombination of the donor members. The candidate member $\mathbf{u}_i$ is constructed element-by-element from the elements y_{ij} of the donor and the elements of the member x_{ij} ($j = 1, \ldots, 5$) according to the following rule. For each element j, we generate a uniform random number U_{ij} and we form the candidate element as

$$u_{ij} = \begin{cases} y_{ij} & \text{if} \quad U_{ij} \leq CR \quad \text{or} \quad j = R \\ x_{ij} & \text{otherwise} \end{cases} \tag{6.13}$$

where R is a randomly chosen integer from 1 to 5 and where CR is a probability called the crossover ratio. The use of R guarantees that the candidate is the not the same as the member, that is, it guarantees that $\mathbf{u}_i \neq \mathbf{x}_i$. This is because, even if all the U_{ij} are very small so that the condition $U_{ij} \leq CR$ is not satisfied for any $j = 1, \ldots, 5$, the condition $j = R$ will be met once and the corresponding element y_{ij} will become the element u_{ij} of the candidate $\mathbf{u}_i$.

Step 4. Selection of the candidate. The member $\mathbf{x}_i$ and its candidate $\mathbf{u}_i$ are each fed into the objective function $f(\mathbf{x})$. If the candidate's value is lower than that of the member, the candidate replaces $\mathbf{x}_i$ as the ith member of the population $\mathbf{P}$ in (6.11). The rule is therefore

$$\mathbf{P} = \begin{cases} (\mathbf{x}_1 \ \cdots \ \mathbf{u}_i \ \cdots \ \mathbf{x}_{N_P}) & \text{if} \ f(\mathbf{u}_i) < f(\mathbf{x}_i) \\ (\mathbf{x}_1 \ \cdots \ \mathbf{x}_i \ \cdots \ \mathbf{x}_{N_P}) & \text{otherwise.} \end{cases} \tag{6.14}$$

When all the members have received the treatment, the population is updated and the next generation starts again at Step 2. The algorithm is thus run over all N_G generations. The parameter estimate is chosen as the member with the lowest value of $f(\mathbf{x})$ from the population of the final generation.

The Differential Evolution algorithm is implemented with the HestonDE.m function. The first part of the function creates the population of members and generates random uniform numbers outside the loop. In the mutation and recombination steps, the function verifies that the candidate (Pnew) falls within the range of acceptable parameter values. If not, a new candidate is created. The population is updated with the candidate, if applicable. At the last generation, the member with the lowest value of the FRFT objective function is returned as the parameter estimate. Note that, at the beginning of each population loop, the candidate Pnew is set so that it automatically violates the range of acceptable parameter values, which ensures that the whole loop is executed at least once.

```
function y = HestonDE(NG,NP,CR,F,Hi,Lo,S,...)
% Step1.  Generate the population of random parameters
P = [kappaL + (kappaU-kappaL)*rand(1,NP); ...
     thetaL + (thetaU-thetaL)*rand(1,NP); ...
```

```
     sigmaL + (sigmaU-sigmaL)*rand(1,NP); ...
        v0L + (   v0U-   v0L)*rand(1,NP); ...
       rhoL + (  rhoU-  rhoL)*rand(1,NP)];
% Generate the random numbers outside the loop
U = rand(5,NP,NG);
for k=1:NG
    for i=1:NP
        % Select the i-th member of the population
        P0 = P(:,i);
        Pnew = -ones(1,5);
        Condition = sum(Lo < Pnew & Pnew < Hi);
        while Condition < 5
            % Select random indices
            I = randperm(NP);
            I = I(find(I~=i));
            r = I(1:3);
            % The three distinct members
            Pr1 = P(:,r(1));
            Pr2 = P(:,r(2));
            Pr3 = P(:,r(3));
            R = randperm(5);
            Pnew = zeros(1,5);
            % Steps 2 and 3.  Mutation & recomb
            for j=1:5
                Ri = R(1);
                u = U(j,i,k);
                if u<=CR || j==Ri
                    Pnew(j) = Pr1(j) + F*(Pr2(j) - Pr3(j));
                else
                    Pnew(j) = P0(j);
                end
            end
            Condition = sum(Lo < Pnew & Pnew < Hi);
        end
        % Step 4.  Selection
        f0   = HestonObjFunFRFT(P0  ,...);
        fnew = HestonObjFunFRFT(Pnew,...);
        % Verify whether the candidate should replace
        if fnew < f0
            P(:,i) = Pnew;
        end
    end
end
for i=1:NP
    f(i) = HestonObjFunFRFT(P(:,i),...);
end
% Find the member with the lowest obj fun
J = find(f==min(f));
y = P(:,J)';
```

In the HestonObjFunFRFT.m function, we perform linear interpolation of the call prices using the LinearInterpolate.m function described in the previous section.

The C# code for the Differential Evolution algorithm is very similar to the Matlab code presented earlier, so we do not present it here. In the code, however, we need the followings functions for calculating random numbers, for random permutations, and for removing indices from a vector. The C# functions RandomNum() and RandomInt() generate random numbers and random integers, respectively.

```
private static readonly Random U = new Random();
private static readonly object sync = new object();
public static double RandomNum(double a,double b) {
    int divisor = 1000000000;
    lock(sync) { return a + (b-a)*U.Next(0,divisor)/
                divisor; } }
// Random integer in (a,b)
private static readonly Random U1 = new Random();
private static readonly object sync1 = new object();
public static int RandomInt(int a,int b) {
    lock(sync1) { return U1.Next(a,b); }}
```

The RandomPerm() function generates a random permutation of a vector of integers.

```
public static int[] RandomPerm(int[] a) {
    int N = a.Length;
    int[][] F = new int[N][];
    for(int i=0;i<=N-1;i++) F[i] = new int[2] { 0,0 };
    for(int j=0;j<=N-1;j++) {
        for(int i=0;i<=N-1;i++) {
            F[j][0] = RandomInt(0,100);
            F[j][1] = j; }
        }
    // Sort the F array w.r.t column 0
    int column = 0;
    Array.Sort(F,delegate(int[] w1,int[] w2)
        {return (w1[column] as IComparable).
         CompareTo(w2[column]);});
    int[] b = new int[N];
    for(int j=0;j<=N-1;j++) b[j] = F[j][1];
return b;}
```

Finally, the RemoveIndex() function creates a vector of integers with one of the indices removed.

```
public static int[] RemoveIndex(int[] a,int position) {
    int N = a.Length;
    int[] b = new int[N-1];
    if(position == 0) {
        for(int i=1;i<=N-1;i++) b[i-1] = a[i];}
    else if(position == N-1) {
        for(int i=0;i<=N-2;i++) b[i] = a[i]; }
    else {
        for(int i=0;i<=position-1;i++) b[i] = a[i];
        for(int i=position;i<=N-2;i++) b[i] = a[i+1]; }
return b;}
```

TABLE 6.4 Comparison of Estimation Methods

Estimation Method	IVMSE	$\hat{\kappa}$	$\hat{\theta}$	$\hat{\sigma}$	$\hat{v}_0$	$\hat{\rho}$	Estimation Time (sec)
FRFT	9.57×10^{-6}	1.6691	0.0932	0.9076	0.0339	−0.8013	1.88
DE	5.95×10^{-6}	1.6167	0.0969	0.9665	0.0345	−0.7734	120.36

The Differential Evolution algorithm is particularly useful when we have very poor starting values. This is because, even with poor values, the algorithm will converge to the global optimum, albeit at the requirement of many iterations. To illustrate, we run the HestonDE.m function on the S&P500 data used to create Table 6.1, and using the MSE loss function. Following Vollrath and Wendland (2009), we set the number of population parameters equal to 15 times the number of parameters so that $N_P = 75$, we set the crossover ratio to $CR = 0.5$, the mutation factor to $F = 0.8$, and the number of generations as $N_G = 200$. We use starting values equal to 1 for all parameters. We compare the DE parameter estimates to those obtained using the FRFT. The results are in Table 6.4.

As expected, the DE method is much slower than estimation using the FRFT. The DE parameter estimates, however, are more accurate since their IVMSE is smaller. Moreover, they are consistent with the estimates in Table 6.1.

MAXIMUM LIKELIHOOD ESTIMATION

When there exists a set of liquid and reliable market quotes of option prices or implied volatilities, then estimation through loss functions is feasible. If there are no such quotes, however, then alternate methods must be used. Atiya and Wall (2009) show how to obtain the maximum likelihood estimates of the physical parameters of the Heston model using a time series of historical stock prices. Recall that, under the risk-neutral measure, the log-stock price $x_t = \ln S_t$ and variance v_t follow the bivariate stochastic differential equation

$$\begin{aligned} dx_t &= \left(r - q - \frac{1}{2}v_t\right)dt + \sqrt{v_t}dW_{1,t} \\ dv_t &= \kappa(\theta - v_t)dt + \sigma\sqrt{v_t}dW_{2,t} \end{aligned} \tag{6.15}$$

with $E^{\mathbb{Q}}[dW_{1,t}dW_{2,t}] = \rho dt$. Since the Brownian motions are correlated normal random variables, the transition probability density for the joint log-stock price/variance process from time t to $t+1$ is bivariate normal

$$p(x_{t+1}, v_{t+1}|x_t, v_t) = \Phi_2(\boldsymbol{\mu}_{t+1}, \boldsymbol{\Sigma}_{t+1})$$

where $\Phi_2(\boldsymbol{\mu}_{t+1}, \boldsymbol{\Sigma}_{t+1})$ is the bivariate normal density with mean vector

$$\boldsymbol{\mu}_{t+1} = \begin{pmatrix} x_t + \left(r - q - \frac{1}{2}v_t\right)dt \\ v_t + \kappa(\theta - v_t)dt \end{pmatrix}$$

and covariance matrix

$$\boldsymbol{\Sigma}_{t+1} = v_t dt \begin{pmatrix} 1 & \rho\sigma \\ \rho\sigma & \sigma^2 \end{pmatrix}$$

and where dt is the time increment between t and $t+1$. Suppose we are given a time series of log-stock prices $x_1, x_2, \ldots, x_N$ observed at equal time increments dt. If the observations are daily, for example, then $dt = 1/252$. Atiya and Wall (2009) apply a filtering argument to show that the likelihood for the unobserved variances can be approximated from the likelihood of stock prices. The likelihood at time $t+1$, given a value v_t at time t, is

$$L_{t+1}(v_{t+1}) \propto d_t (ab_t)^{-1/4} e^{-2\sqrt{ab_t}} L_t \left(\sqrt{\frac{b_t}{a}} \right). \tag{6.16}$$

The log-likelihood is therefore

$$\ell_{t+1}(v_{t+1}) \propto \ln d_t - \frac{1}{4} \ln(ab_t) - 2\sqrt{ab_t} + \ell_t \left(\sqrt{\frac{b_t}{a}} \right). \tag{6.17}$$

These expressions use the following quantities, defined as Equations (14) through (16) in Atiya and Wall (2009)

$$\begin{aligned} a &= \frac{(\kappa')^2 + \rho\sigma\kappa' dt + \sigma^2 (dt)^2/4}{2\sigma^2(1-\rho^2)dt} \\ b_t &= \frac{(v_{t+1} - \alpha dt)^2 - 2\rho\sigma(v_{t+1} - \alpha dt)(\Delta x_{t+1} - \mu dt) + \sigma^2(\Delta x_{t+1} - \mu dt)^2}{2\sigma^2(1-\rho^2)dt} \\ d_t &= \frac{1}{D} \exp\left(\frac{(2\kappa' + \rho\sigma dt)(v_{t+1} - \alpha dt) - (2\rho\sigma\kappa' + \sigma^2 dt)(\Delta x_{t+1} - \mu dt)}{2\sigma^2(1-\rho^2)dt} \right) \end{aligned} \tag{6.18}$$

with $\mu = r - q$ the drift, $\Delta x_{t+1} = x_{t+1} - x_t$ the increment between log-stock prices, $\kappa' = 1 - \kappa dt$, $\alpha = \kappa\theta$, and $D = 2\pi\sigma\sqrt{1-\rho^2}dt$.

The likelihood Equation (6.16) depends also on v_{t+1}, through the terms b_t and d_t. To evaluate v_{t+1} from v_t, Atiya and Wall (2009) note that $v_t = \sqrt{b_t/a}$. Inverting this expression and applying the quadratic formula produces the solution

$$v_{t+1} = \sqrt{B^2 - C} - B \tag{6.19}$$

where

$$\begin{aligned} B &= -\alpha dt - \rho\sigma(\Delta x_{t+1} - \mu dt), \\ C &= (\alpha dt)^2 + 2\rho\sigma\alpha dt(\Delta x_{t+1} - \mu dt) + \sigma^2(\Delta x_{t+1} - \mu dt)^2 - 2v_t^2 a\sigma^2(1-\rho^2)dt. \end{aligned}$$

Hence, to evaluate the likelihood Equation (6.16) or the log-likelihood (6.17), we start with initial values $L_0(v_0)$ or $\ell_0(v_0)$. To evaluate $L_{t+1}(v_{t+1})$ or $\ell_{t+1}(v_{t+1})$ given $L_t(v_t)$ or $\ell_t(v_t)$, we first obtain v_{t+1} from (6.19). We then apply Equation (6.16) or

(6.17). We continue until time T, at which time we have $L_T(v_T)$ or $\ell_T(v_T)$, to which we apply an optimization routine to find the maximum. The initial value suggested by Atiya and Wall (2009) is $L_0(v_0) = e^{-v_0}$, where v_0 is the initial variance parameter from the Heston model.

The likelihood function is implemented using the Matlab function LikelihoodAW.m. The function returns the negative of the likelihood or log-likelihood, since fmincon.m is designed for minimization.

```
function [y v] = LikelihoodAW(param,x,r,q,dt,method);
alpha = kappa*theta;
beta  = kappa;
v(1)  = v0;
if method==1
    L(1) = exp(-v(1));      % Construct Likelihood
elseif method==2
    L(1) = -v(1);           % Construct log-likelihood
end
% Construction the likelihood for time t = 1 through t = T
for t=1:T-1
    % Stock price increment
    dx  = x(t+1) - x(t);
    % Equations (31), (32), and (30)
    B = -alpha*dt - rho*sigma*(dx-mu*dt);
    C = alpha^2*dt^2 + 2*rho*sigma*alpha*dt*(dx-mu*dt) + ...;
    % Equation (30) to update the variance
    if B^2 - C > 0;
        v(t+1) = sqrt(B^2 - C) - B;
    else
        % If v(t+1) is imaginary use Equation (33)
        bt = ((v(t)-alpha*dt)^2 - 2*rho*sigma* ...;
        if bt/a > 0
            v(t+1) = sqrt(bt/a);
        else
            % If v(t+1) is negative take previous value
            v(t+1) = v(t);
        end
    end
    % Equation (15) and (16)
    bt = ((v(t+1)-alpha*dt)^2 - 2*rho*sigma* ...;
    x1 = ((2*betap+rho*sigma*dt)*(v(t+1)-alpha*dt) ...;
    x2 = -2*sqrt(a*bt);
    % Combined exponent for Equation (34)
    E = exp(x1 + x2) / D;
    if method==1
        % Equation (34) for the likelihood L(t+1)
        L(t+1) = (a*bt)^(-1/4) * E * L(t);
    elseif method==2
        % Alternatively, use the log-likelihood
        L(t+1) = -1/4*log(a*bt) + x1 + x2 -log(D) + L(t);
    end
end
% Negative likelihood is the last term.
y = -real(L(T));
```

The C# code to implement the Atiya and Wall (2009) likelihood function is very similar and is not presented here.

To illustrate, we continue with the example involving the S&P500 Index. Recall that the example involved SPY option quotes on April 13, 2012, with maturities of 45, 98, 261, and 348 days and seven strikes, running from 120 to 150 in increments of 5. The MSE loss function estimates are calculated first. To compare the performance of Atiya and Wall's (2009) method we obtain, for each maturity separately, the parameter MLEs by minimizing the log-likelihood in Equation (6.17). We obtain implied volatilities using the set of parameter estimates, and repeat for the remaining maturities. This following code obtains both sets of estimates.

```
T = [45 98 261 348]./365;
% Obtain the estimates w option prices and loss functions
[true feval] = fmincon(@(p) HestonObjFun(p,...),start,...);
% Choose the number of days to use in the MLE.
% Run again with t>1
t = 1;
% Historical stock prices.  Use D days before May 7, 2010.
D = T(t)*365;
S = xlsread('SPY Prices.xls', 'table',['G2:G' num2str(D+1)]);
% Put oldest prices first and calculate log prices
S = flipud(S);
x = log(S);
% Obtain the estimates using Atiya and Wall MLE
param = fmincon(@(p) LikelihoodAW(p,...),start,...);
```

We then obtain option prices and implied volatilities from each set of parameters, along with the IVRMSE error for each maturity.

```
for t=1:NT
    for k=1:NK
        PriceAW(k,t) = HestonPriceGaussLaguerre(K(k),T(t)...);
        IVAW(k,t) = BisecBSIV(K(k),T(t),PriceAW(k,t),...);
        Error(k,t) = abs(IVAW(k,t) - MktIV(k,t))/
                     MktIV(k,t)*100;
    IVRMSE(t) = sum(Error(:,t))/N(t);
end
IVRMSE = sum(IVRMSE)/NK;
```

The parameter estimates are presented in Table 6.5 and indicate variability in the set of parameter estimates, depending on the length of the time series used to obtain the MLEs.

Figure 6.2 plots the implied volatilities generated with the 98-day maturity parameter estimates.

The plots of implied volatilities using MLEs from the other time series of stock prices are not as attractive as they illustrate a much poorer fit to the market implied volatilities. Finally, the results in Table 6.5 and Figure 6.2 are for illustrative

TABLE 6.5 MLE and Loss Function Estimates

Days	Method	$\hat{\kappa}$	$\hat{\theta}$	$\hat{\sigma}$	$\hat{v}_0$	$\hat{\rho}$	IVRMSE
45	Atiya-Wall	13.1798	0.0118	1.9961	0.0011	−0.9829	0.007
98	Atiya-Wall	10.6384	0.0222	1.0586	0.0325	−0.9057	0.002
261	Atiya-Wall	3.4827	0.0763	0.7690	0.0007	−0.9631	0.001
348	Atiya-Wall	15.5095	0.0207	0.9444	0.0260	0.0460	0.003
All	Loss Function	1.7704	0.0927	0.9812	0.0344	−0.7791	

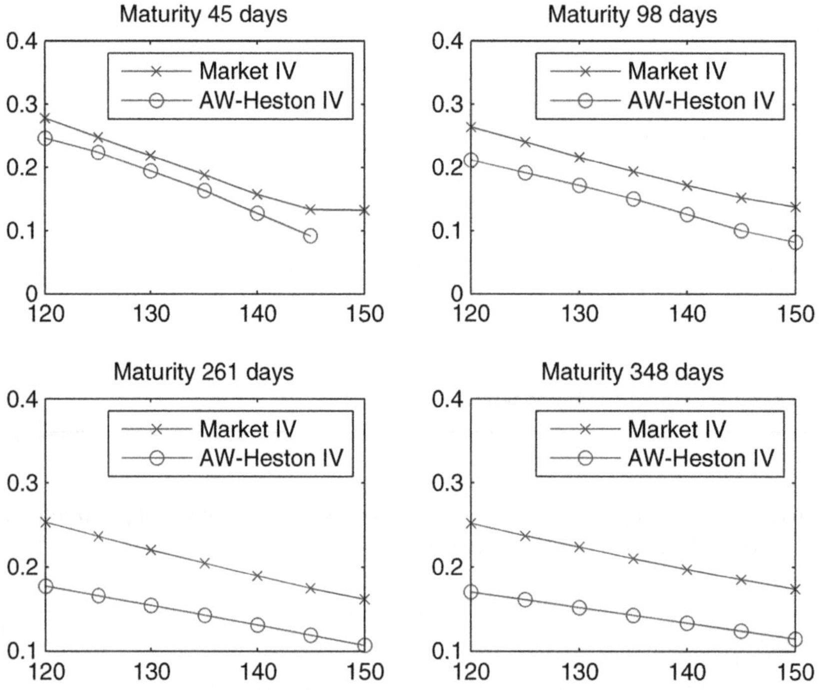

FIGURE 6.2 Implied Volatilities from MLE and Loss Function Estimates

purposes only. Indeed, if a set of market option prices is available, then parameter estimation can be done using loss functions and the MLE method of Atiya and Wall (2009) is not needed.

RISK-NEUTRAL DENSITY AND ARBITRAGE-FREE VOLATILITY SURFACE

With estimated parameters, the question arises whether the volatility surface generated from the parameter values is able to produces price that are arbitrage-free. An example of an implied volatility surface generated by the model appeared in Figure 2.9. Arbitrage can be present along both dimensions of the volatility surface:

strikes and maturities. The absence of arbitrage across strikes is reflected in prices of butterfly spreads that are non-negative. A butterfly spread is a portfolio with three positions: long one call at strike $K - dK$, long another call at strike $K + dK$, and short two calls each struck at K. It is easy to show that as $dK \to 0$ the value of $1/dK^2$ units of the portfolio converges to the discounted risk-neutral density (RND) of Breeden and Litzenberger (1978)

$$e^{-r\tau} f_{S_T}(S) = \left. \frac{\partial^2 C(K)}{\partial K^2} \right|_{K=S} \tag{6.20}$$

where $C(K)$ is the price of a call struck at K generated from the implied volatility, and $f_{S_T}(S)$ is the RND. If we further let the time to maturity expire, $\tau \to 0$, the portfolio value converges to the Dirac delta function, as expected, since that corresponds to a degenerate density at maturity.[1] One convenient way to check for the absence of arbitrage across strikes is to obtain $f_{S_T}(S)$ across a wide domain, and ensure that the following properties hold:

Non-negativity property. The RND must be such that $f_{S_T}(S) \geq 0$ for all $S \geq 0$.

Integrability property. The RND must integrate to unity

$$\int_0^\infty f_{S_T}(S) dS = 1.$$

Martingale property. The RND must be able to recover the market prices of calls.

$$\int_0^\infty \max(S - K, 0) f_{S_T}(S) dS = e^{r\tau} C(K, \tau)$$

where $C(K, \tau)$ is the market price of a call struck at K with maturity $\tau = T - t$. See Brunner and Hafner (2003) and Carr (2004). The first two properties ensure that the RND is a density function. The third property is sometimes expressed with $K = 0$, in which case the left-hand side becomes $E^{\mathbb{Q}}[S_T] = S_t e^{r(T-t)} = F_{t,T}$, where $F_{t,T}$ is the forward price. Hence, the third property is sometimes verified in terms of the ability of the RND to recover forward prices rather than call prices, and as such, it is sometimes called the forward property.

To verify whether a set of estimated parameters $\hat{\Theta}$ produces call prices that are free of arbitrage across strikes for a given maturity, we use these estimates to generate a set of Heston (1993) call prices at a finely spaced grid of strikes. We then use central finite differences to approximate the second derivative in Equation (6.20), generate the RND, and verify whether the earlier properties hold. Jondeau et al. (2006), however, caution that the RND estimated with finite differences can be inaccurate and unstable, since even small pricing errors are amplified when finite differences are applied twice. To ensure that the prices are very accurate, it is preferable to use an integration method that uses many abscissas, such as the Gauss-Legendre

[1] If instead we use $1/dK$ units of the portfolio, then convergence is to an Arrow-Debreu security rather than to the Dirac delta function.

multi-domain integration rule, which was covered in Chapter 5. Finite difference approximations to first- and second-order derivatives will be covered in Chapter 10.

The Matlab function ExtractRND.m applies central differences to find the RND. It accepts as inputs a vector of finely spaced strikes and call prices, and returns the same vector of strikes but with four endpoints removed and the value of the RND at each strike.

```
function [RND, K2] = ExtractRND(K,CallPrice)
% Calculate the first derivatives of calls w.r.t. strike K.
for i=2:length(K)-1
    dK = K(i+1) - K(i-1);
    dC = CallPrice(i+1) - CallPrice(i-1);
    dCdK(i-1) = dC/dK;
end
% Calculate the risk neutral density by central finite
% differences.
for i=2:length(dCdK)-1;
    dK  = K(i+1) - K(i-1);
    dC2 = dCdK(i+1) - dCdK(i-1);
    RND(i-1) = dC2/dK;
end
K2 = K(3:end-2);
```

We use the RMSE parameter estimates in the second row of Table 6.1 to illustrate risk neutral density estimation in the Heston (1993) model. The following code is used to generate the RNDs for the four maturities. The call prices are obtained using multi-domain integration using a domain of $A = (0, 500)$ divided into 50 subdomains along with a strike increment of $dK = 0.5$. The strike range increases with increasing maturity, to allow for more dispersion in the RND at higher maturities. The code also uses the Matlab function trapz() to integrate each RND, and calculates the number of negative values of each RND, thus providing a check of the first two properties. The code makes use of Matlab cells, to allow for varying strike ranges in each maturity.

```
T = [45 98 261 348]./365;
NT = length(T);
% RMSE parameters
kappa =  8.9931;
theta =  0.0571;
sigma =  2.0000;
v0    =  0.0405;
rho   = -0.8038;
% Multi-domain integration rule settings
lo = 1e-10;  hi = 500;
Ndomains = 50 ;
dA = (hi - lo)/Ndomains;
A = [lo:dA:hi];
tol = 1e-8;
dK = 0.5;
```

```
% Strike increment and ranges
dK = 0.5;
K{1} = 90:dK:170;
K{2} = 80:dK:180;
K{3} = 40:dK:220;
K{4} = 20:dK:240;
% Extract the RND, integration domain, area, negative values
for t=1:NT;
    NK = length(K{t});
    for k=1:NK;
        [C{t}(k) H(k) N{t}(k)] = HestonPriceGaussLegendreMD
                                  (K{t}(k),T(t),...);
    end
    Domain{t} = max(H);
    [RND{t} ST{t}] = ExtractRND(K{t},C{t});
    Area(t) = trapz(RND{t})*dK;
    Zero(t) = length(find(RND{t}<0));
end
```

The second part of the code uses the RND to recover the market prices of the calls and verify the third property. This is done using the trapezoidal rule, with the built-in Matlab function trapz.m.

```
MktStrike = [120,125,130,135,140,145,150];
NK = length(MktStrike);
for t=1:NT
    for k=1:NK
        Payoff = max(ST{t} - MktStrike(k), 0);
        RNDCall(k,t) = trapz(Payoff.*RND{t}) * dK * exp(-rf*T(t));
    end
end
error = sum(sum(MktPrice - RNDCall));
```

Table 6.6 contains the results of the RND estimates, including the area under each RND, and the upper integration limit and number of integration points calculated by the multi-domain integration method.

All RNDs integrate to unity approximately and have no negative values, which suggest that the first two properties hold. The upper integration limit decreases with increasing maturity, corroborating the observation in Chapter 5 that integrands with

TABLE 6.6 Results of the RND Estimation

Maturity	Area	Upper Limit	# Points
45	0.9959	470	1,536
98	0.9915	290	960
261	0.9977	150	512
348	0.9996	120	416

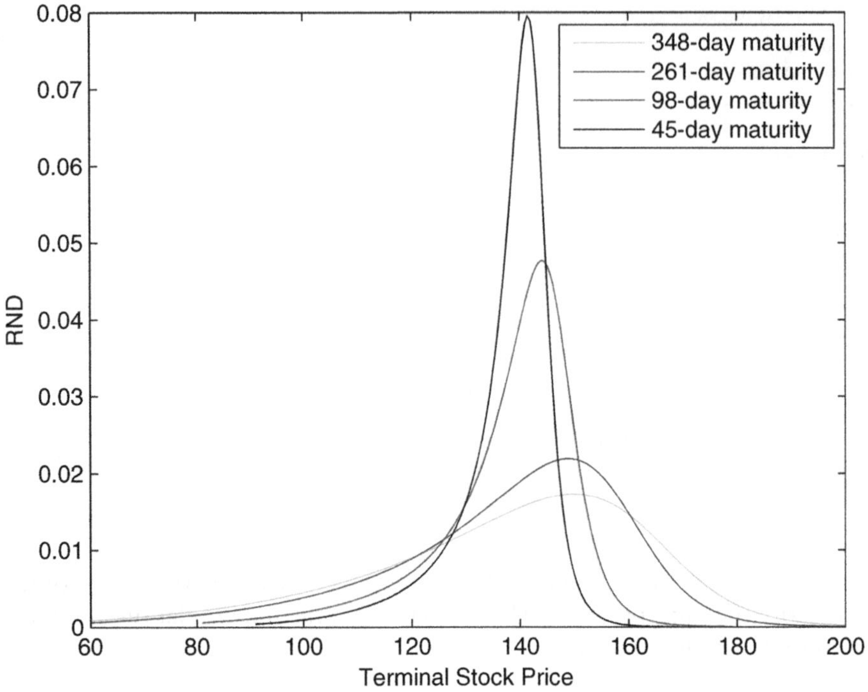

FIGURE 6.3 RNDs for the S&P500 Data

longer maturities are better behaved. To verify the third property, we note that the RND is also able to recover the market prices of the calls fairly well, but these are not shown here to conserve space.

The RNDs of the four maturities are plotted in Figure 6.3. These RNDs behave as expected. In particular, the RNDs for the longer maturities are more spread out than those for the short maturities, reflecting increasing market uncertainty about future prices with increasing maturity. Note also the negative skew in each density, induced by the negative correlation used to generate them.

The parameter estimates used to generate Figure 6.3 were those of the RMSE loss function from the second row of Table 6.1. The RNDs generated using the MSE and IVMSE parameters from Table 6.1 will produce similar results. The Christoffersen et al. (2009) parameters, however, will produce RNDs with a more pronounced skew, owing to the extreme value of the correlation parameter, $\rho = -0.9921$.

The RND is a convenient tool for verifying the absence of arbitrage across strikes, but since it is designed for a single maturity, it cannot verify the absence of arbitrage across maturities. As explained by Carr and Madan (2005), ensuring the absence of calendar arbitrage usually involves verifying that calendar spreads have a non-negative price. Kahalé (2004) and Fengler (2009) show that a test of calendar arbitrage can be formulated in terms of the total implied variance $v^2(K, \tau_i) = IV^2(K, \tau_i) \times \tau_i$, where $IV(K, \tau_i)$ is the implied volatility corresponding to strike K and maturity $\tau_i = T_i - t$. The test stipulates that there is no calendar arbitrage if $v^2(K, \tau_i)$ is a strictly increasing function of τ_i.

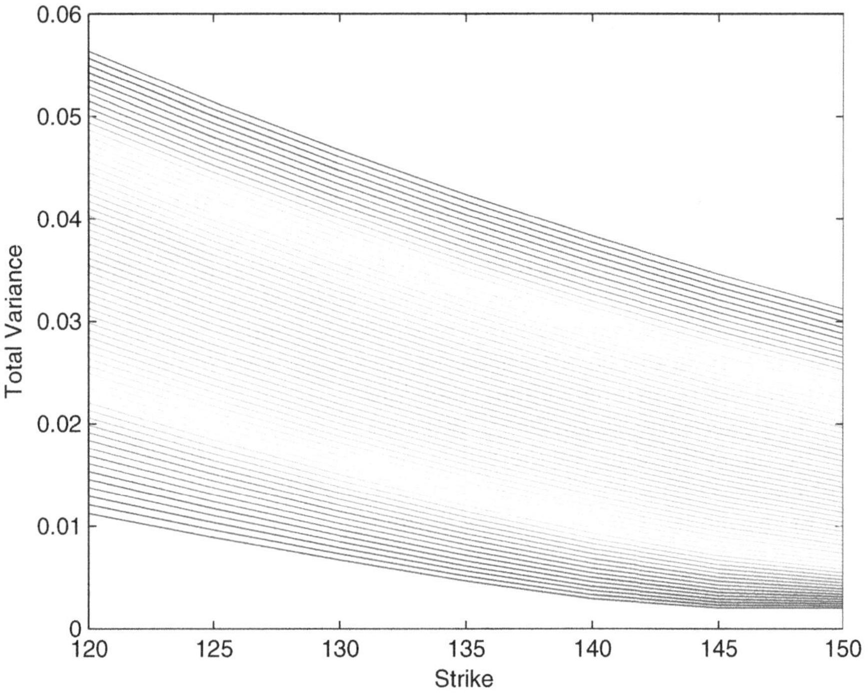

FIGURE 6.4 Total Variance for the S&P500 Data

Continuing with the S&P500 example and the RMSE parameter estimates from Table 6.1, Figure 6.4 plots the total variance for maturities ranging from 45 to 360 days, in 5-day increments. The lines change in color as the maturity increases, from red at the shortest maturities, to yellow, green, and finally blue at the long maturities. The figure clearly shows increasing monotonic total variance with increasing maturity, indicating the absence of calendar arbitrage in the volatility surface generated with the RMSE parameters.

CONCLUSION

In this chapter, we have presented methods to estimate the parameters of the Heston model. Estimation by loss functions is the most popular method to estimate risk-neutral parameters, but it requires a set of market quotes of implied volatilities or prices. The maximum likelihood estimation proposed by Atiya and Wall (2009) is relatively straightforward to implement, but is designed for the Heston model only. This is contrary to other methods that are applicable to a wide range of stochastic volatility models, such as that of Aït-Sahalia and Kimmel (2007). The differential evolution algorithm is able to produce precise estimates, but at the expense of increased computation time. The risk-neutral density and the total variance can be used to verify whether option prices generated from a set estimated parameters admit arbitrage. Finally, the estimation examples in this chapter all use four maturities only and show a good fit of the model to market data. We caution, however, that the Heston (1993) model is usually unable to fit the implied volatility surface over a large range of maturities.[2]

A number of researchers have developed alternate methods to estimate the parameters of diffusions such as those specified by the Heston model. The literature is rich and varied and includes methods for univariate processes, as in Aït-Sahalia (2002), as well as for multivariate processes, as in Singleton (2001). The methods encompass estimation by maximum likelihood (Aït-Sahalia and Kimmel, 2007), estimation by the method of moments (Chernov and Ghysels, 2000), Bayesian estimation (Jones, 2003), and particle filtering (Christoffersen et al., 2010, Johannes et al., 2009). In some studies, returns data are employed exclusively, as in Pan (2002), and sometimes a combination of returns data and option prices is employed, as in Eraker (2004). In this chapter, however, we bypass these methods altogether and focus mostly on estimation with loss functions.

All of the pricing methods covered in this book so far have used the closed-form approach to obtain the value of the call in the Heston model. Another popular method of option valuation is through simulation of the stock price and volatility processes of the model. One advantage of this approach is that these simulated quantities can be used in the algorithm of Longstaff and Schwartz (2001) to obtain the prices of American options. In response, a number of researchers have adapted existing simulation schemes to the Heston model, and have created new schemes designed exclusively for the model. We deal with some of these schemes in the next chapter.

[2]We thank Jim Gatheral for this observation.

CHAPTER 7

Simulation in the Heston Model

Abstract

All the methods we have encountered so far for pricing options under the Heston model have been analytic, in the sense that the option price is expressed in closed-form and involves one or more complex integrals that must be evaluated numerically. This is one standard approach for many option pricing methodologies. Another approach is to use simulation, which we describe in this chapter.

Monte Carlo simulation in the context of the Heston model refers to a set of techniques to generate artificial time series of the stock price and variance over time, from which option prices can be derived. There are several choices available in this regard. The first choice is to apply a standard method such as the Euler, Milstein, or implicit Milstein scheme, as described by Gatheral (2006) and Kahl and Jäckel (2006), for example. The advantage of these schemes is that they are easy to understand, and their convergence properties are well-known. The other choice is to use a method that is better suited, or that is specifically designed for the model. These methods include the IJK scheme of Kahl and Jäckel (2006), the quadratic-exponential scheme of Andersen (2008), the transformed volatility scheme of Zhu (2010), the scheme of Alfonsi (2010), or the moment-matching scheme of Andersen and Brotherton-Ratcliffe (2005). These schemes are designed to have faster convergence to the true option price, and in some cases, to also avoid the negative variances that can sometimes be generated from standard methods. These and other schemes are reviewed by Van Haastrecht and Pelsser (2010).

GENERAL SETUP

Recall that the stock price and its variance are driven by the following bivariate system of stochastic differential equations (SDE)

$$
\begin{aligned}
dS_t &= (r-q)S_t dt + \sqrt{v_t} S_t dW_{1,t} \\
dv_t &= \kappa(\theta - v_t)dt + \sigma\sqrt{v_t} dW_{2,t}
\end{aligned}
\tag{7.1}
$$

where $E[dW_{1,t}dW_{2,t}] = \rho dt$. The processes in Equation (7.1) are specified in continuous time. Simulation, however, is done at discrete time steps. Hence, the first step in a simulation scheme is usually to approximate a continuous-time process with a discrete time process, a task known as discretization. The stock price and its volatility can each be written in the general form

$$dX_t = \mu(X_t, t)dt + \sigma(X_t, t)dW_t \tag{7.2}$$

where W_t is Brownian motion. We simulate X_t over the time interval $[0, \tau]$, which we assume to be divided into N points as $0 = t_1 < t_2 < \cdots < t_N = \tau$, where the time increments are equally spaced with width dt. Equally spaced time increments makes the notation convenient, because it allows us to write $t_i - t_{i-1}$ as simply dt for all $i = 2, \ldots, N$. All the results derived with equally spaced increments are easily generalized to unequal spacing, however. Integrating dX_t from t to $t + dt$ produces

$$X_{t+dt} = X_t + \int_t^{t+dt} \mu(X_u, u)du + \int_t^{t+dt} \sigma(X_u, u)dW_u. \tag{7.3}$$

Equation (7.3) is the starting point for discretization. The idea is that at time t the value of X_t is known, and we wish to obtain the next value X_{t+dt} at time $t + dt$.

To obtain the price of a European option using simulation in the Heston model, we first simulate the bivariate process (S_t, v_t) and generate N paths from $t = 0$ to $t = \tau$. We then retain the last stock price from each stock price path and obtain the payoff of the European option at expiry, take the average over all stock price paths and discount back to time zero. Hence, for example, the call and put price $C(K)$ and $P(K)$ are

$$\begin{aligned} C(K) &= e^{-r\tau}\frac{1}{N}\sum_{i=1}^{N}\max(0, S_T^{(i)} - K) \\ P(K) &= e^{-r\tau}\frac{1}{N}\sum_{i=1}^{N}\max(0, K - S_T^{(i)}) \end{aligned} \tag{7.4}$$

where $S_T^{(i)}$ is the terminal stock price generated by the ith stock price path, $i = 1, \ldots, N$. This requires that we have estimates of the parameters $\kappa, \theta, \sigma, v_0$, and ρ.

There are two issues that arise when simulating the bivariate process (S_t, v_t). The first is the slow speed of convergence. The second, more serious issue, is that since v_t follows a CIR process, many simulation schemes, including the Euler and Milstein schemes, will generate negative values for v_t, even if the Feller condition $2\kappa\theta > \sigma^2$ is met. This is because the Feller condition is valid for continuous time processes, but simulation is done in discrete time and serves only as an approximation to continuous time processes.

The simplest way to deal with negative variances is to override them as they arise. There are at least two ways to do this

- In the *full truncation scheme*, a negative value for v_t is floored at zero. Hence, v_t is replaced by $v_t^+ = \max(0, v_t)$ everywhere in the discretization.
- In the *reflection scheme*, a negative value for v_t is reflected with $-v_t$. Hence, v_t is replaced by $|v_t|$ everywhere in the discretization.

The disadvantage of the full truncation scheme is that it creates zero variances, which is unrealistic because stock prices never exhibit zero variance.

The disadvantage of the reflection scheme is that it reflects a large negative variance to a large positive variance. Hence, it transforms realizations of low volatility into high volatility.

Another way to deal with negative simulated values of v_t is to devise simulation schemes for v_t that do not produce negative values in the first place. Much of the research on simulating the CIR variance process in the Heston model is devoted to this approach. Yet another way is to simulate $\ln v_t$ or $\sqrt{v_t}$, and then exponentiate or square the result. For the stock price, we can simulate S_t itself, but we will see in this chapter that a better approach is to simulate the log price $x_t = \ln S_t$ instead, and then exponentiate.

All of the simulation schemes for the Heston model contain the same basic steps. First, two independent standard normal random variables are generated, and then made dependent by applying Cholesky decomposition. These are multiplied by $\sqrt{dt}$ to make them proxy Brownian motion increments. Second, we obtain the updated value v_{t+dt}. Third, we obtain the updated value S_{t+dt} (or x_{t+dt}).

Step 0. Initialize S_0 to the spot price (or x_0 to the log spot price), and initialize v_0 to the current variance parameter.

Step 1. Generate two independent random variables Z_1 and Z_2, and define $Z_V = Z_1$ and $Z_S = \rho Z_V + \sqrt{1-\rho^2}Z_2$. Proxy the Brownian motion by $dW_{1,t} = \sqrt{dt}Z_S$ and $dW_{2,t} = \sqrt{dt}Z_V$.

Step 2. Obtain the updated value v_{t+dt}.

Step 3. Given v_{t+dt}, obtain the updated value S_{t+dt} (or x_{t+dt}) and return to Step 1.

Note that Z_V and Z_S are constructed so that $E[Z_V] = E[Z_S] = 0$, and so that $E[Z_V Z_S] = \rho E[Z_1^2] + \sqrt{1-\rho^2}E[Z_1 Z_2] = \rho$, as required.

In this chapter, we describe some common discretization schemes for (S_t, v_t). We assume that the time grid is discretized using time increments that are equally spaced with width dt.

EULER SCHEME

The simplest way to discretize the process in Equation (7.3) is to use Euler discretization. This is equivalent to approximating the integrals using the left-point rule. The first integral is approximated as the product of the integrand at time t and the integration domain dt

$$\int_t^{t+dt} \mu(X_u, u)du \approx \mu(X_t, t)\int_t^{t+dt} du = \mu(X_t, t)dt.$$

We use the left-point rule since at time t the value $\mu(X_t, t)$ is known. The right-point rule would require that $\mu(X_{t+dt}, t+dt)$ be known at time t. The second integral is approximated as

$$\int_t^{t+dt} \sigma(X_u, u)du \approx \sigma(X_t, t)$$

$$\int_t^{t+dt} dW_u = \sigma(X_t, t)(W_{t+dt} - W_t) \stackrel{d}{=} \sigma(X_t, t)\sqrt{dt}Z$$

since $W_{t+dt} - W_t$ and $\sqrt{dt}Z$ are identical in distribution, where Z is a standard normal variable. Hence, Euler discretization of Equation (7.3) is

$$X_{t+dt} = X_t + \mu(X_t, t)dt + \sigma(X_t, t)\sqrt{dt}Z. \tag{7.5}$$

In the next subsections, we illustrate Euler discretization of the Heston model.

Euler Scheme for the Variance

The SDE for v_t in Equation (7.1) written in the form of (7.3) is

$$v_{t+dt} = v_t + \int_t^{t+dt} \kappa(\theta - v_u)du + \int_t^{t+dt} \sigma\sqrt{v_u}dW_u. \tag{7.6}$$

In accordance with Equation (7.5), Euler discretization approximates the integrals in (7.6) as

$$\begin{aligned}
&\int_t^{t+dt} \kappa(\theta - v_u)du \approx \kappa(\theta - v_t)dt \\
&\int_t^{t+dt} \sigma\sqrt{v_u}dW_{2,u} \approx \sigma\sqrt{v_t}(W_{t+dt} - W_t) \stackrel{d}{=} \sigma\sqrt{v_t}\sqrt{dt}Z_V.
\end{aligned} \tag{7.7}$$

This implies that Euler discretization for the variance is

$$v_{t+dt} = v_t + \kappa(\theta - v_t)dt + \sigma\sqrt{v_t}\sqrt{dt}Z_V. \tag{7.8}$$

It is well-known that the probability of generating a negative value for v_{t+dt} is

$$\Pr(v_{t+dt} < 0) = \Phi\left(\frac{-(1-\kappa dt)\,v_t - \kappa\theta dt}{\sigma\sqrt{v_t}\sqrt{dt}}\right)$$

where $\Phi(x)$ denotes the standard normal cumulative distribution function, evaluated at x. Hence, when we apply Euler discretization to the variance, we must also apply the full truncation scheme or the reflection scheme to override any negative values that are generated in the simulation.

Euler Scheme for the Stock Price

There are two common approaches to simulating the stock price. We can either simulate S_t directly, or we can simulate $\ln S_t$ and then exponentiate. The SDE for S_t in Equation (7.3) can be written in integral form as

$$S_{t+dt} = S_t + (r-q)\int_t^{t+dt} S_u du + \int_t^{t+dt} \sqrt{v_u}S_u dW_u.$$

Applying Equation (7.5), Euler discretization approximates the integrals as

$$\int_t^{t+dt} S_u du \approx S_t dt$$

$$\int_t^{t+dt} \sqrt{v_u} S_u dW_{1,u} \approx \sqrt{v_t} S_t (W_{t+dt} - W_t) \stackrel{d}{=} \sqrt{v_t} S_t \sqrt{dt} Z_S.$$

So Euler discretization of the stock price is

$$S_{t+dt} = S_t + (r-q)S_t dt + \sqrt{v_t} S_t \sqrt{dt} Z_S. \tag{7.9}$$

To simulate the log stock price, we apply Itō's lemma to the first equation in Equation (7.1). Hence, $\ln S_t$ follows the SDE

$$d\ln S_t = \left(r - q - \frac{1}{2}v_t\right) dt + \sqrt{v_t} dW_{1,t}$$

or in integral form

$$\ln S_{t+dt} = \ln S_t + \int_t^{t+dt} \left(r - q - \frac{1}{2}v_u\right) du + \int_t^{t+dt} \sqrt{v_u} dW_{1,u}. \tag{7.10}$$

Euler discretization of the process for $\ln S_t$ is, thus,

$$\begin{aligned} \ln S_{t+dt} &\approx \ln S_t + \left(r - q - \frac{1}{2}v_t\right) dt + \sqrt{v_t}(W_{1,t+dt} - W_{1,t}) \\ &= \ln S_t + \left(r - q - \frac{1}{2}v_t\right) dt + \sqrt{v_t}\sqrt{dt} Z_S. \end{aligned} \tag{7.11}$$

Euler discretization of S_t is obtained by exponentiation of Equation (7.11)

$$S_{t+dt} = S_t \exp\left(\left(r - q - \frac{1}{2}v_t\right) dt + \sqrt{v_t}\sqrt{dt} Z_S\right). \tag{7.12}$$

Again, to avoid negative variances we must apply the full truncation or reflection scheme by replacing v_t everywhere with v_t^+ or with $|v_t|$.

To implement Euler simulation we start with initial values S_0 (or $x_0 = \ln S_0$) for the stock price and v_0 for the variance. Given the values (S_t, v_t), we obtain v_{t+dt} from Equation (7.8), and we obtain S_{t+dt} from either (7.9) or (7.12).

MILSTEIN SCHEME

This scheme is described in Glasserman (2003) and in Kloeden and Platen (1992) for general processes, and in Kahl and Jäckel (2006) for stochastic volatility models. For the Heston model, the coefficients in Equation (7.2) depend on X_t only, and do not depend on t directly. Hence, for simplicity, we can assume that the stock price and variance are driven by the SDE

$$\begin{aligned} dX_t &= \mu(X_t)dt + \sigma(X_t)dW_t \\ &= \mu_t dt + \sigma_t dW_t. \end{aligned}$$

In integral form

$$X_{t+dt} = X_t + \int_t^{t+dt} \mu_s ds + \int_t^{t+dt} \sigma_s dW_s. \tag{7.13}$$

The idea behind the Milstein scheme is that the accuracy of the discretization can be increased by expanding the coefficients $\mu_t = \mu(X_t)$ and $\sigma_t = \sigma(X_t)$ via Itō's lemma. This is sensible since the coefficients are also functions of X_t. Indeed, we can apply Itō's Lemma to the functions μ_t and σ_t as we would for any differentiable function of X_t. By Itō's lemma, then, the coefficients follow the SDEs

$$\begin{aligned} d\mu_t &= \left(\mu'_t\mu_t + \frac{1}{2}\mu''_t\sigma_t^2\right) dt + (\mu'_t\sigma_t)dW_t \\ d\sigma_t &= \left(\sigma'_t\mu_t + \frac{1}{2}\sigma''_t\sigma_t^2\right) dt + (\sigma'_t\sigma_t)dW_t \end{aligned}$$

where the prime refers to differentiation in X and where the derivatives in t are zero because in the Heston model μ_t and σ_t have no direct dependence on t. The integral form of the coefficients at time s (with $t < s < t + dt$) is

$$\begin{aligned} \mu_s &= \mu_t + \int_t^s \left(\mu'_u\mu_u + \frac{1}{2}\mu''_u\sigma_u^2\right) du + \int_t^s (\mu'_u\sigma_u)dW_u \\ \sigma_s &= \sigma_t + \int_t^s \left(\sigma'_u\mu_u + \frac{1}{2}\sigma''_u\sigma_u^2\right) du + \int_t^s (\sigma'_u\sigma_u)dW_u. \end{aligned}$$

Substitute for μ_s and σ_s inside the integrals of Equation (7.13) to produce

$$\begin{aligned} X_{t+dt} = X_t &+ \int_t^{t+dt} \left(\mu_t + \int_t^s \left(\mu'_u\mu_u + \frac{1}{2}\mu''_u\sigma_u^2\right) du + \int_t^s (\mu'_u\sigma_u)dW_u\right) ds \\ &+ \int_t^{t+dt} \left(\sigma_t + \int_t^s \left(\sigma'_u\mu_u + \frac{1}{2}\sigma''_u\sigma_u^2\right) du + \int_t^s (\sigma'_u\sigma_u)dW_u\right) dW_s. \end{aligned} \tag{7.14}$$

The differentials higher than order one are $dsdu = O(dt^2)$ and $dsdW_u = O(dt^{3/2})$, and are ignored. The term involving $dW_u dW_s$ is retained since it is $O(dt)$, of order one. This implies that (7.14) simplifies to

$$X_{t+dt} = X_t + \mu_t \int_t^{t+dt} ds + \sigma_t \int_t^{t+dt} dW_s + \int_t^{t+dt} \int_t^s (\sigma'_u\sigma_u)dW_u dW_s. \tag{7.15}$$

Apply Euler discretization to the last term in (7.15) to obtain

$$\begin{aligned}\int_t^{t+dt}\int_t^s (\sigma_u'\sigma_u)dW_u dW_s &\approx \sigma_t'\sigma_t\int_t^{t+dt}\int_t^s dW_u dW_s = \sigma_t'\sigma_t\int_t^{t+dt}(W_s - W_t)dW_s \\ &= \sigma_t'\sigma_t\left(\int_t^{t+dt} W_s dW_s - W_t W_{t+dt} + W_t^2\right).\end{aligned} \tag{7.16}$$

To solve the remaining integral in (7.16), define $dY_t = W_t dW_t$. Using Itō's lemma, it is easy to show that Y_t has the solution $Y_t = \frac{1}{2}W_t^2 - \frac{1}{2}t$. Indeed, we have $\partial Y/\partial t = -\frac{1}{2}$, $\partial Y/\partial W = W$ and $\partial^2 Y/\partial W^2 = 1$, so that

$$dY_t = \left(-\frac{1}{2} + 0 + \frac{1}{2}\times 1\times 1\right)dt + (W_t \times 1)dW_t = W_t dW_t.$$

Applying this result, we can write

$$\int_t^{t+dt} W_s dW_s = Y_{t+dt} - Y_t = \frac{1}{2}W_{t+dt}^2 - \frac{1}{2}W_t^2 - \frac{1}{2}dt. \tag{7.17}$$

Substitute back into (7.16) to obtain

$$\begin{aligned}\int_t^{t+dt}\int_t^s (\sigma_u'\sigma_u)dW_u dW_s &\approx \frac{1}{2}\sigma_t'\sigma_t[(W_{t+dt} - W_t)^2 - dt] \\ &= \frac{1}{2}\sigma_t'\sigma_t[(\Delta W_t)^2 - dt]\end{aligned} \tag{7.18}$$

where $\Delta W_t = W_{t+dt} - W_t$, which is equal in distribution to $\sqrt{dt}Z$ with Z distributed as standard normal. Combining Equations (7.15) and (7.18), the general form of Milstein discretization is, therefore,

$$X_{t+dt} = X_t + \mu_t dt + \sigma_t\sqrt{dt}Z + \frac{1}{2}\sigma_t'\sigma_t dt(Z^2 - 1). \tag{7.19}$$

Hence, Milstein discretization of dX_t in Equation (7.19) is identical to Euler discretization in (7.5), except for the extra term $\frac{1}{2}\sigma_t'\sigma_t dt(Z^2 - 1)$ that appears in (7.19). This extra term improves the accuracy of Milstein discretization over Euler discretization.

MILSTEIN SCHEME FOR THE HESTON MODEL

Recall that the Heston model is specified by the bivariate process given in Equation (7.1). In the processes for S_t and v_t, the drift and volatility coefficients do not depend on t directly. Thus Equation (7.19) can be applied to both processes, and to the process for $\ln S_t$ also.

Milstein Scheme for the Variance

The coefficients of the variance process are $\mu(v_t) = \kappa(\theta - v_t)$ and $\sigma(v_t) = \sigma\sqrt{v_t}$ so an application of Equation (7.19) to v_t produces

$$v_{t+dt} = v_t + \kappa(\theta - v_t)dt + \sigma\sqrt{v_t}\sqrt{dt}Z_V + \frac{1}{4}\sigma^2 dt(Z_V^2 - 1) \tag{7.20}$$

which can be written

$$v_{t+dt} = \left(\sqrt{v_t} + \frac{1}{2}\sigma\sqrt{dt}Z_V\right)^2 + \kappa(\theta - v_t)dt - \frac{1}{4}\sigma^2 dt. \tag{7.21}$$

This last equation is also Equation (2.18) of Gatheral (2006). Milstein discretization of the variance process produces far fewer negative values for the variance than Euler discretization. Nevertheless, the full truncation scheme or the reflection scheme must be applied to (7.20) and (7.21) as well.

Milstein Scheme for the Stock Price

The coefficients of the stock price process are $\mu(S_t) = (r - q)S_t$ and $\sigma(S_t) = \sqrt{v_t}S_t$, so Equation (7.19) becomes

$$S_{t+dt} = S_t + (r - q)S_t dt + \sqrt{v_t}\sqrt{dt}S_t Z_S + \frac{1}{2}v_t S_t dt(Z_S^2 - 1). \tag{7.22}$$

We can also discretize the log-stock process, which by Itō's lemma follows the process

$$d\ln S_t = \left(r - q - \frac{1}{2}v_t\right)dt + \sqrt{v_t}dW_{1,t}.$$

The coefficients are $\mu(S_t) = (r - q - v_t/2)$ and $\sigma(S_t) = \sqrt{v_t}$ so that $\mu'_t = \sigma'_t = 0$. Since v_t is known at time t, we can treat it as a constant in the coefficients. An application of Equation (7.19) produces

$$\ln S_{t+dt} = \ln S_t + \left(r - q - \frac{1}{2}v_t\right)dt + \sqrt{v_t}\sqrt{dt}Z_S \tag{7.23}$$

which is identical to Euler discretization in (7.11). Hence, Milstein discretization of $\ln S_t$ in the Heston model does not produce a more accurate approximation than Euler discretization. The stock price is obtained by exponentiation of (7.23). Again, it is necessary to apply the full truncation or reflections schemes to (7.22) and (7.23).

To implement Milstein simulation, we start with initial values S_0 (or $x_0 = \ln S_0$) for the stock price and v_0 for the variance. Given the simulated values (S_t, v_t), we obtain v_{t+dt} from Equation (7.20), and we obtain S_{t+dt} from either (7.22) or by exponentiating (7.23), as in (7.12).

Simulation schemes can serve as a powerful illustrator of how the Heston (1993) parameters affect the behavior of the stock price and the volatility. In Chapter 2, for example, we saw that the parameter ρ drives the correlation between the processes

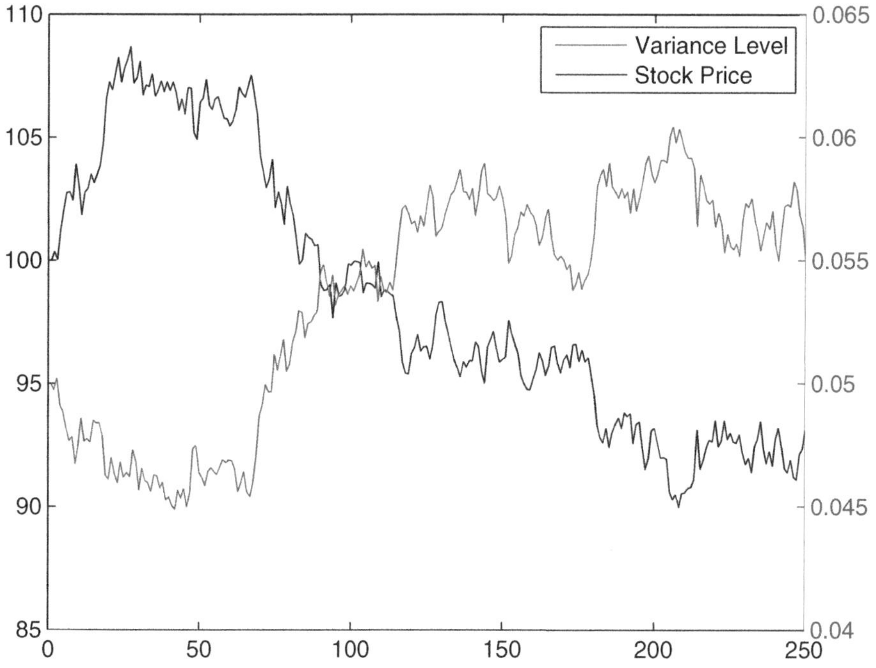

FIGURE 7.1 Stock Price and Variance under Negative Correlation

driving the stock price and the variance. The following figures each contain a single daily simulated stock price path and variance path over 1 trading year (250 days), starting with initial values $(S_0, v_0) = (100, 0.05)$ and using typical values of the parameters. Figure 7.1 uses $\rho = -0.9$ and clearly illustrates the negative relationship between price and variance. Indeed, increases in variance are associated with a decreasing stock price, while the opposite is true for decreases in variance.

Figure 7.2, on the other hand, uses $\rho = +0.9$ and shows the opposite effect, increases in variance are associated with increasing prices, and vice-versa.

Simulation can also be used to illustrate the effect of the other Heston parameters on the stock price and the variance.

IMPLICIT MILSTEIN SCHEME

Recall that, in Equation (7.19) for Milstein discretization of dX_t, the coefficients $\mu_t = \mu(X_t)$ and $\sigma_t = \sigma(X_t)$ are the drift and volatility of the process for X_t and are functions of X_t itself. In the Milstein drift-implicit scheme, or simply implicit scheme, the drift coefficient μ_t is specified to be a function of X_{t+dt}. Hence, under this scheme, the drift coefficient is known only implicitly, and not explicitly, as is the case when it depends on X_t. Under the Itō version of this scheme Equation (7.19) becomes

$$X_{t+dt} = X_t + \mu_{t+dt}dt + \sigma_t\sqrt{dt}Z + \frac{1}{2}\sigma_t'\sigma_t dt(Z^2 - 1) \quad (7.24)$$

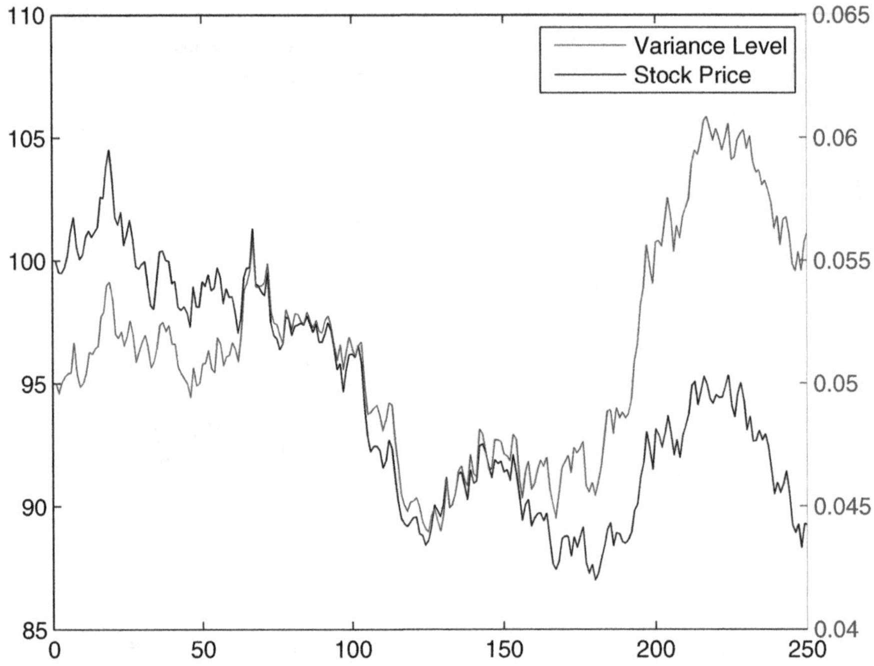

FIGURE 7.2 Stock Price and Variance under Positive Correlation

where $\mu_{t+dt} = \mu(X_{t+dt})$. See Kloeden and Platen (1992) for details. It is also possible to interpolate between explicit and implicit Milstein schemes by taking a weighted average of μ_t and μ_{t+dt}. The weighted implicit-explicit Milstein scheme is therefore

$$X_{t+dt} = X_t + [\alpha\mu_t + (1-\alpha)\mu_{t+dt}]dt + \sigma_t\sqrt{dt}Z + \frac{1}{2}\sigma_t'\sigma_t dt(Z^2 - 1) \tag{7.25}$$

where $\alpha \in (0, 1)$ is the weight. The explicit Milstein scheme corresponds to $\alpha = 1$, and the implicit Milstein scheme to $\alpha = 0$.

To apply the implicit Milstein scheme to the Heston model, in Equation (7.20) we replace the term $\kappa(\theta - v_t)dt$ with $\kappa(\theta - v_{t+dt})dt$. We then bring $\kappa v_{t+dt}dt$ over to the left-hand side of the resulting equation, and we divide by $1 + \kappa dt$ to obtain

$$v_{t+dt} = \frac{v_t + \kappa\theta dt + \sigma\sqrt{v_t}\sqrt{dt}Z_V + \frac{1}{4}\sigma^2 dt(Z_V^2 - 1)}{1 + \kappa dt}. \tag{7.26}$$

If we apply the same steps to the weighted scheme in Equation (7.25) we obtain

$$v_{t+dt} = \frac{v_t + \kappa(\theta - \alpha v_t)dt + \sigma\sqrt{v_t}\sqrt{dt}Z_V + \frac{1}{4}\sigma^2 dt(Z_V^2 - 1)}{1 + (1-\alpha)\kappa dt}. \tag{7.27}$$

The Matlab function EulerMilsteinSim.m applies Euler (7.8), Milstein (7.20), implicit Milstein (7.26), or weighted Milstein (7.27) discretization to the variance, and simulates the log-stock price using (7.12). It allows negative variances to be overridden with either the reflection or full truncation scheme. The function returns the matrices S and V that contain the stock price and volatility paths, and the scalar F for the number of negative variance overrides. To conserve space, parts of the functions have been omitted.

```
function [S V F] = EulerMilsteinSim(scheme,...)
for i=1:N;
    for t=2:T;
        % Generate two dependent N(0,1) variables
        Zv = randn(1);
        Zs = rho*Zv + sqrt(1-rho^2)*randn(1);
        if strcmp(scheme,'E')
            % Euler discretization for the variance
            V(t,i) = V(t-1,i) + kappa*(theta-V(t-1,i)) ...;
        elseif strcmp(scheme,'M')
            % Milstein discretization for the variance.
            V(t,i) = V(t-1,i) + kappa*(theta-V(t-1,i)) ...;
        elseif strcmp(scheme,'IM')
            % Implicit Milstein for the variance.
            V(t,i) = (V(t-1,i) + kappa*theta*dt +  ...;
        elseif strcmp(scheme,'WM')
            % Weighted Explicit-Implicit Milstein Scheme
            V(t,i) = (V(t-1,i) + kappa*(theta-alpha*V(t-1,i)) ...;
        end
        % Apply the full truncation or reflection scheme
        if V(t,i) <= 0
            F = F+1;
            if strcmp(negvar,'R')
                V(t,i) = abs(V(t,i));
            elseif strcmp(negvar,'T')
                V(t,i) = max(0, V(t,i));
            end
        end
        % Discretize the log stock price
        S(t,i) = S(t-1,i)*exp((r-q-V(t-1,i)/2)*dt + ...;
    end
end
```

This function is fed into the EulerMilsteinPrice.m function that uses the simulated price paths as input, and calculates the call or put price from the terminal prices, as in Equation (7.4).

```
function [S V F SimPrice] = EulerMilsteinPrice(scheme,...);
% Obtain the simulated stock price and simulated variance
[S V F] = EulerMilsteinSim(scheme,...);
% Terminal stock prices
ST = S(end,:);
```

```
% Payoff vectors
if strcmp(PutCall,'C')
    Payoff = max(ST - K,0);
elseif strcmp(PutCall,'P')
    Payoff = max(K - ST,0);
end
SimPrice = exp(-r*Mat)*mean(Payoff);
```

The C# code to obtain option prices using the Euler, Milstein, implicit Milstein, and weighted Milstein schemes is very similar to the Matlab code in the snippets stated above. In C#, however, we need to create functions to generate random draws from the standard normal density. We use the RandomNum() and RandomInt() functions that were presented in the Differential Algorithm of Chapter 6 to generate uniform random numbers and random integers, respectively. We use the Box-Muller transformation to convert uniform random numbers into a random draw z from the standard normal density. This involves using the RandomNum() function to generate two random numbers u_1 and u_2 uniformly distributed on $[0, 1]$, and then defining

$$z = \sqrt{-2\ln u_1} \times \sin(2\pi u_2). \tag{7.28}$$

```
public static double RandomNorm() {
    double U1 = RandomNum(0.0,1.0);
    double U2 = RandomNum(0.0,1.0);
    return Math.Sqrt(-2.0*Math.Log(U1)) * Math.Sin(2.0*Math.PI*U2); }
```

To illustrate, the price of a 3-month European call struck at $K = 90$ on a dividend-paying stock with spot price $S = 100$ and dividend yield $q = 0.02$ is \$11.2087 when $r = 0.03$, $\kappa = 6.2$, $\theta = 0.06$, $\sigma = 0.5$, $\rho = -0.7$, and $v_0 = 0.03$. We use 5,000 stock price paths and 100 time steps for each path, and apply the reflection scheme. The price of the call with the Euler scheme is \$11.3855 (an error of 1.6 percent) and requires seven negative variances to be overridden. The Milstein scheme produces a price of \$11.1413 (an error of −0.6 percent), the implicit Milstein scheme a price of \$11.0692 (an error of −1.2 percent), and the weighted implicit-explicit Milstein scheme a price of 11.1566 (an error of −0.5 percent). None of the three Milstein schemes generated negative variances.

TRANSFORMED VOLATILITY SCHEME

One simple way to avoid negative variances is to simulate the volatility rather than the variance, and then square the result. By Itō's lemma, the volatility $\omega_t = \sqrt{v_t}$ follows the process

$$d\omega_t = \frac{\kappa}{2}\left[\left(\theta - \frac{\sigma^2}{4\kappa}\right)\frac{1}{\omega_t} - \omega_t\right]dt + \frac{1}{2}\sigma dW_{1,t}. \tag{7.29}$$

Euler discretization of (7.29) is simply

$$\omega_{t+dt} = \omega_t + \frac{\kappa}{2}\left[\left(\theta - \frac{\sigma^2}{4\kappa}\right)\frac{1}{\omega_t} - \omega_t\right]dt + \frac{1}{2}\sigma\sqrt{dt}Z_V \tag{7.30}$$

while Euler discretization of the log stock price produces

$$S_{t+dt} = S_t \exp\left(\left(r - q - \frac{1}{2}\omega_t^2\right)dt + \omega_t\sqrt{dt}Z_S\right). \tag{7.31}$$

Zhu (2010) points out that, while Euler discretization of the volatility ω_t avoids negative variances, the drawback is that the mean level $\theta_\omega = \left(\theta - \frac{\sigma^2}{4\kappa}\right)/\omega_t$ in (7.29) is stochastic because of the term $1/\omega_t$. This will cause the simulation to be poorly behaved. The transformed volatility scheme proposed by Zhu (2010) applies a robust approximation of θ_ω to rectify this problem. His transformed volatility process is

$$d\omega_t = \frac{\kappa}{2}[\theta_t^* - \omega_t]dt + \frac{\sigma}{2}dW_{2,t} \tag{7.32}$$

which has the mean reversion speed $\kappa/2$ and volatility of variance $\sigma/2$, respectively. The mean reversion level θ_t^* is

$$\theta_t^* = \frac{\beta - \omega_t \exp(-\kappa dt/2)}{1 - \exp(-\kappa dt/2)}$$

where

$$\beta = \sqrt{(E[v_{t+dt}] - \text{Var}[\omega_{t+dt}])^+} = \sqrt{\left(\theta + (v_t - \theta)e^{-\kappa dt} - \frac{\sigma^2}{4\kappa}(1 - e^{-\kappa dt})\right)^+}.$$

Note that the β parameter is set to zero when $E[v_{t+dt}] < \text{Var}[\omega_{t+dt}]$, while the mean reversion level θ_t^* depends on the value of ω_t. Euler discretization of $d\omega_t$ in (7.32) produces

$$\omega_{t+dt} = \omega_t + \frac{\kappa}{2}[\theta^* - \omega_t]dt + \frac{\sigma}{2}\sqrt{dt}Z_V. \tag{7.33}$$

The TransVolSim.m Matlab function simulates the stock price in Equation (7.31), and the volatility in either (7.30) or (7.33). The functions use the parameters κ, θ, σ, and ρ, as in the other simulations, but the parameter for the initial volatility is $\sqrt{v_0}$.

```
function [S v] = TransVolSim(scheme,...)
v(1,:) = v0;          % Heston initial variance
w(1,:) = sqrt(v0);    % Heston initial volatility
for i=1:N;
    for t=2:T;
        % Generate two dependent N(0,1) variables
        Zv = randn(1);
```

```
            Zx = rho*Zv + sqrt(1-rho^2)*randn(1);
            if strcmp(scheme,'Euler')
                % Euler volatility scheme
                w(t,i) = w(t-1,i) + 0.5*kappa
                         *((theta-sigma^2/4/kappa) ...;
            elseif strcmp(scheme,'TV')
                % Transformed Volatility scheme
                m1 = theta + (v(t-1,i) - theta)*exp(-kappa*dt);
                m2 = sigma^2/4/kappa*(1-exp(-kappa*dt));
                beta = sqrt(max(0,m1-m2));
                thetav = (beta - w(t-1,i)*exp(-kappa*dt/2)) ...;
                w(t,i) = w(t-1,i) + 0.5*kappa*(thetav - w(t-1,i)) ...;
            end
            v(t,i) = w(t,i)^2;
            % Discretize the log stock price
            X(t,i) = X(t-1,i) + (r-q-w(t-1,i)^2/2)*dt + w(t-1,i) ...;
            S(t,i) = exp(X(t,i));
        end
    end
```

The simulated stock price values are then passed to the TransVolPrice.m function, which calculates the price of the European call or put. It is almost identical to the pricing function for the Euler and Milstein schemes presented at the end of the previous section.

```
function [S v SimPrice] = TransVolPrice(...)
[S v] = TransVolSim(scheme,params,S0,Mat,r,q,T,N);
ST = S(end,:);
if strcmp(PutCall,'C')
    Payoff = max(ST - K,0);
elseif strcmp(PutCall,'P')
    Payoff = max(K - ST,0);
end
SimPrice = exp(-r*Mat)*mean(Payoff);
```

In numerical experiments Zhu (2010) shows that the accuracy of his transformed volatility scheme is very high and comparable to the Quadratic Exponential scheme, which we cover later in this chapter. The C# code to implement the transformed volatility scheme is very similar to the Matlab code and is not presented here.

Continuing with the example at the end of the previous section, the closed-form call price is 11.2087. Using 5,000 stock price paths and 100 time steps per path, the price using Euler discretization of the volatility in Equation (7.30) is 11.1040. The transformed volatility in (7.33), however, produces a price of 11.1524, which is more accurate.

BALANCED, PATHWISE, AND IJK SCHEMES

In this section, we describe three schemes proposed by Kahl and Jäckel (2006). The Balanced Implicit method of Milstein et al. (1998) introduces implicitness in the diffusion term. The Pathwise Adapted Linearization Quadratic method retains terms up to $(dt)^2$ in a more general expansion for pathwise approximation. Finally, the IJK scheme uses the implicit Milstein scheme for the variance, along with an alternative discretization for the log stock price.

Balanced Implicit Scheme

This scheme is able to preserve positivity of the variance process. It is defined in Platen and Heath (2009) and Kahl and Jäckel (2006) as

$$v_{t+dt} = v_t + \mu_t dt + \sigma_t \Delta W_t + (v_t - v_{t+dt})C(v_t)$$

where

$$C(v_t) = c^0(v_t)dt + c^1(v_t)|\Delta W_t|$$

with c^0 and c^1 suitably chosen positive real valued and bounded functions defined as $c^0(v_t) = \kappa$ and $c^1(v_t) = \sigma/\sqrt{v_t}$. The Balanced Implicit scheme for the Heston model is, therefore,

$$\begin{aligned} v_{t+dt} &= v_t + \kappa(\theta - v_t)dt + \sigma\sqrt{v_t}\sqrt{dt}Z_V + (v_t - v_{t+dt})C(v_t) \\ &= \frac{v_t(1 + C(v_t)) + \kappa(\theta - v_t)dt + \sigma\sqrt{v_t}\sqrt{dt}Z_V}{1 + C(v_t)} \end{aligned} \tag{7.34}$$

with

$$C(v_t) = \kappa dt + \frac{\sigma\sqrt{dt}|Z_V|}{\sqrt{v_t}}.$$

Since the variance is always guaranteed to be positive, reflection and truncation are not needed. Unfortunately, as shown by Kahl and Jäckel (2006), the convergence of this scheme can be very poor. For details please refer to Equations (6.25) through (6.28) in their paper.

Pathwise Adapted Linearization Quadratic

Another scheme for discretization of the variance is the Pathwise Adapted Linearization Quadratic scheme presented in Kahl and Jäckel (2006). Its convergence is fast, especially for small values of σ. The discretization scheme is given by

$$v_{t+dt} = v_t + (\kappa(\widetilde{\theta} - v_t) + \sigma\beta_n\sqrt{v_t})\left(1 + \frac{\sigma\beta_n - 2\kappa\sqrt{v_t}}{4\sqrt{v_t}}dt\right)dt \tag{7.35}$$

where $\widetilde{\theta} = \theta - \sigma^2/(4\kappa)$ and where $\beta_n = Z_V/\sqrt{dt}$. This scheme must be implemented with care, as it can lead to numerical instability for large values of σ.

Kahl-Jäckel IJK Scheme

This was also proposed by Kahl and Jäckel (2006). It involves simulating v_t with the implicit Milstein scheme from Equation (7.26), and simulating $\ln S_t$ with their IJK discretization given by

$$\begin{aligned}\ln S_{t+dt} &= \ln S_t + \left(r - q - \frac{v_t + v_{t+dt}}{4}\right) dt + \rho\sqrt{v_t dt} Z_V \\ &+ \frac{1}{2}(\sqrt{v_t} + \sqrt{v_{t+dt}})(Z_S - \rho Z_V)\sqrt{dt} + \frac{\rho\sigma dt}{2}(Z_V^2 - 1).\end{aligned} \tag{7.36}$$

Since this scheme can also produce negative variances, in (7.36) the full truncation scheme or the reflection scheme should be used. See their paper for details of the derivation.

The Matlab function KahlJackelSim.m implements the Balanced (7.34), Pathwise (7.35), and IJK (7.36) schemes. Parts of the function have been omitted to conserve space.

```
function [S V F] = KahlJackelSim(scheme,...)
for i=1:N;
    for t=2:T;
        if strcmp(scheme,'IJK')
            % Implicit Milstein for the variance.
            V(t,i) = (V(t-1,i) + kappa*theta*dt +...;
            % IJK discretization log stock prices
            S(t,i) = S(t-1,i)*exp((r-q-(V(t,i)+V(t-1,i))/4) ...;
        elseif strcmp(scheme,'PW')
            % Pathwise Adapted Linearization for variance.
            theta2 = theta - sigma^2/4/kappa;
            Bn = Zv/sqrt(dt);
            V(t,i) = V(t-1,i) + (kappa*(theta2-V(t-1,i)) + ...;
            % Euler/Milstein discretization log stock prices
            S(t,i) = S(t-1,i)*exp((r-q-V(t-1,i)/2)*dt + ...;
        elseif strcmp(scheme,'B')
            % Balanced Implicit scheme for the variance
            absdW = sqrt(dt)*abs(Zv);
            C = kappa*dt + sigma/sqrt(V(t-1,i))* ...;
            V(t,i) = (V(t-1,i)*(1+C) + kappa*(theta-V(t-1,i)) ...;
            % Euler/Milstein discretization log stock prices
            S(t,i) = S(t-1,i)*exp((r-q-V(t-1,i)/2)*dt + ...;
        end
    end
end
```

The KahlJackelPrice.m function calculates the price of a European call or put, based on paths simulated using the KahlJackelSim.m function. The C# code to implement these three methods is very similar to the Matlab code and is not presented here.

We continue with the example in earlier sections that use 5,000 simulation paths each with 100 time steps. Recall that the closed-form price is 11.2087. The IJK scheme produces 11.2833 (an error of 0.7 percent), the Pathwise scheme produces 11.2192 (error of 0.1 percent), and the Balanced scheme produces 11.2841 (error of 0.7 percent). These errors are small, and none of the schemes generated negative variances.

QUADRATIC-EXPONENTIAL SCHEME

Recall from Chapter 1 that the value of v_{t+dt} conditional on a realized value v_t follows the non-central chi-square distribution. Andersen (2008) suggests sampling from an approximation to the distribution, depending on whether the non-centrality parameter, $2c_{t+dt}v_te^{-\kappa dt}$, is large or small. Since the non-centrality parameter is proportional to v_t, large or small values of the parameter correspond to large or small values of v_t. The algorithm switches back and forth between two different approximations to the non-central chi-square distribution; the choice of the approximation depends on the magnitude of v_t. The reasoning is as follows:

For moderate or high values of v_t, a non-central chi-square random variable can be approximated by a power function applied to a standard normal variable Z_V

$$v_{t+dt} = a(b + Z_V)^2 \tag{7.37}$$

where a and b are determined by moment-matching using the mean m and variance s^2 of the Cox, Ingersoll, and Ross (CIR) (1985) process presented in Chapter 1.

For small values of v_t, the non-central chi-square density can be approximated by a weighted average of a term involving the Dirac delta function δ and another term involving $e^{-\beta x}$

$$\Pr(v_{t+dt} \in [x, x + dx]) = (p\delta(0) + (1 - p)\beta e^{-\beta x})dx \tag{7.38}$$

where p and β are determined by moment-matching also. Note that $0 \leq p \leq 1$. Integrating (7.38) and inverting produces the inverse distribution function

$$\Psi^{-1}(u) = \begin{cases} 0 & \text{for } 0 \leq u \leq p \\ \dfrac{1}{\beta}\ln\dfrac{1-p}{1-u} & \text{for } p \leq u \leq 1. \end{cases} \tag{7.39}$$

The sampling scheme for small values of v_t is, therefore,

$$v_{t+dt} = \Psi^{-1}(U_V) \tag{7.40}$$

where U_V is a uniform random number.

The Quadratic Exponential (QE) sampling scheme is defined by Equations (7.37) and (7.40). From these equations it is clear that the QE scheme guarantees that only positive values of v_{t+dt} will be generated. Duffy and Kienitz (2009) present a nice explanation of the QE scheme.

Moment-Matching

The parameters a, b, p, and β are obtained by matching the first two moments of the non-central chi-square distribution to those of the approximate distributions. Recall from Chapter 1 that the mean and variance of the CIR process are, respectively,

$$\begin{aligned} m &= E[v_{t+dt}|v_t] = \theta + (v_t - \theta)e^{-\kappa dt} \\ s^2 &= \text{Var}[v_{t+dt}|v_t] = \frac{v_t\sigma^2 e^{-\kappa dt}}{\kappa}(1 - e^{-\kappa dt}) + \frac{\theta\sigma^2}{2\kappa}(1 - e^{-\kappa dt})^2. \end{aligned} \tag{7.41}$$

For moderate or high values of v_t, since $v_{t+dt} = a(b + Z_V)^2$ from (7.37), and since Z_V^2 is distributed chi-squared with one degree of freedom, we have that $E[v_{t+dt}] = a(1 + b^2)$ and $\text{Var}[v_{t+dt}] = 2a^2(1 + 2b^2)$. Equating these to m and s^2 respectively and solving for a and b produces

$$b = \left(\frac{2}{\psi} - 1 + \sqrt{\frac{2}{\psi}\left(\frac{2}{\psi} - 1\right)}\right)^{\frac{1}{2}}, \qquad a = \frac{m}{1 + b^2} \tag{7.42}$$

where $\psi = s^2/m^2$. Note that b is only defined when $\psi \leq 2$.

For low values of v_t, the mean and variance of v_{t+dt} are found by integrating Equation (7.38) directly, which produces $E[v_{t+dt}] = (1 - p)/\beta$ and $\text{Var}[v_{t+dt}] = (1 - p^2)/\beta^2$. Again, equating these to m and s^2 and solving for p and β produces

$$p = \frac{\psi - 1}{\psi + 1} \quad \text{and} \quad \beta = \frac{1 - p}{m}. \tag{7.43}$$

Note that the condition that $p \geq 0$ requires that $\psi \geq 1$. We thus have the restriction that $1 \leq \psi \leq 2$. The value of ψ stipulates which approximation to use. Indeed, the first approximation requires $\psi \leq 2$, while the second requires $\psi \geq 1$. This implies that a critical level $\psi_c \in [1, 2]$ ought to be defined as a threshold to switch between the two approximations. Andersen (2008) uses $\psi_c = 1.5$.

The scheme can be summarized as follows:

Given v_t, obtain m and s^2 from Equation (7.41) using estimates of θ and κ, and define $\psi = s^2/m^2$.

Draw a uniform random number $U_V \in [0, 1]$.

If $\psi \leq \psi_c$ compute a and b from (7.42), and compute $Z_V = \Phi^{-1}(U_V)$. Define $v_{t+dt} = a(b + Z_V)^2$ from (7.37).

If $\psi > \psi_c$ compute β and p from (7.43). Define $v_{t+dt} = \Psi^{-1}(U_V)$ from (7.39).

In the same paper, Andersen (2008) presents the Truncated Gaussian (TG) scheme which uses the approximation $v_{t+dt} = (\mu + \sigma Z_V)^+$ for μ and σ constants. The performance of the TG scheme is inferior to that of the QE scheme, however, and Andersen recommends that the QE scheme be the default choice.

Process for the Log-Stock Price

Andersen (2008) proposes a discretization scheme for $\ln S_t$ that overcomes the problem of "leaky" correlation brought on by Euler discretization. Recall from Chapter 3 that we can use Cholesky decomposition to replace the correlated Brownian motions $W_{1,t}$ and $W_{2,t}$ in the Heston bivariate system of SDEs with two independent Brownian motions $B_{1,t}$ and $B_{2,t}$ by defining $W_{1,t} = \rho B_{2,t} + \sqrt{1-\rho^2} B_{1,t}$ and $W_{2,t} = B_{2,t}$. The integral form of the process for v_t is, therefore,

$$v_{t+dt} = v_t + \kappa\theta dt - \kappa \int_t^{t+dt} v_u du + \sigma \int_t^{t+dt} \sqrt{v_u} dB_{2,u}.$$

Rearranging terms produces

$$\int_t^{t+dt} \sqrt{v_u} dB_{2,u} = \frac{1}{\sigma}\left(v_{t+dt} - v_t - \kappa\theta dt + \kappa \int_t^{t+dt} v_u du \right). \tag{7.44}$$

Applying Cholesky decomposition to Equation (7.10), the integral form of the SDE for $\ln S_t$, produces

$$\begin{aligned} \ln S_{t+dt} &= \ln S_t + (r-q)dt - \frac{1}{2}\int_t^{t+dt} v_u du \\ &+ \int_t^{t+dt} \sqrt{v_u}(\rho dB_{2,u} + \sqrt{1-\rho^2} dB_{1,u}). \end{aligned} \tag{7.45}$$

Now substitute Equation (7.44) into (7.45) to obtain

$$\begin{aligned} \ln S_{t+dt} &= \ln S_t + (r-q)dt + \frac{\rho}{\sigma}(v_{t+dt} - v_t - \kappa\theta dt) \\ &+ \left(\frac{\kappa\rho}{\sigma} - \frac{1}{2}\right) \int_t^{t+dt} v_u du + \sqrt{1-\rho^2} \int_t^{t+dt} \sqrt{v_u} dB_{1,u}. \end{aligned} \tag{7.46}$$

Andersen (2008) uses the approximations

$$\int_t^{t+dt} v_u du \approx dt(\gamma_1 v_t + \gamma_2 v_{t+dt})$$

$$\int_t^{t+dt} \sqrt{v_u} dB_{1,u} \approx Z_V \sqrt{dt} \sqrt{\gamma_1 v_t + \gamma_2 v_{t+dt}}$$

where Z_V is standard normal. Substituting these approximations into (7.46) produces

$$\ln S_{t+dt} = \ln S_t + (r-q)dt + K_0 + K_1 v_t + K_2 v_{t+dt} + \sqrt{K_3 v_t + K_4 v_{t+dt}} Z_V \tag{7.47}$$

where

$$K_0 = -\frac{\kappa\rho\theta}{\sigma}dt,\quad K_1 = \left(\frac{\kappa\rho}{\sigma} - \frac{1}{2}\right)\gamma_1 dt - \frac{\rho}{\sigma},\quad K_2 = \left(\frac{\kappa\rho}{\sigma} - \frac{1}{2}\right)\gamma_2 dt + \frac{\rho}{\sigma}$$

$$K_3 = (1-\rho^2)\gamma_1 dt,\quad K_4 = (1-\rho^2)\gamma_2 dt.$$

The constants γ_1 and γ_2 in these expressions are arbitrary. Setting $\gamma_1 = 1$ and $\gamma_2 = 0$ produces an Euler-type scheme, while $\gamma_1 = \gamma_2 = \frac{1}{2}$ produces a central discretization. With these values, the algorithm to generate a value of S_{t+dt}, given the values S_t, v_t, and v_{t+dt} is evident.

Martingale Correction

Under the risk-neutral measure $\mathbb{Q}$, the discounted asset price will be a martingale in continuous time. On the other hand, the discretized stock price

$$S_{t+dt} = S_t \exp\left((r-q)\,dt + K_0 + K_1 v_t + K_2 v_{t+dt} + \sqrt{K_3 v_t + K_4 v_{t+dt}} Z_V\right) \tag{7.48}$$

will not be a martingale. The resulting bias is minor, since the drift away from the martingale can be controlled by reducing the size of the time increment, dt. Nonetheless, Andersen (2008) shows that the martingale property can be satisfied simply by replacing K_0 with K_0^* given by

$$K_0^* = -\ln M - \left(K_1 + \frac{1}{2}K_3\right) v_t. \tag{7.49}$$

The martingale correction makes use of the term $A = K_2 + \frac{1}{2}K_4$, along with a and b defined in Equation (7.42) and p and β defined in (7.43). When $\psi \leq \psi_c$ we can implement the martingale correction provided that $A < 1/(2a)$, and the expression for M is

$$M = \frac{\exp\left(\frac{Ab^2 a}{1-2Aa}\right)}{\sqrt{1-2Aa}}. \tag{7.50}$$

When $\psi > \psi_c$, we can implement the martingale correction provided that $A < \beta$, and the expression for M is

$$M = p + \frac{\beta(1-p)}{\beta - A}. \tag{7.51}$$

The simulation of stock price paths under Quadratic Exponential scheme is implemented with the QESim.m function. Parts of the function have been removed to conserve space.

```
function [S V] = QESim(params,gamma1,gamma2,...)
% Loop through the simulation runs
for i=1:N;
    % Loop through the time increments
    for t=2:T;
        % Generate two dependent N(0,1) variables
        Zv = randn(1);
        Zs = rho*Zv + sqrt(1-rho^2)*randn(1);
        % QE Agorithm
        m = theta + (V(t-1,i) - theta)*E;
        s2 = V(t-1,i)*sigma^2*E/kappa*(1-E) + ...;
        phi = s2/m^2;
        Uv = rand;
        if phi <= phic
            b = sqrt(2/phi - 1 + sqrt(2/phi*(2/phi-1)));
            a = m/(1+b^2);
            if icdf==1
                Zv = norminv(Uv);
            elseif icdf==2
                Zv = normICDF(Uv);
            end
            V(t,i) = a*(b + Zv)^2;
            % Martingale correction: Define new K0
            if (MC==1) & A<(1/(2*a));
                M = exp(A*b^2*a/(1-2*A*a))/sqrt(1-2*A*a);
                K0 = -log(M) - (K1+0.5*K3)*V(t,i);
            end
            S(t,i) = S(t-1,i)*exp((r-q)*dt + K0 + ...;
        else
            p = (phi-1)/(phi+1);
            beta = (1-p)/m;
            if (0<=Uv) & (Uv<=p);
                phiinv = 0;
            elseif (p<Uv) & (Uv<=1);
                phiinv = 1/beta*log((1-p)/(1-Uv));
            end
            V(t,i) = phiinv;
            % Martingale correction: Define new K0 if possible
            if MC==1 & A<beta;
                M = p + beta*(1-p)/(beta-A);
                K0 = -log(M) - (K1+0.5*K3)*V(t,i);
            end
            S(t,i) = S(t-1,i)*exp((r-q)*dt + K0 + ...;
        end;
    end
end
```

Using the same settings as the example throughout this chapter, we obtain a price of 11.2173, which represents an error of less than 1 percent from the closed-form price of 11.2087.

Inversion of the standard normal CDF using the built-in Matlab function norminv.m slows down the simulation. To rectify this problem we create the Matlab function normICDF, which implements the approximation algorithm of Wichura

(1988). This function is an adaptation of Fortran code AS241 downloaded from StatLib (lib.stat.cmu.edu), a software and data repository hosted by the Department of Statistics at Carnegie Mellon University. In the QESim.m Matlab function, we set the "icdf" argument to 2, which replaces the Matlab function

```
Zv = norminv(Uv);
```

with the function based on the Wichura (1988) approximation

```
Zv = normICDF(Uv);
```

This reduces the simulation time by more than 50 percent. The approximation to $\Phi^{-1}(p)$ considers three cases separately. The first case is for $p \approx 0.5$, the second is for p not close to 0, 0.5, or 1, and the third is for $p \approx 0$ or $p \approx 1$. As usual, most of the function is not presented here.

```
function y = normICDF(p)
q = p - 0.5;
if (abs(q) < 0.425)
    % For p close to 0.5
    y = q*((((((a7*r + a6)*r + a5)*r + a4)*r + a3)...;
else
    if (r <= 5)
        % For p not close to 0, 0.5, or 1
        y = (((((((c7*r + c6)*r + c5)*r + c4)*r + c3)...;
    else
        % For p near 0 or 1
        y = (((((((e7*r + e6)*r + e5)*r + e4)*r + e3)...;
    end
end
```

The C# code to implement the Quadratic Exponential method and the Wichura (1988) approximation is very similar and is not presented here.

ALFONSI SCHEME FOR THE VARIANCE

Alfonsi (2010) proposes a simulation scheme that performs well under the Heston model and that avoids negative variances. Define

$$\Psi = \frac{1 - \exp(-\kappa dt/2)}{\kappa}$$

and define the constant K_2 as

$$K_2 = \exp(\kappa dt/2)\left[\left(\frac{\sigma^2}{4} - \theta\kappa\right)\Psi + \left(\sqrt{e^{\kappa dt/2}\left(\frac{\sigma^2}{4} - \theta\kappa\right)\Psi} + \frac{\sigma}{2}\sqrt{3dt}\right)^2\right]$$

when $\sigma^2 > 4\kappa\theta$, and as $K_2 = 0$ when $\sigma^2 \leq 4\kappa\theta$. At each simulation step, we compare v_t to K_2, and we have a different updated value v_{t+dt} depending on the results of the comparison.

Case 1, $v_t > K_2$ Updating to v_{t+dt} requires two steps. In the first step we need to simulate a discrete random variable $Y \in \{0, \sqrt{3}, -\sqrt{3}\}$ with probabilities 2/3, 1/6, and 1/6, respectively. This can be done by first simulating a uniform random variable U on $(0,1)$ and then assigning a value of Y depending on the realized value of U. In the second step we update to v_{t+dt} using

$$v_{t+dt} = \exp(-\kappa dt/2)\left(\sqrt{\left(\kappa\theta - \frac{\sigma^2}{4}\right)\Psi + e^{-\kappa dt/2}v_t} + \frac{\sigma}{2}\sqrt{dt}Y\right)^2 + \left(\kappa\theta - \frac{\sigma^2}{4}\right)\Psi.$$

Case 2, $v_t \leq K_2$ Denote the first two moments of v_{t+dt} conditional on v_t by

$$u_1 = E[v_{t+dt}|v_t], \quad u_2 = E[v_{t+dt}^2|v_t].$$

The first moment, u_1 was presented in Chapter 1, where it was denoted m. The second moment, u_2 can be obtained as $u_2 = s^2 + u_1^2$, where $s^2 = \text{Var}[v_{t+dt}|v_t]$ is the conditional variance, also presented in Chapter 1. Define the quantity π as

$$\pi = \frac{1}{2} - \frac{1}{2}\sqrt{1 - \frac{u_1^2}{u_2}}.$$

In the first step, we simulate a uniform random variable U on $(0,1)$. In the second step, we update to v_{t+dt} by comparing U to π so that

$$v_{t+dt} = \frac{u_1}{2\pi} \quad \text{if } U \leq \pi$$

$$v_{t+dt} = \frac{u_1}{2(1-\pi)} \quad \text{if } U > \pi.$$

The function CIRmoments.m calculates the moments u_1 and u_2.

```
function [u1 u2] = CIRmoments(param,Vs,dt)
u1 = theta + (Vs - theta)*exp(-kappa*dt);
s2 = Vs*sigma^2*exp(-kappa*dt)/kappa*(1-exp(-kappa*dt)) + ...;
u2 = s2 + u1^2;
```

The algorithm to update v_t is implemented with the Matlab function AlfonsiV.m.

```
function newV = AlfonsiV(param,vt,dt);
phi = (1-exp(-kappa*dt/2))/kappa;
S = (sigma^2/4 - theta*kappa);
E = exp(kappa*dt/2);
if sigma^2 > 4*kappa*theta
    K2 = E*(S*phi + (sqrt(E*S*phi) + sigma ...;
else
   K2 = 0;
end
if vt >= K2
    U = rand(1);
    if U <= 1/6;
        Y = sqrt(3);
    elseif U <= 1/3;
        Y = -sqrt(3);
    else
        Y = 0;
    end
    phi = (1-exp(-kappa*dt/2))/kappa;
    S = (theta*kappa - sigma^2/4);
    E = exp(-kappa*dt/2);
    newV = E*(sqrt(S*phi + E*vt) + sigma/2 ...;
else
    [u1 u2] = CIRmoments(param,vt,dt);
    Pi = 0.5 - 0.5*sqrt(1 - u1^2/u2);
    U = rand(1);
    if U <= Pi
        newV = u1/2/Pi;
    elseif U > Pi
        newV = u1/2/(1-Pi);
    end
end
```

The AlfonsiV.m function is used in the AlfonsiSim.m function, which simulates the stock price in accordance with the Predictor-Corrector scheme, and simulates the variance using the Alfonsi scheme. To conserve space parts of the function are omitted.

```
function [S V] = AlfonsiSim(params,S0,Mat,r,q,T,N)
% Time increment
dt = Mat/T;
% Required quantities
K0 = -rho*kappa*theta*dt/sigma;
K1 = dt/2*(kappa*rho/sigma - 1/2) - rho/sigma;
K2 = dt/2*(kappa*rho/sigma - 1/2) + rho/sigma;
K3 = dt/2*(1-rho^2);
% Generate the stock and volatility paths
for i=1:N;
    for t=2:T;
        % Alfonsi discretization
        V(t,i) = AlfonsiV(params,V(t-1,i),dt);
        % Predictor-Corrector for the stock price
```

```
            B = randn(1);
            logS = log(exp(-r*t*dt)*S(t-1,i)) + K0 ...;
            S(t,i) = exp(logS)*exp(r*(t+1)*dt);
        end
    end
```

The stock price and variance simulated with the AlfonsiSim.m function are then passed to the AlfonsiPrice.m function, which returns the price of a European call or put.

```
function [S V SimPrice] = AlfonsiPrice(params,PutCall,...)
% Obtain the simulated stock price and simulated variance
[S V] = AlfonsiSim(params,S0,Mat,r,q,T,N);
% Terminal stock prices
ST = S(end,:);
% Payoff vectors
if strcmp(PutCall,'C')
    Payoff = max(ST - K,0);
elseif strcmp(PutCall,'P')
    Payoff = max(K - ST,0);
end
% Simulated price
SimPrice = exp(-r*Mat)*mean(Payoff);
```

The C# code to implement the Alfonsi (2010) method is similar and not presented. Continuing with the example throughout this book, the Alfonsi method returns a call price of 11.4065.

MOMENT MATCHING SCHEME

Andersen and Brotherton-Ratcliffe (2005) propose a moment-matched discretization scheme that generates positive variances only. The scheme produces a variance that is distributed as lognormal, so a natural choice of parameterization is one that matches the first two moments of the discretized process to lognormal moments. This produces a discretization of the form

$$v_{t+dt} = (\theta + (v_t - \theta)e^{-\kappa dt}) \exp\left(-\frac{1}{2}\Gamma_t^2 + \Gamma_t Z_V\right) \tag{7.52}$$

where

$$\Gamma_t = \ln\left(1 + \frac{\sigma^2 v_t\left(1 - e^{-2\kappa dt}\right)}{2\kappa(\theta + (v_t - \theta)e^{-\kappa dt})^2}\right).$$

The Moment Matching scheme is implemented with the function MMSim.m. The C# code is very similar and is not presented.

TABLE 7.1 European Call Prices Using Simulation

Scheme	Price	Dollar Error
Exact	11.2087	
Euler	11.3855	0.1768
Milstein	11.1413	−0.0674
Implicit Milstein	11.0692	−0.1395
Weighted Milstein	11.1566	−0.0521
Zhu Euler	11.1040	−0.1047
Zhu Transformed Volatility	11.1524	−0.0563
IJK	11.2833	0.0746
Pathwise Adapted	11.2192	0.0105
Balanced Implicit	11.2841	0.0754
Quadratic Exponential	11.2173	0.0086
Moment Matching	11.1091	0.0996
Alfonsi	11.4065	−0.1978

```
function [S V F] = MMSim(params,S0,Mat,r,q,T,N)
for i=1:N;
    for t=2:T;
        % Generate two dependent N(0,1) variables
        Zv = randn(1);
        Zs = rho*Zv + sqrt(1-rho^2)*randn(1);
        % Matched moment lognormal approximation
        dW = sqrt(dt)*Zv;
        num = 0.5*sigma^2*V(t-1,i)*(1-exp(-2*kappa*dt)) ...;
        den = (exp(-kappa*dt)*V(t-1,i) + (1-exp(-kappa*dt)) ...;
        Gam = log(1 + num/den);
        V(t,i) = (exp(-kappa*dt)*V(t-1,i) + (1-exp(-kappa*dt)) ...;
        % Euler/Milstein discretization log stock prices
        S(t,i) = S(t-1,i)*exp((r-q-V(t-1,i)/2)*dt + ...;
    end
end
```

Using the same settings as the example in this chapter, we obtain a price of 11.1091, which represents an error of less than −1 percent from the true price of 11.2087. Table 7.1 summarizes the call prices obtained using the simulations schemes covered in this chapter.

Table 7.1 suggests that the Quadratic-Exponential and Pathwise Adapted schemes are the most accurate, with many of the other schemes showing moderate to poor accuracy. The prices of Table 7.1, however, are based on only 5,000 simulated paths and 100 time steps per path and are for illustrative purposes only. In practice, the number of simulations would be much larger.

CONCLUSION

In this chapter, we describe several popular simulation schemes for the bivariate system (S_t, v_t) or $(\ln S_t, v_t)$ of the Heston model. Some of these schemes are traditional schemes that are applied to the Heston model, while others are developed specifically for the model to address the problem of slow convergence and negative variances.

The exact simulation scheme of Broadie and Kaya (2006) is not covered in this chapter. It is an important scheme from a theoretical standpoint, but is difficult to implement in practice. See Van Haastrecht and Pelsser (2010) for an explanation. Other notable methods not covered in this chapter include those by Smith (2007), Van Haastrecht and Pelsser (2010), Chan and Joshi (2010a), and additional schemes by Kahl and Jäckel (2006).

One of the most important applications of simulated stock prices is for the calculation of American option prices using the Least Squares Monte Carlo approach of Longstaff and Schwartz (2001). We describe this method as part of the next chapter on American option valuation in the Heston model.

CHAPTER 8

American Options

Abstract

In this chapter, we present methods to value American options in the Heston model. We first present the simulation-based algorithm of Longstaff and Schwartz (2001). Next, we present a finite difference method, the explicit method, for American options. This method will be presented in its entirety in Chapter 10. We present the bivariate tree of Beliaeva and Nawalkha (2010), an adaptation of the trinomial tree in which the stock price and the volatility evolve along separate trees. We also cover the method of Medvedev and Scaillet (2010), which approximates the American option price using an analytic expansion and is thus able to produce option prices very quickly. Finally, we present the method of Chiarella and Ziogas (2006) for the valuation of American calls.

LEAST-SQUARES MONTE CARLO

The Least-Squares Monte Carlo (LSM) algorithm was developed by Longstaff and Schwartz (2001) as a way to price American options using simulation. The algorithm can be applied to any stock price stochastic process that lends itself to simulation. It is especially useful for multi-dimensional processes for which high-dimension trees are difficult to construct. In this section, we implement the method for the Heston model.

Denote by $C(\omega, s; t, T)$ the set of cash flows generated by the option along the stock price path ω, conditional on the option not being exercised prior to time t, and on the holder following the optimal stopping strategy at all times s, $s < t \leq T$. Longstaff and Schwartz (2001) assume that the American option can be exercised only at K discrete times $0 < t_1 \leq t_2 \leq \cdots \leq t_K = T$, where T is the time to maturity. At time t_k, the value $F(\omega, t_k)$ of continuing to hold the option, as opposed to immediate exercise, is the discounted expectation of the remaining cash flows, under all stock price paths and using the risk-neutral measure, $\mathbb{Q}$. Assuming a constant rate of interest r, the value of continuation is, therefore,

$$F(\omega, t_k) = e^{-r(T-t_k)} E^{\mathbb{Q}} \left[\sum_{j=k+1}^{K} C\left(\omega, t_j; t_k, T\right) \middle| \mathcal{F}_{t_k} \right]. \tag{8.1}$$

The American option is valued by comparing the value of immediate exercise, which is known, with $F(\omega, t_k)$, which is unknown. Longstaff and Schwartz (2001) estimate $F(\omega, t_k)$ using least squares on a set of basis functions, which they select to be the weighted Laguerre polynomials we encountered in Chapter 5

$$\begin{aligned} L_0(x) &= e^{-x/2}, \\ L_1(x) &= e^{-x/2}(1-x), \\ L_2(x) &= e^{-x/2}(1-2x+x^2/2), \cdots \\ L_M(x) &= e^{-x/2}\sum_{r=0}^{M}\frac{(-1)^r}{r!}\binom{M}{r}x^r. \end{aligned} \tag{8.2}$$

Using the first M basis functions, $F(\omega, t_k)$ can be approximated by

$$F_M(\omega, t_k) = \sum_{j=0}^{M} a_j L_j(S_k) \tag{8.3}$$

where $S_k = S_k(\omega)$ is the value of the underlying stock price at time t_k along the price path ω. The coefficients a_j are constants that are estimated using least squares. Equation (8.3) can be written in matrix form, as $\mathbf{F} = \mathbf{La}$, where

$$\underset{K\times 1}{\mathbf{F}} = \begin{pmatrix} F_M(\omega, t_1) \\ F_M(\omega, t_2) \\ \vdots \\ F_M(\omega, t_K) \end{pmatrix}, \quad \underset{K\times N}{\mathbf{L}} = \begin{pmatrix} L_0(S_1) & L_1(S_1) & \cdots & L_M(S_1) \\ L_0(S_2) & L_1(S_2) & \cdots & L_M(S_2) \\ \vdots & \vdots & & \vdots \\ L_0(S_K) & L_1(S_K) & \cdots & L_M(S_K) \end{pmatrix}, \quad \underset{N\times 1}{\mathbf{a}} = \begin{pmatrix} a_0 \\ a_1 \\ \vdots \\ a_M \end{pmatrix} \tag{8.4}$$

with $N = M + 1$. Longstaff and Schwartz (2001) emphasize that other basis functions are possible, and that even simple powers of S_k will yield accurate approximations to the American option price.

The cash flows at an arbitrary time t_k depend on whether or not exercise occurs at t_{k+1}. If exercise occurs, the cash flows going forward will change. Hence, it is not possible to determine the cash flows at t_k by going forward. Consequently, Longstaff and Schwartz (2001) apply the LSM algorithm to approximate the cash flows backward, from t_{K-1} to t_1. At time $t_K = T$, the cash flow is simply the payoff. At each time t_k $(2 \le k \le K-1)$, we find all stock price paths that are in-the-money and discount by one period the cash flows at t_{k+1} along the in-the-money paths. We then estimate the $M+1$ coefficients $a_0, \cdots, a_M$ of Equation (8.3) by regression, using the basis functions in a design matrix and using the single-period discounted cash flows as the dependent variable. The least-squares regression estimates are, therefore,

$$\hat{\mathbf{a}} = (\mathbf{L}'\mathbf{L})^{-1}\mathbf{L}'\mathbf{F}. \tag{8.5}$$

See, for example, Kutner et al. (2004). Next, we form the predicted continuation value $\hat{F}(\omega, t_{k-1})$ as the fitted values from the regression

$$\hat{F}(\omega, t_{k-1}) = \hat{a}_0 L_0(S_{k-1}) + \hat{a}_1 L_1(S_{k-1}) + \cdots + \hat{a}_M L_M(S_{k-1}). \tag{8.6}$$

We compare the predicted continuation to the value of exercise, and replace the current cash flows (at time t_k) in those stock paths where it is optimal. We repeat until time t_1 and form the American option value by discounting the time t_1 cash flows by a single period.

To illustrate with a simple example, suppose we have six stock prices, each with seven time steps. These appear at the top of Figure 8.1.

The strike price is $K = 10$ and we wish to value an American put. This implies that at time $t = 6$ there are three paths that are in-the-money: paths 3, 4, and 6. The

```
Spaths =
   10.0000   10.0000   10.0000   10.0000   10.0000   10.0000
    9.7649   10.1610    9.6139    9.5743   10.1996   10.1734
    9.5249   10.2491    9.3050    9.8990   10.5908    9.2473
    9.4070   10.8710    9.2125    9.3057   10.3304    8.8187
    9.9986   11.7387    8.9473    9.5383   10.4294    9.4736
   10.5262   11.6362    9.2696    9.8500   10.0660    9.0414
   11.2665   11.3212    9.6290    9.6288   10.0228    9.3346
t = 6 ----------------------------------------------------------------
In the money indices             3         4          6
In the money prices         9.2696    9.8500     9.0414
Predicted cash flows        0.5053    0.3350     0.5723
Immediate Exercise          0.7304    0.1500     0.9586
Paths of optimal exercise        3                    6
Updated cash flows          0.7304               0.9586
t = 5 ----------------------------------------------------------------
In the money indices             1         3          4         6
In the money prices         9.9986    8.9473     9.5383    9.4736
Predicted cash flows        0.1559    0.9019     0.4826    0.5285
Immediate Exercise          0.0014    1.0527     0.4617    0.5264
Paths of optimal exercise                  3
Updated cash flows                    1.0527
t = 4 ----------------------------------------------------------------
In the money indices             1         3          4         6
In the money prices         9.4070    9.2125     9.3057    8.8187
Predicted cash flows        0.2861    0.5617     0.4296    1.1197
Immediate Exercise          0.5930    0.7575     0.6943    1.1813
Paths of optimal exercise        1         3          4         6
Updated cash flows          0.5930    0.7875     0.6943    1.1813
t = 3 ----------------------------------------------------------------
In the money indices             1         3          4         6
In the money prices         9.5249    9.3050     9.8990    9.2473
Predicted cash flows        0.8003    0.9191     0.5980    0.9503
Immediate Exercise          0.4751    0.6950     0.1010    0.7527
Paths of optimal exercise
Updated cash flows
t = 2 ----------------------------------------------------------------
In the money indices             1         3          4
In the money prices         9.7649    9.6139     9.5743
Predicted cash flows        0.6116    0.7243     0.7538
Immediate Exercise          0.2351    0.3861     0.4257
Paths of optimal exercise
Updated cash flows
```

FIGURE 8.1 Illustration of the LSM Algorithm

least-squares estimates in Equation (8.5) are thus obtained using these three values of the stock price in the design matrix, **L**. Paths 3 and 6 both have a value of immediate exercise that is greater than that of the predicted cash flows from the regression, so early exercise is optimal in those two paths. Consequently, the cash flows from these paths are updated with the value of immediate exercise. The other remaining path 4 has a predicted cash flow greater than immediate exercise, indicating that continuation is optimal for that path. Consequently, its cash flow is not updated. At the next time step $t = 5$ there are four in-the-money paths, so four stock prices points for **L**, but early exercise is optimal only for path 3, so only the third cash flow is updated. At $t = 4$, there are four in-the-money paths, and early exercise is optimal in all of them so the four cash flows are all updated. The regressions for the final two time steps are based on 4 and 3 in-the-money stock prices, respectively, but all of the predicted cash flows are greater than the value of immediate exercise. Early exercise is therefore not optimal in any of the paths in these final time steps, and consequently none of the cash flows is updated.

The accuracy of the American option value can be improved by using the control variate technique. The idea behind this technique is that, if we assume that the error in LSM pricing of an American option from its true value is the same as the error in LSM pricing of a European option from its true value, then we can write

$$\begin{aligned}\text{American Error} &= \text{European Error}\\ \text{American Price}_{\text{True}} - \text{American Price}_{\text{LSM}} &= \text{European Price}_{\text{True}}\\ &\quad - \text{European Price}_{\text{LSM}}.\end{aligned}$$

The control variate price of the American option is, therefore,

$$\begin{aligned}\text{American Put}_{\text{CV}} = \ &\text{European Price}_{\text{True}}\\ &+ (\text{American Price}_{\text{LSM}} - \text{European Price}_{\text{LSM}}).\end{aligned} \tag{8.7}$$

In Equation (8.7), we use the American and European prices obtained from the LSM algorithm, and we use the closed form using the original Heston (1993) formulation obtained with 32-point Gauss-Laguerre quadrature. Note that (8.7) amounts to adding the early exercise premium estimated by the LSM algorithm to the closed form European price. See Hull and White (1988) for a discussion of the control variate technique for pricing American options.

The Matlab function LSM.m implements the Longstaff-Schwartz (2001) algorithm and returns American and European prices. The function requires a matrix of simulated Heston stock prices as input along with a function handle for the regression design matrix. In the example later in this subsection, we use the moment-matching algorithm presented in Chapter 7 to simulate the stock prices. The following code snippet presents a stripped-down version of the LSM.m function, for puts only.

```
function [EuroPrice AmerPrice] = LSM(...,PutCall,XmatrixHandle)
% Initialize the Cash Flows and set the last CF to the
% intrinsic value.
CF = zeros(NS,NT);
```

```
CF(:,NT) = max(K - S(:,NT), 0);
% European price
EuroPrice = exp(-r*T)*mean(CF(:,NT));
% Work backwards through the stock prices until time t=2.
for t = NT-1:-1:2
    % Stock paths in-the-money at time t
    I = find(S(:,t) < K);
    X = S(I,t);
    % Cash flows at time t+1, discounted one period
    Y = CF(I,t+1)*exp(-r*dt);
    % Regression to predict cash flows
    Z = zeros(length(X),NX);
    for k=1:NX
        Z(:, k) = feval(XmatrixHandle{k}, X);
    end
    beta = Z\Y;
    PredCF = Z*beta;
    % Indices for stock paths where immediate exercise is optimal
    J = max(K - X, 0) > PredCF;
    Ex = I(J);
    % All other stock path indices --> continuation is optimal
    Co = setdiff((1:NS),Ex)';
    % Replace cash flows with exercise value where exercise
    % is optimal
    CF(Ex,t) = max(K - X(J), 0);
    % Continued CF are discounted back one period.
    CF(Co,t) = exp(-r*dt)*CF(Co,t+1);
end
% The American option price
AmerPrice = exp(-r*dt)*mean(CF(:,2));
```

The C# code to implement the Longstaff-Schwartz (2001) algorithm is more complicated because we do not have a function for identifying in-the-money stock price paths and for producing the regression estimates in Equation (8.5). In the code for the Matlab LSM.m function, we use the built-in Matlab function find.m to identify in-the-money paths. In C#, we can use indexing to identify the paths and then use the List<> function in Linq to arrange the in-the-money paths into a matrix. The List<> function is convenient, because its dynamic nature accommodates the different number of in-the-money paths at each time point and at each simulation. The following snippet is an extract of the C# function HestonLSM().

```
// Indices for stock paths in-the-money at time t
int[] I = new int[NS];
for(int s=0;s<=NS-1;s++) {
    I[s] = 0;
    if(((PutCall == "P") & (S[s,t] < K)) | ((PutCall == "C")
       & (S[s,t] > K)))
        I[s] = 1; }
// Stock paths in-the-money at time t
int NI = 0;
```

```
List<double> X = new List<double>();
List<int> Xi = new List<int>();
for(int s=0;s<=NS-1;s++)
    if(I[s] == 1) {
        X.Add(S[s,t]);
        Xi.Add(s);
        NI += 1;
}
```

Estimating the coefficients in (8.5) with C# requires a method for matrix inversion. One popular method is to use LU decomposition, as described in Burden and Faires (2010) and Press et al. (2007), among others. Suppose that we wish to obtain the inverse of a square matrix **A**. The LU decomposition requires that **A** be factored into the product of a lower triangular matrix **L** and an upper triangular matrix **U**, so that $\mathbf{A} = \mathbf{LU}$. The inverse of **A** is then $\mathbf{A}^{-1} = \mathbf{U}^{-1}\mathbf{L}^{-1}$. The method requires little computation time because the inverse of a triangular matrix can be obtained very quickly. The C# function LU() performs LU decomposition and returns the upper and lower triangular matrices into the structure LUstruct.

```
static LUstruct LU(double[,] A) {
int N = A.GetLength(0);
double[,] B = new double[N,N];
for(int i=0;i<=N-1;i++)
    for(int j=0;j<=N-1;j++) B[i,j] = A[i,j];
for(int k=0;k<=N-2;k++) {
    for(int i=k+1;i<=N-1;i++) B[i,k] = B[i,k] / B[k,k];
    for(int j=k+1;j<=N-1;j++) {
        for(int i=k+1;i<=N-1;i++) B[i,j] = B[i,j] -
 B[i,k]*B[k,j]; } }
double[,] L = new double[N,N];
double[,] U = new double[N,N];
for(int i=0;i<=N-1;i++) {
    L[i,i] = 1.0;
    for(int j=0;j<=N-1;j++) {
        if(i>j) L[i,j] = B[i,j];
        else U[i,j] = B[i,j]; } }
LUstruct Mats;
Mats.LM = L;
Mats.UM = U;
return Mats;
}
```

The C# functions MatUpTriangleInv() and MatLowTriangleInv() return the inverse of an upper and lower triangular matrix, respectively. These algorithms are described in Burden and Faires (2010).

```
// Inverse of an upper triangular matrix
static double[,] MatUpTriangleInv(double[,] U)
{
int N = U.GetLength(0);
double[,] V = new double[N,N];
for(int j=N-1;j>=0;j--) {
    V[j,j] = 1.0/U[j,j];
    for(int i=j-1;i>=0;i--)
        for(int k=i+1;k<=j;k++)
            V[i,j] -= 1.0 / U[i,i] * U[i,k] * V[k,j]; }
return V; }
// Inverse of a lower triangular matrix
static double[,] MatLowTriangleInv(double[,] L) {
int N = L.GetLength(0);
double[,] V = new double[N,N];
for(int i=0;i<=N-1;i++) {
    V[i,i] = 1.0/L[i,i];
    for(int j=i-1;j>=0;j--)
        for(int k=i-1;k>=j;k--)
            V[i,j] -= 1.0 / L[i,i] * L[i,k] * V[k,j]; }
return V;
}
```

The inverse of a matrix is then found by straightforward matrix multiplication of the inverses of the upper and lower triangular matrices. This is accomplished using the MInvLU() function.

```
// Inverse of a matrix through LU decomposition
static double[,] MInvLU(double[,] A)
{
    LUstruct Mats;
    Mats = LU(A);
    double[,] L = Mats.LM;
    double[,] U = Mats.UM;
    double[,] Uinv = MatUpTriangleInv(U);
    double[,] Linv = MatLowTriangleInv(L);
    double[,] Ainv = MMMult(Uinv,Linv);
    return Ainv;
}
```

Finally, the estimates of the regression coefficients in Equation (8.5) are obtained using the C# function Beta().

```
// Regression parameters
static double[] Beta(double[,] X,double[] y)
{
    double[,] Xt = MTrans(X);
    double[,] XtX1 = MInvLU(MMMult(Xt,X));
    double[] Xty = MVMult(Xt,y);
    return MVMult(XtX1,Xty);
}
```

The C# functions MTrans(), MMMult(), and MVMult() are used to find the transpose of a matrix, to multiply a matrix with another matrix, and to multiply a matrix with a vector, respectively. These three functions are not presented here.

To illustrate, we implement the example of Clarke and Parrott (1999), which uses the settings $K = 10$, $r = 0.1$, and $T = 0.25$ years, with parameter values $\kappa = 5$, $\theta = 0.16$, $\sigma = 0.9$, $\rho = 0.1$, and $v_0 = 0.0625$, and spot prices 8, 9, 10, 11, and 12. We use the value of American puts computed by Ikonen and Toivanen (2008) for the Clarke and Parrott (1999) settings, namely 2.0000, 1.107641, 0.520030, 0.213668, and 0.082036. The following C# code is used to implement the LSM algorithm with these settings. We use the Moment-Matching method of Chapter 7 to simulate a set of stock price paths. The values of the correlated random variables are generated once, and the same values are fed into the Moment Matching and LSM algorithms to obtain each American put price. We use 50,000 stock price paths and 1,000 time steps per path. We also calculate the control variate prices, using the closed-form European price obtained with 32-point Gauss-Laguerre quadrature.

```
// Simulation settings
int NS = 50000;
int NT = 1000;
// Generate the correlated random variables
for(int t=0;t<=NT-1;t++)
    for(int s=0;s<=NS-1;s++)
    {
        Zv[t,s] = RandomNorm();
        Zs[t,s] = rho*Zv[t,s] + Math.Sqrt(1-rho*rho)*RandomNorm();
    }
for(int k=0;k<=M-1;k++)
{
    // LSM Euro and American prices
    settings.S = Spot[k];
    LSMPrice = HestonLSM(MTrans(MMSim(param,settings,NT,NS,
                Zv,Zs)),...);
    LSMEuro[k] = LSMPrice[0];
    LSMAmer[k] = LSMPrice[1];
    // Closed Euro price
    ClosedEuro[k] = HestonPriceGaussLaguerre(param,settings,X,W);
    // Control variate price
    CVAmer[k] = ClosedEuro[k] + (LSMAmer[k] - LSMEuro[k]);
}
```

The RandomNorm() function defined in Chapter 7 is used to generate independent standard normal random variables. The MMSim() function generates the stock price paths, using a different spot price at each "k" iteration. The matrix of paths is first transposed using the MTrans() function before being passed to the HestonLSM() function. To conserve memory these two steps are combined into a single step.

The prices using the control variate technique with the LSM algorithm are 1.99958, 1.103571, 0.519039, 0.226137, and 0.082123, which are all close the prices obtained by Ikonen and Toivanen (2008). The LSM prices are also very close, but slightly less so.

THE EXPLICIT METHOD

In Chapter 10 we will encounter methods to obtain the Heston price of European options by approximating with finite differences the PDE that these options satisfy. It is straightforward to adapt one of these methods, the explicit method, to price American options. Recall from Chapter 1 that the value $U(S,v,t)$ of a derivative with maturity t satisfies the PDE

$$\begin{aligned}\frac{\partial U}{\partial t} &= \frac{1}{2}vS^2\frac{\partial^2 U}{\partial S^2} + \rho\sigma vS\frac{\partial^2 U}{\partial v \partial S} + \frac{1}{2}\sigma^2 v\frac{\partial^2 U}{\partial v^2} - rU \\ &+ (r-q)S\frac{\partial U}{\partial S} + \kappa(\theta - v)\frac{\partial U}{\partial v},\end{aligned} \tag{8.8}$$

where we have defined $\lambda = 0$. Recall also that, since we are using t to represent maturity, the sign of the derivative $\partial U/\partial t$ is the opposite of what it would be if t represented time. We will see in Chapter 10 that the first step in solving the PDE with finite differences is to build discrete grids for the stock price, volatility, and maturity. Denote by $U_{i,j}^n = U(S_i, v_j, t_n)$ the value of the European derivative when the stock price and volatility are at points i and j respectively of their grids, and when the maturity is at the point n, for $i = 0, \cdots, N_S$, for $j = 0, \cdots, N_V$, and for $n = 0, \cdots, N_T$. The explicit method defines the value of the derivative at maturity point $n+1$ as

$$\begin{aligned}U_{i,j}^{n+1} &= U_{i,j}^n + dt\left[\frac{1}{2}v_j S_i^2\frac{\partial^2}{\partial S^2} + \frac{1}{2}\sigma^2 v_i\frac{\partial^2}{\partial v^2}\right. \\ &\left. + \rho\sigma v_j S_i\frac{\partial^2}{\partial v \partial S} + (r-q)\,S_i\frac{\partial}{\partial S} + \kappa(\theta - v_j)\frac{\partial}{\partial v} - r\right]U_{i,j}^n.\end{aligned} \tag{8.9}$$

To evaluate $U_{i,j}^{n+1}$ we need to substitute finite difference approximations of the derivatives. We will see in Chapter 10 that, when a uniform grid is constructed, namely, one that uses equidistant spacing between successive values of the stock price and volatility, the expression for $U_{i,j}^{n+1}$ in (8.9) reduces to a very simple form. A non-uniform grid, however, leads to greater accuracy with fewer grid points, but also to an expression for $U_{i,j}^{n+1}$ that is slightly more complicated.

Since the explicit method works backward in time, we start with the value $U_{i,j}^0$, namely the value of the derivative at maturity. For a put option, we use

$$U_{i,j}^0 = \max(K - S_i, 0) \tag{8.10}$$

This quantity is identical for all points $j = 0, \cdots, N_V$ in the v-direction. We then obtain $U^1_{i,j}, U^2_{i,j}, \ldots$ in succession until we reach the last maturity point, representing zero time to maturity. To price an American put, at each time step we add the early exercise condition

$$U^{n+1}_{i,j} = \max(K - S_i, U^{n+1}_{i,j}) \text{ for } j = 0, \cdots, N_V. \tag{8.11}$$

Finally, to price the option, we need boundary conditions on the maximum and minimum values of S and v. Please refer to Chapter 10 for these boundary conditions.

The Matlab function HestonExplicitPDENonUniformGrid.m calculates the Heston price of an American call or put using the explicit method and a non-uniform grid. To conserve space, parts of the function are omitted. The first part of the function defines the payoff of the option at maturity.

```
function U = HestonExplicitPDENonUniformGrid(params,...,EuroAmer)
% Temporary grid for previous time steps
u = zeros(NS,NV);
% Boundary condition for t=maturity
for s=1:NS
    if strcmp(PutCall,'C')
        U(s,:) = max(S(s) - K, 0);
    elseif strcmp(PutCall,'P')
        U(s,:) = max(K - S(s), 0);
    end
end
```

The middle part of the function loops through time and updates the option value in accordance with Equation (8.9), the derivatives of which are approximated with finite differences.

```
for t=1:NT-1
    U(1,:) = 0;
    % Boundary condition for Vmin.
    if strcmp(PutCall,'C')
        U(NS,:) = max(0, Smax - K)
        U(:,NV) = max(0, S - K);
    elseif strcmp(PutCall,'P')
        U(NS,:) = max(0, K - Smax);
        U(:,NV) = max(0, K - S);
    end
    % Update the temporary grid u(s,t)
    u = U;
    % Boundary condition for Vmin.
    for s=2:NS-1
        derV = (u(s,2)   - u(s,1))   / (V(2)-V(1));
        derS = (u(s+1,1) - u(s-1,1)) / (S(s+1)-S(s-1));
        LHS = - r*u(s,1) + (r-q)*S(s)*derS + ...;
```

```
            U(s,1) = LHS*dt + u(s,1);
        end
        u = U;
        % Interior points of the grid
        for s=2:NS-1
            for v=2:NV-1
                derS  =  (u(s+1,v)  - u(s-1,v)) / (S(s+1)-S(s-1));
                derV  =  (u(s,v+1)  - u(s,v-1)) / (V(v+1)-V(v-1));
                derSS = ((u(s+1,v)  - u(s,v))   / ...;
                derVV = ((u(s,v+1)  - u(s,v))   / ...;
                derSV =  (u(s+1,v+1)  - u(s-1,v+1)  - U(s+1,v-1)  + ...;
                L = 0.5*V(v)*S(s)^2*derSS + rho*sigma*V(v)*S(s) ...;
                U(s,v) = L*dt + u(s,v);
            end
        end
end
```

Finally, the last part of the function applies the condition in Equation (8.11) at each time step to determine whether or not early exercise is optimal.

```
if strcmp(EuroAmer,'A')
    for s=1:NS
        if strcmp(PutCall,'C')
            U(s,:) = max(U(s,:), S(s) - K);
        elseif strcmp(PutCall,'P')
            U(s,:) = max(U(s,:), K - S(s));
        end
    end
end
```

The function returns the entire grid at maturity, namely $U_{i,j}^{N_T}$ for $i = 0, \cdots, N_S$, and $j = 0, \cdots, N_V$. The Matlab function interp2.m employs two-dimensional interpolation to obtain the price of the option for values of (S, v) that lie in between points on the grid.

The C# code for implementing the explicit method is very similar and is not presented here. We do need a function for two-dimensional linear interpolation, however. This is accomplished with the C# function interp2().

```
static double interp2(double[] X,double[] Y,double[,] Z,...) {
// Find the index for X
if(xi == X[0]) {x1 = 0; xflag = 1;}
else if(xi == X[NX-1]) {x1 = NX-1; xflag = 1;}
else
    for(int i=1;i<=NX-1;i++)
        if((X[i-1] <= xi) & (xi < X[i])) {x1 = i-1; x2 = i;}
        // Find the index for Y
```

```
        if(yi == Y[0]) {y1 = 0; yflag = 1;}
        else if(yi == Y[NY-1]) {y1 = NY-1; yflag = 1;}
        else
            for(int i=1;i<=NY-1;i++)
                if((Y[i-1] <= yi) & (yi < Y[i])) { y1 = i-1;
                    y2 = i; }
        // Interpolation: both xi and yi lie off the grid points
        if((xflag==0) & (yflag==0)) {
            double z11 = Z[y1,x1]; double z12 = Z[y1,x2];
            double z21 = Z[y2,x1]; double z22 = Z[y2,x2];
            double px = (xi - Convert.ToDouble(X[x1])) / ...;
            double py = (yi - Convert.ToDouble(Y[y1])) / ...;
            double Y1int = (1.0-py)*z11 + py*z21;
            double Y2int = (1.0-py)*z12 + py*z22;
            IntValue = (1.0-px)*Y1int + px*Y2int;
        }
        // Interpolation: xi lies on the grid point, yi off
        if((xflag==1) &(yflag==0)) {
            double z11 = Z[y1,x1]; double z21 = Z[y2,x1];
            double py = (yi - Convert.ToDouble(Y[y1])) / ...;
            IntValue = (1.0-py)*z11 + py*z21;}
        // Interpolation: xi lies off the grid point, yi on
        if((xflag==0) & (yflag==1)) {
            double z11 = Z[y1,x1]; double z12 = Z[y1,x2];
                double px = (xi-Convert.ToDouble(X[x1]))/...;
            IntValue = (1.0-px)*z11 + px*z12; }
        // Interpolation: both xi and yi lie on the grid;
        if((xflag==1) & (yflag==1))
            IntValue = Z[y1,x1];
        // Return the result
        return IntValue;
}
```

To illustrate, we use the numerical example of Clarke and Parrott (1999) and Ikonen and Toivanen (2008) described in the previous section. The explicit method is implemented with the following code.

```
U = HestonExplicitPDENonUniformGrid(...);
for k=1:length(Spot);
    S0 = Spot(k);
    AmerPrice(k) = interp2(V,S,U,V0,S0);
end
```

Using a grid size of 140 and 90 for the stock price and volatility, respectively, along with 3,000 time steps, we obtain 2.000000, 1.106130, 0.518422, 0.212221, and 0.080802, respectively.

BELIAEVA-NAWALKHA BIVARIATE TREE

Beliaeva and Nawalkha (2010) have developed a path-independent two-dimensional tree for the Heston model. In their approach, separate trees for the stock price and for the variance are constructed independently of one another, and then recombined. This requires a transformation Y_t of S_t that renders Y_t and v_t independent. Recall that the Heston model is defined by the bivariate system of stochastic differential equations (SDEs)

$$\begin{aligned} dS_t &= rS_t dt + \sqrt{v_t} S_t dW_{1,t} \\ dv_t &= \kappa(\theta - v_t)dt + \sigma\sqrt{v_t} dW_{2,t} \end{aligned} \tag{8.12}$$

where $E^{\mathbb{Q}}[dW_{1,t}dW_{2,t}] = \rho dt$ is the correlation between the SDEs. The transformation of S_t is defined by

$$Y_t = \ln S_t - \frac{\rho}{\sigma} v_t - h_t \tag{8.13}$$

where

$$h_t = \left(r - \frac{\rho\kappa\theta}{\sigma} \right) t. \tag{8.14}$$

Applying Itō's lemma produces the SDE for Y_t

$$dY_t = \mu_Y(t)dt + \sigma_Y(t)dW^*_{1,t} \tag{8.15}$$

where the drift and volatility are given by

$$\mu_Y(t) = \left(\frac{\rho\kappa}{\sigma} - \frac{1}{2} \right) v_t, \qquad \sigma_Y(t) = \sqrt{1-\rho^2}\sqrt{v_t}. \tag{8.16}$$

The stochastic term of the SDE in (8.15) is

$$dW^*_{1,t} = \frac{dW_{1,t} - \rho dW_{2,t}}{\sqrt{1-\rho^2}}. \tag{8.17}$$

Since $E^{\mathbb{Q}}[dW^*_{1,t}dW_{2,t}] = 0$ the bivariate process (Y_t, v_t) is uncorrelated. This implies that the processes for Y_t and v_t can each be approximated with trinomial trees that are constructed independently of one another. Moreover, the joint probabilities in the two-dimensional tree for (Y_t, v_t) will be the product of the marginal probabilities for Y_t and v_t.

Given a value Y_t, the stock price can be recovered by inverting (8.13)

$$S_t = \exp\left(Y_t + \frac{\rho}{\sigma} v_t + h_t \right). \tag{8.18}$$

Beliaeva and Nawalkha (2010) build a trinomial tree for the transformed variance x_t defined as

$$x_t = \frac{2\sqrt{v_t}}{\sigma}. \tag{8.19}$$

They recover the variance v_t through the inverse transformation

$$v_t = \frac{1}{4}x_t^2\sigma^2. \tag{8.20}$$

A trinomial tree for the transformed variance x_t is constructed first, and transformed into a tree for the variances v_t through (8.20). Next, a tree for the transformed stock price Y_t is constructed, and transformed into a tree for the stock price S_t through (8.18). Finally, the trees are combined to form a bivariate tree on which American options can be priced. In the following sections, we explain how this is done.

Trinomial Tree for the Variance

By Itō's lemma the transformed variance x_t follows an SDE with drift

$$\mu(x_t, t) = \frac{1}{x_t}\left(\frac{2\kappa\theta}{\sigma^2} - \frac{\kappa x_t^2}{2} - \frac{1}{2}\right). \tag{8.21}$$

The time-zero node of the trinomial tree for x_t is x_0, obtained by substituting the initial variance parameter v_0 into Equation (8.19). At time $t > 0$, given that the process is at node x_t, there are two sets of moves, depending on whether $x_t > 0$ or $x_t = 0$.

Case 1. If $x_t > 0$, the up, middle, and down moves at time $t + dt$ are

$$\begin{aligned} x_{t+dt}^{\mathrm{u}} &= x_t + b(J+1)\sqrt{dt}, \\ x_{t+dt}^{\mathrm{m}} &= x_t + bJ\sqrt{dt}, \\ x_{t+dt}^{\mathrm{d}} &= x_t + b(J-1)\sqrt{dt} \end{aligned} \tag{8.22}$$

where J and b are defined in Equations (8.25) and (8.26) later. The probability of each move is

$$\begin{aligned} p_v^{\mathrm{u}} &= \frac{1}{2b^2} - \frac{J}{2} + \frac{1}{2b}\mu(x_t, t)\sqrt{dt}, \\ p_v^{\mathrm{m}} &= 1 - \frac{1}{b^2}, \\ p_v^{\mathrm{d}} &= \frac{1}{2b^2} + \frac{J}{2} - \frac{1}{2b}\mu(x_t, t)\sqrt{dt}. \end{aligned} \tag{8.23}$$

Case 2. If $x_t = 0$, the up move x^{u}_{t+dt} is defined identically to that in Equation (8.22), the down move is $x^{\mathrm{d}}_{t+dt} = 0$, and the middle move x^{m}_{t+dt} is not used. The probabilities in this case are

$$p^{\mathrm{u}}_{v} = \frac{\kappa\theta dt}{v^{\mathrm{u}}_{t+dt}}, \quad p^{\mathrm{m}}_{v} = 0, \quad p^{\mathrm{d}}_{v} = 1 - p^{\mathrm{u}}_{v} \tag{8.24}$$

where v^{u}_{t+dt} is obtained by substituting x^{u}_{t+dt} into Equation (8.20).

The preceding equations use J and b defined by

$$J = \text{floor}\left(\frac{\mu(x_t, t)\sqrt{dt}}{b} + \frac{1}{b^2}\right) \tag{8.25}$$

and

$$b = \begin{cases} b_c & \text{if } \left|b_c - \sqrt{1.5}\right| < |b_e - \sqrt{1.5}| \\ b_e & \text{otherwise} \end{cases} \tag{8.26}$$

where

$$b_e = \frac{x_0/\sqrt{dt}}{\text{floor}(x_0/\sqrt{1.5dt})}, \qquad b_c = \frac{x_0/\sqrt{dt}}{\text{floor}(x_0/\sqrt{1.5dt} + 1)}. \tag{8.27}$$

The trinomial tree for x_t and v_t are each truncated below zero (they can be truncated above an arbitrary value also, to reduce computation time). The b parameter is defined within the range $1 \leq b \leq \sqrt{2}$ and serves to contract or expand the tree to ensure that the last row of the tree for x_t is exactly zero. The trinomial tree for v_t is obtained by substituting the value of x_t at each node into Equation (8.20).

Trinomial Tree for the Stock Price

In the trinomial tree for the transformed stock price Y_t defined in Equation (8.13), jumps across multiple nodes are allowed. High values of v_t cause Y_t to jump up and down across multiple nodes while low values of v_t allow for jumps across single nodes only. Beliaeva and Nawalkha (2010) define the node span as $k_t\sigma_Y(0)\sqrt{dt}$, which represents the distance between nodes for values of Y_{t+dt}, given that the process is at the node Y_t. The case $k_t = 1$ represents a jump across a single node, while $k_t > 1$ represents a jump across multiple nodes. This parameter is defined as

$$k_t = \begin{cases} \text{Ceiling}\left(\sqrt{v_t/v_0}\right) & \text{if } v_t > 0, \\ 1 & \text{otherwise.} \end{cases} \tag{8.28}$$

Multiple jumps in Y_t are illustrated in Figure 8.2, which reproduces Exhibit 3 of Beliaeva and Nawalkha (2010). The left panel is for the case $k_t = 1$ is analogous

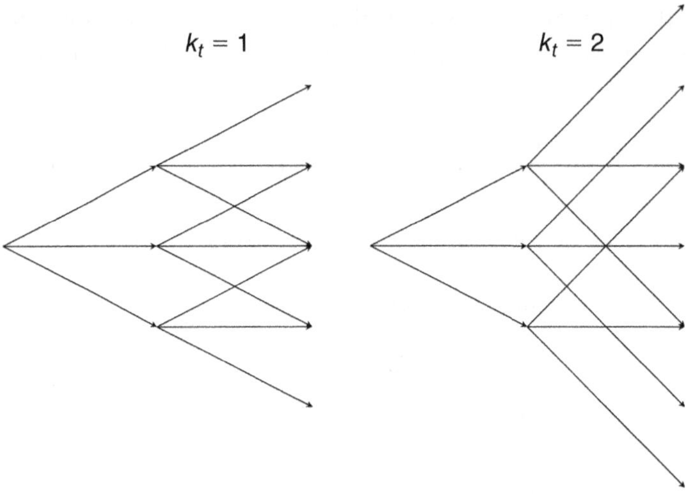

FIGURE 8.2 Jumps in the Transformed Stock Price

to an ordinary trinomial tree. The right panel illustrates the case $k_t = 2$. Note that in both cases, the tree recombines at every time step.

The time-zero value of the tree at the initial node is given by Y_0, obtained by setting $t = 0$ in Equations (8.13) and (8.14). Conditional on Y_t, the up, middle, and down values of Y_{t+dt} are

$$\begin{aligned} Y^{\mathrm{u}}_{t+dt} &= Y_t + (I+1)\cdot k_t\sigma_Y(0)\sqrt{dt}, \\ Y^{\mathrm{m}}_{t+dt} &= Y_t + I\cdot k_t\sigma_Y(0)\sqrt{dt}, \\ Y^{\mathrm{d}}_{t+dt} &= Y_t + (I-1)\cdot k_t\sigma_Y(0)\sqrt{dt} \end{aligned} \tag{8.29}$$

where I is the integer closest in absolute value to

$$\frac{\mu_Y(t)\sqrt{dt}}{k_t\sigma_Y(0)}.$$

In these expressions, $\sigma_Y(0)$ is obtained by setting $t = 0$ in $\sigma_Y(t)$ from Equation (8.16). The probabilities of up, middle, and down moves are given by

$$\begin{aligned} p^{\mathrm{u}}_Y &= \frac{1}{2}\frac{\sigma^2_Y(t)dt + e_{\mathrm{m}}e_{\mathrm{d}}}{(k_t\sigma_Y(0))^2dt}, \\ p^{\mathrm{m}}_Y &= -\frac{\sigma^2_Y(t)dt + e_{\mathrm{u}}e_{\mathrm{d}}}{(k_t\sigma_Y(0))^2dt} \\ p^{\mathrm{d}}_Y &= \frac{1}{2}\frac{\sigma^2_Y(t)dt + e_{\mathrm{u}}e_{\mathrm{m}}}{(k_t\sigma_Y(0))^2dt}, \end{aligned} \tag{8.30}$$

where

$$
\begin{aligned}
e_{\mathrm{u}} &= Y^{\mathrm{u}}_{t+dt} - Y_t - \mu_Y(t)dt = (I+1)\cdot k_t\sigma_Y(0)\sqrt{dt} - \mu_Y(t)dt, \\
e_{\mathrm{m}} &= Y^{\mathrm{m}}_{t+dt} - Y_t - \mu_Y(t)dt = I\cdot k_t\sigma_Y(0)\sqrt{dt} - \mu_Y(t)dt, \\
e_{\mathrm{d}} &= Y^{\mathrm{d}}_{t+dt} - Y_t - \mu_Y(t)dt = (I-1)\cdot k_t\sigma_Y(0)\sqrt{dt} - \mu_Y(t)dt.
\end{aligned}
\tag{8.31}
$$

When the number of time steps is large, I approaches zero and the expressions in (8.30) take on the simpler form given in Equation (18) of Beliaeva and Nawalkha (2010). The tree for the stock price S_t is obtained by applying the inverse transformation of (8.18) at every node of the tree for Y_t. Note that since Y_t depends on k_t, and since k_t depends on v_t, the tree for the variance must be constructed before the tree for the stock price.

Combining the Trinomial Trees

The final step in the approach of Beliaeva and Nawalkha (2010) is to mesh the trinomial trees for v_t and S_t into a single tree. At time zero there is a single node for (S_0, v_0). At each subsequent node (S_t, v_t) of the tree, S_t and v_t each evolve to one of three possible values (up, middle, or down). Hence, each node branches out to $3\times 3 = 9$ potential new nodes. Since these nodes recombine, however, the actual number of nodes does not increase by a factor of nine at each time step. Rather, the number of nodes depends on the values of k_t at the nodes; higher values of k_t require more nodes. The number of nodes can increase very rapidly but the fact that the tree for Y_t recombines mitigates this increase substantially. In Exhibit 11 of Beliaeva and Nawalkha (2010), for example, there are 35 nodes at the second time step.

Each node (S_t, v_t) branches out to nine nodes. Since the trees for Y_t and v_t are uncorrelated, the joint probabilities of these branches are the product of the three marginal probabilities from each tree, defined in Equations (8.23) and (8.30).

$$
\begin{aligned}
p_{\mathrm{uu}} &= p^{\mathrm{u}}_Y \times p^{\mathrm{u}}_v, & p_{\mathrm{mu}} &= p^{\mathrm{m}}_Y \times p^{\mathrm{u}}_v, & p_{\mathrm{du}} &= p^{\mathrm{d}}_Y \times p^{\mathrm{u}}_v, \\
p_{\mathrm{um}} &= p^{\mathrm{u}}_Y \times p^{\mathrm{m}}_v, & p_{\mathrm{mm}} &= p^{\mathrm{m}}_Y \times p^{\mathrm{m}}_v, & p_{\mathrm{dm}} &= p^{\mathrm{d}}_Y \times p^{\mathrm{m}}_v, \\
p_{\mathrm{ud}} &= p^{\mathrm{u}}_Y \times p^{\mathrm{d}}_v, & p_{\mathrm{md}} &= p^{\mathrm{m}}_Y \times p^{\mathrm{d}}_v, & p_{\mathrm{dd}} &= p^{\mathrm{d}}_Y \times p^{\mathrm{d}}_v.
\end{aligned}
\tag{8.32}
$$

With the tree for the stock price S_t and the joint probabilities, pricing American options is done exactly as in an ordinary trinomial tree, by working backward in time from the maturity where the payoff is known, and at each node comparing the value of the American option with the value of immediate exercise. Hence, the price of the American put at time t is

$$
\begin{aligned}
U(S_t, v_t) = e^{-r\times dt}\max\big(K - S_t,& \\
p_{\mathrm{uu}}U\left(S^{\mathrm{u}}_{t+dt}, v^{\mathrm{u}}_{t+dt}\right) + p_{\mathrm{um}}U(S^{\mathrm{u}}_{t+dt}, v^{\mathrm{m}}_{t+dt}) + \cdots + p_{\mathrm{dd}}U(S^{\mathrm{d}}_{t+dt}, v^{\mathrm{d}}_{t+dt})\big)&.
\end{aligned}
\tag{8.33}
$$

Beliaeva and Nawalkha (2010) also compute the price of American puts using the control variate technique

$$\begin{aligned}\text{American Put}_{\text{CV}} &= \text{European Put}_{\text{True}} \\ &\quad + (\text{American Put}_{\text{Bivariate Tree}} - \text{European Put}_{\text{Bivariate Tree}}).\end{aligned} \tag{8.34}$$

In (8.34), we use the American and European puts obtained from the tree, and we use the closed form using the original Heston (1993) formulation with 32-point Gauss-Laguerre integration.

Computer Implementation

The Matlab function BuildVolTree.m builds the trees for the transformed variance x_t and the variance v_t. The first part of the function computes the b parameter from Equation (8.26), finds the number of required rows (NR) and the middle row (M) where the first node x_0 is placed, and initializes the first two columns of the tree, corresponding to time zero and time one, respectively. To conserve space portions of the function have been removed.

```
function [X V RBound M] = BuildVolTree(...)
X0 = 2*sqrt(V0)/sigma;
NR = 2*NT-1;
M = (NR+1)/2;
X(M,1) = X0;
% Time 1 node for X.  Equations (22) and (30)
muX = 1/X(M,1)*(0.5*kappa*(4*theta/sigma^2-X(M,1)^2)-0.5);
J = floor(muX*sqrt(dt)/b + 1/b^2);
X(M-1,2) = X(M,1) + b*(J+1)*sqrt(dt);
X(M+0,2) = X(M,1) + b*(J+0)*sqrt(dt);
X(M+1,2) = X(M,1) + b*(J-1)*sqrt(dt);
```

The second part of the function creates the remaining nodes x^{u}_{t+dt}, x^{m}_{t+dt} and x^{d}_{t+dt}, based on the current node x_t and using Equation (8.22). Values of x_t smaller than a user-defined threshold are assumed to be zero. Next, a parameter (RBound) is created that identifies the row at which x_t becomes zero. Finally, the tree for the variances v_t is constructed using (8.20).

```
% Remaining nodes for X
for t=2:M-1
    for n=M-t+1:M+t-1
        muX = 1/X(n,t)*(0.5*kappa*(4*theta/sigma^2 ...;
        J = floor(muX*sqrt(dt)/b + 1/b^2);
        if X(n,t)>threshold && X(n,t)^2*sigma^2/4>threshold
            % Case 1: Nodes where X > 0 -- Equation (27)
```

```
            X(n-1,t+1) = X(n,t) + b*(J+1)*sqrt(dt);
            X(n+0,t+1) = X(n,t) + b*(J+0)*sqrt(dt);
            X(n+1,t+1) = X(n,t) + b*(J-1)*sqrt(dt);
            % Case 2: Nodes where X = 0
        else
              X(n-1,t+1) = X(n-1,t);
              X(n-0,t+1) = X(n-0,t);
              X(n+1,t+1) = X(n+1,t);
        end
    end
end
% Identify row of the tree where X = 0
RBound = 1;
while X(RBound,M)>=threshold && RBound < NR;
    RBound = RBound+1;
end
% Build the volatility tree V(n,t)
for t=1:NT
    for n=1:NR
        V(n,t) = X(n,t)^2*sigma^2/4;
        if V(n,t) < threshold
            V(n,t) = 0;
        end
        if X(n,t) < threshold
            X(n,t) = 0;
        end
    end
end
```

The probabilities for v_t are calculated using the Matlab function probV.m. The function applies Equation (8.23) for the case $x_t > 0$ and (8.24) for the case $x_t = 0$.

```
function [pu pm pd] = probV(X,X0,dt,kappa,theta,sigma)
muX = 1/X*(0.5*kappa*(4*theta/sigma^2 - X^2) - 0.5);
J =  floor(muX*sqrt(dt)/b + 1/b^2);
if X > 0
    % Probabilities where X > 0 (Equation 28)
    pu = 1/2/b^2 - J/2 + 1/2/b*muX*sqrt(dt);
    pm = 1 - 1/b^2;
    pd = 1/2/b^2 + J/2 - 1/2/b*muX*sqrt(dt);
else
    % Probabilities where X = 0 (Equation 33)
    Xu = X + b*(J+1)*sqrt(dt);
    Vu = Xu^2*sigma^2/4;
    pu = kappa*theta*dt/Vu;
    pm = 0;
    pd = 1 - pu;
end
```

The probabilities for S_t are calculated using the Matlab function probY.m, which applies Equation (8.30).

```
function [pu pm pd] = probY(Vt,V0,Yt,dt,rho,sigma,kappa)
% Equation 11
if Vt > 0
    k = ceil(sqrt(Vt/V0));
else
    k = 1;
end
% Equations 9 and 6
muY = (rho/sigma*kappa - 0.5)*Vt;
sigmayt = sqrt(1-rho^2)*sqrt(Vt);
sigmay0 = sqrt(1-rho^2)*sqrt(V0);
% Calculate the Yu, Ym, Yd from Equation 13
I = (round(muY/k/sigmay0*sqrt(dt)));
Yu = Yt + (I+1)*k*sigmay0*sqrt(dt);
Ym = Yt + (I+0)*k*sigmay0*sqrt(dt);
Yd = Yt + (I-1)*k*sigmay0*sqrt(dt);
% Equations 17 and 16
eu = Yu - Yt - muY*dt;
em = Ym - Yt - muY*dt;
ed = Yd - Yt - muY*dt;
pu = 0.5*(sigmayt^2*dt + em*ed)/k^2/sigmay0^2/dt;
pm =     -(sigmayt^2*dt + eu*ed)/k^2/sigmay0^2/dt;
pd = 0.5*(sigmayt^2*dt + eu*em)/k^2/sigmay0^2/dt;
```

The transformed stock price tree Y_t, the stock prices S_t and the American and European prices are all built using the BuildBivariateTree.m function. The structure of Y_t is upper triangular and constructed by placing Y_0 in the top left-hand corner of the matrix for Y_t. The values at the first time step are placed in the first nine rows of the second column of the matrix, the values at the second time step are placed in the third column starting from the top row, and so on.

The first part of the function generates the tree for the variance, finds the value of k_t at each node of v_t, and finds the number of rows needed at each time step based on the maximum value of k_t and the number of variance nodes at that step. The value of k_t at each node is obtained from Equation (8.28).

```
function [EuroPrice AmerPrice ... Branch] = BuildBivariateTree(...)
dt = T/NT;
sigmay0 = sqrt(1-rho^2)*sqrt(V0);
% Generate the volatility tree
[X V RBound M] = BuildVolTree(...);
ColChange = RBound - M + 2;
% The values of k(t) from Equation (11) and I(t) from (14)
k = zeros(2*NT-1,NT);
for t=1:NT
    for n=M-(t-1):M+(t-1);
```

```
        if V(n,t) > 0
            k(n,t) = ceil(sqrt(V(n,t)/V0));
        else
            k(n,t) = 1;
        end
    end
end
% Find dimensions of the tree
maxK = max(k);
numY = [1 3];
numV = [1 3];
numRows = [1 9];
for t=3:NT
    numY(t) = numY(t-1) + 2*maxK(t);
    numV(t) = 2*t - 1;
    numRows(t) = numV(t)*numY(t);
end
NR = max(numRows);
```

The next part of the function finds the nine branch indices at each node, and stores these in a Matlab cell. The indices depend on the current values of Y_t and k_t. In Exhibit 11 of Beliaeva and Nawalkha (2010), for example, at the first time step the top node (denoted V_{11}, Y_{11} in their exhibit) has a jump size $k_{11} = 2$. This node therefore branches out to nodes 1, 3, 5 for V_{21}, to nodes 8, 10, 12 for V_{22}, and to nodes 15, 17, and 19 for V_{23}. These nodes are placed two steps apart. The last node at the first time step (denoted V_{13}, Y_{13}) has a jump size $k_{13} = 1$. The node therefore branches out to nodes 17, 18, 19 to nodes 25, 26, 27, and to nodes 32, 33, and 34. These nodes are placed one step apart.

```
Branch = cell(numRows(NT-1),NT-1);
Branch(1,1) = {[1:9]};
B = zeros(numV(NT-1)*numY(NT-1),9);
% To Branches
for t=2:NT-1
    nY = numY(t);
    First = maxK(t)+1;
    K = k(M-(t-1):M+(t-1),t);
    for n = 1:numRows(t);
        a = ceil(n/nY);
        b = mod(n-1,nY);
        % Find the middle-to-middle branches
        B(n,2) = First + (a-1)*numY(t+1) + b;
        B(n,5) = B(n,2) +      numY(t+1);
        B(n,8) = B(n,2) +    2*numY(t+1);
        % Find the rest of the branches
        B(n,1) = B(n,2) - K(a);  B(n,3) = B(n,2) + K(a);
        B(n,4) = B(n,5) - K(a);  B(n,6) = B(n,5) + K(a);
        B(n,7) = B(n,8) - K(a);  B(n,9) = B(n,8) + K(a);
        Branch(n,t) = {B(n,:)};
    end
end
```

```
clear B;
% Adjust the last branch upward
for t=ColChange:NT-1
    for j=7:9
        Branch{numRows(t),t}(j) = Branch{numRows(t)-1,t}(j);
    end
end
```

The next part of the function creates the tree for Y_t, based on the branch indices defined earlier, and creates the joint probabilities in Equation (8.32). At each node defined by time ("t" loop), volatility ("j" loop), and transformed stock price ("r" loop), several quantities are needed: the current values of Y_t, x_t, v_t, and k_t, the values of $\mu(x_t, t)$ and I, and the branch indices to where Y_t evolves to Y_{t+dt}. These indices are in the Matlab array NewBranch. At each node, nine future values of Y_{t+dt} are created whenever $Y_t > 0$; if $Y_t = 0$ then no branches evolve from that node, and a probability of zero is assigned to each joint probability. In Exhibit 11 of Beliaeva and Nawalkha (2010) at the second time step, no branches originate from nodes (V_{24}, Y_{21}), (V_{24}, Y_{27}), (V_{25}, Y_{21}), or (V_{25}, Y_{27}). In our notation, these are rows number 22, 28, 29, and 35 in the third column of the matrix for Y_t. Finally, the joint probabilities are stored in the Matlab cell Prob.

```
% Log stock tree (Yt), (St), and (Prob)
Yt = zeros(NR,NT);
Y0 = log(S0) - rho*V0/sigma;
Yt(1,1) = Y0;
Prob = cell(numRows(NT-1),NT-1);
X0 = X(M,1);
for t=1:NT-1;
    n = 0;
    J = -(t-1):(t-1);
    for j=1:numV(t);
        for r=1:numY(t);
            n = n + 1;
            Vt = V(M+J(j),t);
            Xt = X(M+J(j),t);
            Kt = k(M+J(j),t);
            NewBranch = cell2mat(Branch(n,t));
            muy = (rho*kappa/sigma - 0.5)*Vt;
            I = round(muy/Kt/sigmay0*sqrt(dt));
            if Yt(n,t) > 0;
                for s=1:9
                    if s==2 || s==5 || s==8 % Middle node
                        Yt(NewBranch(s),t+1) = Yt(n,t) + (I+0)...;
                    elseif s==1 || s==4 || s==7 % Up node
                        Yt(NewBranch(s),t+1) = Yt(n,t) + (I+1)...;
                    elseif s==3 || s==6 || s==9 % Down node
                        Yt(NewBranch(s),t+1) =Yt(n,t) + (I-1)...;
                    end
                end
            else
```

```
                Branch(n,t) = {['No branch from (' ...]};
            end
            if Yt(n,t) == 0;
                Prob(n,t) = {zeros(1,9)};
            else
                [pvu pvm pvd] = probV(Xt,X0,...);
                [pyu pym pyd] = probY(Vt,V0,Yt(n,t),...);
                prob = [pvu*pyu pvu*pym pvu*pyd pvm*pyu ...];
                Prob(n,t) = {prob};
            end
        end
    end
end
```

The last part of the function calculates the European and American prices in the usual fashion, by working backward from maturity where the payoff is known. At each time step, the probabilities are needed to calculate the option price, and the branches are needed to link the option prices from the previous step. The function produces the price of an American option by calculating the value of S_t at each node, and comparing the value of the option with the value of immediate exercise, in accordance with Equation (8.33).

```
% Last column for the stock price and payoff at maturity
t = NT;
ht = (rf - rho*kappa*theta/sigma)*(t-1)*dt;
n = 0;
J = -(t-1):(t-1);
ST = zeros(numRows(t),1);
for j=1:numV(t);
    for r=1:numY(t);
        n = n + 1;
        Vt = V(M+J(j),t);
        if Yt(n,t) > 0
            ST(n) = exp(Yt(n,t) + rho/sigma*Vt + ht);
        end
    end
end
if strcmp(PutCall,'C')
    Euro(:,NT) = max(ST - Strike, 0);
    Amer(:,NT) = max(ST - Strike, 0);
elseif strcmp(PutCall,'P')
    Euro(:,NT) = max(Strike - ST, 0);
    Amer(:,NT) = max(Strike - ST, 0);
end
for t = NT-1:-1:1
    n = 0;
    ht = (rf - rho*kappa*theta/sigma)*(t-1)*dt;
    J = -(t-1):(t-1);
    for j=1:numV(t);
        for r=1:numY(t);
            n = n + 1;
```

```
                Vt = V(M+J(j),t);
                if Yt(n,t) > 0
                    St = exp(Yt(n,t) + rho/sigma*Vt + ht);
                    P = cell2mat(Prob(n,t));
                    B = cell2mat(Branch(n,t));
                    Euro(n,t) = P(1)*Euro(B(1),t+1) + ...;
                    Euro(n,t) = exp(-rf*dt)*Euro(n,t);
                    Amer(n,t) = P(1)*Amer(B(1),t+1) + ...;
                    Amer(n,t) = exp(-rf*dt)*Amer(n,t);
                end
                if strcmp(PutCall,'C')
                    Amer(n,t) = max(St - Strike, Amer(n,t));
                elseif strcmp(PutCall,'P')
                    Amer(n,t) = max(Strike - St, Amer(n,t));
                end
            end
        end
end
EuroPrice = Euro(1,1);
AmerPrice = Amer(1,1);
```

We use three possible versions of the BuildBivariateTree.m functions, each of which are identical except for how the branch indices and nine joint probabilities are stored. The function presented in the earlier snippets use Matlab cells for the probabilities and the branches. This simplifies the coding in Matlab, but increases the computation time. The function BuildBivariateTree2.m uses Matlab cells for the probabilities but arrays for the branches. Finally, BuildBivariateTree3.m uses arrays for the probabilities and the cells. This last function runs faster than the other two. Moreover, since it does not employ Matlab cells, it is more easily translated into C#. The disadvantage is that for the purposes of building the bivariate tree, arrays are more difficult to work with than cells. The C# code to calculate American option prices using the method of Beliaeva and Nawalkha (2010) is similar to the Matlab code and the BuildBivariateTree3.m function and is not presented here.

To illustrate, we reproduce the American put prices of Clarke and Parrott (1999) and Ikonen and Toivanen (2008). Using 50 time steps and the control variate technique, we obtain 1.996724, 1.105855, 0.519488, 0.213408, and 0.081948, all of which are accurate to within less than one penny.

MEDVEDEV-SCAILLET EXPANSION

Medvedev and Scaillet (2010) develop a method in which the American put price can be expressed analytically, as an asymptotic expansion. Their method is applicable to a wide class of stochastic volatility models. In this section, we first introduce their method for American puts under the Black-Scholes model, and then present their expansion for the Heston model. The advantage of their method is that the American put price is available in an expansion which involves analytic terms only. Hence, the method is able to generate Black-Scholes and Heston American option prices very quickly.

Medvedev-Scaillet for Black-Scholes

Under the assumptions of the Black-Scholes model the price $\mathbf{P}(S(t), t)$ at time t of an American put option with time to maturity $\tau = T - t$ follows the PDE

$$\mathbf{P}_t + (r - q)S\mathbf{P}_S + \frac{1}{2}\sigma^2 S^2 \mathbf{P}_{SS} - r\mathbf{P} = 0 \tag{8.35}$$

with boundary conditions

$$\begin{aligned} \mathbf{P}(\infty, t) &= 0 \\ \mathbf{P}(S(T), T) &= \max(K - S(T), 0) \\ \mathbf{P}(\overline{S}(\tau), t) &= \max(K - \overline{S}(\tau), 0) \\ \mathbf{P}_S(\overline{S}(\tau), t) &= -1 \end{aligned} \tag{8.36}$$

where $\overline{S}(\tau)$ is the early exercise price. See, for example, Albanese and Campolieti (2006). In Equations (8.35) and (8.36), the subscripts denote differentiation, r and q are the risk-free rate and dividend yield, and σ is the stock price volatility.

Medvedev and Scaillet (2010) construct a modified version of the PDE in (8.35) in terms of the modified price $P(\theta, \tau) = \mathbf{P}(Ke^{-\sigma\theta\sqrt{\tau}}, T - \tau)$, where θ is the normalized moneyness

$$\theta = \frac{\ln(K/S)}{\sigma\sqrt{\tau}}. \tag{8.37}$$

The modified version of the PDE still follows Equation (8.35) but replaces the last condition in (8.36) with the requirement that the early exercise price satisfy $\overline{S}(\tau) = Ke^{-\theta y\sqrt{\tau}}$. The unique solution to this modified problem is the price of a barrier option that is exercised immediately as θ reaches the barrier level y, where $y \approx 2$.

By applying the chain rule and using the PDE (8.35), it is straightforward to obtain the modified PDE, namely, (8.35) expressed in terms of $P(\theta, \tau)$

$$\theta P_\theta + P_{\theta\theta} + \frac{1}{\sigma}[\sigma^2 + 2(q - r)]P_\theta\sqrt{\tau} - 2(P_\tau + rP)\tau = 0. \tag{8.38}$$

Again, subscripts denote differentiation. The boundary conditions to the modified PDE are

$$\begin{aligned} P(-\infty, \tau) &= 0, \\ P(y, \tau) &= K(1 - e^{-\sigma y\sqrt{\tau}}). \end{aligned} \tag{8.39}$$

The main result of Medvedev and Scaillet (2010) is that the solution to the modified PDE (8.38) is the expansion

$$P(\theta, \tau) = \sum_{n=1}^{\infty} P_n(\theta)\tau^{n/2}. \tag{8.40}$$

The terms inside the sum are defined as

$$
\begin{aligned}
P_n(\theta) &= C_n[p_n^0(\theta)\Phi(\theta) + q_n^0(\theta)\phi(\theta)] + p_n^1(\theta)\Phi(\theta) + q_n^1(\theta)\phi(\theta) \\
&= C_n P_n^0(\theta) + P_n^1(\theta)
\end{aligned}
\tag{8.41}
$$

where $\Phi(\theta)$ and $\phi(\theta)$ denote the standard normal cumulative distribution function and density, respectively. We will see later that the coefficients C_n in (8.41) are evaluated at $\theta = \widetilde{y}$. To obtain the American put price $P(\theta,\tau)$, we first find the polynomials p_n^0, q_n^0, p_n^1 and q_n^1, and the coefficients C_n. We then find non-negative values of the barrier $\widetilde{y} \geq \theta$ as

$$
\widetilde{y} = \underset{y\geq\theta, y\geq 0}{\arg\max}\, P(\theta,\tau,y) \tag{8.42}
$$

where $P(\theta,\tau,y)$ is $P(\theta,\tau)$ in (8.40), but with the extra argument to emphasize the dependence of $P(\theta,\tau)$ on y through C_n. The approximation of Medvedev and Scaillet (2010) for the price of an American put, $P(\theta,\tau,\widetilde{y})$, given p_n^0, q_n^0, p_n^1, q_n^1, and C_n is the following.

Construct $P(\theta,\tau,y)$ using Equation (8.40) with $C_n = C_n(y)$.
Find $\widetilde{y}$ using (8.42), under the constraint $\widetilde{y} \geq \theta$.
Use $C_n = C_n(\widetilde{y})$ in $P(\theta,\tau,\widetilde{y})$ to find the price, using (8.40) and (8.41).

In the derivation of the quantities required of (8.40), we will need the following first- and second-order derivatives of $P_n^0(\theta)$, obtained using the chain rule

$$
\begin{aligned}
P_{n\theta}^0 &= p_{n\theta}^0\Phi + (p_n^0 + q_{n\theta}^0 - \theta q_n^0)\phi \\
P_{n\theta\theta}^0 &= p_{n\theta\theta}^0\Phi + (2p_{n\theta}^0 - \theta p_n^0 + q_{n\theta\theta}^0 - 2\theta q_{n\theta}^0 - q_n^0 + \theta^2 q_n^0)\phi.
\end{aligned}
\tag{8.43}
$$

The derivatives $P_{n\theta}^1$ and $P_{n\theta\theta}^1$ are identical to those in Equation (8.43) but in terms of p_n^1 and q_n^1 and their first- and second-order derivatives. To obtain the solution in (8.40), the polynomials p_n^0, q_n^0, p_n^1 and q_n^1 in (8.41) are found first, and the coefficients C_n are obtained afterward. First, p_n^0 and q_n^0 are defined recursively in Appendix A of Medvedev and Scaillet (2010) as

$$
\begin{aligned}
p_n^0(\theta) &= \pi_{n0}^0\theta^n + \pi_{n1}^0\theta^{n-2} + \pi_{n2}^0\theta^{n-4} + \cdots \\
q_n^0(\theta) &= x_{n0}^0\theta^{n-1} + x_{n1}^0\theta^{n-3} + x_{n2}^0\theta^{n-5} + \cdots
\end{aligned}
\tag{8.44}
$$

with coefficients $\pi_{n0}^0 = x_{n0}^0 = 1$, and with

$$
\begin{aligned}
\pi_{n,i+1}^0 &= \frac{(n-2i)(n-2i-1)}{2i+2}\pi_{n,i}^0 \\
x_{n,i+1}^0 &= \frac{x_{n,i}^0(n-1-2i)(n-2-2i) + 2\pi_{n,i+1}^0(n-2i-2)}{2n-2i-2}
\end{aligned}
\tag{8.45}
$$

for $i = 0,1,2,\cdots$. Note the dependence of $x_{n,i+1}^0$ on $\pi_{n,i+1}^0$. Obtaining p_n^0 and q_n^0 is done through a straightforward application of (8.45). The coefficients of these polynomials for $n \leq 7$ appear in Tables 8.1 and 8.2.

TABLE 8.1 Coefficients for the Polynomials p_n^0

N	θ^7	θ^6	θ^5	θ^4	θ^3	θ^2	θ^1	θ^0
1	0	0	0	0	0	0	1	0
2	0	0	0	0	0	1	0	1
3	0	0	0	0	1	0	3	0
4	0	0	0	1	0	6	0	3
5	0	0	1	0	10	0	15	0
6	0	1	0	15	0	45	0	15
7	1	0	21	0	105	0	105	0

TABLE 8.2 Coefficients for the Polynomials q_n^0

N	θ^7	θ^6	θ^5	θ^4	θ^3	θ^2	θ^1	θ^0
1	0	0	0	0	0	0	0	1
2	0	0	0	0	0	0	1	0
3	0	0	0	0	0	1	0	2
4	0	0	0	0	1	0	5	0
5	0	0	0	1	0	9	0	8
6	0	0	1	0	14	0	33	0
7	0	1	0	20	0	87	0	48

The polynomials p_n^1 and q_n^1 are of the form

$$\begin{aligned} p_n^1(\theta) &= \pi_{n0}^1\theta^n + \pi_{n1}^1\theta^{n-2} + \pi_{n2}^1\theta^{n-4} + \cdots \\ q_n^1(\theta) &= x_{n0}^1\theta^{n-1} + x_{n1}^1\theta^{n-3} + x_{n2}^1\theta^{n-5} + \cdots \end{aligned} \tag{8.46}$$

with $\pi_{n0}^1 = x_{n0}^1 = 0$. Obtaining p_n^1 and q_n^1 is more involved and is done by substituting separate solutions into the PDE of Equation (8.38). The expansion (8.40) is substituted into (8.38) and terms common to $\tau^{n/2}$ are collected. This produces Equation (29) of Medvedev and Scaillet (2010)

$$-nP_n + \theta P_{n\theta} + P_{n\theta\theta} + \widetilde{\sigma} P_{n-1\theta} - 2rP_{n-2} = 0 \tag{8.47}$$

where $\widetilde{\sigma} = [\sigma^2 - 2\mu]/\sigma$ and $\mu = r - q$. The solution to (8.47) is obtained by separating the PDE into its homogeneous and non-homogeneous part, and finding a solution for each part separately.

1. The homogeneous part of Equation (8.47) has the solution $P_n^1(\theta)$.
2. The non-homogenous part of Equation (8.47) has solution $P_n(\theta) = C_n P_n^0(\theta) + P_n^1(\theta)$.

The homogenous part of (8.47) involves the first three terms only, those with P_n and its derivatives. In the homogeneous part, substitute $P_n^1(\theta)$ from (8.41) and make use of the derivatives in (8.43) to obtain

$$(p_{n\theta\theta}^1 + \theta p_{n\theta}^1 - np_n^1)\Phi(\theta) + (-(n+1)q_n^1 - \theta q_{n\theta}^1 + q_{n\theta\theta}^1 + 2p_{n\theta}^1)\phi(\theta) = 0. \tag{8.48}$$

In the non-homogenous part of Equation (8.47), which involves only the last two terms on the left-hand side of (8.47), substitute $C_n P_n^0(\theta) + P_n^1(\theta)$ and apply the chain rule again to obtain

$$\begin{aligned}&\left(\tilde{\sigma} C_{n-1} p_{n-1,\theta}^0 + \tilde{\sigma} p_{n-1,\theta}^1 - 2rC_{n-2} p_{n-2}^0 - 2rp_{n-2}^1\right)\Phi(\theta)\\&\quad + \left(\tilde{\sigma} C_{n-1} p_{n-1}^0 + \tilde{\sigma} C_{n-1} q_{n-1,\theta}^0 - \tilde{\sigma} C_{n-1} q_{n-1}^0 \theta + \tilde{\sigma} p_{n-1}^1\right.\\&\quad \left.+ \tilde{\sigma} q_{n-1,\theta}^1 - \tilde{\sigma} q_{n-1}^1 \theta - 2rC_{n-2} q_{n-2}^0 - 2rq_{n-2}^1\right)\phi(\theta) = 0.\end{aligned} \tag{8.49}$$

Regroup (8.48) and (8.49) into terms common to $\Phi(\theta)$ and $\phi(\theta)$, which produces the system of two equations

$$\begin{aligned}&p_{n\theta\theta}^1 + \theta p_{n\theta}^1 - np_n^1 + \tilde{\sigma} C_{n-1} p_{n-1,\theta}^0 + \tilde{\sigma} p_{n-1,\theta}^1 - 2r(C_{n-2} p_{n-2}^0 + p_{n-2}^1) = 0,\\&\quad - (n+1) q_n^1 - \theta q_{n\theta}^1 + q_{n\theta\theta}^1 + 2p_{n\theta}^1 + \tilde{\sigma} C_{n-1}(p_{n-1}^0 + q_{n-1,\theta}^0 - \theta q_{n-1}^0)\\&\quad + \tilde{\sigma}(p_{n-1}^1 + q_{n-1,\theta}^1 - \theta q_{n-1}^1) - 2r(C_{n-2} q_{n-2}^0 + q_{n-2}^1) = 0.\end{aligned} \tag{8.50}$$

For each n, the first PDE in Equation (8.50) is solved for p_n^1; all other quantities are known. Similarly, the second PDE in (8.50) is solved for q_n^1. At the end of this section, we should how this can be done using the symbolic module in Matlab.

Once the polynomials p_n^0, q_n^0 are obtained by recursion, and p_n^1, q_n^1 obtained through the set of two PDEs in Equation (8.50), the coefficients C_n can be obtained by evaluating (8.40) at $\theta = y$, substituting the Taylor series expansion for $e^{-\sigma y \sqrt{\tau}}$ in (8.39), and equating the two equations for successive powers of $\tau^{n/2}$. After cancelling $\tau^{n/2}$ from both sides, this produces the following equation, which is readily solved for C_n

$$C_n[p_n^0(y)\Phi_0 + q_n^0(y)\phi_0] + p_n^1(y)\Phi_0 + q_n^1(y)\phi_0 = (-1)^{n+1}\frac{K}{n!}\sigma^n y^n \tag{8.51}$$

where $\Phi_0 = \Phi(\tilde{y})$ and $\phi_0 = \phi(\tilde{y})$ are the standard normal distribution and density, respectively, evaluated at $\theta = \tilde{y}$, the optimized value from (8.42). For example, when $n = 1$ we will see that $p_1^0 = \theta$, $q_1^0 = 1$, and $p_1^1 = q_1^1 = 0$. Hence C_1 is obtained as

$$C_1 = \frac{Ky\sigma}{\tilde{y}\Phi_0 + \phi_0}. \tag{8.52}$$

The first step in implementing the Medvedev and Scaillet (2010) expansion to the Black-Scholes price of an American put is to generate the coefficients for the polynomials p_n^0 and q_n^0. This is done with the following code, taken from the Matlab file GeneratePQ.m. The code finds coefficients up to $n = 7$, but can easily be modified for higher n.

```
p0n = inline('(n-2*i)*(n-2*i-1)/(2*i+2)*pi','n','i','pi');
q0n = inline('(qi*(n-1-2*i)*(n-2-2*i) + 2*pi*(n-2*i-2)) ...');
Q = {'q01','q02','q03','q04','q05','q06','q07'};
P = {'p01','p02','p03','p04','p05','p06','p07'};
N = 7;
```

```
% Coefficients for p0n
p0 = zeros(N,N+1);
for n=1:N
    p0(n,N-n+1) = 1;
    i = 0;
    for j=N-n+3:2:N+1
        p0(n,j) = p0n(n,i,p0(n,j-2));
        i = i+1;
    end
end
% Coefficients for q0n
q0 = zeros(N,N+1);
for n=1:N
    q0(n,N-n+2) = 1;
    i = 0;
     for j=N-n+4:2:N+1
         q0(n,j) = q0n(n,i,q0(n,j-2),p0(n,j-1));
         i = i+1;
     end
end
```

The code automatically generates the coefficients for powers of θ in p_n^0 and q_n^0, up to $n = 7$. These are represented in Tables 8.1 and 8.2.

Using the tables, it is simple to evaluate the polynomials at any desired power. Hence, for example, $p_5^0 = \theta^5 + 10\theta^3 + 15\theta$ and $q_5^0 = \theta^4 + 9\theta^2 + 8$.

The Matlab function PQ.m uses the symbolic calculator in Matlab to generate symbolic representations of the required polynomials and their derivatives, which are needed to solve the two PDE in Equation (8.50). These polynomials are

$$\begin{gathered}p_n^0, q_n^0, p_n^1, q_n^1, p_{n-1}^1, q_{n-1}^1, p_{n-2}^1, q_{n-2}^1, p_{n-1}^0, q_{n-1}^0, p_{n-2}^0, q_{n-2}^0, \\ p_{n\theta}^1, p_{n\theta\theta}^1, p_{n-1,\theta}^0, p_{n-1,\theta}^1, q_{n\theta}^1, q_{n\theta\theta}^1, q_{n-1,\theta}^0, q_{n-1,\theta}^1.\end{gathered} \tag{8.53}$$

The polynomial $q_{n\theta\theta}^1$, for example, denotes the second-order derivative $d^2q_n^1(\theta)/d\theta^2$, where $q_n^1(\theta)$ is defined by (8.46). To conserve space parts of the PQ.m function have been omitted.

```
function [p0n q0n ... dq0n_1 dq1n_1] = PQ(n,N,p0,q0)
syms theta
thet = [theta^7 theta^6 theta^5 theta^4 theta^3 theta^2 ...];
% Generate the polynomials p0n and q0n
for i=1:N
    pp(i,:) = sym(p0(i,:));
    qq(i,:) = sym(q0(i,:));
end
p0n = dot(pp(n,:),thet);
q0n = dot(qq(n,:),thet);
% Generate the polynomial p1n
syms pi11 pi12 pi13 pi14 pi15 pi16 pi17 % add more as needed
pis = [pi11 pi12 pi13 pi14 pi15 pi16 pi17; ...
syms pi
```

```
for i=1:N
    for k=1:N-i+2
        pi(i,k) = 0;
    end
    j = N-i+3;
    k = 1;
    while j<=N+1
        pi(i,j) = pis(i,k);
        k = k+1;
        j = j+2;
    end
end
p1n = dot(pi(n,:)',thet);
% Generate the polynomial q1n
syms qi11 qi12 qi13 qi14 qi15 qi16 qi17 % add more as needed
qis = [qi11 qi12 qi13 qi14 qi15 qi16 qi17; ...
syms qi
for i=1:N;
    for k=1:N-i+3;
        qi(i,k) = 0;
    end
    j = N-i+4;
    k = 1;
    while j<=N+1
        qi(i,j) = qis(i,k);
        k = k+1;
        j = j+2;
    end
    qi = qi(:,1:N+1);
end
q1n = dot(qi(n,:)',thet);
% Generate the past polynomials p0n-1 and p0n-2, etc.
if n>=2
    p0n_1 = dot(pp(n-1,:) ,thet);
    q0n_1 = dot(qq(n-1,:) ,thet);
    p1n_1 = dot(pi(n-1,:)',thet);
    q1n_1 = dot(qi(n-1,:)',thet);
else
    p0n_1 = 0;  q0n_1 = 0;
    p1n_1 = 0;  q1n_1 = 0;
end
if n>=3
    p0n_2 = dot(pp(n-2,:) ,thet);
    q0n_2 = dot(qq(n-2,:) ,thet);
    p1n_2 = dot(pi(n-2,:)',thet);
    q1n_2 = dot(qi(n-2,:)',thet);
else
    p0n_2 = 0;  q0n_2 = 0;
    p1n_2 = 0;  q1n_2 = 0;
end
% Create the derivatives
dp1n   = diff(p1n,theta);   d2p1n  = diff(dp1n,theta);
dp0n_1 = diff(p0n_1,theta); dp1n_1 = diff(p1n_1,theta);
dq1n   = diff(q1n,theta);   d2q1n  = diff(dq1n,theta);
dq0n_1 = diff(q0n_1,theta); dq1n_1 = diff(q1n_1,theta);
```

The PQ.m function is used in the GeneratePQ.m Matlab file, which generates symbolic representations of the polynomials p_n^1 and q_n^1 by solving Equation (8.50), and representations of the coefficients C_n by using (8.51). The polynomials for $n = 1$ are generated by calling the PQ.m function.

```
n = 1;
[p0n q0n ... dq0n_1 dq1n_1] = PQ(n,N,p0,q0);
p01 = p0n;
p11 = p1n;
q01 = q0n;
q11 = q1n;
```

This generates $p_1^0 = \theta$, $q_1^0 = 1$ and $p_1^1 = q_1^1 = 0$. The code becomes more complicated for higher powers. For $n = 2$, we obtain $p_2^0 = \theta^2 + 1$ and $q_2^0 = \theta$ directly from the PQ.m function, and from Equation (8.46), we know that $q_2^1 = 0$ and that $p_2^1 = \pi_{21}^1$. To obtain the unknown coefficient π_{21}^1, we create a symbolic object for the first PDE in (8.50) and solve the PDE using the Matlab built-in function solve.m. This produces $\pi_{21}^1 = C_1(\sigma^2 - 2\mu)/(2\sigma)$, where $\mu = r - q$. We then define $p_2^1 = \pi_{21}^1$.

```
n = 2;
[p0n q0n ... dq0n_1 dq1n_1] = PQ(n,N,p0,q0);
p02 = p0n;
q02 = q0n;
% Solve the first PDE for p12
syms sigma mu C1 C0 r pi21 sigma_
sigma_ = (sigma^2-2*mu)/sigma;
PDE1 = d2p1n + theta*dp1n -
n*p1n + sigma_*C1*dp0n_1 + sigma_*dp1n_1 ...;
pi21 = solve(PDE1,pi21);
p12 = pi21;
% Set q12 to known value of 0
q12 = 0;
```

For higher powers of n, the code involves cutting and pasting from the Matlab output window. The polynomials p_n^0 and q_n^0 are generated by the PQ.m function, as shown below for $n = 5$.

```
n = 5;
[p0n q0n ... dq0n_1 dq1n_1] = PQ(n,N,p0,q0);
p05 = p0n;
q05 = q0n;
```

From Equation (8.46), we know that $p_5^1 = \pi_{51}^1\theta^3 + \pi_{52}^1\theta$. Using the Matlab function subs.m, we substitute all previous values of the coefficients (for $n \leq 4$) in the first PDE in (8.50) so that π_{51}^1 and π_{52}^1 are the only unknowns remaining. We then use the collect.m function to regroup terms common to θ^3 and θ. We cut and paste the resulting two PDEs from the Matlab output into the code, and solve the first and second PDE for π_{51}^1 and π_{52}^1 respectively, using the solve.m function and the simplify.m function. With the values of π_{51}^1 and π_{52}^1 we then create p_5^1.

```
% Solve the first PDE for p15
syms pi51 C4 C3
PDE1 = d2p1n + theta*dp1n - n*p1n + sigma_*C4*dp0n_1 + ...;
PDE1 = subs(PDE1);
collect(PDE1,theta);
pi51 = solve('-2*pi51-2*r*C3+4*(sigma^2-2*mu) ... ','pi51');
pi52 = solve('6*pi51-4*pi52+2*r*(-C2*sigma^2  ... ','pi52');
pi52 = subs(pi52);
pi52 = simplify(pi52);
p15 = pi51*theta^3 + pi52*theta;
```

Finding q_5^1 is done in the same fashion. We know from Equation (8.46) that $q_5^1 = x_{51}^1\theta^2 + x_{52}^1$. We substitute all previous values of the coefficients in the second PDE in (8.50) using the subs.m function and regroup terms using the collect.m function, cut and paste into the code, solve the two resulting equations for x_{51}^1 and x_{52}^1, and create q_5^1.

```
% Solve the second PDE for q15
syms qi51
PDE2 = -(n+1)*q1n - theta*dq1n + d2q1n + 2*dp1n + sigma_*C4*p0n_1 ...;
PDE2 = subs(PDE2);
collect(PDE2,theta);
qi51 = solve('(1/48*sigma^2-1/24*mu)/sigma^4 ... ','qi51');
qi52 = solve('(-6*r*C3*sigma^2+12*C4 ... ','qi52');
qi51 = simplify(qi51);
qi52 = simplify(qi52);
q15 = qi51*theta^2 + qi52;
```

Finally, the last part of the GeneratePQ.m function finds the C_n coefficients using (8.51). For example, with $n = 2$ the code is

```
Exp2 = -sigma^2*y^2*K/2;
C2 = (Exp2 - p12*cdf - q12*pdf)/(p02*cdf + q02*pdf);
C2 = subs(C2,theta,y);
C2 = simplify(C2);
```

Note that we do not need to invoke the solve.m function to obtain C_n, because it is readily available from Equation (8.51). The code produces the coefficient

$$C_2 = -\frac{C_1\Phi_0\sigma^2 - 2C_1\Phi_0\mu + K\sigma^3y^2}{2\sigma(\Phi_0y^2 + \Phi_0 + \phi_0y)}.$$

The output of the GeneratePQ.m function is a list of all the required coefficients, which allows an expansion of $P(\theta, \tau)$ in (8.40) up to $n = 5$ terms. This output is presented in the following snippet for $n = 3$.

```
Set 1 polynomials
-----------------
p01 = theta;
p11 = 0;
q01 = 1;
q11 = 0;

Set 2 polynomials
p12 is of the form p12 = pi21
-----------------
p02 = theta^2+1;
p12 = -1/2*(-sigma^2+2*mu)*C1/sigma;
q02 = theta;
q12 = 0;

Set 3 polynomials
p13 is of the form p13 = pi31*theta
q13 is of the form q13 = qi31
-----------------
p03 = theta^3+3*theta;
p13 = -theta*(-sigma^2*C2+2*C2*mu+r*C1*sigma)/sigma;
q03 = theta^2+2;
q13 = -1/8*(-8*C2*sigma^3+16*C2*mu*sigma ...;

"C" Coefficients
----------------
C1 = sigma*y*K/(y*cdf+pdf);
C2 = -1/2*(cdf*sigma^2*C1-2*mu*C1*cdf+sigma^3*y^2*K) ...;
C3 = 1/24*(-24*y*cdf*sigma^3*C2+48*y*cdf*sigma*C2*mu ...;
```

The coefficients are copied and pasted from the Matlab output window into the Matlab function MSPutBS.m for pricing an American call option under Black-Scholes, shown here only up to $n = 2$ to conserve space.

```
function Price = MSPutBS(y,theta,K,sigma,r,q,T)
mu = r-q;
% The "C" coefficients evaluated at theta = y
cdf = normcdf(y);
pdf = normpdf(y);
```

```
C1 = sigma*y*K/(y*cdf+pdf);
C2 = -1/2*(C1*cdf*sigma^2-2*C1*cdf*mu+sigma^3*y^2*K) ...;
% Set 1 polynomials
p01 = theta ;
p11 = 0 ;
q01 = 1 ;
q11 = 0 ;
% Set 2 polynomials
p02 = theta^2+1 ;
p12 = -1/2*C1*(-sigma^2+2*mu)/sigma ;
q02 = theta ;
q12 = 0 ;
% The Black-Scholes American put approximation
cdf = normcdf(theta);
pdf = normpdf(theta);
Price = (C1*(p01*cdf + q01*pdf) + p11*cdf + q11*pdf)*T^(1/2) ...
      + (C2*(p02*cdf + q02*pdf) + p12*cdf + q12*pdf)*T^(2/2);
```

We do not create C# code to obtain the polynomials and their derivatives in Equation (8.53), because C# does not have a symbolic calculator that allows us to solve the PDEs. We do, however, create the C# function MSPutBS(), which is very similar to the MSPutBS.m function presented in the earlier code snippet. This C# function is not presented here.

Finally, obtaining American put prices is done in two steps. In the first step, we find the barrier $\widetilde{y}$ using Equation (8.42). In the second step, we feed $\widetilde{y}$ into $P(\theta, \tau, y)$ in (8.40). In Matlab, this is accomplished with the MSPriceBS.m function, which uses the built-in function fmincon.m for the first step. The moneyness θ is used for the lower bound for $\widetilde{y}$ in the fmincon.m function.

```
function [Price y theta] = MSPriceBS(S,K,T,sigma,r,q)
% Moneyness and optimization settings
theta = log(K/S)/sigma/sqrt(T);
start = 2;
options = optimset('LargeScale','off');
% Find the barrier
[y feval] = fmincon(@(p) -MSPutBS(p,...),start,...,theta);
Price = MSPutBS(y,theta,K,sigma,r,q,T);
```

We can use the bisection algorithm to find the barrier $\widetilde{y}$ in C#, by setting the objective function to be the derivative of (8.42) and finding its zero. The following function creates the derivative.

```
static double MSPutBSdiff(double y,MSset mssettings,double dy) {
    return (MSPutBS(y+dy,mssettings) - MSPutBS
           (y-dy,mssettings))/2.0/dy;
}
```

The C# function Bisection() presented in Chapter 2 is easily modified to find the zero of this objective function and is not presented here. Prices of American puts are generated in C# using the MSPriceBS() function.

```
static double MSPriceBS(double S,double K,double T,...) {
    mssettings.theta = Math.Log(K/S)/sigma/Math.Sqrt(T);
    double a = 0.5*mssettings.theta;
    double y = Bisection(mssettings,a,b,Tol,MaxIter,dt);
    if(y<mssettings.theta)
        y = mssettings.theta;
    return MSPutBS(y,mssettings);
}
```

To illustrate, we reproduce Table 2 of Medvedev and Scaillet (2010). The settings are $S = 40$, $r = 0.0488$, and $q = 0$ for various values of volatility (σ) and maturity (τ). We benchmark the results to the American put prices obtained using a trinomial tree with 500 steps. European puts are obtained using the Black-Scholes formula. This is done with the following Matlab code.

```
% Black Scholes European price
BSP = @(s,K,rf,q,v,T) (K*exp(-rf*T)*normcdf(-(log(s/K) + ...;
% Find the tree and M-S prices for Table 2
K = [35 40 45];
for k=1:3
    for i=1:9
        BSPut(k,i) = BSP(S,K(k),r,q,sigma(i),T(i));
        MSPut(k,i) = MSPriceBS(S,K(k),T(i),sigma(i),r,q);
        BTPut(k,i) = TrinomialTree(S,K(k),r,q,sigma(i),T(i),...);
    end
end
```

The portion of Table 2 for $K = 45$ from Medvedev and Scaillet (2010) is reproduced in Table 8.3. The table indicates close agreement between the American put prices obtained under the trinomial tree and those obtained using the Medvedev

TABLE 8.3 American Put Prices Under Black-Scholes

	$\tau = \frac{1}{12}$ $\sigma = 0.2$	$\tau = \frac{1}{3}$ $\sigma = 0.2$	$\tau = \frac{7}{12}$ $\sigma = 0.2$	$\tau = \frac{1}{12}$ $\sigma = 0.3$	$\tau = \frac{1}{3}$ $\sigma = 0.3$	$\tau = \frac{7}{12}$ $\sigma = 0.3$	$\tau = \frac{1}{12}$ $\sigma = 0.4$	$\tau = \frac{1}{3}$ $\sigma = 0.4$	$\tau = \frac{7}{12}$ $\sigma = 0.4$
European	4.840	4.780	4.840	4.980	5.529	5.972	5.236	6.377	7.165
M.-S.	5.000	5.085	5.261	5.059	5.702	6.237	5.286	6.506	7.377
Tree	5.000	5.088	5.267	5.060	5.706	6.243	5.287	6.510	7.383

and Scaillet (2010) expansion with five terms. The results in Table 8.3 are nearly identical to those obtained by the authors in their Table 2.

The entries in the last row of Table 8.3 are calculated with the Matlab function TrinomialTree.

```
function y = TrinomialTree(Spot,K,r,q,v,T,N,PutCall,EuroAmer)
% Trinomial tree parameters and probabilities.
dt = T/N;
u = exp(v*sqrt(2*dt));
d = 1/u;
pu = (exp((r-q)*dt/2) - exp(-v*sqrt(dt/2)))^2/
     (exp(v*sqrt(dt/2)) ... ;
pd = (exp(v*sqrt(dt/2)) - exp((r-q)*dt/2))^2/
     (exp(v*sqrt(dt/2)) ...;
pm = 1 - pu - pd;
% Calculate all the stock prices.
S = zeros(2*N+1,N+1);
S(N+1,1) = Spot;
for j=2:N+1
    for i=N-j+2:N+j
        S(i,j) = Spot*u^(N+1-i);
    end
end
% Calculate terminal option prices.
V = zeros(2*N+1,N+1);
V(:,N+1) = max(K - S(:,N+1), 0);
% Calculate remaining entries
for j=N:-1:1
    for i=N-j+2:N+j
        V(i,j) = max(K - S(i,j), exp(-r*dt)*(pu*V(i-1,j+1)
                 + pm*V(i,j+1) + ...;
    end
end
% Option price is at the first node.
y = V(N+1,1);
```

The C# code for the trinomial tree is similar and not presented here.

Medvedev-Scaillet for Heston

The Medvedev and Scaillet (2010) approximation for the American put price under the Heston (1993) model is identical in form to that for the Black-Scholes model in Equation (8.40)

$$P(\theta,\tau,v) = \sum_{n=1}^{\infty} P_n(\theta,v)\tau^{n/2}. \tag{8.54}$$

The terms inside the sum are defined as

$$\begin{aligned}P_n(\theta, v) &= C_n(v)[p_n^0(\theta)\Phi(\theta) + q_n^0(\theta)\phi(\theta)] + p_n^1(\theta, v)\Phi(\theta) + q_n^1(\theta, v)\phi(\theta)\\ &= C_n(v)P_n^0(\theta) + P_n^1(\theta, v).\end{aligned} \tag{8.55}$$

Note that the polynomials superscripted with 1 now depend on v as well as on θ, and that the C_n coefficients depend on v. To simplify the notation, we write $p_n^1 = p_n^1(\theta, v)$, $q_n^1 = q_n^1(\theta, v)$, $p_n^0 = p_n^0(\theta)$, $q_n^0 = q_n^0(\theta)$, and $C_n = C_n(v)$.

Recall the Heston PDE from Chapter 1, written here using the notation of Medvedev and Scaillet (2010) and using $\overline{\theta}$ to denote the mean reversion level of the variance process

$$\mathbf{P}_t + (r-q)S\mathbf{P}_S + \frac{1}{2}vS^2\mathbf{P}_{SS} - r\mathbf{P} + \rho\sigma vS\mathbf{P}_{vS} + \frac{1}{2}\sigma^2 v\mathbf{P}_{vv} + \kappa(\overline{\theta} - v)\mathbf{P}_v = 0. \tag{8.56}$$

Redefine the normalized moneyness as

$$\theta = \frac{\ln(K/S)}{\sqrt{v}\sqrt{\tau}} \tag{8.57}$$

and consider the transformation from $\mathbf{P}(S, v, t)$ to $P(\theta, v, t)$. We need the following derivatives, obtained as total derivatives and by applying the chain rule

$$\begin{aligned}
\mathbf{P}_t &= \frac{\theta}{2\tau}P_\theta - P_\tau,\\
\mathbf{P}_S &= P_\theta\theta_S = \frac{-1}{S\sqrt{v}\sqrt{\tau}}P_\theta,\\
\mathbf{P}_{SS} &= P_{\theta\theta}(\theta_S)^2 + P_\theta\theta_{SS} = \frac{1}{S^2 v\tau}P_{\theta\theta} + \frac{1}{S^2\sqrt{v}\sqrt{\tau}}P_\theta,\\
\mathbf{P}_v &= P_v + P_\theta\theta_v = P_v - \frac{\theta}{2v}P_\theta,\\
\mathbf{P}_{vS} &= P_{v\theta}\theta_S - \frac{1}{2v}(\theta_S P_\theta + \theta P_{\theta\theta}\theta_S) = \frac{-1}{S\sqrt{v}\sqrt{\tau}}P_{v\theta} + \frac{1}{2Sv^{3/2}\sqrt{\tau}}P_\theta + \frac{\theta}{2Sv^{3/2}\sqrt{\tau}}P_{\theta\theta},\\
\mathbf{P}_{vv} &= P_{vv} - \frac{\theta}{v}P_{v\theta} + \frac{\theta^2}{4v^2}P_{\theta\theta} + \frac{3\theta}{4v^2}P_\theta.
\end{aligned} \tag{8.58}$$

We have used the following derivatives of θ

$$\begin{aligned}
\theta_S &= \frac{-1}{S\sqrt{v}\sqrt{\tau}}, \qquad \theta_{SS} = \frac{1}{S^2\sqrt{v}\sqrt{\tau}}, \qquad \theta_{Sv} = \frac{1}{2Sv^{3/2}\sqrt{\tau}},\\
\theta_v &= \frac{-\theta}{2v}, \qquad \theta_{vv} = \frac{\theta - \theta_v v}{v^2} = \frac{3\theta}{4v^2}.
\end{aligned} \tag{8.59}$$

Substitute the derivatives in Equation (8.58) into the Heston PDE of (8.56), multiply by 2τ, and group terms common to $\sqrt{\tau}$ and τ to obtain

$$\begin{aligned}
&P_{\theta\theta} + \theta P_\theta - 2\tau P_\tau \\
&+ \sqrt{\tau}\left[\frac{1}{\sqrt{v}}\left(v + 2\left(q - r\right)\right)P_\theta + \rho\sigma\sqrt{v}\left(-2P_{v\theta} + \frac{1}{v}P_\theta + \frac{\theta}{v}P_{\theta\theta}\right)\right] \\
&+ \tau\left[\kappa\left(\overline{\theta} - v\right)\left(2P_v - \frac{\theta}{v}P_\theta\right) + \sigma^2 v\left(P_{vv} - \frac{\theta}{v}P_{v\theta} + \frac{\theta^2}{4v^2}P_{\theta\theta} + \frac{3\theta}{4v^2}P_\theta\right) - 2rP\right] \\
&= 0.
\end{aligned} \tag{8.60}$$

As before, express the PDE of Equation (8.60) in terms of $P_n(\theta, v)$. Terms that are multiplied by $\sqrt{\tau}$ get shifted back once in n, while those multiplied by τ get shifted back twice in n. After re-arranging this produces

$$\begin{aligned}
&P_{n\theta\theta} + \theta P_{n\theta} - nP_n \\
&\quad + \frac{1}{\sqrt{v}}(v + 2(q - r))P_{n-1,\theta} + \rho\sigma\sqrt{v}\left(-2P_{n-1,v\theta} + \frac{1}{v}P_{n-1,\theta} + \frac{\theta}{v}P_{n-1,\theta\theta}\right) \\
&\quad + \kappa(\overline{\theta} - v)\left(2P_{n-2,v} - \frac{\theta}{v}P_{n-2,\theta}\right) \\
&\quad + \sigma^2 v\left(P_{n-2,vv} - \frac{\theta}{v}P_{n-2,v\theta} + \frac{\theta^2}{4v^2}P_{n-2,\theta\theta} + \frac{3\theta}{4v^2}P_{n-2,\theta}\right) - 2rP_{n-2} = 0.
\end{aligned} \tag{8.61}$$

The solution to the PDE in Equation (8.61) is found using the same reasoning that was applied to solve the Black-Scholes PDE in (8.47), by considering the homogeneous and non-homogeneous portions of the PDE separately. Hence, the first three terms of (8.61) comprise the homogeneous part, and the remaining terms comprise the non-homogeneous part. As in the Black-Scholes case the homogeneous part assumes a solution of the form

$$P_n^1(\theta, v) = p_n^1(\theta, v)\Phi(\theta) + q_n^1(\theta, v)\phi(\theta) \tag{8.62}$$

while the non-homogeneous part assumes a solution of the form

$$\begin{aligned}
P_n(\theta, v) &= C_n(v)P_n^0(\theta) + P_n^1(\theta, v) \\
&= C_n(v)[p_n^0(\theta)\Phi(\theta) + q_n^0(\theta)\phi(\theta)] + p_n^1(\theta, v)\Phi(\theta) + q_n^1(\theta, v)\phi(\theta).
\end{aligned} \tag{8.63}$$

We will need the following derivatives of $P_n(\theta, v)$, obtained by applying the chain rule

$$\begin{aligned}
P_{n\theta} &= C_n[p_{n\theta}^0\Phi + p_n^0\phi + q_{n\theta}^0\phi - q_n^0\theta\phi] + p_{n\theta}^1\Phi + p_n^1\phi + q_{n\theta}^1\phi - q_n^1\theta\phi, \\
P_{n\theta\theta} &= C_n[p_{n\theta\theta}^0\Phi + 2p_{n\theta}^0\phi - p_n^0\theta\phi + q_{n\theta\theta}^0\phi - 2q_{n\theta}^0\theta\phi - q_n^0\phi + q_n^0\theta^2\phi] \\
&\quad + p_{n\theta\theta}^1\Phi + 2p_{n\theta}^1\phi - p_n^1\theta\phi + q_{n\theta\theta}^1\phi - 2q_{n\theta}^1\theta\phi - q_n^1\phi + q_n^1\theta^2\phi, \\
P_{nv} &= C_{nv}[p_n^0\Phi + q_n^0\phi] + p_{nv}^1\Phi + q_{nv}^1\phi,
\end{aligned}$$

$$
\begin{aligned}
P_{nvv} &= C_{nvv}[p_n^0\Phi + q_n^0\phi] + p_{nvv}^1\Phi + q_{nvv}^1\phi, \\
P_{nv\theta} &= C_{nv}[p_{n\theta}^0\Phi + p_n^0\phi + q_{n\theta}^0\phi - q_n^0\theta\phi] + p_{nv\theta}^1\Phi + p_{nv}^1\phi + q_{nv\theta}^1\phi - q_{nv}^1\theta\phi.
\end{aligned}
\tag{8.64}
$$

Substitute these derivatives into the solutions for Equations (8.62) and (8.63) of the homogeneous and non-homogeneous parts, respectively, and collect terms common to $\Phi(\theta)$ and to $\phi(\theta)$. The terms common to $\Phi(\theta)$ are

$$
\begin{aligned}
& p_{n\theta\theta}^1 + \theta p_{n\theta}^1 - np_n^1 \; + \frac{1}{\sqrt{v}}(v + 2(q-r))\{C_{n-1}p_{n-1,\theta}^0 + p_{n-1,\theta}^1\} \\
& + \rho\sigma\sqrt{v}\left(-2\left\{C_{n-1,v}p_{n-1,\theta}^0 + p_{n-1,v\theta}^1\right\} + \frac{1}{v}\{C_{n-1}p_{n-1,\theta}^0 + p_{n-1,\theta}^1\}\right) \\
& + \rho\sigma\sqrt{v}\left(\frac{\theta}{v}\left\{C_{n-1}p_{n-1,\theta\theta}^0 + p_{n-1,\theta\theta}^1\right\}\right) \\
& + \kappa(\overline{\theta} - v)\left(2\left\{C_{n-2,v}p_{n-2}^0 + p_{n-2,v}^1\right\} - \frac{\theta}{v}\{C_{n-2}p_{n-2,\theta}^0 + p_{n-2,\theta}^1\}\right) \\
& + \sigma^2 v\left(C_{n-2,vv}p_{n-2}^0 + p_{n-2,vv}^1 - \frac{\theta}{v}\left\{C_{n-2,v}p_{n-2,\theta}^0 + p_{n-2,v\theta}^1\right\}\right) \\
& + \sigma^2 v\left(\frac{\theta^2}{4v^2}\left\{C_{n-2}p_{n-2,\theta\theta}^0 + p_{n-2,\theta\theta}^1\right\} + \frac{3\theta}{4v^2}\{C_{n-2}p_{n-2,\theta}^0 + p_{n-2,\theta}^1\}\right) \\
& - 2r\{C_{n-2}p_{n-2}^0 + p_{n-2}^1\} = 0.
\end{aligned}
\tag{8.65}
$$

The terms common to ϕ are

$$
\begin{aligned}
& -(n+1)q_n^1 - \theta q_{n\theta}^1 + q_{n\theta\theta}^1 + 2p_{n\theta}^1 \\
& + \frac{1}{\sqrt{v}}(v + 2(q-r))(C_{n-1}[p_{n-1}^0 + q_{n-1,\theta}^0 - q_{n-1}^0\theta] + p_{n-1}^1 + q_{n-1,\theta}^1 - q_{n-1}^1\theta) \\
& + \rho\sigma\sqrt{v}\left(\begin{matrix} -2\left\{\begin{matrix} C_{n-1,v}\left[p_{n-1}^0 + q_{n-1,\theta}^0 - q_{n-1}^0\theta\right] \\ +p_{n-1,v}^1 + q_{n-1,v\theta}^1 - \theta q_{n-1,v}^1 \end{matrix}\right\} + \frac{1}{v}\left\{\begin{matrix} C_{n-1}\left[p_{n-1}^0 + q_{n-1,\theta}^0 - q_{n-1}^0\theta\right] \\ +p_{n-1}^1 + q_{n-1,\theta}^1 - q_{n-1}^1\theta \end{matrix}\right\} \\ + \frac{\theta}{v}\left\{\begin{matrix} C_{n-1}\left[2p_{n-1,\theta}^0 - p_{n-1}^0\theta + q_{n-1,\theta\theta}^0 - 2q_{n-1,\theta}^0\theta - q_{n-1}^0 + q_{n-1}^0\theta^2\right] \\ +2p_{n-1,\theta}^1 - p_{n-1}^1\theta + q_{n-1,\theta\theta}^1 - 2q_{n-1,\theta}^1\theta - q_{n-1}^1 + q_{n-1}^1\theta^2 \end{matrix}\right\} \end{matrix}\right) \\
& + \kappa(\overline{\theta} - v)\left(2\left\{C_{n-2,v}q_{n-2}^0 + q_{n-2,v}^1\right\} - \frac{\theta}{v}\left\{\begin{matrix} C_{n-2}\left[p_{n-2}^0 + q_{n-2,\theta}^0 - q_{n-2}^0\theta\right] \\ +p_{n-2}^1 + q_{n-2,\theta}^1 - q_{n-2}^1\theta \end{matrix}\right\}\right) \\
& + \sigma^2 v\left(\begin{matrix} \left\{C_{n-2,vv}q_{n-2}^0 + q_{n-2,vv}^1\right\} - \frac{\theta}{v}\left\{\begin{matrix} C_{n-2,v}\left[p_{n-2}^0 + q_{n-2,\theta}^0 - q_{n-2}^0\theta\right] \\ +p_{n-2,v}^1 + q_{n-2,v\theta}^1 - \theta q_{n-2,v}^1 \end{matrix}\right\} \\ + \frac{\theta^2}{4v^2}\left\{\begin{matrix} C_{n-2}\left[2p_{n-2,\theta}^0 - p_{n-2}^0\theta + q_{n-2,\theta\theta}^0 - 2q_{n-2,\theta}^0\theta - q_{n-2}^0 + q_{n-2}^0\theta^2\right] \\ +2p_{n-2,\theta}^1 - p_{n-2}^1\theta + q_{n-2,\theta\theta}^1 - 2q_{n-2,\theta}^1\theta - q_{n-2}^1 + q_{n-2}^1\theta^2 \end{matrix}\right\} \\ + \frac{3\theta}{4v^2}\{C_{n-2}[p_{n-2}^0 + q_{n-2,\theta}^0 - q_{n-2}^0\theta] + p_{n-2}^1 + q_{n-2,\theta}^1 - q_{n-2}^1\theta\} \end{matrix}\right) \\
& - 2r(C_{n-2}q_{n-2}^0 + q_{n-2}^1) = 0.
\end{aligned}
\tag{8.66}
$$

Note that the homogeneous parts of Equations (8.65) and (8.66) are identical to that for the Black-Scholes case, so combining these two parts produces (8.48) from the previous section.

Equations (8.65) and (8.66) form the system of two equations to be solved, done in a manner analogous to that used to solve the two equations in (8.50) for the Black-Scholes American put. For each n, the PDE in (8.65) is solved for p_n^1 as all other quantities are known. Similarly, the PDE in (8.66) is solved for q_n^1 as all other quantities are known. The polynomials p_n^0 and q_n^0 are obtained by recursion and are identical to those in Tables 8.1 and 8.2, respectively. The polynomials p_n^1 are identical in form to those in (8.46), reproduced here for convenience

$$p_n^1(\theta, v) = \pi_{n0}^1 \theta^n + \pi_{n1}^1 \theta^{n-2} + \pi_{n2}^1 \theta^{n-4} + \cdots \tag{8.67}$$

The polynomials q_n^1, on the other hand, now take the form

$$q_n^1(\theta, v) = x_{n1}^1 \theta^{3n-5} + x_{n2}^1 \theta^{3n-7} + x_{n3}^1 \theta^{3n-9} + x_{n4}^1 \theta^{3n-11} + \cdots \tag{8.68}$$

For example

$$\begin{aligned} q_4^1 &= x_{41}^1 \theta^7 + x_{42}^1 \theta^5 + x_{43}^1 \theta^3 + x_{44}^1 \theta, \\ q_5^1 &= x_{51}^1 \theta^{10} + x_{52}^1 \theta^8 + x_{53}^1 \theta^6 + x_{54}^1 \theta^4 + x_{55}^1 \theta^2 + x_{56}^1. \end{aligned}$$

Once the polynomials p_n^1, q_n^1, p_n^0, and q_n^0 have been obtained, the coefficients $C_n(v)$ are constructed by evaluating Equation (8.55) at $\theta = y$ and substituting a Taylor series expansion for $\exp(\sqrt{v}y\sqrt{\tau})$. After canceling $\tau^{n/2}$ from both sides, this produces the following equation, which is readily solved for C_n

$$C_n(v)[p_n^0(y)\Phi_0 + q_n^0(y)\phi_0] + p_n^1(y, v)\Phi_0 + q_n^1(y, v)\phi_0 = \frac{(-1)^{n+1}K}{n!} v^{n/2} y^n. \tag{8.69}$$

As in the Black-Scholes case the coefficients C_n are evaluated at $\theta = \tilde{y}$. To obtain the American put price $P(\theta, \tau, v)$, we first find the polynomials p_n^0, q_n^0, p_n^1 and q_n^1, and the coefficients $C_n(v)$. We then find the barrier y as

$$\tilde{y} = \underset{y \geq \theta, y \geq 0}{\arg\max} P(\theta, \tau, v, y) \tag{8.70}$$

where $P(\theta, \tau, y, v)$ is $P(\theta, \tau, v)$ in Equation (8.54) but with the extra argument to emphasize the dependence of $P(\theta, \tau, v)$ on y through $C_n(v)$. The first approximation of Medvedev and Scaillet (2010) for the price of an American put, $P(\theta, \tau, v, \tilde{y})$, given p_n^0, q_n^0, p_n^1, q_n^1, and C_n is analogous to that in the Black-Scholes case.

Approximation 1:
Construct $P(\theta, \tau, v, y)$ using (8.54) with $C_n = C_n(v, y)$.
Find $\tilde{y}$ using (8.70), under the constraint $\tilde{y} \geq \theta$.
Use $C_n = C_n(v, \tilde{y})$ in $P(\theta, \tau, v, \tilde{y})$ to find the price.

Medvedev and Scaillet (2010) point out that the case of an infinite barrier, $\widetilde{y} = \infty$, corresponds to a European put. They recommend obtaining the price of an American put as the European put obtained using a closed-form, such as those covered in Chapters 1, 3, or 4, plus the early exercise premium. Their second approximation for the American put is, therefore, the control variate price.

Approximation 2:

Find the price of the European put $P(K)$ using a closed-form solution.

Find $\widetilde{y}$ as in the first approximation.

Obtain the early exercise premium as $\varepsilon = P(\theta, \tau, v, \widetilde{y}) - P(\theta, \tau, v, \infty)$.

Obtain the American put price as $P_A(K) = P(K) + \varepsilon$.

We illustrate the maximization problem in Equation (8.70) in Figure 8.3 by plotting $P(\theta, \tau, v, y)$ over various values of y, using the settings of Clarke and Parrott (1999) for the spot prices 8, 9, and 11. The optimal values $\widetilde{y}$ are represented by dashed lines and all lie within the vicinity $\widetilde{y} \approx 2$. The curves have been rescaled so to make the graph more illustrative.

In the remainder of this section, we present the Matlab code for obtaining the Medvedev and Scaillet (2010) approximation for the American put under the Heston

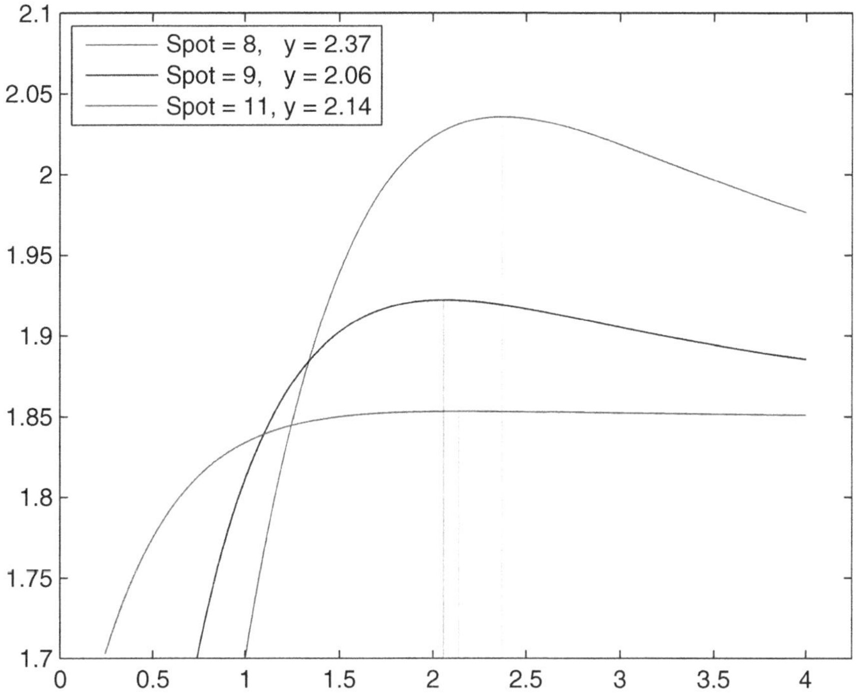

FIGURE 8.3 Barrier Levels for the Medvedev-Scaillet Approximation

model. The Matlab function PQHeston.m creates the polynomials p_n^0, q_n^0, p_n^1, q_n^1, in the same way that was done with the PQ.m function for the Black-Scholes model in the previous section. It is nearly identical to PQ.m, and similarly requires the coefficients for p_n^0 and q_n^0, taken from Tables 8.1 and 8.2, as inputs.

```
function [p0n q0n p1n q1n ...] = PQHeston(n,N,p0,q0)
syms theta
thet = [theta^7 theta^6 theta^5 theta^4 theta^3 theta^2
       theta^1 theta^0];
% Generate the coefficients p0n and q0n
for i=1:N
    pp(i,:) = sym(p0(i,:));
    qq(i,:) = sym(q0(i,:));
end
% Generate the polynomials p0n and q0n
p0n = dot(pp(n,:),thet);
q0n = dot(qq(n,:),thet);
```

The PQHeston.m function is used in the GeneratePQHeston.m Matlab file. This file is analogous to the GeneratePQ.m file for the Black-Scholes model presented in the previous section. The code generates symbolic representations of the polynomials p_n^1 and q_n^1 by solving Equations (8.65) and (8.66), and the coefficients C_n by solving (8.69). For each n, the code works in the same manner as in the Black-Scholes case: by generating symbolic representations of the polynomials using the PQHeston.m function, forming two PDEs, collecting terms common to powers of θ, and solving for p_n^1, q_n^1, and C_n. This requires that output from the collect.m function be cut and pasted into the Matlab file GeneratePQHeston.m itself.

The portion of the GeneratePQHeston for $n = 4$ is presented later for illustration. The first part of the code uses the GeneratePQ.m function to generate symbolic representations of the polynomials p_4^0 and q_4^0, and also generates the required first- and second-order derivatives of the polynomials.

```
n = 4;
[p0n q0n p1n q1n p1n_1 q1n_1 ...] = PQHeston(n,N,p0,q0);
p04 = p0n;
q04 = q0n;
dp1n_1   = diff(p1n_1,theta);    % Der of p1(n-1) wrt theta
dq1n_1   = diff(q1n_1,theta);    % Der of q1(n-1) wrt theta
d2p1vt_1 = diff(dp1n_1,v);       % Der of p1(n-1) wrt theta & v
```

The second part of the code sets $C_{n-1} = C_3$ and $C_{n-2} = C_2$, takes the volatility derivatives of both, and creates the first PDE in (8.65). Terms common to powers of θ (namely θ^2 and θ^0 for $n = 4$) are collected using the collect.m function, and the expressions resulting from this collection are cut and paste into the solve.m function. The solve.m functions are used to solve the expressions for π^1_{41} and π^1_{42}, and p^1_4 is formed as $p^1_4(\theta, v) = \pi^1_{41}\theta^2 + \pi^1_{42}$, in accordance with Equation (8.67).

```
Cn_1 = C3;
Cn_2 = C2;
Cvn_1  = diff(Cn_1,v);
Cvn_2  = diff(Cn_2,v);
Cvvn_2 = diff(Cn_2,v,2);
syms pi41 pi42
PDE1 = d2p1n + theta*dp1n - n*p1n + 1/sqrt(v)*(v - 2*mu) ... ;
collect(subs(PDE1),theta)
pi41 = solve(' (3/v*(v-2*mu)*(2*cdf^2*y*mu^2 ... ',pi41);
pi42 = solve('2*pi41+rho*sigma*v^(1/2) ... ',pi42);
p14 = pi41*theta^2 + pi42;
```

Similarly, the next part of the code defines the second PDE and collects terms common to powers of θ. The resulting expressions are cut and paste and solved for x^1_{41}, x^1_{42}, x^1_{43}, and x^1_{44}. The polynomial q^1_4 is the formed as $q^1_4(\theta, v) = x^1_{41}\theta^7 + x^1_{42}\theta^5 + x^1_{43}\theta^3 + x^1_{44}\theta$, in accordance with Equation (8.68).

```
syms qi41 qi42 qi43 qi44
PDE2 = -(n+1)*q1n - theta*dq1n + d2q1n + 2*dp1n ...;
collect(subs(PDE2),theta)
qi41 = solve('(-12*qi41+1/32*rho^3*sigma^3 ... ',qi41);
qi42 = solve('(rho*sigma/v^(1/2) ... ',qi42);
qi43 = solve('(rho*sigma/v^(1/2)*(1/4*y* ... ',qi43);
qi44 = solve('(-6*qi44+3/4*sigma^2/v ... ',qi44);
q14 = qi41*theta^7 + qi42*theta^5 + qi43*theta^3 + qi44*theta;
```

The last part of the code for $n = 4$ uses p^0_4, q^0_4, p^1_4 and q^1_4 to obtain the coefficient C_4, in accordance with Equation (8.69). Note that the code substitutes $\widetilde{y}$ for θ, using the subs.m function.

```
syms C4
Put4 = C4*(p04*cdf + q04*pdf) + p14*cdf + q14*pdf;
Exp4 = -v^(4/2)*y^4*K/24;
C4 = solve(Put4 - Exp4,C4);
C4 = subs(C4,theta,y);
```

The code in the GeneratePQHeston.m file, thus, generates polynomials and coefficients up to and including $n = 5$. The expressions for these quantities are cut and paste from the Matlab output screen into the function MSPutHeston.m, which is similar to the MSPutBS.m function defined in the previous section for pricing American puts under the Black-Scholes model. The function can accommodate an expansion up to and including fifth order, but can be reduced to third or fourth orders to reduce computational time.

```
function Price = MSPutHeston(y,theta,K,params,r,q,T,NumTerms)
cdf = normcdf(y);
pdf = normpdf(y);
% First set of polynomials
p11 = 0 ;
q11 = 0 ;
p01 = theta ;
q01 = 1 ;
C1 = v^(1/2)*y*K/(y*cdf+pdf) ;
% Second set of polynomials
p12 = 1/2*(v-2*mu)*y*K/(y*cdf+pdf) ;
q12 = 1/4*rho*sigma*theta*y*K/(y*cdf+pdf) ;
p02 = theta^2+1 ;
q02 = theta ;
C2 = -1/4*y*K*(2*v*cdf-4*cdf*mu+y*rho*sigma*pdf ... ;
% Fifth set of polynomials
if NumTerms == 5
    p15 = -1/192*y*K/v^(3/2)*(-16*v*y^2*sigma^3 ... ;
    q15 = 1/6144*rho^4*sigma^4/v^(3/2)*y*K ... ;
    p05 = theta^5+10*theta^3+15*theta ;
    q05 = theta^4+9*theta^2+8 ;
    C5 = -1/645120*(-40320*y^13*cdf^2*v^6 ...;
end
% The Heston American put approximation
cdf = normcdf(theta);
pdf = normpdf(theta);
Price = (C1*(p01*cdf + q01*pdf) + p11*cdf + q11*pdf)*T^(1/2)...
      + (C2*(p02*cdf + q02*pdf) + p12*cdf + q12*pdf)*T^(2/2)...
      + (C3*(p03*cdf + q03*pdf) + p13*cdf + q13*pdf)*T^(3/2);
if NumTerms == 4
    Price = Price + (C4*(p04*cdf + q04*pdf) + p14*cdf
          + q14*pdf)*T^(4/2);
elseif NumTerms == 5
    Price = Price + (C4*(p04*cdf + q04*pdf) + p14*cdf
          + q14*pdf)*T^(4/2) ...
                + (C5*(p05*cdf + q05*pdf) + p15*cdf
                  + q15*pdf)*T^(5/2);
end
```

The Matlab function MSPrice.m returns the second approximation of Medvedev and Scaillet (2010) of the American put price. Recall that this approximation uses the expansion to find the early exercise premium, and obtains the price of the American put as the price of the European put obtained under a closed-form solution plus the early exercise premium. The built-in Matlab function fminbnd.m for bounded optimization in a single variable is used to find $\widetilde{y}$ from Equation (8.70), using $(\max(\theta,2),3)$ as the bounds.

```
function [EuroPutClosed AmerPutMS AmerPut EEP theta y] = MSPrice(...)
% Closed-form European put
EuroPutClosed = HestonPriceNewtonCoates('P',...);
% Find the barrier level, y
theta = log(Strike/S)/sqrt(v0)/sqrt(T);
lo = max(2,theta);
y = fminbnd(@(p) -MSPutHeston(p,...,NumTerms),lo,3);
% Euro and Amer put by MS expansion, and early ex. premium
EuroPutMS = MSPutHeston(yinf,...,NumTerms);
AmerPutMS = MSPutHeston(y,    ...,NumTerms);
EEP = AmerPutMS - EuroPutMS;
% American put terms using Approximation 2
AmerPut = EuroPutClosed + EEP;
```

With these functions, generating American put prices using the second approximation of Medvedev and Scaillet (2010) is straightforward. The C# code to generate the American put price is similar and not presented. In C#, however, we use the bisection algorithm to find $\widetilde{y}$. We, therefore, need the following C# function for the derivative of the put price.

```
static double MSPutDiff(y,...,dy)
{
    return (MSPutHeston(y+dy,...) - MSPutHeston(y-dy,...))/2.0/dy;
}
```

The MSPrice() function uses the MSPutHeston() function, which contains the expansion terms, to generate the American put price as the closed-form European put, plus the early exercise premium.

```
static double[] MSPrice(HParam param,...,int NumTerms,double yinf)
// Closed-form European put
double EuroPutClosed = HestonPriceNewtonCoates(param,opset,
       method,A,B,N);
// Moneyness
double theta = Math.Log(K/S)/Math.Sqrt(v0)/Math.Sqrt(T);
// Lower point for the bisection algorithm
double a = Math.Max(2.0,theta);
// Find the barrier level
```

```
double y = Bisection(a,b,theta,K,param,r,q,T,NumTerms,tol,
           MaxIter,dy);
if(y<theta)
    y = theta;
// Find the early exercise premium
double AmerPutMS = MSPutHeston(y,theta,K,param,r,q,T,NumTerms);
double EuroPutMS = MSPutHeston(yinf,theta,K,param,r,q,T,NumTerms);
double EEP = AmerPutMS - EuroPutMS;
// Control variate American put
double AmerPut = EuroPutClosed + EEP;
```

To illustrate, we continue with the example of Clarke and Parrott (1999) and Ikonen and Toivanen (2008). This is accomplished with the following Matlab code, which uses five terms in the expansion.

```
% Settings from Clarke and Parrott
S = [8 9 10 11 12];
TruePrice = [2.00 1.107641 0.520030 0.213668 0.082036];
Strike = 10;
% Find the Medvedev-Scaillet Heston price
NumTerms = 5;
yinf = 1e4
for k=1:5
    [EuroPut AmerPutMS AmerPut(k) EEP theta(k) y(k)]
     = MSPrice(S(k),...);
    error(k) = TruePrice(k)—AmerPut(k);
end
```

The results with five expansion terms are in the last row of Table 8.4, along with the same prices obtained using the other methods described earlier in this chapter and the total absolute error of each method. For comparison, the last row contains the European put prices, obtained with Simpson's three-eighths rule.

All of the methods produce American put prices that are fairly accurate. The method of Medvedev and Scaillet (2010) forgoes accuracy slightly, especially

TABLE 8.4 Clarke and Parrott (1999) American Put Prices Under Various Models

	$S_t = 8$	$S_t = 9$	$S_t = 10$	$S_t = 11$	$S_t = 12$	Abs(Error)
Clarke-Parrott Price	2.0000	1.1076	0.5200	0.2137	0.0820	—
L.S. Monte Carlo	1.9996	1.1036	0.5190	0.2261	0.0821	0.0179
Explicit Method	2.0000	1.1061	0.5184	0.2122	0.0808	0.0058
Bivariate Tree	1.9967	1.1059	0.5195	0.2134	0.0819	0.0059
M.S. Approximation	2.0030	1.1111	0.5202	0.2137	0.0830	0.0077
European Put Price	1.8389	1.0483	0.5015	0.2082	0.0804	—

compared to the explicit method or the bivariate tree, but it is able to produce prices much faster than the other methods.

Parameter Estimation

The fact that the Medvedev and Scaillet (2010) expansion produces American put prices with little computation time makes it feasible to estimate Heston parameters for pricing American options. We illustrate this with American puts written on IBM on May 7, 2010. The closing price of IBM was \$122.10. We use the Medvedev and Scaillet (2010) method to obtain Black-Scholes implied volatilities for American puts. This is accomplished with the Matlab function BisecMSIV.m function, which is similar to the BisecBSIV.m function presented in Chapter 2. The difference is that model prices are obtained using the MSPriceBS.m function for the Medvedev-Scaillet-Black-Scholes pricing of American puts, rather than using the Black-Scholes European closed form.

```
function y = BisecMSIV(S,K,rf,q,T,a,b,MktPrice,Tol,MaxIter)
lowCdif  = MktPrice - MSPriceBS(S,K,T,a,rf,q);
highCdif = MktPrice - MSPriceBS(S,K,T,b,rf,q);
if lowCdif*highCdif > 0
    y = -1;
else
    for x=1:MaxIter
        midP = (a+b)/2;
        midCdif = MktPrice - MSPriceBS(S,K,T,midP,rf,q);
        ... ;
    end
    y = midP;
end
```

The following code snippet extracts implied volatilities from the IBM American put prices.

```
% Settings for the bisection algorithm
a = 0.01;
b = 2.0;
Tol = 1e-5;
MaxIter = 1000;
% American implied volatilities
for t=1:NT
    for k=1:NK
        MktIV(k,t) = BisecMSIV(K(k),T(t),MktPrice(k,t),...);
    end
end
```

The BisecMSIV.m function can easily be modified to allow for an alternate pricing model for Black-Scholes American puts, such as the trinomial tree or the approximation of Barone-Adesi and Whaley (1987).

The function HestonObjFunMS.m applies the RMSE loss function discussed in Chapter 6. Prices and implied volatilities are obtained with the MSPrice.m and BisecMSIV.m functions, respectively.

```
function y = HestonObjFunMSIV(param,MktIV,...)
for k=1:NK
    for t=1:NT
         ModelPrice(k,t)  = MSPrice(K(k),T(t),...,yinf);
         ModelIV(k,t)  = BisecMSIV(K(k),T(t),
                            ModelPrice(k,t),...);
         error(k,t)  =  (ModelIV(k,t)  - MktIV(k,t))^2 /
                        MktIV(k,t);
    end
end
% MSE loss function
y = sum(sum(error));
```

Parameter estimation is done by passing the HestonObjFunMS.m function to the built-in Matlab function fmincon.m for constrained minimization.

```
% kappa theta sigma v0 rho
start = [1.0, 0.01, 3.2, 0.12, -0.5];
% Estimation bounds
e = 1e-3;
lb = [e    e   e   e -.99];
ub = [20   2   5   2  .99];
% Constrained minimization
[param feval] = fmincon(@(p) HestonObjFunMSIV(p, MktIV,...),
                start,...,lb,ub);
```

The C# code to obtain the parameter estimates is similar to the Matlab code and not presented here.

We estimate parameters using IBM American put prices on the first maturity, 14 days. We then fit Medvedev and Scaillet (2010) prices using four terms in the expansion, and extract implied volatilities from these prices. Both sets of implied volatilities appear in Figure 8.4. The mean square error between both sets of implied volatilities is 3.15×10^{-5}.

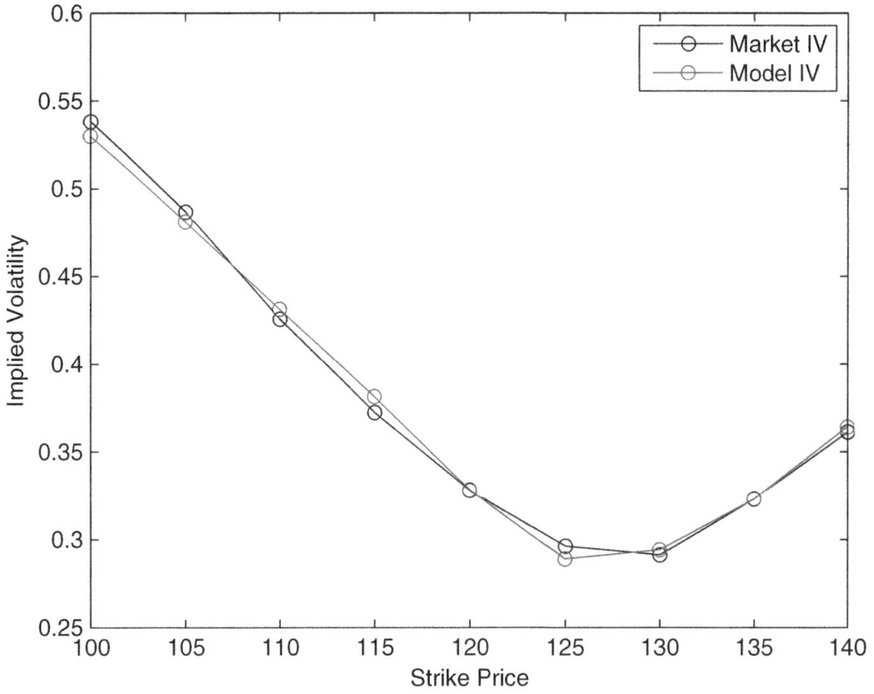

FIGURE 8.4 Implied Volatility From American Puts

CHIARELLA AND ZIOGAS AMERICAN CALL

In this section, the last of this chapter, we present the method of Chiarella and Ziogas (2006) for pricing American calls in the Heston (1993) model. Their method requires an estimate of the early exercise boundary. The early exercise boundary and other features of American options are discussed in Kwok (2008), for example.

Early Exercise Boundary Approximation

Recall from Chapter 1 that the price $U(S, v, \tau)$ a European option satisfies the Heston (1993) PDE, subject to certain boundary conditions. We saw in the previous sections that an American option satisfies the same PDE, but with different boundaries. For an American call option $C_A(S, v, \tau)$, we can therefore write

$$\begin{aligned}\frac{\partial C_A}{\partial \tau} &= \frac{1}{2}vS^2\frac{\partial^2 C_A}{\partial S^2} + \rho\sigma vS\frac{\partial^2 C_A}{\partial v\partial S} + \frac{1}{2}\sigma^2 v\frac{\partial^2 C_A}{\partial v^2} \\ &\quad - rC_A + (r-q)S\frac{\partial C_A}{\partial S} + [\kappa(\theta - v) - \lambda v]\frac{\partial C_A}{\partial v}\end{aligned} \tag{8.71}$$

where τ is the time until maturity. The PDE holds for $0 \leq \tau < T$, where T is the maturity calendar time, and for $0 < S \leq b(v,\tau)$, where $b(v,\tau)$ is the early exercise boundary. Essentially, this means that as long as the stock price is within the early exercise boundary, the American call option behaves like its European counterpart and the PDE in Equation (8.71) holds.

Building on the work of Tzavalis and Wang (2003), Chiarella and Ziogas (2006) approximate the early exercise boundary $b(v,\tau)$ with the log-linear function

$$b(v,\tau) \approx \exp(b_0(\tau) + b_1(\tau)v_0). \tag{8.72}$$

In the following section we explain how $b(v,\tau)$ is estimated, and how the American call price is obtained.

The American Call Price

To implement the method of Chiarella and Ziogas (2006), we need to introduce an additional time variable t into the characteristic function, by replacing τ with $\tau - t$, and an additional integration variable ψ. They write the characteristic function f_2 as

$$f_2(\phi,\psi x_0,v_0,\tau-t) = \exp(C_2(\tau-t,\phi,\psi) + D_2(\tau-t,\phi,\psi)v_0 + i\phi x_0) \tag{8.73}$$

where the coefficients are

$$\begin{aligned} C_2(\tau-t,\phi,\psi) &= (r-q)i\phi(\tau-t) \\ &\quad + \frac{a}{\sigma^2}\left[(b_2 - \rho\sigma i\phi + d_2)(\tau-t) - 2\ln\left(\frac{1-g_2e^{d_2(\tau-t)}}{1-g_2}\right)\right], \\ D_2(\tau-t,\phi,\psi) &= i\psi + \frac{b_2 - \rho\sigma i\phi - \sigma^2 i\psi + d_2}{\sigma^2}\left(\frac{1-e^{d_2(\tau-t)}}{1-g_je^{d_2(\tau-t)}}\right). \end{aligned} \tag{8.74}$$

The required quantities are

$$g_2 = \frac{b_2 - \rho\sigma i\phi - \sigma^2 i\psi + d_2}{b_2 - \rho\sigma i\phi - \sigma^2 i\psi - d_2}, \quad d_2 = \sqrt{(\rho\sigma i\phi - b_2)^2 - \sigma^2(2u_2 i\phi - \phi^2)}. \tag{8.75}$$

Note that, when $t = \psi = 0$, the coefficients reduce to those of the original Heston (1993) model. As before, we have $b_2 = \kappa + \lambda$, $u_2 = -\frac{1}{2}$, and $a = \kappa\theta$. The characteristic function f_1 is

$$f_1(\phi,\psi;x_0,v_0,\tau-t) = \exp(-x_0 - (r-q)(\tau-t)) \times f_2(\phi-i,\psi;x_0,v_0,\tau-t) \tag{8.76}$$

where $x_0 = \ln S_0$ the log spot price, and v_0 is the initial variance. Obtaining the European call price $C(x_0,v_0,\tau)$ is straightforward, by setting $\psi = 0$ and $t = 0$ into the characteristic functions. The calculation is identical to that in the original Heston (1993) model

$$C(x_0, v_0, \tau) = S_0 e^{-q\tau} P_1 - K e^{-r\tau} P_2 \tag{8.77}$$

where, for $j = 1, 2$

$$P_j = \frac{1}{2} + \frac{1}{\pi} \int_0^\infty \text{Re}\left(\frac{e^{-i\phi \ln K}}{i\phi} f_j(\phi, 0; x_0, v_0, \tau) \right) d\phi. \tag{8.78}$$

Chiarella and Ziogas (2006) show that the early exercise premium $V(x_0, v_0, \tau)$ on an American call with strike K and maturity is τ is

$$\begin{aligned} V(x_0, v_0, \tau) &= \frac{1}{2}[S_0(1 - e^{-q\tau}) - K(1 - e^{-r\tau})] \\ &+ \frac{S_0}{\pi} q e^{-q\tau} \int_0^\tau \int_0^\infty e^{qt} \text{Re}\left(\frac{\exp(-b_0(t)\, i\phi)}{i\phi} f_1(\phi, -b_1(t)\phi; x_0, v_0, \tau - t) \right) d\phi dt \\ &- \frac{K}{\pi} r e^{-r\tau} \int_0^\tau \int_0^\infty e^{rt} \text{Re}\left(\frac{\exp(-b_0(t)\, i\phi)}{i\phi} f_2(\phi, -b_1(t)\phi; x_0, v_0, \tau - t) \right) d\phi dt. \end{aligned} \tag{8.79}$$

Finally, the control variate price of an American call is obtained by adding the early exercise premium to the price of the European call

$$C_A(S_0, v_0, \tau) = C(x_0, v_0, \tau) + V(x_0, v_0, \tau). \tag{8.80}$$

To evaluate the integral for the European call $C(x_0, v_0, \tau)$, we can use Gauss-Laguerre quadrature. To evaluate the double integrals in the early exercise premium $V(x_0, v_0, \tau)$, we can use either composite Gauss-Legendre quadrature or the composite trapezoidal rule. Both of these rules were presented in Chapter 5. As explained in that chapter, Gauss-Legendre quadrature requires a transformation of the integration domain from $(-1, +1) \times (-1, +1)$ to $(0, \tau) \times (0, M)$, where M is a large number that replaces ∞ in the upper limit of the ϕ integrals in (8.79).

The Matlab functions CZCharFun.m implements the characteristic functions in Equations (8.73) and (8.76).

```
function y = CZCharFun(S0,tau,t,params,K,rf,q,phi,psi,FunNum)
x = log(S0);
a = kappa*theta;
b = kappa + lambda;
d = sqrt((rho*sigma*i*phi - b)^2 + sigma^2*phi*(phi+i));
g = (b - rho*sigma*i*phi - sigma^2*i*psi + d) ...;
% The components of the affine characteristic function.
G = (1-g*exp(d*(tau-t)))/(1-g);
C = (rf-q)*i*phi*(tau-t) + a/sigma^2* ...;
F = (1-exp(d*(tau-t)))/(1-g*exp(d*(tau-t)));
```

```
D = i*psi + (b - rho*sigma*i*phi - sigma^2*i*psi ...;
% The second characteristic function
f2 = exp(C + D*v0 + i*phi*x);
if (FunNum == 2)
    y = f2;
else
    d = sqrt((rho*sigma*i*(phi-i) - b)^2 + sigma^2*(phi-i)*phi);
    ...
    F2 = exp(C + D*v0 + i*(phi-i)*x);
    % The first characteristic function
    y = 1/S0 * exp(-(rf-q)*(tau-t)) * F2;
end
```

The first part of the function calculates the coefficients $C_2(\tau - t, \phi, \psi)$ and $D_2(\tau - t, \phi, \psi)$, and returns the second characteristic function, f_2. The second part of the function calculates $C_2(\tau - t, \phi - i, \psi)$ and $D_2(\tau - t, \phi - i, \psi)$, and returns the first characteristic function, f_1. The function is identical to that for the characteristic functions of the Heston (1993) model, except for the additional integration variable and the fact that τ is replaced by $\tau - t$.

The function CZEuroCall.m calculates the European call price in Equation (8.77). The first part of the function sets $\psi = t = 0$ in the characteristic functions, as required by (8.78), and calculates the European call price exactly as in the original Heston (1993) model.

```
function y = CZEuroCall(S0,tau,params,K,rf,q,x,w)
t   = 0;
psi = 0;
% Create the integrands
for k=1:length(x);
    phi = x(k);
    Int1(k)  = w(k)*real(exp(-i*phi*log(K))*CZCharFun(...,1) ...;
    Int2(k)  = w(k)*real(exp(-i*phi*log(K))*CZCharFun(...,2) ...;
end
P1 = 1/2 + (1/pi)*sum(Int1);
P2 = 1/2 + (1/pi)*sum(Int2);
% The call price
y = S0*exp(-q*tau)*P1 - K*exp(-rf*tau)*P2;
```

The function CZEarlyExercise.m implements the early exercise premium in Equation (8.79) using either composite Gauss-Legendre quadrature or the composite trapezoidal rule. The arguments (a, b) represent the integration domain for time, and (c, d) represent the integration domain for the stock price.

```
function V = CZEarlyExercise(...,a,b,c,d,DoubleType)
% The integrals
if strcmp(DoubleType,'GLe')
    Int1 = DoubleGaussLegendre(...,1);
    Int2 = DoubleGaussLegendre(...,2);
```

```
elseif strcmp(DoubleType,'Trapz')
    ht = (b-a)/Nt;
    hs = (d-c)/Nt;
    X = zeros(Nt,1);
    T = zeros(Nt,1);
    for j=1:Nt+1;
        T(j) = a + (j-1)*ht;
        X(j) = c + (j-1)*hs;
    end
    Int1 = DoubleTrapezoidal(...,b0,b1,X,T,1);
    Int2 = DoubleTrapezoidal(...,b0,b1,X,T,2);
end
% The early exercise premium
V1 = S0*(1-exp(-q*tau))/2 + (1/pi)*S0*q*exp(-q*tau)*Int1;
V2 = K*(1-exp(-rf*tau))/2 + (1/pi)*K*rf*exp(-rf*tau)*Int2;
V = V1 - V2;
```

The function DoubleGaussLegendre.m calculates the double integrals for the exercise premium using composite Gauss-Legendre quadrature. The function exploits the fact that the double integrals in Equation (8.79) are identical in form, except that the first contains e^{qt} while the second contains e^{rt}.

```
function y = DoubleGaussLegendre(...,a,b,c,d,funNum)
y = 0;
if (funNum == 1)
    qr = q;
elseif (funNum == 2)
    qr = rf;
end
for t=1:Nt;
    time = h1*xt(t) + h2;
    for x=1:Ns
        phi = k1*xs(x) + k2;
        fun = real(exp(-b0*i*phi)*CZCharFun(...,funNum) ...;
        y = y + h1*k1*wt(t)*ws(x) * exp(qr*time)*fun;
    end
end
```

The function DoubleTrapezoidal.m calculates the double integrals using the composite trapezoidal rule. It is similar to that presented in Chapter 5 and is not presented here.

Finally, the function CZAmerCall.m adds the early exercise premium to the European call to obtain the American call.

```
function [Amer Euro] = CZAmerCall(...,b0,b1,a,b,c,d,DoubleType)
Euro    = CZEuroCall(S0,tau,params,K,rf,q,xs,ws);
Premium = CZEarlyExercise(...,b0,b1,a,b,c,d,DoubleType);
Amer    = Euro + Premium;
```

The C# code to calculate the American call using the method of Chiarella and Ziogas (2006) is similar and not presented here.

Estimating the Early Exercise Boundary

The European call in Equation (8.77) requires no new quantities beyond those of the original Heston (1993) model, but the early exercise premium $V(x_0, v_0, \tau)$ requires estimates of the two unknowns $b_0(\tau)$ and $b_1(\tau)$ in (8.72). Using two distinct values $v_0 = v_0(\tau)$ and $v_1 = v_1(\tau)$ of the variance, along with the boundary condition for the call at $b(v, \tau)$, Chiarella and Ziogas (2006) obtain the following system of two equations

$$\begin{aligned} C_A(b(v_0, \tau), v, \tau) &= \exp(b_0(\tau) + b_1(\tau)v_0(\tau)) - K \\ C_A(b(v_1, \tau), v, \tau) &= \exp(b_0(\tau) + b_1(\tau)v_1(\tau)) - K \end{aligned} \tag{8.81}$$

and suggest an iterative method to solve this system. The method works by dividing the time interval $(0, T)$ into N subintervals of increasing length $\tau_1, \ldots, \tau_N$, where $\tau_n = n \cdot d\tau$, $n = 1, \ldots, N$ and $d\tau = \tau/N$ is the time increment. Denote $b_0^n = b_0(\tau_n)$, $b_1^n = b_1(\tau_n)$, $v_0^n = v_0(\tau_n)$, and $v_1^n = v_1(\tau_n)$. The starting values for b_0^0 and b_1^0 at time zero are

$$b_0^0 = \max\left(\ln \frac{rK}{q}, \ln K\right) \quad \text{and} \quad b_1^0 = 0 \tag{8.82}$$

and the starting values for values for v_0^0 and v_1^0 are

$$\begin{aligned} v_0^0 &= E[v_\tau | v_0] + \frac{\sigma}{\kappa}\sqrt{\frac{\kappa\theta}{2}} \\ v_1^0 &= E[v_\tau | v_0] - \frac{\sigma}{\kappa}\sqrt{\frac{\kappa\theta}{2}}. \end{aligned} \tag{8.83}$$

The conditional expectation for the variance was presented in Chapter 2

$$E[v_t | v_s] = \theta + (v_s - \theta)e^{-\kappa(t-s)}. \tag{8.84}$$

At each time step n, the variances v_0^n and v_1^n are updated using Equation (8.83) with $v_s = v_0$, and using $t = \tau$ and $s = \tau_n$ in (8.84). This specification ensures that v_0^n and v_1^n will be distinct, as indicated in Figure 8.5, which reproduces Figure 1 of Chiarella and Ziogas (2006).

The coefficients b_0^n and b_1^n are updated iteratively, by obtaining a successive set of coefficients $b_{0,k}^n$ and $b_{1,k}^n$ that are the roots of the non-linear equations g_1 and g_0 defined as

$$\begin{aligned} g_1(b_{1,k}^n) &= \frac{1}{v_0^n}\{\ln[C_A(\exp(b_{0,k-1}^n + v_0^n b_{1,k}^n), v_0^n, \tau) + K] - b_{0,k-1}^n\} - b_{0,k-1}^n \\ g_0(b_{0,k}^n) &= \ln[C_A(\exp(b_{0,k}^n + v_1^n b_{1,k}^n), v_1^n, \tau) + K] - v_1^n b_{1,k}^n - b_{0,k}^n. \end{aligned} \tag{8.85}$$

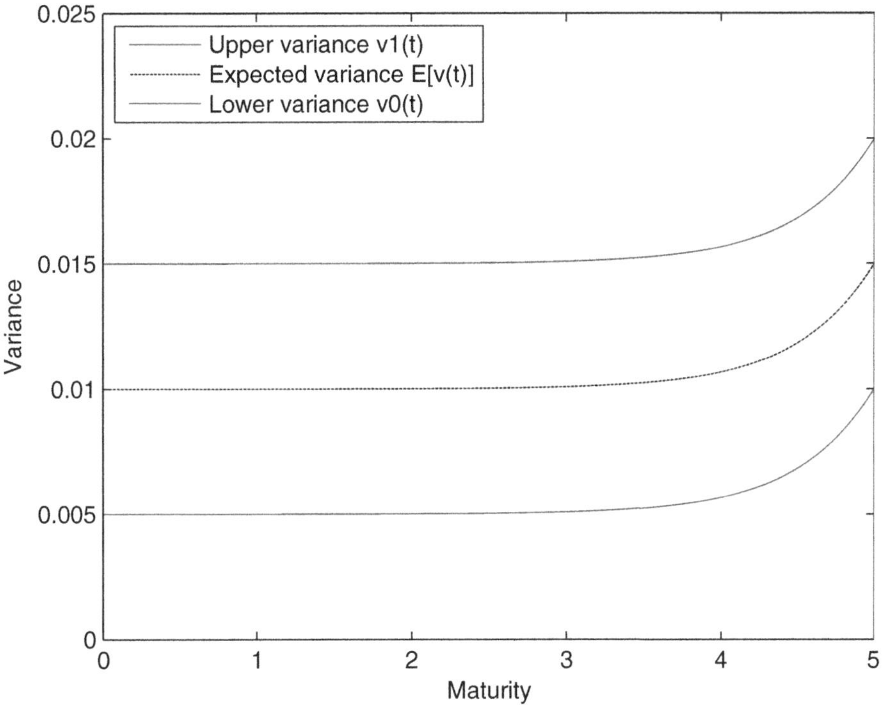

FIGURE 8.5 Sample Values of Variances

The starting values in (8.85) are the values of the coefficients in the previous time step, so that $b^n_{1,0} = b^{n-1}_1$ and $b^n_{0,0} = b^{n-1}_0$. At step k, the quantities $b^n_{0,k-1}$, v^n_0, and τ are substituted into g_1 and Newton's method is used to find $b^n_{1,k}$. Then $b^n_{1,k}$, v^n_1, and τ are substituted into g_2 and Newton's method is used to find $b^n_{0,k}$. The iterations stop when both $|b^n_{0,k} - b^n_{0,k-1}| < \varepsilon_0$ and $|b^n_{1,k} - b^n_{1,k-1}| < \varepsilon_1$, where ε_0 and ε_1 are tolerance levels. Chiarella and Ziogas (2006) use $\varepsilon_1 = \varepsilon_2 = 5 \times 10^{-4}$, and $N = 25$ time steps. The values of b^n_0 and b^n_1 are the last values of $b^n_{0,k}$ and $b^n_{1,k}$ returned in the iteration. The values of $b_0(\tau)$ and $b_1(\tau)$ are the values at the last time step, so that $b_0(\tau) = b^N_0$ and $b_1(\tau) = b^N_1$.

The function CZNewton.m uses Newton's method to find the roots the functions g_1 or g_0 defined in (8.85). The derivatives required of Newton's method are obtained with central differences.

```
function b = CZNewton(v0,v1,B0,B1,gNum,...)
params0 = [kappa theta sigma v0 rho lambda];
params1 = [kappa theta sigma v1 rho lambda];
B = mat;
% Newton's method
while (abs(diff) > tol)
    if gNum == 1
        % First set of functions and derivative
        [CallA1 Euro] = CZAmerCall(exp(B0 + b*v0),...,B0,b);
```

```
        g0 = (log(CallA1 + K) - B0)/v0 - b;
        [CallA1 Euro] = CZAmerCall(exp(B0 + (b+db)*v0),...,B0,b+db);
        g  = (log(CallA1 + K) - B0)/v0 - (b+db);
        [CallA1 Euro] = CZAmerCall(exp(B0 + (b-db)*v0),...,B0,b-db);
        g_ = (log(CallA1 + K) - B0)/v0 - (b-db);
    else
        % Second set of functions and derivatives
        [CallA0 Euro] = CZAmerCall(exp(b + B1*v1),...,b,B1);
        g0 = (log(CallA0 + K) - v1*B1) - b;
        [CallA0 Euro] = CZAmerCall(exp(b+db + B1*v1),...,b+db,B1);
        g  = (log(CallA0 + K) - v1*B1) - (b+db);
        [CallA0 Euro] = CZAmerCall(exp(b-db + B1*v1),...,b-db,B1);
        g_ = (log(CallA0 + K) - v1*B1) - (b-db);
    end
    % The derivative by finite difference
    dg = (g - g_)/2/db;
    % Newton's method
    b_new = b - f0/dg;
    diff = b_new - b;
    b = b_new;
end
```

The findB.m function loops through the time steps and applies the iterative procedure to the functions g_1 and g_0 at each time step. It returns the vectors b_0^n and b_1^n for $n = 0, \cdots, N$.

```
function [b0 b1] = findB(...,a,b,c,d,DoubleType)
% Conditional expected value of variance and time increment
EV = @(Vt,theta,kappa,T,t) (theta + (Vt - theta)* ...;
dtau = tau/Ntau;
for n=2:Ntau
    % Maturity
    mat = n*dtau;
    Evt = EV(v0t,theta,kappa,tau,mat);
    v0(n) = Evt + sigma/kappa*sqrt(kappa*theta/2);
    v1(n) = Evt - sigma/kappa*sqrt(kappa*theta/2);
    % Starting values for Newton's method
    b0k_ = b0(n-1);
    b1k_ = b1(n-1);
    % Set the counter and the initial differences
    diff0 = 1.1*tol0;
    diff1 = 1.1*tol1;
    % Loop through until Newton's method returns bk and bk(-1)
    while (diff0>tol0) && (diff1>tol1)
        b1k = CZNewton(b1k_,v0(n),v1(n),...,b0k_,b1k_,1);
        b0k = CZNewton(b0k_,v0(n),v1(n),...,b0k_,b1k ,0);
        b0(n) = b0k;
        b1(n) = b1k;
        diff0 = abs(b0k_ - b0k);
        diff1 = abs(b1k_ - b1k);
        b0k_ = b0k;
        b1k_ = b1k;
    end
end
```

The C# code is very similar and not presented here. To illustrate, we use the settings $S = K = 100$, a maturity of 3 months, $r = 0.01$, $q = 0.12$, along with the parameter values $\kappa = 4$, $\theta = 0.09$, $\sigma = 0.1$, $v_0 = 0.04$, and $\rho = 0$. The findB.m function returns $b_0(\tau) = 4.7237$, $b_1(\tau) = 0.1674$, and the American call price using these values is 3.6256, which is 0.10 less than the price of 3.7301 produced by the explicit method covered in this chapter. The Heston (1993) European put price is 3.5058.

CONCLUSION

In this chapter, we have presented several methods to value American options in the Heston model. The Least-Squares Monte Carlo (LSM) algorithm can be applied to the model in this regard, and as will be shown in Chapter 12, to the double Heston model of Christoffersen et al. (2009) as well. The explicit method, which will be covered in Chapter 10 when we present finite difference methods, can easily be adapted to handle American options also.

In this chapter, we have reviewed the bivariate tree of Beliaeva and Nalwalkha (2010). Other multivariate trees for pricing American options in a stochastic volatility framework are those of Ruckdeschel et al. (2013) and Vellekoop and Nieuwenhuis (2009), which are designed for the Heston model, and Leisen (2000) which can handle more general models. Finally, Zhylyevskyy (2010) extends the Geske and Johnson (1984) approximation to the Heston model. We also reviewed the approximation of Medvedev and Scaillet (2010), which is able to produce option prices very quickly, and the method of Chiarella and Ziogas (2006), which is designed for American calls and borrows from the method of Tzavalis and Wang (2003). In a recent paper, AitSahlia et al. (2012) adapt the method of Chiarella and Ziogas (2006) to American puts.

All of the methods presented so far have assumed the Heston parameters to be static, as in the original formulation of Heston (1993). As shown in Chapter 6, however, the Heston model with static parameters is sometimes unable to provide a good fit to the volatility surface at short maturities. A number of researchers have modified the original Heston (1993) model to allow for parameters to be time-dependent. This enrichment of the model makes it more flexible and better able to fit the volatility surface at all maturities. We introduce the Heston model with time-dependent parameters in the next chapter.

CHAPTER 9

Time-Dependent Heston Models

Abstract

The Heston model is sometimes unable to provide a good fit to short-maturity market implied volatilities. One common remedy to this problem is to enrich the model with additional parameters by specifying a more realistic volatility process, which is the approach of the double Heston model covered in Chapter 12. Another approach is to allow the parameters to be time-dependent. This latter approach is the one adopted by Mikhailov and Nögel (2003), Elices (2009), Benhamou, Gobet, and Miri (2010) and others. In this chapter, we present these time-dependent models. First, we introduce a generalization of the Riccati equation from Chapter 1 that allows for non-zero initial conditions. Then we introduce the bivariate characteristic function, and we show that the generalization of the Riccati equation arises as a special case. We then present the models with time-dependent parameters and show how to estimate these parameters using loss functions.

GENERALIZATION OF THE RICCATI EQUATION

Recall from Chapter 1 that the general solution to the Riccati equation for $D_j(\phi,\tau)$ is

$$D_j(\phi,\tau) = -\frac{2}{\sigma^2}\left(\frac{K_j\alpha_j e^{\alpha_j\tau} + \beta_j e^{\beta_j\tau}}{K_j e^{\alpha_j\tau} + e^{\beta_j\tau}}\right). \tag{9.1}$$

Recall also that the initial condition $D_j(\phi,0)=0$ at expiry $\tau=0$ produced $K_j = -\beta_j/\alpha_j$ and the solution for D_j given by

$$D_j(\phi,\tau) = \frac{b_j - \rho\sigma i\phi + d_j}{\sigma^2}\left(\frac{1-e^{d_j\tau}}{1-g_je^{d_j\tau}}\right). \tag{9.2}$$

This expression uses the quantities

$$d_j = \sqrt{(\rho\sigma i\phi - b_j)^2 - \sigma^2(2u_j i\phi - \phi^2)},\qquad g_j = \frac{b_j - \rho\sigma i\phi + d_j}{b_j - \rho\sigma i\phi - d_j} = \frac{\beta_j}{\alpha_j} \tag{9.3}$$

with $u_1 = \frac{1}{2}$, $u_2 = -\frac{1}{2}$, $a = \kappa\theta$, $b_1 = \kappa+\lambda-\rho\sigma$, and $b_2 = \kappa+\lambda$.

Similarly, the general solution for $C_j(\phi,\tau)$ was

$$C_j(\phi,\tau) = (r-q)i\phi\tau + \frac{a}{d_j}\left(\frac{Q_j+d_j}{\sigma^2}\right)\int_1^{\exp(d_j\tau)}\left(\frac{1-x}{1-g_jx}\right)\frac{1}{x}dx + k_1 \tag{9.4}$$

for a constant k_1. The initial condition $C_j(\phi,0)=0$ produced $k_1=0$ and the solution for $C_j(\phi,\tau)$ given by

$$C_j(\phi,\tau) = (r-q)i\phi\tau + \frac{a}{\sigma^2}\left[(b_j-\rho\sigma i\phi+d_j)\tau - 2\ln\left(\frac{1-g_je^{d_j\tau}}{1-g_j}\right)\right]. \tag{9.5}$$

Suppose that instead of the initial conditions $C_j(\phi,0)=D_j(\phi,0)=0$, we use the general non-zero initial conditions

$$C_j(\phi,0)=C_j^0,\quad D_j(\phi,0)=D_j^0. \tag{9.6}$$

This generalization is illustrated by Mikhailov and Nögel (2003) and Elices (2009). Letting $\tau=0$ in Equation (9.1), equating the result to the initial condition D_j^0, and solving for K_j produces

$$\widetilde{K}_j = -\left(\frac{2\beta_j + D_j^0\sigma^2}{2\alpha_j + D_j^0\sigma^2}\right) = -\left(\frac{b_j-\rho\sigma i\phi+d_j-D_j^0\sigma^2}{b_j-\rho\sigma i\phi-d_j-D_j^0\sigma^2}\right). \tag{9.7}$$

Now define $\tilde{g}_j=-\widetilde{K}_j$. Substituting $\widetilde{K}_j$ back into (9.1), it is easy to see that the solution for D_j when the general, non-zero initial condition in (9.6) holds is

$$\widetilde{D}_j(\phi,\tau) = \frac{(b_j-\rho\sigma i\phi+d_j)-(b_j-\rho\sigma i\phi-d_j)\tilde{g}_je^{d_j\tau}}{\sigma^2(1-\tilde{g}_je^{d_j\tau})}. \tag{9.8}$$

The notation $\widetilde{D}_j(\phi,\tau)$ is meant to distinguish it from its time-static counterpart $D_j(\phi,\tau)$. The general condition $C_j(\phi,0)=C_j^0$ produces $k_1=C_j^0$ and the solution for $C_j(\phi,\tau)$ given by

$$\widetilde{C}_j(\phi,\tau) = (r-q)i\phi\tau + \frac{a}{\sigma^2}\left[(b_j-\rho\sigma i\phi+d_j)\tau - 2\ln\left(\frac{1-\tilde{g}_je^{d_j\tau}}{1-\tilde{g}_j}\right)\right] + C_j^0. \tag{9.9}$$

Note that the solution for $\widetilde{C}_j(\phi,\tau)$ is identical to $C_j(\phi,\tau)$, except that g_j is replaced by $\tilde{g}_j$, and $k_1=0$ is replaced by $k_1=C_j^0$. Note also that setting $C_j^0=D_j^0=0$ in Equations (9.8) and (9.9) reduces $\widetilde{C}_j(\phi,\tau)$ and $\widetilde{D}_j(\phi,\tau)$ to their original Heston (1993) forms $C_j(\phi,\tau)$ and $D_j(\phi,\tau)$, respectively.

BIVARIATE CHARACTERISTIC FUNCTION

In Chapter 1, it was shown that the characteristic function of the log asset price at maturity, $x_T=\ln S_T$, is of the following form (dropping the j subscripts on f_j,

$C_j(\tau,\phi)$ and $D_j(\tau,\phi)$ for notational convenience)

$$f(\phi,\tau;x_t,v_t) = E[\exp(i\phi x_T)] = \exp(C(\tau,\phi) + D(\tau,\phi)v_t + i\phi x_t). \tag{9.10}$$

Recall that the initial conditions $C(0,\phi) = D(0,\phi) = 0$ were used to find analytic expressions for $C(\tau,\phi)$ and $D(\tau,\phi)$, based on a Riccati equation and an ordinary differential equation.

In this section, the bivariate characteristic function of the joint process (x_T, v_T) is derived. This function is defined as

$$f(\phi_1,\phi_2;v_t,x_t) = E[\exp(i\phi_1 x_T + i\phi_2 v_T)]. \tag{9.11}$$

Duffie, Pan, and Singleton (2000) show that the characteristic function of a wide class of multivariate affine models (of which the Heston model is a special case) has a log linear form and can be obtained as the solution of a system of Riccati equations. Singleton (??) illustrates this with the Heston model, which he shows to be affine in (x_t, v_t). The Heston model can be written in terms of two independent Brownian motions $B_{1,t}$ and $B_{2,t}$ as

$$d\mathbf{x}_t = \boldsymbol{\mu}(\mathbf{x}_t)dt + \boldsymbol{\sigma}(\mathbf{x}_t)d\mathbf{B}_t \tag{9.12}$$

where

$$\boldsymbol{\mu}_t = \begin{pmatrix} r - \frac{1}{2}v_t \\ \kappa\left(\theta - v_t\right) \end{pmatrix}, \quad \boldsymbol{\sigma}(\mathbf{x}_t) = \begin{pmatrix} \sqrt{v_t} & 0 \\ \sigma\rho\sqrt{v_t} & \sigma\sqrt{1-\rho^2}\sqrt{v_t} \end{pmatrix}, \quad d\mathbf{B}_t = \begin{pmatrix} dB_{1,t} \\ dB_{2,t} \end{pmatrix}. \tag{9.13}$$

The drift $\boldsymbol{\mu}$ and the matrix $\boldsymbol{\sigma}\boldsymbol{\sigma}^T$ in the Heston model can both be written in the affine form

$$\begin{aligned} \boldsymbol{\mu}(\mathbf{x}_t) &= \mathbf{K}_0 + \mathbf{K}_1 x_t + \mathbf{K}_2 v_t \\ \boldsymbol{\sigma}(\mathbf{x}_t)\boldsymbol{\sigma}(\mathbf{x}_t)^T &= \mathbf{H}_0 + \mathbf{H}_1 x_t + \mathbf{H}_2 v_t \end{aligned} \tag{9.14}$$

with

$$\mathbf{K}_0 = \begin{pmatrix} r \\ \kappa\theta \end{pmatrix}, \quad \mathbf{K}_1 = \begin{pmatrix} 0 \\ 0 \end{pmatrix}, \quad \mathbf{K}_2 = \begin{pmatrix} -\frac{1}{2} \\ -\kappa \end{pmatrix},$$

$$\mathbf{H}_0 = \mathbf{H}_1 = \begin{pmatrix} 0 & 0 \\ 0 & 0 \end{pmatrix}, \quad \mathbf{H}_2 = \begin{pmatrix} 1 & \rho\sigma \\ \rho\sigma & \sigma^2 \end{pmatrix}.$$

The result of Duffie, Pan, and Singleton (2000) is that the characteristic function has the log-linear form

$$f\left(\phi_1,\phi_2;x_t,v_t\right) = \exp\left(A(\tau,\phi_1,\phi_2) + B(\tau,\phi_1,\phi_2)x_t + C(\tau,\phi_1,\phi_2)v_t\right) \tag{9.15}$$

where $\tau = T - t$ is the time remaining until expiry. Moreover, the coefficients of the characteristic function can be obtained by solving the system of Riccati equations

$$\begin{aligned}\frac{\partial A}{\partial t} &= -\mathbf{K}_0^T\boldsymbol{\beta} - \frac{1}{2}\boldsymbol{\beta}^T\mathbf{H}_0\boldsymbol{\beta}\\ \frac{\partial B}{\partial t} &= -\mathbf{K}_1^T\boldsymbol{\beta} - \frac{1}{2}\boldsymbol{\beta}^T\mathbf{H}_1\boldsymbol{\beta}\\ \frac{\partial C}{\partial t} &= -\mathbf{K}_2^T\boldsymbol{\beta} - \frac{1}{2}\boldsymbol{\beta}^T\mathbf{H}_2\boldsymbol{\beta}\end{aligned} \tag{9.16}$$

subject to the boundary conditions $B(0) = i\phi_1$, $C(0) = i\phi_2$, and $A(0) = 0$, and where $\boldsymbol{\beta}^T = (B, C)$. After substituting, this produces the set of differential equations

$$\begin{aligned}\frac{\partial A}{\partial t} &= -rB - \kappa\theta C\\ \frac{\partial B}{\partial t} &= 0\\ \frac{\partial C}{\partial t} &= -\frac{1}{2}\sigma^2C^2 - (\rho\sigma B - \kappa)C - \frac{1}{2}B^2 + \frac{1}{2}B.\end{aligned} \tag{9.17}$$

For the Heston model, it is straightforward to find the equations in (9.17) and their boundary conditions directly, without using the result of Duffie, Pan, and Singleton (2000). First, note that, as in the univariate case, at expiry ($\tau = 0$) the expected value in Equation (9.11) disappears, since (x_T, v_T) is known. Hence, at expiry, $f(\phi_1, \phi_2; x, v)$ in (9.15) must be equal to

$$f(\phi_1, \phi_2; x, v) = \exp(i\phi_1 x_T + i\phi_2 v_T). \tag{9.18}$$

This implies the following initial conditions

$$A(0, \phi_1, \phi_2) = 0,\ \ B(0, \phi_1, \phi_2) = i\phi_1,\ \ C(0, \phi_1, \phi_2) = i\phi_2. \tag{9.19}$$

Recall from Chapter 1 the partial differential equation (PDE) for the second characteristic function f_2, which we denote simply by f

$$\begin{aligned}&-\frac{\partial f}{\partial \tau} + \rho\sigma v\frac{\partial^2 f}{\partial v\partial x} + \frac{1}{2}v\frac{\partial^2 f}{\partial x^2} + \frac{1}{2}\sigma^2 v\frac{\partial^2 f}{\partial v^2}\\ &+\left(r - \frac{1}{2}v\right)\frac{\partial f}{\partial x} + \kappa(\theta - v)\frac{\partial f}{\partial v} = 0.\end{aligned} \tag{9.20}$$

Note that we have substituted for $u_2 = -\frac{1}{2}$, $a = \kappa\theta$, and $b_2 = \kappa + \lambda$ with $\lambda = 0$. The PDE in (9.20) holds for the bivariate characteristic function also. We proceed exactly as in Chapter 1, by obtaining the derivatives of $f(\phi_1, \phi_2; x, v)$ in (9.15) with respect to x, v, and τ, substituting them into the PDE (9.20), and eliminating f from both sides of the resulting equation, which produces

$$
\begin{aligned}
&-\left(\frac{\partial A}{\partial \tau}+\frac{\partial B}{\partial \tau}x+\frac{\partial C}{\partial \tau}v\right)+\rho\sigma vBC+\frac{1}{2}vB^2+\frac{1}{2}\sigma^2 vC^2 \\
&+\left(r-\frac{1}{2}v\right)B+\kappa(\theta-v)C=0.
\end{aligned}
\tag{9.21}
$$

Grouping terms common to x and common to v, and equating each set of terms to zero results in the equations

$$
\begin{aligned}
\frac{\partial A}{\partial \tau}&=rB+\kappa\theta C \\
\frac{\partial B}{\partial \tau}&=0 \\
\frac{\partial C}{\partial \tau}&=\frac{1}{2}\sigma^2 C^2+(\rho\sigma B-\kappa)C+\frac{1}{2}B^2-\frac{1}{2}B.
\end{aligned}
\tag{9.22}
$$

These equations are identical to those given by the result of Duffie, Pan, and Singleton (2000) in Equation (9.17), except for the sign which has been reversed. This is because, in (9.22), we are differentiating with respect to the time to maturity $\tau=T-t$, but, in (9.17), the derivative is with respect to t.

To solve the system of equations in (9.22), first note that the second equation along with the boundary condition $B(0,\phi_1,\phi_2)=i\phi_1$ implies that $B(\tau,\phi_1,\phi_2)=i\phi_1$. After substituting for B, this leaves us with two equations

$$
\begin{aligned}
\frac{\partial A}{\partial \tau}&=ri\phi_1+\kappa\theta C \\
\frac{\partial C}{\partial \tau}&=-\frac{1}{2}\phi_1(\phi_1+i)-(\kappa-\rho\sigma i\phi_1)C+\frac{1}{2}\sigma^2 C^2.
\end{aligned}
\tag{9.23}
$$

The second equation in Equation (9.23) is a Riccati equation that can be solved using the method described in Chapter 1. We can write this equation as

$$
\frac{\partial C}{\partial \tau}=P_2-Q_2C+RC^2 \tag{9.24}
$$

where

$$
P_2=-\frac{1}{2}\phi_1(\phi_1+i),\ \ Q_2=\kappa-\rho\sigma i\phi_1,\ \ R=\frac{1}{2}\sigma^2. \tag{9.25}
$$

The coefficients in (9.25) are exactly those of the Riccati coefficients P_j, Q_j, and R_j for $j=2$ described in Chapter 1 that lead to a solution for $D_2(\tau,\phi)$ for the univariate characteristic function, reproduced in Equation (9.1). Note that, in the univariate case, the coefficient for v_t is denoted $D_2(\tau,\phi)$ in Equation (9.10), while in the bivariate case the coefficient for v_t is denoted $C(\tau,\phi_1,\phi_2)$ in Equation (9.15). Recall that, in the bivariate case, the initial condition for the Riccati equation is different. Hence, to solve for the v_t coefficient in the bivariate characteristic function, first we set $\tau = 0$ along with $C(0,\phi_1,\phi_2) = i\phi_2$ in the general solution of Equation (9.1) to obtain

$$i\phi_2 = -\frac{2}{\sigma^2}\left(\frac{K_2\alpha_2 + \beta_2}{K_2 + 1}\right). \tag{9.26}$$

We then solve for K_2

$$\widetilde{K}_2 = -\left(\frac{2\beta_2 + i\phi_2\sigma^2}{2\alpha_2 + i\phi_2\sigma^2}\right) = -\left(\frac{b_2 - \rho\sigma i\phi_1 + d_2 - i\phi_2\sigma^2}{b_2 - \rho\sigma i\phi_1 - d_2 - i\phi_2\sigma^2}\right). \tag{9.27}$$

Since α_2 and β_2 are constructed from the quantities in (9.25), they are functions of ϕ_1 but not of ϕ_2

$$\alpha_2 = \frac{-b_2 + \rho\sigma i\phi_1 + d_2}{2}, \quad \beta_2 = \frac{-b_2 + \rho\sigma i\phi_1 - d_2}{2}. \tag{9.28}$$

Note that $\widetilde{K}_2$ in Equation (9.27) is identical to $\widetilde{K}_2$ in (9.7) for $j = 2$, with D_2^0 replaced by $i\phi_2$. Defining $\tilde{g}_2 = -\widetilde{K}_2$ and substituting in the general solution of Equation (9.1) produces the solution for $C(\tau,\phi_1,\phi_2)$, in which we have set $\lambda = 0$ in b_2

$$C(\tau,\phi_1,\phi_2) = \frac{(\kappa - \rho\sigma i\phi_1 + d_2) - (\kappa - \rho\sigma i\phi_1 - d_2)\tilde{g}_2 e^{d_2\tau}}{\sigma^2(1 - \tilde{g}_2 e^{d_2\tau})}. \tag{9.29}$$

In this expression, $C(\tau,\phi_1,\phi_2)$ is identical to $\widetilde{D}(\phi,\tau)$ defined in (9.8) for $j = 2$, but again, with D_j^0 replaced by $i\phi_2$.

We obtain $A(\tau,\phi_1,\phi_2)$ by integrating the first equation in (9.23), and by using the initial condition $A(0,\phi_1,\phi_2) = 0$, exactly as in Chapter 1

$$\begin{aligned} A(\tau,\phi_1,\phi_2) = (r-q)i\phi_1\tau + \kappa\theta\Bigg[&\frac{Q_2 + d_2}{\sigma^2}\int_0^\tau \frac{1}{1 - \tilde{g}_2 e^{d_2 y}}dy \\ &- \frac{Q_2 - d_2}{\sigma^2}\int_0^\tau \frac{\tilde{g}_2 e^{d_2 y}}{1 - \tilde{g}_2 e^{d_2 y}}dy + k_1\Bigg]. \end{aligned} \tag{9.30}$$

Both integrals in (9.30) can be evaluated by substitution of $x = \exp(d_2 y)$ and partial fractions, exactly as in Chapter 1. After substituting for the integrals and for d_2 and Q_2, and applying the initial condition $A(0,\phi_1,\phi_2) = 0$ to produce $k_1 = 0$ we end up with the solution for $A(\tau,\phi_1,\phi_2)$

$$A(\tau,\phi_1,\phi_2) = (r-q)i\phi_1\tau + \frac{\kappa\theta}{\sigma^2}\left[(\kappa - \rho\sigma i\phi_1 + d_2)\tau - 2\ln\left(\frac{1 - \tilde{g}_2 e^{d_2\tau}}{1 - \tilde{g}_2}\right)\right]. \tag{9.31}$$

Finally, we note that $A(\tau,\phi_1,\phi_2)$ is equivalent to $\widetilde{C}_j(\phi,\tau)$ in Equation (9.9), but with $C_j^0 = 0$ and $D_j^0 = i\phi_2$.

LINKING THE BIVARIATE CF AND THE GENERAL RICCATI EQUATION

The univariate characteristic function for x_T in the Heston model is Equation (9.10)

$$f(\phi, \tau; x_t, v_t) = \exp\left(C(\tau, \phi) + i\phi x_t + D(\tau, \phi) v_t\right) \tag{9.32}$$

with $C(\tau,\phi)$ given by (9.5) and $D(\tau,\phi)$ given by (9.2). The bivariate characteristic function for (x_T, v_T), on the other hand, is (9.15)

$$f(\phi_1, \phi_2; x, v) = \exp\left(A(\tau, \phi_1, \phi_2) + i\phi_1 x_t + C(\tau, \phi_1, \phi_2) v_t\right) \tag{9.33}$$

with $A(\tau,\phi_1,\phi_2)$ given by (9.31) and $C(\tau,\phi_1,\phi_2)$ given by (9.29). The two characteristic functions are clearly similar in form. We showed in the previous subsection that the coefficients are different, however. The difference arises from the choice of initial conditions for the general solution of the Riccati equation presented earlier. To obtain the univariate characteristic function, we set $C_j^0 = 0$ and $D_j^0 = 0$ in Equation (9.6), but to obtain the bivariate characteristic function we set $C_j^0 = 0$ and $D_j^0 = i\phi_2$.

If we set $\phi_2 = 0$ and write $\phi = \phi_1$ in the bivariate characteristic function (9.11) we obtain $f(\phi, 0; x, v) = E[\exp(i\phi x_T)]$, which is the univariate characteristic function $f_2(\phi; x, v)$ for x_T, and we also obtain $D_j^0 = 0$. Hence, when we set $\phi_2 = 0$ in the coefficients of the bivariate characteristic function, we should recover the coefficients of the univariate characteristic function $f_2(\phi; x, v)$. In other words, we should obtain

$$A(\tau, \phi, 0) = C_2(\tau, \phi), \quad C(\tau, \phi, 0) = D_2(\tau, \phi). \tag{9.34}$$

It is easy to verify that setting $\phi_2 = 0$ in Equation (9.27) produces $g_2 = (Q_2 + d_2)/(Q_2 - d_2)$, exactly as in Chapter 1, and consequently, that $C(\tau,\phi,0)$ in (9.29) becomes

$$C(\tau, \phi, 0) = \frac{\kappa - \rho\sigma i\phi + d_2}{\sigma^2}\left(\frac{1 - e^{d_2\tau}}{1 - g e^{d_2\tau}}\right) \tag{9.35}$$

which is exactly $D_2(\tau,\phi)$ from Chapter 1. Furthermore, with $g_2 = (Q + d_2)/(Q_2 - d_2)$, $A(\tau,\phi,0)$ in (9.31) becomes $C_2(\tau,\phi)$.

Finally, the coefficients of the bivariate characteristic function can be written in an equivalent form that is consistent with the "Little Trap" formulation of Albrecher et al. (2006), as in Kahl (2008). Indeed, by defining $\tilde{c}_2 = 1/\tilde{g}_2$ we can write $C(\tau,\phi_1,\phi_2)$ in Equation (9.29) as

$$C(\tau, \phi_1, \phi_2) = \frac{(\kappa - \rho\sigma i\phi_1 - d_2) - (\kappa - \rho\sigma i\phi_1 + d_2)\tilde{c}_2 e^{-d_2\tau}}{\sigma^2(1 - \tilde{c}_2 e^{-d_2\tau})}. \tag{9.36}$$

This is the definition of Kahl (2008) with $c = G(u)$ from his Equation (2.119), $D(u)$ in his Equation (2.120) equivalent to d_2, and with u_1 replacing ϕ_1, and u_2

replacing ϕ_2. Similarly, using (9.31) we can write $A(\tau, \phi_1, \phi_2)$ as

$$A(\tau, \phi_1, \phi_2) = (r - q)i\phi_1\tau + \frac{\kappa\theta}{\sigma^2}\left[\left(\kappa - \rho\sigma i\phi_1 - d_2\right)\tau - 2\ln\left(\frac{1 - \tilde{c}_2 e^{-d_2\tau}}{1 - \tilde{c}_2}\right)\right] \quad (9.37)$$

which is Equation (2.118) of Kahl (2008).

The bivariate characteristic function is implemented using the HestonBivariateCF.m Matlab function.

```
function y = HestonBivariateCF(phi1,phi2,...,trap);
x0 = log(S);
b = lambda + kappa;
d = sqrt((rho*sigma*i*phi1 - b)^2 - sigma^2* ...;
g = (b - rho*sigma*i*phi1 + d - sigma^2*i*phi2) ...;
c = 1/g;
B = i*phi1;
if trap==1
    % Little Trap formulation in Kahl (2008)
    G = (c*exp(-d*tau)-1)/(c-1);
    A = (r-q)*i*phi1*tau + a/sigma^2 ...;
    C = ((b - rho*sigma*i*phi1 - d) ...;
elseif trap==0
    % Original Heston formulation.
    G = (1-g*exp(d*tau))/(1-g);
    A = (r-q)*i*phi1*tau + a/sigma^2 ...;
    C = ((b - rho*sigma*i*phi1 + d) ...;
end
% The characteristic function.
y = exp(A + B*x0 + C*v0);
```

This function can be passed to the HestonGaussLaguerre.m function, which illustrates that the call price can be identically obtained with either the univariate or bivariate characteristic function. This is accomplished by setting the second argument to zero in the HestonBivariateCF.m function.

```
function y = HestonPriceGaussLaguerre(...,CF)
for k=1:length(x);
    phi    = x(k);
    weight = w(k);
    if CF==1
        % Univariate CF
        f2(k) = HestonCF(phi  ,kappa,...);
        f1(k) = HestonCF(phi-i,kappa,...)/(S*exp((r-q)*T));
    elseif CF==2
        % Bivariate CF
        f2(k) = HestonBivariateCF(phi  ,0,kappa,...);
        f1(k) = HestonBivariateCF(phi-i,0,kappa,...)/(S*exp((r-q)*T));
    end
```

```
    int2(k) = weight * real(exp(-i*phi*log(K))*f2(k)/i/phi);
    int1(k) = weight * real(exp(-i*phi*log(K))*f1(k)/i/phi);
end
P1 = 1/2 + 1/pi*sum(int1);
P2 = 1/2 + 1/pi*sum(int2);
```

MIKHAILOV AND NÖGEL MODEL

This model introduces time dependency in the Heston model by allowing the parameters in the model to be piecewise constant. The model makes use of the general Riccati equation defined earlier in this chapter. We denote the coefficients of the characteristic function by $\widetilde{C}_j(\phi, \tau_1; \Theta)$ and $\widetilde{D}_j(\phi, \tau_1; \Theta)$ to emphasize their dependence on the parameters $\Theta = (\kappa, \theta, \sigma, v_0, \rho)$.

Suppose we are given the N maturities $0 < T_1 < T_2 < \cdots < T_N < \infty$. Divide the time axis $[0, T_N]$ into the maturity increments $\tau_1, \tau_2, \ldots, \tau_N$, where $\tau_k = T_k - T_{k-1}$ for $k = 2, \ldots, N$, and with $\tau_1 = T_1$. The idea is to obtain expressions for $\widetilde{C}_j$ and $\widetilde{D}_j$ recursively. In first estimation step, we obtain $\widetilde{C}_j(\phi, \tau_1; \Theta)$ and $\widetilde{D}_j(\phi, \tau_1; \Theta)$ for the first maturity τ_1 using the static initial conditions $C_j^0 = 0$ and $D_j^0 = 0$, exactly as in the ordinary Heston model. We then construct the characteristic functions and the Heston model option prices, and estimate Θ. This produces the first set of estimates $\Theta_1 = (\kappa^{(1)}, \theta^{(1)}, \sigma^{(1)}, v_0^{(1)}, \rho^{(1)})$ corresponding to the first maturity τ_1. In the subsequent steps, the estimation is modified since we are using general $C_j^k \neq 0$ and $D_j^k \neq 0$. Hence, in the second estimation step, substitute Θ_1 into the expressions for $\widetilde{C}_j$ and $\widetilde{D}_j$ to produce the second set of initial conditions C_j^1 and D_j^1. Then construct $\widetilde{C}_j(\phi, \tau_2; \Theta)$ and $\widetilde{D}_j(\phi, \tau_2; \Theta)$ for the second maturity τ_2, construct the characteristic functions and the Heston model option prices, and produce the parameter estimate $\Theta_2 = (\kappa^{(2)}, \theta^{(2)}, \sigma^{(2)}, v_0^{(2)}, \rho^{(2)})$. We continue in this recursive fashion until the last maturity, τ_N. The following steps summarize this recursive method.

Step 1. Use $C_j^0 = D_j^0 = 0$ to form $\widetilde{C}_j(\phi, \tau_1; \Theta)$ and $\widetilde{D}_j(\phi, \tau_1; \Theta)$ as

$$\widetilde{C}_j(\phi, \tau_1; \Theta) = (r - q)i\phi\tau_1 + \frac{a}{\sigma^2}\left[\left(b_j - \rho\sigma i\phi + d_j\right)\tau_1 - 2\ln\left(\frac{1 - g_j e^{d_j\tau_1}}{1 - g_j}\right)\right]$$

$$\widetilde{D}_j(\phi, \tau_1; \Theta) = \frac{b_j - \rho\sigma i\phi + d_j}{\sigma^2}\left(\frac{1 - e^{d_j\tau_1}}{1 - g_j e^{d_j\tau_1}}\right)$$

where d_j and g_j are from Equation (9.3). Obtain the characteristic functions f_j $(j = 1, 2)$ at time τ_1

$$f_j(\phi; x, v, \Theta) = \exp(\widetilde{C}_j(\phi, \tau_1; \Theta) + \widetilde{D}_j(\phi, \tau_1; \Theta)v_0 + i\phi x)$$

where $x = \ln S_0$, the log spot price. Form the Heston option prices, and use them or the Heston implied volatilities to obtain $\Theta_1 = (\kappa^{(1)}, \theta^{(1)}, \sigma^{(1)},$

$v_0^{(1)}, \rho^{(1)})$, the set of parameter estimates for maturity τ_1. In this first step, the estimation of Θ is exactly the same as that for the ordinary Heston model, using the maturity τ_1.

Step $k \geq 2$. Substitute the parameter estimates $\Theta_{k-1} = (\kappa^{(k-1)}, \theta^{(k-1)}, \sigma^{(k-1)}, v_0^{(k-1)}, \rho^{(k-1)})$ from the previous step into the expressions for $\widetilde{C}_j$ and $\widetilde{D}_j$ to obtain the next initial conditions $C_j^{k-1} = \widetilde{C}_j(\phi, \tau_{k-1}; \Theta_{k-1})$ and $D_j^{k-1} = \widetilde{D}_j(\phi, \tau_{k-1}; \Theta_{k-1})$, using Equations (9.9) and (9.8), respectively. Construct $\widetilde{C}_j(\phi, \tau_k; \Theta)$ and $\widetilde{D}_j(\phi, \tau_k; \Theta)$ for the maturity τ_k, again using (9.9) and (9.8)

$$\widetilde{C}_j(\phi, \tau_k; \Theta) = (r-q)i\phi\tau_k + \frac{a}{\sigma^2}\left[(b_j - \rho\sigma i\phi + d_j)\,\tau_k - 2\ln\left(\frac{1-\tilde{g}_j e^{d_j\tau_k}}{1-\tilde{g}_j}\right)\right] + C_j^{k-1}$$

$$\widetilde{D}_j(\phi, \tau_k; \Theta) = \frac{(b_j - \rho\sigma i\phi + d_j) - (b_j - \rho\sigma i\phi - d_j)\tilde{g}_j\exp(d_j\tau_k)}{\sigma^2(1-\tilde{g}_j\exp(d_j\tau_k))} \tag{9.38}$$

where $\tilde{g}_j$ was defined after Equation (9.7)

$$\tilde{g}_j = \left(\frac{b_j - \rho\sigma i\phi + d_j - D_j^{k-1}\sigma^2}{b_j - \rho\sigma i\phi - d_j - D_j^{k-1}\sigma^2}\right) \tag{9.39}$$

and where d_j is defined in (9.3). Use the characteristic function

$$f_j(\phi; x, v, \Theta) = \exp(\widetilde{C}_j(\phi, \tau_k; \Theta) + \widetilde{D}_j(\phi, \tau_k; \Theta)v_0 + i\phi x)$$

to form the integrand for the probabilities P_1 and P_2, obtain the Heston prices with maturity τ_k, and obtain the parameter estimates $\Theta_k = (\kappa^{(k)}, \theta^{(k)}, \sigma^{(k)}, v_0^{(k)}, \rho^{(k)})$.

Final Step. At the final time τ_N we have the parameter estimates $\Theta_N = (\kappa^{(N)}, \theta^{(N)}, \sigma^{(N)}, v_0^{(N)}, \rho^{(N)})$, which we use to form the characteristic function

$$f_j(\phi; x, v, \Theta_N) = \exp(\widetilde{C}_j(\phi, \tau_N; \Theta_N) + \widetilde{D}_j(\phi, \tau_N; \Theta_N)v_0^{(N)} + i\phi x). \tag{9.40}$$

We use this characteristic function to form the integrand for the probabilities P_1 and P_2, and obtain the Heston prices with maturity τ_N.

Note that the estimation in Step $k \geq 2$ is for the current parameter set Θ only. The parameter set from the previous iteration, Θ_{k-1}, is fixed and used in the initial conditions C_j^{k-1} and D_j^{k-1}. Hence, the initial conditions do not impact the estimation of Θ directly. Note, however, that even though the initial conditions are not functions of the current parameter set Θ, they are functions of the integration variable ϕ. For the purposes of integration, the initial conditions cannot be treated as constants.

Note that $\widetilde{D}_j(\phi, \tau_k; \Theta)$ in Equation (9.38) depends on D_j^{k-1} through $\tilde{g}_j$ in (9.39). On the other hand, $\widetilde{C}_j(\phi, \tau_k; \Theta)$ in (9.38) also depends on D_j^{k-1} through $\tilde{g}_j$, and depends on C_j^{k-1} also.

The Matlab function MNProb.m implements the integrand for the time-dependent Heston model of Mikhailov and Nögel (2003). The function accepts as inputs a vector of parameter estimates obtained in the prior time steps, stored in the matrix param0, with the parameter estimates arranged in rows. The estimates from the most recent time step are in the top row, and the oldest estimates are in the bottom row. It also accepts vector of prior maturities (tau0), with the most recent maturity on top, and the oldest at the bottom. The function returns the integrand for the probabilities P_1 and P_2.

```
function y = MNProb(phi,param,param0,tau,tau0,...)
N = length(tau0);
C = 0;
% Create the past Cj and Dj values for the old maturities
for t=1:N
    kappa = param0(t,1);
    theta = param0(t,2);
    sigma = param0(t,3);
    v0    = param0(t,4);
    rho   = param0(t,5);
    T = tau0(t);
    if t==1
        D0 = 0; C0 = 0;
    else
        D0 = D; C0 = C;
    end
    C = Ct(phi,...,C0,D0);
    D = Dt(phi,...,C0,D0);
end
% Cj and Dj values for a single maturity
if N==0
    D0 = 0; C0 = 0;
else
    D0 = D; C0 = C;
end
C = Ct(phi,...,C0,D0);
D = Dt(phi,...,C0,D0);
f = exp(C + D*v0 + i*phi*x);
y = real(exp(-i*phi*log(K))*f/i/phi);
```

The function makes use of the Matlab functions Ct.m and Dt.m, which construct $\widetilde{C}_j(\phi, \tau_k; \Theta)$ and $\widetilde{D}_j(\phi, \tau_k; \Theta)$, respectively, from (9.38).

```
function C = Ct(phi,...,C0,D0)
d = sqrt((rho*sigma*i*phi - b)^2 - sigma^2* ...;
g = (b - rho*sigma*i*phi + d - D0*sigma^2)  ...;
G = (1 - g*exp(d*T))/(1-g);
C = (rf-q)*i*phi*T + kappa*theta/sigma^2 ...;

function D = Dt(phi,...,C0,D0)
d = sqrt((rho*sigma*i*phi - b)^2 - sigma^2* ...;
g = (b - rho*sigma*i*phi + d - D0*sigma^2)  ...;
G = (1 - g*exp(d*T))/(1-g);
D = ((b - rho*sigma*i*phi)*(1-g*exp(d*T)) + ...;
```

Finally, the MNProb.m function is passed to the MNPriceGaussLaguerre.m function, which uses Gauss-Laguerre integration to obtain the call price.

```
function y = MNPriceGaussLaguerre(param,param0,tau,tau0,...)
N = length(x)
for k=1:N;
    int1(k) = w(k)*HestonProbTD(x(k),...,1);
    int2(k) = w(k)*HestonProbTD(x(k),...,2);
end
P1 = 1/2 + 1/pi*sum(int1);
P2 = 1/2 + 1/pi*sum(int2);
Call = S*exp(-q*tau)*P1 - K*exp(-rf*tau)*P2;
if strcmp(PutCall,'C')
    y = Call;
else
    y = Call-S*exp(-q*tau) + K*exp(-rf*tau);
end
```

The C# code to implement the model is similar to the Matlab code and is not presented here.

To illustrate, we reproduce Table 1 of Mikhailov and Nögel (2003). They use $S = 1$, $r = 0$ and a maturity of $T = 5$ years. The parameters $\theta = v_0 = 0.1$, $\sigma = 0.2$, $\rho = -0.3$ are fixed, and κ varies from $\kappa = 1, 2, 4$ in the three periods, which we assume to be equal in length. This is implemented with the following code.

```
tau = [5/3 5/3  5/3];
param0 = [4 theta sigma v0 rho; ...
          2 theta sigma v0 rho];
param  = [1 theta sigma v0 rho];
tau0 = [5/3 5/3];
tau  =  5/3;
K = [0.5:.25:1.5];
[x w] = GenerateGaussLaguerre(32);
for k=1:length(K)
    NM(k) = MNPriceGaussLaguerre(param,param0,tau,tau0,...);
end
```

The results are presented in the second column of Table 9.1. For comparison, the result of Mikhailov and Nögel (2003) is presented in the third column. The table indicates that both sets of prices are in close agreement.

Parameter Estimation

In this section, we use loss functions to estimate the time-dependent parameters of the Mikhailov and Nögel (2003) model. The Matlab function MNObjFun.m

TABLE 9.1 Replication of Table 1 of Mikhailov and Nögel (2003)

Strike	Matlab Price	Mikhailov-Nögel Price
0.50	0.5429	0.5430
0.75	0.3852	0.3851
1.00	0.2737	0.2733
1.25	0.1960	0.1954
1.50	0.1420	0.1412

allows for piecewise constant parameters, and also accommodates three types of loss functions, MSE, RMSE, and the proxy IVMSE of Christoffersen, Heston, and Jacobs (2009).

```
function y = MNObjFun(param,param0,tau,tau0,...);
[NK,NT] = size(MktPrice);
for k=1:NK
    MPrice(k) = MNPriceGaussLaguerre(param,param0,tau,tau0,...);
    switch ObjFun
        case 1 % MSE
            error(k) =  (MPrice(k) - MktPrice(k))^2;
        case 2 % RMSE
            error(k) =  (MPrice(k) - MktPrice(k))^2 / MktPrice(k);
        case 3 % CHJ (2009)
            Vega(k) = BSV(S,K(k),rf,q,MktIV(k),tau);
            error(k) = sqrt((MPrice(k) - MktPrice(k))^2) / Vega(k);
    end
end
y = sum(sum(error))/(NT*NK);
```

The loss function allows for past values of parameters and maturities to be used as inputs, stored in the matrix param0 and in the vector tau0, respectively. To initialize time-dependent parameter estimation, we use the MNObjFun.m function with empty matrices [ ] in the place of param0 and tau0. This produces the first set of estimates at the first maturity.

```
ParamTD = fmincon(@(p) MNObjFun(p,[],tau(1),[],MktPrice(:,1),...)...);
oldparam = [];
oldtau   = [];
```

We then loop through the remaining maturities, using the previous maturity's parameter estimates as starting values for the next estimation.

```
for t=2:NT
    oldparam = [oldparam; ParamTD(t-1,:)];
    oldtau   = [oldtau, tau(t-1)];
    start = ParamTD(t-1,:);
    ParamTD(t,:) = fmincon(@(p)MNObjFun(p,oldparam,tau(t),oldtau,
                                          MktPrice(:,t),...)...);
end
```

The time-dependent parameters are stored in the matrix ParamTD, with the parameters estimates obtained from the shortest maturity in the first row. To obtain the time-dependent prices for a given strike K, we loop through the maturities, and construct a matrix of previous parameter values (oldparam) and previous maturities (oldtau) at each step. The parameter estimates are appended at the bottom of the ParamTD matrix, so that estimates from the shortest maturity appear in the top row, and those from the longest maturity in the bottom row. The time-dependent prices are stored in the matrix PriceTD, again with the top row corresponding to the shortest maturity. The prices with static parameters are in the matrix PriceTI.

```
oldparam = [];
oldtau   = [];
for t=1:NT
    PriceTI(t) = MNPriceGaussLaguerre(ParamTI,[],T(t),[],...);
    if t==1
        PriceTD(t) = MNPriceGaussLaguerre(ParamTD(t,:),[],tau(t),[],...);
    else
        oldparam = [oldparam; ParamTD(t-1,:)];
        oldtau   = [oldtau, tau(t-1)];
        PriceTD(t) = MNPriceGaussLaguerre(ParamTD(t,:),oldparam,
                                           tau(t),...);
  end
end
```

The C# code to implement the estimation is very similar and is not presented here. One key feature is that we use the ArrayList() function to allow for allocation of the maturities into a dynamic array.

```
// Arrays for old maturities and parameters
ArrayList OldTau = new ArrayList ();
for(int mat=1;mat<=NT-1;mat++)
{
    OldTau.Add(tau[mat-1]);
    tau0 = OldTau.ToArray();
}
```

TABLE 9.2 Estimates from Mikhailov and Nögel (2003) Model, DIA Data

Maturity (days)	κ	θ	σ	v_0	ρ	Estimation Error
37	1.9946	0.0073	1.2699	0.0423	−0.2733	1.44×10^{-6}
72	2.0340	0.2157	1.0430	0.0156	−0.4787	
135	1.9857	0.0010	1.1213	0.0486	−0.5022	
226	1.9877	0.0194	1.1452	0.0837	−0.5347	
All	1.9967	0.0942	1.2056	0.0314	−0.4695	2.02×10^{-5}

We illustrate the estimation of time-dependent parameters in the model of Mikhailov and Nögel (2003) by using puts on the Dow Jones Industrial Average EFT (DIA) on May 10, 2012. The spot price is $S = 129.14$, the strikes range from $K = 124$ to $K = 136$ in increments of \$1, and there are four maturities. We assess the estimation error using IVMSE

$$\frac{1}{N}\sqrt{\sum_{t,k}(IV_{tk} - IV_{tk}^{\Theta})^2} \tag{9.41}$$

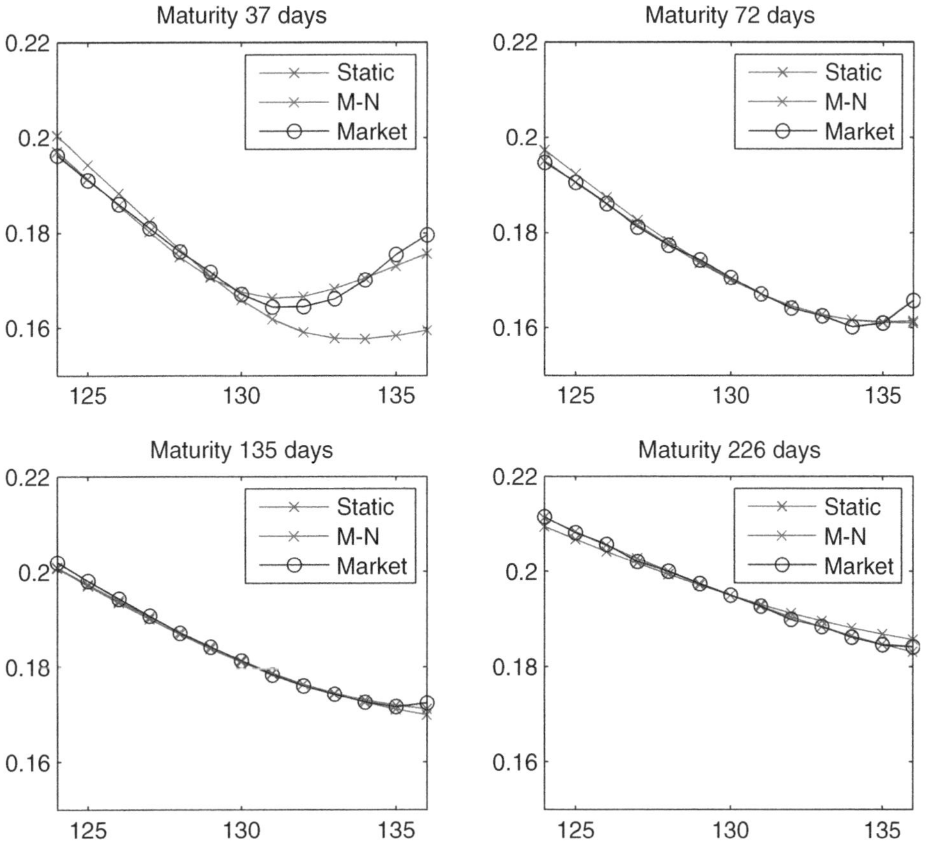

FIGURE 9.1 Implied Volatilities from the Mikhailov and Nögel (2003) Model, DIA Data

where N is the number of quoted implied volatilities used in the estimation, IV_{tk} is the quoted implied volatility at the k-th strike and t-th maturity, and IV_{tk}^{Θ} is the model implied volatility using the piecewise constant parameter estimates.

The MSE parameter estimates obtained from the time-dependent model, and those obtained from the static model, are presented in Table 9.2, along with the estimation error. For each maturity, we fit Heston call prices under both models, and we obtain implied volatilities from each set of prices. These are plotted in Figure 9.1, along with the implied volatility quotes. The table and the figure both suggest that the time-dependent model provides a closer fit to the market volatilities than the static model, especially at short maturities.

ELICES MODEL

The time-dependent models of Elices (2009) and Mikhailov and Nögel (2003) both make use of a recursive calculation on the bivariate characteristic function, presented in Afshani (2010) and Kahl and Lord (2010). In Elices (2009), however, this calculation is more clearly illustrated. Recall from Equations (9.11) and (9.33) that the time-t bivariate characteristic function for (x_T, v_T) is

$$\begin{aligned} f(\phi_1,\phi_2,\tau,x_t,v_t) &= E\left[\exp\left(i\phi_1 x_T + i\phi_2 v_T\right)|\mathcal{F}_t\right] \\ &= \exp(A(\tau,\phi_1,\phi_2) + i\phi_1 x_t + C(\tau,\phi_1,\phi_2)v_t) \end{aligned} \tag{9.42}$$

where $\tau = T - t$ is the time to maturity. As before, suppose that we are given the N maturities $0 < T_1 < T_2 < \cdots < T_N < \infty$ and that the time axis $[0, T_N]$ is divided into the maturity increments $\tau_1, \tau_2, \ldots, \tau_N$, where $\tau_k = T_k - T_{k-1}$ for $k = 2, \ldots, N$ and with $\tau_1 = T_1$. Define x_k, v_k and $\mathcal{F}_k$ to represent x_t, v_t and $\mathcal{F}_t$, but each evaluated at T_k. Lord and Kahl (2010) apply the law of iterated expectations by conditioning on the information set at T_{N-1} to obtain the characteristic function for x_N as

$$\begin{aligned} E\left[\exp\left(i\phi_1 x_N\right)\right] &= E\left[E\left[\exp\left(i\phi_1 x_N\right)|\mathcal{F}_{N-1}\right]\right] \\ &= E\left[f\left(\phi_1, 0, \tau_N, x_{N-1}, v_{N-1}\right)\right] \\ &= E\left[\exp\left(A\left(\tau_N,\phi_1,0\right) + i\phi_1 x_{N-1} + C(\tau_N,\phi_1,0)v_{N-1}\right)\right] \\ &= \exp(A(\tau_N,\phi_1,0))E\left[\exp\left(i\phi_1 x_{N-1} + i\left[-iC\left(\tau_N,\phi_1,0\right)\right]v_{N-1}\right)\right] \\ &= \exp(A(\tau_N,\phi_1,0))E\left[\exp\left(i\phi_1 x_{N-1} + i\phi_2^{N-1} v_{N-1}\right)\right] \end{aligned} \tag{9.43}$$

where $\phi_2^{N-1} = -iC(\tau_N, \phi_1, 0)$. Recognizing that the second argument of the bivariate characteristic can be written in this form is the trick that makes the recursive calculation possible. Now apply the law of iterated expectations again to the last term of the last equation in (9.43), conditioning this time on $\mathcal{F}_{N-2}$. We obtain

$$\begin{aligned} E[e^{i\phi_1 x_N}] &= \exp(A(\tau_N,\phi_1,0))E[E[\exp(i\phi_1 x_{N-1} + i\phi_2^{N-1}v_{N-1})|\mathcal{F}_{N-2}]] \\ &= \exp(A(\tau_N,\phi_1,0))E[f(\phi_1,\phi_2^{N-1},\tau_{N-1},x_{N-2},v_{N-2})] \end{aligned}$$

$$= \exp(A(\tau_N, \phi_1, 0) + A(\tau_{N-1}, \phi_1, \phi_2^{N-1}))$$
$$\times E[\exp(i\phi_1 x_{N-2} + C(\tau_{N-1}, \phi_1, \phi_2^{N-1})v_{N-2})]$$
$$= \exp(A(\tau_N, \phi_1, 0) + A(\tau_{N-1}, \phi_1, \phi_2^{N-1}))E[\exp(i\phi_1 x_{N-2} + i\phi_2^{N-2} v_{N-2})]$$

where $\phi_2^{N-2} = -iC(\tau_{N-1}, \phi_1, \phi_2^{N-1})$. Continuing in this manner, by repeated application of the law of iterated expectations and the trick, the characteristic function for $x_N = x_{T_N}$ can be written

$$f(\phi_1, x_0, v_0) = E[\exp(i\phi_1 x_N)]$$
$$= \exp\left(\sum_{k=0}^{N-1} A\left(\tau_{N-k}, \phi_1, \phi_2^{N-k}\right)\right) \exp(i\phi_1 x_0 + C(\tau_1, \phi_1, \phi_2^0)v_0) \quad (9.44)$$

with $\phi_2^{N-k} \equiv -iC(\tau_{N-k+1}, \phi_1, \phi_2^{N-k+1})$ and $\phi_2^N \equiv 0$.

As explained in Chapter 2, we use $f(\phi, x_0, v_0)$ in (9.44) directly for the second characteristic function, but for the first characteristic function we must use $f(\phi - i, x_0, v_0)/(Se^{(r-q)T_N})$.

Elices (2009) estimates v_0 at the first maturity, and restricts this parameter to remain constant throughout the remaining maturities. The other parameters are piecewise constant and change their value at the maturities. Denote by $\Theta_k = (\kappa^{(k)}, \theta^{(k)}, \sigma^{(k)}, \rho^{(k)})$ the parameter set estimated in the time increment (T_{k-1}, T_k). The model of Elices (2009) is implemented from the first maturity to the last, using the following steps.

Step 1. Construct the characteristic function at the first maturity, which depends on the parameter set Θ_1, as

$$\exp(A(\tau_1, \phi_1, 0; \Theta_1)) \times \exp(i\phi_1 x_0 + C(\tau_N, \phi_1, 0; \Theta_1)v_0)$$

Obtain the parameter estimates v_0 and Θ_1 by minimizing the loss function using market prices or implied volatilities at the first maturity.

Step 2. Construct the characteristic function at the second maturity, which depends on the parameter sets Θ_1 and Θ_2, as

$$\exp(A(\tau_2, \phi_1, 0; \Theta_2) + A(\tau_1, \phi_1, \phi_2^1; \Theta_1)) \times \exp(i\phi_1 x_0 + C(\tau_1, \phi_1, \phi_2^0; \Theta_1)v_0)$$

where $\phi_2^1 = -iC(\tau_2, \phi_1, 0; \Theta_2)$ and $\phi_2^0 = -iC(\tau_1, \phi_1, \phi_2^1; \Theta_1)$. Obtain the parameter estimates Θ_2 by minimizing the loss function using prices or volatilities at the second maturity, keeping Θ_1 and v_0 fixed.

Step *k*. Construct the characteristic function at maturity k, which depends on the parameter sets set $\Theta_1, \Theta_2, \ldots, \Theta_k$, as

$$\exp(A(\tau_k, \phi_1, 0; \Theta_k) + A(\tau_{k-1}, \phi_1, \phi_2^{k-1}; \Theta_{k-1}) + \cdots + A(\tau_1, \phi_1, \phi_2^1; \Theta_1))$$
$$\times \exp(i\phi_1 x_0 + C(\tau_1, \phi_1, \phi_2^0; \Theta_1)v_0)$$

where

$$\begin{aligned}
\phi_2^k &= 0 \\
\phi_2^{k-1} &= -iC(\tau_k, \phi_1, \phi_2^k; \Theta_k) \\
&\vdots \\
\phi_2^1 &= -iC(\tau_2, \phi_1, \phi_2^2; \Theta_2) \\
\phi_2^0 &= -iC(\tau_1, \phi_1, \phi_2^1; \Theta_1).
\end{aligned}$$

Obtain the estimates Θ_k by minimizing the loss function using prices or volatilities at the kth maturity, keeping $\Theta_1, \Theta_2, \ldots, \Theta_{k-1}$ and v_0 fixed.

At the final step, we have the characteristic function in Equation (9.44) at the last maturity, written here to emphasize its dependence on the parameter sets $\Theta_1, \Theta_2, \ldots, \Theta_N$

$$\begin{aligned}
f(\phi_1, x_0, v_0) = \exp\left(\sum_{k=0}^{N-1} A\left(\tau_{N-k}, \phi_1, \phi_2^{N-k}; \Theta_{N-k}\right)\right) \\
\times \exp(i\phi_1 x_0 + C(\tau_1, \phi_1, \phi_2^0; \Theta_1) v_0).
\end{aligned} \tag{9.45}$$

The coefficients $A(\tau_j, \phi_1, \phi_2^j; \Theta_j)$ and $C(\tau_j, \phi_1, \phi_2^j; \Theta_j)$ are implemented with the Matlab functions A.m and C.m, respectively.

```
function y = A(phi1,phi2,param,tau,r,q,trap)
if trap==1
    % Little Trap formulation
    G = (c*exp(-d*tau)-1)/(c-1);
    AA = (r-q)*i*phi1*tau + a/sigma^2 ...;
elseif trap==0
    % Original Heston formulation.
    G = (1-g*exp(d*tau))/(1-g);
    AA = (r-q)*i*phi1*tau + a/sigma^2 ...);
end
y = AA;
```

```
function y = C(phi1,phi2,param,tau,S,trap)
if trap==1
    % Little Trap formulation
    G = (c*exp(-d*tau)-1)/(c-1);
    CC = ((b - rho*sigma*i*phi1 - d) ...;
elseif trap==0
    % Original Heston formulation.
    G = (1-g*exp(d*tau))/(1-g);
    CC = ((b - rho*sigma*i*phi1 + d) ...;
end
y = CC;
```

These are used in the Matlab function ElicesCF.m, which calculates the characteristic function in Equation (9.45). The parameters for the current maturity are passed in the vector param, while the parameters of the prior maturities are passed in the matrix paramfixed. The initial variance parameter estimate is passed as an argument to the function. The maturity increments are passed in the vector tau, with the increment for the shortest maturity in the top position of the vector. The first portion of the function calculates the coefficients ϕ_2^k recursively, going backwards from the last maturity value $\phi_2^N = 0$.

```
function y = ElicesCF(phi1,param,paramfixed,v0,tau,...)
% Maturity increments
N = length(tau);
% phi2 coefficients vector.
phi2(N) = 0;
if N>=2
    phi2(N-1) = -i*C(phi1,phi2(N),param,tau(N),S,trap);
end
if N>=3
    for t=N-2:-1:1
        phi2(t) = -i*C(phi1,phi2(t+1),paramfixed(t+1,:),tau(t+1),...);
    end
end
if N>=2
    phi20 = -i*C(phi1,phi2(1),paramfixed(1,:),tau(1),...);
else
    phi20 = -i*C(phi1,phi2(1),param,tau(1)...;
end
```

The next part of the function calculates the coefficients $A(\tau_j, \phi_1, \phi_2^j; \Theta_j)$ and $C(\tau_1, \phi_1, \phi_2^0; \Theta_1)$, and returns the characteristic function.

```
% A coefficients.
Ah(N) = A(phi1,0,param,tau(N),r,q,trap);  % Current params
if N>=2
    for t=N-1:-1:1
        Ah(t) = A(phi1,phi2(t),paramfixed(t,:),tau(t),r,q,trap);
    end
end
% C coefficient
if N>=2
    Ch = C(phi1,phi20,paramfixed(1,:),tau(1),...);
else
    Ch = C(phi1,phi20,param,tau(1),...);
end
% Characteristic function
y = exp(sum(Ah) + i*phi1*x0 + Ch*v0);
```

The function ElicesPrice.m uses the characteristic function to produce the Heston call or put price with time-dependent parameters. The current parameters are in the vector param, while the fixed parameters from the previous periods are in the matrix paramfixed.

```
function y = ElicesPrice(...,param,paramfixed)
Mat = T(end);
% Numerical integration
for k=1:length(x);
    phi    = x(k);
    weight = w(k);
    f2(k)  = ElicesCF(phi   ,param,paramfixed);
    f1(k)  = ElicesCF(phi-i,param,paramfixed)/(S*exp((r-q)*Mat));
    int2(k) = weight * real(exp(-i*phi*log(K))*f2(k)/i/phi);
    int1(k) = weight * real(exp(-i*phi*log(K))*f1(k)/i/phi);
end
% Probabilities
P1 = 1/2 + 1/pi*sum(int1);
P2 = 1/2 + 1/pi*sum(int2);
% Call and Put price
HestonC = S*exp(-q*Mat)*P1 - K*exp(-r*Mat)*P2;
HestonP = HestonC - S*exp(-q*Mat) + K*exp(-r*Mat);
if strcmp(PutCall,'C')
    y = HestonC;
else
    y = HestonP;
end
```

Finally, the function ElicesObjFun.m produces an objective function for loss function estimation of the time-dependent parameters. Note that, since the estimation is done for a single maturity, only at each maturity step, the function includes only a loop for strikes.

```
function y = ElicesObjFun(param,paramfixed,v0,,MktPrice,MktIV,)
[NK,NT] = size(MktPrice);
% BlackScholes vega
BSV = @(S,K,r,q,v,T) (S*exp(-q*T)*normpdf((log(S/K) + ...;
for k=1:NK
    MPrice(k) = ElicesPrice(K(k),param,paramfixed,v0,...);
    switch ObjFun
        case 1
            % MSE
            error(k) = (MktPrice(k) - MPrice(k))^2;
        case 2
            % RMSE
            error(k) = (MktPrice(k) - MPrice(k))^2 / MktPrice(k);
```

```
        case 3
            % CHJ (2009)
            Vega(k) = BSV(S,K(k),rf,q,MktIV(k),T(end));
            error(k) = sqrt((MPrice(k) - MktPrice(k))^2) / Vega(k);
    end
end
y = sum(sum(error));
```

The C# code to implement the Elices (2009) time-dependent model is similar to the Matlab code and is not presented.

To illustrate piecewise constant parameter estimation in the model of Elices (2009), we use the same Dow Jones Industrial Average (DJIA) data used to generate Table 9.2 for the Mikhailov and Nögel (2003) model. This is accomplished with the following code. The first snippet defines the starting values and choice of loss function, and obtains the original Heston (1993) static parameter estimates across all maturities, for comparative purposes with the piecewise constant estimates. Prices and implied volatilities are obtained using these static parameter estimates. The code also estimates the parameter v_0 using the market data at the first maturity only.

```
% Static parameter estimates, prices, and implied vol
start = [2 0.1 1.2 0.05 -.5];
e = 1e-3;
lb = [e   e   e   e   -.999];  % Lower bound on the estimates
ub = [20  10  10  10  .999];   % Upper bound on the estimates
ObjFun = 1;
% Parameter estimation
ParamTI = fmincon(@(b) HestonObjFun(b,T,MktPrice,...),start,...,lb,ub);
% Prices and implied vol
for t=1:NT
    for k=1:NK
        PriceTI(k,t) = HestonPriceGaussLaguerre(K(k),T(t),...);
        IVTI(k,t) = BisecBSIV(K(k),T(t),PriceTI(k,t),...);
    end
end
% Volatility estimated from first maturity only
ParamTemp = fmincon(@(b) HestonObjFun(b,MktPrice(:,1),T(1),...),...);
v0 = ParamTemp(4);
```

The next portion of the code obtains the piecewise constant estimates, which are stored in the matrix ParamTD. At each maturity step, the starting values for the minimization are the parameter estimates from the previous maturity. During the optimization for the first maturity, the empty array [ ] is passed to the argument in the ElicesObjFun.m function corresponding to the fixed parameters.

```
% Time dependent parameter estimates, prices, and implied vol
% Remove v0 from subsequent parameter estimation.
start(4) = [];
lb(4)    = [];
ub(4)    = [];
% Elices (2009) model for remaining parameters
ParamTD(1,:) = fmincon(@(b) ElicesObjFun(b,[],tau(1),MktIV(:,1));
start = ParamTD(1,:);
ParamTD(2,:) = fmincon(@(b) ElicesObjFun(b,ParamTD(1,:),
                    tau(1:2),MktIV(:,2));
start = ParamTD(2,:);
ParamTD(3,:) = fmincon(@(b) ElicesObjFun(b,ParamTD(1:2,:),
                    tau(1:3),MktIV(:,3));
start = ParamTD(3,:);
ParamTD(4,:) = fmincon(@(b) ElicesObjFun(b,ParamTD(1:3,:),
                    tau(1:4),MktIV(:,4));
```

The final portion of the code uses the piecewise constant parameter estimates to obtain the piecewise constant prices, and implied volatilities extracted from those prices.

```
% Prices and implied vol
HParam = [ParamTD(1,1) ParamTD(1,2) ParamTD(1,3) v0 ParamTD(1,4)];
for k=1:NK
    PriceTD(k,1) = ElicesPrice(K(k),tau(1),   ParamTD(1,:),
                               []           ,v0);
    PriceTD(k,2) = ElicesPrice(K(k),tau(1:2),ParamTD(2,:),
                               ParamTD(1,:)  ,v0);
    PriceTD(k,3) = ElicesPrice(K(k),tau(1:3),ParamTD(3,:),
                               ParamTD(1:2,:),v0);
    PriceTD(k,4) = ElicesPrice(K(k),tau(1:4),ParamTD(4,:),
                               ParamTD(1:3,:),v0);
end
for t=1:NT
    for k=1:NK
        IVTD(k,t) = BisecBSIV(K(k),T(t),PriceTD(k,t));
    end
end
```

The Elices (2009) piecewise parameter estimates based on the DJIA data and the MSE loss function are in Table 9.3. The table also includes in the last row the static parameter estimates of the original Heston (1993) model.

The model and quoted implied volatilities are in Figure 9.2. The time-dependent model shows a good fit to the data, most notably at the short maturity.

TABLE 9.3 Parameter Estimates From the Elices (2009) Model, DJIA Data

Maturity (days)	κ	θ	σ	v_0	ρ	Estimation Error
37	5.8947	0.0067	1.0246	0.0341	−0.2686	1.14×10^{-6}
72	5.3900	0.1736	3.7798	0.0341	−0.6429	
135	4.1022	0.1544	5.9139	0.0341	−0.4599	
226	3.7900	0.1760	5.8142	0.0341	−0.5475	
All	1.8887	0.1065	1.4756	0.0340	−0.4418	1.41×10^{-5}

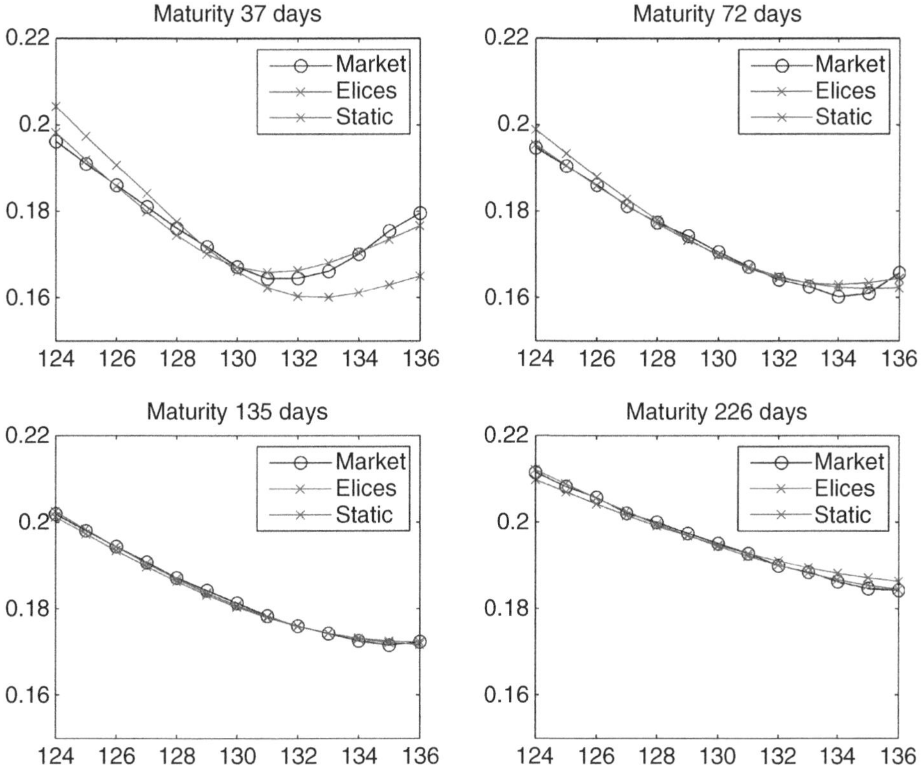

FIGURE 9.2 Implied Volatilities from the Elices (2009) Model, DIA Data

BENHAMOU-MIRI-GOBET MODEL

Benhamou, Gobet, and Miri (2010) use a volatility of variance expansion similar to the one employed by Lewis (2000) to derive an expression for the European put price that is not only very fast but also allows for the parameters θ, σ, and ρ to be piecewise constant. The remaining two parameters, v_0 and κ, are assumed constant.

Denote the time-t log forward price by $X_t = \ln(Se^{(r-q)\tau})$, where $\tau = T - t$ is the time to maturity. Applying Itō's lemma, the bivariate process for the time-dependent Heston model of Benhamou et al. (2010) is

$$dX_t = -\frac{v_t}{2}dt + \sqrt{v_t}dW_{1,t}$$

$$dv_t = \kappa(\theta_t - v_t)dt + \sigma_t\sqrt{v_t}dW_{2,t} \tag{9.46}$$

$$E^{\mathbb{Q}}[dW_{1,t}dW_{2,t}] = \rho_t dt$$

where v_0 is the initial variance. Using a perturbed version of the model and Malliavin calculus, they show that the put price in the Heston model can be expressed as a sum of the Black-Scholes put price and a set of correction terms involving derivatives of the Black-Scholes put. Assuming a constant rate of interest and dividend yield, the Black-Scholes put price can be expressed in terms of the total variance $y = \sigma^2\tau$ and the log-spot price $x = \ln S$ as[1]

$$P_{BS}(x,y) = Ke^{-r\tau}\Phi(f(x,y)) - Se^{-q\tau}\Phi(g(x,y)) \tag{9.47}$$

where

$$f(x,y) = \frac{1}{\sqrt{y}}[-x + \ln K - (r-q)T] + \frac{\sqrt{y}}{2},$$

$$g(x,y) = \frac{1}{\sqrt{y}}[-x + \ln K - (r-q)T] - \frac{\sqrt{y}}{2}.$$

Note that $f = g + \sqrt{y}$ and that $g = f - \sqrt{y}$. The put price in the model appears in Theorem 2.2 of Benhamou et al. (2010) as

$$e^{-r\tau}E^{\mathbb{Q}}[(K - e^{r\tau + X_T})^+] = P_{BS}(x, \hat{w}_T) + a_{1,T}\frac{\partial^2 P_{BS}}{\partial x \partial y}(x, \hat{w}_T) + a_{2,T}\frac{\partial^3 P_{BS}}{\partial x^2 \partial y}(x, \hat{w}_T)$$

$$+ b_{0,T}\frac{\partial^2 P_{BS}}{\partial y^2}(x, \hat{w}_T) + b_{2,T}\frac{\partial^4 P_{BS}}{\partial x^2 \partial y^2}(x, \hat{w}_T) \tag{9.48}$$

where

$$\hat{w}_T = \int_0^T v_{0,t}dt \tag{9.49}$$

and

$$v_{0,t} = e^{-\kappa t}\left(v_0 + \int_0^t \theta_s \kappa e^{\kappa s} ds\right). \tag{9.50}$$

[1] Benhamou et al. (2010) use a time-varying interest rate and dividend yield, but we assume these are constant for notational simplicity. The generalization to the time-varying versions is straightforward.

The coefficients in Equation (9.48) are obtained using the integral operators defined by Benhamou et al. (2010). The coefficients are defined in their Equation (2.13) as

$$a_{1,T} = \int_0^T e^{\kappa t}\rho_t\sigma_t v_{0,t}\left(\int_t^T e^{-\kappa u}du\right)dt, \tag{9.51}$$

$$a_{2,T} = \int_0^T e^{\kappa t}\rho_t\sigma_t v_{0,t}\left(\int_t^T \rho_s\sigma_s\left(\int_s^T e^{-\kappa u}du\right)ds\right)dt, \tag{9.52}$$

$$b_{0,T} = \int_0^T e^{2\kappa t}\sigma_t^2 v_{0,t}\left(\int_t^T e^{-\kappa s}\left(\int_s^T e^{-\kappa u}du\right)ds\right)dt, \tag{9.53}$$

$$b_{2,T} = \frac{a_{1,T}^2}{2}. \tag{9.54}$$

Note that only the parameters θ, σ, and ρ are allowed to vary; κ is assumed constant, and v_0 is an unobserved state variable.

Constant Parameters

If the parameters are assumed constant, then $\theta_t = \theta$, $\sigma_t = \sigma$, and $\rho_t = \rho$. Moving these parameters outside the integrals and evaluating the integrals in (9.51) through (9.53) produces the following expressions, which appear in Proposition 2.4 of Benhamou et al. (2010)

$$\begin{aligned}
a_{1,T} &= \frac{\rho\sigma e^{-\kappa T}}{\kappa^2}\left[v_0\left(-\kappa T + e^{\kappa T} - 1\right) + \theta\left(\kappa T + e^{\kappa T}(\kappa T - 2) + 2\right)\right], \\
a_{2,T} &= \frac{\rho^2\sigma^2 e^{-\kappa T}}{2\kappa^3}[v_0\left(-\kappa T(\kappa T + 2) + 2e^{\kappa T} - 2\right) \\
&\quad + \theta\left(2e^{\kappa T}(\kappa T - 3) + \kappa T(\kappa T + 4) + 6\right)], \\
b_{0,T} &= \frac{\sigma^2 e^{-2\kappa T}}{4\kappa^3}[v_0\left(-4e^{\kappa T}\kappa T + 2e^{2\kappa T} - 2\right) \\
&\quad + \theta\left(4e^{\kappa T}(\kappa T + 1) + e^{2\kappa T}(2\kappa T - 5) + 1\right)], \\
b_{2,T} &= a_{1,T}^2/2.
\end{aligned} \tag{9.55}$$

Note that under constant parameters we have

$$v_{0,t} = \theta + (v_0 - \theta)e^{-kt}, \quad \hat{w}_T = (v_0 - \theta)\left(\frac{1 - e^{-\kappa T}}{\kappa}\right) + \theta T \tag{9.56}$$

so that $\hat{w}_T$ reduces to the form we encountered in Chapter 2. To obtain the put price, substitute the coefficients from Equation (9.55) into (9.48), using the Black-Scholes derivatives presented at the end of this chapter. The call price is obtained by put-call parity.

As noted by Benhamou et al. (2010), the put price expansion in Equation (9.48) under constant parameters is identical to the volatility of variance expansion of Lewis (2000) covered in Chapter 4. Indeed, it is straightforward to verify that

$a_{1,T} = \sigma J_1(v,T)$, $a_{2,T} = \sigma^2 J_4(v,T)$, and $b_{0,T} = \sigma^2 J_3(v,T)$, and that identical put prices are produced.

The Matlab function BGMApproxPrice.m implements the approximation to the Heston put in (9.48) assuming constant parameters. To conserve space, parts of the function have been omitted. The function also returns the price of a call obtained by put-call parity.

```
function y = BGMApproxPrice(params,S,K,rf,q,T,trap,PutCall)
g = y^(-1/2) * (-x + log(K) - (rf-q)*T) - (1/2)*sqrt(y);
f = y^(-1/2) * (-x + log(K) - (rf-q)*T) + (1/2)*sqrt(y);
BSPut = K*exp(-rf*T)*normcdf(f) - S*exp(-q*T)*normcdf(g);
a1T = (rho*sigma*ekTm/k^2) * (v0*(-kT+ekT-1) ... ;
a2T = (rho^2*sigma^2*ekTm/2/k^3) * (v0*(-kT*(kT+2)+2*ekT-2) ...;
b0T = (sigma^2*exp(-2*kT)/4/k^3) * (v0*(-4*ekT*kT+ ...;
b2T = a1T^2/2;
dPdxdy   = K*exp(-rf*T)*PHIfxy   - exp(-q*T)*S ...;
dPdx2dy  = K*exp(-rf*T)*PHIfx2y  - exp(-q*T)*S ...;
dPdy2    = K*exp(-rf*T)*PHIfy2   - exp(-q*T)*S ...;
dPdx2dy2 = K*exp(-rf*T)*PHIfx2y2 - exp(-q*T)*S ...;
Put = BSPut + a1T*dPdxdy + a2T*dPdx2dy + b0T*dPdy2 + b2T*dPdx2dy2;
if strcmp(PutCall(1),'P')
    y = Put;
else
    y = Put - K*exp(-rf*T) + S*exp(-q*T);
end
```

The C# code to implement the model under constant parameters is very similar and is not presented here.

To illustrate, in Table 9.4 we reproduce the call prices and implied volatilities in Tables 4 and 3, respectively, of Benhamou et al. (2010).[2] Their tables use $S = 100$, $\theta = 0.06$, $\kappa = 3$, $\sigma = 0.3$, and $\rho = 0$. To conserve space, only the at-the-money column is presented in Table 9.4. For each maturity the implied volatility and call price is presented, each obtained using the closed-form Heston model with 32-point Gauss-Laguerre integration and using the approximation in Equation (9.48).

The entries in Table 9.4 are identical to those obtained by Benhamou et al. (2010) in their Tables 9.3 and 9.4.

Piecewise Constant Parameters

Suppose that there are N maturities $0 < T_1 < T_2 < \cdots < T_N < \infty$. Benhamou et al. (2010) assume that κ and v_0 are constant over $[0, T_N]$, but that θ, σ, and ρ have the piecewise constant values θ_{i+1}, σ_{i+1} and ρ_{i+1} respectively, over the interval $[T_i, T_{i+1}]$. They provide recursive expressions for the price coefficients $a_{1,T_{i+1}}$, $a_{2,T_{i+1}}$ and $b_{0,T_{i+1}}$ by separating the domain of integration in Equations (9.51) through (9.53) over

[2]Note that the prices in Tables 3 and 4 of Benhamou et al. (2010) are those of calls, not puts. We thank Emmanuel Gobet for pointing this out.

TABLE 9.4 ATM Call Prices and Implied Volatility, Closed Form and Approximation

Maturity	Closed Form Call Price	Approximate Call Price	Closed Form Implied Vol	Approximate Implied Vol
3M	4.23	4.22	21.19	21.19
6M	6.20	6.19	21.99	21.98
1Y	9.12	9.11	22.90	22.89
2Y	13.26	13.26	23.61	23.61
3Y	16.39	16.39	23.89	23.89
5Y	21.26	21.26	24.12	24.12
7Y	25.14	25.14	24.23	24.22
10Y	29.92	29.92	24.30	24.30

$(0,T_i)$ and (T_i,T_{i+1}). Hence, for $a_{1,T_{i+1}}$ we have, from (9.51) and the proof of proposition 2.5 of Benhamou et al. (2010)

$$\begin{aligned} a_{1,T_{i+1}} &= \int_0^{T_{i+1}} e^{\kappa t}\rho_t\sigma_t v_{0,t}\left(\int_t^{T_{i+1}} e^{-\kappa u}du\right)dt \\ &= \int_0^{T_i} e^{\kappa t}\rho_t\sigma_t v_{0,t}\left(\int_t^{T_{i+1}} e^{-\kappa u}du\right)dt + \int_{T_i}^{T_{i+1}} e^{\kappa t}\rho_t\sigma_t v_{0,t}\left(\int_t^{T_{i+1}} e^{-\kappa u}du\right)dt. \end{aligned} \tag{9.57}$$

The first term in the second line of (9.57) can be separated into two parts by breaking up the domain (t,T_{i+1}) of the inner integral into (t,T_i) and (T_i,T_{i+1})

$$\int_0^{T_i} e^{\kappa t}\rho_t\sigma_t v_{0,t}\left(\int_t^{T_i} e^{-\kappa u}du\right)dt + \int_0^{T_i} e^{\kappa t}\rho_t\sigma_t v_{0,t}\left(\int_{T_i}^{T_{i+1}} e^{-\kappa u}du\right)dt. \tag{9.58}$$

The first term in (9.58) is a_{1,T_i}. This implies that we can write $a_{1,T_{i+1}}$ as

$$\begin{aligned} a_{1,T_{i+1}} = a_{1,T_i} &+ \int_0^{T_i} e^{\kappa t}\rho_t\sigma_t v_{0,t}\left(\int_{T_i}^{T_{i+1}} e^{-\kappa u}du\right)dt \\ &+ \int_{T_i}^{T_{i+1}} e^{\kappa t}\rho_t\sigma_t v_{0,t}\left(\int_t^{T_{i+1}} e^{-\kappa u}du\right)dt. \end{aligned} \tag{9.59}$$

Since the parameters are piecewise constant over the intervals (T_i,T_{i+1}), we need to break up the integral over the $(0,T_i)$ domain into integrals over domains (T_i,T_{i+1}). Hence Equation (9.59) becomes

$$\begin{aligned} a_{1,T_{i+1}} = a_{1,T_i} &+ \rho_1\sigma_1\int_0^{T_1} e^{\kappa t}v_{0,t}\left(\int_{T_i}^{T_{i+1}} e^{-\kappa u}du\right)dt \\ &+ \rho_2\sigma_2\int_{T_1}^{T_2} e^{\kappa t}v_{0,t}\left(\int_{T_i}^{T_{i+1}} e^{-\kappa u}du\right)dt + \cdots \\ &+ \rho_i\sigma_i\int_{T_{i-1}}^{T_i} e^{\kappa t}v_{0,t}\left(\int_{T_i}^{T_{i+1}} e^{-\kappa u}du\right)dt \\ &+ \rho_{i+1}\sigma_{i+1}\int_{T_i}^{T_{i+1}} e^{\kappa t}v_{0,t}\left(\int_t^{T_{i+1}} e^{-\kappa u}du\right)dt \end{aligned} \tag{9.60}$$

which can be written

$$\begin{aligned} a_{1,T_{i+1}} &= a_{1,T_i} + \sum_{j=1}^{i} \rho_j\sigma_j \int_{T_{j-1}}^{T_j} e^{\kappa t} v_{0,t} \left(\int_{T_i}^{T_{i+1}} e^{-\kappa u} du \right) dt \\ &\quad + \rho_{i+1}\sigma_{i+1} \int_{T_i}^{T_{i+1}} e^{\kappa t} v_{0,t} \left(\int_{t}^{T_{i+1}} e^{-\kappa u} du \right) dt \end{aligned} \tag{9.61}$$

where $T_0 = 0$. The other recursive coefficients are obtained in a similar fashion. From Equation (9.52)

$$\begin{aligned} a_{2,T_{i+1}} &= a_{2,T_i} + \int_0^{T_i}\int_t^{T_i}\int_{T_i}^{T_{i+1}} + \int_0^{T_i}\int_{T_i}^{T_{i+1}}\int_s^{T_{i+1}} + \int_{T_i}^{T_{i+1}}\int_t^{T_{i+1}}\int_s^{T_{i+1}} \\ &= a_{2,T_i} + \sum_{j=1}^{i} (\rho_j\sigma_j)^2 \int_{T_{j-1}}^{T_j} e^{\kappa t} v_{0,t} \int_t^{T_i} \left(\int_{T_i}^{T_{i+1}} e^{-\kappa u} du \right) ds dt \\ &\quad + \sum_{j=1}^{i} (\rho_j\sigma_j)^2 \int_{T_{j-1}}^{T_j} e^{\kappa t} v_{0,t} \int_{T_i}^{T_{i+1}} \left(\int_{s}^{T_{i+1}} e^{-\kappa u} du \right) ds dt \\ &\quad + (\rho_{i+1}\sigma_{i+1})^2 \int_{T_i}^{T_{i+1}} e^{\kappa t} v_{0,t} \int_t^{T_{i+1}} \left(\int_{s}^{T_{i+1}} e^{-\kappa u} du \right) ds dt. \end{aligned} \tag{9.62}$$

In the first line of (9.62), the integrands are suppressed to simplify the equation. From Equations (9.53) and (9.54)

$$\begin{aligned} b_{0,T_{i+1}} &= b_{0,T_i} + \int_0^{T_i}\int_t^{T_i}\int_{T_i}^{T_{i+1}} + \int_0^{T_i}\int_{T_i}^{T_{i+1}}\int_s^{T_{i+1}} + \int_{T_i}^{T_{i+1}}\int_t^{T_{i+1}}\int_s^{T_{i+1}} \\ &= b_{0,T_i} + \sum_{j=1}^{i} \sigma_j^2 \int_{T_{j-1}}^{T_j} e^{2\kappa t} v_{0,t} \int_t^{T_i} e^{-\kappa s} \left(\int_{T_i}^{T_{i+1}} e^{-\kappa u} du \right) ds dt \\ &\quad + \sum_{j=1}^{i} \sigma_j^2 \int_{T_{j-1}}^{T_j} e^{2\kappa t} v_{0,t} \int_{T_i}^{T_{i+1}} e^{-\kappa s} \left(\int_{s}^{T_{i+1}} e^{-\kappa u} du \right) ds dt \\ &\quad + \sigma_{i+1}^2 \int_{T_i}^{T_{i+1}} e^{2\kappa t} v_{0,t} \int_t^{T_{i+1}} e^{-\kappa s} \left(\int_{s}^{T_{i+1}} e^{-\kappa u} du \right) ds dt, \\ b_{2,T_{i+1}} &= a_{1,T_{i+1}}^2/2. \end{aligned} \tag{9.63}$$

In these expressions, we use the following form for $v_{0,t}$, the piecewise constant version of Equation (9.50)

$$v_{0,t} = e^{-\kappa t} \left(v_0 + \theta_{i+1} \int_0^t \kappa e^{\kappa s} ds \right) = e^{-\kappa t}(v_0 - \theta_{i+1}) + \theta_{i+1}. \tag{9.64}$$

Although these integrals can be evaluated by hand, it is convenient to evaluate them with the symbolic toolbox in Matlab. For $a_{2,T_{i+1}}$, this is accomplished with the following code.

```
% Coefficients for a2T(T+1)
% First element in the first sum
f10 = int(exp(kappa*t)*v0t
    * int(int(exp(-kappa*u),u,s,Tip1),s,Ti,Tip1),t,0,Tj);
% Remaining elements in the first sum
f11 = int(exp(kappa*t)*v0t
    * int(int(exp(-kappa*u),u,s ,Tip1),s,Ti,Tip1),t,Tjm1,Tj);
% First element in the second sum
f20 = int(exp(kappa*t)*v0t
    * int(int(exp(-kappa*u),u,Ti,Tip1),s,t,Ti),t,0,Tj);
% Remaining elements in the second sum
f21 = int(exp(kappa*t)*v0t
     * int(int(exp(-kappa*u),u,Ti,Tip1),s,t,Ti),t,Tjm1,Tj);
% Final term
f3 = int(exp(kappa*t)*v0t
   * int(int(exp(-kappa*u),u,s,Tip1),s,t,Tip1),t,Ti,Tip1);
```

Once the code is run, the symbolic terms must be changed into Matlab arrays where applicable, using the search and replace feature in a word processor. For example, Tj must be changed to T(j), and Tip1 to T(t+1). The code to obtain the remaining coefficients is similar.

To evaluate the put price under piecewise constant parameters, we first evaluate a_{1,T_1}, a_{2,T_1}, b_{0,T_1} and b_{2,T_1} using Equations (9.55) with parameters κ, v_0, θ_1, σ_1 and ρ_1. We then evaluate a_{1,T_2}, a_{2,T_2}, b_{0,T_2} and b_{2,T_2} using Equations (9.60) through (9.64) with parameters κ, v_0, θ_2, σ_2 and ρ_2, and θ_1, σ_1 and ρ_1. We continue to apply (9.60) through (9.64) until we reach the last maturity T_N, and we substitute a_{1,T_N}, a_{2,T_N}, b_{0,T_N} and b_{2,T_N} into (9.48) to obtain the put price.

Recall that the parameters κ and v_0 are fixed for all maturities, but θ, σ, and ρ are allowed to vary. Hence, if there are N maturities, there will be $2 + 3N$ parameters. It is convenient to stack the parameters in a vector. We use κ and v_0 in the first two positions, and θ_j, σ_j, and ρ_j (in that order) for the remaining positions. For example, for three maturities, the vector is

$$(\kappa, v_0, \theta_1, \sigma_1, \rho_1, \theta_2, \sigma_2, \rho_2, \theta_3, \sigma_3, \rho_3). \tag{9.65}$$

To implement the price in Matlab, it is convenient to break up the sums in the expressions for $a_{1,T_{i+1}}$, $a_{2,T_{i+1}}$ and $b_{0,T_{i+1}}$ into the first term of the sum and the remaining terms. For example, $a_{1,T_{i+1}}$ in Equation (9.61) is written as

$$\begin{aligned} a_{1,T_{i+1}} &= a_{1,T_i} + \rho_1\sigma_1 \int_0^{T_1} e^{\kappa t} v_{0,t} \left(\int_{T_i}^{T_{i+1}} e^{\kappa u} du \right) dt \\ &+ \sum_{j=2}^{i} \rho_j\sigma_j \int_{T_{j-1}}^{T_j} e^{\kappa t} v_{0,t} \left(\int_{T_i}^{T_{i+1}} e^{-\kappa u} du \right) dt \\ &+ \rho_{i+1}\sigma_{i+1} \int_{T_i}^{T_{i+1}} e^{\kappa t} v_{0,t} \left(\int_{t}^{T_{i+1}} e^{-\kappa u} du \right) dt. \end{aligned} \tag{9.66}$$

The function BGMApproxPriceTD.m calculates the approximate put value under piecewise constant maturities. We illustrate the function with the code for the coefficient $a_{1,T_{i+1}}$ in (9.66). The code for the other coefficients is similar. The beginning of the function stacks the parameters in the order specified by (9.65) and calculates the first component of the coefficients, corresponding to the first time step. The first component is the term a_{1,T_i} in (9.66), obtained using (9.55).

```
function y = BGMApproxPriceTD(param,T,S,K,rf,q,PutCall)
NT = length(T);
Nparam = 2 + 3*NT;
kappa = param(1);
v0    = param(2);
for i=3:3:Nparam
    j = floor(i/3);
    theta(j)  = param(i);
    sigma(j)  = param(i+1);
    rho(j)    = param(i+2);
end
% First set of coefficients
a1T(1)  = -rho(1)*sigma(1)*(2*theta(1)*exp(kappa*T(1))+ ...;
a2T(1)  = -1/2*rho(1)^2*sigma(1)^2*(kappa^2*v0*T(1)^2+ ...;
b0T(1)  = -1/4*sigma(1)^2*(5*theta(1)*exp(kappa*T(1))^2+ ...;
b2T(1)  = a1T(1)^2/2;
```

The second part calculates the remaining portion of the coefficients. The terms A1 correspond to the integrals in (9.66), in the same order.

```
% Remaining sets of coefficients
A1 = 0;
if NT>=2
    for t=1:NT-1
        % Coefficients for a1T(T+1)
        for j=1
            A1 = A1 + rho(j)*sigma(j)*(-exp(-kappa*T(t))+ ...;
        end
        for j=2:t
            A1 = A1 - rho(j)*sigma(j)*(-exp(-kappa*T(t))+ ...;
        end
        for j=t+1
            A1 = A1 - rho(j)*sigma(j)*(-v0*exp(kappa*T(t+1)) ...;
        end
        a1T(t+1) = a1T(t) + A1;
    end
end
```

The third and final part retains the last element of the arrays for the coefficients, calculates the required derivatives, and calculates the put price in Equation (9.48). The function returns the call price by put-call parity.

```
% Coefficients for the expansion are the last ones in the iterations
A1T = a1T(end);
A2T = a2T(end);
B0T = b0T(end);
B2T = b2T(end);
% Integrated variance
wT = (v0-theta(end))*(1-exp(-kappa*T(end)))/kappa + ...;
% Derivatives of Black-Scholes Put
dPdxdy    = K*exp(-rf*T(end))*PHIfxy    - ...;
dPdx2dy   = K*exp(-rf*T(end))*PHIfx2y   - ...;
dPdy2     = K*exp(-rf*T(end))*PHIfy2    - ...;
dPdx2dy2 = K*exp(-rf*T(end))*PHIfx2y2 - ...;
% Benhamou, Gobet, Miri expansion
Put = BSPut + A1T*dPdxdy + A2T*dPdx2dy + B0T*dPdy2 + B2T*dPdx2dy2;
```

The C# code is similar and not presented here.

To illustrate pricing with time-dependent parameters in the model of Benhamou et al. (2010), we reproduce the at-the-money ($K = 100$) put prices in their Table 8. This is done with the following snippets of code. The first snippet constructs the time-varying parameters across 40 time periods.

```
% Construct the parameters
for i=1:40;
    T(i)     =  i/4;
    theta(i) =  0.04 + (i-1)*0.05/100;
    sigma(i) =  0.30 + (i-1)*0.50/100;
    rho(i)   = -0.20 + (i-1)*0.35/100;
end;
```

The second snippet constructs the Benhamou et al. (2010) prices, concatenating the parameter vector with the piecewise constant parameters at each time step.

```
% BGM (2010) model prices
param = [kappa v0];
for t=1:40;
    param = [param theta(t) sigma(t) rho(t)];
    ApproxPW(t) = BGMApproxPriceTD(param,T(1:t),...;
end
```

The next snippet constructs the Mikhailov and Nögel (2003) prices. At the first time step these are the closed-form prices. In the next time steps, the parameter and maturity vectors are updated by concatenation. Only time steps corresponding to the maturities are retained.

```
% Mikhailov-Nogel (2003) model prices
for t=1:40;
    if t==1
        ClosedPW(t) = HestonPriceGaussLaguerre(T(1),theta(1),
                                                sigma(1),...);
    else
        MNparam0 = [kappa theta(t-1) sigma(t-1) v0 rho(t-1); MNparam0];
        tau0 = [tau(t-1) tau0];
        MNparam = [kappa theta(t) sigma(t) v0 rho(t)];
        ClosedPW(t) = HestonPriceGLTD(MNparam,MNparam0,tau(t),...);
    end
end
I = ismember(T,[3/12 6/12 1 2 3 5 7 10]);
ApproxPW = ApproxPW(I);
ClosedPW = ClosedPW(I);
```

Finally, the last snippet obtains the Heston (1993) closed form prices, using the averaged parameter values of Benhamou et al. (2010).

```
% The averaged parameter values.  Note: v0(5) has been changed
v0     =  [.04 .0397 .0328 .0464 .05624 .2858 .8492 .1454]';
theta  =  [.04 .0404 .0438 .0402 .0404  .0268 .0059 .0457]';
sigma  =  [.30 .3012 .3089 .3112 .3210  .3363 .3541 .3998]';
rho    = -[.20 .1993 .1972 .1895 .1820  .1652 .1480 .1232]';
% The time-static prices using the averaged parameter values
for t=1:N;
    ClosedAvg(t) = HestonPriceGaussLaguerre(T(t), theta(t),...);
end
```

The prices generated from this code are in Table 9.5. The first column contains the closed form Heston prices using 32-point Gauss-Laguerre integration and the

TABLE 9.5 Comparison of Put Prices

Maturity (years)	Heston, Averaged Parameters	Mikhailov & Nögel, Piecewise Parameters	Benhamou et al., Piecewise Parameters	Benhamou et al., True Prices
0.25	3.93	3.93	3.93	3.93
0.5	5.53	5.54	5.54	5.53
1.0	7.84	7.86	7.80	7.85
2.0	11.23	11.24	11.11	11.23
3.0	13.92	13.93	13.78	13.92
5.0	18.35	18.37	18.24	18.37
7.0	22.13	22.16	21.99	22.15
10.0	27.14	27.17	26.77	27.17

averaged parameter values that appear in Table 6 of Benhamou et al. (2010). The second column contains the prices from the Mikhailov and Nögel (2003) formulation described earlier in this chapter. The third column contains prices computed using the model of Benhamou et al. (2010) in Equation (9.47), using the recursive relationships on the coefficients in (9.60) through (9.64). Finally, the last column contains the Benhamou et al. 2010 piecewise prices from Table 8 of their paper. Only the at-the-money ($K = 100$) results are presented.

Parameter Estimation

To estimate constant (not time-dependent) parameters, we use a loss function that estimates κ, v_0, θ, σ, and ρ across all maturities. This is accomplished using the HestonObjFun.m function from Chapter 6.

```
function y = HestonObjFun(...);
for t=1:NT
    for k=1:NK
        MPrice(k,t) = HestonPriceGaussLaguerre(K(k),T(t),...);
        switch ObjFun
            case 1
                error(k,t) = (MPrice(k,t)-MktPrice(k,t))^2;
            case 2
                error(k,t) = (MPrice(k,t)-MktPrice(k,t))^2/
                                   MktPrice(k,t);
        end
    end
end
y = sum(sum(error));
```

To estimate piecewise constant parameters, we use a loss function that simultaneously estimates all these parameters. This is accomplished with the Matlab function HestonBGMObjFun.m. The only difference between this loss function and the HestonObjFun.m one described earlier is that the Benhamou et al. (2010) approximation is used to obtain model prices, rather than the Heston (1993) closed form.

```
function y = HestonBGMObjFun(...);
for t=1:NT
    for k=1:NK
        MPrice(k,t) = BGMApproxPutTD(param,T(1:t),K(k),...);
        switch ObjFun
            case 1
                error(k,t) = (MPrice(k,t)-MktPrice(k,t))^2;
        end
    end
end
y = sum(sum(error));
```

To illustrate, we use the same set of puts on the DJIA index used to generate the time-dependent parameter estimates of Mikhailov and Nögel (2003) in Table 9.2. To estimate the static parameters, we use the usual HestonObjFun.m objective function, along with the same starting values to generate Table 9.3.

```
% Starting values
kappa0 =  2.0;
theta0 =  0.1;
sigma0 =  1.2;
v00    =  0.05;
rho0   = -0.5;
start = [kappa0 theta0 sigma0 v00 rho0];
e = 1e-3;
lb = [e    e    e    e   -.999];  % Lower bound on the estimates
ub = [20   10   10   10   .999];  % Upper bound on the estimates
% Static parameter estimates
ParamTI = fmincon(@(p) HestonObjFun(p,..), start,...,lb,ub);
```

To estimate the piecewise constant parameters, we use the HestonBGMObjFunTD.m objective function along with the static parameter estimates as starting values.

```
% Starting values
kappa0 = ParamTI(1);
theta0 = ParamTI(2);
sigma0 = ParamTI(3);
v00    = ParamTI(4);
rho0   = ParamTI(5);
start = [kappa0 v00 repmat([theta0 sigma0 rho0],1,length(T))];
% Parameter bounds
lb = [e    e repmat([e  e   -.999],1,length(T))];
ub = [100 2 repmat([10 10   .999],1,length(T))];
% Time dependent parameter estimates
paramTD = fmincon(@(p) HestonBGMObjFun(p,...), start,...,lb,ub);
```

We then separate the piecewise constant parameters into separate vectors, and obtain both sets of prices and implied volatilities. The parameter estimates are in the vector paramTD and stacked in the matrix ParamTD. Parameter estimates for the shortest maturity are stacked on top, and those for the longest maturity on the bottom.

```
% Number of time dependent parameters
Nparam = 2 + 3*length(T);
kappa = paramTD(1);
v0    = paramTD(2);
```

```
for i=3:3:Nparam
    j = floor(i/3);
    theta(j) = paramTD(i);
    sigma(j) = paramTD(i+1);
    rho(j)   = paramTD(i+2);
end
% Static the parameter estimates in a matrix
for t=1:NT
    ParamTD(t,:) = [kappa v0 theta(t) sigma(t) rho(t)];
end
% Obtain prices for both sets of parameters
for k=1:NK
    for t=1:NT
        % Prices using static and piecewise constant params
        PriceTI(k,t) = HestonPriceGaussLaguerre(ParamTI,...);
        PriceTD(k,t) = BGMApproxPutTD(paramTD,T(1:t),...);
        % Implied volatilities
        IVTI(k,t) = BisecBSIV(PriceTI(k,t),...);
        IVTD(k,t) = BisecBSIV(PriceTD(k,t),...);
    end
end
```

The C# code to implement time-dependent parameter estimation in the model of Benhamou et al. (2010) is similar and not presented here. One key difference is that we make use of the List function, which allows us to stack the parameters estimated from previous maturities. These lists are then converted to arrays and passed to the BGMApproxPriceTD() function in C#, which returns the call or put price.

```
List<double> MatList   = new List<double>();
List<double> thetaList = new List<double>();
List<double> sigmaList = new List<double>();
List<double> rhoList   = new List<double>();
double[] Mat,Theta,Sigma,Rho;
for(int t=0;t<NT;t++) {
    // Stack the parameters
    MatList.Add(T[t]);
    thetaList.Add(theta[t]);
    sigmaList.Add(sigma[t]);
    rhoList.Add(rho[t]);
    // Convert to arrays
    Mat   = MatList.ToArray();
    Theta = thetaList.ToArray();
    Sigma = sigmaList.ToArray();
    Rho   = rhoList.ToArray();
    for(int k=0;k<NK;k++) {
        ModelPrice[k,t] = BGMApproxPriceTD(opset,K[k],...);
        ModelIV[k,t] = BisecBSIV(opset,K[k],T[t],ModelPrice[k,t],...);
        Error += Math.Pow(ModelIV[k,t] - MktIV[k,t],2.0);
    }
}
```

TABLE 9.6 Piecewise Constant and Static Parameters, DIA Data

	Maturity (days)	κ	v_0	θ	σ	ρ	Estimation Error
Time	37	1.7850	0.0341	0.2900	2.2764	−0.1640	2.48×10^{-6}
Dependent	72	1.7850	0.0341	0.2579	1.4506	−0.6297	
Model	135	1.7850	0.0341	0.2371	1.2833	−0.0452	
	226	1.7850	0.0341	0.2099	1.1512	−0.3383	
Static Model	All	1.4601	0.0302	0.1048	0.9967	−0.4529	1.87×10^{-5}

The estimates of the piecewise constant and static parameters appear in Table 9.6. As expected, the static estimates in the last rows of Table 9.2 (which contains the estimates from the Mikhailov and Nögel (2003) model) and of Table 9.6 are similar, as is the MSE.

The implied volatilities from the static and piecewise constant models are plotted for each maturity in Figure 9.3, along with the market implied volatilities. As in the other models with time-dependent parameters, the figure indicates that the piecewise constant model provides a better fit to the market implied volatilities than the static model, especially for short maturities.

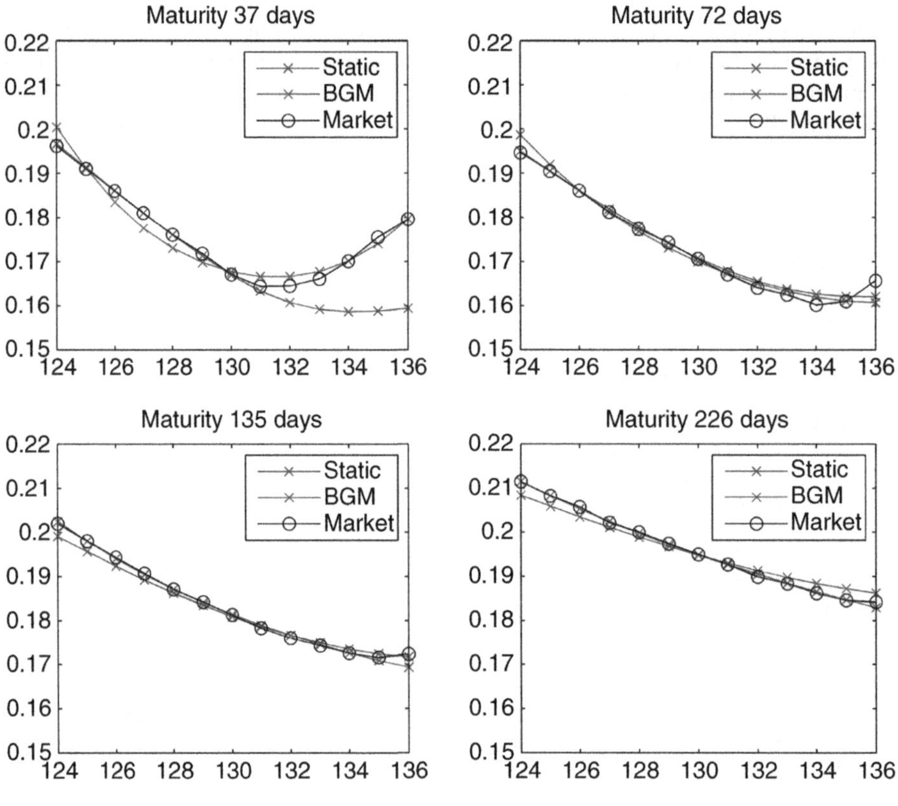

FIGURE 9.3 Implied Volatilities for the Benhamou et al. (2010) Model, DIA Data

BLACK-SCHOLES DERIVATIVES

To obtain the approximated put price of Benhamou et al. (2010) in Equation (9.48), we need high-order derivatives of the Black-Scholes put. The derivative of the standard normal density $\phi(x) = e^{-x^2/2}/\sqrt{2\pi}$ is $\phi_x(x) = -x\phi(x)$. It is easy to verify the derivatives $f_x = g_x = -y^{-1/2}$, $g_y = -\frac{1}{2}y^{-1}f$ and $f_y = -\frac{1}{2}y^{-1}g$.

For the derivatives of $\Phi(f)$ and $\phi(f)$ we have $\Phi(f)_x = -\phi(f)y^{-1/2}$, $\phi(f)_x = y^{-1/2}f\phi(f)$, $\phi(f)_y = \frac{1}{2}y^{-1}fg\phi(f)$, $\Phi(f)_{xy} = \frac{1}{2}y^{-3/2}\phi(f)(1-fg)$, and

$$\Phi(f)_{x^2y} = \frac{1}{2y^2}\phi(f)[2f + g - f^2g],$$

$$\Phi(f)_{y^2} = \frac{1}{2y^2}\phi(f)\left(g + \frac{1}{2}f - \frac{1}{2}fg^2\right),$$

$$\Phi(f)_{y^2x^2} = \frac{1}{2}[(y^{-2}\phi_y - 2y^{-3}\phi)(2f + g - f^2g) + y^{-2}\phi(2f_y + g_y - 2f_yfg - f^2g_y)].$$

Similarly, for derivatives involving $\Phi(g)$ and $\phi(g)$, we have $\Phi(g)_x = -\phi(g)y^{-1/2}$, $\Phi(g)_y = -\frac{1}{2}f\phi(g)y^{-1}$, $\phi(g)_x = y^{-1/2}g\phi(g)$, $\phi(g)_y = \frac{1}{2}y^{-1}fg\phi(g)$, $\Phi(g)_{xy} = \frac{1}{2}y^{-3/2}\phi(g)$ $(1-fg)$, and

$$\Phi(g)_{x^2y} = \frac{1}{2y^2}\phi(g)[2g + f - fg^2],$$

$$\Phi(g)_{y^2} = \frac{1}{2}y^{-2}\phi(g)\left(f + \frac{1}{2}g - \frac{1}{2}f^2g\right),$$

$$\Phi(g)_{xy^2} = \frac{1}{4y^2}[\phi(g)_x(2f + g - f^2g) + \phi(g)(2f_x + g_x - f_xgf - f^2g_x)],$$

$$\Phi(g)_{y^2x^2} = \frac{1}{2}\left[(y^{-2}\phi_y - 2y^{-3}\phi)(2g + f - fg^2) + y^{-2}\phi(2g_y + f_y - 2fgg_y - g^2f_y)\right].$$

The required derivatives of the Black-Scholes put are, therefore,

$$\frac{\partial^2 P_{BS}}{\partial x \partial y} = Ke^{-r\tau}\Phi(f)_{xy} - e^{-q\tau}e^x[\Phi(g)_y + \Phi(g)_{xy}],$$

$$\frac{\partial^3 P_{BS}}{\partial x^2 \partial y} = Ke^{-r\tau}\Phi(f)_{x^2y} - e^{-q\tau}e^x[\Phi(g)_y + 2\Phi(g)_{xy} + \Phi(g)_{x^2y}],$$

$$\frac{\partial^2 P_{BS}}{\partial y^2} = Ke^{-r\tau}\Phi(f)_{yy} - e^{-q\tau}e^x\Phi(g)_{yy},$$

$$\frac{\partial^4 P_{BS}}{\partial x^2 \partial y^2} = Ke^{-r\tau}\Phi(f)_{x^2y^2}$$
$$- e^{-q\tau}e^x[\Phi(g)_y + 2\Phi(g)_{xy} + \Phi(g)_{x^2y} + \Phi(g)_{yy} + 2\Phi(g)_{xy^2} + \Phi(g)_{x^2y^2}].$$

CONCLUSION

In this chapter, we have shown that the univariate characteristic function for x_T and the bivariate characteristic function for (x_T, v_T) are identical in form except for the coefficients in each function. What differentiates the coefficients is solely the initial condition for the Riccati equation that is solved to obtain them. We have also shown that the univariate characteristic function is a special of the bivariate characteristic function that arises by setting the argument for v_T to zero. Next, we have presented the time-dependent parameter models of Mikhailov and Nögel (2003) and Elices (2009). Both of these models rely on a recursive relation on the bivariate characteristic function illustrated by Kahl and Lord (2010). Finally, we have presented the model of Benhamou et al. (2010), which relies on an analytic expansion to obtain prices under time-dependent parameters. As such, it produces option prices much faster than either of the other two time-dependent models covered in this chapter. All the models with time-dependent parameters that we have examined, however, provide a better fit to quoted implied volatilities than the models with constant parameters covered up to now.

In Chapter 8, we introduced the explicit method and we explained that it is an example of methods that approximate the Heston partial differential equation (PDE) with finite differences. We also saw in that chapter that these methods produce a set of option prices along a two-dimensional grid of stock prices and volatility, and not solely for a single value of stock price and volatility. The literature on finite difference methods in option pricing is rich and varied, and we present several popular methods in the next chapter.

CHAPTER 10

Methods for Finite Differences

Abstract

In this chapter, we present methods to obtain the European call price by solving the Heston PDE along a two-dimensional grid representing the stock price and the volatility. We first show how to construct uniform and non-uniform grids for the discretization of the stock price and the volatility, and present formulas for finite difference approximations to the derivatives in the Heston PDE. We then present the weighted method, a popular method which includes the implicit scheme, explicit scheme, and Crank-Nicolson scheme as special cases. We encountered the explicit scheme briefly in Chapter 8, when we applied this method to the pricing of American options. Next, we explain the boundary conditions of the PDE for a European call. Finally, we present the Alternating Direction Implicit (ADI) method, which produces accurate results with very few time points.

The methods can easily be modified to allow for the pricing of European puts, which requires a reformulation of the boundary conditions. In many cases, however, it is simpler to use put-call parity to obtain the put price.

THE PDE IN TERMS OF AN OPERATOR

Recall from Chapter 1 the Heston PDE for the value $U(S, v, t)$ of an option on a dividend-paying stock, with $\lambda = 0$, when the spot price is S and the volatility is v, and when the maturity is t

$$\begin{aligned}\frac{\partial U}{\partial t} &= \frac{1}{2}vS^2\frac{\partial^2 U}{\partial S^2} + \rho\sigma vS\frac{\partial^2 U}{\partial v \partial S} + \frac{1}{2}\sigma^2 v\frac{\partial^2 U}{\partial v^2} \\ &\quad - rU + (r-q)S\frac{\partial U}{\partial S} + \kappa(\theta - v)\frac{\partial U}{\partial v}.\end{aligned} \tag{10.1}$$

Recall also that, since we are using t to represents maturity, the sign of the derivative $\partial U/\partial t$ is the opposite of what it would be if t represented time. Using $U(t) = U(S, v, t)$ as compact notation we can express the PDE as

$$\frac{\partial U}{\partial t} = LU(t) \tag{10.2}$$

where the operator L is defined as

$$L = \frac{1}{2}vS^2\frac{\partial^2}{\partial S^2} + \frac{1}{2}\sigma^2 v\frac{\partial^2}{\partial v^2} + \rho\sigma v S\frac{\partial^2}{\partial v \partial S}$$
$$+ (r-q)S\frac{\partial}{\partial S} + \kappa(\theta - v)\frac{\partial}{\partial v} - r. \tag{10.3}$$

Finite difference methods are techniques to find a numerical approximation to the PDE. To implement finite differences, we first need a discretization grid for the two state variables (the stock price and the variance), and a discretization grid for the maturity. These grids can have equally or unequally spaced increments. Second, we need discrete approximations to the continuous derivatives that appear in the PDE. Finally, we need a finite difference methodology to solve the PDE.

BUILDING GRIDS

Uniform grids are those that have equally spaced increments for the two state variables. These grids have two advantages: first, they are easy to construct, and second, since the increments are equal, the finite difference approximations to the derivatives in the PDE take on a simple form. Non-uniform grids are more complicated to construct, and the finite difference approximations to the derivatives are more complicated. These grids, however, can be made finer around certain points, in particular, around the region $(S, v) = (K, 0)$ where option prices are often required. Hence, non-uniform grids are often preferable since they produce more accurate prices with fewer grid points, and consequently, with less computation time.

We denote the maximum values of S, v, and t as $S_{\max}$, $v_{\max}$ and $t_{\max} = \tau$ (the maturity), and the minimum values as $S_{\min}$, $v_{\min}$, and $t_{\min} = 0$. We denote by $U^n_{i,j} = U(S_i, v_j, t_n)$ the value of a European call at time t_n when the stock price is S_i and the volatility is v_j. We use $N_S + 1$ points for the stock price, $N_V + 1$ points for the volatility, and $N_T + 1$ points for the maturity. For convenience, sometimes we write simply $U(S_i, v_j)$ for $U^n_{i,j}$.

Using the minimum values $S_{\min} = v_{\min} = 0$ a uniform grid for (S, v, t) can be constructed as

$$\begin{aligned} S_i &= i \times ds, & i &= 0, 1, \ldots, N_S \\ v_j &= j \times dv, & j &= 0, 1, \ldots, N_V \\ t_n &= n \times dt, & n &= 0, 1, \ldots, N_T \end{aligned} \tag{10.4}$$

where the increments are $ds = (S_{\max} - S_{\min})/N_S$, $dv = (v_{\max} - v_{\min})/N_V$, and $dt = (t_{\max} - t_{\min})/N_T$. The maximum values are therefore $S_{\max} = N_S ds$ and $v_{\max} = N_V dv$.

Building on the work of Clarke and Parrott (1999) and Kluge (2002), In'T Hout and Foulon (2010) describe a non-uniform grid that is finer around the strike price

K and around the spot volatility $v_0 = 0$. Their grid of size $N_S + 1$ for the stock price is

$$S_i = K + c\sinh(\xi_i), \quad i = 0, 1, \ldots, N_S$$

where they select $c = K/5$, and where

$$\xi_i = \sinh^{-1}(-K/c) + i\Delta\xi$$

with

$$\Delta\xi = \frac{1}{N_S}\left[\sinh^{-1}\left(\frac{S_{\max} - K}{c}\right) - \sinh^{-1}\left(-\frac{K}{c}\right)\right].$$

The grid of size $N_V + 1$ for the volatility is

$$v_j = d\sinh(j\Delta\eta), \quad j = 0, 1, \ldots, N_V$$

with

$$\Delta\eta = \frac{1}{N_V}\sinh^{-1}\left(\frac{V_{\max}}{d}\right).$$

In'T Hout and Foulon (2010) use $d = V_{\max}/500$, and a uniform grid for t. Figure 10.1 illustrates a non-uniform grid using their settings, along with $N_S = 70$, $N_V = 50$ and $K = 10$. The grid for the stock price is represented by blue lines, and the volatility by red lines. Note that in the stock price dimension the grid is finest around the strike price, while in the volatility dimension the grid becomes finer as we progress towards zero.

FINITE DIFFERENCE APPROXIMATION OF DERIVATIVES

Recall that we use the notation $U^n_{i,j}$, $U(S_i, v_j, t_n)$, or $U(S_i, v_j)$ to represent the value of a European call at time t_n when the stock price is S_i and the volatility is v_j. The finite difference approximations to the derivatives are simple when the grids are uniform. The generalization to non-uniform grids is straightforward, but the approximations are a little more complicated. Whenever possible throughout this book, we use central difference approximations to the first- and second-order derivatives in the S and v directions in the PDE for $U^n_{i,j}$ in Equation (10.1). In general, first- and second-order derivatives of $U^n_{i,j}$ at a point (S_i, v_j) on the grid can be written in terms of sums of values of U at points adjacent to (S_i, v_j).

In the following paragraphs, we express the central difference approximation to the derivatives assuming a non-uniform grid. The approximations under a uniform grid arise as a special case and reduce the expressions to much simpler forms. In the remainder of this section, we treat the approximations for the interior and boundary points of the PDE separately.

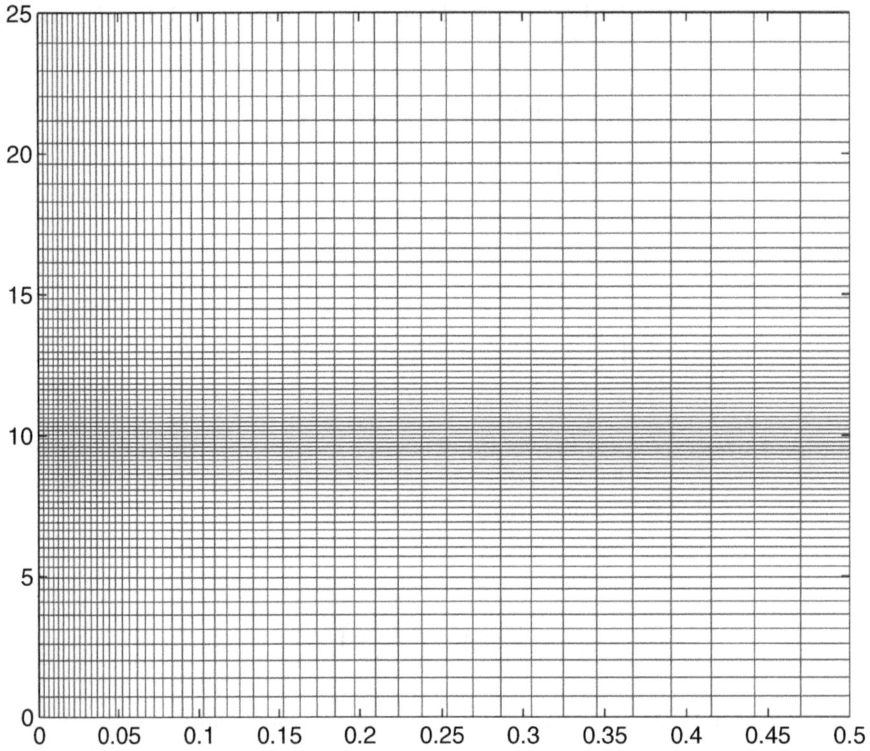

FIGURE 10.1 Non Uniform Grid

Interior points lie on the interior of the grid, so they are off the boundary. The first-order derivatives approximated with central differences for an interior point (S_i, v_j) are

$$\frac{\partial U}{\partial S}(S_i, v_j) = \frac{U^n_{i+1,j} - U^n_{i-1,j}}{S_{i+1} - S_{i-1}}, \quad \frac{\partial U}{\partial v}(S_i, v_j) = \frac{U^n_{i,j+1} - U^n_{i,j-1}}{v_{j+1} - v_{j-1}}. \tag{10.5}$$

When uniform grids are used, the denominators are replaced by $2ds$ and $2dv$, respectively. The central differences for second-order derivatives are in Table 4.1 of Kluge (2002) and also in In'T Hout and Foulon (2010). These are

$$\begin{aligned}\frac{\partial^2 U}{\partial S^2}(S_i, v_j) &= \frac{U^n_{i-1,j}}{(S_i - S_{i-1})(S_{i+1} - S_{i-1})} - \frac{2U^n_{i,j}}{(S_i - S_{i-1})(S_{i+1} - S_i)} \\ &+ \frac{U^n_{i+1,j}}{(S_{i+1} - S_i)(S_{i+1} - S_{i-1})}\end{aligned}$$

and

$$\frac{\partial^2 U}{\partial v^2}(S_i, v_j) = \frac{U^n_{i,j-1}}{(v_j - v_{j-1})(v_{j+1} - v_{j-1})} - \frac{2U^n_{i,j}}{(v_j - v_{j-1})(v_{j+1} - v_j)} + \frac{U^n_{i,j+1}}{(v_{j+1} - v_j)(v_{j+1} - v_{j-1})}.$$

When uniform grids are used, the denominators are replaced by $(ds)^2$ and $(dv)^2$, respectively, and the resulting expressions are much simpler. Finally, the mixed derivative of an interior point appears in Table 4.4 of Kluge (2002) as

$$\begin{aligned}\frac{\partial^2 U}{\partial S \partial v}(S_i, v_j) = {} & a_{-1,-1} U^n_{i-1,j-1} + a_{-1,0} U^n_{i-1,j} + a_{-1,1} U^n_{i-1,j+1} \\ & + a_{0,-1} U^n_{i,j-1} + a_{0,0} U^n_{i,j} + a_{0,1} U^n_{i,j+1} \\ & + a_{1,-1} U^n_{i+1,j-1} + a_{1,0} U^n_{i+1,j} + a_{1,1} U^n_{i+1,j+1}\end{aligned} \tag{10.6}$$

where the coefficients are

$$\begin{aligned}
a_{-1,1} &= \frac{\Delta s_{i+1}}{\Delta s_i(\Delta s_i + \Delta s_{i+1})} \times \frac{\Delta v_{j+1}}{\Delta v_j(\Delta v_j + \Delta v_{j+1})}, \\
a_{-1,0} &= \frac{-\Delta s_{i+1}}{\Delta s_i(\Delta s_i + \Delta s_{i+1})} \times \frac{\Delta v_{j+1} - \Delta v_j}{\Delta v_j \Delta v_{j+1}}, \\
a_{1,0} &= \frac{-\Delta s_{i+1}}{\Delta s_i(\Delta s_i + \Delta s_{i+1})} \times \frac{\Delta v_j}{\Delta v_{j+1}(\Delta v_j + \Delta v_{j+1})}, \\
a_{0,-1} &= \frac{\Delta s_{i+1} - \Delta s_i}{\Delta s_i \Delta s_{i+1}} \times \frac{-\Delta v_{j+1}}{\Delta v_j(\Delta v_j + \Delta v_{j+1})}, \\
a_{0,0} &= \frac{\Delta s_{i+1} - \Delta s_i}{\Delta s_i \Delta s_{i+1}} \times \frac{\Delta v_{j+1} - \Delta v_j}{\Delta v_j \Delta v_{j+1}}, \\
a_{0,1} &= \frac{\Delta s_{i+1} - \Delta s_i}{\Delta s_i \Delta s_{i+1}} \times \frac{\Delta v_j}{\Delta v_{j+1}(\Delta v_j + \Delta v_{j+1})}, \\
a_{1,-1} &= \frac{\Delta s_i}{\Delta s_i(\Delta s_i + \Delta s_{i+1})} \times \frac{-\Delta v_{j+1}}{\Delta v_j(\Delta v_j + \Delta v_{j+1})}, \\
a_{1,0} &= \frac{\Delta s_i}{\Delta s_{i+1}(\Delta s_i + \Delta s_{i+1})} \times \frac{\Delta v_{j+1} \quad \Delta v_j}{\Delta v_j \Delta v_{j+1}}, \\
a_{1,1} &= \frac{\Delta s_i}{\Delta s_{i+1}(\Delta s_i + \Delta s_{i+1})} \times \frac{\Delta v_j}{\Delta v_{j+1}(\Delta v_j + \Delta v_{j+1})}.
\end{aligned}$$

In these coefficients, the increments are $\Delta s_i = S_i - S_{i-1}$ and $\Delta v_j = v_j - v_{j-1}$. These simpler expressions for the second-order derivatives also work but are not as accurate

$$\frac{\partial^2 U}{\partial S^2}(S_i, v_j) = \left(\frac{U^n_{i+1,j} - U^n_{i,j}}{S_{i+1} - S_i} - \frac{U^n_{i,j} - U^n_{i-1,j}}{S_i - S_{i-1}} \right) \frac{1}{S_{i+1} - S_i},$$

$$\frac{\partial^2 U}{\partial v^2}(S_i, v_j) = \left(\frac{U^n_{i,j+1} - U^n_{i,j}}{v_{j+1} - v_j} - \frac{U^n_{i,j} - U^n_{i,j-1}}{v_j - v_{j-1}} \right) \frac{1}{v_{j+1} - v_j},$$

$$\frac{\partial^2 U}{\partial S \partial v}(S_i, v_j) = \left(\frac{U^n_{i+1,j+1} - U^n_{i-1,j+1} - U^n_{i+1,j-1} + U^n_{i-1,j-1}}{(S_{i+1} - S_{i-1})(v_{j+1} - v_{j-1})} \right).$$

When the grid is uniform, the mixed derivative in Equation (10.6) reduces to the much simpler form

$$\frac{\partial^2 U}{\partial S \partial v}(S_i, v_j) = \frac{U^n_{i+1,j+1} + U^n_{i-1,j-1} - U^n_{i-1,j+1} - U^n_{i+1,j-1}}{4\, ds\, dv}. \tag{10.7}$$

Regardless of whether a uniform or non-uniform grid is used, all derivatives at the point (S_i, v_j) can be expressed in terms of sums involving U evaluated at points adjacent to (S_i, v_j), and their coefficients, as

$$\sum_{k,l} a_{k,l} U^n_{i+k,j+l}.$$

See Kluge (2002) or Burden and Faires (2010) for details. On the boundary points of the PDE, which are defined later in this chapter, we need to use approximations which do not involve points off the grid. Hence, we can use forward or backward differences. For the first-order S-derivative, for example, the differences are, respectively

$$\frac{\partial U}{\partial S}(S_i, v_j) = \frac{U^n_{i+1,j} - U^n_{i,j}}{S_{i+1} - S_i}, \quad \frac{\partial U}{\partial S}(S_i, v_j) = \frac{U^n_{i,j} - U^n_{i,j-1}}{S_i - S_{i-1}}. \tag{10.8}$$

The textbook by Duffy (2006) is also an excellent reference for finite difference approximations to PDEs in the context of option pricing.

THE WEIGHTED METHOD

This is a general method that incorporates other finite difference schemes as special cases. Recall that $U^n_{i,j}$ denotes the value of the European call at the grid points (S_i, v_j) and at maturity t_n. Since the two-dimensional grid for (S, v) is of size $N = (N_S + 1)(N_V + 1)$, at each t_n there are N possible values for $U^n_{i,j}$, as indicated in Figure 10.2.

To apply the weighted method, we must construct a vector $\mathbf{U}^n$ of size N with these values, arranged in any way we like. We choose to stack the N_V

v-direction

S-direction	v_0	v_1	...	v_{N_V}
S_0	$U^n_{0,0}$	$U^n_{0,1}$	...	U^n_{0,N_V}
S_1	$U^n_{1,0}$	$U^n_{1,1}$	...	U^n_{1,N_V}
⋮	⋮	⋮	...	⋮
S_{N_S}	$U^n_{N_S,0}$	$U^n_{N_S,1}$	...	$U^n_{N_S,N_V}$

FIGURE 10.2 Value of the European Call Along the Stock Price and Variance Grids

column vectors $\mathbf{u}_0, \mathbf{u}_1, \mathbf{u}_2, \ldots, \mathbf{u}_{N_V}$ in Figure 10.2 on top of one another, so that $\mathbf{U}^n = (\mathbf{u}_0^T, \mathbf{u}_1^T, \ldots, \mathbf{u}_{N_V}^T)^T$ is our vector. The entries of $\mathbf{U}^n$ therefore correspond to the following (S_i, v_j) points

$$\underbrace{(S_0, v_0), (S_1, v_0), \ldots, (S_{NS}, v_0)}_{\text{Values of } S \text{ for } v_0}, \underbrace{(S_0, v_1), (S_1, v_1), \ldots, (S_{NS}, v_1)}_{\text{Values of } S \text{ for } v_1}, \ldots,$$

$$\underbrace{(S_0, v_{NV-1}), (S_1, v_{NV-1}), \ldots, (S_{NS}, v_{NV-1})}_{\text{Values of } S \text{ for } v_{NV-1}}, \underbrace{(S_0, v_{NV}), (S_1, v_{NV}), \ldots, (S_{NS}, v_{NV})}_{\text{Values of } S \text{ for } v_{NV}}. \quad (10.9)$$

The weighted method, also called the θ-method, is defined via the relationship

$$\frac{\mathbf{U}^{n+1} - \mathbf{U}^n}{dt} = \mathbf{L}(\theta \mathbf{U}^{n+1} + (1-\theta)\mathbf{U}^n) \quad (10.10)$$

where $\mathbf{L}$ is a sparse matrix of dimension $N \times N$. This matrix is based on the operator defined in Equation (10.3). The initial condition $\mathbf{U}^0$ is known, since it represents the value of the call at expiry. Hence, we can work from expiry, starting with the initial value $\mathbf{U}^0$, and we use $\mathbf{L}$ to obtain $\mathbf{U}^1$, $\mathbf{U}^2$, and so forth, until we reach $\mathbf{U}^{N_T}$. This is done by solving, at each time, the system

$$(\mathbf{I} - \theta dt \mathbf{L})\mathbf{U}^{n+1} = (\mathbf{I} + (1-\theta) dt \mathbf{L})\mathbf{U}^n \quad (10.11)$$

where $\mathbf{I}$ is the identity matrix of size N. The system can be solved by taking the inverse of the matrix on the left-hand side, so that

$$\mathbf{U}^{n+1} = (\mathbf{I} - \theta dt \mathbf{L})^{-1}(\mathbf{I} + (1-\theta) dt \mathbf{L})\mathbf{U}^n. \quad (10.12)$$

Several algorithms have been proposed that exploit the sparse nature of $\mathbf{L}$ to speed up the inversion. We refer readers to Duffy (2006).

The vector $\mathbf{U}^0$ depends on the option being priced. For a call option, it will contain $S - K$ in the components of $\mathbf{U}$ that correspond to $S > K$, and zero in the components that correspond to $S < K$. The order in which these appear in the vector will depend on how the components of $\mathbf{U}$ are arranged.

A number of finite difference schemes arise as a special case of Equation (10.11), depending on the value of θ. Setting $\theta = 0$ produces the explicit scheme, $\theta = \frac{1}{2}$ produces the Crank-Nicolson scheme, and $\theta = 1$ produces the implicit scheme. See Kluge (2002) for details of a general derivation of the weighted method, and a discussion of the numerical difficulties that can arise when N is large. The explicit Euler scheme is the simplest to deal with numerically, because when we set $\theta = 0$ in (10.12) we no longer need to invert a matrix.

The $\mathbf{L}$ matrix is a square matrix of dimension $N = (N_S + 1)(N_V + 1)$, with rows and columns that depend on how the vector $\mathbf{U}^n$ is constructed. Since we have constructed $\mathbf{U}^n$ by stacking the N_V column vectors $\mathbf{u}_0, \mathbf{u}_1, \ldots, \mathbf{u}_{N_V}$ from Figure 10.2 on top of one another, the row and columns of $\mathbf{L}$ correspond to the entries of the vector $\mathbf{U}^n$ in (10.9).

We modify the matrix $\mathbf{L}$ for the operator L in Equation (10.3) by separating $\partial/\partial v$ in L into two components

$$\begin{aligned} L = {} & \frac{1}{2}vS^2\frac{\partial^2}{\partial S^2} + \frac{1}{2}\sigma^2 v\frac{\partial^2}{\partial v^2} + \rho\sigma vS\frac{\partial^2}{\partial v\partial S} \\ & + (r-q)S\frac{\partial}{\partial S} + \kappa\theta\frac{\partial}{\partial v} - \kappa v\frac{\partial}{\partial v} - r. \end{aligned} \tag{10.13}$$

It is preferable to construct the sub-matrices of $\mathbf{L}$ (namely, the sub-matrices for the first- and second-order derivatives) without the Heston parameters, and add the parameters later when we construct $\mathbf{L}$ from its sub-matrices. In this way, we can construct the sub-matrices once, and then obtain $\mathbf{L}$ for any values of the Heston parameters we desire. Note that, to separate the Heston parameters from the construction of the sub-matrices, two separate matrices are required for $\partial/\partial v$, as indicated in (10.13).

To summarize, we construct the following sub-matrices

$$\mathbf{L}_{SS} \text{ for } vS^2\frac{\partial^2}{\partial S^2}, \quad \mathbf{L}_{vv} \text{ for } v\frac{\partial^2}{\partial v^2}, \quad \mathbf{L}_{vS} \text{ for } vS\frac{\partial^2}{\partial v\partial S}$$

$$\mathbf{L}_S \text{ for } S\frac{\partial}{\partial S}, \quad \mathbf{L}_{v1} \text{ for } \frac{\partial}{\partial v}, \quad \mathbf{L}_{v2} \text{ for } v\frac{\partial}{\partial v}, \quad \text{and } \mathbf{I} \text{ for } r.$$

Coding the sub-matrices of $\mathbf{L}$ in a programming language is tricky, since some values adjacent to a point (S_i, v_j) on the grid in Figure 10.2 will no longer be adjacent in the v-direction when we arrange the grid into the vector $\mathbf{U}^n$, although they will still be adjacent in the S-direction. Hence, we lose the convenient indexing of having $U_{i,j}^n$ represented in a two-dimensional grid.

To illustrate how these sub-matrices are constructed with finite differences, suppose we are at the point (S_i, v_j) on the stock price/volatility grid, and suppose that this point corresponds to cell (r, c) in the $\mathbf{L}$ matrix. We use the sub-matrices $\mathbf{L}_S$

and $\mathbf{L}_{v2}$ in the illustration. When a uniform grid is used the central difference for the S-derivative is

$$\frac{\partial U}{\partial S}(S_i, v_j) = \frac{U(S_{i+1}, v_j) - U(S_{i-1}, v_j)}{2ds}.$$

From Equation (10.9), the points (S_{i-1}, v_j) and (S_{i+1}, v_j) in $\mathbf{U}^n$ lie immediately below and above the point (S_i, v_j), respectively, as indicated in (10.14).

$$\mathbf{U}^n = \begin{pmatrix} \mathbf{u}_0 \\ \hline \mathbf{u}_1 \\ \hline \vdots \\ \hline U^n_{0,j} \\ \vdots \\ U^n_{i-1,j} \\ U^n_{i,j} \\ U^n_{i+1,j} \\ \vdots \\ U^n_{NS,j} \\ \hline \vdots \\ \hline \mathbf{u}_{NV} \end{pmatrix} \quad \begin{matrix} \text{Column vector } 0 \\ \hline \text{Column vector } 1 \\ \hline \vdots \\ \hline \\ \\ \\ \text{Column vector } j \\ \\ \\ \\ \hline \vdots \\ \hline \text{Column vector } N_V \end{matrix} \quad \begin{matrix} \\ \\ \\ \\ \\ r-1 \\ r \\ r+1 \\ \\ \\ \\ \\ \end{matrix} \qquad (10.14)$$

Since the point $U^n_{i,j}$ itself is not used in the central difference approximation to the S-derivative, the entries of $\mathbf{L}_S$ are simply

$$\begin{aligned} \mathbf{L}_{SS}(r-1, c) &= -\frac{1}{2ds} \times S_i \\ \mathbf{L}_{SS}(r, c) &= 0 \\ \mathbf{L}_{SS}(r+1, c) &= \frac{1}{2ds} \times S_i. \end{aligned} \qquad (10.15)$$

Since the sub-matrix $\mathbf{L}_S$ is for the operation $(\partial/\partial S) \times S$ evaluated at the point (S_i, v_j), the terms involving $2ds$ are for differentiation and the terms S_i are for S. When a non-uniform grid is used then $2ds$ in the denominators in Equation (10.15) are replaced with $(S_{i+1} - S_{i-1})$. The central difference for the v-derivative is more complicated to deal with. It is given by

$$\frac{\partial U}{\partial v}(S_i, v_j) = \frac{U(S_i, v_{j+1}) - U(S_i, v_{j-1})}{2dv}.$$

The points (S_i, v_{j-1}) and (S_i, v_{j+1}) in $\mathbf{U}^n$ lie $N_V + 1$ positions below and above (S_i, v_j) respectively, as indicated in Equation (10.16)

$$\mathbf{U}^n = \begin{pmatrix} \mathbf{u}_0 \\ \vdots \\ \hline \vdots \\ U^n_{i,j-1} \\ \vdots \\ \hline \vdots \\ U^n_{i,j} \\ \vdots \\ \hline \vdots \\ U^n_{i,j+1} \\ \vdots \\ \hline \vdots \\ \hline \mathbf{u}_{NV} \end{pmatrix} \begin{matrix} \text{Column vector } 0 \\ \vdots \\ \\ \\ \text{Column vector } j-1 \\ \\ \\ \\ \text{Column vector } j \\ \\ \\ \\ \text{Column vector } j+1 \\ \\ \\ \vdots \\ \text{Column vector } N_V \end{matrix} \begin{matrix} \\ \\ \\ \\ r - N_S - 1 \\ \\ \\ \\ r \\ \\ \\ \\ r + N_S + 1 \\ \\ \\ \\ \\ \end{matrix} \tag{10.16}$$

The entries of $\mathbf{L}_{v2}$ are therefore

$$\begin{aligned} \mathbf{L}_{v2}(r - N_s - 1, c) &= \frac{-1}{2dv} \times v_j \\ \mathbf{L}_{v2}(r, c) &= 0 \\ \mathbf{L}_{v2}(r + N_S + 1, c) &= \frac{1}{2dv} \times v_j. \end{aligned} \tag{10.17}$$

When a non-uniform grid is used then $2dv$ in the denominators of (10.17) are replaced with $(v_{j+1} - v_{j-1})$.

The Matlab function BuildDerivatives.m is a lengthy program that creates the sub-matrices of L. It requires three grids as inputs: for the stock price, volatility, and maturity. It assumes that these are built using uniform grids. To conserve space we present the most important parts only.

The first section identifies the elements of U that correspond to boundary points for S and v.

```
function [derS ... derSV R] = BuildDerivatives(S,V,T)
N = NS*NV;
Si = repmat(S',NV,1);
Vi = reshape(kron(V,ones(NS,1)),N,1);
```

```
VminB = zeros(N,1); VmaxB = zeros(N,1);
SminB = zeros(N,1); SmaxB = zeros(N,1);
VminB(1:NS-1) = 1;
VmaxB(N-NS+2:N) = 1;
for i=NS+1:N
    if mod(i,NS)==0 & (i~=N)
        SmaxB(i) = 1;
    end
    if mod(i,NS)==1 & (i~=1)
        SminB(i) = 1;
    end
end
```

The second section identifies non-boundary points, and identifies which elements of **U** receive forward, backward, or central differences.

```
NB = zeros(N,1);
for b=2:NV-1
    for k=b*NS-(NS-2):b*NS-1;
        NB(k) = 1;
    end
end
NB(NS) = 1;
Cs = zeros(N,1);   % Central differences
Fs = zeros(N,1);   % Forward differences
Bs = zeros(N,1);   % Backward differences
for b=2:NV-1
    for k=b*NS-(NS-3):b*NS-2;
        Cs(k) = 1;
    end
end
Fs((2:NV-1)*NS-(NS-2)) = 1;
Bs((2:NV-1)*NS-1) = 1;
Cv = zeros(N,1);   % Central differences
Fv = zeros(N,1);   % Forward differences
Bv = zeros(N,1);   % Backward differences
for b=3:NV-2
    for k=b*NS-(NS-2):b*NS-1;
        Cv(k) = 1;
    end
end
Fv(2*NS-(NS-2):2*NS-1) = 1;
Bv((NV-1)*NS-(NS-2):(NV-1)*NS-1) = 1;
Csv = zeros(N,1);
for b=2:NV-1
    for k=b*NS-(NS-2):b*NS-1
        Csv(k) = 1;
    end
end
```

The final section loops through the identified points, and attributes the coefficients for central, forward, or backward differences to each of the first- and second-order matrices. To conserve space, only the central differences of the interior points are shown.

```
I = find(Cs==1);
for k=1:length(I)
    % Create the matrix for S-derivatives
    derS(I(k),I(k)-1)  =  -1/2/ds * Si(I(k));
    derS(I(k),I(k))    =   0;
    derS(I(k),I(k)+1)  =   1/2/ds * Si(I(k));
    derSS(I(k),I(k)-1) =   1/ds^2 * Vi(I(k))*Si(I(k))^2;
    derSS(I(k),I(k))   =  -2/ds^2 * Vi(I(k))*Si(I(k))^2;
    derSS(I(k),I(k)+1) =   1/ds^2 * Vi(I(k))*Si(I(k))^2;
end
I = find(Cv==1);
for k=1:length(I)
    % Create the matrix for V-derivatives
    derV1(I(k),I(k)-NS)  = -1/2/dv;
    derV1(I(k),I(k))     =  0;
    derV1(I(k),I(k)+NS)  =  1/2/dv;
    derV2(I(k),I(k)-NS)  = -1/2/dv * Vi(I(k));
    derV2(I(k),I(k))     =  0;
    derV2(I(k),I(k)+NS)  =  1/2/dv * Vi(I(k));
    derVV(I(k),I(k)-NS)  =  1/dv^2 * Vi(I(k));
    derVV(I(k),I(k))     = -2/dv^2 * Vi(I(k));
    derVV(I(k),I(k)+NS)  =  1/dv^2 * Vi(I(k));
end
I = find(Csv==1);
for k=1:length(I)
    % Create the matrix for SV-derivatives
    derSV(I(k),I(k)+NS+1) =  1/(4*ds*dv)*Vi(I(k))*Si(I(k));
    derSV(I(k),I(k)+NS-1) = -1/(4*ds*dv)*Vi(I(k))*Si(I(k));
    derSV(I(k),I(k)-NS-1) =  1/(4*ds*dv)*Vi(I(k))*Si(I(k));
    derSV(I(k),I(k)-NS+1) = -1/(4*ds*dv)*Vi(I(k))*Si(I(k));
end
```

The BuildDerivatives.m function is used in the WeightedMethod.m function, which applies Equation (10.12) and updates **U** at every time step iteration. The value of the derivative is returned by interpolating **U** at the desired point (S_0, v_0).

```
function WPrice = WeightedMethod(thet,...)
u = zeros(NS*NV,1);
Si = repmat(S',NV,1);
U  = max(0, Si - K);
for t=2:NT
    u = U;
```

```
    if thet==0
        U = B*u;            % Explicit Method
    elseif thet==1
        U = invA*u;         % Implicit Method
    else
        U = A\B*u;          % Weighted Method
    end
end
U = reshape(U,NS,NV);
WPrice = interp2(V,S,U,V0,S0);
```

To illustrate the weighted method we use the parameter values defined in Case 1 of Table 1 of In'T Hout and Foulon (2010), namely $\kappa = 1.5$, $\theta = 0.04$, $\sigma = 0.3$, $\rho = -0.9$, $r = 0.02$, $\lambda = 0$, and a strike price of $K = 100$. In addition, we use $v_0 = 0.05$, $q = 0.05$, and a maturity of $\tau = 0.15$ years. We wish to obtain the price at the spot $S = 101.52$ when the volatility is $v = 0.05412$. The following Matlab code builds a uniform grid of size 40×40 and uses 20 time steps. It obtains prices from the explicit, implicit, and Crank-Nicolson schemes, all from the same WeightedMethod.m function, but with different settings for the parameter θ.

```
nS = 39;         % Stock price
nV = 39;         % Volatility
nT = 19;         % Maturity
[derS derSS derV1 derV2 derVV derSV R] = BuildDerivatives(S,V,T);
L = (r-q).*derS + kappa.*theta.*derV1 - kappa.*derV2 + ...;
I = eye(NS*NV);
S0 = 101.52;
V0 = 0.05412;
thet = 0;
A = (I - thet.*dt*L);
B = (I + (1-thet).*dt.*L);
invA = inv(A);
EPrice = WeightedMethod(thet,S0,V0,K,S,V,T,A,invA,B);
```

In this example, the exact price using the Heston closed-form solution is 4.1086. The explicit scheme price is 4.1679, which as expected, is a poor approximation because of the small number of steps. The implicit and Crank-Nicolson schemes produce 4.1023 and 4.1350, respectively, which are both much more accurate.

The Matlab function BuildDerivativesNonUniform.m is a version of the function BuildDerivatives.m that accepts a non-uniform grid and returns the sub-matrices of **L**. For each entry of the sub-matrices, the divisors ds and dv are specified in accordance with the values of (S, v), and must respect the non-adjacent positions of successive values in the vector that stores the volatilities.

```
function [derS ... derSV R] = BuildDerivativesNonUniform(S,V,T)
I = find(Cs==1);
for k=1:length(I)
    ds = Si(I(k)) - Si(I(k)-1);
    derS(I(k),I(k)-1)  =  -1/2/ds * Si(I(k));
    derSS(I(k),I(k)-1) =   1/ds^2 * Vi(I(k))*Si(I(k))^2;
    ds = Si(I(k)+1) - Si(I(k));
    derS(I(k),I(k)+1)  =   1/2/ds * Si(I(k));
    derSS(I(k),I(k)+1) =   1/ds^2 * Vi(I(k))*Si(I(k))^2;
    ds = (Si(I(k)+1) - Si(I(k)-1))/2;
    derS(I(k),I(k))    =   0;
    derSS(I(k),I(k))   =  -2/ds^2 * Vi(I(k))*Si(I(k))^2;
end
I = find(Cv==1);
for k=1:length(I)
    dv = Vi(I(k)) - Vi(I(k)-NS);
    derV1(I(k),I(k)-NS)  = -1/2/dv;
    derV2(I(k),I(k)-NS)  = -1/2/dv * Vi(I(k));
    derVV(I(k),I(k)-NS)  =  1/dv^2 * Vi(I(k));
    dv = Vi(I(k)+NS) - Vi(I(k));
    derV1(I(k),I(k)+NS)  =  1/2/dv;
    derV2(I(k),I(k)+NS)  =  1/2/dv * Vi(I(k));
    derVV(I(k),I(k)+NS)  =  1/dv^2 * Vi(I(k));
    dv = (Vi(I(k)+NS) - Vi(I(k)-NS))/2;
    derV2(I(k),I(k))     =  0;
    derV1(I(k),I(k))     =  0;
    derVV(I(k),I(k))     = -2/dv^2 * Vi(I(k));
end
```

To illustrate, we use the same settings as in the example under the uniform case, but use a smaller grid size of 30×30 along with 20 time steps. This produces results with similar accuracy, but requires much less computation time. The Heston closed-form solution is 4.1086. The explicit scheme price is 4.1577, the implicit scheme price is 4.0901, and the Crank-Nicolson scheme price is 4.1241, which is fairly accurate. The prices obtained under the uniform and non-uniform grids are summarized in Table 10.1.

The C# code to construct the **L** matrix and to implement the weighted method is very similar and is not presented here. The code does require, however, a routine for matrix inversion. We use the MInvLU() function for this purpose, which applies LU decomposition to calculate the inverse of $(\mathbf{I} - \theta dt\mathbf{L})$ in (10.12) when $\theta \neq 0$. This is

TABLE 10.1 Value of the European Call Using Uniform and Non-Uniform Grids

	Uniform Grid Price	Error	Non-Uniform Grid Price	Error
Closed-Form	4.1086		4.1086	
Explicit	4.1679	0.0593	4.1577	0.0491
Implicit	4.1023	−0.0062	4.0901	−0.0184
Crank-Nicolson	4.1350	0.0264	4.1241	0.0156

the same C# function we used in the Longstaff and Schwartz (2001) algorithm to price American options in Chapter 8. We also need the C# function interp2() for two-dimensional interpolation. Please refer to Chapter 8 for an explanation of both functions.

BOUNDARY CONDITIONS FOR THE PDE

Boundary conditions for the PDE in Equation (10.1) for a European call are explained by Heston (1993) and by In'T Hout and Foulon (2010), among others. We describe them in the following paragraphs for a European call option.

Boundary Condition at Maturity

At maturity ($t = 0$) the value of the call is its intrinsic value (the payoff)

$$U(S_i, v_j, 0) = \max(0, S_i - K).$$

This implies that the boundary condition for $t = 0$ is $U^0_{i,j} = (S_i - K)^+$ for $i = 0, 1, \ldots, N_S$ and $j = 0, 1, \ldots, N_V$. The vector $\mathbf{U}^0$ will contain zeros and $S_i - K$, depending on how the components of $\mathbf{U}$ are arranged. A boundary condition for $\mathbf{L}$ at $t = 0$ is not required since $\mathbf{L}$ is not used to obtain $\mathbf{U}^0$.

Boundary Condition for $S = S_{\min}$

When $S = S_{\min} = 0$, the call is worthless. Hence, we have $U(0, v_j, t_n) = 0$ and the boundary condition is $U^n_{0,j} = 0$ for $n = 0, \ldots, N_T$ and $j = 0, 1, \ldots, N_V$. The entries of $\mathbf{L}$ corresponding to the points $U^n_{0,j}$ are therefore zero as well.

Boundary Condition for $S = S_{\max}$

As S becomes large, delta for the call option approaches one. Hence, for $S = S_{\max}$, we have

$$\frac{\partial U}{\partial S}(S_{\max}, v_j, t_n) = 1.$$

The boundary condition for $S_{\max}$ is, therefore, $U^n_{N_S,j} = S_{\max}$ for $n = 0, \ldots, N_T$ and $j = 0, \ldots, N_V$. The sub-matrix $\mathbf{L}_S$ takes on the value $S_{\max}$ at the boundary points, while the sub-matrices $\mathbf{L}_{SS}$ and $\mathbf{L}_{vS}$ take on the value zero.

Boundary Condition for $v = v_{\max}$

When v becomes large, we have $U(S_i, v_{\max}, t_n) = S_i$. The boundary condition for $v_{\max}$ is, therefore, $U^n_{i,N_V} = S_i$ for $n = 0, \ldots, N_T$, and $i = 0, \ldots, N_S$. Since at $v_{\max}$ we have $U = S_i$ and, therefore, $\partial U/\partial S = 1$, the sub-matrix $\mathbf{L}_S$ takes on the value S_i at the $v_{\max}$ boundary points. The sub-matrices $\mathbf{L}_{SS}$, $\mathbf{L}_{vS}$, $\mathbf{L}_{v1}$, and $\mathbf{L}_{v2}$ all take on the value zero.

Boundary Condition for $v = v_{\min}$

When $v = v_{\min} = 0$, the boundary condition is a little more complicated. When $v = 0$ the PDE in (10.1) becomes

$$\frac{\partial U}{\partial t} = -rU + (r - q)S\frac{\partial U}{\partial S} + \kappa\theta\frac{\partial U}{\partial v}.$$

We can use central differences for $\partial U/\partial S$

$$\frac{\partial U}{\partial S}(S_i, 0, t_n) = \frac{U^n_{i+1,0} - U^n_{i-1,0}}{S_{i+1} - S_{i-1}}$$

but for $\partial U/\partial v$, we must use forward differences, for example, the simple form

$$\frac{\partial U}{\partial S}(S_i, 0, t_n) = \frac{U^n_{i,1} - U^n_{i,0}}{v_1}$$

since $v_0 = 0$. Remember that in this context we are using v_0 to denote the first point on the grid for the variance, and not the Heston parameter for the spot variance. The sub-matrices $\mathbf{L}_{SS}$, $\mathbf{L}_{vS}$, and $\mathbf{L}_{vv}$ take on the value zero at the boundary points.

EXPLICIT SCHEME

The explicit scheme produces an expression for the PDE that is very simple when the grids are uniform. It is a special case of the weighted method that arises by setting $\theta = 0$ in Equation (10.11)

$$\mathbf{U}^{n+1} = (\mathbf{I} + dt\mathbf{L})\mathbf{U}^n. \tag{10.18}$$

Hence, given the matrix $\mathbf{L}$, we can obtain $\mathbf{U}^{n+1}$ directly from $\mathbf{U}^n$, without requiring matrix inversion. The element of $\mathbf{U}^{n+1}$ corresponding to $U^{n+1}_{i,j}$ is

$$\begin{aligned} U^{n+1}_{i,j} = U^n_{i,j} + dt\Bigg[\frac{1}{2}v_j S_i^2 \frac{\partial^2}{\partial S^2} + \frac{1}{2}\sigma^2 v_j \frac{\partial^2}{\partial v^2} \\ + \rho\sigma v_j S_i \frac{\partial^2}{\partial v \partial S} + (r-q)S_i \frac{\partial}{\partial S} + \kappa(\theta - v_j)\frac{\partial}{\partial v} - r\Bigg] U^n_{i,j}. \end{aligned} \tag{10.19}$$

This is the same expression for $U^{n+1}_{i,j}$ that we encountered in Chapter 8, when we used the explicit scheme to price American options. To implement the explicit scheme, we need to substitute finite difference approximations of the derivatives. The simplest implementation arises when we use a uniform grid for (S_i, v_j). In that case, the expression for $U^n_{i,j}$ can be reduced to a simple expression that involves only the parameters, the index values, points adjacent to $U^n_{i,j}$, and the increments. We substitute the approximations to the derivatives under a uniform grid to obtain

$$\begin{aligned} U^{n+1}_{i,j} = U^n_{i,j} + dt\Bigg[\frac{1}{2}v_j S_i^2 \frac{U^n_{i+1,j} - 2U^n_{i,j} + U^n_{i-1,j}}{(ds)^2} \\ + \rho\sigma v_j S_i \frac{U^n_{i+1,j+1} + U^n_{i-1,j-1} - U^n_{i-1,j+1} - U^n_{i+1,j-1}}{4\,ds\,dv} \\ + \frac{1}{2}\sigma^2 v_j \frac{U^n_{i,j+1} - 2U^n_{i,j} + U^n_{i,j-1}}{(dv)^2} \\ + \frac{1}{2}(r-q)S_i \frac{U^n_{i+1,j} - U^n_{i-1,j}}{2ds} + \kappa(\theta - v_j)\frac{U^n_{i,j+1} - U^n_{i,j-1}}{2dv} - r\Bigg] U^n_{i,j}. \end{aligned}$$

Grouping common terms and simplifying, noting that $S_i = i \times ds$ and $v_j = j \times dv$ produces

$$\begin{aligned}
U_{i,j}^{n+1} &= \left[1 - dt\left(i^2 j dv + \frac{\sigma^2 j}{dv} + r\right)\right] U_{i,j}^n \\
&+ \left[\frac{idt}{2}\left(ijdv - r + q\right)\right] U_{i-1,j}^n + \left[\frac{idt}{2}\left(ijdv + r - q\right)\right] U_{i+1,j}^n \\
&+ \left[\frac{dt}{2dv}\left(\sigma^2 j - \kappa(\theta - jdv)\right)\right] U_{i,j-1}^n + \left[\frac{dt}{2dv}\left(\sigma^2 j + \kappa(\theta - jdv)\right)\right] U_{i,j+1}^n \\
&+ \frac{ijdt\sigma}{4}\left(U_{i+1,j+1}^n + U_{i-1,j-1}^n - U_{i-1,j+1}^n - U_{i+1,j-1}^n\right). \qquad (10.20)
\end{aligned}$$

The Matlab function HestonExplicitPDE.m returns the matrix that contains all the elements $U_{i,j}^{N_T}$. All the intermediate time values $U_{i,j}^t$ for $t < N_T$ are discarded. The function requires as inputs the grids for S, v, and t. To conserve space some steps of the function have been removed.

```
function U = HestonExplicitPDE(params,...)
for s=1:NS
    for v=1:NV
        U(s,v) = max(S(s) - K, 0);
    end
end
for t=1:NT-1
    for v=1:NV-1
        U(1,v) = 0;
        U(NS,v) = max(0, Smax - K);
    end
    for s=1:NS
        U(s,NV) = max(0, S(s) - K);
    end
    u = U; % Update the temporary grid u(s,t)
    for s=2:NS-1
        DerV = (u(s,2) - u(s,1)) / dv;
        DerS = (u(s+1,1) - u(s-1,1))/2/ds;
        U(s,1) = u(s,1)*(1 - r*dt - kappa*theta*dt/dv) ...;
    end
    u = U;
    for s=2:NS-1
        for v=2:NV-1
            A = (1 - dt*(s-1)^2*(v-1)*dv - sigma^2*(v-1) ...);
            B = (1/2*dt*(s-1)^2*(v-1)*dv - 1/2*dt*(r-q)*(s-1));
            C = (1/2*dt*(s-1)^2*(v-1)*dv + 1/2*dt*(r-q)*(s-1));
            D = (1/2*dt*sigma^2*(v-1)/dv - 1/2*dt*kappa ...);
            E = (1/2*dt*sigma^2*(v-1)/dv + 1/2*dt*kappa ...);
            F = 1/4*dt*sigma*(s-1)*(v-1);
            U(s,v) = A*u(s,v) + B*u(s-1,v) + C*u(s+1,v) ...;
        end
    end
end
```

When we use a non-uniform grid, simplification of Equation (10.19) to (10.20) is not possible, and we work with (10.19) directly. This is illustrated with the Matlab function HestonExplicitPDENonUniformGrid.m. Again, only the terminal values of $U_{i,j}^{N_T}$ are retained.

```
function U = HestonExplicitPDENonUniformGrid(params,...)
for s=1:NS
    for v=1:NV
        U(s,v) = max(S(s) - K, 0);
    end
end
for t=1:NT-1
    for v=1:NV-1
        U(1,v) = 0;
        U(NS,v) = max(0, Smax - K);
    end
    for s=1:NS
        U(s,NV) = max(0, S(s) - K);
    end
    u = U;
    for s=2:NS-1
        derV = (u(s,2)   - u(s,1))   / (V(2)-V(1));
        derS = (u(s+1,1) - u(s-1,1)) / (S(s+1)-S(s-1));
        LHS = - r*u(s,1) + (r-q)*S(s)*derS + kappa*theta*derV;
        U(s,1) = LHS*dt + u(s,1);
    end
    u = U;
    for s=2:NS-1
        for v=2:NV-1
            derS  =  (u(s+1,v) - u(s-1,v)) / (S(s+1)-S(s-1));
            derV  =  (u(s,v+1) - u(s,v-1)) / (V(v+1)-V(v-1));
            derSS = ((u(s+1,v) - u(s,v))   / (S(s+1)-S(s)) ...;
            derVV = ((u(s,v+1) - u(s,v))   / (V(v+1)-V(v)) ...;
            derSV =  (u(s+1,v+1) - u(s-1,v+1) - U(s+1,v-1) ...;
            L = 0.5*V(v)*S(s)^2*derSS + rho*sigma*V(v)*S(s) ...;
            U(s,v) = L*dt + u(s,v);
        end
    end
end
```

Although we can use the non-uniform grid function with a uniform grid, the function made for a uniform grid is slightly faster. The functions HestonExplicitPDE.m and HestonExplicitPDENonUniformGrid both return the grid $U_{i,j}^{N_T}$ of terminal values, corresponding to values S_i and v_j along the grids. To obtain a value of U^{N_T} between points on the grid, we apply the Matlab function interp2.m for two-dimensional interpolation.

The C# code to implement the explicit method using uniform and non-uniform grids is similar to the Matlab code and is not presented here. As explained earlier in this chapter, however, we need to use the C# function interp2() presented in Chapter 8 for two-dimensional linear interpolation.

To illustrate, suppose we use the parameter values above, namely $\kappa = 1.5$, $\theta = 0.04$, $\sigma = 0.3$, $\rho = -0.9$, $r = 0.02$, $q = 0.05$, $\lambda = 0$, $K = 100$, $v_0 = 0.05$, and $\tau = 0.15$ years. We wish to obtain the price at the spot $S = 101.52$ when the volatility is $v = 0.05412$. The following Matlab code builds a uniform grid of size 80×40 and uses 3,000 time steps.

```
Smin = 0;  Smax = 2*K;
Vmin = 0;  Vmax = 0.5;
Tmin = 0;  Tmax = Mat;
nS = 79;        % Stock price
nV = 39;        % Volatility
nT = 3000;      % Maturity
ds = (Smax-Smin)/nS;
dv = (Vmax-Vmin)/nV;
dt = (Tmax-Tmin)/nT;
S = [0:nS].*ds;
V = [0:nV].*dv;
T = [0:nT].*dt;
```

The grid and parameters are then passed to the HestonExplicitPDE.m function, and the price is obtained by two-dimensional interpolation with the Matlab function interp2.m.

```
U = HestonExplicitPDE(params,...);
S0 = 101.52;
V0 = 0.05412;
UniformPrice = interp2(V,S,U,V0,S0);
```

The following Matlab code constructs the non-uniform grid described by In'T Hout and Foulon (2010) and presented earlier in this chapter, and also returns the price.

```
c = K/5;
dz = 1/nS*(asinh((Smax-K)/c) - asinh(-K/c));
for i=1:nS+1;
    z(i) = asinh(-K/c) + (i-1)*dz;
    S(i) = K + c*sinh(z(i));
end
d = Vmax/500;
dn = asinh(Vmax/d)/nV;
for j=1:nV+1
    n(j) = (j-1)*dn;
    V(j) = d*sinh(n(j));
end
U = HestonExplicitPDENonUniformGrid(params,...);
NonUniformPrice = interp2(V,S,U,V0,S0);
```

The exact price, using the closed-form solution, is 4.1086. The uniform grid produces a price of 4.0543, while the non-uniform grid produces a price of 4.1100, which is much more accurate. Even with 10,000 time points, the accuracy of the uniform grid does not improve much. To increase the accuracy of the uniform grid, we must use larger grid sizes for the stock price and volatility, which increases computational time.

Error Analysis

It is informative to investigate the convergence of the explicit scheme to the true price as the number of grid points for the stock price and the volatility both increase. We illustrate this using the same settings as in the previous section, and using uniform and non-uniform grids.

The exact price of a European call, using the Heston closed form, is 4.1086. We examine the convergence of the PDE price to the true price, as the number of points for the stock price grid, N_S, ranges from 20 to 40 in increments of 5, and as the number of points for the volatility grid, N_V, ranges from 10 to 40 in increments in 10. We use $N_T = 1,000$ for the number of time points. The non-uniform grid and the maximum number of points, $N_S = 40$ and $N_V = 40$, produces a price of 4.1151, a difference of less than 1 penny from the true price of 4.1086.

If we use the non-uniform grid with the same maximum number of points, we obtain a price of 4.5811, which is far closer to the true price of 4.5802 than the price of 4.5511 obtained using an even grid. The convergence to the true price using a non-uniform grid is also must faster, as indicated in Figure 10.3.

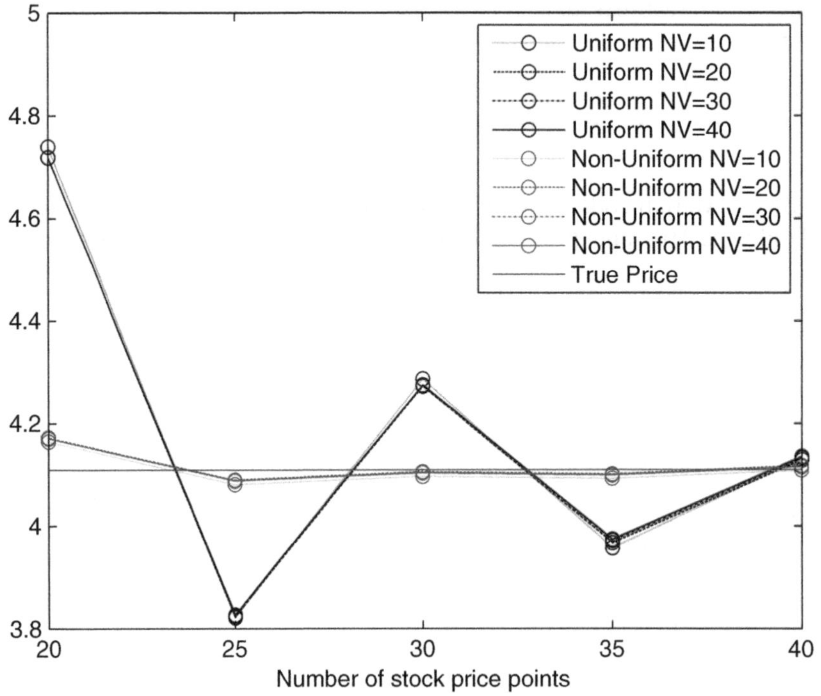

FIGURE 10.3 Pricing Error of the Explicit Scheme

In general, it is best not to implement the explicit scheme for European options using a three-dimensional array for $U(S, v, t)$, since this requires a substantial allocation of memory. The Matlab and C# code in this chapter both use a two-dimensional array for $U(S, v)$, and overwrite successive time values of $U(S, v)$ so that only the value at maturity $t_{\max}$ is retained. Storing values of $U_{i,j}^n$ at intermediate time steps is wasteful since only the values at maturity are needed to price European options.

ADI SCHEMES

Alternating Direction Implicit (ADI) schemes have the advantage of being stable and showing good convergence for a small number of time points. Recall that, in the weighted method, we constructed the matrix **L** from components corresponding to the first- and second-order derivatives. We also constructed the vector $\mathbf{U}^n$ using the components of $U_{i,j}^n$ on the (S, v) grid illustrated in Figure 10.2. The idea behind ADI schemes is that the components of **L** are treated separately, so that certain components are treated explicitly, and others implicitly. We decompose **L** into three matrices $\mathbf{A}_0$, $\mathbf{A}_1$, and $\mathbf{A}_2$ each of size $N \times N$, so that

$$\mathbf{L} = \mathbf{A}_0 + \mathbf{A}_1 + \mathbf{A}_2 \tag{10.21}$$

where $\mathbf{A}_0$ contains all entries of **L** corresponding to the mixed derivative $\partial^2 U/\partial S \partial v$, $\mathbf{A}_1$ contains all entries corresponding to $\partial U/\partial S$ and $\partial^2 U/\partial S^2$, and $\mathbf{A}_2$ contains all entries corresponding to $\partial U/\partial v$ and $\partial^2 U/\partial v^2$. The entries of **L** corresponding to $rU_{i,j}^n$ are split evenly between $\mathbf{A}_1$ and $\mathbf{A}_2$. Hence, we construct the matrices as

$$\begin{aligned}
\mathbf{A}_0 &= \rho\sigma v S\left(\frac{\partial U}{\partial S \partial v}\right)_{N\times N} \\
\mathbf{A}_1 &= (r-q)S\left(\frac{\partial U}{\partial S}\right)_{N\times N} + \frac{1}{2}vS^2\left(\frac{\partial^2 U}{\partial S^2}\right)_{N\times N} - \frac{1}{2}r(U)_{N\times N} \\
\mathbf{A}_2 &= \kappa(\theta - v)\left(\frac{\partial U}{\partial v}\right)_{N\times N} + \frac{1}{2}\sigma^2 v\left(\frac{\partial^2 U}{\partial v^2}\right)_{N\times N} - \frac{1}{2}r(U)_{N\times N}.
\end{aligned} \tag{10.22}$$

From Equation (10.2) we can write

$$\mathbf{U}'(t) = \mathbf{L}\mathbf{U}(t). \tag{10.23}$$

This system of equations can be solved using various ADI schemes that all work iteratively, by updating a given $\mathbf{U}_{t-1} = \mathbf{U}(t-1)$ to a new value $\mathbf{U}_t = \mathbf{U}(t)$. All the schemes require an initial value $\mathbf{U}_0$. For the call option, this initial value is exactly the same as that described in previous sections of this chapter. Denote by **I** the identity matrix of dimension N. The schemes covered by In'T Hout and Foulon (2010) are the following.

Douglas Scheme

This is the simplest ADI scheme under consideration. Given $\mathbf{U}_{t-1}$, we update to $\mathbf{U}_t$ using the following steps.

Step 1. $\mathbf{Y}_0 = [\mathbf{I} + dt\mathbf{L}]\mathbf{U}_{t-1}$.
Step 2. $\mathbf{Y}_k = [\mathbf{I} - \theta dt\mathbf{A}_k]^{-1}[\mathbf{Y}_0 - \theta dt\mathbf{A}_k\mathbf{U}_{t-1}]$ for $k = 1, 2$.
Step 3. Set $\mathbf{U}_t = \mathbf{Y}_2$.

Craig-Sneyd Scheme

This scheme is similar to the Douglas scheme, expect that two additional steps are added.

Step 1. $\mathbf{Y}_0 = [\mathbf{I} + dt\mathbf{L}]\mathbf{U}_{t-1}$.
Step 2. $\mathbf{Y}_k = [\mathbf{I} - \theta dt\mathbf{A}_k]^{-1}[\mathbf{Y}_{k-1} - \theta dt\mathbf{A}_k\mathbf{U}_{t-1}]$ for $k = 1, 2$.
Step 3. $\tilde{\mathbf{Y}}_0 = \mathbf{Y}_0 + \frac{1}{2}dt[\mathbf{A}_0\mathbf{Y}_2 - \mathbf{A}_0\mathbf{U}_{t-1}]$.
Step 4. $\tilde{\mathbf{Y}}_k = [\mathbf{I} - \theta dt\mathbf{A}_k]^{-1}[\tilde{\mathbf{Y}}_{k-1} - \theta dt\mathbf{A}_k\mathbf{U}_{t-1}]$.
Step 5. Set $\mathbf{U}_t = \tilde{\mathbf{Y}}_2$.

Modified Craig-Sneyd Scheme

Step 1. $\mathbf{Y}_0 = [\mathbf{I} + dt\mathbf{L}]\mathbf{U}_{t-1}$.
Step 2. $\mathbf{Y}_k = [\mathbf{I} - \theta dt\mathbf{A}_k]^{-1}[\mathbf{Y}_{k-1} - \theta dt\mathbf{A}_k\mathbf{U}_{t-1}]$.
Step 3. $\hat{\mathbf{Y}}_0 = \mathbf{Y}_0 + \theta dt[\mathbf{A}_0\mathbf{Y}_2 - \mathbf{A}_0\mathbf{U}_{t-1}]$.
Step 4. $\tilde{\mathbf{Y}}_0 = \hat{\mathbf{Y}}_0 + \left(\frac{1}{2} - \theta\right) dt[\mathbf{L}\mathbf{Y}_2 - \mathbf{L}\mathbf{U}_{t-1}]$.
Step 5. $\tilde{\mathbf{Y}}_k = [\mathbf{I} - \theta dt\mathbf{A}_k]^{-1}[\tilde{\mathbf{Y}}_{k-1} - \theta dt\mathbf{A}_k\mathbf{U}_{t-1}]$.
Step 6. Set $\mathbf{U}_t = \tilde{\mathbf{Y}}_2$.

Hundsdorfer-Verwer Scheme

Step 1. $\mathbf{Y}_0 = [\mathbf{I} + dt\mathbf{L}]\mathbf{U}_{t-1}$.
Step 2. $\mathbf{Y}_k = [\mathbf{I} - \theta dt\mathbf{A}_k]^{-1}[\mathbf{Y}_{k-1} - \theta dt\mathbf{A}_k\mathbf{U}_{t-1}]$.
Step 3. $\tilde{\mathbf{Y}}_0 = \mathbf{Y}_0 + \frac{1}{2}dt[\mathbf{L}\mathbf{Y}_2 - \mathbf{L}\mathbf{U}_{t-1}]$.
Step 4. $\tilde{\mathbf{Y}}_k = [\mathbf{I} - \theta dt\mathbf{A}_k]^{-1}[\tilde{\mathbf{Y}}_{k-1} - \theta dt\mathbf{A}_k\mathbf{Y}_2]$.
Step 5. $\tilde{\mathbf{Y}}_2 = [\mathbf{I} - \theta dt\mathbf{A}_2]^{-1}[\tilde{\mathbf{Y}}_1 - \theta dt\mathbf{A}_2\mathbf{Y}_2]$.
Step 6. Set $\mathbf{U}_t = \tilde{\mathbf{Y}}_2$.

The parameter θ controls the type of weighing being implemented, exactly as in the weighted method. Hence, $\theta = 0$ produces the fully explicit scheme, $\theta = \frac{1}{2}$ produces the Crank-Nicolson scheme, and $\theta = 1$ produces the fully implicit scheme. Hence, an ADI scheme is specified by the scheme itself and the value of the parameter θ.

Once the **L** matrix is constructed, it is straightforward to implement the ADI schemes. This is done with the ADIPrice.m function. The first part of the function builds the required matrices of derivatives, which can be constructed with either a uniform or non-uniform grid. The functions used to build the matrices are the same that were used for the weighted method presented earlier in this chapter.

```
function y = ADIPrice(scheme,GridType,...)
if strcmp(GridType,'NonUniform')
    [derS ... derSV R] = BuildDerivativesNonUniform(S,V,T);
else
    [derS ... derSV R] = BuildDerivatives(S,V,T);
end
```

The second part uses the derivatives matrices to construct the matrices $\mathbf{A}_0$, $\mathbf{A}_1$, and $\mathbf{A}_2$, in accordance with (10.22), creates a vector stock prices from the grid, and initializes the vector $\mathbf{U}^n$ as the value of the European call at maturity.

```
A0 = rho.*sigma.*derSV;
A1 = (r-q).*derS + (1/2).*derSS - r.*R./2;
A2 = kappa.*theta.*derV1 - kappa.*derV2 + ...;
Si = repmat(S',NV,1);
U = max(0, Si - K);
```

Finally, the last part of the function loops through time and applies the desired ADI scheme. It then re-arranges the vector $\mathbf{U}^n$ into a matrix, and interpolates the matrix to find the European call price at the desired values of S_0 and v_0.

```
for t=2:NT
    u  = U;
    Y0 = (I + dt.*(A0+A1+A2))*u;
    Y1 = (I - thet.*dt.*A1) \ (Y0 - thet.*dt.*A1*u);
    Y2 = (I - thet.*dt.*A2) \ (Y1 - thet.*dt.*A2*u);
    if strcmp(scheme,'DO')
        U  = Y2;
    elseif strcmp(scheme,'CS')
        Y0_ = Y0 + (1/2).*dt.*(A0*Y2 - A0*u);
        Y1_ = (I - thet.*dt.*A1) \ (Y0_ - thet.*dt.*A1*u);
        Y2_ = (I - thet.*dt.*A2) \ (Y1_ - thet.*dt.*A2*u);
        U = Y2_;
    elseif strcmp(scheme,'MCS')
        Y0h = Y0 + thet.*dt.*(A0*Y2 - A0*u);
        Y0_ = Y0h + (1/2-thet).*dt.*((A0+A1+A2)*Y2 - (A0+A1+A2)*u);
        Y1_ = (I - thet.*dt.*A1) \ (Y0_ - thet.*dt.*A1*u);
        Y2_ = (I - thet.*dt.*A2) \ (Y1_ - thet.*dt.*A2*u);
        U = Y2_;
    elseif strcmp(scheme,'HV')
        Y0_ = Y0 + (1/2).*dt.*((A0+A1+A2)*Y2 - (A0+A1+A2)*u);
        Y1_ = (I - thet.*dt.*A1) \ (Y0_ - thet.*dt.*A1*Y2);
        Y2_ = (I - thet.*dt.*A2) \ (Y1_ - thet.*dt.*A2*Y2);
        U = Y2_;
    end
end
U = reshape(U,NS,NV);
y = interp2(V,S,U,V0,S0);
```

The C# code to implement the ADI schemes is very similar to the Matlab code and is not presented here. As required for the C# code for the weighted method, however, we need the C# functions MInvLU() and interp2() for matrix inversion and two-dimensional interpolation, respectively. We also need functions for vector and matrix operations. The ADIPrice() function calculates the option price under a selected ADI scheme. The following snippet of code contains the portion of the ADIPrice() function for the Hundsdorfer-Verwer scheme.

```
elseif(scheme == "HV")
{    // Hundsdorfer-Verwer ADI scheme
     double[] A0Y2 = MVMult(SumA,Y2);
     double[] A0u = MVMult(SumA,u);
     double[] A0A0 = VSub(A0Y2,A0u);
     double[] dtA = VMultS(A0A0,dt*0.5);
     Y0_ = VAdd(Y0,dtA);
     double[] A1Y2 = VMultS(MVMult(A1,Y2),thet*dt);
     double[] Y0_minusA1Y2 = VSub(Y0_,A1Y2);
     Y1_ = MVMult(MInvLU(IminusA1),Y0_minusA1Y2);
     double[] A2Y2 = VMultS(MVMult(A2,Y2),thet*dt);
     double[] Y1_minusA2Y2 = VSub(Y1_,A2Y2);
     Y2_ = MVMult(MInvLU(IminusA2),Y1_minusA2Y2);
     U = Y2_;
}
```

We continue with the example earlier in this chapter, using $N_T = 20$ time steps and a uniform grid with $N_S = N_v = 40$. The exact price is 4.1086. With the Modified Craig-Sneyd method the prices under the explicit ADI, implicit ADI, and Crank-Nicolson schemes are 4.1123, 4.1124, and 4.1132, respectively, all of which

TABLE 10.2 ADI Prices Under a Uniform Grid, Size 40 × 40 × 20

Scheme	Explicit	Error	Implicit	Error	C.-N.	Error
Douglas	4.1467	0.038	4.0928	−0.016	4.1197	0.011
C.S.	4.1400	0.031	4.0864	−0.022	4.1132	0.005
M.C.S.	4.1123	0.004	4.1124	0.004	4.1132	0.005
H.V.	4.1123	0.004	4.1124	0.004	4.1132	0.005

TABLE 10.3 ADI Prices Under a Non-Uniform Grid, Size 20 × 20 × 10

Scheme	Explicit	Error	Implicit	Error	C.-N.	Error
Douglas	4.2133	0.105	4.1042	−0.004	4.1582	0.050
C.S.	4.1946	0.086	4.0856	−0.023	4.1395	0.031
M.C.S.	4.1363	0.028	4.1360	0.028	4.1395	0.031
H.V.	4.1363	0.028	4.1357	0.027	4.1395	0.031

are accurate to roughly 1 penny. If a non-uniform grid is used, then the grid size can be reduced to 20×20 and the time steps reduced to 10. This produces results that are comparable in accuracy but that require much less computational time. The complete results are in Table 10.2 for the uniform grid and in Table 10.3 for the non-uniform grid.

CONCLUSION

In this chapter, we have presented some of the finite difference methods that are commonly used to obtain European prices in the Heston model. These methods have been extended to obtain the prices of American options also. As we saw in Chapter 8, the explicit method is particularly simple to adapt for American options. Pricing models that employ finite differences are varied and have been applied in a stochastic volatility framework by Clarke and Parrott (1999), In'T Hout and Foulon (2010), and Ikonen and Toivanen (2008), among many others. Please see Tavella and Randall (2000) and Duffy (2006) for an overview of finite differences for pricing European and American options.

All of the methods we have encountered up to this chapter have dealt with either the European or American price. Central to option pricing theory, however, are the option price sensitivities to the inputs used in the price: the Greeks. This is the subject of the next chapter.

CHAPTER 11

The Heston Greeks

Abstract

In this chapter, we present the option sensitivities—the Greeks—from the Heston model. We first derive analytic expressions for the most popular Greeks. We illustrate the Heston Greeks by comparing them to Greeks from Black-Scholes prices that are close to the Heston prices. We show that finite differences produce very good approximations to analytic Greeks, at the expense of increased computation time. We do this for Greeks obtained from the original Heston (1993) model, but also with Greeks from the Attari (2004), Lewis (2000, 2001), and Carr and Madan (1999) formulations. We show that fast Fourier transform (FFT) of Carr and Madan (1999) and that the fractional FFT of Chourdakis (2005), both covered in Chapter 5, are able to very quickly produce a set of Greeks across a wide range of strikes, in the same way that these methods produce prices. Finally, we show that Greeks of American options can be obtained from simulation methods presented in Chapter 7, from the Medvedev and Scaillet (2010) expansion covered in Chapter 8, and from the explicit method covered in Chapter 10.

ANALYTIC EXPRESSIONS FOR EUROPEAN GREEKS

The prices of European calls and puts in the Heston model are available in closed form. It is, therefore, possible to differentiate the call or put price and obtain expressions for most of the Greeks in closed form also. Recall that the call and put price are, respectively,

$$C(K) = S_t e^{-q\tau} P_1 - K e^{-r\tau} P_2, \quad P(K) = C(K) + K e^{-r\tau} - S_t e^{-q\tau} \tag{11.1}$$

where

$$P_j = \frac{1}{2} + \frac{1}{\pi} \int_0^\infty \mathrm{Re}\left[\frac{e^{-i\phi \ln K} f_j\,(\phi; x_t, v_t)}{i\phi} \right] d\phi. \tag{11.2}$$

Hence, the sensitivity of calls and puts to a parameter or input y usually involves first- and second-order derivatives of the in-the-money probabilities P_j

$$\frac{\partial P_j}{\partial y} = \frac{1}{\pi} \int_0^\infty \mathrm{Re}\left[\frac{\partial f_j}{\partial y} \times \frac{e^{-i\phi \ln K}}{i\phi} \right] d\phi, \quad \frac{\partial^2 P_j}{\partial y^2} = \frac{1}{\pi} \int_0^\infty \mathrm{Re}\left[\frac{\partial^2 f_j}{\partial y^2} \times \frac{e^{-i\phi \ln K}}{i\phi} \right] d\phi. \tag{11.3}$$

In the following subsections, we use (11.3) to derive analytic expressions for most of the popular first- and second-order Greeks.

Delta, Gamma, Rho, Theta, and Vega

Delta, gamma, rho and theta are obtained by differentiating Equation (11.1) and applying (11.3) when required. Vega is more arbitrary, since there are several parameters that affect the volatility smile in the Heston model. The second-order volatility Greeks vanna and volga will be covered in the next section.

As explained by Bakshi, Cao, and Chen (1997), Reiss and Wystup (2000), and Bakshi and Madan (2000), and others, delta for the call and put and are given by, respectively

$$\Delta_C = \frac{\partial C}{\partial S} = e^{-q\tau} P_1 \quad \text{and} \quad \Delta_P = \frac{\partial P}{\partial S} = e^{-q\tau}(P_1 - 1). \tag{11.4}$$

Gamma is found by differentiating delta. By definition, it is the same for calls and puts. Using $\partial f_1/\partial S = i\phi f_1/S_t$ in Equation (11.3) to obtain $\partial P_1/\partial S$, we can express gamma as

$$\Gamma = \frac{\partial^2 C}{\partial S^2} = e^{-q\tau} \frac{\partial P_1}{\partial S} = \frac{e^{-q\tau}}{\pi S_t} \int_0^\infty \text{Re}[e^{-i\phi \ln K} f_1(\phi; x_t, v_t)]\, d\phi. \tag{11.5}$$

Rho is found by differentiating (11.1) with respect to the risk-free rate, r. For calls and puts rho is, respectively

$$\rho_C = \frac{\partial C}{\partial r} = Ke^{-r\tau}\tau P_2 \quad \text{and} \quad \rho_P = \frac{\partial P}{\partial r} = Ke^{-r\tau}\tau(P_2 - 1). \tag{11.6}$$

Theta is the negative of the derivative with respect to maturity, τ. For calls and puts, theta is, respectively,

$$\begin{aligned} \Theta_C &= -\frac{\partial C}{\partial \tau} = -S_t e^{-q\tau}\left(-qP_1 + \frac{\partial P_1}{\partial \tau}\right) + Ke^{-r\tau}\left(-rP_2 + \frac{\partial P_2}{\partial \tau}\right) \\ \Theta_P &= -\frac{\partial P}{\partial \tau} = \Theta_C + Kre^{-r\tau} - qS_t e^{-q\tau} \end{aligned} \tag{11.7}$$

where

$$\frac{\partial f_j}{\partial \tau} = \exp(C_j + D_j v_t + i\phi x_t)\left(\frac{\partial C_j}{\partial \tau} + \frac{\partial D_j}{\partial \tau} v_t\right) \tag{11.8}$$

and

$$\begin{aligned} \frac{\partial C_j}{\partial \tau} &= (r-q)\phi i + \frac{\kappa\theta}{\sigma^2}\left[b_j - \rho\sigma\phi i + d_j + \frac{2g_j d_j e^{d_j\tau}}{1 - g_j e^{d_j\tau}}\right], \\ \frac{\partial D_j}{\partial \tau} &= \frac{b_j - \rho\sigma\phi i + d_j}{\sigma^2} \times \frac{(g_j - 1)d_j e^{d_j\tau}}{(1 - g_j e^{d_j\tau})^2}. \end{aligned} \tag{11.9}$$

In Equation (11.8), $x_t = \ln S_t$ is the log spot price, and v_t is the initial variance, which is unobserved and estimated as the parameter v_0. The quantities b_j, g_j, and d_j are given in Chapter 1 for $j = 1, 2$.

Vega is defined as the derivative of the call and put price with respect to the implied volatility. In the Black-Scholes model, the implied volatility is represented by the volatility parameter σ_{BS}, so vega for the call is readily obtained as $\partial C_{BS}/\partial \sigma_{BS}$, where C_{BS} is the Black-Scholes call price. Recall from Chapter 1 that in the Heston model, however, the shape of the implied volatility surface is determined by the parameters driving the process for the variance, namely the mean reversion speed κ, the mean reversion level θ, the initial level of the variance v_0, and the correlation ρ. Since v_0 and θ are responsible for the initial and long-term level of the variance, Zhu (2010) recommends basing vega on those two parameters. Both parameters represent variance, so to create measures of sensitivity to volatility, Zhu (2010) defines two vegas, one based on $\upsilon = \sqrt{v_0}$ and the other based on $\omega = \sqrt{\theta}$. The vegas for the call are, therefore, the derivatives

$$\mathcal{V}_1 = \frac{\partial C}{\partial \upsilon} = \frac{\partial C}{\partial v_0} 2\sqrt{v_0} \quad \text{and} \quad \mathcal{V}_2 = \frac{\partial C}{\partial \omega} = \frac{\partial C}{\partial \theta} 2\sqrt{\theta}. \tag{11.10}$$

The first vega is

$$\mathcal{V}_1 = Se^{-q\tau} \frac{\partial P_1}{\partial v_0} 2\sqrt{v_0} - Ke^{-r\tau} \frac{\partial P_2}{\partial v_0} 2\sqrt{v_0} \tag{11.11}$$

where

$$\frac{\partial P_j}{\partial v_0} = \frac{1}{\pi} \int_0^\infty \text{Re}\left[\frac{e^{-i\phi \ln K} f_j(\phi; x_t, v_t)\, D_j(\tau, \phi)}{i\phi}\right] d\phi. \tag{11.12}$$

The second vega is

$$\mathcal{V}_2 = Se^{-q\tau} \frac{\partial P_1}{\partial \theta} 2\sqrt{\theta} - Ke^{-r\tau} \frac{\partial P_2}{\partial \theta} 2\sqrt{\theta} \tag{11.13}$$

where

$$\frac{\partial P_j}{\partial \theta} = \frac{1}{\pi} \int_0^\infty \text{Re}\left[\frac{e^{-i\phi \ln K} f_j(\phi; x_t, v_t)\, \partial C_j/\partial \theta}{i\phi}\right] d\phi \tag{11.14}$$

and

$$\frac{\partial C_j}{\partial \theta} = \frac{\kappa}{\sigma^2}\left[(b_j - \rho\sigma i\phi + d_j)\,\tau - 2\ln\left(\frac{1 - g_j e^{d_j \tau}}{1 - g_j}\right)\right]. \tag{11.15}$$

By examination of Equation (11.1), it is easy to verify that $\mathcal{V}_1$ and $\mathcal{V}_2$ for the put are the same as those for the call.

Vanna, Volga, and Other Greeks

The most popular second-order Greeks are vanna, the derivative of vega with respect to the spot price, and volga, the derivative of vega with respect to volatility. In this subsection, we focus only the first vega, $\mathcal{V}_1$ in Equation (11.11). Hence, vanna and volga are

$$\text{Vanna} = \frac{\partial^2 C}{\partial v \partial S} = \frac{\partial^2 C}{\partial v_0 \partial S} 2\sqrt{v_0} \quad \text{and} \quad \text{Volga} = \frac{\partial^2 C}{\partial v^2} \tag{11.16}$$

where $v = \sqrt{v_0}$. Again, it is easy to verify that vanna and volga for the put are identical. Vanna can be obtained from delta as

$$\text{Vanna} = \frac{\partial}{\partial v}\left(\frac{\partial C}{\partial S}\right) = 2e^{-q\tau}\sqrt{v_0}\frac{\partial P_1}{\partial v_0} \tag{11.17}$$

where we use the derivative in (11.12). Volga can be obtained from vega, by using (11.10)

$$\text{Volga} = \frac{\partial \mathcal{V}_1}{\partial v} = Se^{-q\tau}\frac{\partial^2 P_1}{\partial v^2} - Ke^{-r\tau}\frac{\partial^2 P_2}{\partial v^2} \tag{11.18}$$

where

$$\begin{aligned}\frac{\partial^2 P_j}{\partial v^2} &= 4\left(\frac{\partial^2 P_j}{\partial v_0^2}v_0 + \frac{1}{2}\frac{\partial P_j}{\partial v_0}\right) \\ &= \frac{1}{\pi}\int_0^\infty \text{Re}\left[\frac{e^{-i\phi \ln K}}{i\phi}2D_j(\tau,\phi)f_j(\phi;x_t,v_t)(2D_j(\tau,\phi)v_0+1)\right]d\phi.\end{aligned} \tag{11.19}$$

Equivalently,

$$\text{Volga} = \frac{\partial \mathcal{V}_1}{\partial v_0}2\sqrt{v_0} = 4\sqrt{v_0}\left(\frac{\partial^2 C}{\partial v_0^2}\sqrt{v_0} + \frac{\mathcal{V}_1}{4v_0}\right) = 4\left(\frac{\partial^2 C}{\partial v_0^2}v_0 + \frac{1}{2}\frac{\partial C}{\partial v_0}\right). \tag{11.20}$$

We need the second order derivative

$$\frac{\partial^2 C}{\partial v_0^2} = Se^{-q\tau}\frac{\partial^2 P_1}{\partial v_0^2} - Ke^{-r\tau}\frac{\partial^2 P_2}{\partial v_0^2} \tag{11.21}$$

with, from Equation (11.12)

$$\frac{\partial^2 P_j}{\partial v_0^2} = \frac{1}{\pi}\int_0^\infty \text{Re}\left[\frac{e^{-i\phi \ln K}f_j(\phi;x_t,v_t)\,D_j(\tau,\phi)^2}{i\phi}\right]d\phi. \tag{11.22}$$

We have defined vega ($\mathcal{V}_1$), vanna, and volga all in terms of the spot volatility, $v = \sqrt{v_0}$. On the other hand, the Heston PDE for the option price $U(S_t, v_t, t)$, which we encountered in Chapter 1, contains derivatives expressed in terms of the variance, v_0. If we redefine vega, vanna, and volga in terms of v_0 instead of v, then we can substitute the Greeks into the PDE and show that it is satisfied. Hence, we obtain

$$\begin{aligned}\Theta + \frac{1}{2}v_0 S_0^2 \Gamma + (r-q)S_0\Delta - rU \\ \rho\sigma v_0 S_0 \text{Vanna} + \frac{1}{2}\sigma^2 v_0 \text{Volga} + \kappa(\theta - v_0)\text{Vega}_1 = 0\end{aligned} \tag{11.23}$$

where we have set $\lambda(S_t, v_t, t) = 0$ and where S_0 is the spot price. The first line in (11.23) is the Black-Scholes PDE, and the second line adds correction terms for stochastic volatility, as specified in the Heston model. It is easy to verify that the PDE with Greeks holds for both the Black-Scholes and Heston models, provided that vega, vanna, and volga are constructed in terms of variance rather than in terms of volatility. This is accomplished with the following snippet of code. The code makes use of the HestonGreeks.m function, which we introduce later in this chapter.

```
% Heston Greeks and PDE
Price = HestonPriceGaussLaguerre(...);
Delta = HestonGreeks(...,'Delta');
Gamma = HestonGreeks(...,'Gamma');
Theta = HestonGreeks(...,'Theta');
Vega1 = HestonGreeks(...,'Vega1') / (2*sqrt(v0));
Vanna = HestonGreeks(...,'Vanna') / (2*sqrt(v0));
Volga = HestonGreeks(...,'Volga');
Volga = (1/4/sqrt(v0)*Volga - Vega1/2/sqrt(v0))/sqrt(v0);
Heston = Theta + 0.5*v0*S0^2*Gamma + (r-q)*S0*Delta ...;
% Black Scholes Greeks and PDE
Theta = BSGreeks(PutCall,S0,K,r,q,T,sigma,'Theta');
Gamma = BSGreeks(PutCall,S0,K,r,q,T,sigma,'Gamma');
Delta = BSGreeks(PutCall,S0,K,r,q,T,sigma,'Delta');
Price = BSPrice(PutCall,S0,K,r,q,T,sigma);
BS = Theta + 0.5*sigma^2*S0^2*Gamma + (r-q)*S0*Delta ...;
```

In the above code snippet, we invert Equations (11.10), (11.16), and (11.18) to express the derivatives in terms of v_0 rather than v before substituting these derivatives into the Heston PDE. See Zhu (2010) for a further discussion of the Heston PDE with Greeks.

As mentioned in Chapter 2, the correlation ρ and the volatility of variance σ control the slope and curvature, respectively, of the implied volatility backed out from Heston model prices, while κ controls the speed of reversion to the mean level θ of volatility. When $\rho < 0$, the slope of the implied volatility curve is negative, and when $\rho > 0$, it is positive. The curvature increases as σ increases. The sensitivity of the call price to these parameters is

$$\frac{\partial C}{\partial \xi} = Se^{-q\tau}\frac{\partial P_1}{\partial \xi} - Ke^{-r\tau}\frac{\partial P_2}{\partial \xi} \tag{11.24}$$

with

$$\frac{\partial P_j}{\partial \xi} = \frac{1}{\pi}\int_0^{\infty} \text{Re}\left[\frac{\partial f_j}{\partial \xi} \times \frac{e^{-i\phi \ln K}}{i\phi}\right] d\phi \tag{11.25}$$

and

$$\frac{\partial f_j}{\partial \xi} = \exp(C_j + D_j v_t + i\phi x_t)\left(\frac{\partial C_j}{\partial \xi} + \frac{\partial D_j}{\partial \xi} v_j\right) \tag{11.26}$$

for $\xi \in (\rho, \sigma, \kappa)$. Obtaining the derivatives of C_j and D_j in Equation (11.26) is complicated, but can be easily handled with a symbolic calculator such as Matlab. By examination of (11.1) it is easy to verify that the sensitivities of the put to ρ, σ, and κ are the same as those for the call.

Finally, recall from Chapter 1 that we can consolidate the integrals for P_1 and P_2 into a single integral, and from Chapter 2 that we can express the first characteristic function, $f_1(\phi)$, in terms of the second, $f_2(\phi)$, as $f_1(\phi) = f_2(\phi - i)/(S_t e^{(r-q)\tau})$. This implies that we can write the call price as

$$C(K) = \frac{1}{2}S_t e^{-q\tau} - \frac{1}{2}Ke^{-r\tau} + \frac{1}{\pi}\int_0^{\infty} \text{Re}\left[\frac{e^{-i\phi \ln K - r\tau}}{i\phi}\left(f_2(\phi - i) - Kf_2(\phi)\right)\right] d\phi. \tag{11.27}$$

The Greeks can be obtained by straightforward differentiation of $C(K)$, in the same manner as described earlier in this section.

FINITE DIFFERENCES FOR THE GREEKS

In the previous section, we derived analytic expressions for the Greeks from the Heston call or put price. Recall that, in the last chapter, we used finite differences to approximate the derivatives that appear in the Heston PDE. We can apply finite differences to find the Greeks and other option sensitivities also. When this approach is used to calculate Greeks, however, the computation time is increased because the option price must be calculated more than once, multiple times in the case of the second-order Greeks. For the first-order Greeks, delta (Δ), theta (Θ), rho (ρ), vega1 ($\mathcal{V}_1$), and vega2 ($\mathcal{V}_2$), as well as for the first-order sensitivities $\partial U/\partial \xi$, for $\xi \in (\rho, \sigma, \kappa)$, the sensitivity of the option price to a parameter or variable can be approximated with first-order central differences. For example, delta for the call $C(S, v, t)$ is approximated as

$$\Delta_C \approx \frac{C(S + dS, v, t) - C(S - dS, v, t)}{2dS}.$$

As another example, to approximate the first vega in Equation (11.10) we approximate the derivative with respect to v_0 by a central difference and we multiply the result by $2\sqrt{v_0}$

$$\mathcal{V}_1 \approx \frac{C(S, v, t; v_0 + dv) - C(S, v, t; v_0 - dv)}{2dv} \times 2\sqrt{v_0}. \tag{11.28}$$

For the second-order Greeks, gamma (Γ) and volga, we can use the second-order central differences for a single variable. Hence, for example, gamma is approximated as

$$\Gamma \approx \frac{C(S+dS,v,t) - 2C(S,v,t) + C(S-dS,v,t)}{(dS)^2}.$$

For volga, which we express in terms of $v = \sqrt{v_0}$, we first approximate the following second order derivative in v_0 as

$$\frac{\partial^2 C}{\partial v_0^2} \approx \frac{C(S,v,t;v_0+dv) - 2C(S,v,t;v_0) + C(S,v,t;v_0-dv)}{(dv)^2}. \quad (11.29)$$

We then approximate $\mathcal{V}_1$ using Equation (11.28) and substitute it along with (11.29) into (11.20). Finally, for vanna, we use the second-order central difference in two variables. We first approximate the second order derivative in (11.16), and then multiply by $2\sqrt{v_0}$. Hence, vanna is approximated as

$$\begin{aligned}\text{Vanna} \approx 2\sqrt{v_0}\big[C\left(S+dS,v,t;v_0+dv\right) - C(S+dS,v,t;v_0-dv) \\ -C\left(S-dS,v,t;v_0+dv\right) + C(S-dS,v,t;v_0-dv)]/(4dSdv)\big]. \quad (11.30)\end{aligned}$$

NUMERICAL IMPLEMENTATION OF THE GREEKS

The Matlab function HestonGreeksProb.m contains the integrands to compute the Greeks in closed form. The first part of the function calculates the coefficients $C_j(\tau,\phi)$ and $D_j(\tau,\phi)$, and calculates the characteristic functions $f_j(\phi)$ in the usual way. The second part of the function returns the integrands. Delta in Equation (11.4) and rho in (11.6) require P_j, so the function simply returns the integrand for P_j.

```
function y = HestonGreeksProb(phi,...,Greek);
f = exp(C + D*v + i*phi*x);
if strcmp(Greek,'Delta') | strcmp(Greek,'Rho')
    y = real(exp(-i*phi*log(K))*f/i/phi);
```

Gamma requires the integrand specified in (11.5).

```
elseif strcmp(Greek,'Gamma')
    y = real(exp(-i*phi*log(K))*f);
```

Theta is slightly more complicated because the derivatives for $C_j(\tau,\phi)$ and $D_j(\tau,\phi)$ in (11.9) need to be obtained.

```
elseif strcmp(Greek,'Theta')
    dD = d*exp(d*tau)*(b-rho*sigma*phi*i+d)*(g-1) ...;
    dC = (r-q)*phi*i + kappa*theta/sigma^2 ...;
    df = f*(dC + dD*v);
    y = real(exp(-i*phi*log(K))*df/i/phi);
```

The first vega ($\mathcal{V}_1$) is straightforward since only the integrand in (11.12) is required.

```
elseif strcmp(Greek,'Vega1')
    y = real(exp(-i*phi*log(K))*f*D/i/phi);
```

The second vega ($\mathcal{V}_2$) is straightforward also, and uses the integrand in (11.15). It allows for the "Little Trap" formulation of Albrecher et al. (2007).

```
elseif strcmp(Greek,'Vega2')
    if Trap==1
        dC = kappa/sigma^2*((b - rho*sigma*i*phi - d)*tau ...);
    elseif Trap==0
        dC = kappa/sigma^2*((b - rho*sigma*i*phi + d)*tau ...);
    end
    df =f*dC;
    y = real(exp(-i*phi*log(K))*df/i/phi);
```

Volga in Equation (11.18) requires the integrand in (11.22).

```
elseif strcmp(Greek,'Volga')
    y = real(exp(-i*phi*log(K))*f*D^2/i/phi);
```

Finally, the risk sensitivities with respect to ρ, σ, κ in Equation (11.24) require the derivatives in (11.26) which are lengthy and, therefore, not presented in their entirety. The integrand for the correlation sensitivity, for example, is the following.

```
elseif strcmp(Greek,'Corr')
    if Pnum==1
        dCdr = kappa*theta/sigma^2*((-sigma-sigma  ...;
        dDdr = (-sigma-sigma*i*phi+1/2/(rho^2*sigma ...;
    elseif Pnum==2
        dCdr = kappa*theta/sigma^2*((-sigma*i*phi+1 ...;
        dDdr = (-sigma*i*phi+1/2/(rho^2*sigma^2*i^2 ...;
    end
    y = real(exp(-i*phi*log(K))*f*(dCdr + dDdr*v)/i/phi);
```

The derivatives in (11.26) were evaluated symbolically using the Matlab file SymbolicDerivatives.m, and pasted into the HestonGreeksProb.m function described above.

To calculate the Greeks, the HestonGreeksProb.m function is then passed to the HestonGreeks.m function, which performs the required integration using Gauss-Laguerre integration, and returns the desired Greek. To conserve space, parts of the function have been removed.

```
function y = HestonGreeks(PutCall,...,Greek)
if strcmp(Greek,'Delta')
   for k=1:length(x);
      int1(k) = w(k)*HestonGreeksProb(x(k),...1,'Delta');
   end
   P1 = 1/2 + 1/pi*sum(int1);
   y = exp(-q*T)*P1;
elseif strcmp(Greek,'Volga')
   for k=1:length(x)
      int1(k) = w(k)*HestonGreeksProb(x(k),...,1,'Vega1');
      int2(k) = w(k)*HestonGreeksProb(x(k),...,2,'Vega1');
   end
   dP1 = 1/pi*sum(int1)*2*sqrt(v0);
   dP2 = 1/pi*sum(int2)*2*sqrt(v0);
   Vega1 = S*exp(-q*T)*dP1 - K*exp(-r*T)*dP2;
   for k=1:length(x);
      int1(k) = w(k)*HestonGreeksProb(x(k),...,1,'Volga');
      int2(k) = w(k)*HestonGreeksProb(x(k),...,2,'Volga');
   end
   dP1 = 1/pi*sum(int1);
   dP2 = 1/pi*sum(int2);
   dC2 = S*exp(-q*T)*dP1 - K*exp(-r*T)*dP2;
   y = 4*sqrt(v0)*(dC2*sqrt(v0) + Vega1/4/v0);
elseif strcmp(Greek,'Corr') | strcmp(Greek,'Sigma') ...;
   for k=1:length(x)
      int1(k) = w(k)*HestonGreeksProb(x(k),...,1,Greek);
      int2(k) = w(k)*HestonGreeksProb(x(k),...,2,Greek);
   end
   dP1 = 1/pi*sum(int1);
   dP2 = 1/pi*sum(int2);
   y = S*exp(-q*T)*dP1 - K*exp(-r*T)*dP2;
end
```

The C# code for the Heston Greeks is very similar and is not presented here. The only difference is that, in C#, we do not calculate the sensitivity with respect to ρ, κ, and σ in closed form, but using finite differences only.

To illustrate the calculation of the Greeks, recall from Chapter 1 that when we set $\sigma = 0$ and $\theta = v_0$ in the Heston model, we retrieve the Black-Scholes model exactly. We also saw in that chapter that we cannot simply set $\sigma = 0$ in the Heston characteristic function, since that will entail division by zero. We can, however, set σ to be small, and set $\theta = v_0$. We will then obtain Heston prices that are close to Black-Scholes prices, and we can compare the Heston Greeks with the Black-Scholes Greeks, which are all available in closed form, in Haug (2006), for example.

TABLE 11.1 Comparison of Greeks Under Heston and Black-Scholes

Greek	Closed Form	Finite Differences	Black-Scholes
Delta (Δ_C)	0.5501	0.5501	0.5501
Gamma (Γ)	0.0208	0.0208	0.0208
Rho (ρ_C)	23.6031	23.6031	23.6030
Theta (Θ_C)	−7.9833	−7.9837	−7.9834
Vega #1 ($\mathcal{V}_1$)	27.4908	27.4908	27.4909
Vanna	0.0589	0.0589	0.0589
Volga	−0.6153	−0.6154	−0.6123

TABLE 11.2 Comparison of Heston Parameter Sensitivities

Parameter	Closed Form	Finite Differences
Vega #2 ($\mathcal{V}_2$)	17.4217	17.4217
Correlation (ρ)	0.0726	0.0726
Mean Reversion (κ)	0.0169	0.0169
Volatility (σ)	−0.4900	−0.4899

We use the following settings: $S = K = 100$, $r = 0.05$, $q = 0.03$, and a maturity of 6 months. In addition, we set $\kappa = 0$, $\theta = v_0 = 0.07$, $\rho = -0.8$, and $\sigma = 0.0001$. The Heston and Black-Scholes price of a call with these features are each 7.8057. The Heston Greeks obtained using their closed forms, the Heston Greeks by finite differences, and the Black-Scholes Greeks, are all presented in Table 11.1.

The three sets of Greeks are all very close, which suggests that the closed form expressions and their finite difference equivalents are sensible. To generate Vega #2 and the sensitivities to ρ, σ, and κ in Equation (11.24), we keep the same settings but change $\kappa = 5$ and $\sigma = 0.35$. Since there are no Black-Scholes counterparts, only the closed form and finite difference equivalents are presented in Table 11.2.

Again, the Greeks produced by both methods are very close. Finally, the Matlab function HestonGreeksConsolidated.m implements the Greeks by differentiation of the consolidated form of the call price in (11.27). The function is similar to the HestonGreeks.m function and is not presented in its entirety.

```
function y = HestonGreeksConsolidated(...,Greek)
for j=1:N
    phi = x(j);
    f1 = HestonCF(phi-i,...);
    f2 = HestonCF(phi  ,...);
    if strcmp(Greek,'Price')
        int(j) = w(j) * real(exp(-i*phi*log(K) ...;
    elseif strcmp(Greek,'Delta')
        df1 = f1 * (i*phi+1)/S;
        df2 = f2 * i*phi/S;
        int(j) = w(j) * real(exp(-i*phi*log(K) ...;
    end
end
```

```
Integral = sum(int);
if strcmp(Greek,'Price')
    y = S*exp(-q*tau)/2 - K*exp(-r*tau)/2 + (1/pi)*Integral;
elseif strcmp(Greek,'Delta')
    y = exp(-q*tau)/2 + (1/pi)*Integral;
end
```

For convenience, the coefficient $D_2(\tau,\phi)$ is calculated in a separate function, D.m.

```
function y = D(phi,...)
if Trap==1
    % "Little Heston Trap" formulation
    c = 1/g;
    y = (b - rho*sigma*i*phi - d)/sigma^2 ...;
elseif Trap==0
    % Original Heston formulation.
    y = (b - rho*sigma*i*phi + d)/sigma^2 ...;
end
```

The DiffTau.m function returns the derivatives of $C_2(\tau,\phi)$ and $D_2(\tau,\phi)$ with respect to τ.

```
function [dC dD] = DiffTau(phi,...)
if trap==1
    C = (r-q)*i*phi*tau + a/sigma^2 ...;
    D = (b - rho*sigma*i*phi - d)/sigma^2 ...;
elseif trap==0
    C = (r-q)*i*phi*tau + a/sigma^2 ...;
    D = (b - rho*sigma*i*phi + d)/sigma^2 ...;
end
dD = d*exp(d*tau)*(b-rho*sigma*phi*i+d)*(g-1) ...;
dC = (r-q)*phi*i + kappa*theta/sigma^2 ...;
```

The C# code to calculate Greeks for the consolidated form in Equation (11.27) is similar and is not presented here.

It is informative to present visual illustrations of the Greeks. Figure 11.1 presents a plot of gamma from the Heston model. The mesh with black squares represents gamma with $\rho = -0.9$ and the smooth-colored surface, gamma with $\rho = 0.9$.

Figure 11.2 presents theta with the same parameter settings. Again, the mesh with black squares corresponds to negative correlation.

In Chapter 2, we saw that the correlation parameter introduces skewness in the Heston (1993) terminal stock price density, with negative correlation

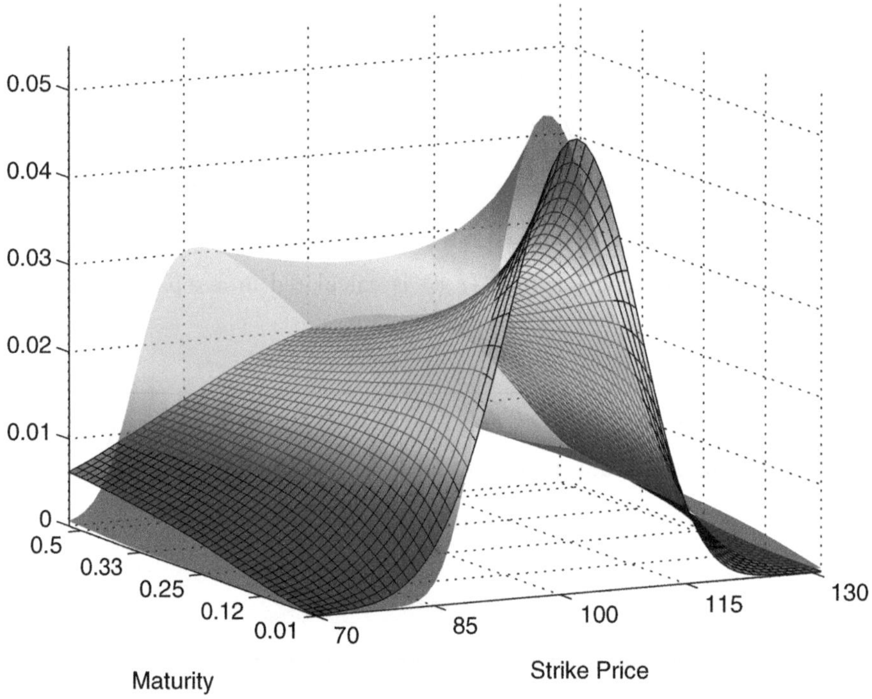

FIGURE 11.1 Gamma from the Heston Model

leading to a negative skew, and positive correlation, to a positive skew. This effect is introduced in the Heston Greeks also, and the skewed patterns are discernible in Figures 11.1 and 11.2.

The figures were created with the following Matlab code.

```
[x w] = GenerateGaussLaguerre(32);
T = [1/12:.01:.5];
S = [70:130];
GreekChoice = 'Gamma';
rhop =  0.9;
rhon = -0.9;
for s=1:length(S);
    for t=1:length(T);
        GreekP(s,t) = HestonGreeks(rhop,GreekChoice,...);
        GreekN(s,t) = HestonGreeks(rhon,GreekChoice,...);
    end
end
```

The code can be easily modified to plot the other Greeks described in this section.

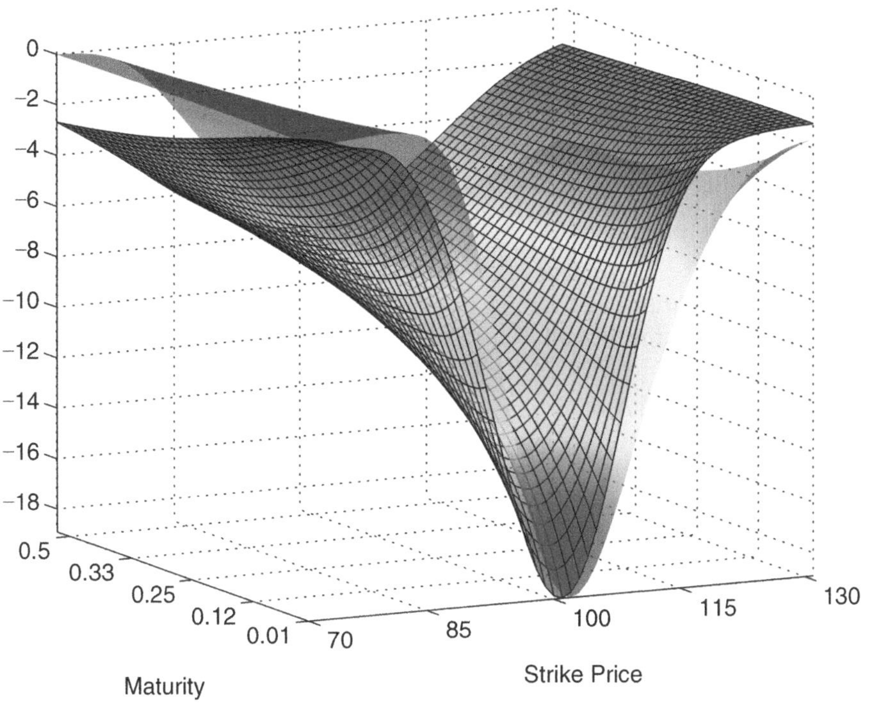

FIGURE 11.2 Theta from the Heston Model

GREEKS UNDER THE ATTARI AND CARR-MADAN FORMULATIONS

In the previous sections, we derived and implemented the Greeks under the original Heston (1993) formulation of the call price. It is also possible to derive analytic expressions for the Greeks under alternate formulations, such as those encountered in previous chapters. It is straightforward to obtain delta and gamma using the Attari (2004) expression for the call price, as explained by Zhu (2010). Recall from Chapter 3 that the call price in this model is given by

$$C(K) = S_t - \frac{1}{2}Ke^{-r\tau} - \frac{Ke^{-r\tau}}{\pi}\int_0^\infty A(u)du.$$

The integrand is

$$\begin{aligned} A(u) &= \frac{\left(R_2 + \frac{I_2}{u}\right)\cos(\ell u) + \left(I_2 - \frac{R_2}{u}\right)\sin(\ell u)}{1+u^2} \\ &= \frac{F(u)\cos(\ell u) + G(u)\sin(\ell u)}{1+u^2} \end{aligned} \tag{11.31}$$

where $\ell = \ln(Ke^{-r\tau}/S_t)$. In the integrand (11.31), $R_2 = \text{Re}[\varphi_2(u)]$ and $I_2 = \text{Im}[\varphi_2(u)]$ denote the real and imaginary parts, respectively, of the Attari (2004) characteristic function $\varphi_2(u)$ given by

$$\varphi_2(u) = \exp(C_2(\tau,u) + D_2(\tau,u)v_0 - iur\tau). \tag{11.32}$$

In (11.32), the coefficients $C_2(\tau,u)$ and $D_2(\tau,u)$ are those of the Heston (1993) characteristic function, $f_2(u)$, and v_0 is the spot variance parameter. We saw in Chapter 3 that $\varphi_2(u)$ is independent of the spot price S_t. The dependency of $A(u)$ on S_t arises through the parameter ℓ only. Consequently, it is straightforward to derive the expression for delta for the call

$$\Delta_C = 1 - \frac{Ke^{-r\tau}}{\pi}\int_0^\infty \frac{\partial A(u)}{\partial S}du. \tag{11.33}$$

By applying the chain rule, we obtain the integrand in (11.33) as

$$\frac{\partial A(u)}{\partial S} = \frac{-F(u)\sin(\ell u) + G(u)\cos(\ell u)}{1+u^2} \times \left(-\frac{u}{S}\right) \tag{11.34}$$

since $\partial(\ell u)/\partial S = -u/S$. Gamma is given by

$$\Gamma = -\frac{Ke^{-r\tau}}{\pi}\int_0^\infty \frac{\partial^2 A(u)}{\partial S^2}du \tag{11.35}$$

with integrand

$$\frac{\partial^2 A(u)}{\partial S^2} = \frac{-F(u)(\cos(\ell u)u + \sin(\ell u)) + G(u)(-\sin(\ell u)u + \cos(\ell u))}{1+u^2} \times \left(\frac{u}{S^2}\right). \tag{11.36}$$

In the Attari (2004) formulation of the call price, delta and gamma are easily obtained in closed form because $\varphi_2(u)$ does not depend on the spot price S_t. It is not practical to obtain the other Greeks in this manner, because the parameter for the Greek will appear in $\varphi_2(u)$. Indeed, to obtain the derivatives of $A(u)$, we would need to separate the real and imaginary parts of $\varphi_2(u)$, as specified in Equation (11.31), and obtain the derivatives of these parts separately. We can still obtain the Greeks in the model using finite differences, however.

The Matlab function AttariProbGreeks.m calculates the integrand required for delta and gamma in Equations (11.34) and (11.36). It is very similar to the AttariProb.m function presented in Chapter 3 and is, therefore, not presented here in its entirety.

```
function A = AttariProbGreeks(u,...,Greek)
% The c.f. for Attari and L function.
f = exp(C + D*v0 - i*u*r*tau);
L  = log(exp(-r*tau)*K/S0);
```

```
% The coefficients
F = (real(f) + imag(f)/u);
G = (imag(f) - real(f)/u);
% Return the integrand for the chosen Greek
if strcmp(Greek,'Delta');
    A = (F*sin(L*u) - G*cos(L*u)) * u/S0/(1+u^2);
elseif strcmp(Greek,'Gamma');
    y = (-F*(cos(L*u)*u + sin(L*u)) + ...;
    A = y * u/S0^2/(1+u^2);
end
```

This function is passed to the AttariGreeks.m function, which uses numerical integration to calculate delta using Equation (11.33), or gamma using (11.35).

```
function y = AttariGreeks(PutCall,...,Greek)
for j=1:length(x);
    if strcmp(Greek,'Delta')
        A(j) = w(j)*AttariProbGreeks(x(j),...,'Delta');
    elseif strcmp(Greek,'Gamma')
        A(j) = w(j)*AttariProbGreeks(x(j),...,'Gamma');
    end
end
Integral = sum(A);
if strcmp(Greek,'Gamma')
    y = -exp(-r*T)*K/pi*Integral;
elseif strcmp(Greek,'Delta')
    if strcmp(PutCall,'C')
        y = 1 - exp(-r*T)*K/pi*Integral;
    else
        y = - exp(-r*T)*K/pi*Integral;
    end
end
```

Using finite difference approximations, it is easy to verify that the AttariGreeks.m function produces values of delta and gamma that are quite accurate. Finally, the C# code for these two Greeks in the Attari (2004) model is similar and not presented.

We can also derive closed-form expressions for the Greeks under the Carr and Madan (1999) formulation of the call price, which we first encountered in Chapter 3. Recall that the call price under their formulation is

$$C(k) = \frac{e^{-\alpha k}}{\pi} \int_0^\infty \mathrm{Re}\left[e^{-ivk} \frac{e^{-r\tau} f_2 \left(v - (\alpha + 1)\, i\right)}{\alpha^2 + \alpha - v^2 + iv(2\alpha + 1)} \right] dv \tag{11.37}$$

where α is the damping factor, k is the logarithm of the strike price, and f_2 is the Heston (1993) characteristic function for $x_T = \ln S_T$. To obtain the Greeks, we simply differentiate f_2, substitute into (11.37) and evaluate the integral. Theta and rho are slightly more complicated, because we need to apply the product rule to $e^{-r\tau}f_2$ in (11.37). Theta, for example, is obtained as

$$\Theta_C = -\frac{e^{-\alpha k}}{\pi}\int_0^{\infty} \text{Re}\left[e^{-ivk}\frac{e^{-r\tau}\left(-rf_2 + \partial f_2/\partial\tau\right)}{\alpha^2+\alpha-v^2+iv(2\alpha+1)}\right]dv \tag{11.38}$$

where f_2 and $\partial f_2/\partial\tau$ are both evaluated at $v-(\alpha+1)i$. To calculate volga for $\upsilon = \sqrt{v_0}$, note that an application of the chain rule produces $\partial^2 f_2/\partial\upsilon^2 = 2D_2f_2(2D_2v_0+1)$, where $D_2 = D_2(\tau, v)$ is the coefficient for the Heston characteristic function.

The Matlab function HestonCFGreek.m returns the derivative of f_2, which is required to obtain the Greeks for the Carr and Madan (1999) call price. The function also returns the call price, if desired, by returning f_2 itself rather than a derivative. It is similar to the HestonGreeksProb.m function defined earlier in this chapter.

```
function df = HestonCFGreek(phi,...,Greek)
% The characteristic function.
f = exp(C + D.*v0 + i.*phi.*x0);
% Derivatives of f2 required for the Greeks
if strcmp(Greek,'Price');
    df = f;
elseif strcmp(Greek,'Delta')
    df = f*i*phi/S;
elseif strcmp(Greek,'Gamma')
    df = i*phi*f*(i*phi - 1)/S^2;
elseif strcmp(Greek,'Theta')
    dDdT = d*exp(d*tau)*(b-rho*sigma*phi*i+d)...;
    dCdT = r*phi*i + kappa*theta/sigma^2...;
    df = r*f - f*(dCdT + dDdT*v0);
elseif strcmp(Greek,'Rho')
    dCdr = i*phi*tau;
    df = (f*dCdr - tau*f);
elseif strcmp(Greek,'Vega1')
    df = f*D;
elseif strcmp(Greek,'Vanna')
    df = f*i*phi*D/S;
elseif strcmp(Greek,'Volga')
    df = 2*D*f*(2*D*v0 + 1);
end
```

The derivatives are then passed to the CarrMadanGreeks.m function, which uses numerical integration and returns delta, gamma, theta, rho, vega1, vanna, and volga, or the call price. Both functions can be easily modified to return additional option sensitivities.

```
function y = CarrMadanGreeks(alpha,...,Greek)
% Perform the numerical integration
for j=1:length(x)
    u    = x(j);
    I(j) = exp(-i*u*log(K))*HestonCFGreek(u-(alpha+1)*i,...,Greek) ...;
    I(j) = w(j)*real(I(j));
end
% Calculate the desired Greek
if strcmp(Greek,'Delta') || strcmp(Greek,'Gamma') ...
    y = exp(-alpha*log(K))*sum(I)/pi;
elseif strcmp(Greek,'Vega1') || strcmp(Greek,'Vanna')
    y = exp(-alpha*log(K))*sum(I)/pi * 2*sqrt(v0);
end
```

It is straightforward to verify that the Greeks calculated with this function produce values that are close to their finite difference approximations. The C# code to implement the Greeks under the Carr and Madan (1999) formulation is similar to the Matlab code and not presented here.

GREEKS UNDER THE LEWIS FORMULATIONS

Recall from Chapter 4 that the Lewis (2000) expressions for the call price can be written in terms of the fundamental transform $\hat{H}(k, v, \tau)$ as

$$C_1(K) = -\frac{Ke^{-r\tau}}{\pi}\int_0^\infty \mathrm{Re}\left[\frac{e^{-ikX}}{k^2 - ik}\hat{H}\left(k, v, \tau\right)\right] dk \tag{11.39}$$

for $1 < k_i < \beta$, and as

$$C_2(K) = S_t e^{-q\tau} - \frac{Ke^{-r\tau}}{\pi}\int_0^\infty \mathrm{Re}\left[\frac{e^{-ikX}}{k^2 - ik}\hat{H}\left(k, v, \tau\right)\right] dk \tag{11.40}$$

for $\max(0, \alpha) < k_i < \min(1, \beta)$ and where $X = \ln(S_t/K) + (r - q)\tau$. We can readily differentiate the integrands for $C_1(K)$ and $C_2(K)$ to obtain analytical expressions for the Greeks, as we did in the previous sections. Gamma, for example, is given by

$$\Gamma = \frac{Ke^{-r\tau}}{\pi S^2}\int_0^\infty \mathrm{Re}[e^{-ikX}\hat{H}(k, v, \tau)]\, dk. \tag{11.41}$$

The Matlab function LewisIntegrandGreek.m is a modification of the function LewisIntegrand.m from Chapter 4 and returns the integrand required for the calculation of Greeks using either $C_1(K)$ or $C_2(K)$. It also returns the integrand for the price itself.

```
function y = LewisIntegrandGreek(k,...,Greek)
% The fundamental transform, H(k,S,t)
H = exp(C + D*v0);
% Return the real part of the integrand
if strcmp(Greek,'Price')
    y = real(exp(-X*i*k-r*tau)/(k^2-i*k)*H);
elseif strcmp(Greek,'Delta')
    y = real(exp(-X*i*k-r*tau)/(k^2-i*k)*H*(-i*k/S));
elseif strcmp(Greek,'Gamma')
    y = -real(exp(-X*i*k-r*tau)*H/S^2);
elseif strcmp(Greek,'Vega1')
    y = real(exp(-X*i*k-r*tau)/(k^2-i*k)*H*D)*2*sqrt(v0);
elseif strcmp(Greek,'Rho')
    y = real(exp(-X*i*k-r*tau)*(-i*k*tau-tau)/(k^2-i*k)*H);
elseif strcmp(Greek,'Theta')
    dC = kappa*theta*((kappa+d)/2 + g*d*exp(d*t) ...;
    dD = (kappa+d)/2*exp(d*t)*d*(g-1)/(1-g*exp(d*t)) ...;
    y =  real((-i*k*(r-q)-r + (dC+dD*v0))*H*exp(-X*i ...;
elseif strcmp(Greek,'Volga')
    I = exp(-X*i*k-r*tau)/(k^2-i*k)*H*D*D*sqrt(v0) ...
    y = real(I)*4*sqrt(v0);
elseif strcmp(Greek,'Vanna')
    y = real(exp(-X*i*k-r*tau)/(k^2-i*k)*H*D*(-i*k/S))*2*sqrt(v0);
end
```

The function is passed to the Matlab function HestonLewisGreekPrice.m. The C# code is similar and not presented here.

The option price $C(S_t)$ derived by Lewis (2001) that uses Parseval's identity was covered in Chapter 4 also. The form that uses $k_i = \frac{1}{2}$ is Equation (3.11) of Lewis (2001)

$$C(S_t) = S_t e^{-q\tau} - \frac{\sqrt{KS_t}e^{-(r+q)\tau/2}}{\pi}\int_0^\infty \text{Re}\left[e^{iuX}\varphi\left(u-\frac{1}{2}i\right)\frac{1}{u^2+\dfrac{1}{4}}\right]du$$

$$= S_t e^{-q\tau} - \frac{\sqrt{K}}{\pi}\int_0^\infty \text{Re}\left[\frac{K^{-iu}e^{-r\tau}f_2\left(u-\dfrac{1}{2}i\right)}{u^2+\dfrac{1}{4}}\right]du$$

where X is defined after (11.40). We have used the fact from Chapter 4 that $\varphi(u) = f_2(u)e^{-iuY}$, where $Y = \ln S_t + (r-q)\tau$ and f_2 is the Heston (1993) characteristic function. Again, by straightforward differentiation of $C(S_t)$ we can obtain the Greeks for this form of the Lewis (2001) price. The Matlab function LewisGreeks311.m and the C# function LewisGreeks311() are used to implement the Greeks for the call price $C(S_t)$ from Equation (3.11) of Lewis (2001). These functions are similar to the ones presented in earlier sections and are not presented.

Table 11.3 presents Greeks calculated using the closed forms derived in this chapter. We use the following settings: $S = K = 100$, $\tau = 0.25$, $r = 0.05$, and $q = 0$, along with the parameter values $\kappa = 2$, $\theta = v_0 = 0.05$, $\sigma = 0.1$, and $\rho = -0.9$.

TABLE 11.3 Closed-Form Greeks Under Various Forms

Greek	Heston (1993)	Attari (2004)	Carr and Madan (1999)	Lewis (2000)	Lewis (2001)
Price	5.0836	5.0836	5.0837	5.0747	5.0796
Delta	0.5833	0.5833	0.5833	0.5666	0.5833
Gamma	0.0347	0.0347	0.0347	0.0353	0.0347
Theta	−11.3995	–	−11.4004	−11.3464	−11.4009
Rho	13.3128	–	13.3127	12.8969	13.3133
Vega 1	15.3911	–	15.3909	15.4812	15.3915
Vanna	−0.1257	–	−0.1257	0.0516	−0.1257
Volga	15.5081	–	15.4273	15.7285	15.4054

GREEKS USING THE FFT AND FRFT

We saw in Chapter 5 that the fast Fourier transform (FFT) and fractional fast Fourier transform (FRFT) are both able to produce call prices very quickly and for a wide range of strikes simultaneously. It is straightforward to adapt these methods to produce the Greeks in the same manner. Recall from Chapter 5 that to implement the FFT on the call price, we construct the integration grid $\{v_j\}_{j=1}^N$ and the log-strike grid $\{k_u\}_{u=1}^N$, and calculate the points $x_j = \exp(i(b - \ln S_t)v_j)\psi(v_j)w_j$ for $j = 1, \ldots, N$. We then obtain $\hat{x}_u = C(k_u)$, the call price evaluated at the log-strike point k_u, as the sum

$$\hat{x}_u = \frac{\eta e^{-\alpha k_u}}{\pi} \sum_{j=1}^{N} \text{Re}\left[e^{-i\frac{2\pi}{N}(j-1)(u-1)} x_j\right] \quad \text{for } u = 1, \ldots, N. \tag{11.42}$$

To obtain a set of Greeks with the FFT, in x_j we simply replace the term

$$\psi(v_j) = \frac{e^{-r\tau} f_2(v_j - (\alpha + 1)i)}{\alpha^2 + \alpha - v_j^2 + iv_j(2\alpha + 1)} \tag{11.43}$$

with a modified version that uses the derivative of f_2 instead of f_2, such as that for theta in Equation (11.38), for example. We use this modification to obtain the Greeks under the fractional fast Fourier transform also.

Implementing the Greeks with the FFT requires a slight modification of the code presented in Chapter 5. The Matlab function HestonCallFFTGreek.m is nearly identical to the HestonCallFFT.m function from that chapter, except that it uses the Matlab function HestonCFGreek.m for the characteristic function. This function returns either the characteristic function or its derivatives through an extra function argument.

```
function [CallFFT K lambdainc eta] = HestonCallFFTGreek(...,Greek)
if fast==1
    % Implement the FFT - fast algorithm
    U = [0:N-1];
    J = [0:N-1];
```

```
    psi = HestonCFGreek(v-(alpha+1).*i,...,Greek);
    phi = exp(-r*tau).*psi ./ (alpha.^2 + alpha - v.^2 + ...;
    x = exp(i.*(b-s0).*v).*phi.*w;
    e = exp(-i*2*pi/N.*(U'*J))*x;
    CallFFT = eta.*exp(-alpha.*k)./pi .* real(e);
end
```

The Matlab function HestonCallFRFTGreek.m is used to implement the fractional FFT Greeks and incorporates the same modification.

The following code snippet implements the FFT or FRFT Greeks for the Carr and Madan (1999) formulation using Simpson's rule. It also uses the CarrMadanGreeks.m function defined in an earlier section to compare the accuracy of the Greeks obtained in this manner.

```
rule = 'S';
Greek = {'Price','Delta','Gamma','Theta','Rho','Vega1','Vanna','Volga'};
% FFT or FRFT
for j=1:8;
    if strcmp(method,'FFT')
        [GreeksFFT(:,j) ...] = HestonCallFFTGreek(...,Greek(j));
    else
        [GreeksFFT(:,j) ...] = HestonCallFRFTGreek(...,Greek(j));
    end
end
% Closed form Greeks and errors
GreeksCM = zeros(length(ATM),8);
for k=1:length(K);
    for j=1:8
        GreeksCM(k,j)  = CarrMadanGreeks(...,Greek(j));
    end
end
for j=1:8
    error(j) = sum(abs(GreeksCM(:,j) - GreeksFFT(:,j)));
end
```

The C# code to implement Greeks using the FFT and FRFT is similar and not presented here.

To illustrate, we run the FRFT Greeks using a spot price of $S_0 = 100$ and a maturity of 6 months, with 2^9 points. The strikes are in increments of \$0.50. The results are in Table 11.4, along with the sum of absolute errors from the true Greek values obtained from the Carr and Madan (1999) formulation.

The table indicates that the Greeks obtained from the fractional FFT are very accurate. The Greeks from the FFT itself are not presented in Table 11.4, but they are very accurate also.

AMERICAN GREEKS USING SIMULATION

Recall that in Chapter 8 we used the Least-Squares Monte Carlo (LSM) algorithm of Longstaff and Schwartz (2001) to value American options in the Heston model.

TABLE 11.4 Greeks from the Fractional Fast Fourier Transform

Strike	Price	Delta	Gamma	Theta	Rho	$Vega_1$	Vanna	Volga
98.02	9.21	0.649	0.021	−9.25	27.85	16.63	−0.188	27.77
98.51	8.93	0.638	0.021	−9.27	27.46	16.80	−0.163	27.44
99.00	8.66	0.628	0.022	−9.28	27.06	16.96	−0.137	27.14
99.50	8.39	0.617	0.022	−9.29	26.64	17.11	−0.111	26.88
100.00	8.12	0.606	0.022	−9.29	26.23	17.25	−0.084	26.66
100.50	7.86	0.595	0.022	−9.29	25.80	17.37	−0.056	26.49
101.01	7.61	0.583	0.023	−9.28	25.36	17.48	−0.028	26.36
Error	4.5×10^{-6}	5.2×10^{-6}	5.2×10^{-7}	1.8×10^{-4}	4.5×10^{-6}	5.2×10^{-6}	5.2×10^{-7}	1.8×10^{-4}

This algorithm can be modified to calculate American Greeks also. In order for the Greeks to be accurate, however, we must store the values of the correlated normal random variables used to generate the stock price and volatility paths, and apply these same random variables when we generate the paths under the shifted values of the inputs. This ensures that any differences between the original paths and the shifted paths are due to the shifts themselves, and not to simulation noise.

It is straightforward to modify the simulation functions of Chapter 7 to obtain Greeks for American options with the LSM algorithm. The first task is to create matrices of simulated correlated random variables outside of the functions, and pass these matrices as function arguments. The Matlab function MMSimGreeks.m is a simple modified version of the MMSim.m function encountered in Chapter 7 for the moment-matching simulation scheme of Andersen and Brotherton-Ratcliffe (2005). The only difference is that the correlated random variables Z_S and Z_V are generated outside the function and passed to the function in its argument.

```
function [S V] = MMSimGreeks(params,...,Zv,Zs)
% Generate the stock and volatility paths
for i=1:N;
    for t=2:T;
        % Matched moment lognormal approximation
        dW = sqrt(dt)*Zv(t,i);
        num = 0.5*sigma^2*V(t-1,i)*(1-exp(-2*kappa*dt)) ...;
        den = (exp(-kappa*dt)*V(t-1,i) + (1-exp(-kappa ...;
        Gam = log(1 + num/den);
        V(t,i) = (exp(-kappa*dt)*V(t-1,i) + (1-exp ...;
        % Euler/Milstein discretization log stock prices
        S(t,i) = S(t-1,i)*exp((r-q-V(t-1,i)/2)*dt + ...;
    end
end
```

To calculate the Greeks, we generate the matrices of correlated random variables, and we generate a series of stock price paths using the same random variables but using shifted values of the inputs. Hence, if we wish to estimate delta and gamma with central differences, we need to shift the spot price twice to obtain two sets of shifted stock price paths. This is accomplished with the Matlab function LSMGreeks.m.

```
function [Euro Amer] = LSMGreeks(...,NT,NS,Zv,Zs,Greek)
ds = 0.01*S;
dv = 0.01*v0;
if strcmp(Greek,'delta') || strcmp(Greek,'gamma')
    [Spathsp V] = MMSimGreeks(params,S+ds,...);
    [Spathsm V] = MMSimGreeks(params,S-ds,...);
    [EuroPricep AmerPricep] = LSM(Spathsp',...);
    [EuroPricem AmerPricem] = LSM(Spathsm',...);
    if strcmp(Greek,'delta')
        Euro = (EuroPricep - EuroPricem)/2/ds;
        Amer = (AmerPricep - AmerPricem)/2/ds;
    else
        [Spaths V] = MMSimGreeks(params,S,...);
        [EuroPrice AmerPrice] = LSM(Spaths',...);
        Amer = (AmerPricep - 2*AmerPrice + AmerPricem)/ds^2;
        Euro = (EuroPricep - 2*EuroPrice + EuroPricem)/ds^2;
    end
end
if strcmp(Greek,'vega1')
    paramsp = [kappa theta sigma v0+dv rho lambda];
    paramsm = [kappa theta sigma v0-dv rho lambda];
    [Spathsp V] = MMSimGreeks(paramsp,S,...);
    [Spathsm V] = MMSimGreeks(paramsm,S,...);
    [EuroPricep AmerPricep] = LSM(Spathsp',...);
    [EuroPricem AmerPricem] = LSM(Spathsm',...);
    Euro = (EuroPricep - EuroPricem)/2/dv*2*sqrt(v0);
    Amer = (AmerPricep - AmerPricem)/2/dv*2*sqrt(v0);
end
```

The LSMGreeks.m function is used in the following code, which generates delta and gamma only.

```
% Matrices for the correlated N(0,1) random variables
Zv = randn(NT,NS);
Zs = rho.*Zv + sqrt(1-rho.^2).*randn(NT,NS);
[EuroDelta AmerDelta] = LSMGreeks(...,'delta');
[EuroGamma AmerGamma] = LSMGreeks(...,'gamma');
```

The C# code to obtain Greeks of American puts using the LSM algorithm of Longstaff and Schwartz (2001) is very similar and is not presented here. The only difference is that we need to create C# functions for obtaining regression parameter estimates and for generating random numbers. These functions are identical to those from Chapter 8, where they were used in the LSM algorithm to generate prices of American options.

To illustrate, we run the LSM algorithm on American puts, using the settings in Clarke and Parrott (1999) with the prices computed by Ikonen and Toivanen (2008), namely $K = 100$, $\tau = 0.25$, $r = 0.1$, $\kappa = 5$, $\theta = 0.16$, $\sigma = 0.9$, and $\rho = 0.1$, with spot price running from 8 to 12. We use $N_T = 1,000$ time steps and $N_S = 50,000$ stock price steps. The results are in Table 11.5.

TABLE 11.5 Prices and Greeks for American Puts, LSM Algorithm

Spot	Price	Delta	Gamma	Theta	Rho	Vega_1	Vanna
8	2.000	−0.999	0.006	0.006	0.005	−0.005	−0.480
9	1.111	−0.731	0.056	−0.835	−1.094	0.848	1.227
10	0.537	−0.431	0.255	−1.255	−0.726	0.983	−0.465
11	0.225	−0.211	0.168	−1.026	−0.427	0.675	−0.481
12	0.083	−0.086	0.089	−0.575	−0.240	0.317	−0.462

TABLE 11.6 Prices and Greeks for European Puts, LSM Algorithm

Spot	Closed Price	LSM Price	Closed Delta	LSM Delta	Closed Gamma	LSM Gamma	Closed Vega1	LSM Vega1
8	1.839	1.834	−0.880	−0.875	0.139	0.174	0.358	0.367
9	1.048	1.057	−0.681	−0.663	0.253	0.252	0.714	0.729
10	0.502	0.522	−0.411	−0.409	0.264	0.241	0.857	0.859
11	0.208	0.221	−0.193	−0.206	0.164	0.155	0.662	0.693
12	0.080	0.081	−0.078	−0.085	0.074	0.085	0.383	0.415

To evaluate the accuracy of the Greeks computed in this way, we can use the LSM algorithm to generate European option prices, using the same settings as those in Table 11.5 and compare the Greeks from the LSM algorithm to the closed form Greeks described previously. The prices and Greeks are in Table 11.6.

The results indicate that the Greeks calculated under the LSM algorithm are fairly close to their closed-form counterparts.

AMERICAN GREEKS USING THE EXPLICIT METHOD

Recall from Chapter 10 that when the Heston PDE is solved with finite differences, a matrix in the stock price and volatility dimensions is obtained that contains a complete set of option prices. Hence, the matrix contains shifted values of the call value in price and volatility, and finite differences can readily be applied to obtain the Greeks. This requires two-dimensional interpolation using the Matlab function interp2.m to obtain the call prices at the shifted values. In this manner, all the Greeks representing sensitivities in S and v_0 can be obtained, namely delta, gamma, vega1, vanna, and volga. The following code shows how this is done in Matlab for European options, using the explicit method along a non-uniform grid. The code uses the Matlab function HestonExplicitPDENonUniformGrid.m presented in Chapter 10 to approximate the Heston PDE along the two-dimensional grid.

```
PutCall = 'P';
EuroAmer = 'E';
[U u] = HestonExplicitPDENonUniformGrid(...,PutCall,EuroAmer);
PDEPrice = interp2(V,S,U,V0,S0);
% Delta and Gamma
dS = 1;
```

```
D1 = interp2(V,S,U,V0,S0+dS);
D2 = interp2(V,S,U,V0,S0-dS);
DeltaPDE = (D1-D2)/2/dS;
GammaPDE = (D1 - 2*PDEPrice + D2)/dS^2;
% Vega #1
dV = 1e-2;
V1 = interp2(V,S,U,V0+dV,S0);
V2 = interp2(V,S,U,V0-dV,S0);
Vega1PDE = (V1-V2)/2/dV*2*sqrt(V0);
C1 = interp2(V,S,U,V0+dV,S0+dS);
C2 = interp2(V,S,U,V0-dV,S0+dS);
C3 = interp2(V,S,U,V0+dV,S0-dS);
C4 = interp2(V,S,U,V0-dV,S0-dS);
% Vanna and Volga
VannaPDE = (C1 - C2 - C3 + C4)/4/dV/dS*2*sqrt(V0);
dC2 = (V1 - 2*PDEPrice + V2)/dV^2;
VolgaPDE = 4*sqrt(V0)*(dC2*sqrt(V0) + Vega1PDE/4/V0);
```

Theta can be obtained by recognizing that the HestonExplicitPDENonUniformGrid.m function retains the value of $U(S, v, t)$ in the previous time step, $U(S, v, t - dt)$, but overwrites this value only until maturity. This provides the time-shifted value of the derivative that is required for a finite difference approximation to theta. The code to obtain theta is the following.

```
[U u] = HestonExplicitPDENonUniformGrid(...);
% Theta
T1 = interp2(V,S,U,V0,S0);  % Obtain U(S,v,T)
T2 = interp2(V,S,u,V0,S0);  % Obtain U(S,v,T-dt)
ThetaPDE = -(T1 - T2)/dt;
```

Note that, in the first line, the function is modified to return both $U(S, v, \tau)$ and $U(S, v, \tau - dt)$, rather than $U(S, v, \tau)$ alone.

The explicit method can also be used to obtain Greeks of American options. The following code calculates American put prices and Greeks for the set of option prices of Clarke and Parrott (1999). A separate non-uniform grid is built for each spot price, and centered about the spot price.

```
S0 = [8 9 10 11 12];
for s=1:length(S0);
    % The stock price grid
    c = S0(s)/5;    % Instead of K/5
    dz = 1/nS*(asinh((Smax-S0(s))/c) - asinh(-S0(s)/c));
                                                % Instead of K/c
```

```
        for i=1:nS+1;
            z(i) = asinh(-S0(s)/c) + (i-1)*dz;     % Instead of K/c
            S(i) = S0(s) + c*sinh(z(i));
        end
        % The volatility grid
        d = Vmax/500;
        dn = asinh(Vmax/d)/nV;
        for j=1:nV+1
            n(j) = (j-1)*dn;
            V(j) = d*sinh(n(j));
        end
        % Solve the PDE
        [U u] = HestonExplicitPDENonUniformGrid(...);
        dS = 0.01*S0(s);
        dv = 0.01*v0;
        % Price, Delta, and Gamma
        PDEPrice(s) = interp2(V,S,U,v0,S0(s));
        D1 = interp2(V,S,U,v0,S0(s)+dS);
        D2 = interp2(V,S,U,v0,S0(s)-dS);
        DeltaPDE(s) = (D1 - D2)/2/dS;
        GammaPDE(s) = (D1 - 2*PDEPrice(s) + D2)/dS^2;
        % Vega #1
        V1 = interp2(V,S,U,v0+dv,S0(s));
        V2 = interp2(V,S,U,v0-dv,S0(s));
        dCdv0 = (V1 - V2)/2/dv;
        Vega1PDE(s) = dCdv0 * 2.0 * sqrt(v0);
        % Theta
        T1 = interp2(V,S,U,v0,S0(s));      % U(S,v,T)
        T2 = interp2(V,S,u,v0,S0(s));      % U(S,v,T-dt)
        Theta(s) = -(T1 - T2)/dt;
end
```

The C# code to generate Greeks of American options using the explicit method is very similar and uses the C# function HestonExplicitPDENonUniformGrid() introduced in Chapter 10 to approximate the PDE. This function must be modified to return both $U(S, v, \tau)$ and $U(S, v, \tau - dt)$ also. In C#, this can be done by creating a structure. The other difference is that we have created the C# function interp2() for two-dimensional linear interpolation. This function was presented in Chapter 10 also.

```
public struct Uu
{
    public double[,] bigU;
    public double[,] smallU;
}
```

```
for(int k=0;k<=N-1;k++)
{
    // Solve the PDE and return U(S,v,T) and U(S,v,T-dt);
    Uu output = HestonExplicitPDENonUniformGrid(...);
    double[,] U = output.bigU;
    double[,] u = output.smallU;
    // Price, Delta, Gamma
    PDEPrice[k] = interp2(V,S,U,V0,S0[k]);
    D1 = interp2(V,S,U,V0,S0[k]+dS);
    D2 = interp2(V,S,U,V0,S0[k]-dS);
    DeltaPDE[k] = (D1-D2)/2.0/dS;
    // Theta
    T1 = interp2(V,S,U,V0,S0[k]);        // U(S,v,T)
    T2 = interp2(V,S,u,V0,S0[k]);        // U(s,v,T-dt)
    ThetaPDE[k] = -(T1 - T2)/dt;
}
```

We use the settings of Clarke and Parrott (1999) and the prices of Ikonen and Toivanen (2008) that were used to generate Table 11.5, along with a stock price grid size of 80, a volatility grid size of 40, and 3,000 time steps. The results are in Table 11.7 and are close to those in Table 11.5. Note, however, that the Explicit Method is unable to accurately calculate vega1, volga, and theta for the deep in-the-money put in the first row.

AMERICAN GREEKS FROM MEDVEDEV AND SCAILLET

In Chapter 8, we presented the American put approximation of Medvedev and Scaillet (2010) and noted that one key advantage of this method is its ability to generate American put prices very quickly. Hence, calculating the Greeks in this model with finite differences does not require excessive computation time. This is accomplished with the Matlab function MSGreeks.m, which uses the MSPrice.m function for the Medvedev and Scaillet (2010) expansion presented in Chapter 8. As usual, parts of the function have been omitted.

TABLE 11.7 Greeks for American Puts, Explicit Method

Spot	Price	Delta	Gamma	Vega1	Vanna	Volga	Theta
8	2.0000	−0.9998	0.0058	0.0000	0.0408	0.0000	−0.0000
9	1.1042	−0.7483	0.3348	0.6662	0.4653	2.6647	−0.6497
10	0.5188	−0.4349	0.2797	0.8624	−0.0515	3.4496	−1.1288
11	0.2134	−0.2028	0.1721	0.6655	−0.2911	2.6620	−0.9875
12	0.0814	−0.0812	0.0780	0.3841	−0.2515	1.5362	−0.6198

```
function y = MSGreeksFD(params,...,Greek)
if strcmp(Greek,'price')
    [EuroPut AmerPutMS AmerPut EEP theta y] = MSPrice(...);
    y = EuroPut + EEP;
end
if (strcmp(Greek,'delta') || strcmp(Greek,'gamma'))
    ds = 0.01*S;
    AmerPutp = MSPrice(S+ds,...);
    AmerPutm = MSPrice(S-ds,...);
    if strcmp(Greek,'gamma')
        AmerPut = MSPrice(S,...);
        y = (AmerPutp - 2*AmerPut + AmerPutm)/ds^2;
    else
        y = (AmerPutp - AmerPutm)/2/ds;
    end
end
if strcmp(Greek,'theta')
    dt = 0.01*T;
    AmerPutp = MSPrice(T+dt,..);
    AmerPutm = MSPrice(T-dt,..);
    y = -(AmerPutp - AmerPutm)/2/dt;
end
if strcmp(Greek,'vega1') | strcmp(Greek,'volga')
    dv = 0.01*v0;
    AmerPutp = MSPrice(v0+dv,...);
    AmerPutm = MSPrice(v0-dv,...);
    Vega1 = (AmerPutp - AmerPutm)/2/dv*2*sqrt(v0);
    if strcmp(Greek,'volga')
        AmerPut = MSPrice(v0,...);
        dC2 = (AmerPutp - 2*AmerPut + AmerPutm)/(dv^2);
        y = 4*sqrt(v0)*(dC2*sqrt(v0) + Vega1/4/v0);
    else
        y = Vega1;
    end
end
```

The C# code to generate Greeks for the Medvedev and Scaillet (2010) American puts is similar and not presented here.

To illustrate, we use the settings of Clarke and Parrott (1999) that were used to generate Tables 11.6 and 11.7. Four terms are used in the expansion. The results are in Table 11.8.

TABLE 11.8 Greeks for American Puts, Medvedev-Scaillet Expansion

Spot	Price	Delta	Gamma	Vega1	Vanna	Volga	Theta
8	2.0008	−0.9642	0.1117	−0.0140	0.4316	4.7165	−0.2162
9	1.1238	−0.7585	0.2924	0.5790	0.6082	3.6768	−0.7937
10	0.5230	−0.4416	0.3030	0.9014	−0.0105	2.2742	−1.1837
11	0.2133	−0.1997	0.1755	0.6830	−0.3256	2.7095	−1.0098
12	0.0822	−0.0792	0.0757	0.3819	−0.2498	2.0886	−0.6288

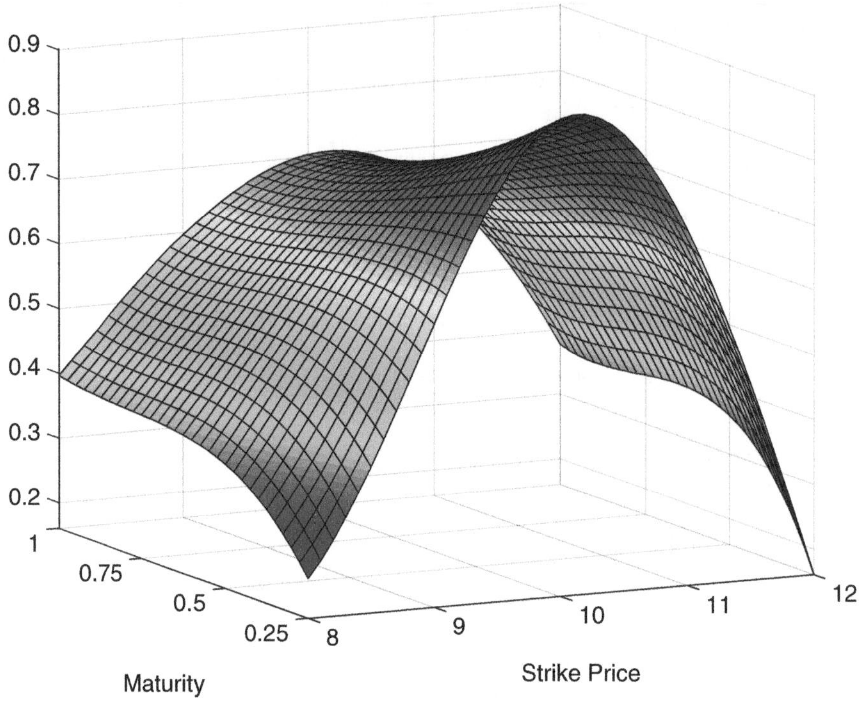

FIGURE 11.3 Vega from American put.

We continue with the settings of Clarke and Parrott (1999) to generate the surface for the first vega ($\mathcal{V}_1$). This plot appears as Figure 11.3. Three terms are used in the Medvedev and Scaillet (2010) expansion.

CONCLUSION

In this chapter, we have presented formulas for the Greeks of the Heston (1993) model. All of the closed-form pricing formulas can be differentiated analytically to yield Greeks. The fast Fourier transform and its fractional counterpart can both produce a large set of Greeks very quickly. In addition, it is straightforward to obtain Greeks from American options with the explicit finite difference method, the expansion of Medvedev and Scaillet (2010), and the LSM algorithm. Glasserman (2003), however, cautions that obtaining Greeks with simulation can cause difficulties for all but the simplest derivatives. Other methods to compute Greeks include the pathwise method and likelihood ratio method of Broadie and Glasserman (1996) described in Glasserman (2003) and Chan and Joshi (2010b). Broadie and Kaya (2004) obtain pathwise and likelihood ratio Greeks under their exact simulation scheme (Broadie and Kaya, 2006). Benhamou (2002) and Davis and Johansson (2005), among others, apply Malliavin calculus to obtain simulation-based Greeks in the Heston model.

In Chapter 9, it was shown that one way to make the Heston model more flexible is to introduce time-dependent parameters. It was shown also that these models can sometimes provide a better fit to the implied volatility surface than the original Heston (1993) model, especially at short maturities. Another way to introduce flexibility into the model is to enrich the volatility dynamics in the model so that the model allows for two regimes of volatility. This is the idea behind the double Heston model that we review in the final chapter.

CHAPTER 12

The Double Heston Model

Abstract

The original Heston (1993) model is not always able to fit the implied volatility smile very well, especially at short maturities. One remedy is to add additional parameters, which allows the model to be more flexible. This can be accomplished by allowing the parameters to be time dependent, as was illustrated by the methods covered in Chapter 9. Another approach is to enrich the variance process. One simple way to do this is to specify a two-factor structure for the volatility. This is the approach of Christoffersen et al. (2009) in their double Heston model, which we present in this chapter.

In this chapter, we first present the multi-dimensional Feynman-Kac theorem, and we show that the double Heston model is affine in the sense of Duffie et al. (2000). These results are used to obtain the characteristic function of the double Heston model. We then show how the double Heston model is a simple extension of its univariate counterpart, and how its extra parameters allow for a better fit of the implied volatility smile at multiple maturities. We also show that the "Little Trap" formulation of the characteristic function of Albrecher et al. (2007) can be applied to the double Heston model. Finally, we present different simulation schemes that can be applied to the double Heston model. Most of these schemes are extensions of univariate schemes presented in Chapter 7.

MULTI-DIMENSIONAL FEYNMAN-KAC THEOREM

The bivariate version of this theorem was presented in Chapters 2 and 9. In this section, we state the multi-dimensional version. Suppose that the vector $\mathbf{x}_t$ follows the n-dimensional stochastic process

$$d\mathbf{x}_t = \boldsymbol{\mu}(\mathbf{x}_t, t) + \boldsymbol{\sigma}(\mathbf{x}_t, t)d\mathbf{B}_t^{\mathbb{Q}} \tag{12.1}$$

where $\mathbf{x}_t$ and $\boldsymbol{\mu}(\mathbf{x}_t, t)$ are each vectors of dimension n, $\mathbf{B}_t^{\mathbb{Q}}$ is a vector of m-dimension independent $\mathbb{Q}$-Brownian motion, and $\boldsymbol{\sigma}(\mathbf{x}_t, t)$ is a volatility matrix of size $n \times m$. We can write Equation (12.1) as

$$\begin{pmatrix} dx_1(t) \\ \vdots \\ dx_n(t) \end{pmatrix} = \begin{pmatrix} \mu_1(\mathbf{x}_t, t) \\ \vdots \\ \mu_n(\mathbf{x}_t, t) \end{pmatrix} dt + \begin{pmatrix} \sigma_{11}(\mathbf{x}_t, t) & \cdots & \sigma_{1m}(\mathbf{x}_t, t) \\ \vdots & \ddots & \vdots \\ \sigma_{n1}(\mathbf{x}_t, t) & \cdots & \sigma_{nm}(\mathbf{x}_t, t) \end{pmatrix} \begin{pmatrix} dB_1^{\mathbb{Q}}(t) \\ \vdots \\ dB_m^{\mathbb{Q}}(t) \end{pmatrix}. \tag{12.2}$$

Analogous to the univariate case, the generator $\mathcal{A}$ of the process is defined as the operator

$$\mathcal{A} = \sum_{i=1}^{n} \mu_i \frac{\partial}{\partial x_i} + \frac{1}{2}\sum_{i=1}^{n}\sum_{j=1}^{n} (\sigma\sigma^T)_{ij} \frac{\partial^2}{\partial x_i \partial x_j} \tag{12.3}$$

where, for notational convenience, $\mu_i = \mu_i(\mathbf{x}_t, t)$, $\sigma = \sigma(x_t, t)$, and $(\sigma\sigma^T)_{ij}$ is element (i, j) of the matrix $\sigma\sigma^T$ of size $n \times n$. The multi-dimensional version of the Feynman-Kac theorem states that the partial differential equation of a function $f(\mathbf{x}_t, t)$ given by

$$\frac{\partial f}{\partial t} + \mathcal{A}f(\mathbf{x}_t, t) - r(\mathbf{x}_t, t)f(\mathbf{x}_t, t) = 0 \tag{12.4}$$

and with boundary condition $f(\mathbf{x}_T, T)$, has the solution

$$f(\mathbf{x}_t, t) = E^{\mathbb{Q}}\left[\exp\left(-\int_t^T r(\mathbf{x}_u u)\, du\right) f(\mathbf{x}_T, T)\middle| \mathcal{F}_t\right].$$

In the following section, we use this result to obtain the PDE and characteristic function of the double Heston model, and the double Heston call price.

DOUBLE HESTON CALL PRICE

The double Heston model proposed by Christoffersen et al. (2009) introduces a second factor for the variance, driven by its own SDE

$$\begin{aligned} dS &= (r-q)Sdt + \sqrt{v_1}SdW_1 + \sqrt{v_2}SdW_2 \\ dv_1 &= \kappa_1(\theta_1 - v_1)dt + \sigma_1\sqrt{v_1}dZ_1 \\ dv_2 &= \kappa_2(\theta_2 - v_2)dt + \sigma_2\sqrt{v_2}dZ_2. \end{aligned} \tag{12.5}$$

The following correlation structure is specified

$$\begin{aligned} E[dW_1 dZ_1] &= \rho_1 dt \\ E[dW_2 dZ_2] &= \rho_2 dt \\ E[dW_1 dW_2] &= E[dZ_1 dZ_2] = E[dW_1 dZ_2] = E[dW_2 dZ_1] = 0. \end{aligned} \tag{12.6}$$

Note that we have suppressed the time subscript for notational simplicity. The idea behind this model is that the additional volatility factor provides more flexibility in modeling the volatility surface. Recall from Chapter 2 that the correlation between the returns and their variance (ρ) controls the slope of the implied volatility. When $\rho \approx 0$, the smile is symmetric, but as ρ moves toward ± 1 the smile becomes highly asymmetric, with $\rho \approx -1$ corresponding to a negative slope and $\rho \approx +1$ to a positive slope. In the single-factor Heston model, ρ is constant over maturities, which means that model has trouble providing an adequate fit to market implied volatilities when the slope of the smile varies substantially across maturities, although it does a good job when the slopes are all relatively flat or all relatively steep. Incorporating a second volatility factor allows for two different correlations and, hence, for two different regimes of volatility.

To derive the PDE for the double Heston model, first apply Itō's lemma to obtain the SDE for $x_t = \ln S_t$

$$dx = \left(r - q - \frac{1}{2}(v_1 + v_2)\right) dt + \sqrt{v_1} dW_1 + \sqrt{v_2} dW_2.$$

In Equation (12.5), if we set

$$\begin{aligned} W_1 &= B_1 \\ W_2 &= B_2 \\ Z_1 &= \rho_1 B_1 + \sqrt{1 - \rho_1^2} B_3 \\ Z_2 &= \rho_2 B_2 + \sqrt{1 - \rho_2^2} B_4 \end{aligned} \tag{12.7}$$

where B_j are independent Brownian motion, then we can write the system of SDEs for $\mathbf{x}_t = (x, v_1, v_2)$ as in Equation (12.2). To do this, we note that the correlation structure in (12.6) corresponds to the volatility matrix of size $n \times m = 3 \times 4$

$$\boldsymbol{\sigma}(\mathbf{x}_t, t) = \begin{pmatrix} \sqrt{v_1} & \sqrt{v_2} & 0 & 0 \\ \sigma_1 \sqrt{v_1} \rho_1 & 0 & \sigma_1 \sqrt{v_1 (1 - \rho_1^2)} & 0 \\ 0 & \sigma_2 \sqrt{v_2} \rho_2 & 0 & \sigma_2 \sqrt{v_2 (1 - \rho_2^2)} \end{pmatrix}$$

and drift

$$\mu = \begin{pmatrix} r - q - \frac{1}{2}(v_1 + v_2) \\ \kappa_1(\theta_1 - v_1) \\ \kappa_2(\theta_2 - v_2) \end{pmatrix}.$$

We have

$$\boldsymbol{\sigma}\boldsymbol{\sigma}^T = \begin{pmatrix} v_1 + v_2 & \sigma_1 v_1 \rho_1 & \sigma_2 v_2 \rho_2 \\ \sigma_1 v_1 \rho_1 & \sigma_1^2 v_1 & 0 \\ \sigma_2 v_2 \rho_2 & 0 & \sigma_2^2 v_2 \end{pmatrix}$$

so the generator for the double Heston model is, from Equation (12.3)

$$\begin{aligned} \mathcal{A} = &\left[r - q - \tfrac{1}{2}(v_1 + v_2)\right] \frac{\partial}{\partial x} + \kappa_1(\theta_1 - v_1) \frac{\partial}{\partial v_1} + \kappa_2(\theta_2 - v_2) \frac{\partial}{\partial v_2} \\ &+ \frac{1}{2}(v_1 + v_2) \frac{\partial^2}{\partial x^2} + \rho_1 \sigma_1 v_1 \frac{\partial^2}{\partial x \partial v_1} + \rho_2 \sigma_2 v_2 \frac{\partial^2}{\partial x \partial v_2} \\ &+ \frac{1}{2} \sigma_1^2 v_1 \frac{\partial^2}{\partial v_1^2} + \frac{1}{2} \sigma_2^2 v_2 \frac{\partial^2}{\partial v_2^2}. \end{aligned} \tag{12.8}$$

The PDE follows from (12.4) with $r(\mathbf{x}_t, t) = r$, a constant. Note that, when one of the volatility terms drops out, the generator in (12.8) reduces to that of the univariate Heston model presented in Chapter 1.

The double Heston system of equations in (x, v_1, v_2) can be written in affine form as

$$\boldsymbol{\mu}(\mathbf{x}_t) = \mathbf{K}_0 + \mathbf{K}_1 x + \mathbf{K}_2 v_1 + \mathbf{K}_3 v_2$$
$$\boldsymbol{\sigma}(\mathbf{x}_t)\boldsymbol{\sigma}(\mathbf{x}_t)^T = \mathbf{H}_0 + \mathbf{H}_1 x + \mathbf{H}_2 v_1 + \mathbf{H}_3 v_2$$

with

$$\mathbf{K}_0 = \begin{pmatrix} r-q \\ \kappa_1\theta_1 \\ \kappa_2\theta_2 \end{pmatrix}, \quad \mathbf{K}_1 = \begin{pmatrix} 0 \\ 0 \\ 0 \end{pmatrix}, \quad \mathbf{K}_2 = \begin{pmatrix} -\frac{1}{2} \\ -\kappa_1 \\ 0 \end{pmatrix}, \quad \mathbf{K}_3 = \begin{pmatrix} -\frac{1}{2} \\ 0 \\ -\kappa_2 \end{pmatrix}$$

and

$$\mathbf{H}_0 = \mathbf{H}_1 = \begin{pmatrix} 0 & 0 & 0 \\ 0 & 0 & 0 \\ 0 & 0 & 0 \end{pmatrix}, \quad \mathbf{H}_2 = \begin{pmatrix} 1 & \sigma_1\rho_1 & 0 \\ \sigma_1\rho_1 & \sigma_1^2 & 0 \\ 0 & 0 & 0 \end{pmatrix}, \quad \mathbf{H}_3 = \begin{pmatrix} 1 & 0 & \sigma_2\rho_2 \\ 0 & 0 & 0 \\ \sigma_2\rho_2 & 0 & \sigma_2^2 \end{pmatrix}.$$

We can therefore use the result of Duffie et al. (2000) that the characteristic function for $(x_T, v_{1,T}, v_{2,T})$ has the log linear form

$$\begin{aligned} f(\phi_0, \phi_1, \phi_2; x_t, v_{1,t}, v_{2,t}) &= E[\exp(i\phi_0 x_T + i\phi_1 v_{1,T} + i\phi_2 v_{2,T})] \\ &= \exp(A(\tau) + B_0(\tau)x_t + B_1(\tau)v_{1,t} + B_2(\tau)v_{2,t}) \end{aligned} \tag{12.9}$$

where $\tau = T - t$ is the time remaining until expiry. In this expression, the coefficients A, B_0, B_1, and B_2 depend not only on τ but also on ϕ_0, ϕ_1, and ϕ_2 but this has been omitted for notational convenience. Recall from Chapter 9 that the result of Duffie et al. (2000) also states that the coefficients of the characteristic function are given by the system of Riccati equations

$$\begin{aligned} \frac{\partial A}{\partial t} &= -\mathbf{K}_0^T\boldsymbol{\beta} - \frac{1}{2}\boldsymbol{\beta}^T\mathbf{H}_0\boldsymbol{\beta} \\ \frac{\partial B_0}{\partial t} &= -\mathbf{K}_1^T\boldsymbol{\beta} - \frac{1}{2}\boldsymbol{\beta}^T\mathbf{H}_1\boldsymbol{\beta} \\ \frac{\partial B_1}{\partial t} &= -\mathbf{K}_2^T\boldsymbol{\beta} - \frac{1}{2}\boldsymbol{\beta}^T\mathbf{H}_2\boldsymbol{\beta} \\ \frac{\partial B_2}{\partial t} &= -\mathbf{K}_3^T\boldsymbol{\beta} - \frac{1}{2}\boldsymbol{\beta}^T\mathbf{H}_3\boldsymbol{\beta} \end{aligned} \tag{12.10}$$

subject to the boundary conditions $B_0(0) = i\phi_0$, $B_1(0) = i\phi_1$, $B_2(0) = i\phi_2$, and $A(0) = 0$, where $\boldsymbol{\beta}^T = (B_0, B_1, B_2)$. As in Chapter 9, we note that the second equation in (12.10) along with its initial condition leads immediately to the solution $B_0(\tau) = i\phi_0$. After substituting for the other terms in (12.10), and reversing the sign because we need derivatives with respect to time-to-maturity τ rather than t, we are left with the set of differential equations

$$\begin{aligned}\frac{\partial A}{\partial \tau} &= (r-q)i\phi_0 + \kappa_1\theta_1 B_1 + \kappa_2\theta_2 B_2 \\ \frac{\partial B_1}{\partial \tau} &= \frac{1}{2}\sigma_1^2 B_1^2 - (\kappa_1 - i\phi_0\rho_1\sigma_1)B_1 - \frac{1}{2}\phi_0(\phi_0 + i) \\ \frac{\partial B_2}{\partial \tau} &= \frac{1}{2}\sigma_2^2 B_2^2 - (\kappa_2 - i\phi_0\rho_2\sigma_2)B_2 - \frac{1}{2}\phi_0(\phi_0 + i).\end{aligned} \tag{12.11}$$

Since we are interested in the characteristic function for x_T only, and not in the joint characteristic function for $(x_T, v_{1,T}, v_{2,T})$, we set $\phi_1 = \phi_2 = 0$ in Equation (12.9). The initial conditions for Equation (12.11) become $B_1(0) = B_2(0) = 0$, while $B_0(0) = i\phi$ and $A(0) = 0$ remain unchanged (we write ϕ for ϕ_0). Hence, the Ricatti equations for B_1 and B_2 are identical to their univariate counterparts in Chapter 1, so their solutions are

$$B_j(\tau,\phi) = \frac{\kappa_j - \rho_j\sigma_j\phi i + d_j}{\sigma_j^2}\left[\frac{1-e^{d_j\tau}}{1-g_j e^{d_j\tau}}\right]$$

where

$$g_j = \frac{\kappa_j - \rho_j\sigma_j\phi i + d_j}{\kappa_j - \rho_j\sigma_j\phi i - d_j},\quad d_j = \sqrt{(\kappa_j - \rho_j\sigma_j\phi i)^2 + \sigma_j^2\phi(\phi+i)}.$$

Note that d_j and g_j both refer to the second form for d and g, which we covered in Chapter 1, corresponding to the second characteristic function f_2. In this chapter, the subscript on d_j and g_j refers to that of the volatility v_j.

The solution for $A(\tau,\phi)$ is

$$A(\tau,\phi) = (r-q)\phi i\tau + \sum_{j=1}^{2}\frac{\kappa_j\theta_j}{\sigma_j^2}\left[(\kappa_j - \rho_j\sigma_j\phi i + d_j)\,\tau - 2\ln\left(\frac{1-g_j e^{d_j\tau}}{1-g_j}\right)\right].$$

By defining $c_j = 1/g_j$, we can also use the "Little Trap" formulation of Albrecher et al. (2007), which expresses the coefficients of the characteristic function in terms of $\exp(-d_j\tau)$ rather than $\exp(d_j\tau)$, as in Gauthier and Possamaï (2010). This produces the alternate forms of the coefficients

$$B_j(\tau,\phi) = \frac{\kappa_j - \rho_j\sigma_j\phi i - d_j}{\sigma_j^2}\left[\frac{1-e^{-d_j\tau}}{1-c_j e^{-d_j\tau}}\right]$$

and

$$A(\tau,\phi) = (r-q)\phi i\tau + \sum_{j=1}^{2}\frac{\kappa_j\theta_j}{\sigma_j^2}\left[(\kappa_j - \rho_j\sigma_j\phi i - d_j)\,\tau - 2\ln\left(\frac{1-c_j e^{-d_j\tau}}{1-c_j}\right)\right].$$

As in the univariate case, this formulation avoids the discontinuity problems that can arise with the original formulation. Once the coefficients are obtained, either with the original formulation or the "Little Trap" formulation, the characteristic function is

$$f(\phi; x_t, v_{1,t}, v_{2,t}) = \exp\left(A(\tau,\phi) + i\phi x_t + B_1(\tau,\phi)v_{1,t} + B_2(\tau,\phi)v_{2,t}\right) \tag{12.12}$$

where x_t is the log spot price of the underlying, and $v_{1,t}$ and $v_{2,t}$ are the initial variances, which can be estimated as the parameters v_{01} and v_{02}, as in the univariate case. The call price is obtained in the usual fashion

$$C(K) = S_t e^{-q\tau} P_1 - K e^{-r\tau} P_2 \tag{12.13}$$

where

$$\begin{aligned} P_1 &= \frac{1}{2} + \frac{1}{\pi}\int_0^\infty \text{Re}\left[\frac{e^{-i\phi \ln K} f\left(\phi - i; x_t, v_{1,t}, v_{2,t}\right)}{i\phi S_t e^{(r-q)\tau}}\right] d\phi, \\ P_2 &= \frac{1}{2} + \frac{1}{\pi}\int_0^\infty \text{Re}\left[\frac{e^{-i\phi \ln K} f\left(\phi; x_t, v_{1,t}, v_{2.t}\right)}{i\phi}\right] d\phi. \end{aligned} \tag{12.14}$$

Note that to allow for the stock to pay a continuous dividend yield q, in the first term of the expression for $A(\tau,\phi)$ we include $r - q$ rather than r alone. Similarly, the first term of the call price in Equation (12.13) is $S_t e^{-q\tau} P_1$, and in the denominator of P_1 in (12.14), we use $S_t e^{(r-q)\tau}$ rather than $S_t e^{r\tau}$.

Implementing the double Heston model is only slightly more complicated than implementing its univariate counterpart. In the computer code, we order the parameters as

$$\Theta = (\kappa_1, \theta_1, \sigma_1, v_{10}, \rho_1, \kappa_2, \theta_2, \sigma_2, v_{20}, \rho_2) \tag{12.15}$$

The Matlab file DoubleHestonCF.m returns the characteristic function for the double Heston model.

```
function y = DoubleHestonCF(phi,...);
if trap==1
  d1 = sqrt((kappa1-rho1*sigma1*i*phi)^2 + ...;
  d2 = sqrt((kappa2-rho2*sigma2*i*phi)^2 + ...;
  G1 = (kappa1-rho1*sigma1*phi*i-d1) ...;
  G2 = (kappa2-rho2*sigma2*phi*i-d2) ...;
  B1 = (kappa1-rho1*sigma1*phi*i-d1)*(1-exp(-d1*tau)) ...;
  B2 = (kappa2-rho2*sigma2*phi*i-d2)*(1-exp(-d2*tau)) ...;
  X1 = (1-G1*exp(-d1*tau))/(1-G1);
  X2 = (1-G2*exp(-d2*tau))/(1-G2);
  A  = (rf-q)*phi*i*tau + ...;
else
   ...
end
y = exp(A + i*phi*x0 + B1*v01 + B2*v02);
```

The following Matlab function calculates the call price using the trapezoidal rule, and returns either the call price itself, or the put price by put-call parity.

TABLE 12.1 Double Heston Call Prices

Strike Price	Maturity	Call Price
61.90	1 yr	19.4538
61.90	10 yrs	41.3940
43.33	1 yr	27.6047
43.33	10 yrs	45.2793
80.47	1 yr	13.9276
80.47	10 yrs	38.2719

```
function y = DoubleHestonPriceTrapezoidal(...,a,b,N)
h = (b-a)/(N-1);
phi = [a:h:b];
w = h.*[1/2 ones(1,N-2) 1/2];
for k=1:length(phi);
    u = phi(k);
    f2(k) = DoubleHestonCF(u  ,...);
    f1(k) = DoubleHestonCF(u-i,...);
    int2(k) = w(k)*real(exp(-i*u*log(K))*f2(k)/i/u);
    int1(k) = w(k)*real(exp(-i*u*log(K))*f1(k)/i/u ...);
end
P1 = 1/2 + 1/pi*sum(int1);
P2 = 1/2 + 1/pi*sum(int2);
HestonC = S*exp(-q*T)*P1 - K*exp(-rf*T)*P2;
```

The C# code to implement the double Heston model is very similar and is not presented here.

To illustrate the double Heston model, we use Matlab to reproduce Table 3 of Gauthier and Possamaï (2010). The call prices using the trapezoidal rule are presented in Table 12.1 and are almost identical to those of Gauthier and Possamaï.

In practice, we use Gauss-Laguerre quadrature, since this is almost as accurate as the trapezoidal rule, but much faster.

DOUBLE HESTON GREEKS

In this section, we derive analytic expressions for the Greeks in the double Heston model. We saw in Chapter 11 that many of the Greeks for the Heston (1993) model are available analytically, by straightforward differentiation of the call price. We also saw that by using finite difference approximations to the Greeks, it is easy to verify the accuracy of the analytic Greeks. This approach can be used with the double Heston model as well, by differentiation of the call price in (12.13). The Greeks in the double Heston model are straightforward generalizations of their univariate counterparts. Gamma, for example, is $\Gamma = e^{-q\tau}\partial P_1/\partial S$, where from Equation (12.14)

$$\frac{\partial P_1}{\partial S} = \frac{1}{\pi}\int_0^\infty \text{Re}\left[\frac{e^{-i\phi\ln K}f\left(\phi - i; x_t, v_{1,t}, v_{2,t}\right)}{S_t^2 e^{(r-q)\tau}}\right]d\phi.$$

Theta requires

$$\frac{\partial P_1}{\partial \tau} = \frac{1}{\pi}\int_0^\infty \text{Re}\left[\frac{e^{-i\phi \ln K}}{i\phi S_t e^{(r-q)\tau}}\left(\frac{\partial f}{\partial \tau} - (r-q)f\right)\right] d\phi$$

where f and its τ-derivative are both evaluated at $\phi - i$. It also requires

$$\frac{\partial P_2}{\partial \tau} = \frac{1}{\pi}\int_0^\infty \text{Re}\left[\frac{e^{-i\phi \ln K}}{i\phi}\left(\frac{\partial f}{\partial \tau}\right)\right] d\phi$$

where the τ-derivative of f is evaluated at ϕ. The expression for theta is identical to that in Chapter 11. In the derivatives of P_1 and P_2, we have

$$\frac{\partial f}{\partial \tau} = \exp(A + i\phi x_t + B_1 v_{1,t} + B_2 v_{2,t})\left(\frac{\partial A}{\partial \tau} + \frac{\partial B_1}{\partial \tau}v_{1,t} + \frac{\partial B_2}{\partial \tau}v_{2,t}\right)$$

where the τ-derivative of $A(\tau,\phi)$ is analogous to that for $C(\tau,\phi)$ in Chapter 11, and where the τ-derivative of $B_1(\tau,\phi)$ and $B_2(\tau,\phi)$ both correspond to that for $D(\tau,\phi)$. Recall that $v_{1,t}$ and $v_{2,t}$ are the initial variances, which are estimated as the parameters v_{01} and v_{02}.

We saw in Chapter 11 that Zhu (2010) defines the first vega $\mathcal{V}_1$ to be based on $v = \sqrt{v_0}$. Since there are two initial variance parameters in the double Heston model, there are two such vegas, $\mathcal{V}_{11}$ based on $v_1 = \sqrt{v_{01}}$, and $\mathcal{V}_{12}$ based on $v_2 = \sqrt{v_{02}}$. These can be easily obtained, by noting that since $\partial f/\partial v_{0j} = f \times B_j$, we have the derivatives

$$\begin{aligned}
\frac{\partial P_1}{\partial v_{0j}} &= \frac{1}{\pi}\int_0^\infty \text{Re}\left[\frac{e^{-i\phi \ln K}}{i\phi S_t e^{(r-q)\tau}} f(\phi - i; x_t, v_{1,t}, v_{2,t}) B_j(\tau, \phi - i)\right] d\phi, \\
\frac{\partial P_2}{\partial v_{0j}} &= \frac{1}{\pi}\int_0^\infty \text{Re}\left[\frac{e^{-i\phi \ln K}}{i\phi} f\left(\phi; x_t, v_{1,t}, v_{2,t}\right) B_j(\tau,\phi)\right] d\phi.
\end{aligned} \tag{12.16}$$

The two vegas are identical to the form derived in Chapter 11

$$\mathcal{V}_{1j} = Se^{-q\tau}\frac{\partial P_1}{\partial v_{0j}}2\sqrt{v_{0j}} - Ke^{-r\tau}\frac{\partial P_2}{\partial v_{0j}}2\sqrt{v_{0j}} \tag{12.17}$$

for $j = 1, 2$. Similarly, the two volgas are obtained with $\partial^2 f/\partial v_{0j}^2 = f \times B_j^2$. Using the relationship derived in Chapter 11, $\partial^2 P_1/\partial v_j^2$ is

$$\begin{aligned}
\frac{\partial^2 P_1}{\partial v_j^2} &= 4\left(\frac{\partial^2 P_1}{\partial v_{0j}^2}v_{0j} + \frac{1}{2}\frac{\partial P_1}{\partial v_{0j}}\right) \\
&= \frac{1}{\pi}\int_0^\infty \text{Re}\left[\frac{e^{-i\phi \ln K}}{i\phi S_t e^{(r-q)\tau}} 2B_1 f(2B_1 v_{0j} + 1)\right] d\phi
\end{aligned}$$

where f and B_1 are both evaluated at $\phi - i$. The expression for $\partial^2 P_2/\partial v_j^2$ is identical, except that $S_t e^{(r-q)\tau}$ is not included in the denominator and f and B_1 are both evaluated at ϕ. The volgas are then

$$\text{Volga}_j = Se^{-q\tau}\frac{\partial^2 P_1}{\partial v_j^2} - Ke^{-r\tau}\frac{\partial^2 P_2}{\partial v_j^2}. \tag{12.18}$$

There are also two vannas, based on v_1 and v_2

$$\text{Vanna}_j = 2e^{-q\tau}\sqrt{v_{0j}}\frac{\partial P_1}{\partial v_{0j}}. \tag{12.19}$$

The Matlab function DoubleHestonGreeks.m calculates the analytical Greeks of the double Heston model. The function calls the B.m function to calculate the coefficients $B_1(\tau,\phi)$ and $B_2(\tau,\phi)$ required for vega, vanna, and volga, as well as the DiffTau.m function to calculate the τ-derivatives of $A(\tau,\phi)$, $B_1(\tau,\phi)$, and $B_2(\tau,\phi)$ required for theta. To conserve space, most of the function has been omitted. The first part of the function creates the integrands for the selected Greek.

```
function y = DoubleHestonGreeks(...,Greek)
for k=1:N;
    u = x(k);
    f2 = DoubleHestonCF(u  ,...);
    f1 = DoubleHestonCF(u-i,...);
    if strcmp(Greek,'Price')
        int2(k) = w(k) * real(exp(-i*u*log(K))/i/u*f2);
        int1(k) = w(k) * real(exp(-i*u*log(K))/i/u ...);
    elseif strcmp(Greek,'Gamma')
        int1(k) = w(k) * real(exp(-i*u*log(K))/exp((rf-q)*T)...);
    elseif strcmp(Greek,'Vega11') || strcmp(Greek,'Vega12')
        if strcmp(Greek,'Vega11') v0choice = 1;
        else v0choice = 2; end
        B1 = B(u-i,param,T,trap,v0choice);
        B2 = B(u  ,param,T,trap,v0choice);
        df1 = f1*B1;
        df2 = f2*B2;
        int2(k) = w(k) * real(exp(-i*u*log(K))/i/u*df2);
        int1(k) = w(k) * real(exp(-i*u*log(K))/i/u ...);
    elseif strcmp(Greek,'Theta')
        int2(k) = w(k) * real(exp(-i*u*log(K))/i/u*f2);
        int1(k) = w(k) * real(exp(-i*u*log(K))/i/u ...);
        v01 = param(4);
        v02 = param(9);
        [dA1 dB11 dB21] = DiffTau(u-i,param,T,S,rf,q);
        df1 = f1*(dA1 + dB11*v01 + dB21*v02) - (rf-q)*f1;
        [dA2 dB12 dB22] = DiffTau(u  ,param,T,S,rf,q);
        df2 = f2*(dA2 + dB12*v01 + dB22*v02);
        dint2(k) = w(k) * real(exp(-i*u*log(K))/i/u*df2);
        dint1(k) = w(k) * real(exp(-i*u*log(K))/i/u ...);
    end
end
```

The second part of the function calculates the integrals and returns the price or the Greek.

```
if strcmp(Greek,'Price')
    P1 = 1/2 + 1/pi*sum(int1);
    P2 = 1/2 + 1/pi*sum(int2);
```

```
    y = S*exp(-q*T)*P1 - K*exp(-rf*T)*P2;
elseif strcmp(Greek,'Gamma')
    y = exp(-q*T)*sum(int1)/pi;
elseif strcmp(Greek,'Vega11') || strcmp(Greek,'Vega12')
    if strcmp(Greek,'Vega11') v0 = param(4);
    else v0 = param(9); end
    dP1 = 1/pi*sum(int1);
    dP2 = 1/pi*sum(int2);
    dC = S*exp(-q*T)*dP1 - K*exp(-rf*T)*dP2;
    y = dC*2*sqrt(v0);
elseif strcmp(Greek,'Rho')
    P2 = 1/2 + 1/pi*sum(int2);
    y = K*T*exp(-rf*T)*P2;
elseif strcmp(Greek,'Theta')
    P1 = 1/2 + 1/pi*sum(int1);
    P2 = 1/2 + 1/pi*sum(int2);
    dP1 = 1/pi*sum(dint1);
    dP2 = 1/pi*sum(dint2);
    y = -S*exp(-q*T)*(-q*P1+dP1) + K*exp(-rf*T)*(-rf*P2+dP2);
end
```

The Matlab function DiffTau.m returns the τ-derivatives of $A(\tau,\phi)$, $B_1(\tau,\phi)$, and $B_2(\tau,\phi)$.

```
function [dA dB1 dB2] = DiffTau(phi,...)
d1 = sqrt((kappa1-rho1*sigma1*phi*i)^2 + ...;
g1 = (kappa1-rho1*sigma1*phi*i+d1) ...;
dC1 = kappa1*theta1/sigma1^2 ...;
% The derivatives
dA = (rf-q)*phi*i + dC1 + dC2;
dB1 = d1*exp(d1*tau)*(kappa1-rho1*sigma1*phi*i+d1)*(g1-1) ...;
dB2 = d2*exp(d2*tau)*(kappa2-rho2*sigma2*phi*i+d2)*(g2-1) ...;
```

The Matlab function B.m returns the coefficient $B_1(\tau,\phi)$ or $B_2(\tau,\phi)$, depending on the choice of "j" in the function argument. The function allows for the original Heston (1993) formulation, or for the "Little Trap" formulation of Albrecher et al. (2007).

```
function y = B(phi,...,j)
if trap==1
    B1 = (kappa1-rho1*sigma1*phi*i-d1)*(1-exp(-d1*tau)) ...;
    B2 = (kappa2-rho2*sigma2*phi*i-d2)*(1-exp(-d2*tau)) ...;
else
    B1 = (kappa1-rho1*sigma1*phi*i+d1)*(1-exp(d1*tau))/ ...;
    B2 = (kappa2-rho2*sigma2*phi*i+d2)*(1-exp(d2*tau))/ ...;
```

```
end
if j==1
    y = B1;
else
    y = B2;
end
```

The C# code to calculate the analytical Greeks of the double Heston model is very similar to the Matlab code and is not presented here.

To illustrate the double Heston Greeks, we use the same settings as those in Table 12.1 and generate the Greeks of the at-the-money call price with a maturity of 1 year. The results are in Table 12.2. Recall from Table 12.1 that the price with these settings is 19.4538. The analytic Greeks are all accurate, as indicated by their absolute difference with their finite difference counterparts. This difference appears in the last column of Table 12.2.

We saw in Chapter 11 that the Greeks satisfy the PDE of the univariate Heston model, provided that the PDE be expressed in terms of S rather than $x = \ln S$, and provided that vega, vanna, and volga be in terms of the variance v_0 rather than the volatility $v = \sqrt{v_0}$. It is straightforward to demonstrate this for the PDE of the double Heston model also. Using the generator in Equation (12.8) for S along with (12.4), and substituting the Greeks for the derivatives in S, v_{01}, and v_{02} of the resulting PDE produces

$$\begin{aligned}\Theta &+ (r-q)S_0\Delta + \kappa_1(\theta_1 - v_{01})\text{Vega}_1 + \kappa_2(\theta_2 - v_{02})\text{Vega}_2 \\ &+ \frac{1}{2}(v_{01}+v_{02})S_0^2\Gamma + \rho_1\sigma_1 v_{01}S_0\text{Vanna}_1 + \rho_2\sigma_2 v_{02}S_0\text{Vanna}_2 \\ &+ \frac{1}{2}\sigma_1^2 v_{01}\text{Volga}_1 + \frac{1}{2}\sigma_2^2 v_{02}\text{Volga}_2 - rC = 0.\end{aligned} \tag{12.20}$$

TABLE 12.2 Double Heston Greeks

Greek	Analytic	Difference
Price	19.4538	
Delta	0.6730	3.3×10^{-7}
Gamma	0.0075	4.2×10^{-9}
Rho	22.2029	4.1×10^{-6}
Theta	−7.0594	1.8×10^{-6}
Vega11	11.2973	1.8×10^{-6}
Vega12	11.5147	1.4×10^{-6}
Vanna1	0.0745	2.6×10^{-7}
Vanna2	0.0816	2.7×10^{-7}
Volga1	10.4625	1.3×10^{-7}
Volga2	7.7954	2.1×10^{-7}

The following snippet of code demonstrates that the PDE in (12.20) holds.

```
Vega1lp = Vega11 / (2*sqrt(v01));
Vega12p = Vega12 / (2*sqrt(v02));
Vanna1p = Vanna1 / (2*sqrt(v01));
Vanna2p = Vanna2 / (2*sqrt(v02));
Volga1p = (1/4/sqrt(v01)*Volga1 - Vega11p/2/sqrt(v01))/sqrt(v01);
Volga2p = (1/4/sqrt(v02)*Volga2 - Vega12p/2/sqrt(v02))/sqrt(v02);
% The double Heston PDE
A = (rf-q)*S*Delta ...
    + kappa1*(theta1-v01)*Vega11p ...
    + kappa2*(theta2-v02)*Vega12p ...
    + 0.5*(v01+v02)*S^2*Gamma ...
    + rho1*sigma1*v01*S*Vanna1p ...
    + rho2*sigma2*v02*S*Vanna2p ...
    + 0.5*sigma1^2*v01*Volga1p ...
    + 0.5*sigma2^2*v02*Volga2p;
PDE = Theta + A - rf*Price;
```

Note that we express the derivatives of the PDE (12.20) in terms of v_0 rather than v, before substituting these derivatives into the Heston PDE, as we did in Chapter 11. With the settings used to generate Table 12.2, the code returns 1.1×10^{-7} for the value of the PDE.

PARAMETER ESTIMATION

Christoffersen et al. (2009) estimate the volatility parameters v_{01} and v_{02} as daily spot volatilities $v_{01,t}$ and $v_{02,t}$, and the remaining parameters $\Omega = \{\kappa_j, \theta_j, \sigma_j, \rho_j\}_{j=1,2}$ on a yearly basis. Their estimation works in two steps. In the first step, a given value of the fixed parameters $\Omega = \{\kappa_j, \theta_j, \sigma_j, \rho_j\}_{j=1,2}$ is used in their loss function with options available on day t to obtain estimates $\hat{v}_{01,t}$ and $\hat{v}_{02,t}$. This is repeated until a yearly time series $\{\hat{v}_{01,t}\}_{t=1}^{T}$ and $\{\hat{v}_{02,t}\}_{t=1}^{T}$ of spot volatilities is obtained. In the second step, these time series are fed into the same objective function, but using options across the entire year, to obtain an updated estimate of Ω. The two steps are repeated until there is no significant reduction in the value of the objective function at the second step. This approach requires a longitudinal set of option prices.

In this section, we employ the simpler approach of treating v_{01} and v_{02} as fixed parameters, analogous to what is done in Chapter 6 for the univariate Heston model. Recall from that chapter that there are many possible loss functions that can be used in the estimation, but if the intent is to minimize the fit of the model to market implied volatilities, then it is preferable to use a loss function that involves implied volatilities. One such example is the IVRMSE loss function

$$\frac{1}{N}\sum_{t,k} w_{tk}\frac{(IV_{tk} - IV_{tk}^{\Theta})^2}{IV_{tk}} \tag{12.21}$$

where IV_{tk} and IV_{tk}^{Θ} are the market and model implied volatilities respectively, w_{tk} is an optional weight, and N is the total number of observations used in the estimation.

As first mentioned in Chapter 6, the problem with using IVRMSE and other objective functions that use implied volatility is that the model implied volatility IV_{tk}^{Θ} must be obtained at every iteration of the optimization, which is computationally intensive. To address this issue, in Chapter 6 we introduced the Christoffersen et al. (2009) proxy of (12.21)

$$\frac{1}{N}\sum_{t,k} w_{tk}\left(\frac{C_{tk} - C_{tk}^{\Theta}}{\text{BSVega}_{tk}}\right)^2 \tag{12.22}$$

where C_{tk} and C_{tk}^{Θ} are the market and model call prices, respectively, and where BSVega_{tk} is the Black-Scholes vega evaluated at the strike K_k, at the maturity τ_t, and using the market implied volatility IV_{tk} as the volatility input. The Black-Scholes vega is given by

$$\text{BSVega}_{tk} = S\exp(-q\tau_t)n(d_{tk})\sqrt{\tau_t} \tag{12.23}$$

where

$$d_{tk} = \frac{\ln(S/K_k) + (r - q + IV_{tk}^2/2)\tau_t}{IV_{tk}\sqrt{\tau_t}} \tag{12.24}$$

and where $n(x) = \exp(-x^2/2)/\sqrt{2\pi}$ is the standard normal density. The loss function in Equation (12.22) is implemented with the Matlab function DoubleHestonObjFun.m.

```
function y = DoubleHestonObjFun(...)
for t=1:NT
  for k=1:NK
   MP(k,t)= DoubleHestonPriceGaussLaguerre(K(k),T(t),...);
   BSVega(k,t) = BSV(K(k),MktIV(k,t),T(t),...);
   error(k,t) = (MP(k,t) - MktPrice(k,t))^2 ...;
  end
end
y = sum(sum(error));
```

The function also allows for MSE and RMSE loss functions, and can be easily modified to accept additional loss functions. The BSV function is a Matlab function that computes vega in (12.23).

We can also use the Strike Vector Computation method of Kilin (2007) described in Chapter 6 to estimate the parameters of the double Heston model, which reduces the estimation time dramatically. This is accomplished with the Matlab function DoubleHestonObjFunSVC.m.

```
function y = DoubleHestonObjFunSVC(param,...)
for t=1:NT
    for j=1:length(x)
        phi = x(j);
```

```
        f2(j) = DoubleHestonCF(phi   ,...);
        f1(j) = DoubleHestonCF(phi-i,...);
    end
    for k=1:NK
        for j=1:length(x);
            phi = x(j);
            int2(j) = w(j)*real(exp(-i*phi*log(K(k)))*f2(j)...);
            int1(j) = w(j)*real(exp(-i*phi*log(K(k)))*f1(j)...);
        end
        P1 = 1/2 + 1/pi*sum(int1);
        P2 = 1/2 + 1/pi*sum(int2);
        CallPrice = S*exp(-q*T(t))*P1 - K(k)*exp(-rf*T(t))*P2;
        if strcmp(PutCall(k,t),'C')
            ModelPrice(k,t) = CallPrice;
        else
            ModelPrice(k,t) = CallPrice - S*exp(-q*T(t)) + ...;
        end
        d = (log(S/K(k)) + (rf-q+MktIV(k,t)^2/2)*T(t))...;
        BSVega(k,t) = S*normpdf(d)*sqrt(T(t));
        error(k,t) = (ModelPrice(k,t) - MktPrice(k,t))^2 ...;
    end
end
y = sum(sum(error));
```

The C# code to estimate parameters in the double Heston model is very similar to the Matlab code and is not presented. The main difference is that, in C#, we need the NelderMead() function presented in Chapter 6 to minimize the objective function and return the parameters. Please refer to that chapter for details on the NelderMead() function.

To illustrate parameter estimation under the double Heston model, we use the same Dow Jones Industrial Average implied volatilities quoted on May 10, 2012, that were used to estimate the time-dependent model of Mikhailov and Nögel (2003) in Chapter 9. The fit of each model is evaluated using the IVMSE estimation error

$$\frac{1}{N}\sqrt{\sum_{t,k}(IV_{tk} - IV_{tk}^{\hat{\Theta}})^2}. \tag{12.25}$$

The parameter estimates $\hat{\Theta}$ from the univariate and double Heston models, along with their estimation error and estimation time, are in Table 12.3. Parameters are estimated using the Christoffersen et al. (2009) loss function (12.22) and the ordinary summation of the terms in the objective function. We also repeat the estimation using (12.22) but with Kilin's (2007) Strike Vector Computation method of summation.

The estimates are consistent with a double regime of volatility described by Christoffersen et al. (2009). The first volatility factor has a low mean reversion level and corresponds to a mildly steep smile for long maturities, while the second factor has much higher reversion and corresponds to a smile that is much steeper for shorter maturities. The fact that the double Heston model can capture the time-varying nature of the smile is reflected in an estimation error that is lower than that

TABLE 12.3 Univariate and Double Heston Parameter Estimates, DIA Data

	$\hat{\kappa}$	$\hat{\theta}$	$\hat{\sigma}$	$\hat{v}_0$	$\hat{\rho}$	Estimation Error	Estimation Time (sec)
Univariate Heston	1.3750	0.1254	1.3185	0.0332	−0.4436	5.13×10^{-4}	29.5
Double	3.0590	0.0317	1.9850	0.0258	0.0643	1.56×10^{-4}	41.5[a]
Heston	1.8467	0.0605	0.7149	0.0092	−0.9750		5.0[b]

[a]Using ordinary estimation method
[b]Using Strike Vector Computation method

of the univariate Heston model. This is also illustrated in Figure 12.1, which plots the market implied volatilities and the implied volatilities extracted from each model. Finally, the estimates produced using the ordinary and SVC methods of summation in the objective function are identical, but the latter reduces the estimation time by nearly 90 percent.

The implied volatility surface and local volatility surface, obtained using the finite difference approximation presented in Chapter 2, are plotted in Figure 12.2. The figure uses the parameter estimates of the double Heston model from Table 12.3. As expected, local volatility shows much more variability than implied volatility.

We can also extract the risk-neutral densities (RND) from the Heston call prices generated with the estimated parameters in Table 12.3. These appear in Figure 12.3.

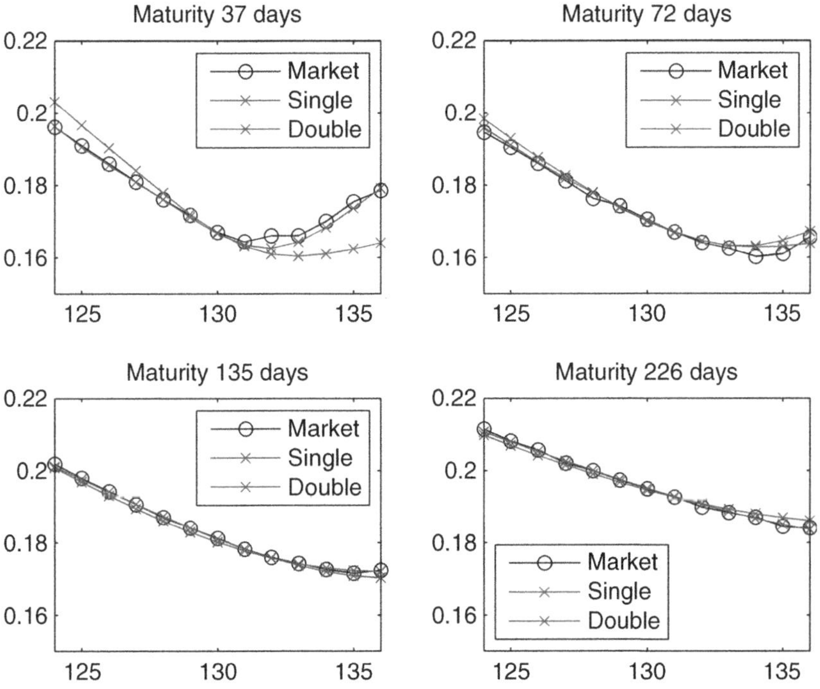

FIGURE 12.1 Implied Volatilities from Univariate and Double Heston Models

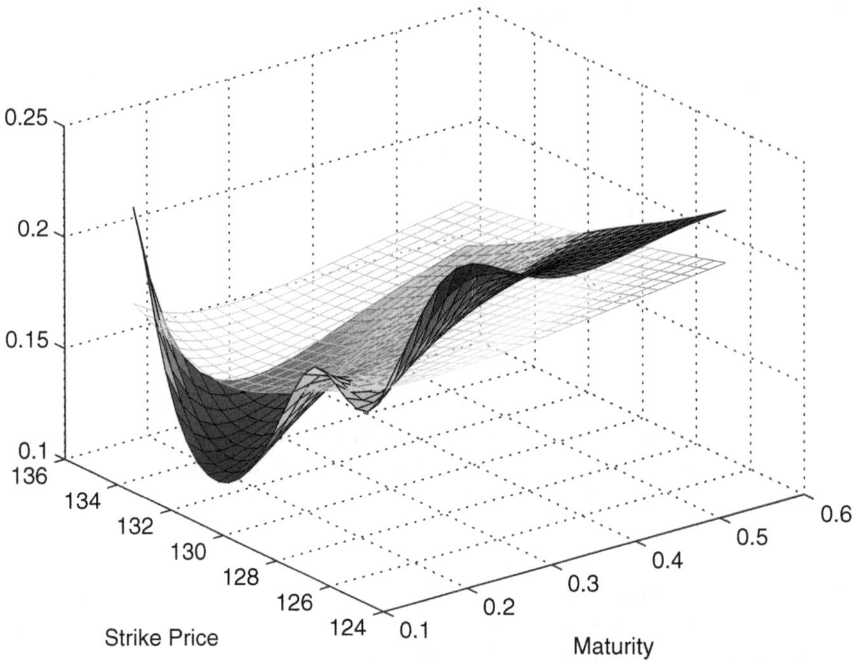

FIGURE 12.2 Implied and Local Volatilities from the Double Heston Model, DJIA Data

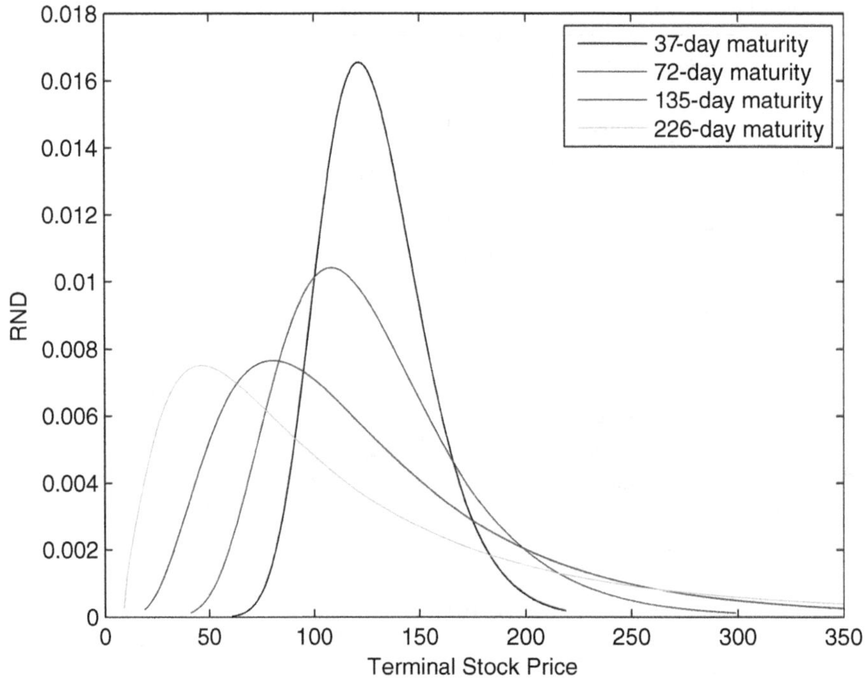

FIGURE 12.3 Risk Neutral Densities, DJIA Data

Figure 12.3 is generated with the following Matlab code, which is very similar to that in Chapter 6 for extracting RNDs from call prices obtained with original Heston (1993) model.

```
% Strike increment and ranges
dK = 0.5;
K{1} = 60:dK:220;
K{2} = 40:dK:300;
K{3} = 18:dK:380;
K{4} = 8:dK:600;

% Extract the RNDs, areas, and zeros
for t=1:NT
    NK = length(K{t});
    for k=1:NK
        Calls{t}(k) = DoubleHestonPriceGaussLaguerre(K{t}(k),T(t),...);
    end
    [RND{t} Strike{t}] = ExtractRND(K{t},Calls{t});
    Area(t) = trapz(RND{t})*dK;
    Zero(t) = length(find(RND{t}<0));
end
```

SIMULATION IN THE DOUBLE HESTON MODEL

In Chapter 7, we presented a set of discretization and simulation schemes for the Heston (1993) model, many of which are designed specifically for the model. Gauthier and Possamaï (2010) adapt many of these schemes to the double Heston model. In this section, we present a few of these simulation schemes. In most cases, the generalization of the scheme from the Heston model to the double Heston model is straightforward and intuitive. In each scheme, it is possible to apply a martingale correction to improve the accuracy of the scheme, but these are not covered.

Simulation of the Stock Price

Rather than simulating the log stock price $\ln S_t$, Gauthier and Possamaï (2010) suggest simulating the discounted log price $\ln(e^{-rt}S_t)$ and applying the Predictor-Corrector scheme. This scheme is given in terms of two standard Brownian motion $W_{1,t}$ and $W_{2,t}$ as

$$\begin{aligned}\ln(e^{-r(t+dt)}S_{t+dt}) &= \ln(e^{-rt}S_t) \\ &\quad + K_0^1 + K_1^1 v_{1,t} + K_2^1 v_{1,t+dt} + \sqrt{K_3^1(v_{1,t} + v_{1,t+dt})}W_{1,t} \\ &\quad + K_0^2 + K_1^2 v_{2,t} + K_2^2 v_{2,t+dt} + \sqrt{K_3^2(v_{2,t} + v_{2,t+dt})}W_{2,t}\end{aligned} \tag{12.26}$$

where the constants are, for $j = 1, 2$

$$K_0^j = -\frac{\rho_j \kappa_j \theta_j}{\sigma_j} dt, \quad K_1^j = \frac{dt}{2}\left(\frac{\kappa_j \rho_j}{\sigma_j} - \frac{1}{2}\right) - \frac{\rho_j}{\sigma_j}$$

$$K_2^j = \frac{dt}{2}\left(\frac{\kappa_j \rho_j}{\sigma_j} - \frac{1}{2}\right) + \frac{\rho_j}{\sigma_j}, \quad K_3^j = \frac{dt}{2}(1 - \rho_j^2).$$

Note that the Brownian motions $W_{1,t}$ and $W_{2,t}$ are independent, but the discretization scheme preserves correlation through the constants K_i^j. The stock price is then found by exponentiating $\ln(e^{-r(t+dt)} S_{t+dt})$ and multiplying the result by $e^{r(t+dt)}$.

Euler Scheme for the Variance

This is a straightforward extension of the univariate case. Under the full truncation scheme, for example, each variance $v_{j,t+dt}$ is generated independently of the other using the current value $v_{j,t}$ as

$$v_{j,t+dt} = v_{j,t}^+ + \kappa_j(\theta_j - v_{j,t}^+)dt + \sigma_j \sqrt{v_{j,t}^+} \sqrt{dt} Z_{j,V} \tag{12.27}$$

for $j = 1, 2$ and where $Z_{1,V}$ and $Z_{2,V}$ are independent Brownian motion. The current and updated values $v_{j,t}$ and $v_{j,t+dt}$ are then fed into the simulation of Equation (12.26), and the process is repeated. Note that $v_{j,t}^+ = \max(0, v_{j,t})$ so that in (12.27), negative variances are avoided. It is also possible to use the reflective scheme instead, by replacing $v_{j,t}^+$ in (12.27) with $|v_{j,t}|$.

Alfonsi Scheme for the Variance

Gauthier and Possamaï (2010) adapt the second-order discretization scheme of Alfonsi (2010) to the double Heston model. For notational simplicity, we drop the "j" subscript from all the parameters and variances. As in Chapter 7, define

$$\Psi = \frac{1 - \exp(-\kappa dt/2)}{\kappa}$$

and define the constant K_2 as

$$K_2 = \exp(\kappa dt/2)\left[\left(\frac{\sigma^2}{4} - \theta\kappa\right)\Psi + \left(\sqrt{e^{\kappa dt/2}\left(\frac{\sigma^2}{4} - \theta\kappa\right)\Psi} + \frac{\sigma}{2}\sqrt{3dt}\right)^2\right] \tag{12.28}$$

when $\sigma^2 > 4\kappa\theta$, and as

$$K_2 = 0 \tag{12.29}$$

when $\sigma^2 \leq 4\kappa\theta$. At each simulation step, we compare v_t to K_2, and we have a different updated value v_{t+dt}, depending on the results of the comparison. Hence, in this scheme, two cases are considered separately, exactly as in Chapter 7.

Case 1, $v_t > K_2$

Updating to v_{t+dt} requires two steps. In the first step, we simulate a discrete random variable $Y \in \{0, \sqrt{3}, -\sqrt{3}\}$ with probabilities 2/3, 1/6, and 1/6, respectively. In the second step, we update to v_{t+dt} using

$$v_{t+dt} = \exp(-\kappa dt/2)\left(\sqrt{\left(\kappa\theta - \frac{\sigma^2}{4}\right)\Psi + e^{-\kappa dt/2}v_t} + \frac{\sigma}{2}\sqrt{dt}Y\right)^2 + \left(\kappa\theta - \frac{\sigma^2}{4}\right)\Psi. \quad (12.30)$$

Case 2, $v_t \le K_2$

Denote the first two moments of v_{t+dt} conditional on v_t by

$$u_1 = E[v_{t+dt}|v_t]$$
$$u_2 = E[v_{t+dt}^2|v_t].$$

Define the quantity π as

$$\pi = \frac{1}{2} - \frac{1}{2}\sqrt{1 - \frac{u_1^2}{u_2}}.$$

In the first step, we simulate a uniform random variable U on $(0, 1)$. In the second step, we update to v_{t+dt} by comparing U to π so that

$$\begin{aligned} v_{t+dt} &= \frac{u_1}{2\pi} && \text{if } U \le \pi \\ v_{t+dt} &= \frac{u_1}{2(1-\pi)} && \text{if } U > \pi. \end{aligned} \quad (12.31)$$

The function CIRmoments.m calculates the moments u_1 and u_2. The algorithm to update v_t is implemented with the Matlab function AlfonsiV.m. These functions are identical to those presented in Chapter 7. Please refer to that chapter for details.

The AlfonsiV.m function is used in the DHEulerAlfonsiSim.m function, which simulates the stock price in accordance with the Predictor-Corrector scheme in Equation (12.26), simulates the variance using the Euler scheme under full truncation in (12.27) or the Alfonsi scheme in (12.30) and (12.31), and returns the simulated value of the call or put. To conserve space, parts of the function are omitted.

```
function [S ... Price] = DHEulerAlfonsiSim(scheme,...)
S(1,:)  = S0;
V1(1,:) = v01;
V2(1,:) = v02;
for i=1:N;
    for t=2:T;
        if strcmp(scheme, 'Euler')
            % Generate two independent N(0,1) variables
            G1 = randn(1);
            G2 = randn(1);
```

```
            % Euler discretization with full truncation
            V1(t,i) = V1(t-1,i) + kappa1*(theta1-V1(t-1,i)) ...;
            V1(t,i) = max(0,V1(t,i));
        elseif strcmp(scheme,'Alfonsi')
            % Alfonsi discretization
            V1(t,i) = AlfonsiV(params1,V1(t-1,i),dt);
        end
        % Predictor-Corrector for the stock price
        B1 = randn(1);
        B2 = randn(1);
        logS = log(exp(-r*t*dt)*S(t-1,i)) + K01 + K11*V1(t-1,i) + ...; ...;
        S(t,i) = exp(logS)*exp(r*(t+1)*dt);
    end
end
ST = S(end,:);
if strcmp(PutCall,'C')
    Payoff = max(ST - Strike,0);
elseif strcmp(PutCall,'P')
    Payoff = max(Strike - ST,0);
end
Price = exp(-r*Mat)*mean(Payoff);
```

The C# code to implement the Alfonsi (2010) method on the double Heston model is similar and not presented here.

Zhu Scheme for the Transformed Variance

We saw in Chapter 7 that one way to avoid negative variances is to simulate the volatility instead of the variance, and then square the volatility before using it as an input to the stock price process. It is straightforward to apply this approach to the double Heston model also. Recall from Chapter 7 that an application of Itō's lemma produces the process for the volatility $\omega_{j,t} = \sqrt{v_{j,t}}$, and that Euler discretization of the volatility produces

$$\omega_{j,t+dt} = \omega_{j,t} + \frac{\kappa_j}{2}\left[\left(\theta_j - \frac{\sigma_j^2}{4\kappa_j}\right)\frac{1}{\omega_{j,t}} - \omega_{j,t}\right]dt + \frac{1}{2}\sigma_j\sqrt{dt}Z_{j,V} \tag{12.32}$$

for $j = 1, 2$. Hence, we first simulate $(\omega_{1,t}, \omega_{2,t})$ and then obtain the variances as $v_{1,t} = \omega_{1,t}^2$ and $v_{2,t} = \omega_{2,t}^2$. These are then fed into the Predictor-Method of Equation (12.26) to obtain S_{t+dt}. Note that this method suffers the same problem of numerical instability as the univariate version, due to the fact that the mean levels $\theta_{\omega,j} = [\theta_j - \sigma_j^2/(4\kappa_j)]/\omega_{j,t}$ are stochastic.

We saw in Chapter 7 that the remedy proposed by Zhu (2010) to this numerical instability is the transformed volatility scheme. Gauthier and Possamaï (2010) show how to apply this scheme to the double Heston model also. The transformed volatilities are defined analogously to those in Chapter 7

$$\omega_{j,t+dt} = \omega_{j,t} + \frac{\kappa_j}{2}[\theta_j^* - \omega_{j,t}]dt + \frac{1}{2}\sigma_j\sqrt{dt}Z_{j,V} \tag{12.33}$$

for $j = 1, 2$, where

$$\theta_j^* = \frac{\beta_j - \omega_{j,t} \exp(-\kappa_j dt/2)}{1 - \exp(-\kappa_j dt/2)}$$

and

$$\beta_j = \sqrt{\left(\theta_j + \left(v_{j,t} - \theta_j\right) e^{-\kappa_j dt} - \frac{\sigma_j^2}{4\kappa_j}(1 - e^{-\kappa_j dt})\right)^+}.$$

Implementing the transformed volatility scheme for the double Heston model is no more complicated than in the univariate case described in Chapter 7. This is accomplished with the DHTransVolSim.m function, which simulates values of the stock price using the Predictor-Corrector method in Equation (12.26), and volatilities in either (12.32) or (12.33). It is important to remember that the square root of the initial variance parameters must be used to initialize the volatilities, and that the volatilities must be squared before they are fed into the stock price process at the end of the function. To conserve space, part of the function has been omitted.

```
function [S ... Price] = DHTransVolSim(scheme,...)
S(1,:)  = S0;
w1(1,:) = sqrt(v01);
w2(1,:) = sqrt(v02);
for i=1:N;
    for t=2:T;
        Zv1 = randn(1);
        Zv2 = randn(1);
        if strcmp(scheme,'Euler')
            % Euler volatility scheme
            w1(t,i) = w1(t-1,i) + 0.5*kappa1 ...;
        elseif strcmp(scheme,'TV')
            % Zhu (2010) process for t.v.
            m11 = theta1 + (v1(t-1,i) - theta1)*exp(-kappa1*dt);
            m12 = sigma1^2/4/kappa1*(1-exp(-kappa1*dt));
            beta1 = sqrt(max(0,m11-m12));
            thetav1 = (beta1 - w1(t-1,i)*exp(-kappa1*dt/2)) ...;
            w1(t,i) = w1(t-1,i) + 0.5*kappa1*(thetav1 ...;
        end
        v1(t,i) = w1(t,i)^2;
        v2(t,i) = w2(t,i)^2;
        % Predictor-Corrector for the stock price
        logS = log(exp(-r*t*dt)*S(t-1,i)) + K01 ...;
        S(t,i) = exp(logS)*exp(r*(t+1)*dt);
    end
end
```

The C# code is similar and is therefore not presented here.

Quadratic Exponential Scheme

The last simulation scheme we cover in this chapter is the Quadratic Exponential (QE) scheme developed by Andersen (2008) and adapted to the double Heston model by Gauthier and Possamaï (2010). It is implemented in the same manner as in the univariate case described in Chapter 7. Denote the conditional means by $m_j = E[v_{j,t+dt}|v_{j,t}]$ and the conditional variances by $s_j^2 = \text{Var}[v_{j,t+dt}|v_{j,t}]$. Also, denote the ratio by $\psi_j = s_j^2/m_j^2$. Define the quantities

$$b_j = \left(\frac{2}{\psi_j} - 1 + \sqrt{\frac{2}{\psi_j}\left(\frac{2}{\psi_j} - 1\right)}\right)^{\frac{1}{2}}, \quad a_j = \frac{m_j}{1+b_j^2}, \tag{12.34}$$

$$p_j = \frac{\psi_j - 1}{\psi_j + 1}, \quad \beta_j = \frac{1-p_j}{m_j}$$

and

$$\Psi_j^{-1}(u) = \begin{cases} 0 & \text{for } 0 \le u \le p_j \\ \dfrac{1}{\beta_j}\ln\left(\dfrac{1-p_j}{1-u}\right) & \text{for } p_j \le u \le 1. \end{cases} \tag{12.35}$$

The scheme proceeds as follows

- Given $v_{j,t}$, obtain m_j and s_j^2, and set $\psi_j = s_j^2/m_j^2$.
- Draw a uniform random number $U_V \in [0,1]$.
- If $\psi_j < \psi_c$ compute $Z_V = \Phi^{-1}(U_V)$ and define $v_{j,t+dt} = a_j(b_j + Z_V)^2$.
- If $\psi_j > \psi_c$ define $v_{j,t+dt} = \Psi_j^{-1}(U_V)$.

As in the univariate case, we use the value of $\psi_c = 1.5$ recommended by Andersen (2008). The QE simulation scheme for the double Heston model is implemented using the DHQuadExpSim.m Matlab function. The function calls the normICDF.m function described in Chapter 7 for inversion of the standard normal distribution function, which applies the algorithm of Wichura (1988) and leads to a considerable reduction in simulation time.

```
function [S ... Price] = DHQuadExpSim(params,...)
for i=1:N;
    for t=2:T;
        m1 = theta1 + (V1(t-1,i) - theta1)*exp(-kappa1*dt);
        s1 = V1(t-1,i)*sigma1^2*exp(-kappa1*dt) ...;
        phi1 = s1/(m1^2);
        p1 = (phi1-1)/(phi1+1);
        U1 = rand(1);
        if phi1 < 1/2
            b1 = sqrt(2/phi1 - 1 + sqrt(2/phi1*(2/phi1-1)));
            a1 = m1/(1+b1^2);
            Zv1 = normICDF(U1);
```

```
            V1(t,i) = a1*(b1+Zv1)^2;
        elseif phi1 >= 1/2
            if U1 <= p1
                V1(t,i) = 0;
            elseif U1 > p1
                beta1 = (1-p1)/m1;
                V1(t,i) = log((1-p1)/(1-U1))/beta1;
            end
        end
        m2 = theta2 + (V2(t-1,i) - theta2)*exp(-kappa2*dt);
        s2 = V2(t-1,i)*sigma2^2*exp(-kappa2*dt)/kappa2 ...;
        phi2 = s2/(m2^2);
        p2 = (phi2-1)/(phi2+1);
        U2 = rand(1);
        if phi2 < 1/2
            b2 = sqrt(2/phi2 - 1 + sqrt(2/phi2*(2/phi2-1)));
            a2 = m2/(1+b2^2);
            Zv2 = normIcdf(U2);
            V2(t,i) = a2*(b2+Zv2)^2;
        elseif phi2 >= 1/2
            if U2 <= p2
                V2(t,i) = 0;
            elseif U2 > p2
                beta2 = (1-p2)/m2;
                V2(t,i) = log((1-p2)/(1-U2))/beta2;
            end
        end
    end
end
```

The C# code to implement the quadratic-exponential of Andersen (2008) for the double Heston model is similar and not presented here.

To illustrate the different simulation schemes covered in this chapter, we use the same settings as those in Gauthier and Possamaï (2010) that were used to generate Table 12.1, with a maturity of one year. We use 50,000 simulations and 1,000 time steps per simulation. This is accomplished with the following code.

```
NS = 50000;
NT =  1000;
trap = 1;
[x w] = GenerateGaussLaguerre(32);
True = DoubleHestonPriceGaussLaguerre(...);
[S V1 V2 Alfonsi] = DHEulerAlfonsiSim('Alfonsi',...);
[S V1 V2 Euler]   = DHEulerAlfonsiSim('Euler',...);
[S v1 v2 ZEuler]  = DHTransVolSim('ZhuEuler',...);
[S v1 v2 ZhuTV]   = DHTransVolSim('ZhuTV',...);
[S V1 V2 QE]      = DHQuadExpSim(...);
```

The results of the simulation are in Table 12.4.

TABLE 12.4 Double Heston Call Prices

Method	Price	Dollar Error	Percent Error
Closed Form	19.4538	—	—
Euler	19.6286	0.17	0.90
Alfonsi	19.5271	0.07	0.38
Zhu-Euler	19.5231	0.07	0.36
Zhu Transformed Vol	19.4650	−0.01	−0.06
Quadratic Exponential	19.3214	−0.13	−0.68

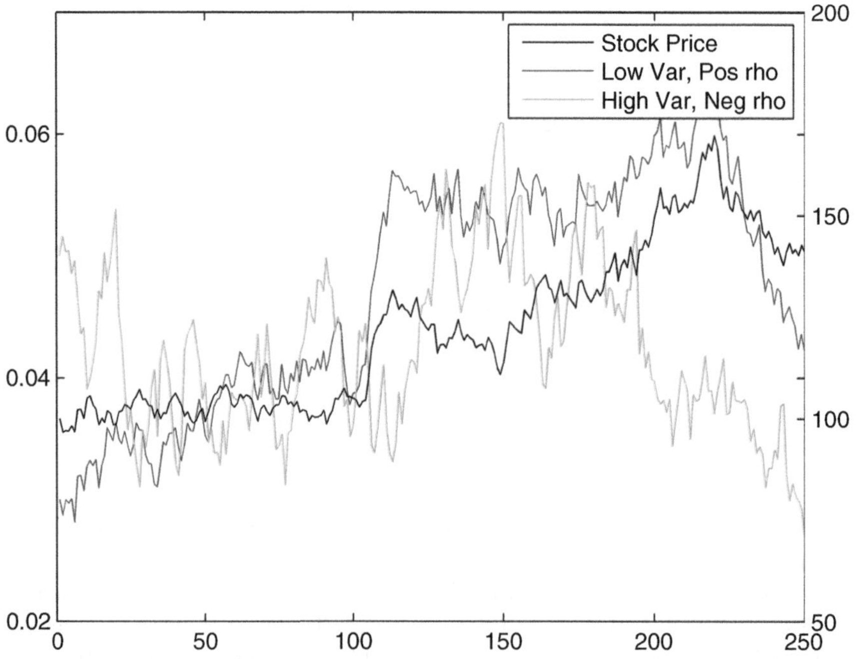

FIGURE 12.4 Simulated Stock Price and Variances with the Double Heston Model

As expected, the Euler scheme is the least accurate of the schemes. The other schemes perform well, with the transformed volatility scheme of Zhu (2010) the most accurate, in this example at least.

It is instructive to plot the effect of double variances on a single simulated stock price path. This is illustrated in Figure 12.4. The stock price starts at $S_0 = 100$ and is represented by the black line. The high variance path (green line) uses $\sigma = 0.3$, $\rho = -0.9$, and starts at $v_{01} = 0.05$, while the low variance path (red line) uses $\sigma = 0.1$, $\rho = 0.9$, and starts at $v_{02} = 0.03$. The effect of the correlations on the price-volatility relationships is evident.

AMERICAN OPTIONS IN THE DOUBLE HESTON MODEL

In the previous sections, we covered a number of simulation schemes adapted to the double Heston model by Gauthier and Possamaï (2010). We can use these schemes along with the Least-Squares Monte-Carlo (LSM) algorithm of Longstaff and Schwartz (2001) to obtain the prices of American options, in the same way that the LSM algorithm was applied to the univariate Heston (1993) model in Chapter 8. We can also apply the control variate technique described by Hull and White (1988) and used by Beliaeva and Nawalkha (2010) in their bivariate tree, which we encountered in Chapter 8 also. The control variate price of the American put is

$$\text{American Put}_{\text{True}} = \text{European Put}_{\text{True}} + (\text{American Put}_{\text{LSM}} - \text{European Put}_{\text{LSM}})$$

We use the closed form of the double Heston model to calculate the true price of the European put.

To implement the pricing of American puts with the LSM algorithm and the double Heston model, we first choose a simulation scheme among those covered in this chapter to generate a set of stock price paths. We then feed these stock price paths into the LSM functions to obtain the simulated prices of American and European puts. Finally, we apply the control variate technique to obtain the price of the American put. The required Matlab and C# functions for the LSM algorithm are those described earlier in this chapter and in Chapter 8, and are not presented here.

For example, suppose we use $N_S = 50{,}000$ simulations along with $N_T = 1{,}000$ time steps per simulation to obtain the price of an American price, using the same settings as those used to create Table 12.2. This is accomplished with the following C# code.

```
// Simulation settings
string PutCall = "P";
int NS = 50000;
int NT = 1000;
// Select the simulation scheme
string scheme = "QE";
double LSMEuro,LSMAmer,Premium,CVPrice;
DHSim Soutput = new DHSim();
if((scheme == "Alfonsi") || (scheme == "Euler"))
    Soutput = DHEulerAlfonsiSim(scheme,...);
else if((scheme=="ZhuEuler") || (scheme=="ZhuTV"))
    Soutput = DHTransVolSim(scheme,...);
else if(scheme == "QE")
    Soutput = DHQuadExpSim(...);
double[,] S = Soutput.S;
double SimEuro = Soutput.EuroPrice;
// LSM algorithm
double[] LSMoutput = new double[2];
double[,] St1 = MTrans(S);
LSMoutput = HestonLSM(St1,K,rf,q,Mat,NT,NS,PutCall);
LSMEuro = LSMoutput[0];
LSMAmer = LSMoutput[1];
Premium = LSMAmer - LSMEuro;
// Control variate American price
double TrueEuroPrice = DoubleHestonPriceGaussLaguerre(...);
CVPrice = TrueEuroPrice + Premium;
```

TABLE 12.5 Double Heston Prices of an American Put

Method	Price	Exercise Premium
Closed-form European	17.6244	—
Euler	17.8278	0.2034
Alfonsi	17.8095	0.1851
Zhu-Euler	17.8068	0.1824
Zhu Transformed Vol	17.8372	0.2128
Quadratic Exponential	17.8185	0.1941

The closed form European price is 17.6244, and the American prices obtained under the simulation schemes covered in this chapter are in Table 12.5.

The schemes all point to an early exercise premium of roughly \$0.20 and a price of roughly \$17.82 for the American option using the control variate technique.

CONCLUSION

The double Heston model is a convenient way to introduce flexibility in the model by allowing for additional parameters. The characteristic function of the double Heston model is a natural extension of its univariate counterpart. As such, obtaining the call price and Greeks in the double Heston model is only slightly more complicated than in the original Heston (1993) model. Moreover, simulation schemes specifically designed for the original model translate easily to the double version. With these simulation schemes, it is straightforward to obtain American option prices with the LSM algorithm of Longstaff and Schwartz (2001).

Other investigations of the double Heston model, or multifactor volatility versions of the model, include the double-lattice approach of Costabile et al. (2012), the multifactor volatility Wishart process of da Fonseca et al. (2008), and the variance curve approach of Buehler (2006).

Bibliography

Afshani, S. (2010). "Complex Logarithms and the Piecewise Constant Extension of the Heston Model." Working Paper, Standard Bank.

AitSahlia, F., Goswami, M., and S. Guha. (2012). "Are There Critical Levels of Stochastic Volatility for Early Option Exercise?" Working Paper, University of Florida.

Aït-Sahalia, Y. (2002). "Maximum Likelihood Estimation of Discretely Sampled Diffusions: A Closed-Form Approximation Approach." *Econometrica*, 70(1): 223–62.

Aït-Sahalia, Y., and R. Kimmel. (2007). "Maximum Likelihood Estimation of Stochastic Volatility Models." *Journal of Financial Economics*, 83:413–52.

Albanese, C., and G. Campolieti. (2006). *Advanced Derivatives Pricing and Risk Management: Theory, Tools, and Hands-On Programming Applications*, London, UK: Elsevier Academic Press.

Albrecher, H., Mayer, P., Schoutens, W., and Tistaert, J. (2007) "The Little Heston Trap." *Wilmott Magazine*, January 2007, 83–92.

Alfonsi, A. (2010). "High Order Discretization Schemes for the CIR Process: Application to Affine Term Structure and Heston Models." *Mathematics of Computation*, 79:209–37.

Andersen, L. (2008). "Efficient Simulation of the Heston Stochastic Volatility Model." *Journal of Computational Finance*, 11(3):1–42.

Andersen, L.B.G., and R. Brotherton-Ratcliffe. (2005). "Extended Libor Market Models with Stochastic Volatility." *Journal of Computational Finance*, 9(1):1–40.

Andersen, L.B.G., and V.V. Piterbarg. (2007). "Moment Explosions in Stochastic Volatility Models." *Finance and Stochastics*, 11(1):29–50.

Atiya, A.F., and S. Wall (2009). "An Analytic Approximation of the Likelihood Function for the Heston Model Volatility Estimation Problem." *Quantitative Finance*, 9(3):289–96.

Attari, M. (2004). "Option Pricing Using Fourier Transforms: A Numerically Efficient Simplification." Working Paper, Charles River Associates, Boston, MA.

Backus D., Foresi, S., and L. Wu. (2004) "Accounting for Biases in Black-Scholes." Working Paper, Stern School of Business, New York University.

Bagby, R.J. (1995). "Calculating Normal Probabilities." *The American Mathematical Monthly*, 102(1):46–9.

Bakshi, G., Cao, C., and Z. Chen. (1997). "Empirical Performance of Alternative Option Pricing Models." *Journal of Finance*, 52(5):2033–49.

Bakshi, G., and D. Madan. (2000). "Spanning and Derivative-Security Valuation." *Journal of Financial Economics*, 55:205–38.

Bams, D., Lehnert, T., and C.C.P. Wolff. (2009). "Loss Functions in Option Valuation: A Framework for Selection." *Management Science*, 55:853–62.

Barone-Adesi, G., and R.E. Whaley. (1987). "Efficient Analytic Approximation of American Option Values." *Journal of Finance*, 42(2):301–20.

Beerends, R.J., ter Morsche, H.G., van den Berg, J.C., and E.M. van de Vrie. (2003). *Fourier and Laplace Transforms*. Cambridge, UK: Cambridge University Press.

Beliaeva, N.A., and S.K. Nawalkha. (2010). "A Simple Approach to Pricing American Options Under the Heston Stochastic Volatility Model." *Journal of Derivatives*, 17(4):25–43.

Benaim, S., and P. Friz. (2008). "Smile Asymptotics II: Models With Known Moment Generating Functions." *Journal of Applied Probability*, 45(1):16–32.

Benhamou, E. (2002). "Smart Monte Carlo: Various Tricks Using Malliavin Calculus." *Quantitative Finance*, 2(5):329–36.

Benhamou, E., Gobet, E., and M. Miri. (2010). "Time Dependent Heston Model." *SIAM Journal on Financial Mathematics*, 1:289–325.

Bollerslev, T., Gibson, M., and H. Zhou (2011). "Dynamic Estimation of Volatility Risk Premia and Investor Risk Aversion From Option-Implied and Realized Volatilities." *Journal of Econometrics*, 160(1):235–45.

Borak, S., Detlefsen, K., and W. Härdle. (2011). "FFT Based Option Pricing." SFB Discussion Paper 2005–11, Humboldt University.

Breeden, D. (1979). "An Intertemporal Asset Pricing Model With Stochastic Consumption and Investment Opportunities." *Journal of Financial Economics*, 7:265–96.

Breeden, D., and R. Litzenberger. (1978). "Prices of State-Contingent Claims Implicit in Option Prices." *Journal of Business*, 51:621–51.

Brigo, D., and F. Mercurio. (2006). *Interest Rate Models - Theory and Practice: With Smile, Inflation, and Credit*. Second Edition. New York, NY: Springer.

Broadie, M., and P. Glasserman. (1996). "Estimating Security Price Derivatives Using Simulation." *Management Science*, 42(2):269–85.

Broadie, M., and Ö. Kaya. (2006). "Exact Simulation of Stochastic Volatility and Other Affine Jump Diffusion Processes." *Operations Research*, 54(2):217–31.

Broadie, M., and Ö. Kaya. (2004). "Exact Simulation of Option Greeks Under Stochastic Volatility and Jump Diffusion Models." In Ingalls, R.G., Rossetti, M.D., Smith, J.S., and B.A. Peters, eds. *Proceedings of the 2004 Winter Simulation Conference*, pp. 1607–15.

Brunner, B., and R. Hafner. (2003). "Arbitrage-Free Estimation of the Risk-Neutral Density From the Implied Volatility Smile." *Journal of Computational Finance*, 7(1):75–106.

Buehler, H. (2006). "Consistent Variance Curve Models." *Finance & Stochastics*, 10(2): 178–203.

Burden, R.L., and J.D. Faires. (2010). *Numerical Analysis*. Ninth Edition. Boston, MA: Brooks Cole.

Carr, P. (2004). "Implied Vol Constraints." Working Paper, Bloomberg.

Carr, P., and D. Madan. (1999). "Option Valuation Using the Fast Fourier Transform." *Journal of Computational Finance*, 2(4):61–73.

Carr, P., and D. Madan. (2005). "A Note on Sufficient Conditions for no Arbitrage." *Finance Research Letters*, 2:125–30.

Carr, P., Madan, D., and E.C. Chang. (1998). "The Variance Gamma Process and Option Pricing." *European Finance Review*, 2:79–105.

Chacon, P. (1991). "Applications of the Fourier Transform to Probability Theory and Stochastic Processes." *International Journal of Mathematical Education in Science and Technology*, 22(5):695–708.

Chan, J.H., and M.S. Joshi. (2010a). "Fast and Accurate Long Stepping Simulation of the Heston Stochastic Volatility Model." Working Paper, University of Melbourne.

Chan, J.H., and M.S. Joshi. (2010b). "First and Second Order Greeks in the Heston Model." Working Paper, University of Melbourne.

Chensey, M., and L. Scott. (1989). "Pricing European Currency Options: a Comparison of the Modified Black-Scholes Model and a Random Variance Model." *Journal of Financial and Quantitative Analysis*, 24(3):267–84.

Chernov, M., and E. Ghysels. (2000). "A Study Towards a Unified Approach to the Joint Estimation of Objective and Risk Neutral Measures for the Purpose of Options Valuation." *Journal of Financial Economics*, 56:407–58.

Chiarella, C., and A. Ziogas. (2006). "Pricing American Options Under Stochastic Volatility." Working Paper, University of Technology, Sydney.

Chourdakis, K. (2005). "Option Pricing Using the Fractional FFT." *Journal of Computational Finance*, 8(2):1–18.

Chriss, N.A. (1996). *Black-Scholes and Beyond: Option Pricing Models.* New York, NY: McGraw-Hill.

Christoffersen, P., Jacobs, K., and K. Mimouni. (2010) "Volatility Dynamics for the S&P500: Evidence from Realized Volatility, Daily Returns, and Options Prices." *Review of Financial Studies*, 23(8):3141–89.

Christoffersen, P., Heston, S., and K. Jacobs. (2009). "The Shape and Term Structure of the Index Option Smirk: Why Multifactor Stochastic Volatility Models Work so Well." *Management Science*, 55:1914–32.

Christoffersen, P., and K. Jacobs. (2004) "The Importance of the Loss Function in Option Valuation." *Journal of Financial Economics*, 72:291–318.

Clarke, N., and K. Parrott. (1999) "Multigrid for American Option Pricing With Stochastic Volatility." *Applied Mathematical Finance*, 6:177–95.

Cohen, H. (2011) *Numerical Approximation Methods.* New York: Springer.

Corrado, C.J., and T. Su. (1997). "Implied Volatility Skews and Stock Index Skewness and Kurtosis Implied by S&P500 Index Option Prices." *Journal of Derivatives*, 4(4):8–19.

Costabile, M., Massabò, I., and E. Russo. (2012). "On Pricing Contingent Claims Under the Double Heston Model." *International Journal of Theoretical and Applied Finance*, 15(5):1250033-1-1250033-27.

Cox, J.C., Ingersoll, J.E., and S.A. Ross (1985). "A Theory of the Term Structure of Interest Rates." *Econometrica*, 53(2):385–408.

Da Fonseca, J., Grasselli, M., and C. Tebaldi. (2008). "A MultiFactor Volatility Heston Model." *Quantitative Finance*, 8(6):591–604.

Davis, M.H.A., and M.P. Johansson. (2005). "Malliavin Monte Carlo Greeks for Jump Diffusions." Working Paper, Imperial College.

Demeterfi, K., Derman, E., Kamal, M., and J. Zhou. (1999). "A Guide to Volatility and Variance Swaps," *Journal of Derivatives*, 6(4):9–32.

Derman, E., Kani, I., and J.Z. Zhou. (1995). "The Local Volatility Surface: Unlocking the Information in Index Option Prices." Goldman Sachs Quantitative Strategies Research Notes. December, 1995.

Dréo, J., Nunes, J.-C., and P. Siarry. (2009)."Metaheuristics for Continuous Variables." In Siarry, P. (ed). *Optimization in Signal and Image Processing.* Hoboken, NJ: John Wiley & Sons.

Duffie, D., Pan, J., and K. Singleton. (2000). Transform Analysis and Asset Pricing for Affine Jump-Diffusions. *Econometrica*, 68:1343–76.

Duffy, D.J. (2006) *Finite Difference Methods in Financial Engineering: A Partial Differential Equation Approach.* Hoboken, NJ: John Wiley & Sons.

Duffy, D.J., and J. Kienitz. (2009). *Monte Carlo Frameworks: Building Customisable High-Performance C++ Applications.* Hoboken, NJ: John Wiley & Sons.

Dupire, B. (1994). "Pricing With a Smile." *Risk*, 7:18–20.

Elices, A. (2009) "Affine Concatenation." *Wilmott Journal*, 1(3):155–62.

Eraker, B. (2004). "Do Stock Prices and Volatility Jump? Reconciling Evidence from Spot and Option Prices". *Journal of Finance*, 59(3):1367–403.

Fang, F., and C.W. Oosterlee (2008). "A Novel Pricing Method for European Options Based on Fourier-Cosine Series Expansions." *SIAM Journal on Scientific Computing*, 31(2):826–48.

Fengler, M. (2009). "Arbitrage-Free Smoothing of the Implied Volatility Surface." *Quantitative Finance*, 9(4):417–28.

Forde, M., and A. Jacquier. (2009). "Small-Time Asymptotics for Implied Volatility Under the Heston Model." *International Journal of Theoretical and Applied Finance*, 12(6):861–876.

Forde, M., Jacquier, A., and A. Mijatovic. (2010). "Asymptotic Formulae for Implied Volatility in the Heston Model." *Proceedings of the Royal Society*, 466(2124):3593–3620.

Galiotos, V. (2008). "Stochastic Volatility and the Volatility Smile." Working Paper, Department of Mathematics, Uppsala University.

Gatheral, J. (2006). *The Volatility Surface: A Practitioner's Guide.* Hoboken, NJ: John Wiley & Sons.

Gauthier, P., and D. Possamaï. (2010). "Efficient Simulation of the Double Heston Model." Working Paper, Pricing Partners (www.pricingpartners.com).

Gauthier, P., and P.-Y. H. Rivaille (2009). "Fitting the Smile: Smart Parameters for SABR and Heston." Working Paper, Pricing Partners (www.pricingpartners.com).

Geske, R., and H.E. Johnson. (1984). "The American Put Option Valued Analytically." *Journal of Finance*, 39(5):1511–24.

Gil-Pelaez, J. (1951). "Note on the Inversion Theorem." *Biometrika*, 38(3-4):481–2.

Gilli, M., and E. Schumann. (2011). Calibrating Option Pricing Models with Heuristics. In Brabazon, A., O'Neill, M., and D. Maringer, eds. *Natural Computing in Computational Finance*, Volume 4. Berlin: Springer-Verlag.

Glasserman, P. (2003). *Monte Carlo Methods in Financial Engineering.* New York, NY: Springer.

Guillaume, F., and W. Schoutens. (2012). "Use a Reduced Heston or Reduce the Use of Heston?" *Wilmott Journal*, 2(4):171–92.

Haug, E.G. (2006). *The Complete Guide to Option Pricing Formulas.* Second Edition. New York, NY: McGraw-Hill.

Heston, S.L. (1993). "A Closed-Form Solution for Options with Stochastic Volatility with Applications to Bond and Currency Options." *Review of Financial Studies*, 6:327–43.

Hogg, R.V., and S. Klugman. (1984) *Loss Distributions.* New York, NY: John Wiley & Sons.

Hull, J.C. (2011). *Options, Futures, and Other Derivatives.* Eighth Edition. New York, NY: Prentice-Hall.

Hull, J.C., and A. White. (1987). "The Pricing of Options on Assets with Stochastic Volatilities." *Journal of Finance*, 42:281–300.

Hull, J.C., and A. White. (1988) "The Use of the Control Variate Technique in Option Pricing." *Journal of Financial and Quantitative Analysis*, 23(3):237–51.

Ikonen, S., and J. Toivanen. (2008). "Efficient Numerical Methods for Pricing American Options Under Stochastic Volatility." *Numerical Methods for Partial Differential Equations*, 24(1):104–26.

In 'T Hout, K.J., and S. Foulon. (2010). "ADI Finite Difference Schemes for Option Pricing in the Heston Model with Correlation." *International Journal of Numerical Analysis and Modeling*, 7(2):303–320.

Itkin, A. (2010). Pricing Options With VG Model Using FFT. Working Paper, Department of Mathematics, Rutgers University.

Janek, A., Kluge, T., Weron, R., and U. Wystup. (2010). FX Smile in the Heston Model. SFB 649 Discussion Paper 2010-047, Humboldt University, Berlin. Also in Cizek, P., Härdle, W.K., and R. Weron, eds. *Statistical Tools for Finance and Insurance.* New York: Springer.

Jarrow, R., and A. Rudd. (1982). "Approximate Option Valuation for Arbitrary Stochastic Processes." *Journal of Financial Economics*, 10:347–69.

Johannes, M.S., Polson, N.G., and J.R Stroud. (2009) "Optimal Filtering of Jump Diffusions: Extracting Latent States from Asset Prices." *Review of Financial Studies*, 22(7):2759–99.

Jondeau, E., Poon, S.-H., and M. Rockinger. (2007). *Financial Modeling Under Non-Gaussian Distributions.* New York, NY: Springer.

Jones, C.S. (2003). "The Dynamics of Stochastic Volatility: Evidence From Underlying and Options Markets." *Journal of Econometrics*, 116:181–224.

Joshi, M. (2008) *The Concepts and Practice of Mathematical Finance.* Second Edition. Cambridge, UK: Cambridge University Press.

Kahalé, N. (2004). "An Arbitrage-Free Interpolation of Volatilities." *Risk*, May 2004: 102–106.

Kahl, C. (2008). *Modeling and Simulation of Stochastic Volatility in Finance*. Published by Dissertation.com.

Kahl, C., and P. Jäckel. (2005). "Not-so-Complex Logarithms in the Heston Model." *Wilmott Magazine*, September 2005:94–103.

Kahl, C., and P. Jäckel. (2006). "Fast Strong Approximation Monte-Carlo Schemes for Stochastic Volatility Models." *Quantitative Finance*, 6(6):513–36.

Kahl, C., and R. Lord. (2010). "Fourier Inversion Methods in Finance." Working Paper, Commerzbank, and Cardano.

Kilin, F. (2007). "Accelerating the Calibration of Stochastic Volatility Models." Working Paper, Frankfurt School of Finance and Management.

Kloeden, P.E., and E. Platen. (1992). *Numerical Solution of Stochastic Differential Equations*. New York, NY: Springer.

Kluge, T. (2002). "Pricing Derivatives in Stochastic Volatility Models Using the Finite Difference Method." Diploma Thesis, Chemnitz University of Technology, Chemnitz, Germany.

Kutner, M.H., Nachtsheim, C.J., Neter, J., and W. Li. (2004). *Applied Linear Statistical Models with Student CD-ROM*. Fifth Edition. New York, NY: McGraw-Hill Education.

Lee, R. (2004a). "Option Pricing by Transform Methods: Extensions, Unification, and Error Control." *Journal of Computational Finance*, 7(3):51–86.

Lee, R. (2004b). "The Moment Formula for Implied Volatility at Extreme Strikes." *Mathematical Finance*, 14(3):469–80.

Leisen, D. (2000). "Stock Evolution Under Stochastic Volatility: A Discrete Approach." *Journal of Derivatives*, 8(2):9–27.

Lewis, A.L. (2000). *Option Valuation Under Stochastic Volatility: With Mathematica Code*. Finance Press.

Lewis, A.L. (2001). "A Simple Option Formula for General Jump-Diffusion and Other Exponential Levy Processes." www.optioncity.net.

Lin, S. (2008). "Finite Difference Schemes for the Heston Model." M.Sc. Dissertation, University of Oxford.

Lipton, A. (2002). "The Vol Smile Problem." *Risk* (February 2002), pp. 61–65.

Longstaff, F.A., and E.S. Schwartz. (2001). Valuing American Options by Simulation: A Simple Least-Squares Approach. *Review of Financial Studies*, 14(1):113–47.

Lord, R., and C. Kahl. (2007). "Optimal Fourier Inversion in Semi-Analytical Option Pricing." Working Paper, Rabobank International and ABN AMRO.

Lord, R., Fang, F., Bervoets, F., and C.W. Oosterlee (2008). "A Fast and Accurate FFT-Based Method for Pricing Early-Exercise Options Under Lévy Processes." *SIAM Journal on Scientific Computing*, 30(4):1678–1705.

McNamee, J.M. (2007). *Numerical Methods for Roots of Polynomials, Part I*. Studies in Computational Mathematics 14. Amsterdam, the Netherlands: Elsevier.

Medvedev, A., and O. Scaillet (2010). "Pricing American Options Under Stochastic Volatility and Stochastic Interest Rates." *Journal of Financial Economics*, 98(1):145–59.

Mikhailov, S., and U. Nögel. (2003). "Heston's Stochastic Volatility Model: Implementation, Calibration, and Some Extensions." *Wilmott Magazine*, July 2003:74–9.

Milstein, G.N., Platen, E., and H. Schurz. (1998). "Balanced Implicit Methods for Stiff Stochastic Systems." *SIAM Journal on Numerical Analysis*, 35(3):1010–9.

Musiela, M., and M. Rutkowsi. (2011). *Martingale Methods in Financial Modelling*. Second Edition. New York, NY: Springer.

Nelder, J.A., and R. Mead. (1965). "A Simplex Method for Function Minimization." *The Computer Journal*, 7(4):308–13.

Nykvist, J. (2009). "Time Consistency in Option Pricing Models." Doctoral Thesis, KTH Royal Institute of Technology.

Pan, J. (2002). "The Jump-Risk Premia Implicit in Options: Evidence From an Integrated Time-Series Study." *Journal of Financial Economics*, 63(1):3–50.

Platen, E., and D. Heath. (2009). *A Benchmark Approach to Quantitative Finance*, Volume 13. New York, NY: Springer.

Press, W.H., Teukolsky, S.A., Vetterling, W.T., and B.P. Flannery. (2007). *Numerical Recipes Third Edition: The Art of Scientific Computing*. New York, NY: Cambridge University Press.

Raible, S. (2000). "Lévy Processes in Finance: Theory, Numerics, and Empirical Facts." Ph.D. dissertation, Albert Ludwig University of Freiburg.

Reiss, O., and U. Wystup. (2000). "Efficient Computation of Option Price Sensitivities Using Homogeneity and Other Tricks." *Working Paper*, Commerzbank.

Ruckdeschel, P., Sayer, T., and A. Szimayer (2013). "Pricing American Options in the Heston Model: A Close Look at Incorporating Correlation." *The Journal of Derivatives*, 20(3):9–29.

Rudin, W. (1986). *Real and Complex Analysis*. Third Edition. New York, NY: McGraw-Hill.

Schmelzle, M. (2010). Option Pricing Formulae Using Fourier Transforms: Theory and Applications. www.pfadintegral.com.

Schoutens, W., Simons, E., and J. Tistaert. (2004). "A Perfect Calibration! Now What?" *Wilmott Magazine*, March 2004:66–78.

Scott, L.O. (1987). "Option Pricing When the Variance Changes Randomly: Theory, Estimation, and an Application." *Journal of Financial and Quantitative Analysis*, 22:419–38.

Shephard, N.G. (1991) "From Characteristic Function to Distribution Function: a Simple Framework for the Theory." *Economic Theory*, 7:519–29.

Shimko, D. (1993) Bounds of Probability. *Risk*, 6(4):33–7.

Singleton, K.J. (2001). "Estimation of Affine Asset Pricing Models Using the Empirical Characteristic Function." *Journal of Econometrics*, 102(1):111–41.

Smith, R.D. (2007). "An Almost Exact Simulation Method for the Heston Model." *Journal of Computational Finance*, 11(1):115–25.

Stein, E.M., and J.C. Stein, (1991). "Stock Price Distributions with Stochastic Volatility: An Analytic Approach." *Review of Financial Studies*, 4:727–52.

Storn, R., and K. Price. (1997). Differential Evolution—A Simple and Efficient Heuristic for Global Optimization Over Continuous Spaces. *Journal of Global Optimization*, 11:341–59.

Stroud, A.H., and D. Secrest. (1966) *Gaussian Quadrature Formulas*. Upper Saddle River, NJ: Prentice-Hall.

Stuart, A. (2010). *Kendall's Advanced Theory of Statistics, Three Volume Set*. Hoboken, NJ: John Wiley & Sons.

Tavella, D., and C. Randall. (2000). *Pricing Financial Instruments: The Finite Difference Method*. New York, NY: John Wiley & Sons.

Tzavalis, E., and S. Wang. (2003). "Pricing American Options Under Stochastic Volatility: A New Method Using Chebyshev Polynomials to Approximate the Early Exercise Boundary." Working Paper 488, Queen Mary, University of London.

Van Haastrecht, A., and A. Pelsser. (2010). "Efficient, Almost Exact Simulation of the Heston Stochastic Volatility Model." International Journal of Theoretical and Applied Finance, 13(1):1–43.

Vellekoop, M., and H. Nieuwenhuis. (2009). "A Tree-Based Method to Price American Options in the Heston Model." *Journal of Computational Finance*, 13(1):1–21.

Vollrath, I., and J. Wendland. (2009). "Calibration of Interest Rate and Option Models Using Differential Evolution." Working Paper, FINCAD Corporation.

Whaley, R.E. (2006). *Derivatives: Markets, Valuation, and Risk Management*. Hoboken, NJ: John Wiley & Sons.

Wichura, M.J. (1988). "Algorithm AS241: The Percentage Points of the Normal Distribution." *Applied Statistics*, 37(3):477–84.

Wiggins, J.B. (1987). "Option Values Under Stochastic Volatility: Theory and Empirical Estimates." *Journal of Financial Economics*, 19:351–72.

Wu, L. (2008) "Modeling Financial Security Returns Using Lévy Processes." In Birge, J.R., and V. Linetsky, (eds.). *Financial Engineering*, Volume 15. Amsterdam: North-Holland Elsevier.

Zhu, J. (2010). *Applications of Fourier Transform to Smile Modeling: Theory and Implementation*. Second Edition. New York, NY: Springer.

Zhylyevskyy, O. (2010). "A Fast Fourier Transform Technique for Pricing American Options Under Stochastic Volatility." *Review of Derivatives Research*, 13(1):1–24.

Zwillinger, D. (1997). *Handbook of Differential Equations*. Third Edition. Orlando, FL: Academic Press.

About the Website

The website that accompanies this book contains extensive libraries of Matlab and C# code. The code includes dozens of functions for implementing all the methods covered in the book. It also includes scripts and market data to reproduce examples in the book. The code assumes intermediate-level familiarity with Matlab and C# as well as an understanding of basic programming principles.

File names have chosen in an intuitive fashion, so that, for example, the file "BisectionBSIV" implements the bisection algorithm for finding Black-Scholes implied volatilities, while "GenerateGaussLaguerre" generates abscissas and weights for Gauss-Laguerre quadrature. Whenever possible, the filenames are identical in Matlab and in C#, except for the file extension.

CODE FUNCTIONALITY BY CHAPTER

All of the functions and examples in the book have been coded in both Matlab and C#. The following table describes the functionality of the code, chapter-by-chapter. Please note that some functions, such as linear regression or interpolation, are not built into C#, and are included with the C# code. In Matlab, however, these are available as built-in functions and are therefore not coded. In some cases, usually to speed up computations, built-in Matlab functions are not used and separate functions are coded instead. The code also includes scripts to generate most of the figures in the book, but in Matlab only.

Chapter	Code Functionality
1. The Heston Model for European Options	Obtaining the original Heston characteristic function
	Obtaining the original Heston price using Newton-Cotes integration
	Consolidating the integrals into a single integral
	Obtaining the Black-Scholes price as a special case of the Heston model
	Generating the figure for the Heston integrand (Matlab only)
2. Integration Issues, Parameter Effects, and Variance Modeling	Calculating the Heston characteristic function under the "Little Trap" formulation of Albrecher et al.
	Obtaining the Heston price using one or two characteristic functions and Gauss-Laguerre quadrature

(continues)

Chapter	Code Functionality
	Obtaining Black-Scholes prices of European options
	Obtaining implied volatility from Heston prices
	Finding the Roger Lee moment formulas and the Andersen and Piterbarg time to moment explosion
	Obtaining local volatility in the Heston model using the Dupire formulation and the Gatheral approximation
	Calculating the fair strike of variance swaps in the Heston model
	Calculating linear interpolated values along a single dimension (C# only)
	Obtaining the standard normal CDF using Bagby's approximation (C# only)
	Generating figures for implied and local volatility surfaces; discontinuities and oscillations in the integrand; effects of parameters on Heston prices and implied volatility; and total volatility (Matlab only)
3. Derivations Using the Fourier Transform	Obtaining the Heston price under the Attari formulation
	Obtaining the Heston price under Carr and Madan formulation for calls, puts, and for OTM options under general values of the spot price
	Finding the Roger Lee admissible values for the Carr and Madan alpha, and the Lord and Kahl optimal value of alpha
	Generating figures for the Attari integrand; alpha bounds; optimal alpha; and Carr and Madan integrands (Matlab only)
4. The Fundamental Transform for Pricing Options	Obtaining the Heston price using Lewis' Fundamental Transform
	Obtaining the Heston price using Parseval's identity as applied by Lewis
	Obtaining the Heston price using Lewis' volatility of volatility expansion
	Generating figures for the payoff transform and prices under the volatility of volatility expansions (Matlab only)

Chapter	Code Functionality
5. Numerical Integration Schemes	Obtaining the Heston price using Newton-Cotes integration schemes
	Generating abscissas and weights for Gauss-Laguerre, Gauss-Legendre, and Gauss-Lobatto quadrature.
	Obtaining the Heston price using Gauss-Laguerre, Gauss-Legendre, and Gauss-Lobatto quadrature
	Obtaining double integrals using the composite Gauss-Legendre and composite trapezoidal rule
	Obtaining the Heston price using the fast Fourier transform (FFT) and the fractional fast Fourier transform (FRFT)
	Obtaining the Heston price using the Kahl and Jackel transformation of the integration domain and Gauss-Lobatto quadrature
	Obtaining the Heston price using Zhu's multi-domain integration algorithm
	Finding roots of polynomials using Sturm sequences (C# only)
	Obtaining the FFT and inverse FFT (C# only)
	Generating figures for the Laguerre polynomial; integrand and maturity comparison; and Kahl and Jackel integrand (Matlab only)
6. Parameter Estimation	Obtaining parameter estimates using loss functions, with the original Heston call price, with the FTT and FRFT formulations, with the Attari formulation, and with the Lewis formulations
	Modifying loss function estimation using Kilin's Strike Vector Computation algorithm
	Obtaining parameter estimates using the Differential Evolution algorithm; with the original Heston call price and with the FRFT formulation
	Obtaining the Gauthier and Rivaille "smart parameter" starting values
	Obtaining parameter estimates using Atiya and Wall's MLE algorithm
	Obtaining the risk neutral density and total implied volatility
	Implementing the Nelder-Mead minimization algorithm (C# only)
	Performing operations on vectors, such as multiplication, addition, and subtraction (C# only)

(continues)

Chapter	Code Functionality
	Generating figures for market and model implied volatility comparisons; risk neutral density; and total volatility (Matlab only)
7. Simulation in the Heston Model	Obtaining the Heston price under various simulation schemes, including Euler, Milstein, Kahl and Jackel, Quadratic Exponential, Moment Matching, and Transformed Volatility.
	Calculating the inverse standard normal distribution
	Generate uniform and standard normal random numbers (C# only)
	Generating figures to illustrate simulated stock price paths and volatility paths (Matlab only)
8. American Options	Obtaining American option prices under the Heston model using the Longstaff-Schwartz LSM simulation algorithm; the Beliaeva-Nawalkha bivariate tree, the Medvedev-Scaillet expansion; and the Explicit finite difference method.
	Obtaining American option prices under the Black-Scholes model using the Medvedev-Scaillet expansion and the trinomial tree
	Symbolic code to solve the Medvedev-Scaillet PDE and find the expansion terms (Matlab only)
	Obtaining American call prices using the Chiarella and Ziogas algorithm
	Estimating parameters of the Heston model using the Medvedev-Scaillet expansion and market prices of American options
	Calculating linear interpolated values along two dimensions (C# only)
	Implementing linear regression, and matrix inversion using LU-decomposition (C# only)
	Generating figures for the illustration of the LSM algorithm; optimization in the Medvedev-Scaillet expansion; comparison of estimated and market implied volatilities; and Chiarella and Ziogas variance convergence (Matlab only)
9. Time-Dependent Heston Models	Obtaining parameter estimates and prices under the Mikhailov and Nogel time-dependent version of the Heston model
	Obtaining parameter estimates and prices under the Elices time-dependent version of the Heston model

Chapter	Code Functionality
	Obtaining parameter estimates and prices under the Benhamou, Gobet and Miri time-dependent version of the Model Symbolic code to obtain coefficients of the Benhamou, Gobet, and Miri model (Matlab only) Illustrating how the univariate characteristic function arises as a special case of the bivariate characteristic function Generating figures for comparing market implied volatilities and implied volatilities from the time-dependent models (Matlab only)
10. Methods for Finite Differences	Obtaining Heston prices using the Explicit, Alternating Direction Implicit (ADI), and Weighted Methods, including the Implicit and Crank-Nicolson methods as special case Obtaining the matrix for the Heston generator required for the ADI and Weighted Methods Constructing uniform and non-uniform grids Generating figures for non-uniform grid and for accuracy analysis of the Explicit Method (Matlab only)
11. The Heston Greeks	Obtaining American Greeks under the Explicit Method, the Longstaff-Schwartz Method, and the Medvedev-Scaillet Method Obtaining European Greeks under the original Heston, Attari, Carr Madan FFT and FRFT, and Lewis formulations, using analytic forms and finite difference approximations Generating figures for the Greeks (Matlab only)
12. The Double Heston Model	Obtaining prices under the double Heston model Obtaining prices under the double Heston model using the simulation schemes of Gauthier and Possamai Estimating parameters of the model using loss functions and Kilin's Strike Vector Computation modification Obtaining American option prices under the double Heston model using the Longstaff-Schwartz algorithm Obtaining Greeks under the double Heston model in analytic form and using finite differences

(*continues*)

Chapter	Code Functionality
	Extracting the risk neutral density from double Heston call prices
	Obtaining local and implied volatilities from the double Heston model
	Generating figures to compare market and estimated implied volatilities; for local volatility; for the risk neutral density; and for the simulated stock price and variances (Matlab only)

ACCESS TO THE CODE AND FILE FORMATS

To access the code, go to www.wiley.com/go/hestonmodel (password: rouah13).

The code files are arranged in directories that correspond to the chapters in which the code is used. The files are then arranged in subdirectories that correspond to the type of analysis for which the files are used. Some files are used in several chapters, so these are included multiple times in the directories.

To access Matlab files, navigate towards the subdirectory that contains the files you are seeking, and download them to a subdirectory on your local machine.

To access C# files, navigate towards the subdirectory that contains the files you are seeking, and proceed in one of two ways:

1. Download only the source code files, including the solution files (.sln extension), project files (.csproj extension), source files (.cs extension), as well as text files (.txt extension) where applicable, to your machine. Create a new project in C# and cut and paste the content of these files into your project.
2. Download the entire subdirectory including the \bin, \obj, and \Properties subdirectories, and copy the entire subdirectory onto your local machine. Double-click on the solution file to open and run the code in C#.

Index

Printed and bound by CPI Group (UK) Ltd, Croydon, CR0 4YY

23/04/2025

14660932-0002